## Pure Economic Loss in Europe

Pure economic loss is one of the most discussed and controversial legal issues in Europe today, raising complex questions which affect the law of tort and contract. How far can tort liability expand without imposing excessive burdens upon individual activity? Should the recovery of pure economic loss be the domain principally of the law of contract? And is there a common core of principles, policies and rules governing tortious liability for pure economic loss in Europe?

This is the first comprehensive study of the subject, using a fact-based comparative method and in-depth research into the laws of thirteen European countries. Following a historical and analytical introduction to economic loss, experts from most European countries consider how their national systems would deal with the same practical problem, highlighting similarities and differences in a range of comprehensive issues. This is the third publication of The Common Core of European Private Law Project.

MAURO BUSSANI is Professor of Law at the University of Trieste. His recent publications include *Il problema del patto commissorio: studio di diritto comparato* (2000), *As peculiaridades da noção de culpa* (2000) and *Making European Law: Essays on the 'Common Core' Project* (co-edited with Ugo Mattei, 2002).

VERNON VALENTINE PALMER is Thomas Pickles Professor of Law at the Tulane University School of Law. He is author and editor of *Louisiana: Microcosm of a Mixed Jurisdiction* (1999) and *Mixed Jurisdictions Worldwide: the Third Legal Family* (2001).

CAMBRIDGE STUDIES IN INTERNATIONAL AND COMPARATIVE LAW

## The Common Core of European Private Law Project

*General Editors*
Mauro Bussani, Università di Trieste
Ugo Mattei, Università degli Studi di Torino

*Late Honorary Editor*
Rudolph B. Schlesinger, Cornell University and University of California, Hastings

*Honorary Editor*
Rodolfo Sacco

*Divisional Editors*
Antonio Gambaro (Property), Centro Studi di Diritto Privato Università degli Studi di Milano
James Gordley (Contract), University of California, Berkeley
Mathias Reimann (Tort), University of Michigan Law School, Ann Arbor

For the transnational lawyer the present European situation is equivalent to that of a traveller compelled to cross legal Europe using a number of different local maps. To assist lawyers in the journey beyond their own locality *The Common Core of European Private Law Project* was launched in 1993 at the University of Trento under the auspices of the late Professor Rudolph B. Schlesinger.

The aim of this collective scholarly enterprise is to unearth what is already common to the legal systems of European Union member states. Case studies widely circulated and discussed between lawyers of different traditions are employed to draw at least the main lines of a reliable map of the law of Europe.

*Books in the Series*

*Pure Economic Loss in Europe*
Edited by Mauro Bussani and Vernon Valentine Palmer
0 521 82464 8 Hardback

*The Enforceability of Promises in European Contract Law*
Edited by James Gordley
0 521 79021 2 Hardback

*Good Faith in European Contract Law*
Edited by Reinhard Zimmermann and Simon Whittaker
0 521 77190 0 Hardback

# Pure Economic Loss in Europe

Edited by
Mauro Bussani
and
Vernon Valentine Palmer

CAMBRIDGE UNIVERSITY PRESS

CAMBRIDGE UNIVERSITY PRESS
Cambridge, New York, Melbourne, Madrid, Cape Town, Singapore,
São Paulo, Delhi, Dubai, Tokyo, Mexico City

Cambridge University Press
The Edinburgh Building, Cambridge CB2 8RU, UK

Published in the United States of America by Cambridge University Press, New York

www.cambridge.org
Information on this title: www.cambridge.org/9780521180054

© Cambridge University Press 2003

This publication is in copyright. Subject to statutory exception
and to the provisions of relevant collective licensing agreements,
no reproduction of any part may take place without the written
permission of Cambridge University Press.

First published 2003
Reprinted 2005
First paperback edition 2010

*A catalogue record for this publication is available from the British Library*

*Library of Congress Cataloguing in Publication data*
Pure economic loss in Europe / edited by Mauro Bussani and Vernon Valentine Palmer.
    p.   cm. – (Cambridge studies in international and comparative law; [28]. The Common
core of European private law project)
Includes bibliographical references and index.
ISBN 0 521 82464 8 (hbk.)
1. Damages–European Union countries.   I. Bussani, Mauro.   II. Palmer, Vernon V.
III. Cambridge studies in international and comparative law (Cambridge, England:
1996); 28.   IV. Cambridge studies in international and comparative law (Cambridge,
England: 1996). Common core of European law project.
KJC1620.P87   2003   346.03'094 – dc21   2002031345

ISBN 978-0-521-82464-4 Hardback
ISBN 978-0-521-18005-4 Paperback

Cambridge University Press has no responsibility for the persistence or
accuracy of URLs for external or third-party internet websites referred to in
this publication, and does not guarantee that any content on such websites is,
or will remain, accurate or appropriate.

# Contents

|  |  |  |
|---|---|---|
| *General editors' preface* | | page xi |
| *Preface* | | xiii |
| *List of contributors* | | xv |
| *Table of legislation* | | xvii |
| *Relevant statutory and codified provisions (in translation)* | | xxvi |
| *List of abbreviations* | | xl |

### Part I: Situating the frontier

| 1 | **The notion of pure economic loss and its setting**<br>Mauro Bussani and Vernon Valentine Palmer | 3 |
|---|---|---|
| | Introduction | 3 |
| | Pure vs. consequential economic loss | 5 |
| | Actor's state of mind: intention vs. negligence | 9 |
| | The standard cases: a taxonomy | 10 |
| | Present vs. future loss | 14 |
| | Basic arguments for an exclusionary rule | 16 |
| 2 | **The rule against recovery in negligence for pure economic loss: an historical accident?**<br>James Gordley | 25 |
| | Introduction | 25 |
| | Continental law before the nineteenth century | 26 |
| | The nineteenth and twentieth centuries | 36 |
| | Conclusion | 55 |
| 3A | **Pure economic loss: an economic analysis**<br>Jürgen G. Backhaus | 57 |
| | Introduction | 57 |

|  |  |  |
|---|---|---|
|  | Basic institutions of the market economy | 58 |
|  | Procedural guarantees | 64 |
|  | Externalities, rent seeking and dynamic markets | 65 |
|  | Looking at the cases | 70 |
|  | Conclusion | 73 |
| 3B | **Liability for pure financial loss: revisiting the economic foundations of a legal doctrine**<br>*Francesco Parisi* | 75 |
|  | The economics of pure economic loss | 77 |
|  | Pure economic loss: towards an economic restatement | 81 |
|  | Conclusion | 92 |
| 4 | **American tort law and the (supposed) economic loss rule**<br>*Gary T. Schwartz* | 94 |
|  | Introduction: the relative unimportance of an exclusionary rule in the United States | 94 |
|  | Products liability as an exception | 96 |
|  | Rationales of the rule | 101 |
|  | Contexts and cases | 108 |
|  | Conclusion | 118 |
| 5 | **The liability regimes of Europe – their façades and interiors**<br>*Mauro Bussani and Vernon Valentine Palmer* | 120 |
|  | Introduction | 120 |
|  | Two alternative formulas: from façades to operative rules | 121 |
|  | General vs. specific characteristics | 123 |
|  | The liberal, pragmatic and conservative regimes of tort | 123 |
|  | The liberal regimes of France, Belgium, Italy, Spain and Greece | 126 |
|  | The pragmatic regimes of England, Scotland and the Netherlands | 139 |
|  | The conservative regimes of Germany, Austria, Portugal, Sweden and Finland | 148 |
|  | Conclusion | 158 |

Part II: The comparative evidence: case responses and editors' comparative comments

| 6 | Preliminary remarks on methodology | 163 |
|---|---|---|
| | *Mauro Bussani and Vernon Valentine Palmer* | |
| | Aim and method of the study | 163 |
| | The common core approach | 163 |
| | The three-level response | 166 |
| 7 | The case studies | 171 |
| | *National Reporters and Editors Commentary* | 171 |
| | Case 1: cable I – the blackout | 171 |
| | Case 2: cable II – the factory shutdown | 192 |
| | Case 3: cable III – the day-to-day workers | 208 |
| | Case 4: convalescing employee | 222 |
| | Case 5: requiem for an Italian all star | 241 |
| | Case 6: the infected cow | 255 |
| | Case 7: the careless architect | 271 |
| | Case 8: the cancelled cruise | 291 |
| | Case 9: fire in the projection booth | 308 |
| | Case 10: the dutiful wife | 328 |
| | Case 11: a maestro's mistake | 344 |
| | Case 12: double sale | 362 |
| | Case 13: subcontractor's liability | 385 |
| | Case 14: poor legal services | 403 |
| | Case 15: a closed motorway – the value of time | 418 |
| | Case 16: truck blocking entrance to business premises | 435 |
| | Case 17: auditor's liability | 453 |
| | Case 18: wrongful job reference | 473 |
| | Case 19: breach of promise | 488 |
| | Case 20: an anonymous telephone call | 507 |

Part III: Much ado about something

| 8 | Summary and survey of the cases and results | 523 |
|---|---|---|
| | *Mauro Bussani and Vernon Valentine Palmer* | |
| | Introduction | 523 |
| | Three comparative tables | 524 |
| | Reappraising the divides | 525 |
| | Certainty vs. uncertainty | 528 |

| | | |
|---|---|---|
| 9 | **General conclusions of the study**<br>*Mauro Bussani and Vernon Valentine Palmer* | 530 |
| | Irrelevance of legal families | 530 |
| | Absence of methodological common core | 530 |
| | Awareness of the time factor | 531 |
| | The substantive common core | 532 |
| | Summary on the 'limited common core' | 536 |
| 10 | **The recoverability of pure economic loss within the perspective of a European codification**<br>*Mauro Bussani and Vernon Valentine Palmer* | 537 |
| | Introduction | 537 |
| | Pure economic loss astride private law frontiers | 538 |
| | The place of pure economic loss within different possible frames of a tort law codification | 540 |
| | Possible basic scenarios | 541 |
| | A destiny to be interpreted | 546 |
| | *Bibliography* | 549 |
| | *Index* | 576 |

# General editors' preface

This is the third book in the series The Common Core of European Private Law which will publish its results within Cambridge Studies in International and Comparative Law. The project was launched in 1993 at the University of Trento under the auspices of the late Professor Rudolf B. Schlesinger. The methodology used in the Trento project is novel. By making use of case studies it goes beyond mere description to detailed inquiry into how most European Union legal systems resolve specific legal questions in practice, and to thorough comparison between those systems. It is our hope that these volumes will provide scholars with a valuable tool for research in comparative law and in their own national legal systems. The collection of materials that the Common Core Project is offering to the scholarly community is already quite extensive and will become even more so when more volumes are published. The availability of materials attempting a genuine analysis of how things are is, in our opinion, a prerequisite for an intelligent and critical discussion on how they should be. Perhaps in the future European private law will be authoritatively restated or even codified. The analytical work carried on today by the almost 200 scholars involved in the Common Core Project is a precious asset of knowledge and legitimization for any such normative enterprise.

We must thank not only the editors and contributors to these first published results but also all the participants who continue to contribute to The Common Core of European Private Law Project. With a sense of deep gratitude we also wish to recall our late Honorary Editor, Professor Rudolf B. Schlesinger. We are sad that we have not been able to present him with the results of a project in which he believed so firmly. No scholarly project can survive without committed sponsors. The Dipartimento di Scienze Giuridiche of the University of Trento, its past and present directors and its excellent staff must first be thanked. The European Commission is partially sponsoring our annual general meetings, having included them in their High Level Conferences Program. The Italian Ministry of Scientific Research is now also funding the project, having recognized it as a 'research of national interest'. The Consiglio Nazionale delle Ricerche, the Istituto Subalpino per l'Analisi e l'Insegnamento del Diritto delle Attività Transnazionali, the University of Torino, the Fromm Chair in International and Comparative Law at the University of California and the Hastings College of Law have all contributed to the funding of this project. Last but not least, we must encourage all those involved in our ongoing Trento projects in contract law, property, tort and other areas whose results will be the subject of future published volumes. Our home page on the internet is at http://www.jus.unitn.it/dsg/common-core. There you can follow our progress in mapping the common core of European private law.

*General Editors*:
Mauro Bussani (University of Trieste)
Ugo Mattei (University of Turin and University of California, Hastings College of Law)

*Honorary Editor*:
Rodolfo Sacco (University of Turin)

*Late Honorary Editor*:
Rudolf B. Schlesinger (Cornell University – University of California, Hastings)

# Preface

Prefaces, happily, are written last when the difficult work is already done. We only take the occasion to say a word about the timing of this project, and to thank those who contributed to it.

As the reader will appreciate, a case study of thirteen European jurisdictions involving the collaboration of twenty-two scholars takes considerable time to complete. This collective enterprise began more than six years ago. The selection of our reporters and contributors, the development of our questionnaire and the refinement of our working method were all settled and agreed upon in our initial meetings in Trento, Italy in 1996. First drafts of the national reports were written and completed in the period 1997–9, and then began a process of study, editing and redrafting which continued for several years thereafter. The introductory chapters, as well as the editors' comparative remarks, were not completed until 2001. Even if this delay could be considered normal, we recognize that it entails the risk that perhaps some recent information or writings in a particular European system may not have been cited. Nevertheless, the general editors of this volume, together with the national reporters, can assure the reader that no material changes in the law have been omitted and that the work is generally current and reliable. For example, important recent developments, such as passage of the Act to modernize the Law of Obligations in Germany (effective 2002) and the most recent decisions of the European Court of Justice, have been taken into account and were added. Thus we are confident that the essential picture of pure economic loss in Europe has been captured.

It remains only to acknowledge our gratefulness to those who have made this book possible.

We express our deepest thanks to all our national reporters and contributors for undertaking this work in the spirit of international cooperation. We sadly note that our colleague Gary Schwartz passed away soon after writing his brilliant chapter on the American view of pure economic loss. In Gary, the world has surely lost one of its greatest tort scholars.

We must also thank Mrs Carla Boninsegna not only for her general role in organizing our meetings in Trento, but for her generous technical assistance with the bibliography and the submission of the manuscript in proper form to Cambridge University Press.

We are grateful to the deans of Tulane Law School, the directors of the Eason-Weinmann Center for Comparative Law of the same law school, the directors of the law departments of Trento and Trieste Universities, the Italian Ministry of Education and Scientific Research, the Italian National Research Council and the European Commission. Without the efforts and the contributions of all these institutions this book would not be what it is.

Finally, we wish to thank our colleagues Francesca Fiorentini, Christina Hultmark, Jane Stapleton, Walter van Gerven Konstantinos D. Kerameus and Tony Weir, whose friendship and patience encouraged us and eased the path towards the publication of the results of our research.

*Mauro Bussani and Vernon Palmer*
*Trieste and New Orleans*
*December 2002*

# Contributors

*Jürgen Backhaus*, Professor, Krupp Chair in Public Finance and Fiscal Sociology, University of Erfurt, Germany

*Estathios Banakas*, Professor of Law, Director of European Private Law Programme, Norwich Law School, University of East Anglia, England

*Willem H. van Boom*, Senior Lecturer in Law, Tilburg University, the Netherlands

*Mauro Bussani*, Professor of Law, University of Trieste, Italy; General Editor of the Common Core Project

*Kostas Christodoulou*, Lecturer in Law, University of Athens, Greece

*Lloyd Embleton*, Solicitor; Scotland

*James Gordley*, Cecil Shannon Professor of Law, University of California, Berkeley, USA

*Pier Giuseppe Monateri*, Professor of Law, University of Turin, Italy

*Alberto Musy*, Professor of Law, University of Piemonte Orientale, Italy

*Christel de Noblet*, Adjunct Professor of Law, Tulane University, New Orleans, USA and member of the Barreau de Paris, France

*Pedro del Olmo*, Professor of Law, University Carlos III, Madrid, Spain

*Vernon Valentine Palmer*, Thomas Pickles Professor of Law, Director of European Legal Studies, Director of Paris Institute of European Legal Studies, Tulane University, New Orleans, USA

*Fernando Pantaleón*, Professor of Law, University Carlos III, Madrid, Spain

*Francesco Parisi*, Professor of Law, George Mason University, School of Law and Co-Director, J. M. Buchanan Center for Political Economy, Program in Economics and the Law, Arlington, USA

*Willibald Posch*, Professor of Law, University of Graz, Austria

*Mathias Reimann*, Professor of Law, University of Michigan, Ann Arbor, USA

*Bernd Schilcher*, Professor of Law, University of Graz, Austria

*Gary T. Schwartz*, late Warren Professor of Law, University of California at Los Angeles, USA
*Alessandro Simoni*, Professor of Law, University of Florence, Italy
*Jorge Sinde Monteiro*, Professor of Law, University of Coimbra, Portugal
*Joseph Thomson*, Regius Professor of Law, University of Glasgow, Scotland
*Jean-Marc Trigaux*, Public Prosecutor and formerly Assistant Professor of Law, Catholic University of Louvain, Belgium

## Contributors to the case studies

| | |
|---|---|
| Austria: | Willibald Posch and Bernd Schilcher |
| Belgium: | Jean-Marc Trigaux |
| England: | Estathios Banakas |
| France: | Vernon Valentine Palmer and Christel de Noblet |
| Germany: | Mathias Reimann |
| Greece: | Kostas Christodoulou |
| Italy: | Pier Giuseppe Monateri and Alberto Musy |
| Portugal: | Jorge Sinde Monteiro |
| Scotland: | Joseph Thomson and Lloyd Embleton |
| Spain: | Pedro del Olmo and Fernando Pantaleón |
| Sweden and Finland: | Alessandro Simoni |
| The Netherlands: | Willem van Boom |

# Table of legislation

## Austria
*Civil Code*

| | |
|---|---|
| 1295 | 168, 323, 339, 378, 379 |
| 1299 | 154, 245–413 |
| 1300 | 154, 245–517 |
| 1311 | 429 |
| 1320 | 267 |
| 1325 | 339 |
| 1329 | 429, 448, 449 |
| 1330 | 154, 245, 468, 484, 485, 517 |
| 1331 | 301, 323, 429, 448 |
| 1332 | 323, 429, 448 |

## Belgium
*Civil Code*

| | |
|---|---|
| 1382 | 131, 132, 173, 192, 209, 210, 224, 241–2, 256, 293, 311, 364, 457, 474, 490, 507, 508, 545 |
| 1383 | 131, 241 |
| 1384 | 209, 210 |
| 1385 | 256 |
| 1386 | |

L. 3 July 1978 (*Employment Contracts*)

| | |
|---|---|
| 18 | 173, 192 |
| 54 | 223 |

L. 10 March 1925 (*Distribution of Electric Energy*)

| | |
|---|---|
| 27 | 173, 192 |

L. 20 February 1939     272
L. 10 April 1971     224
*Product Liability Law*, 25 February 1991     310

## England

*Misrepresentation Act* 1967     140, 242
*Consumer Credit Act* 1979     512
*Data Protection Act* 1984     512
*Consumer Protection Act* 1987     316
*Social Security Act* 1992     231

## Finland

*Tort Liability Act* 1974
chapter 5, §1, 3, 4, 5     156, 238, 246, 253, 269, 382, 416, 451, 486, 505
*Consumer Protection Act* 1978
Chapter 5, §10     401
*Traffic Insurance Act* 1959     432
*Auditors Act* 1994     470
*Act on Personal Information* 1999     519

## France

*Civil Code*
212     328
1141     192
1149     132, 241–92
1165     385
1382     126, 127, 168, 172–3, 192, 241, 255–6, 291, 308, 328, 344, 362, 363, 385, 403, 418–19, 420, 435, 456, 473, 488–9, 507
1383     126, 127, 168, 192, 241–419, 473, 507
1384     172–3, 222, 291, 435–6
1385     255–6
1386     308
1641     309
1648     309
2279     363
*Labour Code*
L.351     208
L.352     208

*Ordinance* of 1681
| | |
|---|---|
| L. III | 291 |
| T. VII | 291 |
| *Convention de Bruxelles* of 1910 | 291 |

*Special law* of 24 July 1966
| | |
|---|---|
| 234 | 453 |

*Law* of 7 July 1967
| | |
|---|---|
| 2 | 291 |
| 3 | 291 |

*Special strict liability law* of 5 July 1985, L no. 85–677
| | |
|---|---|
| 3 | 418–19 |
| 5 | 418–19 |
| 6 | 419 |
| 29 | 222 |
| 30 | 222 |
| 31 | 222 |

# Germany

*German Constitution*
| | |
|---|---|
| 14 | 302 |

*Civil Code*
| | |
|---|---|
| 241 | 151, 245, 355, 484, 502 |
| 242 | 151, 245, 484 |
| 249 | 302 |
| 252 | 185 |
| 278 | 150, 243 |
| 280 | 355 |
| 293 | 218 |
| 296 | 218 |
| 311 | 151, 244, 354–5 |
| 421 | 285 |
| 426 | 284, 285 |
| 427 | 285 |
| 615 | 218 |
| 630 | 484 |
| 633 | 285 |
| 634 | 285 |
| 635 | 285 |
| 675 | 288 |

| | |
|---|---|
| 823 | 8, 39, 40, 41, 42, 43–4, 45, 125, 127, 134, 148, 149, 154, 157, 171–85, 200–1, 204, 218, 234, 241–2, 243–5, 246, 250, 266–323, 327, 338, 354, 377, 378, 396, 402, 427–8, 466, 483, 502, 515, 543 |
| 824 | 134, 242, 466, 483–4, 515 |
| 825 | 134, 242 |
| 826 | 42, 134, 149, 234, 242, 243–377, 378, 396, 502, 543 |
| 831 | 185 |
| 833 | 266–323 |
| 840 | 285 |
| 843 | 218, 338, 354 |
| 844 | 218, 338 |
| 845 | 234, 250, 338, 355 |
| 929 | 378 |
| 931 | 378 |
| 1360 | 338 |
| *Animal Diseases Law* 1995 | 266–323 |
| *Commercial Code* | |
| 323 | 472 |
| *Federal Notary Law* 1961 | |
| 19 | 413 |
| *Pay Continuation Statute* 1994 | |
| 3 | 234 |
| 6 | 234 |
| *Products Liability Law* | |
| 1 | 327 |
| *Road Traffic Act* 1952 | |
| 7 | 428 |

## Greece

| | |
|---|---|
| *Civil Code* | |
| 57 | 260, 422, 438, 477, 510 |
| 59 | 477, 511 |
| 138 | 214 |
| 140 | 348 |
| 142 | 461 |
| 143 | 461 |
| 144 | 348 |
| 147 | 461 |
| 178 | 368 |

| | |
|---|---|
| 197 | 460 |
| 198 | 460 |
| 239 | 367 |
| 281 | 260, 348, 389–90 |
| 288 | 260, 314, 348, 389–90, 478 |
| 298 | 195 |
| 330 | 177 |
| 334 | 389–90 |
| 335 | 367, 478 |
| 336 | 315 |
| 342 | 315 |
| 361 | 276 |
| 363 | 315 |
| 656 | 214 |
| 678 | 478 |
| 729 | 347–8 |
| 914 | 178, 185, 195, 213, 229, 295, 332, 389–90, 406, 422, 459, 477, 510 |
| 919 | 347–8, 368 |
| 922 | 178, 195, 389–90, 460 |
| 926 | 195, 389–90 |
| 929 | 213, 332 |
| 932 | 477, 511 |
| 967 | 422, 478 |
| 1033 | 367 |
| 1034 | 367 |

Penal Code

| | |
|---|---|
| 42 | 260 |
| 242 | 406 |
| 308 | 260 |

Code of Civil Procedure

| | |
|---|---|
| 72 | 230, 276, 315 |
| 455 | 406 |
| 559 | 315 |

L. 2112/ 1920 (Regulation of Labour Matters)

| | |
|---|---|
| 2 | 478 |

L. 2190/ 1920 (Companies)

| | |
|---|---|
| 34 | 459 |

Royal Decree 16–18/07/1920

L. 2472/ 1997 (Data Protection)

| | |
|---|---|
| 4 | 511 |
| 23 | 511 |

## Italy

*Civil Code*

| | |
|---|---|
| 1153 | 365 |
| 1176 | 273 |
| 1223 | 174 |
| 1226 | 294 |
| 1227 | 437 |
| 1337 | 311, 491, 492–3, 509 |
| 1483 | 364–5 |
| 1669 | 387 |
| 2043 | 175–6, 194, 211, 224, 243–4, 273, 294, 330, 346, 387, 405, 437, 457, 475, 509, 510 |
| 2050 | 174 |
| 2110 | 224 |
| 2644 | 364–5 |
| D.p.r., 24.5.1988, no. 224 (*Products Liability Act*) | 311 |
| D.lg. 24.2.1998, no. 58 (*Accountant Liability Act*) | 457 |

## Portugal

*Civil Code*

| | |
|---|---|
| 2 | 238 |
| 70 | 155, 219, 245 |
| 227 | 450–86, 504 |
| 246 | 358 |
| 281 | 381 |
| 334 | 155, 245–357 |
| 407 | 304 |
| 408 | 381 |
| 443 | 286 |
| 483 | 154, 187, 203, 245, 268, 304, 325, 431 |
| 484 | 155, 245–518 |
| 485 | 155, 245–87 |
| 487 | 187 |
| 493 | 188, 268 |
| 495 | 237, 340 |
| 500 | 187 |
| 502 | 268 |
| 503 | 251, 431 |

| | |
|---|---:|
| 592 | 236 |
| 606 | 400 |
| 609 | 400 |
| 809 | 325 |
| 875 | 380 |
| 879 | 381 |
| 1213 | 400 |
| 1301 | 381 |
| 1305 | 450–86 |
| 1311 | 381 |
| 1674 | 340 |
| 1878 | 340 |
| *Code of Land Registration* 1984 | |
| 4–5 | 380, 381 |
| *Stock Market Code (Código do Mercado de Valores Mobiliários)* 1991 | |
| 161–165 | 469–70 |
| *DL no. 48051/67* | |
| 3 | 414–15 |
| *DL no. 519/F2 of 29 December 1979 (Registration and Conveying Services)* | |
| *L. 28/84* | |
| 16 | 237 |
| *DL no. 383/89 of 6 November 1989 (Defective Products Liability)* | 324 |
| *DL 329/95 of 9 December 1995 (Pleasure Boats Act)* | |
| 43 | 303 |
| *L. no. 100/97 of 13 September 1997 (Occupational Accidents)* | 236 |

## Scotland

| | |
|---|---:|
| *Sale of Goods Act* 1979 | 374–5 |
| *Land Registration (Scotland) Act* 1979 | 374 |
| *Administration of Justice Act* 1982 | 335 |
| *Consumer Protection Act* 1987 | 320 |
| *Law Reform (Miscellaneous Provisions) (Scotland) Act* 1990 | 335 |
| *Requirements of Writing (Scotland) Act* 1995 | 497, 498, 499 |

## Spain

| | |
|---|---:|
| *Civil Code* | |
| 609 | 366 |
| 705 | 405–6 |

| | |
|---|---:|
| 1103 | 246, 259, 295, 438 |
| 1111 | 389 |
| 1186 | 228 |
| 1473 | 366–7 |
| 1902 | 135, 227, 228, 242, 295, 387, 405–6, 437, 458–9 |
| 1905 | 258 |
| 1906 | 258 |//
*Criminal Code*
| | |
|---|---:|
| 113 | 225–7 |

*Auditing of Accounts Act* no. 19, 12 July 1988
| | |
|---|---:|
| 11.1 | 458–9 |
| 15.1 | 458–9 |

*Labour Contract Act* 1944
| | |
|---|---:|
| 75.5 | 475 |

| | |
|---|---:|
| *Real Decreto* no. 1636, 20 December 1990 | 458–9 |

*Civil Liability for Damage Caused to Defective Products Act* no. 22, 6 July 12 1994
| | |
|---|---:|
| 10 | 312 |

# Sweden

| | |
|---|---:|
| *Tort Liability Act* 1972 | 156, 157, 246 |
| chapter 2, §1, 4 | 157–8, 246 |
| chapter 4, §2 | 269, 382, 416, 486, 505 |
| chapter 5, §2, 7 | 238, 253 |
| *Consumer Services Act* 1985 | |
| §33 | 401 |
| *Traffic Damages Act* 1975 | 432 |
| *Companies Act* 1975 | 470 |
| *Act on Credit Information* 1973 | 519 |

# The Netherlands

*Civil Code*
| | |
|---|---:|
| 3:89 | 376 |
| 3:90 | 376 |
| 3:114–115 | 376 |
| 6:74 | 376 |
| 6:98 | 147, 243 |
| 6:101 | 184, 200–338 |

| | |
|---|---|
| 6:102 | 283 |
| 6:107 | 233–4, 240, 336–8 |
| 6:109 | 146, 243 |
| 6:162 | 145, 184, 199, 242, 283, 300, 376, 426 |
| 6:163 | 146, 243, 426 |
| 6:179 | 264 |
| 7:22 | 300 |
| 7:420 | 395 |
| 7:424 | 395 |

# Relevant statutory and codified provisions
*(In translation)*

## Austria

*Civil Code*

*Article 1295*
(1) A person is entitled to demand indemnification for the damage from a person causing an injury by his fault; the damage may have been caused either by the violation of a contractual duty or without regard to a contract.
(2) A person who intentionally injures another in a manner in violation of public morals, is liable therefor; however, if the injury was caused in the exercise of legal rights, the person causing it shall be liable therefor only when the exercise of this right obviously has the purpose to cause damage to the other.

*Article 1299*
A person who claims publicly an office, art, trade or handicraft, or who assumes voluntarily without necessity a business which demands specialized knowledge or extraordinary diligence, warrants thereby that he trusts himself to possess the necessary diligence and extraordinary knowledge; therefore, such person is liable for the lack thereof. However, if the person who entrusted the business to him knew of his inexperience, or could have known thereof by applying the usual attention, such person is also guilty of negligence.

*Article 1300*
An expert is liable when he negligently gives, for a consideration, bad advice in matters of his art or science. In other cases, a person giving advice is liable only for damage which he has knowingly caused to another by giving the advice.

*Article 1311*
Mere accidents affect only the person to whose property or person they occur. However, if another person has occasioned the accident by his fault, or if such person has acted in violation of a law in endeavouring to prevent incidental injuries, or if he has interfered unnecessarily with the business of another, he is liable for any damages which would not otherwise have occurred [...]

*Article 1330*
(1) If a person has suffered actual damage or loss of profit through libel and slander he is entitled to demand indemnity therefor.
(2) This provision is also applicable where a person makes notorious matters which might endanger the credit, business or property of another person and which he knew or should have known were untrue. In such a case, the public revocation thereof may also be demanded. However, a person who makes a secret communication the untruth of which he does not know is not liable if he or the addressee has a legal interest therein.

## Belgium

*Civil Code*

*Article 1382*
Any act whatever of man which causes damage to another obliges him by whose fault it occurred to make reparation.

*Article 1383*
Each one is liable for the damage which he causes not only by his own act but also by his negligence or imprudence.

*Article 1384*
One is liable not only for the damage which he caused by his own act but also for that which is caused by the act of persons for whom he is responsible, or by things which he has in his keeping.
 The father and the mother are liable for damage caused by their minor children.
 Masters and principals [are liable] for damage caused by their domestics and employees in the functions for which they have been employed.
 Teachers and artisans [are liable] for damage caused by their pupils and apprentices during the time when they are under their surveillance.

The above liability arises unless the father and mother and the teachers and the artisans prove that they could not prevent the act which gave rise to such liability.

*Article 1385*
The owner of an animal or he who avails himself of it while it is being put to his use is liable for the damage which the animal causes, whether the animal was in his keeping or whether it had strayed or escaped.

*Article 1386*
The owner of a building is liable for the damage caused by its collapse when it happens as a result of default of maintenance or through a defect in its construction.

## Finland

*Tort Liability Act 1974*

*Chapter 2 § 1*
One who by intent or by negligence causes another a damage shall compensate it, as far as this Act does not prescribe otherwise.

*Chapter 5 § 1*
Compensation includes recovery for personal injury and property damage. If damage has been caused through an act sanctioned by criminal law or through an act of authority or if in other cases there are specially important reasons, compensation includes also recovery of such economic losses which are not in connection with personal injury or property damage.

## France

*Civil Code*

*Article 212*
Spouses mutually owe each other fidelity, aid, assistance.

*Article 1141*
If the thing which one is obligated to give or to deliver to two persons successively is purely movable property, that one of the two who has been put in actual possession of it is preferred and remains owner of it, although his title is subsequent in date, provided, however, that the possession is in good faith.

*Article 1149*
Damages to a creditor are in general due for the loss which he incurred and for the gain of which he was deprived, apart from the exceptions and modifications hereinafter.

*Article 1151*
Even in the case where the inexecution of the agreement results from the wilfulness of the debtor, damages are to include, with regard to the loss incurred by the creditor and the gain of which he has been deprived, only what is an immediate and direct consequence of the inexecution of the agreement.

*Article 1165*
Agreements are effective only between the contracting parties; they do not harm a third party, and they benefit him only in the case provided in Article 1121.

*Article 1382*
Any act whatever of man which causes damage to another obliges him by whose fault it occurred to make reparation.

*Article 1383*
Each person is liable for the damage which he causes not only by his own act but also by his negligence or imprudence.

*Article 1384*
He is liable not only for the damage which he caused by his own act, but also for that which is caused by the act of persons for whom he is responsible, or by things which he has in his keeping. [...]
    Masters and principals [are liable] for damage caused by their domestics and employees in the functions for which they have been employed.

*Article 1385*
The owner of an animal or he who avails himself of it while it is being put to his use is liable for the damage which the animal causes, whether the animal was in his keeping or whether it had strayed or escaped.

*Article 1641*
The seller is held to a guaranty against hidden defects in the thing sold which render it unsuitable to the use for which it is intended, or which so diminish such use that the buyer would not have purchased it, or would have given only a lesser price for it, had he known of them.

*Article 2279*

As to movable property, possession is equivalent to title.

Nevertheless, one who has lost or from whom was stolen a thing may claim it during three years, counting from the day of the loss or theft, against the one in whose hands he finds it, saving to that one his recourse against him from whom he holds it.

## Germany

*Civil Code*

*Article 823*

(1) A person who, wilfully or negligently, unlawfully injures the life, body, health, freedom, property or other right of another is bound to compensate him for any damages arising therefrom.

(2) The same obligation is placed upon a person who infringes a statute intended for the protection of others. If, according to the provisions of the statute, an infringement is possible even without fault, the duty to make compensation arises only in the event of fault.

*Article 824*

(1) A person who declares or publishes, contrary to the truth, a statement which is likely to endanger the credit of another, or to injure his earnings or prosperity in any manner, shall compensate the other for any damage arising therefrom, even if he does not know of its untruth, but should know of it.

(2) A person who makes a communication, the untruth of which is unknown to him, does not thereby render himself liable to make compensation, if he or the receiver of the communication has a lawful interest in it.

*Article 825*

A person who by cunning, by threats, or by the abuse of a relationship of dependence, induces a woman to permit extra-marital cohabitation, is bound to compensate her for any damages arising therefrom.

*Article 826*

A person who wilfully causes damage to another in a manner contrary to public policy is bound to compensate the other for the damage.

# Greece

## Civil Code

### Article 57
A person who has suffered an unlawful offence to his personality has the right to claim the cessation of such offence as also the non-recurrence thereof in the future. If the offence was directed against the personality of a deceased person the right referred to above shall belong to the spouse the descendants the ascendants the brothers and sisters and the legatees appointed by testament. Tortious liability for damages is not excluded when true claim is based on the provision governing unlawful acts.

### Article 59
In the cases referred to in the two preceding sections the Court may at the request of the person harmed and having regard to the nature of the offence order the person responsible to furnish reparation of the moral prejudice suffered by the person offended. Such reparation may consist of the payment of a sum of money of a publication or any other appropriate measure in the circumstances.

### Article 197
In the course of negotiations for the conclusion of a contract the parties shall be reciprocally bound to adopt the conduct which is dictated by good faith and business usages.

### Article 198
A person who in the course of negotiations for the conclusion of a contract has through his fault caused prejudice to the other party shall be liable for compensation even if the contract has not been concluded.

For the prescription of such claim shall be applicable by analogy the provisions governing prescription in the matter of claims arising from unlawful acts.

### Article 281
The exercise of a right shall be prohibited if such exercise obviously exceeds the limits imposed by good faith or morality or by the social or economic purpose of the right.

*Article 288*
A debtor shall be bound to perform the undertaking in accordance with the requirements of good faith taking into consideration business usages.

*Article 298*
Damages shall comprise the decrease in the existing *patrimonium* of the creditor (positive damage) as well as loss of profit. Such profit shall be that which can be reasonably anticipated in the usual course of things or by reference to the special circumstances having regard to the preparatory steps taken.

*Article 335*
If at the time of furnishing of the performance such furnishing is in whole or in part impossible for reasons either of a general nature or relating to the debtor the latter shall be bound to compensate the prejudice resulting therefrom for the creditor.

*Article 362*
A person who promised a performance which at the time of the conclusion of the contract is not possible by reason either of general considerations or of considerations relating to the promissor shall be liable to compensate the damage caused to the creditor by non-performance. The provisions of section 337 are also applicable in this case by analogy.

*Article 914*
A person who through his fault has caused in a manner contrary to the law prejudice to another shall be liable for compensation.

*Article 919*
A person who has intentionally caused prejudice to another in a manner contrary to morality shall be liable for damages.

*Article 929*
In case of harm to the body or health of a person the compensation shall include in addition to medical expenses and the prejudice hitherto caused everything of which the victim shall be deprived in the future or the further burden he shall bear by reason of an increase in his expenses. An obligation to compensate shall also arise in regard to a third party who being entitled by the law to rely on the performance of a service by the victim has been deprived of such service.

# Italy

## Civil Code

### Article 1153
He to whom movable property is conveyed by one who is not the owner, acquires full ownership by means of possession, provided that he be in good faith at the moment of consignment and there be an instrument or transaction capable of transferring ownership.

Ownership is acquired free of rights of others in the thing, if they do not appear in the instrument of transaction and the acquirer is in good faith.

### Article 1176
In performing the obligation the debtor shall observe the diligence of a good *pater familias*.

In the performance of obligations inherent in the exercise of a professional activity, diligence shall be evaluated with respect to the nature of that activity.

### Article 1218
The debtor who does not exactly render due performance is liable for damages unless he proves that the non-performance or delay was due to impossibility of performance for a cause not imputable to him.

### Article 1223
The measure of damages arising from non-performance or delay shall include the loss sustained by the creditor and the lost profits insofar as they are a direct and immediate consequence of the non-performance or delay.

### Article 1226
If damages cannot be proven in their exact amount, they are equitably liquidated by the court.

### Article 1227
When the negligent behaviour by the creditor has contributed to cause the damage, compensation will be reduced according to the degree of negligence and the actual consequence suffered therefrom.

### Article 1256
An obligation is extinguished when its performance becomes impossible for a cause not imputable to the debtor.

If the impossibility is only temporary the debtor is not liable for delay in performance as long as it continues to exist. However, the obligation is extinguished if the impossibility continues until, depending on the source of the obligation or the nature of its subject matter, the debtor can no longer be held bound to perform the obligation or the creditor is no longer interested in the performance.

*Article 1337*
The parties, in the conduct of negotiations and the formation of the contract, shall conduct themselves according to good faith.

*Article 1483*
If the buyer suffers total eviction from the thing as a result of rights enforced in it by a third person, the seller is bound to compensate him for damage according to Article 1479.

*Article 2043*
Any fraudulent, malicious, or negligent act that causes an unjustified injury to another obliges the person who has committed the act to pay damages.

*Article 2050*
Whoever causes injury to another in the performance of an activity dangerous by its nature or by reason of the instrumentalities employed, is liable for damages, unless he proves that he has taken all suitable measures to avoid the injury.

*Article 2059*
Non-economic damages are recoverable only in cases where a statute so provides.

*Article 2644*
(2) After first transcription, any successive transcription or registration of titles against the author cannot be enforced, even if the title had been acquired at a prior date.

## Decreto Legislativo 58/1998

*Article 164*
The rule of article 2407, section 1, civil code, applies to account societies.

The auditor and its employees are jointly liable with the auditing company, towards the client company or third parties, for damages due to their mistakes and torts.

# Portugal

## Civil Code

*Article 70*
The law protects individuals against any unlawful offence or threat of offence to his physical or moral entity.

*Article 227*
Whoever negotiates with another to conclude a contract must, in the preliminary stages as well as during its formation, proceed according to the rules of good faith, on pain of being liable for the damage that may be negligently caused to the other party.

*Article 246*
The declaration is without any effect if the declarant is unaware that he is making a transactional declaration or was coerced by physical force to issue it; but, if lack of awareness of the declaration was through fault, the declarant is obliged to compensate the declaree.

*Article 483*
(1) Whoever, whether by wilful misconduct (*dolus*) or by negligence unlawfully infringes the rights of another person or any legal provision intended to safeguard the interests of others must compensate the injured party for damage arising from such violation.

*Article 484*
Whoever affirms or disseminates a fact capable of prejudicing the credit or good name of any person, private individual or legal person, is responsible for the damage caused.

*Article 485*
(1) Mere advice, recommendation or information do not confer liability on whoever gives it, even though there may be negligence on their part.
(2) The obligation to compensate exists, however, when the responsibility for damage has been assumed, when there is a legal duty to give advice, recommendation or information and this has been done with negligence or intent to harm, or when the behaviour of the agent constitutes a punishable act.

*Article 494*
If the liability is based upon negligence compensation may be equitably settled at a lesser amount so as to correspond to the damage caused, as

long as the degree of culpability of the agent, his financial conditions and those of the injured party and other circumstances justify it.

*Article 495*
(2) Those who render assistance to the injured party [have a right to compensation] as well as hospitals, doctors or other persons or entities who may have contributed to the treatment or assistance of the victim.
(3) Those who might claim the injured party for alimonies or those to whom the injured party was paying them as a natural obligation [have a right to compensation].

*Article 609*
Subrogation exercised by one of the creditors profits to all the others.

*Decree-Law no. 383/89 of 6 November 1989*

*Article 8*
Damage resulting in death or physical injury and damage *in rem* different from the defective product are recoverable, where it is normally intended for private use or consumption and the injured party had principally attributed this end to it.

## Spain

*Civil Code*

*Article 1103*
The responsibility arising from negligence can be claimed in all kinds of obligations; but the Courts can moderate the compensation according to the circumstances of each case.

*Article 1111*
The creditors, once they have seized the debtor's assets, can make use of any action or remedy the debtor may have to collect what he owes them, with the only exception of the rights that are strictly personal to the debtor.

*Article 1186*
Having extinguished the obligation for loss of the asset, the creditor shall have access to all actions against third parties the debtor may be entitled to.

*Article 1902*
He who causes damages to another by act or omission, through fault or negligence, shall be obliged to compensate the damage caused.

*Auditing of Accounts Act no. 19 of 12 July 1988*

*Article 11.1*
Account auditors shall be directly and jointly and severally liable to the audited companies or entities and to third parties, for damages derived from the unfulfilment of their obligations.

*Article 15.1*
Civil or criminal responsibility which (auditors) may incur shall be claimed from them according to legal provisions.

*Criminal Code*

*Article 104 of the former Criminal Code* (Art. 113 of the current Criminal Code reproduces this exact legal content):
Compensation for material damages and pain and suffering shall not only include those caused to the injured party, but also those derived from criminal activity and caused to his family or to a third party.

## Sweden

*Tort Liability Act 1972*

*Chapter 1 § 2*
By pure economic loss in this Act is to be understood such economic loss arising without connection with anybody suffering bodily injury or property damage.

*Chapter 2 § 1*
Anybody who intentionally or negligently causes a personal injury or a damage to things shall compensate it, as far as this Act does not prescribe otherwise.

*Chapter 2 § 4*
Who causes pure economic loss through the commission of a crime shall compensate it according to what is established in §§ 1–3 concerning personal injury or damage to things.

## The Netherlands

*Civil Code*

*Article 6:98*
Compensation can only be claimed insofar as the damage is related to the event giving rise to liability in such a fashion that the damage, also taking into account its nature and that of the liability, can be imputed to the debtor as a result of this event.

*Article 6:101*
Where circumstances which can be imputed to the injured have contributed to the damage, the obligation to repair is reduced by apportioning the damage between the injured and the injurer in proportion to the degree in which the circumstances which can be imputed to each of them, have contributed to the damage. [...]

*Article 6:107*
(1) If a person suffers physical or mental injury as a result of an event for which another person is liable, that other person is not only obliged to repair the damage of the injured person himself, but also to indemnify a third person for costs [...] incurred for the benefit of the injured, which the latter, had he incurred them himself, would have been able to claim from that other person.
(2) He who has been held responsible by the third party pursuant to the preceding paragraph can raise the same defences as he would have had against the injured person.

*Article 6:109*
(1) The judge may reduce the obligation to repair damage if awarding full reparation would lead to clearly unacceptable results in the given circumstances, including the nature of the liability, the legal relationship between the parties, and their respective financial capacities.
(2) The reduction may not exceed the amount for which the debtor has covered his liability by insurance or was obliged to maintain such a cover.
(3) Any stipulation derogating from paragraph 1 is null.

*Article 6:162*
(1) A person who commits an unlawful act vis-à-vis another person, which can be imputed to him, is obliged to repair the damage suffered by the other person as a consequence of the act.

(2) Save grounds for justification, the following acts are deemed to be unlawful: the infringement of a subjective right, an act or omission violating a statutory duty, or conduct contrary to the standard of conduct acceptable in society.

(3) An unlawful act can be imputed to its author if it results from his fault or from a cause for which he is answerable according to law or common opinion.

*Article 6:163*
No obligation to repair damages arises whenever the violated norm does not purport to protect against damage such as that suffered by the injured.

*Article 6:179*
The possessor of an animal is liable for the damage caused by the animal, unless, pursuant to the preceding section, there would have been no liability if the possessor would have had control over the behaviour of the animal by which the damage was caused.

*Article 7:424*
If an agent has, in his own name, contracted with a party who does not fulfil his contractual obligations, then this party is also obliged [...] to repair the damage suffered by the principal.

# Abbreviations

| | |
|---|---|
| A. | Corte di Appello |
| AA | Ars Aequi |
| ABGB | Allgemeines Bürgerliches Gesetzbuch |
| AC | Appeal Cases |
| | Archivio civile |
| | Arresten van het Hof van Cassatie |
| ACirc. | Archivio circolazione |
| Ac P | Archiv für die civilistische Praxis |
| AG | Aktiengesellschaft |
| AGBG | Gesetz zur Regelung des Rechts der Allgemeinen Geschäftsbedingungen |
| AID | Archeion Idiotikou Dikaiou |
| AJCL | American Journal of Comparative Law |
| AJDA | Les actualités juridiques – Droit administratif |
| AK | Astikos Kodikas |
| All ER | All England Reports |
| AMG | Arzneimittelgesetz |
| AngG | Angestelltengesetz |
| AP | Areios Pagos |
| App. Cas. | Law Reports Appeal Cases, House of Lords |
| Arc | Archeio Nomologias |
| Arm | Armenopoulos |
| Arr. Verbr. | Arresten van het Hof van Verbreking |
| Ass. Plén. | Cour de Cassation, Assemblée Plénière |
| AtomG | Atomgesetz |
| B&S | Best & Smith's Queen Bench Reports |
| BAG | Bundesarbeitsgericht |

| | |
|---|---|
| BB | *Der Betriebsberater* |
| BBergG | *Bundesbergbaugesetz* |
| BBTC | *Banca borsa e titoli di credito* |
| BergG | *Berggesetz* |
| BGB | *Bürgerliches Gesetzbuch* |
| BGBl | *Bundesgesetzblatt* |
| BGH | *Bundesgerichtshof* |
| BGH-GS | *Bundesgerichtshof – Großer Senat für Zivilsachen* |
| BGHSt. | *Entscheidungen des Bundesgerichtshofes in Strafsachen* |
| BGHZ | *Entscheidungen des Bundesgerichtshofes in Zivilsachen* |
| Bing NC | *Bingham, New Cases, English Common Pleas* |
| BNatSchG | *Bundesnaturschutzgesetz* |
| BNotO | *Bundesnotarordnung* |
| BPflV | *Bundespflegesatzverordnung* |
| BR | *Bouwrecht* |
| BS/MB | *Belgisch Staatsblad/Moniteur belge* |
| BT Drucks | *Drucksachen des Deutschen Bundestages* |
| Bull. Civ. | *Bulletin des arrêts de la Cour de Cassation, chambres civiles* |
| Bull. Crim. | *Bulletin des arrêts de la Cour de Cassation, chambre criminelle* |
| Bull. Joly | *Bulletin Joly* |
| BVerfG | *Bundesverfassungsgericht* |
| BVerfGE | *Entscheidungen des Bundesverfassungsgerichtes* |
| BW | *Burgerlijk Wetboek* |
| CA | *Court of Appeal* |
| CAA | *Cour Administrative d'Appel* |
| Camb LJ | *Cambridge Law Journal* |
| Cass. | *Cour de Cassation/Corte di Cassazione, sezione civile* |
| Cass. 1e civ. | *Cour de Cassation, première chambre civile* |
| Cass. 2e civ. | *Cour de Cassation, deuxième chambre civile* |
| Cass. 3e civ. | *Cour de Cassation, troisième chambre civile* |
| Cass. ass. plén. | *Cour de Cassation, assemblée plénière* |
| Cass. com. | *Cour de Cassation, chambre commerciale et financière* |
| Cass. crim. | *Cour de Cassation, chambre criminelle* |
| Cass. pen. | *Corte di Cassazione, sezione penale* |
| Cass. soc. | *Cour de Cassation, chambre sociale* |
| cc/CC/C.civ. | *Codice Civile/Code civil/Civil Code/Código Civil* |
| CCPr. | *Code of Civil Procedure* |

| | |
|---|---|
| CÉ | *Conseil d'État* |
| CG | *Corriere giuridico* |
| Ch | Law Reports, Chancery |
| Ch D | Chancery Division of the High Court |
| Ch. mixte | Cour de Cassation, Mixed Chambers |
| Ch. réun. | Cour de Cassation, Joined Chambers |
| CI | *Contratto e impresa* |
| Cir. | Circuit Court |
| CJ | *Colectânea de Jurisprudência* |
| Cm. | Command Paper |
| Cmnd | Command Papers, 5th series |
| c. Nap. | *Code Napoléon* |
| CP | *Corte di Cassazione penale* |
| C&P | Carrington & Payne's Nisi Prius Reports |
| Curr. Legal Prob. | Current Legal Problems |
| D | *Dike* |
| | *Recueil Dalloz et Sirey* |
| DA | *Recueil analitique Dalloz* |
| DAR | *Deutsches Autorecht* |
| DB | *Der Betrieb* |
| DC | Divisional Court |
| | *Recueil critique Dalloz* |
| DF | *Diritto fallimentare* |
| DH | *Recueil hebdomadaire Dalloz* |
| Dig. | Digest of Justinian |
| Dig. It. | *Digesto Italiano* |
| DII | *Diritto informazione e informatica* |
| Dir. e Prat. Lav. | *Diritto e pratica del lavow* |
| DJZ | *Deutsche Juristenzeitung* |
| d.lgvo. | *Decreto legislativo* |
| DP | *Recueil périodique et critique Dalloz* (until 1940) |
| d.p.r. | *Decreto Presidente della Repubblica* |
| DR | *Danno e responsabilità* |
| | *Deutsches Recht* |
| D. somm. | *Recueil Dalloz, Dalloz-Sirey, Sommaires Commentés* |
| East | East's Term Reports, King's Bench |
| ecolex | *Ecolex – Fachzeitschrift für Wirtschaftsrecht* |
| EEDSTh | *Epistimoniki Epetiris Dikigorikou Sillogou Thessalonikis* |
| EEmbD | *Epitheorisi Emborikou Dikaiou* |

| | |
|---|---|
| EEN | Efimeris Ellinon Nomikon |
| EErgD or EED | Epitheorisi Ergatikou Dikaiou |
| EfAth | Efeteio Athinon |
| EfSlg | Ehe- und familienrechtliche Entscheidungen |
| EfThes | Efeteio Thessalonikis |
| EGLR | Estates Gazette Law Reports |
| EKHG | Eisenbahn- und Kraftfahrzeug-Haftpflichtgesetz |
| El & Bl | Ellis & Blackburn's Queen's Bench Reports |
| EllDni | Helliniki Dikaiosyni |
| EmbN | Emporikos Nomos |
| ER | English Reports |
| ErmAK | Commentary interpreting the Civil Code (Greece) |
| EuGRZ | Europäische Grundrechte Zeitschrift |
| EuZW | Europäische Zeitschrift für Wirtschaftsrecht |
| eV | eingetragener Verein |
| EvBl | Evidenzblatt |
| Ex | Court of Exchequer |
| Ex. Ch. | Court of Exchequer Chamber |
| Fam. Law | Family Law |
| FI | Il Foro Italiano |
| FLR | Family Law Reports |
| ForstG | Forstgesetz |
| FP | Il Foro Padano |
| FSR | Fleet Street Reports |
| GA | Goltdammer's Archiv für Strafrecht |
| Gaz. Pal. | Gazette du Palais |
| GC | Giustizia civile |
| GenTG | Gentechnikgesetz |
| GG | Grundgesetz |
| GI | Giurisprudenza Italiana |
| GlUNF | Sammlung von Entscheidungen des k.k. Obersten Gerichtshofes, Neue Folge |
| Giur. Comm. | Giurisprudenza commerciale |
| GM | Giurisprudenza di merito |
| GmbH | Gesellschaft mit beschränkter Haftung |
| GU | Gazzetta Ufficiale |
| HaftpltG | Haftpflichtgesetz |
| HC | High Court |
| HD | Högsta domstolen |
| HdBW | Handbuch des Bau- und Wohnungsrechts |

| | |
|---|---|
| HGB | Handelsgesetzbuch |
| HL | House of Lords |
| HLR | Housing Law Reports |
| HR | Hoge Raad der Nederlanden |
| ICLQ | International and Comparative Law Quarterly |
| ICR | Industrial Cases Reports |
| ILRM | Irish Law Reports Monthly |
| IPRax | Praxis des internationalen Privat- und Verfahrensrechts |
| IR | Irish Reports |
| JBl | Juristische Blätter |
| JCP | Semaine Juridique or Juris-classeur périodique, Edition générale |
| JCP(E) | Juris-classeur périodique, Edition Entreprise |
| JLSS | Journal of the Law Society of Scotland |
| Jour. Soc. lég. comp. | Journées de la Société de législation comparée |
| JR | Juristische Rundschau |
| JT | Journal des tribunaux |
| Juris-Data | Recueil Dalloz, Juris-Data |
| JuS | Juristische Schulung |
| JZ | Juristenzeitung |
| KB | King's Bench |
| | Koninklijk Besluit |
| KBD | King's Bench Division |
| KCLJ | King's College Law Journal |
| KKO | Korkein oikeus |
| LAG | Landesarbeitsgericht |
| LC | Lord Chancellor |
| Leb. | Recueil des décisions du Conseil d'État (Recueil Lebon) |
| LM | Lindenmaier-Möhring, Nachschlagewerk des Bundesgerichtshofes |
| LQR | Law Quarterly Review |
| LR | Law Reports |
| LuftVG | Luftverkehrsgesetz |
| M | Macpherson's Series, Court of Session Reports |
| Macq | Macqueen's Scots Appeal Cases |
| MDR | Monatsschrift für Deutsches Recht |
| MGC | Giustizia civile: massimario annotato della Cassazione |

| | |
|---|---|
| MGLav. | Massimario Giustizia Lavoro |
| MinD | Ministerial Decision |
| MJ | Maastricht Journal of European and Comparative Law |
| Mod. LR | Modern Law Review |
| MprThes | Monomeles Protdikeio Thesalonikis |
| MR | Master of the Rolls |
| M & R | Milieu en Recht |
| NBW | Nieuw Burgerlijk Wetboek |
| NDik | Neon Dikaion |
| NGCC | Nuova giurisprudenza civile commentata |
| NILR | Netherlands International Law Review |
| NJ | Nederlandse Jurisprudentie |
| NJA | Nytt Juridiskt Arkiv avd.I |
| NJB | Nederlands Juristenblad |
| NJW | Neue juristische Wochenschrift |
| NJW-RR | Neue juristische Wochenschrift – Rechtsprechungsreport Zivilrecht |
| NoB | Nomiko Vima |
| NRDCo | Nuora Rivista di diritto Commerciale |
| NTBR | Kwartaalbericht Nieuw BW |
| N.V. | Naamloze Vennootschap |
| NZ | Notariatszeitung |
| NZA | Neue Zeitschrift für Arbeits- und Sozialrecht |
| NZV | Neue Zeitschrift für Verkehrsrecht |
| ÖBA | Österreichisches Bankarchiv |
| ÖBl | Österreichische Blätter für gewerblichen Rechtsschutz und Urheberrecht |
| OGH | Oberster Gerichtshof |
| OJ | Official Journal (of the EC/EU) |
| OJLS | Oxford Journal of Legal Studies |
| ÖJZ | Österreichische Juristenzeitung |
| OLG | Oberlandesgericht |
| OR | Pasicrisie/Pasinomie |
| PC | Judicial Committee of the Privy Council Penal Code |
| Pin Chr | Pinika Chronika |
| PrD | Presidential Decree |
| Pret. | Pretura |

| | |
|---|---|
| ProdHaftG | *Produkthaftungsgesetz* |
| Pub L | *Public Law* |
| pVV | *positive Vertragsverletzung* |
| QB | *Queen's Bench Reports* |
| QBD | *Queen's Bench Division of the High Court* |
| R | *Rettie* |
| Rass DC | *Rassegna di diritto civile* |
| RCDP | *Rivista critica di diritto privato* |
| RCJB | *Revue critique de jurisprudence belge* |
| RCP | *Responsabilità civile e previdenza* |
| R.D. | *Royal Decree* |
| Rd.-Nr. | *Randnummer* |
| RDC/RDComm. | *Rivista di diritto commerciale* |
| RdW | *Österreichisches Recht der Wirtschaft* |
| Rec. | *Recueil des décisions du Conseil d'État* |
| Rep.Not.Defr. | *Répertoire du notariat Defrénois* |
| Req. | *Cour de Cassation, chambre des requêtes* |
| Resp. Ass. | *Responsabilité civile et assurances* |
| Rev. trim. dr. civ. | *Revue trimestrielle de droit civil* |
| RFDA | *Revue française de droit administratif* |
| RFL | *Rivista Finanza Locale* |
| RG | *Reichsgericht* |
| RGAR | *Revue générale des assurances et des responsabilités* |
| RGBl | *Reichsgesetzblatt* |
| RGCirc. | *Rivista giuridica circolazione e trasporti* |
| RGEnel | *Rassegna giuridica Enel* |
| RGRK | *Reichsgerichtsrätekommentar* |
| RGZ | *Entscheidungen des Reichsgerichtes in Zivilsachen* |
| RHDI | *Revue hellénique de droit international* |
| RHG | *Reichshaftpflichtgesetz* |
| RICO | *Racketeer-Influenced and Corrupt Organizations* |
| RIDC | *Revue internationale de droit comparé* |
| Riv. dir. civ. | *Rivista di diritto civile* |
| Riv.Soc. | *Rivista delle Società* |
| Riv. trim. dir. civ. | *Rivista trimestrale di diritto e procedura civile* |
| RM Themis | *Rechtsgeleerd Magazijn Themis* |
| RohrlG | *Rohrleitungsgesetz* |
| RSC | *Rules of the Supreme Court* |
| RTDCiv. | *Revue trimestrielle de droit civil* |

| | |
|---|---|
| RTR | Road Traffic Reports |
| RvdW | Rechtspraak van de Week |
| RW | Rechtskundig Weekblad |
| RZ | Richterzeitung |
| S | Recueil Sirey (until 1962) |
| SA | Société Anonyme |
| S. Jur. | Recueil Dalloz, Sirey, Jurisprudence |
| SkadestL | Skadeståndslag |
| SLT | Scottish Law Times Reports |
| SOU | Statens offentlig utredning |
| StGB | Strafgesetzbuch |
| STJ | Supremo Tribunal de Justiça |
| StPO | Strafprozeßordnung |
| StVG | Straßenverkehrsgesetz |
| StVO | Straßenverkehrsordnung |
| StVZO | Straßenverkehrszulassungsordnung |
| SU | Sezioni Unite |
| SV | Sozialversicherungsrechtliche Entscheidungssammlung |
| SZ | Entscheidungen des österreichischen Obersten Gerichtshofes in Zivilsachen |
| T | Temi |
| TBBR | Tijdschrift voor Belgisch burgerlijk recht |
| TBP | Tijdschrift voor bestuurswetenschappen en publiek recht |
| TGI | Tribunal de grande instance |
| Them | Themis |
| Trib. | Tribunal |
| Trib. com. Paris | Tribunal de chambre commerciale et financière à Paris |
| T Romana | Temi Romana |
| TvC | Tijdschrift voor Consumentenrecht |
| TVvS | Maandblad voor ondernemingsrecht en rechtspersonen |
| UCC | Uniform Commercial Code |
| UHG | Umwelthaftungsgesetz |
| UWG | Gesetz gegen unlauteren Wettbewerb |
| VersR | Versicherungsrecht |
| VersVG | Versicherungsvertragsgesetz |

| | |
|---|---|
| VR | *Verkeersrecht* |
| WBl | *Wirtschaftsrechtliche Blätter* |
| WHG | *Wasserhaushaltsgesetz* |
| WLR | *Weekly Law Reports* |
| WM | *Wertpapiermitteilungen* |
| WPNR | *Weekblad voor privaatrecht, notariaat en registratie* |
| ZAS | *Zeitschrift für Arbeits- und Sozialrecht* |
| ZEuP | *Zeitschrift für Europäisches Privatrecht* |
| ZIP | *Zeitschrift für Wirtschaftsrecht* |
| ZPO | *Zivilprozeßordnung* |
| ZRP | *Zeitschrift für Rechtspolitik* |
| ZVR | *Zeitschrift für Verkehrsrecht* |
| ZZP | *Zeitschrift für Zivilprozess* |

PART I • SITUATING THE FRONTIER

# 1 The notion of pure economic loss and its setting

MAURO BUSSANI AND VERNON VALENTINE PALMER

## Introduction

Pure economic loss is one of the most discussed topics of European tort law scholarship. Fascination with the subject (which may at first glance appear dry and technical) has developed into a wealth of literature about this frontier notion.[1] It stands at the cutting edge of many questions: how far can tort liability expand without imposing excessive burdens upon individual activity (or, as some may wish, to what extent should tort rules be compatible with the market orientation of the legal system)?[2] How should the tort law of the twenty-first century – or the provisions of a projected European code – approach this issue? As a

---

[1] The literature is overwhelmingly weighted to those countries where the concept is well recognized by practitioners, judge and scholars. See E. K. Banakas, *Civil Liability for Pure Economic Loss* (Kluwer, 1996); J. M. Barendrecht, 'Pure Economic Loss in the Netherlands', in E. H. Hondius (ed.) *Netherlands Reports to the Fifteenth International Congress of Comparative Law* (1998), at pp. 115–35; R. Bernstein, *Economic Loss* (2nd edn, Sweet & Maxwell, London, 1998); B. Feldthusen, *Economic Negligence: The Recovery of Pure Economic Loss* (Carswell, 1989); J. Kleineman, *Ren förmögenhetsskada* (1987); C. Lapoyade Deschamps, 'La reparation du prejudice pur en droit français' in Banakas, *Civil Liability*, pp. 89–101; W. Posch and B. Schilcher, 'Civil Liability for Pure Economic Loss: An Austrian Perspective', in Banakas, *Civil Liability*, at pp. 149–76; J. Spier (ed.) *The Limits of Liability: Keeping the Floodgates Shut* (Kluwer, 1996) (discussion of eight 'Tilburg Hypotheticals' – four of which concern pure economic loss); C. von Bar, 'Liability for Information and Opinions Causing Pure Economic Loss to Third Parties: A Comparison of English and German Case Law', in B. Markesinis (ed.) *The Gradual Convergence* (Oxford University Press, Oxford, 1994), pp. 99 ff.; B. Markesinis, *The German Law of Obligations*, vol. II *The Law of Torts* (3rd edn, Oxford University Press, Oxford, 1997); J. M. Thomson, 'Delictual Liability for Pure Economic Loss: Recent Developments', 1995 SLT 139; J. Herbots, 'Le "duty of care" et le dommage purement financier en droit comparé', (1985) 62 *Revue de Droit International et de Droit Comparé* 7–33; L. Khoury, 'The Liability of Auditors Beyond Their Clients: A Comparative Study', (2001) 46 *McGill Law Journal* 413.

[2] P. Benson, 'The Basis for Excluding Liability for Economic Loss in Tort Law', in D. G. Owen, *The Philosophical Foundations of Tort Law* (Clarendon, Oxford, 1995), pp. 427, 431.

matter of policy, should the recovery of pure economic loss be the domain principally of the law of contract? To these and others we add our own modest question: is there a common core of principles, policies and rules governing tortious liability for pure economic loss in Europe? There has never been a universally accepted definition of 'pure economic loss'. Perhaps the simplest reason is that a number of legal systems neither recognize the legal category nor distinguish it as an autonomous form of damage. Nevertheless, where the concept is recognized, as in Germany and common law systems, it is apparently associated with a rule of no liability and there a definition is likely to be found.[3] The contrasting approaches here obviously do not follow the familiar common law/civil law divide, for civil law is itself divided to some extent over this question.

Our own approach in this study was to make no supposition in advance about the nature or definition of this notion. We hoped it might be possible to allow a neutral, fact-based questionnaire to flush out the rules and responses of each national system. Therefore, in framing the questionnaire we did not hesitate to mix into the facts instances of property damage, personal injury and other infringements that particular traditions may regard as absolute rights (i.e. rights opposable to the world at large – *erga omnes*). In this way we were attempting to clarify the grey zones that exist between recoverable and non-recoverable loss. Consistent with the Cornell methodology,[4] the questionnaire alleges facts

---

The same author, articulating a well-known *tòpos* among tort lawyers (see e.g. G. Viney, 'Introduction à la responsabilité', in J. Ghestin (ed.), *Traité de droit civil* (1995), p. 21; P. G. Monateri, *La responsabilità civile* (UTET, Turin, 1998) pp. 8 ff.), writes: '[T]he fact that every individual is somewhere and is making use of some external objects, with the result that he or his property is put into relation with them and is subject to being affected by conduct that affects them, is an inevitable incident of being active in the world ... [considered as] beings who exist in space and time and who are inescapably active and purposive, persons are necessarily and always connected in manifold ways with other things which they can affect and which in turn can affect them as part of a causal sequence.' Benson, 'Excluding Liability', at p. 443 (emphasis and footnotes omitted).

[3] Gary Schwartz refers to 'the general economic loss no liability doctrine' in his essay 'The Economic Loss Doctrine in American Tort Law: Assessing the Recent Experience', in Banakas *Civil Liability*, at pp. 103–30.

[4] The 'Cornell methodology' refers to the research project on 'Formation of Contracts' which Rudolph Schlesinger directed from 1957–68, R. B. Schlesinger (ed.), *Formation of Contracts* (2 vols, Oceana, New York, 1968). For Schlesinger's later views, see 'The Past and Future of Comparative Law', (1995) 43 *American Journal of Comparative Law* 477, 479. See also M. Bussani and U. Mattei, 'The Common Core Approach to European Private Law', (1997–98) 3 *Columbia Journal of European Law* 339 and, M. Bussani and U. Mattei, 'Le fonds commun du droit privé Européen', (2000) 52 *Revue Internationale de Droit Comparé* 29. M. Bussani, 'Current Trends in European Comparative Law: The Common Core Approach', in (1998) 21 *Hastings International and Comparative Law Review* 785.

and avoids the use of what could be classified as legal artifacts such as the expression 'pure economic loss' itself. Because there is no recognition of the term in some systems, and in any event less than complete consensus about its meanings in others, we rigorously excluded all use of the term in the hypotheticals.

For example, in the not-so-hypothetical 'cable cases', we posed variant forms of loss to see where and when the negative objection, if any, arises. To throw light on the rule from different patrimonial angles, we took the same facts but varied the victim, or varied the tortfeasor's state of mind.[5] Obtaining these permutations and combinations in collecting the data was an important objective of this study.[6]

## Pure vs. consequential economic loss

The outcome of the research about the underlying notion of 'pure economic loss' can be shortly stated as follows. What is made clear by the national reports is twofold: the negative cast and the patrimonial character of that loss. In countries where the term is well recognized, its meaning is essentially explained in a negative way. It is loss without antecedent harm to plaintiff's person or property. Here the word 'pure' plays a central role, for if there is economic loss that is connected to the slightest damage to person or property of the plaintiff (provided that all other conditions of liability are met) then the latter is called *consequential* economic loss and the whole set of damages may be recovered without question.[7] *Consequential* economic loss (sometimes also termed

---

[5] Thus the same negligent act might cause recoverable physical damage to one, but pure economic loss to another which is non-recoverable unless, perhaps, the act was intentional. The instructions to the national reporters asked them to assume that the conduct in the hypothetical was intentional if this would produce a significantly different result. It was recognized that in some cases the claimant might not be entitled to recover for pure economic loss unless in fact the act were intentional.

[6] See particularly, as examples of this factual flexibility, Cases 6 ('The Infected Cow'), 12 ('Double Sale') and 15 ('A Closed Motorway – The Value of Time'). These are the same reasons that account also for the choice of not referring to any pigeonhole framework (such as the ones used, e.g., by I. Englard, *The Philosophy of Tort Law* (Dartmouth, Aldershot, 1993), pp. 211 ff.; Benson, 'Excluding Liability for Economic Loss', at 427 ff.; see also H. Kötz, 'Economic Loss in Tort and Contract', (1994) 58 *Rabels Zeitschrift für ausländisches und internationales Privatrecht* 3, 423; P. Cane, 'Economic Loss in Tort and Contract', (1994) 58 *Rabels Zeitschrift für ausländisches und internationales Privatrecht* 3, at 429 ff.) in presenting the study of the cases.

[7] Perhaps another way to describe pure economic loss is to say that it does not arise as a consequence of some earlier physical loss, and it is not a court's substituted value for physical loss.

parasitic loss[8]) is recoverable because it presupposes the existence of physical injuries, whereas pure economic loss strikes the victim's wallet and nothing else. In Sweden, where the legislator says that only victims of crimes may recover for pure economic loss, the Tort Liability Act 1972, §2, defines the notion exactly in these terms: 'In the present act, "pure economic loss" (*ren förmögenhetsskada*) means such economic loss as arises without connection to personal injury or property damage to anyone.'[9] A similar definition seems to prevail in England and Germany.[10]

One will discern from these preliminary remarks that the distinction under discussion is highly technical, perhaps even artificial. This impression is based upon two technical features of the exclusionary rule. The first feature is that 'consequential' economic loss only describes a relationship of cause and effect *within the same patrimony* (plaintiff's). All relation of cause and effect running *between patrimonies* is technically excluded. Put another way, when pecuniary loss is described as 'pure' (rather than 'consequential') it is apparent that each patrimony is viewed as an interruption of causation. For example, an injury to B (say, the breadwinner of the family) may have an immediate and foreseeable economic consequence upon A (his dependent child). Yet this causal impact is disregarded by the way in which our subject is defined. The child's loss of support will not be called 'consequential' economic loss, though clearly it did arise as a 'consequence' of physical injury to a parent. It is apparent, then, that those legal systems which employ these labels conceive of economic loss as an isolated phenomenon, as if plaintiff's patrimony were a separate world, cut off from all others. It is also apparent that this logic defies economic and social reality. In the real world, 'a practically unlimited range of interests are intertwined in an almost unlimited variety of ways'.[11] The affairs of economic actors are highly interdependent, connected to one another by a web of rights

---

[8] For this usage, see W. L. Prosser, W. P. Keeton, *On the Law of Torts* (5th edn, 1984), 43, at 291.

[9] W. van Gerven, J. Lever and P. Larouche (eds.), *Tort Law: Scope of Protection* (Hart, Oxford, 1998), p. 44.

[10] See Lord Denning's statement that 'it is better to disallow economic loss altogether at any rate when it stands alone, independent of any physical damage'. *Spartan Steel & Alloys Ltd v. Martin & Co. Ltd* [1973] QB 27, (1972) 3 All ER 557. Regarding *reiner vermögensschaden*, van Gerven et al., *Tort Law*, at p. 43, speaks of a 'worsening of one's overall economic position (loss of profit, diminution in the value of property, etc.) that is not directly consequential upon injury to the person or damage to a particular piece of property'.

[11] Benson, 'Excluding Liability for Economic Loss', at p. 431.

and duties that bind together contractual, proprietary and any other sort of legal interests. In these circumstances it is reasonably foreseeable that damage to any one interest may affect other interests. Indeed, it has been rightly said that 'no reverberation from the initial damage, so long as it arises through this interdependence of interests, can intelligibly be distinguished as extraordinary or unforeseeable'.[12] Yet the inevitable effect (of what we might call the exclusionary rule's 'atomistic' approach to causation) is that the scope of 'consequential' loss is artificially narrow, and accordingly the incidence of 'pure' economic loss is greatly multiplied.

A second technical aspect is that, although all countries following the exclusionary rule may be in 'acoustical' agreement on the proposition that 'consequential loss' is recoverable, they actually do not agree in concrete instances how it will be applied. Since consequential loss is a causal construct influenced (in its ultimate results) by policy considerations, it is perhaps unsurprising to find divergent interpretation at the national level. Some national courts have developed rules that require a more stringent connection between antecedent physical loss and the economic harm which results from it. Under such rules the court may conclude that plaintiff's loss was 'pure' (hence unrecoverable) because there was insufficient relation to prior physical harm sustained by plaintiff. Yet judges in other systems, employing less exigent notions, may deem the same loss 'consequential' and thereby permit its recovery.[13]

Despite the foregoing caveats about the artificial and technical aspects of this concept, we must not lose sight of the fact that consequential economic loss (and for the purpose of this generalization we apply this term even to systems which do not actually use it) is in principle recoverable in every European system within this study – whether the source of the loss is intentional or negligent conduct, or an activity subject to strict liability. Ignoring for the moment divergent European views toward the recoverability of 'pure' economic loss, here at least is an area of common ground that is worth noting.

Furthermore, the recoverability of economic loss, even when 'pure', is not regarded as doubtful when such loss stems from the infringement

---

[12] Ibid.
[13] For further details, see Editors' Comparative Comments under Cases 1 ('Cable I – The Blackout') and 9 ('Fire in the Projection Booth'). Cf. C. von Bar, *The Common European Law of Torts*, vol. II (Oxford University Press, Oxford, 2000), pp. 30–5, 487–9.

of statutorily protected interests, such as those we will meet in our case studies,[14] and those protected by antitrust, copyright and patent laws.[15]

Taken in the aggregate, the above considerations lead us to say that consequential loss and 'pure' economic loss are not different in kind or in principle, but distinguishable only by the circumstances in which they originate and the technical limits which have been imposed on their recoverability.[16]

---

[14] See especially the answers to Case 4 ('Convalescing Employee'). Cf. C. von Bar, *Common European Law of Torts*, II, pp. 54–6.

[15] The same could be said as to some other fields, particularly the field of 'business torts'. Although legal systems such as France, the Netherlands, UK and Portugal handle these problems with the help of the general law of obligations (the sixth book of the Dutch Civil Code devotes an entire chapter to unfair advertising), these subjects are not dealt with here. Since the rules in these areas largely depend on policy factors which are only partially common to our field and would deserve detailed investigation, reasons of space compelled the editors to place limits on the research. For a general survey, C. von Bar, *Common European Law of Torts*, II, pp. 4–200, 245–9 and, more closely related to our issue, 52–6; van Gerven et al., *Tort Law*, (Hart, Oxford, 2000), pp. 208–48, 358–94.

[16] It is of interest to note that breach of European Community law may entail liability for pure economic loss. The liability of the Community institutions and its servants in the performance of their duties finds its source in art. 288(2) of the EC Treaty. The liability of a Member State has its origins in the case law of the European Court of Justice (ECJ), particularly the preliminary rulings pursuant to art. 234 of the EC Treaty. It is true that under these provisions, plaintiffs can recover only when they fall within a group of persons which the infringed provision was designed to protect, but no 'in principle' restriction is made regarding the interests that are protected. Indeed, since Community law is primarily concerned with economic matters, breaches of Community law will typically result in economic or purely economic losses. The compensability of these losses when caused by Community institutions has been clearly set forth in an ECJ case, Case C-104/89, 19 May 1992, *Mulder* v. *Council*, [1992] ECR I–3061. With regard to the Member States, their liability has been clearly endorsed by ECJ Case C-49/93, 5 March 1996, *Brasserie du Pêcheur* v. *Germany*, R v. *Secretary of State for Transport, ex p. Factortame*, [1996] ECR I–1029 (wherein the ECJ explicitly rejects the use of German and English national rules which would have prevented individuals from benefiting from the use of Community law to impose liability on Member States. The rejection was particularly important in the case of the English rule requiring proof akin to abuse of power to establish the tort of misfeasance in public office, and in the case of the German hierarchy of protected interests under BGB § 823. For a comparative survey, see van Gerven et al., *Tort Law*, (2000), at p. 889 ff; see *passim*, T. Heukels and A. McDonnell (eds.), *The Action for Damages in Community Law* (Kluwer, The Hague, 1997); P. Craig, 'Once More Unto the Breach: The Community, the State and Damages Liability', (1997) 113 LQR 67. See also Markesinis, *German Law of Obligations*, p. 902 ff.

It is a different, and still open issue, whether individuals are entitled to compensation under national law when other individuals infringe Community law and thereby cause economic loss. Under the laws of the Member States a right to recovery is generally acknowledged in cases of breach of a Community law provision which imposes direct obligations upon individuals – such as Arts. 81 and 82 of the EC

## Actor's state of mind: intention vs. negligence

The exclusionary rule is associated with economic loss caused by negligent behaviour, not intentional wrongdoing. European systems do not begin to diverge until the question becomes one of liability for negligence. Here is a kind of rubicon which some fear to cross and others blithely dismiss. However, all systems agree that intentionally inflicted pure economic loss is recoverable in circumstances where the conduct in question is regarded as culpable, immoral or contrary to public policy. The significance of this point is of more practical importance than it may appear at first sight. Its range of application may be somewhat greater than the narrow, infrequent form of liability which the words 'intentionally inflicted' harm suggests. In some systems a broad, flexible meaning is given to the 'intention' element.[17] Furthermore, though harder to prove than negligence, the incidence of financial fraud is not a rare occurrence. A consistent rule across Europe is therefore an important protection. Secondly, we think it is interesting to observe from the comparative point of view that the shift to higher degrees of culpability tends to broaden the scope of recovery in all systems. This at least suggests that the exclusionary rule should not be conceived as a simple rule based solely on the nature of plaintiff's damage. The material nature of the loss, in our view, is no more than one element in a complex balancing act which decides where and when limits will be imposed in tort. To tailor reasonable limits, judges and legislators must consider other important factors as well, including the actor's state of mind.[18]

---

Treaty, or other provisions having the so-called 'horizontal' direct effect: see W. van Gerven, 'Bridging the Unbridgeable: Community and National Tort Laws after Francovich and Brasserie', (1996) 45 ICLQ 507 and, recently, upholding 'horizontal' direct effect of arts. 81 and 82 of the EC Treaty, *Courage Ltd* v. *Bernard Crehan* and *Bernard Crehan* v. *Courage Ltd and Others*: ECJ, judgment of 20 September 2001, reference for a preliminary ruling: Court of Appeal (England and Wales) (Civil Division) United Kingdom, Case C-453/99, [2000] ECR I-7499.

[17] See, e.g. von Bar 'Liability for Information', at 104.

[18] The existence of a balancing process is not so apparent in open, liberal systems such as the French which appear to make little use of the distinction between intentional and careless fault, but the complex interaction of scienter with other factors clearly surfaces in the English and German systems. In those systems, where harm is intentionally inflicted, restrictions on the recoverability of the type of harm are dropped, and in addition, concepts of remoteness of causation are relaxed. As David Howarth correctly notes, the overall result is that intentionality removes restrictions on liability that do not exist in the first place in other jurisdictions; 'The General Conditions of Unlawfulness', in A. Hartkamp, M. Hesselink, E. Hondius, C. Joustra and E. du Perron (eds.), *Towards a European Civil Code* (2nd edn, Kluwer, 1998), at p. 411.

## The standard cases: a taxonomy

Broadly speaking, pure economic loss arises out of the interdependence of relationships and interests in the modern world. These relationships are sometimes two-dimensional and other times three-dimensional. In this section we attempt to draw up a taxonomy of the principal ways in which it arises within such relationships. Our list will not exhaust all the conceivable ways in which such damage may arise. Our only interest lies in tracing the most recurrent and typical patterns which we refer to as 'standard cases'. Although we have sometimes borrowed and at other times given new names to these standard situations, we have not attempted to explain or employ all of the descriptive labels that writers and judges have used. These diverse and contradictory ideas are not always compatible with the results of our own study and would serve no purpose here. With these provisos in mind, we venture to set forth four categories that seem to be functionally and relationally distinct.[19]

### Ricochet loss

'Ricochet loss' classically arises when physical damage is done to the property or person of one party, and that loss in turn causes the impairment of a plaintiff's right. This situation is three-dimensional and certain authors call it 'relational economic loss'.[20] A direct victim sustains physical damage of some kind, while plaintiff is a secondary victim who incurs only economic harm. To illustrate: A has a contract to tow B's ship. C's negligent act of sinking the ship makes it impossible for A to perform his contract and thus deprives him of expected profits. A's financial loss is the ricochet effect of C's negligence toward B. The loss is purely economic, since no property interest of A's has been impaired.[21] A ricochet loss can also arise from the impairment of an employment contract. For example, B is a key employee in A's business or sporting team. C's negligent driving leads to B's death or incapacity, thus causing A's

---

[19] For a longer taxonomic list consisting of eight categories (in which we think there is considerable overlap), see W. Bishop and J. Sutton, 'Efficiency and Justice in Tort Damages: The Shortcomings of the Pecuniary Loss Rule', (1986) 15 *Journal of Legal Studies* 347, 360–61. Benson's taxonomy consists of five situations, two of which he calls 'exclusionary situations'. His three other situations are called 'non-exclusionary', Benson, 'Excluding Liability for Economic Loss', at pp. 427–30.

[20] See this terminology and analysis in Bernstein, *Economic Loss*, pp. 163 ff. and Feldthusen, *Economic Negligence*, pp. 199 ff.

[21] The example closely follows *La Société Anonyme de Remorquage à Helice v. Bennets* [1911] 1 KB 243.

team or business to lose profits and revenues. Here B's injury is physical, but A's loss is purely financial. The 'Cable Cases',[22] the *Meroni* Case,[23] and certain other hypotheticals studied in this volume[24] are also variations of ricochet harm. Concern about the indeterminate number and size of the claims for losses is often associated with cases falling within this category.

*Transferred loss*

Here, C causes physical damage to B's property or person, but a contract between A and B (or the law itself) transfers a loss that would ordinarily be B's onto A. Thus a loss *ordinarily falling on the primary victim* is passed on to a secondary victim. The transfer of the loss from its 'natural' to an 'accidental' bearer differentiates this from a case of ricochet loss, where the damage in question is not transferred but is a distinct damage to the interests of the secondary victim.[25] These transfers frequently result from leases, sales, insurance agreements and other contracts that separate property rights from rights of use or specifically reallocate risk bearing. To illustrate, A is time charterer of a ship owned by B. The day before the time charter is to go into effect and while the ship is in B's possession, C negligently damages the ship's propeller, thus necessitating repairs and a two-week delay, which causes A to lose all use of the ship. Here B suffers property damage, and ordinarily B as owner would recover for the consequential loss of the ship's use, but the right of use had been transferred to A by the boat charter. So A's loss is purely pecuniary because he has no antecedent property loss.[26] A similar effect can result under a sales contract which reserves title in B (seller) while the goods are in shipment, but places the risk of loss in transit upon the buyer A. If the goods (still technically owned by B)[27] are damaged in

---

[22] See e.g. *Spartan Steel & Alloys* v. *Martin & Co. Ltd.* [1973] QB 27 and Cases 1 ('Cable I – The Blackout'), 2 ('Cable II – Factory Shutdown'), 3 ('Cable III – The Day-to-Day Workers').
[23] *Torino Calcio SpA* v. *Romero*, Cass. Civ., SU 26.1.1971, no. 174, GI, 1971, I, 1, 681. Case 5 ('Requiem for an Italian All Star') is modelled upon the *Meroni* case.
[24] See Case 10 ('The Dutiful Wife').
[25] This category receives extensive consideration in von Bar, *Common European Law of Torts*, I, pp. 507–512.
[26] The illustration is based upon *Robins Dry Dock* v. *Flint*, 13 F 2d 3 (2nd Cir. 1926), 275 US 303 (1927) as well as Case 8 ('The Cancelled Cruise').
[27] As is well known, who should be called the 'owner' of goods in shipment depends on the law applicable to the transfer of ownership, and above all on the validity and extent of the principle of transfer of possession. See von Bar, *Common European Law of Torts*, at p. 509, fn. 499.

transit by the carrier's negligence, then a loss normally incurred by the owner has been transferred to A. A's loss is purely financial since he has no property interest in the goods.[28]

A similar result is reached when the transfer occurs by operation of law. For example B, A's employee, may be injured by the negligent driving of C and thus find himself unable to work for three months. Nevertheless, a statute requires A to continue to pay B's salary, even though no work is received in return. Thus what ordinarily would have been B's loss is statutorily transferred to A as a combined result of C's negligence and the effects of the pay continuation statute.[29]

Transferred loss cases are liability neutral from the perspective of the tortfeasor and should avoid fears of indeterminate liability. An additional argument in favour of an award of compensation is that the tortfeasor who is clearly liable to the primary victim should not benefit from the accidental operation of rules which by pure chance exclude him from liability. According to von Bar, the concept of transferred loss is intended 'to prevent someone appealing to rules whose purpose is not to protect that person, but to protect others'.[30]

## Closure of public markets, transportation corridors and public infrastructures

Here, economic loss arises without a previous injury to anyone's property or person. There may be physical damage, but it is to 'unowned resources' that lie in the public domain.[31] A single negligent act may necessitate the closure of markets, highways and shipping lanes which no person owns, yet the closure inflicts economic loss directly on individuals whose livelihoods closely depend upon the use of these facilities. This category raises the greatest concern about liability to an indeterminate class in an indeterminate amount. A financial ripple effect is then at its height. To illustrate: C negligently spills chemicals into a river, and all traffic on the waterway is suspended for two weeks during a clean-up effort. As a result, shippers must take more expensive overland routes, and marinas, boat suppliers, hotel operators and commercial

---

[28] This illustration is based upon *The Aliakmon* [1985] 2 All ER 44.
[29] The example is taken from Case 4 ('Convalescing Employee').
[30] Von Bar, *Common European Law of Torts*, I, pp. 510–511.
[31] V. Goldberg, 'Recovery For Economic Loss Following the Exxon Valdez Oil Spill', (1994) 23 *Journal of Legal Studies* 1, 37.

fishermen in the area suffer severe economic loss.³² A similar chain of loss may arise when C negligently allows infected cattle to escape from his premises, and the government must order all cattle and meat markets to close. As a result broad classes of plaintiffs will suffer pure economic loss, including cattle breeders who are unable to sell their stock and butchers who are unable to obtain supplies.³³ As we note below, the 'floodgates' argument acquires great force in such contexts.

*Reliance upon flawed data, advice or professional services*

Those who furnish advice, prepare data or render services concerning financial matters often understand that the information will be furnished to a client and then relied upon by third persons with whom they have no contractual relation. If the advice, data or services are carelessly compiled or executed, this may not necessarily breach the provider's contract with their client (even if there is breach, the damage will usually be strictly financial) but the relying third party will sustain pure pecuniary loss. For example: C, an accountant, carelessly conducts an audit of B, a publicly traded company, and vastly overstates the company's net financial worth. Relying upon the accuracy of the audit, investor A buys shares in B at twice their actual value.³⁴ Here, A's loss arises not in consequence of physical damage to B, but on the basis of misplaced reliance.³⁵ Similarly, erroneous information about a

---

³² This illustration resembles the facts of Case 15 ('A Closed Motorway – The Value of Time') as well as *Louisiana ex rel. Guste* v. *M/V Testbank* (*The Testbank*), 752 F 2d 1019 (1985).

³³ See the facts in Case 6 ('The Infected Cow') and the case of *Weller* v. *Foot and Mouth Disease Research Inst.* [1966] 1 QB 569.

³⁴ See Case 17 ('Auditor's Liability').

³⁵ According to Tony Honoré, losses attributed to plaintiffs' 'reliance' pose a causation issue which is different in kind to causation in the context of physical damage. His discussion seems pertinent to the concern of some that this category of pure economic loss opens the floodgates of liability. When a person is said to 'rely' on another's statement, he or she often has two or more (typically many more) reasons or motives for reaching a decision and acting on it. The question whether A's statement 'caused' B's response is highly indeterminate. A potential investor in Eldorado Mines, for example, may be influenced by a false statement in a prospectus as well as by advice from his stockbroker, by his own review of the company books, and so forth. How are we to say that from among all these reasons that the false statement in the prospectus 'caused' his financial loss? T. Honoré, 'Necessary and Sufficient Conditions in Tort Law', in D. G. Owen (ed.), *Philosophical Foundation of Tort Law* (Clarendon Press, Oxford, 1995), at pp. 382–3.

client's solvency may lead to financial losses. Thus A, before extending credit to B, takes the precaution of asking C (the merchant bank where B kept its account) for an assessment of B's creditworthiness. C carelessly replies that B is 'good for its ordinary engagements' (when in fact B would soon go into liquidation), and thereby influences A to advance credit and to lose a large sum.[36] Here, A's loss is purely financial, not because it ricochets off or is transferred from someone else's physical damage, but because it arises directly from A's reliance.

Professional services for a client may cause pecuniary loss to a non-client. B, an elderly man, asks C, his lawyer, to prepare a will in which he will leave £100,000 to A. C takes no action for six months, as a result of which B dies intestate and A receives nothing.[37] A's loss is purely economic.

## Present vs. future loss

Examples given in the preceding paragraphs would suggest that patrimonial injury may take two distinguishable forms. It may relate to the existing – as opposed to the anticipated – wealth of the victim. In the first sense, plaintiff's present wealth may be simply depleted by poor financial advice, or by wasting time and petrol circumnavigating a motorway that was closed due to an accident. In the second sense, plaintiff may instead lose that which s/he expected to acquire, such as the profits from productive machinery suddenly shut down, or a testamentary legacy lost because of a defectively drawn instrument, or a sport club's reduced gate receipts due to the accidental death of its star player. Sometimes, when an expectation is destroyed *in utero* and proof that it would have materialized is difficult, it is called the loss of a chance.[38]

---

[36] These facts are taken from the well-known case of *Hedley Byrne & Co.* v. *Heller & Partners Ltd* [1964] AC 465 (HL). For other instances of pecuniary harm from incorrect information, see Case 18 ('Wrongful Job Reference') and Case 20 ('An Anonymous Telephone Call').

[37] See *White* v. *Jones* [1995] 2 AC 207 (HL); *Lucas* v. *Hamm*, 15 Cal. Rept. 821 (1961) (cert. denied, 368 vs 987); *Ross* v. *Caunters* [1980] Ch. 297; and Case 14 ('Poor Legal Services').

[38] For example: a commission unlawfully rejects a candidate's application for a job or a fellowship. See e.g. Conseil d'Etat, 12.11.1965, in (1965) *Recueil Lebon* 613: 'le réquérant, évincé d'un concours auquel il se serait présenté avec des chances sérieuses de succès en raison de ses titres et travaux, a subi un préjudice'. As to the debate, see G. Viney and P. Jourdain, 'Les conditions de la responsabilité', in J. Ghestin (ed.), *Traité de droit civil* (2nd edn, Paris, 1998), pp. 71 ff.; N. Jansen, 'The Idea of a Lost Chance', (1999) 19 *Oxford Journal of legal Studies*, 271 (discussing German and English experience); P. G. Monateri, 'La responsabilità civile', in R. Sacco (ed.), *Trattato di diritto civile* (Torino, 1998), pp. 283 ff., 583 ff.

As between these types of wealth, it is the loss of expected wealth – unrealised profits, cancelled legacies – which presents the sharpest question for tort systems to deal with. The difficulty is not simply that the demand for proof is more exigent – by definition, expectancies explore a future that only might have occurred – but also the appropriateness of affording protection in tort may be questioned. For when an economic expectation receives legal protection in tort, as in principle it does under French law, plaintiff can be compensated to the same extent *as if* he or she were protected by a contract with the tortfeasor.[39] In countries where an exclusionary rule of tort law exists, we may find a tendency to say that wealth expectancies should be protected in contract.[40] For example, German courts are generally unable to approach the question through tort, but at the same time they willingly stretch contractual concepts that make the defendant liable to plaintiff, although there is no actual contract between the parties.

In these circumstances it becomes difficult to tell where tort ends and contract begins. We seem to be at the frontier where functions meet and merge, for although it has been theorized that contract creates wealth whereas tort only protects that which we already have,[41] the notion of pure economic loss presents, at a European level, a challenge to traditional views about the relationship between contract and tort law. A distinguished Austrian scholar, Helmut Koziol, has pointed out that we must not lose our way in the conceptual shadows of this borderland.

Liability based on tort and liability based on breach of contract usually are taken as clearly separated contrasts. But I think they are the two ends of liability based on fault and that between them there is a connecting chain of intermediate

---

[39] See Viney and Jourdain, 'Conditions de la responsabilité', pp. 71 ff., 195 ff.; Viney, 'Introduction à la responsabilité', pp. 360 ff. See also our comparative Comments to Case 18 ('Wrongful Job Reference') regarding the distinction to be made between cases in which the lost chance is to be understood as a distinct loss in itself (an autonomous loss), as distinguished from the case where the concept is invoked as an equitable means of proving a loss.

[40] Note, for example, the tense unease in the following statement from a British judge: 'I do not consider that damages for loss of an expectation are excluded in cases of negligence arising under the principle in *Hedley Byrne*, simply because the cause of action is classified as tortious. Such damages may in principle be recoverable in cases of contractual negligence; and I cannot see that, for present purposes, any relevant distinction can be drawn between the two forms of action.' *per* Lord Goff of Chieveley in *White* v. *Jones* [1995] AC 207. On this subject see also J. Stapleton, 'The Normal Expectancies Measure in Tort Damages', (1997) 113 *Law Quarterly Review* 257; H. Reece, 'Loss of Chances in the Law', (1996) 59 Mod. LR 188.

[41] J. A. Weir, 'Complex Liabilities', No. 6, *International Encyclopedia of Comparative Law*, XI (1976), p. 5: 'Contract is productive, tort law protective.'

stages. This understanding is important because one has not to sort liability in one of these two categories and, therefore, is able to avoid abruptly different treatment of rather similar cases.[42]

## Basic arguments for the exclusionary rule: the 'floodgates', ordering of human values and lessons of history

It will be useful to set out the fundamental arguments which are usually presented in support of an exclusionary rule. Naturally these arguments were developed by jurists in legal systems which take the position that such losses should not be generally recoverable in tort, except in defined and limited circumstances. However, the experience of other countries may suggest certain difficulties or counter-arguments which we will also mention.

### The 'floodgates'

This is the most important of the three arguments we will discuss. It is not only pervasive but has proved persuasive. It usually links up with, and reinforces, the other arguments. Though not always noticed, there are actually three distinct strands to the floodgates argument, and it is helpful to separate them. The first strand is the belief that to permit recovery of pure economic loss in some cases would unleash an infinity of actions that would burden, if not overwhelm, the courts. If defendant's negligence necessitates the closure of trading markets or shuts down all commerce travelling on a busy motorway, there may be hundreds, perhaps thousands of people who would be financially damaged. Assuming a large number of these cases were to reach the courts, there would be administrative chaos. The justice system could not cope with the sheer numbers of claims.

The second strand is the fear that widespread liability would place an excessive burden upon the defendant who, for purposes of the argument, is treated as the living proxy of human initiative and enterprise. Von Jhering's statement: 'Where would it lead if everyone could be sued...!'[43] is a famous rendition of the argument. The potentially staggering liability would be out of all proportion to the degree to which defendant was negligent. It is also said that it is manifestly impossible

---

[42] H. Koziol (ed.), *Unification of Tort Law: Wrongfulness* (Kluwer, 1998), p. 25.
[43] Quoted below, at p. 120, footnote 1 and accompanying text.

for defendant to predict in advance how many relational economic loss claims he might face when, for example, he injures the property of a primary victim. Whether there is a small or large class of secondary loss sufferers depends, fortuitously, upon the number of parties with economic interests linked to the exploitation of the property.[44]

The danger of disproportionate consequences resulting from minor blameworthiness is of course an issue of fairness, no matter what kind of damages have been caused,[45] but some scholars believe that the danger is far greater in pure financial loss cases. Financial harm is assumed to have a greater propensity to travel far and wide. It has often been pointed out that the laws of Newton do not apply on the road to financial ruin.[46] Physical damage has at least a final resting point, but patrimonial harm is not slowed down by gravity and friction.[47] The harm has often been compared to the recovery of damages for nervous shock, since there too the loss can be 'pure' as opposed to consequential, and there too the danger of reverberating impacts is commonly given as a reason for restrictive rules.[48]

---

[44] The rationales of predictability and practicality are discussed in Bernstein, *Economic Loss*, pp. 201–203.

[45] See, J. Waldron, 'Moments of Carelessness and Massive Loss', in D. Owen (ed.), *Philosophical Foundations of Tort Law* (Oxford, 1995), at p. 387.

[46] Weir, *Encyclopedia of Comparative Law*, no. 14(d). This was also the view of Fleming James who stated that the 'physical consequences of negligence usually have been limited, but the indirect economic repercussions of negligence may be far wider, indeed virtually open-ended'. R. James, 'Limitations on Liability for Economic Loss Caused by Negligence: A Pragmatic Appraisal', (1972) 25 *Vanderbilt Law Review* 43, 45.

[47] See, however, J. Stapleton, 'Legal Cause: Cause-in-Fact and the Scope of Liability for Consequences' (2001) 54 *Vanderbilt Law Review* 941, at 974: 'The reference to the laws of physics reflects a long-standing fallacy in traditional running down cases that control of liability for consequences can be achieved by some "billiard ball" notion of the laws of physics. That is, this reference rests upon the faulty notion that claims for physical damage, whether to person or property, are inherently limited by the laws of physics which teach that physical forces will ultimately come to rest. After I have run you over and broken your leg, we have "come to rest" in a crude sense. Yet if you later suffer negligent treatment at a hospital that damages your other leg, the law may well say this injury is within the appropriate scope of my liability for consequences. What is doing the work in this judgment is not some inherent limit on my liability set by the law of physics but a judgment about the appropriate scope of liability for consequences in light of, among other things, the perceived purpose underlying the recognition of the obligation in the first place.'

[48] However, the analogy must not be pressed too far. Courts in emotional shock cases have been troubled by a number of rather different concerns, particularly the difficulty of defining the threshold harm (what degree of shock should be cognizable? what manifestation of the harm should be required?) and the difficulty of detecting false or fraudulent claims. In the case of pure economic loss, however, the problem of

The third strand of the argument maintains that pure economic loss is simply part of a broad modern trend toward increasing tort liability, a trend that must be kept under control. Allowing exceptions to the exclusionary rule is a slippery slope that may lead to reversal of the rule and may also encourage the development of other types of tort liability. The Tilburg Group, for example, argues that the floodgates must be kept shut in order 'to dam crushing liability' and to resist the general trend toward expansion of liability.[49] Their view may mean that the exclusionary rule should be invoked, even in factual instances where there is no danger of a flood of claims or of disproportionate recovery. No compensation should be made for fear of establishing an exception that erodes the rule and may receive analogical extension in the future.

In assessing the cumulative weight of the argument, there are in our view a number of considerations to bear in mind. To begin with, it should be remembered that the floodgates argument has never purported to be a scientific claim nor a claim based upon comparative law research. It is not very easy to test whether the dire prophecy of the 'nightmare scenario' is dream or reality. Is it founded on blind conservatism or does it have a rational basis?[50] For example, the central assertion that physical damage is different than financial damage because

> defining the threshold of the harm is minimal (the threshold of financial damage always begins at zero); the factual existence of loss is objectively demonstrable and its measurement and proof are not easy but perhaps less problematic. The characteristic uncertainty of financial loss does not consist in defining or verifying the harm, but in establishing the causal link between it and defendant's conduct. The threat of fraud is also of less concern because such loss is free of the danger that claimants may simulate its symptoms. Accordingly, economic loss is less easily feigned than the manifestations of nervous shock. We therefore suggest that the most important similarity between the two areas centres upon judicial concern about expanding liability in favour of an indeterminate number of plaintiffs, for indeterminate amounts of damages. Cf. von Bar, *Common European Law of Torts*, II, pp. 76–84. For a discussion in American law, see R. L. Rabin, 'Tort Liability for Negligently Inflicted Economic Loss: A Reassessment', (1985) 37 *Stanford Law Review* 1513, at 1524–5.

[49] Six of eight hypotheticals chosen for comparative study by the Tilburg Group deal with the subject of pure economic loss. The floodgates metaphor plays a central role in their orientation. See Spier (ed.) *Limits of Liability* and also J. Spier, *The Limits of Expanding Liability* (Kluwer, 1998).

[50] For example, in 1939 the eminent American torts scholar, William Prosser, cuttingly observed: 'It is the business of the law to remedy wrongs that deserve it, even at the expense of a "flood of claims"; and it is a pitiful confession of incompetence on the part of any court of justice to deny relief upon the ground that it will give the courts too much work to do': 'Intentional Infliction of Mental Suffering: a New Tort' (1939) 37 *Michigan Law Review* 874, at 877.

it is more contained and judicially manageable seems increasingly difficult to understand in view of today's mass torts, which sometimes involve innumerable physically injured victims asserting claims sometimes amounting to billions of dollars.[51] These disasters range from single-event catastrophes such as the Exxon Valdez oil spill and the Bhopal gas leak, to multiple-event injuries such as the asbestos and DES (Diethyl Stilbestrol) tragedies which extend over a wide geographic area, producing literally thousands of actual claims that stretched judicial resources to their limits.[52] The Exxon Valdez oil spill by itself produced more than 30,000 litigated claims.[53] The recent outbreak of foot and mouth disease in Europe which spreads physical and/or financial loss by the same prevailing wind may prove to be a bigger disaster. These examples would suggest that the law is normally content to impose liability even though the potential plaintiff class is large.[54] It would sound very odd if the defendant could argue that they should not owe a duty because they would have too many victims.[55] For many scholars, therefore, the justification for a no-recovery rule based upon a supposed difference in ripple effect, or in the sheer size of the plaintiff class, is hard to reconcile with the

---

[51] The point is repeatedly emphasized by H. Bernstein, 'Civil Liability for Economic Loss', (1998) 46 *American Journal of Comparative Law* 111, at 126–8.

[52] For a summary of the American scene, see C. H. Peterson and J. Zekoll, 'Mass Torts', (1994) 42 *American Journal of Comparative Law* 79. For a valuable analysis of the doctrine of pure economic loss in relation to the Exxon Valdez and Amoco Cadiz oil spills, see Goldberg, 'Recovery for Economic Loss'. On its facts, the Exxon Valdez accident caused enormous physical damage to the environment, that is, to things in the public domain such as shoreline, waters and wildlife. The individual litigants were directly affected as fishermen, tour operators, hotel owners. Their claims were viewed as a species of pure economic loss. However, such accidents could just as well occur in places where thousands of private owners would suffer property losses and consequential economic losses. The threat of an avalanche of claims, therefore, is hardly reduced by the metaphysical nature of the damage, and it is questionable that the law can construct a sensible rule based upon such a distinction.

[53] Goldberg, 'Recovery for Economic Loss', at 1.

[54] As Professor Jane Stapleton wrote in a private communication to the authors of these pages: 'we should not forget that modern procedural reforms, such as statutory provisions facilitating class actions, reflect society's concern to address the barriers to justice that might otherwise face the mass of victims that can result in today's complex society from a single piece of wrongdoing. They are a way of addressing, by lowering, the "costs of mass litigation" concern.'

[55] The judgment of *Griffiths* v. *British Coal Corporation* (23 January 1998, QBD.) upheld the largest personal injury claim in British history which led to a record settlement of £2 billion being agreed for the benefit of 100,000 ex-miners suffering from a range of chest illnesses, a sum considerably more than government received from the privatization of the coal industry: see J. Stapleton (2000) 120 *Law Quarterly Review* 506–11.

recovery of extremely large economic losses resulting from negligently caused physical injury.[56]

The geographical distribution of the floodgates argument is another interesting facet of its development. While a perennial in some soils and climates, the argument has failed to take root in others. We have no clear explanation why this occurs. One might say that the theme resonates better in particular legal cultures, but what makes one culture or legal infrastructure more receptive than another? Until research is available, the question is open to speculation and to discussion of interesting clues. For example, litigation rates in Europe are known to be very variable, and it appears that some of the more litigious countries adhere to the no-recovery rule. Is it coincidence that both the exclusionary rule and floodgates argument flourish in Germany and Austria where the rates are among the highest in Europe? Does this factor explain why, in the neighbouring Netherlands, where rates are remarkably low, there is no categorical rule against recovery, nor even – so far as an outside observer can judge – any particular fear of docket inundation?[57] Consider England and Scotland where the floodgates argument has enjoyed significant success. Should we be surprised that an historically small, close-knit coterie of judges may be sensitive to the question of administrative overload? Does institutional structure and conditioning play a role in this question? Another relevant issue may be to investigate the way in which broad arguments of this kind circulate in international channels. The ruling ideas of influential exporting legal cultures (not merely substantive law ideas, but 'soft' formants such as the conventional wisdom

---

[56] See J. Stapleton, 'Duty of Care Factors: a Selection from the Judicial Menus', in P. Cane and J. Stapleton (eds.), *The Law of Obligations: Essays in Celebration of John Fleming* (Oxford University Press, Oxford, 1998), p. 59. The author, at pp. 65–6, argues: 'Concern that, in a particular context, imposition of a duty of care might expose defendants to a large volume of claims (as opposed to an indeterminate number of claims – see below) are unconvincing given that the law is content elsewhere to impose liability where the potential plaintiff class is large. Indeed, it would be very odd if a defendant could argue in favour of his argument that he should not owe a duty that he had many victims!'

[57] For relevant figures, see E. Blankenburg, 'Civil Litigation Rates as Indicators of Legal Culture', in D. Nelkin (ed.), *Comparing Legal Cultures* (Dartmouth, 1997) at pp. 41 ff. where the author discusses the thesis that differences in legal culture may account for the disparities in civil litigation rates between neighbouring countries with very similar legal traditions and socio-economic conditions. For further comparisons, see B. S. Markesinis, 'Litigation Mania in England, Germany and the USA: Are We So Very Different?' (1990) 49 *Cambridge Law Journal* 133; P. Atiyah, 'Tort Law and the Alternatives: Some Anglo-American Comparisons', (1987) 36 *Duke Law Journal* 1002; A.A.S. Zuckerman (ed.), *Civil Justice in Crisis* (Oxford, 1999).

and dominant policy arguments) clearly have extraterritorial scope and impact. It does not seem accidental that in countries where English and German legal cultures have a decisive sphere of influence (e.g. English influence in Commonwealth countries and the United States; Germanic influence in Austria and Portugal), the floodgates argument has been received almost unquestioned. It is interesting that in countries where French leadership is acknowledged, one vainly searches for any trace or mention of floodgates anxiety. As stated earlier, our discussion is purely speculative and the subject merits deeper investigation.

*In the scale of human values*

A second argument is cast in terms of philosophical values. It maintains that intangible wealth is not, and should not, be treated on the same level as protecting bodily integrity or even physical property. People are more important than things, and things are more important than money.[58] Our legal interest in liberty, bodily integrity, land, possessions, reputation, wealth, privacy and dignity are all good interests, 'but they are not equally good'. The law protects interests according to their rank. And so 'a legal system which is concerned with human values (and the law is supposed to reflect the proper values of society) would be right to give greater protection to tangible property than to intangible wealth'.[59] The exclusionary rule is then a reflection of the lower value ascribed to unreified wealth.

It is important to note that this view has a silent premise: these interests must be ranked because the law *cannot* simultaneously protect all interests fully. Even if one accepts, for the sake of argument, that wealth is less important than other values, still there would be no justification for a rule restricting its recovery unless we had to do so in order to protect other, more meritorious interests. Thus the philosophical point is persuasive to the extent that (1) there is indeed a finite limit to the law's ability to protect interests; and (2) giving full protection to pure patrimonial wealth would clearly exceed that capacity, therefore impinging on other protections or the interests of third persons. The

[58] The argument has been made in England that 'The philosophy of the market place presumes that it is lawful to gain profit by causing others economic loss...Certainly there seems to have developed an understanding that economic loss at the hands of others is something we have to accept without legal redress, unless caused by some specifically outlawed conduct such as fraud or duress.' *The Aliakmon* [1985] 2 All ER 44, at p. 73, *per* Lord Goff.
[59] Tony Weir, *A Casebook on Tort* (9th edn, Sweet & Maxwell, London, 2000), p. 6.

first point may be less controversial than the second. No one doubts that resources are finite: judicial resources are not unlimited; tort liability cannot be extended indefinitely without stifling human initiative; and responsible defendants can be bankrupted by financial claims that leave claims for bodily injury unsatisfied. Therefore, it may be argued, that if pure economic loss were freely protected and allowed to compete on an equal footing with other, worthier claims for limited resources, the effect might be to crowd out 'better' interests and leave them unsatisfied. However, that conclusion depends on the answer to the second point, namely whether those limits would be surpassed by a presumption of recoverability. The answer to this question again seems to be conjectural, since it ultimately depends to some extent upon the same unverified assumptions inherent in the floodgates rationale. It also raises the question of how countries such as France and Belgium, which follow a rule of presumptive recovery of economic loss, have managed to avoid what the floodgates argument predicts. Is their experience proof that the argument is a gross exaggeration of the consequences, or does their experience tend to prove that these countries are simply using hidden and indirect means of controlling those consequences?[60]

There is an additional question. The exclusionary rule is associated with the negligence standard. However, all systems in our study permit recovery when pure financial loss is inflicted wrongfully and intentionally. Thus, the exclusionary rule cannot be seen simply as an abstract ordering of interests but as a rule tied to the gradations of blame. It would be difficult to say whether the nature of the interest or the nature of the fault is the more important factor in the equation. Indeed we think it would be essentially misguided to assign such priorities because the rule, when it is applied and to the extent that it is a rule, is really the outcome of many other interacting factors as well.[61] Not the least of these are many metalegal considerations, such as the size of the plaintiff class, the potential scope of the damages, public policy toward professional standards and so forth, which have varying degrees of cogency in actual context. Only through study of these factors in their liability context will we understand why the alleged rule operates selectively

---

[60] Genevieve Viney tends to regard French law in this perspective: 'on a privilégié l'emploi de méthodes indirectes et quasi-occultes', quoted in Spier *Limits of Liability*, at 3.

[61] For a nuanced attempt to use various factors in a sliding scale to explain the lesser protection given to pure economic loss, see Koziol, *Unification of Tort Law: Wrongfulness*, pp. 29–30.

and situationally, never mechanically, and indeed leaves untouched a number of defined situations where one may even speak of a limited core of protection for pure economic loss.

## In historical perspective

Some scholars assert as an historical matter that pure economic loss has traditionally been left unprotected by the law. If the assertion were generally true, it may have important normative implications for the present and the future. Hein Kötz deduces a teleological point in the evolution of tort law: the primary *purpose* of the law in England and Germany, he maintains, has 'always been' to provide protection against personal injuries and harm to physical property. Pure economic loss seems to have been left out of historical development, at least in those two countries.[62] Bruce Feldthusen argues that the rules of tort based on foreseeability were developed for physical damage and are not workable outside of the context for which they were developed. The straightforward application of the foreseeability test to claims of pure financial loss would lead to ruinous levels of liability.[63] Because they are products of history, tort rules today are ill-adapted to the problem of pure economic loss.

However, whether these views do justice to the past is open to question. James Gordley's essay, which explores the history of pure economic loss in some detail, notes that many early civilians said that plaintiff could recover if he suffered 'damage', and damage meant simply a diminution of his *patrimonium*. They did not distinguish between loss of a physical asset and other kinds of loss. They occasionally put cases in which the plaintiff would recover what we today would regard as pure economic loss, though he cautions that they did not know or use this term and did not recognize an autonomous category by that name.[64] For example there was the dependant's action for loss of support due to wrongful death, which clearly existed on the continent in Grotius's time. This was in effect an action for the recovery of pure economic loss sustained by wife and children, but it was not referred to in those

---

[62] H. Kötz, 'Economic Loss in Tort and Contract' (1994) 58 *Rabels Zeitschrift für ausländisches und internationales Privatrecht* 428.
[63] Feldthusen, *Economic Negligence*, pp. 10–11. The author asserts that the 'remoteness' of the damage from the initial conduct of the defendant is the characteristic and endemic issue which distinguishes pure economic loss, as a practical matter, from cases involving physical damage.
[64] See Gordley, below at pp. 26–29, and the citations to the views of Durandus, Baldus, Brunnemann, Lauterbach and Grotius, at pp. xxx.

terms. Evidence of this kind would suggest that there was no *per se* rule against compensation for pure economic harm in the civilian tradition.[65] Indeed, Gordley's account characterizes the rise of the exclusionary rule both in England and Germany as a late development of the nineteenth century[66] and the peculiar outgrowth of analytical thinking. He concludes that the rule is an 'accident' of legal history, not a pervasive feature of it. His highly interesting account follows immediately.

---

[65] See R. Zimmermann, *The Law of Obligations: Roman Foundations of the Civil Law Tradition* (Juta, Cape Town/Johannesburg, 1966), pp. 1024–5; V. Palmer, 'The Fate of the General Clause in a Cross-Cultural Setting: The Tort Experience of Louisiana', (2000) 46 *Loyola Law Review* 535, at 551.

[66] Insurance practices tend also to show the late development of the rule. Development of business interruption insurance, often called 'consequential loss insurance', belongs to the late nineteenth century, and even now the availability of such insurance is still rather limited. A prevalent restriction is that interruption insurance is essentially 'follow-on' coverage to another insured peril, such as fire. Under the wording of standard fire policies, there is no compensation for interruption unless it results from a fire. This is not really compensation for *pure* economic loss, however, but rather compensation for *parasitic* loss. See G. J. R. Hickmott, *Principles and Practice of Interruption Insurance* (Witherby, London, 1982), pp. 3–4; D. C. Jess, *The Insurance of Commercial Risks, Law and Practice* (Butterworths, London, 1986), pp. 244–51.

2   The rule against recovery in negligence for pure economic loss: an historical accident?

JAMES GORDLEY

Introduction

The history of a rule can shed some light on its merits. We may be less inclined to abolish a rule if we discover that legal systems have done so and later had to bring it back, finding that they could not live without it. Bernard Windscheid, the great nineteenth-century German jurist, counselled his contemporaries not to try to abolish the doctrine of changed circumstances in contract law: 'Thrown out the door it comes back in again through the window.'[1] The drafters of the German Civil Code of 1900 did try to abolish it, only to have the German courts bring the doctrine back two decades later. Conversely, we may be more inclined to abolish a rule if we find that it was adopted because of the accident that a certain approach to law, which is now rightly discredited, was in fashion at the time it was adopted. In this chapter, we will see that the rule against recovery for pure economic loss was the result of such an accident. It was adopted comparatively recently, at the turn of the last century in Germany and England, because of a conceptualistic argument about the difference between rights against all the world and rights against a particular contracting party which would not be compelling today. It became enshrined in the German Civil Code and English precedent and lived on largely because of judges' respect for them.

Our first step will be to see that before the turn of the last century, the problem of limiting recovery for negligence either was not faced squarely or was resolved in other ways. It was not resolved by distinguishing between physical harm and economic loss. We will examine only the history of continental law, because this problem did not exist in England

---

[1] B. Windscheid, 'Die Voraussetzung', (1892) 78 *Archiv für die civilistische Praxis* 161, at 197.

until the late nineteenth century when an action for negligence became more clearly recognized.

## Continental law before the nineteenth century

### The Roman texts

Before codification, in much of continental Europe recovery in tort was governed by Roman law, or more precisely, by the interpretation that jurists placed on the Roman texts of the *Corpus iuris civilis* compiled by the Emperor Justinian in the sixth century. In Roman law, the *lex Aquilia*, enacted in the late second century or possibly in the third century BC, was interpreted to allow the plaintiff to recover for harm that the defendant had caused negligently or intentionally. There were originally two limits on recovery but both had disappeared by the Middle Ages.

One limit was that the defendant was liable under the *lex Aquilia* only if the damage was done in a physically direct way. In classical Roman law, this limit had been effectively abolished by granting the plaintiff an *actio in factum* or an *actio utilis* where he could not sue under the *lex* itself.[2] Eventually, Justinian's compilers rationalized this distinction by saying that an action under the *lex* could be brought where the defendant injured the plaintiff *a corpore in corpus*, 'by the body to the body', meaning that the harm had to be physical and to be physically inflicted by the defendant. For example, the defendant would be liable if he struck and broke something that belonged to the plaintiff. The plaintiff was allowed to bring an *actio in factum* for harm that was *a corpore* but not *in corpus*, as for example, if the defendant tossed the plaintiff's ring in the river: the harm was done physically but the ring itself was not damaged but rather put beyond reach. The plaintiff was allowed to bring an *actio utilis* for harm that was neither *a corpore* nor *in corpus*, as for example, if the defendant untied the plaintiff's slave so he could run away; like the ring, the slave was now beyond reach but this time the defendant himself had not physically moved him.[3]

Medieval jurists were not sensitive to the historical meaning of their texts. They tried to reconcile the texts logically, but since there were

---

[2] R. Zimmermann, *The Law of Obligations: Roman Foundations of the Civilian Tradition* (Juta, Cape Town/Johannesburg, 1966), at pp. 993–6.

[3] I. 4.3.16. See Zimmermann, *Law of Obligations*, at pp. 996–7.

different ways that they could be reconciled, the medieval jurists were able to reach results that would have surprised the Romans. Had they wished to limit liability under the *lex Aquilia*, they could have held, for example, that an *actio in factum* or an *actio utilis* did not invariably lie, that the court had some power of discretion in allowing these actions that it did not have if the action were brought directly under the *lex Aquilia*. But they did not do so. The thirteenth-century jurist Accursius, who wrote the Ordinary Gloss on the *Corpus iuris civilis*, did say that an *actio in factum* is given 'if equity persuades that an action be given'.[4] But it is clear from the authority he cites that he meant that, as a matter of equity, the plaintiff should have an action even if the damage is not *a corpore* and *in corpus*. He did not mean that such an action is subject to a special requirement that the plaintiff show it is equitable that he recover.[5] And indeed, a medieval plaintiff bringing an *actio utilis* would frame his complaint in the same terms as one bringing an action that lay squarely within the *lex Aquilia*. He would not add an allegation that his case is especially deserving and therefore he should have relief as a matter of equity.[6] As Brunnemann noted in the eighteenth century, it did not matter which action the plaintiff brought.[7]

---

[4] Accursius, *Glossa ordinaria* (Venice, 1581), to D. 9.2.33.1 to *lege Aquilia* ('et hoc [giving an *actio in factum*] si aequitas suaderet actionem dari').

[5] In modern printed editions, the passage just cited ends 'alioquin contra ut s[upra] eo[dem titulo lex] quaemadmodum § sed et si tanto'. This means that an action is given only when equity so 'persuades' because otherwise there would be a contradiction with the section that begins 'sed et si tanto' of the law that begins 'quaemadmodum' which is to be found in the same title (Dig. 9.2) as the law which Accursius is explaining. That must be a miscitation since there is no passage that exactly fits this description. But there is one that comes close: the passage beginning 'sed si tanto' in Dig. 9.2.29, which does begin 'quaemadmodum'. And that, indeed, is the citation given in several medieval manuscripts. Vat. Lat. 2511 f. 78va; Vat. Lat. 1410 f. 158va; Pal. Lat. 733 f. 180va. This passage says that there is no liability under the *lex Aquilia* if a ship hits another because of the overpowering force of the elements. The context of the passage, and Accursius's gloss to *dominium* make it clear that there would be an action had the navigators been at fault for managing the ship. Accursius says: 'Et sic collige hic a contrario in damnum dari quando non fiat fortuitus casus'. Thus, when he says that an action outside the terms of the *lex Aquilia* is to be given only if equity so 'persuades', all he seems to mean is that one is not to give such an action invariably since then one would do so even if the defendant were not at fault.

[6] For model complaints, see Odofredus, *Summa de formandis libellis in refugium advocatorum* (Vale Argentorael, 1510). The volume is neither folioed nor paginated but the form for an *actio in factum* under the *lex Aquilia* is on what would be f. 11v and the one for an *actio directa* is on what would be f. 40v. The complaints are the same except that the factual situation differs as one might expect from the Roman sources.

[7] J. Brunnemann, *Commentarius in quinquaginta libros pandectarum* (ed. novissima, Coloniae Allogrum, 1762), to D. 2.9.7 no. 11.

A second limitation can be inferred from the texts in which the Roman jurists said that the plaintiff can recover. Nearly always, his tangible property has been damaged physically or else put beyond his reach, as for example, when his ring is thrown into the river or his slave is allowed to escape.[8] Two texts go further and let a father recover for the death of a son who is still *in manus*.[9] Perhaps it seemed odd that the father could recover for the death of a slave but not a son.[10] Or perhaps the loss of the son was seen as an economic loss because legally, as long as the son was *in manus*, the father had a right to any assets that the son possessed.

In any event, this limitation disappeared in the Middle Ages. The two texts just mentioned were generalized. A surviving widow was thus able to recover for economic losses suffered when her husband died.[11]

With this limitation gone, medieval[12] and early modern jurists[13] simply said that the plaintiff could recover if he suffered damage, and that damage meant a diminution in his *patrimonium*. They did not distinguish between loss of a physical asset and other kinds of loss. Indeed, they occasionally put cases in which, they said, the plaintiff will recover although he suffered what we today would call pure economic loss. The

---

[8] See Zimmermann, *Law of Obligations*, 1023–4. One Roman text did allow the plaintiff to recover the value of property he never obtained because the defendant destroyed a will or some other document legally necessary to obtain it. Dig. 9.2.41. In that case, however, the will or the document had been destroyed, which may not have seemed much different than physically destroying any other physical asset. At least, that is how medieval jurists regarded the destruction of such documents in other contexts. E.g. *Glossa ordinaria* to *Decretales Gregorii* ix to 5.36.7.

[9] Dig. 9.2.5.3; Dig. 9.2.7.4. A person could also recover if, not knowing that he was a free man, he served in good faith as someone's slave. Dig. 9.2.13.pr. See Zimmermann, *Law of Obligations*, pp. 1016–17.

[10] Zimmermann, *Law of Obligations*, p. 1015.    [11] Ibid., pp. 1024–5.

[12] Azo, *Summa codicis* (Lyons, 1557), to D. 9.2 ('Et dicit damnum a demo vel a diminuatione patrimonium'); Hostienisis, *Summa aurea* (Lyon, 1556), lib. 5, rubr. 'de damno dato' no. 1 ('Quid sit damnum. Diminutio vel redemptio patrimonii.').

[13] G. A. Struvius, *Syntagma iurisprudentiae secundum ordinem pandectarum* (Jena, 1692), Exerc. XIV, lib. 9, tit. 2, no. xx ('Fundamentum et causa huius actionis est damnum iniuria datum, quod est delictum privatum, quo patrimonium sive re aliena dolo aut culpa diminuitur'); W. A. Lauterbach, *Collegium theorico-practici* (Tübingen, 1707), to D. 9.2 no. vii ('ut itaque hoc delictum dicatur commissum, requiritur ut damnum sit datum pecuniarium, scilicet, quo alterius diminuitur patrimonium'); A. Vinnius, *In quatuor libros institutionem imperialium commentarius* (4th edn, Amsterdam, 1665), to I. 4.3 pr. ('Nam damnum ad ademptione, et quasi diminutione patrimonii dictum est'); G. Heineccius, *Elementa iuris civilis secundum ordinem pandectarum* (5th edn, Traiecti ad Rhenum, 1772), to Dig. 9.2 § clxxxvi ('quia haec actio ad patrimonii diminutionem pertinet').

medieval jurist Durandus said that the plaintiff could recover if the defendant put dung in the street in front of his house, and he therefore had to pay a fine imposed by statute.[14] One of the greatest medieval jurists, Baldus de Ubaldi, said that the plaintiff could recover against his secretary who revealed his secrets.[15] In the sixteenth century, Zasius gave the same opinion in the case of the secretary, citing Baldus.[16] In the eighteenth century, Lauterbach and Brunnemann said that a client could recover from an advocate who harmed him through lack of skill.[17] Horst Kaufmann has found many other examples from the practice of early modern times.[18]

Before the nineteenth century, then, jurists would not deny relief under the lex Aquilia on the grounds that the plaintiff had suffered a purely economic loss. It does not follow that the plaintiff could recover in all the cases jurists put today when they discuss the problem of economic loss.[19] The category of economic loss is ours, not theirs. We cannot assume that these jurists would have seen all cases of economic loss as similar to those in which they said the plaintiff should recover. They did say that the plaintiff could recover for damage, and that damage meant any diminution in his *patrimonium*. But jurists make general statements like this one to address questions that they have consciously in mind. The question before them was one the Romans had already asked and answered: whether he could recover for damages inflicted *non in corpus* and even *non a corpore*. We should be careful about reading their statements as answers to questions they were not asking.

## The natural law schools

Neither the Romans nor the medieval jurists had been concerned with the theory or general principles of tort. The Romans had discussed

---

[14] G. Durandus, *Speculum iuris* (Basil, 1574) lib. iv, par. iv, *De iniuriis et damno dato*, § 2 (sequitur), no. 15.
[15] B. de Ubaldi, *Commentaria corpus iuris civilis* (Venice, 1577), to Dig. 9.2.41 (vulg.9.2.42) pr. in fine.
[16] U. Zasius, 'Commentaria seu lecturas eiusdem in titulos primae Pandectarum' to Dig. 9.2 no. 1 39, in *Opera omnia*, vol. 1 (Lyon, 1550, repr. Scientia Verlag, Aalen, Darmstadt, 1966).
[17] Lauterbach, *Collegium theorico-practici* to Dig. 9.2 no. xv; Brunnemann, *Commentarius* to Dig. 9.2.8 no. 5.
[18] H. Kaufmann, *Rezeption und Usus Modernus der Actio Legis Aquiliae* (Köln, Böhlan, 1958), pp. 46–56.
[19] As noted by Kaufmann, *Rezeption*, p. 58.

concrete instances of recovery, and the medieval jurists had tried to reconcile Roman texts. In contrast, the members of the natural law schools which flourished from the sixteenth through to the eighteenth century were looking for principles. They were the first to ask whether a person should recover, not only when something that already belonged to him was harmed, but when he was prevented from obtaining something of value.

This question was debated in the sixteenth and early seventeenth century by jurists known to historians as the late scholastics or Spanish natural law school.[20] Leaders of the group included Tomasso de Vio, better known as Cajetan (1468–1534), Domingo de Soto (1494–1560), Luis de Molina (1535–1600), Leonard Lessius (1554–1623), and Juan de Lugo (1583–1660). They were self-consciously trying to synthesize Roman law with the moral philosophy of Aristotle and Thomas Aquinas.[21] In the seventeenth and eighteenth century, many of their conclusions were borrowed and disseminated throughout Europe by the northern natural law school founded by Hugo Grotius (1583–1645) and Samuel Pufendorf (1632–94) – paradoxically, since the Aristotelian philosophy on which these conclusions had been based was falling from favour.

The late scholastics developed their theories of tort and contract by drawing on Aristotle's theories of distributive and commutative justice. While distributive justice guarantees each citizen a fair share of whatever resources were to be distributed, commutative justice preserves

---

[20] On the late scholastics generally, see H. Thieme, 'Qu'est-ce que nous, les juristes, devons à la seconde scolastique espagnole?', in P. Grossi (ed.), *La seconda scolastica nella formazione del diritto privato moderno* (Giuffrè Milano, 1973), 20; H. Thieme, 'Natürliches Privatrecht und Spätscholastik' in *Zeitschrift der Savigny-Stiftung für Rechtsgeschichte Rom. Abt.* 70 (1953), p. 230. For their influence on other areas of law, see J. Gordley, *The Philosophical Origins of Modern Contract Doctrine* (Oxford University Press, Oxford, 1991), pp. 69–133; I. Birocchi, *Saggi sulla formazione storica della categoria generale del contratto* (1988); M. Diesselhorst, *Die Lehre des Hugo Grotius vom Versprechen* (Böhlan, Köln, 1959), 6; J. Gordley, 'Tort Law in the Aristotelian Tradition', in D. Owen (ed.), *Philosophical Foundations of Tort Law* (Oxford University Press, Oxford, 1995), p. 131; J. Gordley 'Responsibility in Crime, Tort, and Contract for the Unforeseeable Consequences of an Intentional Wrong: A Once and Future Rule?', in P. Cane and J. Stapleton (eds.), *The Law of Obligations: Essays in Celebration of John Fleming* (Oxford University Press, Oxford, 1998), p. 175; R. Feenstra, 'Grotius' Doctrine of Unjust Enrichment as a Source of Obligation: its Origin and its Influence on Roman-Dutch Law', in E. G. H. Shrage (ed.), *Unjust Enrichment* (Duncker & Humblot, Berlin, 1995), p. 197; J. Gordley, 'The Principle Against Unjustified Enrichment', in H. Schack (ed.), *Gedächtnisschrift für Alexander Lüderitz* (C. H. Beck, Munich, 2000), pp. 213, 217–19.

[21] For a description of their theory of torts, see Gordley, 'The Aristotelian Tradition', For their theories about contract law, see Gordley, *Philosophical Origins*.

what belongs to each citizen. When people exchange resources voluntarily, commutative justice requires that they do so at a just price, a price that preserves each person's share. If one person harms another by taking or destroying something belonging to that person, commutative justice requires that he undo the harm by giving back what he took or by making compensation.[22]

Thomas Aquinas had described what belongs to a person and the types of harm that one could suffer. The harm might be to a 'thing' that belongs to him. It might be to his 'person', and then, either to his person itself or to his dignity. It might be to his relationship with another person such as his wife or his slave.[23] The late scholastics concluded that the Roman distinctions between different actions were mere matters of Roman positive law. In principle, and as a matter of commutative justice, a person should recover whenever he suffered harm. Sometimes they merely stated this principle,[24] and sometimes they classified types of harm in much the same way as Aquinas.[25]

Grotius was merely summarizing their conclusions when he gave his famous description of the basic principles of tort law: 'From...fault, if damage is caused, an obligation arises, namely, that the damage should be made good.' He explained: 'Damage is when a man has less than what is his...' 'Things which a man may regard as his by nature are his life...body, limbs, fame, honor, and his own acts. In the previous part of our treatise we have shown how each man by property right and by agreements possesses his own not only with respect to property but also with respect to the acts of others...'[26]

Anyone who culpably deprived another of any of these 'things' therefore owed compensation. But suppose he prevented the other from obtaining something that might have been his. Did he owe compensation

---

[22] *Nicomachean Ethics*, V.ii, 1130b–1131a.
[23] T. Aquinas, *Summa theologiae*, II–II, Q. 61, a. 3.
[24] E.g. D. Soto, *De iustitia et iure libri decem* (Salamanca, 1553), lib. 4, q. 6, a. 5; L. Molina, *De iustitia et iure tractatus* (Venice, 1614), disps. 315, 724; L. Lessius, *De iustitia et iure ceterisque virtutibus cardinalibus libri quatuor* (Paris, 1628), lib. 2, cap. 12, dubs. 16, 18; cap. 20, dubs. 10–11.
[25] E.g. Lessius, *De iustitia et iure*, lib. 2, caps. 3, 9–12.
[26] H. Grotius, *De iure belli ac pacis libri tres* (eds. B. J. A. de Kanter-van Hettinga Tromp, 1939), II.xvii.1–2. For similar conclusions by other natural lawyers, see S. Pufendorf, *De iure naturae et gentium libri octo* (Amsterdam, 1688), III.i.2, III.i.3, III.i.6; J. Barbeyrac, *Le droit de la nature et des gens, où système général des principes les plus importants de la morale, de la jurisprudence, et de la politique par le baron de Pufendorf* (5th edn, Amsterdam, 1734), no. 1 to III.i.2; no. 1 to III.i.3; no. 4 to III.i.6. See generally Zimmermann, *Law of Obligations*, pp. 1032–4.

then? Aquinas had said yes, adding that the amount to be paid in compensation is not the same:

[A] man is bound to make compensation [*restitutio*] for whatever of another's he harmed. But one is harmed in two ways. One way is that he is harmed because that which he actually has is taken, and compensation must always be made for such a harm by payment of an equivalent. For example, when one person harms another by destroying his house, he is bound to pay the amount that the house is worth. The other way is that someone harms another by preventing him from acquiring what he was on the way (*in via*) to having. And compensation of an equal amount need not be made for such harm, for it is less to have such a thing virtually than to have it actually. One who is on the way to acquiring a thing has it only virtually or potentially. Consequently, if he is paid as though he had the thing actually, he would not receive the value of what was taken as compensation but more, which is not required in making compensation, as noted in article 3. He is bound, however, to make compensation according to the condition of persons and affairs.[27]

In Article 3, which he cites, Aquinas had put the case of someone who unjustly prevents another from obtaining a benefice. He said that compensation must be paid, but not for its entire value 'because the man had not yet obtained the benefice and might have been prevented from doing so in many ways'.[28] Similarly, if one person destroys seeds which belong to another and which have not yet grown, he need not make compensation for the value that the crop would have had at harvest.[29]

Disagreeing with Aquinas, Cajetan tried to distinguish the case of the seeds from that of the benefice. The person claiming compensation for the seeds had a right to them, and it was on this right that his hope to profit at harvest time was based. In the case of the benefice, the claimant never had either the right to it or to anything else. Therefore, Cajetan said, he was not entitled to compensation:

[N]o reason can be seen why I am bound to make compensation in whole or in part for impeding someone from seeking a benefit to which he never had any right. It follows from this – that he never had any right in anything – that nothing was his, and consequently it follows that no compensation is due him. And if it be said that he has a right hoped for [*ius in spe*], that is not a valid consideration because a right in hope is not a right, just as wealth hoped for is not wealth. Moreover, compensation for a thing hoped for is given when a person is deprived of a right on which that hope is founded, as is shown when

---

[27] Aquinas, *Summa theologiae*, II–II, Q. 62, a. 4.   [28] Ibid., a. 3 ad 4.
[29] Ibid. 4 ad 1 and 2.

seeds are destroyed or the tools of a craft are taken away through the use of which a person's family is supported, and in similar cases.[30]

Cajetan's position was rejected by other late scholastics. They failed to see how it could matter from the standpoint of commutative justice whether or not a person's expectations of a benefit were 'founded' on something he presently owned. If he was unjustly deprived of that benefit, as a matter of commutative justice, he was entitled to compensation. Moreover, Cajetan assumed that a person who does not yet have the right to the benefit he is seeking has, at present, no rights at all. Therefore, he cannot have been deprived of a right. In that respect, his argument is conceptualistic: the conclusion follows only if 'having a right' is implicitly defined to exclude a person from having a right to seek a benefit to which he, as yet, does not have the right. Lessius answered that a person could have a right to something he had not yet acquired, for example, to a gift that had not yet been made to him. Such a right was not 'absolute' but 'conditional'. The recipient's right to a gift was 'conditional' on the decision of the potential donor to give it to him.[31] Molina distinguished two meanings of the phrase 'having a right':

[A] person is said to have a right [*ius*] to something in two different ways. First, because it is in some way his or owed to him. When right is used in this sense, we distinguish right in a thing [*ius in re*] and right to a thing (*ius ad rem*). In another sense, a person is said to have a right to something, not because it is owed to him, but because he has the capacity [*facultas*] for it, so that one who contravenes that right does him an injury. In this sense, everyone can be said to have the right to use his own things, for example, to eat his own food, so that injury and injustice is done to him if he is impeded. Indeed, we say that the poor have the right to beg for alms, that one who works for pay has the right to hire out his services, and that everyone has the right to hunt and fish in places where it is not prohibited. Consequently, if anyone impedes them in these matters, he does an injury and injustice and has the duty to make compensation.

Thus a person could have the right to seek what he had not yet acquired, and the violation of this right entitled him to compensation.

While the late scholastics generally agreed that Cajetan was wrong, there was less agreement about how much compensation should be paid in such cases. As we have seen, Aquinas said that one must pay, not the value of the benefice that was never obtained or of the crop never

---

[30] Cajetan, *Commentaria to Thomas Aquinas, Summa theologica* (Padua, 1698), to II–II, Q. 62, a. 2 ad 4.
[31] Lessius, *De iustitia et iure*, lib. 2, cap. 12, dub. 18.

harvested, but a lesser amount, according to the state of 'persons and affairs', since the party entitled to compensation could have been prevented from obtaining these benefits in many ways. Soto disagreed. If the land owner had wanted to sell his crop in the ear he would have done so. If he did not, it was in order to reap the harvest to come, and his loss was therefore the value of the harvest. As Soto put it:

> If the person who has the object in hope [res in spe] does not want to sell it only in hope but to await all risks until he has it, therefore, he who destroys another's thing against his will is not only bound to restore the amount that it is worth in hope but, it appears, the amount it will be worth.[32]

The trouble was, Soto thought, that a person who negligently destroyed another's crop really should not have to pay the full value of the grain at harvest time. So he claimed that only a person who did harm intentionally should have to pay full compensation. A negligent person should pay only the amount that Aquinas had described.[33]

That conclusion was rejected by Lessius, de Lugo and Molina. They thought the amount of compensation to be paid should be the same whether harm is done negligently or intentionally. Lessius and de Lugo explained that if the owner did not want to sell his crop in the ear, admittedly, the wrong done to him was greater than if he did. Even if he is compensated, nevertheless, he was forced against his will to give up his crop and receive its value in money before he wished to sell it. But however great the wrong a person suffers, commutative justice entitles him to recover only an amount equivalent to the harm actually done.[34] That harm, according to Lessius, is the value of the crop at the time it was destroyed 'taking in account the circumstances prevailing then'.[35] Molina argued that if the owner were paid the value of the crop at harvest time, he would be overcompensated. The further off the time of harvest, the less the crop is worth, since the perils to the crop and the labour necessary to produce it are greater.[36] For Molina, this conclusion followed from general principles that determine the value of a thing at any given time. For example, one who destroys a thing need not pay both for the thing and for the fruits it was expected to produce, 'because the value of a thing at the time at which is destroyed

---

[32] Soto, *De iustitia et iure*, lib. 4, q. 6, a. 5.    [33] Ibid.
[34] Lessius, *De iustitia et iure*, lib. 2, cap. 12, dub. 19, no. 137; I. de Lugo, *Disputationum de iustitia et iure* (Lyon, 1670), disp. 18, § 4, no. 79.
[35] Lessius, *De iustitia et iure*, lib. 2, cap. 12, dub. 19, no. 137.
[36] Molina, *De iustitia et iure*, III, disp. 726, no. 4.

is evaluated with regard to the fruits which can be received from it and with regard to the use and benefit that can be received from it in the future'.[37] The value of a crop thus reflects its value at maturity as well as the risk and labour of producing it. Molina consequently came close to the concept that modern economists call the 'expected value' of an asset, although he did not express it mathematically as they do.

De Lugo came closer still. He agreed with Aquinas, Lessius and Molina that compensation should be made 'according to the present value (*secundum valorem praesentem*) of the object in the state in which it was when destroyed'.[38] But he took them to mean that this amount was the price for which the object could then have been sold. De Lugo argued that this is usually the case, but not always. It all depends on whether the owner of the object could have bought another like it. If a person's foal is killed, usually he can buy another. If he does, he will not lose the profit he intended to make by later selling a fully grown horse. If he does not, then the reason he will not make this profit is his own decision not to replace the foal rather than the foal's death. In either case, he should only receive the price of the foal in compensation. However, suppose that he could not replace it because he lacked the money to do so. In that case, the foal's death did deprive him of the profit he would have made on the horse, and so he should recover that profit. Indeed, it may be impossible to buy something equivalent to the object that was destroyed. Buying another foal is easy but if crops are destroyed, it may be impossible to replace them by replanting the field that year. In that event, the owner should receive the profit he lost because he could not raise that crop, not merely the value of the crop when still immature. That conclusion, de Lugo said, was consonant with the principles of Aquinas, Lessius and Molina although it seemed to contradict their views. De Lugo added that the owner's compensation, if he could not replace the crop, should not be the full value of a mature crop. A deduction should be made for the risks the owner would have faced and the expenses he would have incurred.[39]

Indeed, because value in the present depends upon what happens in the future, a person should be compensated for the loss of things that he hopes to obtain but does not yet have. 'You say', de Lugo challenged a hypothetical interlocutor, 'that the hope of this profit from a future object (*spes illa lucri ex rei futuri*) does not increase the value of this object itself.' But if that were so, one who ousted the owner of a field

---

[37] Ibid., no. 3.  [38] De Lugo, *Disputationum*, disp. 18, § 4, no. 81.  [39] Ibid.

and occupied it without raising crops would merely need to give back the field without paying for the crops that the owner could have raised, had he not been ousted. As this example shows:

[T]his hope [of profit] is not based on the field alone, at least when effort and cultivation are wanted in order to profit, but, indeed, on the will of the owner who wants to till the field or to pasture animals and to expend the effort and care by which he adds something to the value of the field alone: the amount, that is, that the hope is worth then of profiting from the effort and care that the owner wants to expend.[40]

In short, the opportunity to profit in the future has a value in the present, and the value of a field in the present depends upon such an opportunity.

Many rules of modern civil law can be traced back to Grotius and Pufendorf who, in turn, had taken them from the late scholastics. If the late scholastics had agreed with Cajetan, perhaps something like the modern German and English rule against the recovery of pure economic loss would have become part of the civil law. Cajetan's position resembled the modern German and English rule although it did not go as far. He wanted to deny compensation to a person who lost his chance to get a benefit to which he 'never had any right'. The modern rule excludes recovery when the person had a right to the benefit under a contract with a third party.

In any event, the late scholastics rejected Cajetan's view, and Grotius and Pufendorf did not mention it. The debate was forgotten as soon as jurists no longer read the works of the late scholastics. As we will now see, the modern rule was formulated by German and English jurists of the late nineteenth and early twentieth century who defended it with an argument as conceptualistic as that of Cajetan. Oddly enough, this argument would have been as vulnerable as Cajetan's to the criticisms of the late scholastics.

## The nineteenth and twentieth centuries

### Germany

Before the code

In Germany, the Roman texts remained in force in many of the German states, and even where they did not, the work of the leading jurists

---

[40] Ibid., no. 82.

centred around them. As we saw earlier, historical study of the texts had pointed out that when the plaintiff recovered under the *lex Aquilia*, he had nearly always lost the physical use of property, although a few texts allowed recovery for injury or death of a son.[41] Therefore the nineteenth-century German jurists found themselves with an alternative to the generalized approach to the texts that had been common since the Middle Ages. Like the Romans, they could limit recovery to certain types of harm.

Most jurists took the latter approach.[42] They said that the defendant was liable for harm to the plaintiff's physical property. Generalizing the few texts in point, they also said he was liable for the plaintiff's physical injuries or death. They justified this limitation by pointing out that it corresponded more closely to the historical meaning of the texts. Some of them also argued that liability would be too extensive if the plaintiff could recover for any type of harm that he suffered. As Rudolf von Jhering said:

Where would it lead if everyone could be sued, not only for intentional wrongdoing [*dolus*] but for gross negligence [*culpa lata*] absent a contractual relationship! A ill-advised statement, a rumor passed on, a false report, bad advice, a poor decision, a recommendation for an unfit serving maid by her former employer, information given at the request of a traveler about the way, the time, and so forth – in short, anything and everything would make one liable to compensate for the damage that ensued if there were gross negligence despite one's good faith...[43]

One consequence of this approach was that a plaintiff could not recover for what we call pure economic loss. Nevertheless, the nineteenth-century jurists had not identified pure economic loss as a particular type of harm for which the plaintiff should not recover. They had proceeded in the opposite fashion by identifying a few limited types of harm for which the plaintiff could recover. Moreover, they gave no reason why recovery for other types of losses would be wrong in principle. A line simply had to be drawn somewhere. When the *Oberlandesgericht* of

---

[41] E.g. J. C. Hasse, *Die Culpa des Römischen Rechts* (2nd edn, A. Marcur, Bonn, 1838), § 8; C. F. Mühlenbruch, *Doctrina Pandectarum* (1838), par. III, § 450.

[42] E.g. B. Windshied, *Lehrbuch des Pandektenrechts*, vol. 2 (7th edn, Rütten & Loening, Frankfurt-am-Main, 1891), §§ 451, 455; K. A. von Vangerow, *Lehrbuch der Pandekten* 3 (6th edn, N. G. Elwert, Marburg, 1863), § 681 no. 1.I (3); K. L. Arndts, *Lehrbuch der Pandekten* (14th edn, Gotha, Stuttgart, 1889), § 324. See Zimmermann, *Law of Obligations*, pp. 1036–8.

[43] R. von Jhering, 'Culpa in contrahendo oder Schadensersatz bei nichtigen oder nicht zur Perfektion gelangten Verträgen', (1861) 4 *Jherings Jahrbücher* 12–13.

Lübeck refused to allow a pilot to recover from a ship captain who had brought criminal charges against him that were ultimately dismissed, it acknowledged:

> The consequence admittedly is that there will be no action for many pecuniary disadvantages that one person suffers through the action of another when they are caused by mere negligence and he is not in a contractual relationship. While this can be a hard result in particular cases, it would have the most serious consequences to grant a claim for every disadvantage that anyone suffers, even in an indirect fashion, from the action of another.[44]

Nevertheless, by the end of the century it seemed as though this approach would be abandoned for a broader one more like the French. It had been challenged by jurists such as Otto von Gierke and Josef Kohler, who argued that the defendant should be liable for violation of a panoply of rights that concerned plaintiff's freedom of action and personality.[45] In 1888, the *Reichsgericht* – the highest German court for civil matters – allowed a plaintiff whose person and property had not been injured to recover. He had been temporarily unable to sell a product because the defendant had raised a claim of patent infringement. The court said his conduct was 'negligent at least'.[46] But then the German Civil Code was drafted.

Codification

Surprising as it may seem in retrospect, a broad approach such as the one just described was taken by the First Commission which produced a draft civil code and did much to give the provisions on tort law their present shape. The preliminary draft (*Vorentwurf*) which was the starting point for their work contained the following provision:

> One who has caused another harm [*Schaden*] by intention or by negligence by an unlawful [*widerrechtlich*] act or omission is obligated to make him compensation.[47]

---

[44] Oberlandesgericht, Lübeck, Decision of 13 October 1838, A. A. Seuffert's (1867) 137 *Archiv für Entscheidungen der obersten Gerichte in den deutschen Staaten* 8.

[45] O. von Gierke, *Der Entwurf eines bürgerlichen Gesetzbuches und das deutsche Recht* (Duncker & Humblot, Leipzig, 1889), p. 264; O. von Gierke, *Deutsches Privatrecht* 3 (1917), 885–7; J. Kohler, 'Recht und Process', (1887) 14 *Zeitschrift für das privat-öffentliche Recht der Gegenwart*, 14 (1887), pp. 4–5; J. Kohler, *Lehrbuch des bürgerlichen Rechts*, 1 (C. Heymann, Berlin, 1904) § 132; 2 (1906), § 190. See K.-H. Fezer, *Teilhabe und Verantwortung* (Beck, Munich, 1986), 456–65.

[46] Decision of 3 December 1888, 22 *Entscheidungen des Reichsgerichts* 208 at 209.

[47] *Teilentwurf des Vorentwurfs zu einem BGB, Recht der Schuldverhältnisse* no. 15, § 1.

The members of the Commission were in agreement with this broad approach. They reported:

Any act is not permitted in the sense of the civil law by which anyone infringes and violates the sphere of rights of another unlawfully in an unauthorized manner. For the sphere of rights of each person must be respected and left untouched by all other persons; whoever acts contrary to this general command of the law without there being any special grounds for justification has by that alone committed a tortious act [literally, a non-permitted act, *unerlaubte Handlung*].[48]

Yet, as we will see, the limitations on recovery that the Code now contains were largely the result of the decisions made by this Commission. Strangely enough, the very drafters who believed in such a general principle wrote these limitations into the Code. To see why, we will describe the limitations in the Code as it was finally enacted, and then their origin.

§ 823(1) of the Code as finally enacted says that

[o]ne who intentionally or negligently unlawfully violates the life, body, health, freedom, property or similar right [*sonstiges Recht*] of another is obligated to compensate him for the harm that thereby ensues.

Economic harm is not recoverable under this provision because it is not one of the enumerated rights, nor a right sufficiently similar to property to count as a 'similar right'. § 823(2) provides in relevant part:

A person is under the same obligation who violates a statute which has the purpose of protecting another.

Economic harm can only be recovered under this provision when it is the subject of a special statute. § 826 provides:

One who intentionally causes another harm in a manner that violates good morals [*gute Sitten*] is obligated to compensate him for the harm.

Economic harm can be recovered under this provision only when it is caused intentionally. Taken together, then, these provisions strictly limit recovery for economic harm. Paradoxically, however, the drafters had not been concerned about limiting the types of harm for which one could recover. They had been concerned about when harm was 'unlawfully' inflicted. The exclusion of recovery for economic harm was a by-product of that concern.

[48] W. Schubert (ed.), *Die Vorlagen der Redaktoren für die erste Kommission zur Ausarbeitung des Entwurfs eines Bürgerlichen Gesetzbuches, Recht der Schuldverhältnisse, Teil 1, Allgemeiner Teil I* (W. de Gruyter, Berlin, 1980), p. 657.

That concern surfaced at an early meeting in which the First Commission discussed 'the requirements for intent or negligence'. The members agreed that these requirements concerned 'not the harm itself but objective unlawfulness', so that it was sufficient that a party knew or foresaw his act was unlawful, whether he intended or foresaw that it would harm anyone.[49] The question then became what actions should be considered unlawful.

The Commission classified unlawful actions into three categories. This threefold classification was eventually reflected in the threefold distinction of §§ 823 (1), 823 (2) and 826 BGB. First, the act might be one that 'includes in itself a violation of right [*Rechtsverletzung*]'.[50] With such an act, the 'doing of the harm [*Schaden*] is among the requirements of objective unlawfulness, or, to put it another way, it belongs to the factual elements that constitute the delict'.[51] Secondly, the act might be a violation of some norm whether or not it results in harm. As the Commission put it, 'the act is unlawful or prohibited also when no harm is done'.[52] An example would be an act prohibited by a criminal statute or police regulation.[53] Thirdly, the act might be unlawful because it was 'unfair' (*illoyal*) in the sense that the defendant wished to cause harm or should have acted differently, given the amount of harm that the plaintiff would suffer: 'liability to make compensation depends, conceptually, on whether the harm was intended or that the extent of it could have been realized'.[54]

The Commission thought that whether the defendant must have been aware that harm would occur turned on which type of unlawful act he committed. Its conclusions passed into its final draft of 1888.[55] In acts of the first type, where the doing of the act is unlawful because it constitutes the 'violation of a right' or 'the doing of harm', the defendant must know or foresee that the victim's rights would be violated, that he would be harmed.[56] Otherwise the defendant would not have been aware that his act was unlawful. This conclusion was expressed in § 704 (2) of the final draft, albeit with a change of terminology. In its early

---

[49] 'Protokolle der Kommission zur Ausarbeitung eines Bürgerlichen Gesetzbuches (1881–89)', in H. H. Jakobs and W. Schubert, *Die Beratung des Bürgerlichen Gesetzbuches*, vol. 3 (W. de Gruyter, Berlin, 1983), p. 969 (hereinafter Protokolle I).
[50] Ibid., 969. [51] Ibid., 973. [52] Ibid., 972–3. [53] Ibid., 970. [54] Ibid.
[55] Erste Entwurf eines Bürgerlichen Gesetzbuches für das Deutsche Reich.
[56] Protokolle I 973. ('hängt zweifellos die Ersatzpflict davon ab, dass der Schaden selbst vorausgesehen (gewollt) oder bei Anwendung der schuldigen Aufmerksamkeit vorauszusehen war, dass also Vorsatz oder Fahrlässigkeit auf den Schaden mit zu beziehen ist').

meetings, the Commission had used the expressions 'violation of a right' and 'the doing of harm' synonymously. Any violation of a right was a doing of harm. § 704(2) of the final draft provided: 'If anyone negligently or intentionally by an unlawful act has violated the rights of another' he shall be liable for any 'harm' that he caused, 'even when it was not foreseeable that any harm would be done'. Used in this sense, 'harm' might or might not arise from the violation of a right. The defendant acted unlawfully whether or not he knew that harm might result because he was aware that he was violating someone's right. When the draft of 1888 was revised, it was realised that the phrase 'even when it was not foreseeable' was unnecessary. It was enough to say, as § 823 (1) now does, that the defendant was liable for any harm he caused in violation of a right.[57]

In the case of acts that were unlawful because of the violation of some independent norm, the Commission thought that the defendant should not be liable for any harm that happens to arise. If he were, 'it would follow that compensation is also to be made for harm when all that can be claimed is that the harm would not have arisen had the statute been obeyed although, nevertheless, the violation had no relationship with the harm, occurred by accident, and could not have been foreseen'.[58] That seemed to go too far. The Commission concluded that the defendant's liability should turn on whether he could foresee the harm, and this conclusion was reflected in § 704 (1) of the final draft. It provided that '[i]f anyone negligently or intentionally by an unlawful act – of commission or omission – causes another harm which he foresaw or must have foreseen would arise', he would be liable 'without distinction as to whether the extent of the harm was foreseeable or not'.[59]

---

[57] Schwitansky believes that the harm must be intended or foreseen under § 704 s. 2 as well as § 704 s. 1 so that the former provision is really an instance of the principle contained in the latter. H. G. Schwitansky, *Deliktsrecht, Unternehmenschutz und Arbeitskampfrecht* (Duncker & Humblot, Berlin, 1986), p. 113. That would be so if the Commission had continued to identify the doing of harm with the violation of a right, as it had in its earlier meetings. Due to the change of terminology, however, all that needs to be intended or foreseen under § 704 s. 2 is the violation of a right, not the ensuing harm. That is consistent with the Commission's consistent position that the requirements of intent and negligence concern, not the harm, but the unlawfulness of an act.

[58] Protokolle I, p. 970.

[59] As Schwitansky points out, it seems clear from the drafting history that this provision is concerned with the violation of a statutory norm even though that is not apparent when the text is taken out of context. Schwitansky, *Deliktsrecht*, p. 112.

Here again, the reference to foreseeability was dropped in later drafts of the Code, this time in response to a suggestion of the *Vorkommission* of the *Reichsjustizamt*. It thought that the scope of liability for violating a statutory prohibition should be determined, not by foreseeability, but by the protective purpose of the statute. Otherwise, someone whom the statute was not designed to protect could recover if harm was foreseeable, and someone whom it was not designed to protect could not recover unless the damages were foreseeable.[60] As a result, what is now § 823 (2) merely says that a person who 'violates a statute which has the purpose of protecting another' is under the same obligation as one who violates a right under § 823 (1).

Acts of the third type which were neither violations of a right nor prohibited by some statute were dealt with in § 705. It provided: 'Acts which are allowed in themselves as a matter of general freedom also count as unlawful when they lead to harm to and their performance violates good morals [*gute Sitten*].' Since the First Commission had in mind acts which violated good morals precisely because of the harm that they caused, it was not necessary to specify that the defendant be aware of this harm.

Thus the threefold classification of §§ 823 (1), 823 (2) and 826 was not devised in order to limit the type of harm for which the plaintiff could recover. It was devised to classify the ways in which an act might be unlawful.[61] That classification was thought to have implications for the extent to which the defendant had to foresee the harm he caused, implications which were reflected in the First Commission's draft although they no longer figure in the Code.

Nevertheless, the classification implied that for the plaintiff to recover, the defendant must have violated one of his rights, or violated a statutory norm, or acted in a way that the Commission described initially

---

[60] 'Protokolle der Vorkommission des Reichsjustizamts' in Jakobs and Schubert, *Beratung*, p. 534.

[61] That, I believe, is why Schmiedel, Schwitansky and Fezer read the drafting history differently. Schmiedel stresses that the First Commission endorsed the very general principle that it did, and so he sees the Commission's concern that the act be unlawful as a formal one which did not put a real limitation on recovery. B. Schmiedel, *Deliktsobligationen nach deutschem Kartellrecht*, vol. 1 (Hob, Tübingen, 1974). p. 23 and p. 23 fn. 75. Schwitansky notes, correctly, that the limitation was a real one: *Deliktsrecht*, pp. 106–14. But then the question arises, why a Commission that believed in such a general principle imposed such a limitation. Fezer believes that they did so as a compromise. Fezer, *Teilhabe*, p. 478. In my own view, because they thought their threefold classification was exhaustive, they were trying to clarify rather than to limit the scope of the general principle.

as *illoyal* and later as a violation of *gute Sitten*. An important question, then, was what should count as a violation of the plaintiff's rights. This question had been discussed at the Commission's first meetings when it had just devised its threefold classification. The question was 'what is to be understood as the "violation of a right": only the violation of a right which receives an absolute protection or any violation of the legal order by an act prohibited by law as contrary to the legal order....'[62] The Commission eventually chose the first of these alternatives. It did not do so, however, by considering the types of harm for which the plaintiff should recover. When the question first arose, the Commission was considering how an act of fraud would fit within its threefold classification. Fraud was, in a sense, a violation of the victim's right not to be defrauded. But it was not in itself a violation of 'a right which receives an absolute protection' such as body or property, since one could commit fraud without injury to the victim's body or property or similar right. Conceived in this way, as the Commission noted, the question was 'of no great practical significance': if fraud was not considered the violation of a right, then the perpetrator would still be liable if harm was foreseeable – which it almost always would be.[63] At a later meeting the Commission noted that, although it did seem odd to treat the defrauder differently than the thief, it would be confusing to devise a broad definition of rights that would include 'those which arise when the legal order prohibits certain actions to be taken against another person'.[64] This problem aside, the Commission seemed to think that the only kind of right that was not 'absolute' and would therefore be left out was a 'right of obligation' (*obligatorisches Recht*), such as a contract right. The Commission noted briefly that such a right should be left out because it 'cannot be violated by anyone except the debtor'.[65]

In response to these considerations, the First Commission added a final sentence to § 704 (1) to clarify the type of right that must be violated. It went without saying that the paradigm case of a violation of a right was an interference with property. But the Commission added: 'The violation of life, body, health, freedom and honor are also to be regarded as the violation of a right in the sense of the previous provision.' This language had mixed fortunes before it passed into what is now § 823 (1). At one point it was deleted as unnecessary. Later it was reinstated, with an explicit mention of the right of property and the subtraction

---

[62] Protokolle I, 971–2.   [63] Ibid, 975.
[64] Ibid, 984–5.   [65] Protokolle I, 984, 986–7.

of 'honor'. The phrase 'or similar right' (*sonstiges Recht*) was added, because it had proven impossible to enumerate all of the ownership-like 'absolute rights' that a defendant could violate.

Thus, by the time the work of the First Commission was done, recovery had been limited in much the same way as in the final Code that came into force in 1900. One further limitation was added by the Second Commission, again in response to a suggestion from the *Vorkommission* of the *Reichsjustizamt*. The *Vorkommission* claimed that one who causes harm by acting contrary to good morals should be liable only if he intended to cause the harm. He should not be liable for negligence. That limitation, it said, reflected the 'view dominant in theory and practice'.[66] The Second Commission which wrote the next draft of the Code adopted this suggestion because 'there is no need to depart from prevailing law in this respect. The negligent violation of another's sphere of interest by an unfair (*illoyal*) act will seldom occur. In any event, one cannot find in it such a serious violation of public morality that the legislator has occasion to step in.'[67] The Second Commission also rejected a proposal to broaden the scope of what is now § 823 so that one who violated another's right would be liable, not only to that person, but to others who were harmed. As they explained the reason:

[T]he provisions over the duty to compensate in tort belong to those provisions which serve to set boundaries to the spheres of rights of individuals within which they may develop their individual freedom and pursue their interests. The spheres of rights of individuals, as has been pointed out, include principally one's own economic rights [*Vermögensrechte*] – both property and obligations – and, however, his so-called rights of personality as well (life, bodily integrity, health, freedom, honor), which, like the right to property, are protected against infringement by a command directed to everyone. The spheres of rights are also bounded in another way: the law places duties on one person in the interest of another, commanding or forbidding a certain course of conduct. But only such commands and prohibitions can be taken into account which have the purpose of protecting the interests of one individual from infringement by another – not those statutory duties which are established in the interest of the community which promote the welfare of each person because they are provided in the interests of all.[68]

Once the German Civil Code came into force, it took German courts very little time to conclude that, indeed, a plaintiff could not recover

---

[66] Ibid, 535.
[67] Protokolle der Kommission für die zweite Lesung des Entwurfs des Bürgerlichen Gesetzbuchs, 2 (1898), p. 576.
[68] Ibid, 567–8.

for pure economic harm. In 1901, it held that a defendant who interfered with the plaintiff's economic freedom of action had not violated his 'freedom' within the meaning of § 823 (1).[69] In 1904, it held that economic harm (*Vermögensschädigung*) was not in itself harm to a right protected by § 823 (1). Therefore, the defendant was not liable for causing it unintentionally unless he violated a statute or a right that was protected under § 823 (1). The German rule against recovery for pure economic loss had taken its modern form.[70]

The courts' interpretation does seem to be consistent with its drafting history. The First Commission had decided that the defendant was liable only for violating 'absolute' rights such as property, life, body and freedom. The Second Commission had decided that the defendant who violated good morals was not liable unless he intended to harm the plaintiff. Yet what is extraordinary is that the problem of recovery for economic harm as such, had not shown up clearly on the radar screens of either Commission. The First Commission had been concerned about 'unlawfulness', and out of this concern grew the tripartite classification of the final Code: violation of a right, violation of a statute and violation of good morals. Rights were then identified with 'absolute rights', and a negligent offence to good morals was said not to be a sufficiently serious violation. And out of these considerations came the modern German rule against recovery for pure economic loss.

Therefore, this rule was the result of more than one historical accident. It was an accident that drafters who were trying to define 'unlawfulness' would end up limiting the types of harm for which a plaintiff could recover. It was an accident that their decision about how to do so was made at a time when a certain argument seemed persuasive. The argument turned on the distinction between an absolute right such as property, and relative right or right of obligation such as contract. An absolute right was a right against all the world. A relative right was a right against a particular person, such as the other party to a contract. So it seemed to follow that to be liable, the defendant must violate an absolute right of the plaintiff since, unless the defendant had a contract with the plaintiff, the plaintiff's relative rights were not rights against the defendant but against someone else. *A fortiori*, the plaintiff could not recover if the defendant had not even interfered with a contract right but a mere economic expectation.

---

[69] Reichsgericht, Decision of 11 April 1901, *Entscheidungen des Reichsgerichts in Zivilsachen* 48, 114.
[70] Reichsgericht, Decision of 27 February 1904, *Entscheidungen des Reichsgerichts in Zivilsachen* 58, 24.

This argument is typical of the conceptualism of the nineteenth century – of what the Germans call *Begriffsjurisprudenz*. It does not consider what principle or purpose might be served by limiting the plaintiff's recovery. It tries to extract limits from the definitions of concepts, in this instance, from the concepts of absolute and relative rights. The late scholastics had rejected the equally conceptualistic argument of Cajetan because they could not see why, in principle, a person who was prevented from obtaining some benefit should not recover. They noted that things may have value in the present precisely because they enable a person to acquire other things in the future. Instead of defining a right, as Cajetan implicitly had done, they said that a person could have a right to seek a benefit, not merely rights to benefits he had already acquired. These objections would have been equally telling against the conceptualist argument of the nineteenth century. Today, *Begriffsjurisprudenz* is in disrepute. It is generally recognized that one cannot find a solution to a problem, such as limiting recovery in tort, by consulting definitions that were framed without that problem in mind, such as the definitions of absolute and relative right. It is an historical accident that the Code was enacted when conceptualism was still in flower.

Then there is one more accident. If the defendant should be liable for negligence only if he violates plaintiff's absolute rights, how can he be liable for intentionally causing the plaintiff an economic loss, as he sometimes is in Germany? If the drafters had seen a contradiction here, they might have rethought limiting recovery in negligence to the violation of absolute rights. They did not see a contradiction because of the way in which they had classified 'unlawfulness'. When the defendant who intentionally caused economic harm was held liable, it was not because he had violated plaintiff's rights but because he had violated good morals. And that settled that. If the defendant had not violated any of the plaintiff's rights, no one asked why intentionally causing him an economic loss should ever be considered a violation of good morals.

## *England*

In England, it also came to be accepted that one could not normally recover in negligence for pure economic loss.[71] The case commonly cited

---

[71] W. V. H. Rogers, *Winfield and Jolowicz on Tort* (15th edn, Sweet & Maxwell, London, 1998), p. 134; K. M. Stanton, *The Modern Law of Tort* (Sweet & Maxwell, London, 1994), pp. 332, 353–4. See generally M. Furmston (ed.), *The Law of Tort Policies and Trends in Liability for Damage to Property and Economic Loss* (Duckworth, London, 1986).

today to illustrate this rule is *Spartan Steel & Alloys Ltd* v. *Martin & Co. (Contractors) Ltd*.[72] The defendants cut the power line to plaintiff's factory causing material to solidify in its furnace. The plaintiff recovered for the loss it suffered because the material solidified, but not for the profit it lost because it could not melt other material while the power was off. This rule pre-dated *Spartan Steel*. It was judge-made, not statutory, and was established by a series of cases rather than a single decision. Unlike Germany, one cannot find a single moment in which the rule became accepted. Nevertheless, one can see a turning point: a point at which the courts began to say that relief would not be given because of the kind of harm that the plaintiff had suffered. At this turning point, a critical role was played by the same conceptualistic argument that influenced the German drafters.

Before this point had been reached, English courts had refused to allow recovery of what we now call pure economic loss in a number of important cases. In 1875 in *Cattle* v. *The Stockton Waterworks Co.*,[73] defendant's negligence caused the flooding of a third party's land on which the plaintiff was building a tunnel. The court refused to allow him to recover for his extra expenses. In 1877, in *Simpson & Co.* v. *Thomson*,[74] an insurance company was denied recovery for the insurance money it had to pay for insured cargo that was lost when one of defendant's ships negligently struck one of his own ships containing the cargo. In 1908, in *Anglo-Algerian Steamship Co. Ltd* v. *The Houlder Line, Ltd.*,[75] defendant had negligently damaged a third party's dock. Plaintiff was not allowed to recover for the loss he suffered when his ship was unable to use it.

Nevertheless, as Robby Bernstein has noted, the rationale of *Cattle* and *Simpson* 'had nothing to do with the fact that the plaintiff's loss was economic',[76] and the same can be said of *Anglo-Algerian Steamship*. One consideration, mentioned in *Cattle* and *Anglo-Algerian Steamship*, was that the damage was too 'remote'.[77] Another, mentioned in *Cattle*, *Simpson* and *Anglo-Algerian Steamship*, was that recovery would unduly multiply the number of possible plaintiffs: if a mine were flooded, those who worked there could recover their lost wages;[78] a doctor who had contracted to treat a man for a fixed fee for a year could recover from the negligent driver of a carriage who had injured his patient;[79] a traveller forced to find other accommodation could recover against a person who

---

[72] [1973] 1 QB 27.   [73] (1875) LR 10 QB 453.   [74] [1877] 3 AC 279 (HL).
[75] [1908] 1 KB 659.   [76] R. Bernstein, *Economic Loss* (2nd edn., 1998), p. 11.
[77] LR 10 QB at 457; [1908] 1 KB at 665.   [78] LR 10 QB at 457.
[79] [1877] 3 AC at 289.

negligently damaged the inn where he planned to stay.[80] The first of these considerations has to do with causation; the second with a pragmatic desire to avoid an indefinite number of plaintiffs. Neither suggests that the plaintiff cannot recover what we now call economic loss. Indeed, in *Anglo-Algerian Steamship*, Walton J indicated that under some circumstances, he could.[81]

Nevertheless, at the turn of the twentieth century, a number of leading treatise writers placed a different interpretation of such cases. According to J. F. Clerk and W. H. B. Lindsell, *Cattle* stood for the principle that 'interference with rights of service or with rights of contract generally is not actionable'.[82] In that respect, such rights were different from rights such as property which were 'unqualified'.[83]

A similar interpretation was adopted in the eighth edition of C. G. Addison's treatise on torts which was published in 1906 after his death by William Gordon and Walter Griffith. Although they styled themselves 'editors', they had found it necessary to rewrite the treatise extensively because it was unsystematic, they said, compared with the treatises of Sir Frederick Pollock and Clerk and Lindsell.[84] Since it contained 'little or nothing about the law of Negligence', they had written the chapter on that subject from scratch.[85] In it they explained that negligence was the breach of a duty, and that therefore the plaintiff is liable only where there is 'an obligation toward the plaintiff'.[86] 'It follows', they said, 'that if there is no duty to be careful there is no action for negligence', citing *Cattle* as an illustration.

Sir John Salmond adopted a similar interpretation of *Cattle* and of *Anglo-Algerian Steamship* in the second edition of his treatise on torts published in 1910. In *Cattle*, the principle was that 'nuisance is actionable only at the suit of the occupier or owner of the land affected by it; not at the suit of strangers whatever pecuniary interest they may have

---

[80] [1908] 1 KB at 668.
[81] [1908] 1 KB at 664–5. He was speaking of what are now called cases of public nuisance in which the plaintiff is specially affected. As will be noted later, today the rule is said to be different in nuisance than in negligence, but Walton J. was writing before that difference came to be accepted.
[82] J. F. Clerk and W. H. B. Lindsell, *The Law of Torts* (ed. W. Paine, 3rd edn, Sweet & Maxwell, London, 1904), p. 11. At another point they do suggest that the case turned on the remoteness of the damage. Ibid, p. 133.
[83] Ibid, 11.
[84] C. G. Addison, *A Treatise on the Law of Torts or Wrongs and Their Remedies* (8th edn, eds. W. E. Gordon and W. H. Griffith, Stevens, London, 1906), p. viii.
[85] Ibid, vii.   [86] Ibid, 701.

in the non-existence of the nuisance'.[87] In *Anglo-Algerian Steamship*, the principle was that '[n]egligent injury to property gives an action to the owner of that property, or to other persons having some proprietary interest therein, but not to mere strangers who are thereby subjected to pecuniary loss'.[88] Both cases were instances of *damnum sine iniuria*.[89] In later editions, he generalized the principle: 'He who does a wrongful act is liable only to the person whose rights are violated.'[90] As illustrations, he cited *Cattle* and *Anglo-Algerian Steamship Co*.[91]

Such an interpretation was adopted by Justice Hamilton in 1911 in deciding the case of *La Société Anonyme de Remorquage à Hélice* v. *Bennets*.[92] The defendant had negligently rammed and sunk a ship owned by a third party which the plaintiff had been towing under contract. The plaintiff was not allowed to recover the money he would have made under the contract. The plaintiff's attorney had argued that he should recover because the damage was not 'too remote'.[93] Instead of arguing whether it was or not, the defendant's attorney said, that '[a]lthough there was a breach of duty followed by damage to the owner of the tow, there was only *iniuria sine damno* so far as the tug was concerned'.[94] Justice Hamilton agreed. Although the headnote to the case said that the plaintiff's harm was not the 'direct consequence of the negligence', Hamilton said that the plaintiffs must 'shew not only an *iniuria*, namely, the breach of the defendant's obligation, but also *damnum* to themselves in the sense of damage recognized by law'.[95] He thus inverted the words of Salmond, who had spoken of *damnum sine iniuria*, although the principle was the same. Salmond meant that the plaintiff had suffered on economic loss but not a wrong that the law would redress. Like the treatise writers, he cited *Cattle* as authority.

After *Remorquage* came a long series of cases in which courts said that what mattered was not remoteness, but the type of harm that the plaintiff had suffered. In 1922, in *Elliott Steam Tug Co. Ltd* v. *Shipping Controller*, the plaintiff did not recover under the common law for the profits he lost when the Admiralty requisitioned his tug. The reason, according to Scrutton J is 'not because the loss of profits during repairs is not the

---

[87] J. W. Salmond, *The Law of Torts: A Treatise on the English Law of Liability for Civil Injuries* (2nd edn, Stevens & Hayer, London, 1910), p. 10.
[88] Ibid, 10.    [89] Ibid, 8, 11.
[90] Salmond, *The Law of Torts* (8th edn, ed. W. T. S. Stallybrass, Sweet & Maxwell, London, 1934), p. 133.
[91] Ibid, 134, 135.    [92] [1911] 1 KB 243.    [93] Ibid, at 245.
[94] Ibid, at 246.    [95] Ibid, at 248.

direct consequence of the wrong, but because the common law rightly or wrongly does not recognise him as able to sue for such an injury to his merely contractual rights'.[96] In 1947, by way of dictum, Lord Roche said of *Remorquage* that '[i]f it was correctly decided, on which I express no opinion, I think it must depend on a view that one vessel (A) does not owe to the tug which is towing vessel (B) any duty not negligently to collide with (B)'.[97] Lord Simonds said of the plaintiff in *Simpson* that '[t]he reason why he cannot recover is not because it could not be reasonably foreseen that he, or at least some insurer, would suffer, but because his loss is of a kind that the law does not regard as recoverable'.[98] He cited with approval *Remorquage* and its statement about *iniuria* without *damno*.[99] In 1952, in *Best v. Samuel Fox & Co. Ltd*, a wife was denied recovery for loss of consortium when her husband had been injured. Lord Goddard said that '[n]egligence, if it is to give rise to legal liability, must result from a breach of duty owed to a person who thereby suffers damage. But what duty was owed here by the employers of the husband to the wife?'[100] In 1955, in *Attorney-General for New South Wales v. Perpetual Trustee Co. (Ltd)*, the government was not allowed to recover for loss of the services of a policeman whom the defendant had tortiously killed. Citing *Remorquage*, Lord Simonds said: 'It is fundamental...that the mere fact that an injury to A. prevents a third party from getting from A. a benefit which he would otherwise have obtained, does not invest the third party with a right of action against the wrongdoer...'[101] In 1966, in *Weller & Co. v. Foot and Mouth Disease Research Institute*, plaintiff could not recover for harm suffered to his business of auctioning cattle when the market for cattle was closed due to the escape of a virus from the defendant institute. Justice Widgery said that 'a duty of care which arises from a risk of direct injury to person or property is owed only to those whose person or property may foreseeably be injured by a failure to take care'.[102] In *Electrochrome Ltd v. Welsh Plastics Ltd*, plaintiff could not recover when defendant negligently cut off the supply of water from his factory. Justice Geoffrey Lane said that '[a] person who suffers *damnum* cannot recover compensation on the basis of *iniuria* suffered by another'.[103] In 1969, in *Margarine Union GmbH v. Cambay Prince Steamship Co. Ltd*, plaintiff failed

---

[96] [1922] 1 KB 127, 140. A few years later, Oliver Wendell Holmes decided a leading American case on the same rationale, citing this language with approval. *Robbins Dry Dock and Repair v. Flint*, 275 US 303 (1927).
[97] *Morrison Steamship Co. Ltd v. Greystoke Castle* [1947] AC 265, 280 (HL).
[98] [1947] AC at 305. [99] Ibid, at 306. [100] [1952] AC 716, 730–1.
[101] [1955] AC 457, 484. [102] [1966] QB 569, 587. [103] [1968] 2 All ER 205, 206.

to recover the loss that he suffered when goods were damaged that he did not own at the time that they were harmed. Justice Roskill said that he agreed with 'every word' of Widgery's judgment in *Weller*.[104]

As P. S. Atiyah observed,[105] and as we have just seen, in these cases the courts did not formulate a rule expressly stating that a plaintiff could not recover for pure economic loss. Nevertheless, this was an implication of what they had said. If the plaintiff could not recover when the defendant interfered with a contractual right, then surely he could not be liable when he interfered with a mere expectation of receiving some benefit.

What is striking is the consistency not only in result but in the way in which this result was explained during this period of over fifty years. Supposedly, the fact that the plaintiff has a contract with a third party cannot change the rights and duties of the plaintiff and defendant to each other. To be liable, the defendant must violate a right such as property which the plaintiff has against all the world, not merely against a third party. This is the same argument that we have seen in Germany.[106] It exemplifies a logical or conceptualist style of reasoning that seemed persuasive at the beginning of the century, but has since been generally discredited. Even at the beginning of the last century, the argument was not decisive. Then, as now, the plaintiff could recover for economic loss in a variety of cases in which the defendant had caused the loss intentionally: for example, by threatening potential customers.[107] For

---

[104] [1969] 1 QB 219, 251.
[105] P. S. Atiyah, 'Negligence and Economic Loss', (1967) 83 *Law Quarterly Review* 248 at 248.
[106] Whether the English treatise writers who first put forward this argument knew that German jurists had already done so is another question. That is certainly a possibility for Salmond. He was surely familiar with the German Civil Code and may have known of the work of the First Commission as well. His select bibliography in his book *Jurisprudence, or the Theory of the Law* shows a thorough knowledge of German writing on private law and a special admiration for Bernard Windscheid, one of the most distinguished members of the First Commission. He described Windscheid as 'one of the most distinguished German exponents of modern Roman law' and his book, *Lehrbuch des Pandektenrechts*, as 'an admirable example of the scientific study of a legal system'. J. Salmond, *Jurisprudence, or the Theory of the Law* (Stevens & Haynes, London, 1902), p. 654. Some have suggested that he used ideas taken from Windscheid in that book. J. Stone, *Legal Systems and Lawyers' Reasonings* (Stanford University Press, Stanford, CA, 1964), p. 141. See A. Frame, *Salmond: Southern Jurist* (Victoria University Press, Wellington, NZ, 1995), 63.
[107] Rogers, *Winfield and Jolowicz on Tort*, p. 133. The classic early case is *Tarleton v. M'Gawley* [1794] 170 ER 153 (KB). Nevertheless, there is no general principle that anyone who intentionally causes another economic loss is liable. The plaintiff must sue for deceit, passing off, or some other particular tort. See M. Brazier, *The Law of Torts* (8th edn, Butterworths, London, 1988), pp. 103–50.

example, they could recover if the defendant created a public nuisance by blocking the street, and the plaintiff suffered some special economic harm that was not suffered by users of the street generally, such as a loss of customers.[108] Today, treatise writers simply say that the plaintiff can recover for such harm in nuisance, but not in negligence, without explaining why there should be such a difference.[109] Such cases can be distinguished in various ways from the ones which we have just described. But if, as a matter of logic, the defendant should not be liable unless he violates a right that the plaintiff has against all the world, it is hard to see why he should ever be liable for preventing the plaintiff from entering into contracts or for interfering with their performance.

Sometimes it seemed that a crack might be opening in the wall, but it has been plastered over. In 1964, in *Hedley Byrne & Co. Ltd* v. *Heller & Partners Ltd* for example, the defendants were held liable for pure economic loss. They were bankers who had negligently given incorrect information about a company's creditworthiness. Lord Devlin claimed that there was 'neither logic nor common sense' in granting recovery only when a financial loss was caused by physical injury.[110] But later courts held that this statement only applied to cases of negligently provided information. They did not change the rule in cases such as *Remorquage*.

Bernstein used the phrase 'historical accident' to describe the shift in rationale from *Cattle* to *Remorquage*.[111] As we can now see, it was the same sort of historical accident that occurred in Germany. The shift occurred because of the accident that a decision was made at a time when this conceptualistic rationale could find favour. In England, judges repeated it for over half a century, either because they still found it persuasive, or out of respect for precedent and the opinion of prior judges.

One might have expected that when this rationale no longer seemed persuasive, judges would react as Lord Devlin did in *Hedley Byrne* and throw out the rule. Instead, Lord Denning kept the rule and threw out

---

[108] *Fritz* v. *Hobson* (1879) 14 Ch. D. 542 (obstruction in the highway costs plaintiff customers); *Rose* v. *Miles* [1815] 1 KB 405 (obstruction of navigable creek forces plaintiff to move his goods by land).

[109] Rogers, *Winfield and Jolowicz on Tort*, p. 493; Stanton, *Modern Law of Tort*, p. 402. Thesiger, J did the same in *SCM*. Thesiger says that the economic loss rule applies in negligence but not in nuisance. *SCM (United Kingdom) Ltd* v. *W. J. Whittall & Son Ltd* [1970] 2 All ER 417, 430.

[110] [1964] AC 465, 517.   [111] Bernstein, *Economic Loss*, p. 11.

the rationale in his decisions in *SCM (United Kingdom) Ltd v. W. J. Whittall & Son Ltd*[112] in 1971 and *Spartan Steel* in 1973.

In both cases, the plaintiffs tried to recover the profits they lost when defendants negligently severed a cable, cutting off the power to their factory. *SCM* reached Lord Denning on appeal from a decision by Justice Thesiger which seems to have influenced his own thinking. Thesiger allowed the plaintiffs to recover, and acknowleged that he did so, in the case before him, because the loss of power had not only cost them profits but also damaged their machines. But in doing so, he gave a new explanation of the prior decisions. As we have seen, they rested on a rationale that was logical and conceptualist. According to Thesiger, however, these decisions could not be explained logically: 'it is not always possible for the law to be logical'.[113] Indeed, these decisions had not been the product of logic but of commonsense groping for reasonable results: 'the common law has always developed by experience rather than logic and by dealing with situations as they arise in what seems a reasonable way'.[114] One indication that judges had been 'dealing with situations as they arise' was the fact that they had stated the principle at stake in two different ways. Sometimes they had said that there was no duty, but sometimes that the harm was too remote.[115] The question should be whether it was reasonable for the plaintiffs to recover in this particular situation. Thesiger thought it was, because the plaintiffs were 'so closely and directly affected' by the act of the defendant.

In this case, on appeal and again in *Spartan Steel*, Lord Denning also gave a new explanation of the prior decisions. The core of his analysis was much like that of Thesiger: he claimed that the rule followed in these decisions was not logical nor based on logic but on common sense. Thus Lord Devlin was only partially right when he said it could be defended by 'neither logic nor common sense'. 'There may be no difference in logic, but I think there is a great deal of difference in common sense. The law is the embodiment of common sense: or, at any rate, it should be.'[116] If we ask why the law has refused to allow the plaintiff to recover for pure economic loss, '[t]he reason is public policy'.[117] In deciding *SCM*, he observed that courts had sometimes said there was no duty and sometimes that the harm was too remote. He claimed 'it was plain' that the defendants owed a duty to the plaintiffs,[118] and seemed

---

[112] [1971] 1 QB 337.  [113] [1970] 2 All ER 417, 431.  [114] Ibid.
[115] Ibid.  [116] [1971] 1 QB at 344.  [117] Ibid.  [118] Ibid, at 343.

at one point to think that the policy concerns that are relevant might be captured by the phrase 'too remote'.[119] In *Spartan Steel*, however, like Thesiger, Denning said that both expressions masked the considerations that had been truly important in the prior cases:

> Sometimes I say: 'There was no duty.' In others I say, 'The damage was too remote.' So much so that I think the time has come to discard those tests which have proved so elusive. It seems to me better to consider the particular relationship in hand, and see whether or not, as a matter of policy, economic loss should be recoverable, or not.[120]

He was less clear about the policy at stake. In *SCM*, he said, '[i]t is not sensible to saddle losses on this scale onto one sole contractor'. 'The risk should be borne by the whole community who suffer the losses, rather than rest on one pair of shoulders...There is not much logic in this, but still it is the law.'[121] In *Spartan Steel* he mentioned this concern, and also the risk of too many claims, the belief 'most people' have that power shortages are 'a thing they must put up with', and the way such risks are allocated by legislation governing the industry.[122]

The account that Justice Thesiger and Lord Denning gave of the history of the rule is history as a common law judge would like it to have occurred. Focusing on the situation before them, judges decide a case as common sense suggests, unsure as yet of the rule or principle to be followed, grasping it dimly but formulating it as best they can. Finally, after many cases are decided, experience makes it possible to see what is at stake more clearly than if one had tried to work out a rule or principle abstractly. Indeed, one may ultimately discover that the problem cannot be solved by a rule or principle that is logically satisfying but must be resolved, case by case, through the exercise of common sense.

I do not deny that sometimes the common law does work that way. I have argued elsewhere that an advantage of the common law method is that it sometimes does.[123] But this time it did not. The courts had not been deciding cases on commonsense grounds. They had been deciding them according to a rationale that had appealed on logical grounds to Clerk, Lindsell, Salmond and the editors of Addison, and before them to the German First Commission. Doubtless, the courts were relieved that

---

[119] Ibid, at 344–5.   [120] [1973] 1 QB at 37.
[121] [1971] 1 QB at 344.   [122] [1973] 1 QB at 38–9.
[123] J. Gordley, 'European Codes and American Restatements: Some Difficulties', (1981) 81 *Columbia Law Review* 140.

this rationale imposed some limit on liability, a concern they sometimes mentioned. Their decisions may have been a product of that concern as well as the logical appeal of the rationale that they adopted. But it does not follow that they placed the limit on recovery where they did by consulting common sense or experience.

Having adopted that rationale in 1911, the courts adhered to it thereafter. To show that they had shifted back and forth between this rationale and a concern for remoteness, Justice Thesiger and Lord Denning only cited pre-*Remorquage* cases such as *Cattle* and *Remorquage* itself which only mentioned remoteness in the headnote, and cases which do not deal with pure economic loss but with physical harm occurring in some improbable way,[124] or nervous shock on witnessing an injury to one's child.[125]

It is an historical accident that rule was adopted at a time when the conceptualistic rationale for it seemed persuasive. To scrap the rationale and keep the rule as though it were the product of experience and common sense is to perpetuate the accident. I agree that there should be a limit on recovery in tort.[126] The fact that this rule was adopted by accident does not prove that it sets the wrong limit. By coincidence, it might be the best rule from the standpoint of policy, common sense and experience. But that would be a remarkable coincidence.

## Conclusion

As we have seen, the rule against recovery for economic loss was adopted in Germany and in England on the strength of an argument that would not be persuasive today. Indeed, three centuries earlier, jurists had shown what the matter was with such an argument in dealing with one that was different but equally conceptualistic. The rule was then preserved by the deference of German judges to the Civil Code and of English judges to precedent. Just as the way in which it was adopted should encourage us to re-examine the rule, the way in which it was preserved should encourage us to re-examine our ideas about the authority of codes and precedents. It is one thing to say that they should have

---

[124] *Woods v. Duncan* [1946] AC 410, 421 (submarine sunk due to an 'extraordinary combination of circumstances'), cited by Thesiger, J in *SCM* [1970] 2 All ER 431.
[125] *King v. Phillips* [1953] 1 QB 429, cited by Lord Denning in *Spartan Steel* [1973] 1 QB at 36.
[126] I suggest a limit that cuts across the distinction between physical and merely economic harm in J. Gordley, 'Contract and Delict: Toward a Unified Law of Obligations', (1997) 1 *Edinburgh Law Review* 345.

authority. It is another to say that courts should defer to a rule founded on academic ideas, now discredited, in the minds of drafters and treatise writers long dead. The courts could instead take a critical and historical approach to their authorities. Otherwise they may find themselves deferring to a fossilized error.

# 3A Pure economic loss: an economic analysis

JÜRGEN G. BACKHAUS

## Introduction

In trying to provide understanding of the concept of pure economic loss from an economic point of view we take the legal concept of pure economic loss for granted but, given the diversity of the issue involved and how it is being dealt with, we are also seeking to establish basic economic considerations which allow us to integrate the salient economic considerations into the discussion of the legal case material.

When parties enter into a contract, or when, without a contract, market participants interfere with each other and losses are inflicted, liability will ensue. Economically, the phenomenon is explained in terms of externalities. In principle, externalities are to be internalized so as to make sure that the true costs of any particular activity are borne by whoever undertook the activity and was therefore responsible for it. It is the purpose of the rule of law to establish appropriate forms of liability which, with a minimum of transaction costs, ascribe liability in tort to the tortfeasor.

However, from a dynamic point of view, not every external effect is to be discouraged. When a new technology is discovered, the owners of the old technology or the machinery which embodies the old technology suffer a purely financial loss which is not to be compensated for, as such compensation would stand in the way of economic progress. Hence, the category of pure economic loss has an important economic meaning. The pure economic loss is the loss imposed in the course of dynamic market activities which is not to be compensated.

In a legal sense, it is difficult to distinguish between the two cases, as they sometimes lie very close to each other. From an economic point of view, however, sharp distinctions can be drawn. The necessary concepts involve the theory of external effects, the theory of rent seeking and the theory of economic development. This chapter first discusses the basic institutions of the market economy necessary for its appropriate functioning. Then the relevant concepts of external effects, rent seeking and dynamic economic development are introduced. The validity of the approach is tested with respect to several of the twenty cases discussed in this study.

## Basic institutions of the market economy

'The division of labour is limited by the extent of the market.' This basic dictum sharply expressed by Adam Smith focuses our attention on those factors which are responsible for limiting the extent of the market, thereby limiting depth and breadth of the division of labour in the economy and, by implication, the creation of wealth.

One can identify eight basic institutions which must be present and workable in order for any market economy to function well, irrespective of the specific style of that economy. Hence, these institutions must be present in an unfettered free market economy, in a socialist market economy, in a co-operative market economy, in a market economy with syndicalist elements or variously in one with strong state market participation. All these forms – and many more – are potentially feasible, provided these basic institutions are firmly in place and can fulfil their functions well.

If these institutions are weakened and impaired, such as when property rights are being diluted, this market will work with high transaction costs and only to the extent that the gains from market exchange outweigh those transaction costs.

### *Basic rights*

Freedom of contract

From an economic point of view, freedom of contract is an important guarantee because it ensures as a necessary condition that all the information available in a society enters economically relevant decisions and all the resources available in a society will be put to their most efficient use. This implies that every infringement of freedom of contract has to be judged in terms of the losses imposed on society due to ignorance and wasted resources. From an economic point of view, it is not sufficient to weigh freedom of contract against some other guarantee such as the principle of equality as such, without paying attention to the full consequences of the trade-off. For example, if it is observed that in a certain society members of a minority are not represented in a particular profession according to their numerical share in that society, from an economic point of view it is not justified to pit the observed end-state inequality against the guarantee of freedom of contract, since a rational choice in the interest of all parties concerned may have led to the unequal outcome. An economic analysis would have to inquire into the reasons for the observed inequality, and it would lay the foundation for assessing the trade-off between the social (opportunity) costs of constraining freedom of contract on the one hand, and the gains in terms of economic equality on the other. Based on the inquiry into the causes of the observed inequalities, an alternative strategy to improve the chances of the minority in question in all likelihood can be derived. It is in this instance that the economic analysis of constitutional guarantees can have implications for constitutional law. Many constitutions require that basic rights can only be curtailed if less onerous measures are not available. To the extent that economic analysis can yield the design of such less onerous measures, it changes the constitutionality of particular policies.

Private property

The guarantee of private property is often thought to be the most important with respect to the means of production. Again, from an economic point of view, the guarantee goes far beyond the protection of people's possession of goods and services. The reason for this wider scope is fairly straightforward. In economics, property rights define and circumscribe alternatives for meaningful actions. Hence, the mere property title to some commodity, such as land, is meaningless if it does not imply discretionary alternatives and options that can be exercised.

In particular, the guarantee of private property rights implies the right to exercise private property prerogatives within workable institutions. The guarantee is violated if, for instance, the contractual forms in which a property right can be exercised are unworkable or impractical, thereby destroying the value of the property right or seriously reducing it. The institutions in which private property rights can be exercised have to provide for the possibility that the four standard options of economic conduct[1] remain open. These options include:

(1) exit: the right to end an economic relationship;
(2) voice: the option to meaningfully improve upon a relationship by changing it through negotiations;
(3) loyalty: the ability to foster the growth of trust and goodwill in a relationship, even in the face of serious problems; and
(4) avoidance: the option to ignore a particular relationship altogether without facing sanctions.

Although these four options exhaust the set of feasible alternatives from an economic point of view, legally they differ in important respects. Exit from an existent relationship is likely to result in the severance of a contract. Since the whole point of exercising the exit option is to contain the costs of a contractual relationship which is no longer mutually beneficial, the party left behind will suffer a loss. Compensating for this loss increases the costs of exit and thereby increases the transaction costs of a contractual relationship in the first place. The mission of minimizing transaction costs would then require curtailing compensation requirements in the case of exit. The alternative is to maintain the exchange relationship by investing in it through communication (voice). Again, this will be the more effective the lower the cost of exit. Hence, again, compensation requirements upon severing the exchange relationship should be contained if transaction costs are to be minimized. Loyalty is an option only if there is hope for repairing an exchange relationship. Compensation requirements upon contract severance will be an *ex ante* tax on loyalty and hence make the contractual relationship more fragile.

Compulsory exchange relationships are particularly frequent in the public sector. The motivation tends to consist in issues of free riding. If free riding is allowed, the supply of a public good or goods laden with externalities may be suboptimally low. However, exit, voice, loyalty and avoidance are less about the quantity of goods and services exchanged than about the quality of service and performance. These need to be weighed against each other. Likewise, minimization of transaction costs is intended to improve the quality of performance. If property is taken to include the right not to enter into exchange relationships, such as not

---

[1] For an analysis of the importance of the first three options see Albert O. Hirschman, *Exit, Voice, and Loyalty: Responses to Decline in Firms, Organizations, and States* (Harvard University Press, Cambridge, MA, 1970).

to enter into a compulsory health insurance scheme, then the provider has to make particular efforts to win over those recalcitrant clients. This, in turn, can only be taken to imply that compensation of a pure economic loss claimed by non-participating legal entities should be held to a minimum.

Liability

This theoretical approach to choice is based on the economic theory of costs as set out in James M. Buchanan's classic *Cost and Choice*.[2] Economics can be broadly described as the science of choices that individuals make either by themselves or in a context of organizations such as firms or state organizations, or else in the context of institutions and networks. To speak of cost in an economic sense is to first identify the decision in which or by which the cost in question arose. The next step is to identify the alternatives to choices that had to be made. The highest valued opportunity foregone is called the opportunity cost. For example, if a case of foot and mouth disease is found on any particular farm, the cost imposed by the requisite sanitary matters depends on the animal holdings of other farmers and on the political discretion of those authorities maintaining public safety. These may face largely different alternatives with different costs attached, and they may be in competition with the other. A single incidence of an animal contaminated with foot and mouth disease may set in motion a sequence of events with heavy losses imposed, notably on owners of similar animal herds, but also gains to be had by competitors (for example, of poultry farms) and in the political sector. The economic losses imposed may be commensurate with the economic windfall profits gained, but liability cannot be established as there is no contractual or tort link anywhere to be found. That is, the decisions of those setting in motion the sequence of events that ultimately determine the size and extent of windfall losses and gains and, of course, where they fall (the incidence) are totally unrelated with the decisions of the original farmer in whose herd the disease had been detected. Hence any standard of due care that might be applicable, for example, to this farmer trading cattle with a neighbour, cannot be carried over into the larger picture. The farmer trading cattle with his neighbour knows both his own herds and roughly the conditions of his neighbours; he will know the trade and other links

---

[2] James M. Buchanan, *Cost and Choice* (Markham, Chicago, 1966).

established between different farms, and therefore he can judge the risk of contamination. This is not so in the wider spectrum where the large losses and gains will fall. The political gains and losses earned and suffered in the process of elevating the case of contamination onto the political scene are completely incommensurate with the original economic gains and losses occurring. As the political sector and the market-place interact, the pursuit of votes and public support translates into political action, perhaps duly exercising legal and political discretion, which is totally out of control from the point of view of the individual actors where the original problem, the contamination, had occurred.

While this cost and choice-based approach calls for a judicious use of granting relief for pure economic losses, the analysis also points to the possibility of recovering such extreme losses through the political sector.

The two basic rights of freedom of contract and private property need to be complemented by the institution of liability in order to be at all meaningful. The faithful observance of contractual terms requires a protective shield of liability for failure to live up to contractual terms, just as much as the respective private property rights require a need to make the intruder liable. Although this principle is straightforward, from an economic point of view the implications can be far-reaching. In particular, liability can only be assigned if the agent to be held liable was indeed in control of events that led to the liability. If this is not the case, the claim has to be followed all the way through to those who were either in control or created the situation that made control impossible. For example, if a patient suffers a serious injury due to a doctor's failure to administer the necessary treatment, because according to state regulations he needed the written consent of two colleagues whom he could not reach because they were tied up in meetings, this doctor is not liable for the injury imposed on the patient; nor is the full damage to remain with the patient; rather, the principle of synchronizing control and liability requires making those jointly and severally liable who contributed to passing the regulations causing the problem – tying up doctors in meetings and requiring written consent to engage in professional activities – in the first place.[3]

---

[3] The legal implications of this rather apodictic statement will be further explored below.

## Stable legal environment

The following three basic guarantees are more or less ancillary to the first three, the classical threesome of economic basic rights. Constancy and predictability of economic policy is required in order to be able to enter into contracts covering not only the present but also the future. The same is true with respect to the exercise of property rights with consequences in the future, notably investment decisions. For private property rights, however, the predictability of economic policy is crucial because it affects the adjustment costs necessarily borne by the private sector and falling onto property, conceivably reducing its value. This requirement does not affect the range and domain of economic policy, but only the time frame within which it can be carried out. The more predictable economic policies are, the smaller the adjustment costs. The corollary statement requires that the more drastic a policy change, the longer its implementation has to be delayed, and the more carefully the precise contours of the new policy have to be explained in order to allow for smooth adjustments in the private sector. A policy may be unconstitutional simply because the legislature did not take the requisite care in spelling it out in time and providing for reasonable adjustment periods before implementation.

## Stable currency

Contractual relationships that are entered into for longer periods of time typically require for some kind of payment to be made by one or the other party. The benefits from contractual relationships can be seriously impaired if there is no common language in which to express the duties of the different parties. The problem is most serious in the case of payments, if there is no stable unit in which to express the size of payments to be made and received. The more uncertainty there is, the smaller the gains from trade can be, and consequently the lower the potential is for economic progress in that society. This is why, from an economic point of view, the guarantee of a stable currency is important as an ancillary right. Again, what is really required is not one particular monetary policy, but rather an institutional arrangement which stabilizes the unit of account. It should be noted here that this requirement does not prescribe any particular monetary policy for a central bank, such as a European central bank; nor does it require only one currency to circulate in a particular market. Leading monetary theorists have shown that a variety of currencies circulating may not only be compatible with the principle of keeping the unit of account stable; it may even be in the interest of enforcing this principle.[4]

*Open markets*

Finally, access to markets has to remain open in order to allow for other basic human rights to be exercised in a meaningful way. This is obvious for the right of freedom of contract, but also extends into such classical basic rights as the freedom of the press, freedom of political expression, of exercising the religion of one's choice, of exercising the profession of one's choice, the academic privileges of freedom of instruction and research, etc. Incidentally, the problem is most serious if a particular government or some private agents suppress the existence of a market altogether. The guarantee of freedom of access to markets obviously includes the guarantee to have such markets established, which does not predetermine the shape that such markets take, so long as they provide for an open forum to communicate and exchange, which is what a market basically is about.[5]

## Procedural guarantees

Basic rights and procedural guarantees are equally important, since basic rights can only be exercised if certain procedural guarantees are observed. The importance of procedural guarantees is not reflected in the amount of space that they receive in this chapter, due to space limitations. Essentially, there are two types of procedural guarantees: guarantees regulating the relationship between public bodies; and guarantees regulating the relationship between public bodies and citizens.

*Relationship between public bodies*

The procedural principles regulating the relationships between public bodies consist of at least three groups. They include all those rules regulating the domains of competence of the various public bodies with

---

[4] See, for example, for a short statement L. B. Yeager, 'Deregulation and Monetary Reform', in *American Economic Review, Papers and Proceedings*, 75.2 (1985), pp. 103–7 with further references.

[5] See A. Schwartze, LLM Thesis, European University Institute, Florence (1990), pp. 30–3.

respect to each other, including the areas of co-operation, mutual consent or hierarchical control. A second group consists of principles of budgeting such as the principles of timeliness, completeness of budgets, etc. A third involves principles of legislation. One is that legislation always has to be of a general character, and that acts are invalid if they address one case only. Another economically relevant principle involves the requirement that legislation which has turned out to be faulty, unjust or seriously impractical and has thereby emerged as in violation of basic rights needs to be corrected.

## Relationships between public bodies and citizens

The second set of procedural rules typically found in constitutions involves the question of how the private citizen or other legal entity relates to public bodies. Into this category fall essentially two sets of rules. One set again governs the separation of the domains of competence. A typical example is the separation of church and state. But here, again, forms of co-operation, of mutual consent or of hierarchical orderings are clearly available. The second set of rules, generally described by the extremely comprehensive term of due process, lays down the rules of the game between public bodies and private citizens or legal entities. These include information rights, notification rights, and the right to have access to courts and bodies of appeal in meaningful ways that go beyond merely procedural ceremonies without content, since the important benchmark is the effectiveness of these procedures in safeguarding the six basic economic rights outlined above.

## Externalities, rent seeking and dynamic markets

Once the basic institutions of the market economy have been established, it is the purpose of legal authority, i.e. the legislature, the judiciary, the legal profession and all those institutions upholding the custom of the land to ensure as smooth an operation of the market economy as possible. More specifically, this implies attempts to reduce all those costs that have to be incurred in order to effect the exchange of goods and services, either inside organizations or through the market, in the public sector or through other networks allowing for exchange. However, when there is exchange which is not captured by the legal framework or the customs and institutions of the land, we speak of external effects which can be either positive or negative. If the band of the local guard or sports club marches through town making music, people may enjoy it or may dislike it, but the exchange (the band making the music and the citizens listening to it or suffering through it) is not subject to any *quid pro quo*. It can be, of course, if the band plays within a confined area where admission charges can be levied. But sometimes, the intention is to leave an effect uncovered by the legal system in the sense that the music is given away free of charge. This is typically done when the costs of protecting the property in the service – here, the music – exceeds the benefit from doing so. Likewise, people will suffer through the music if the nuisance is not worth the trouble of protecting against the noise. This illustrates that there are costs in establishing legal boundaries, and hence some effects are left where they fall. When it can be shown therefore that efforts could be undertaken to protect against a nuisance, or else claim property in a good or service which has not been undertaken, then no compensation can be claimed in the case of a particular external effect, such as the nuisance of the noise stemming from the marching band. This is the simple case of an externality, where the effect is small relative to the transaction costs that would be necessary in order to internalize it with whoever caused it, such as the marching band in our example.

Quite generally, we distinguish between three types of transaction costs: costs necessary to gather information about a particular transaction, costs of contracting the circumstances of a particular transaction and costs of monitoring the contract that regulates the exchange. When the sum of these is greater than the value itself, the externality falls where it may happen to be.

A different type of externality which in a market economy is supposed to occur is what we refer to as the pure monetary or financial externality. If a particular product which requires a certain technology can be produced at a given price $p$, at a particular time $t$ by a particular entrepreneur $e$, then customers will demand a particular quantity $q$ given the price $p$ for the good in question. However, as we can see, there is still unsatisfied demand in that if the price were lower, a larger quantity would be demanded. Here lies the opportunity of a new market entrant. If a second entrepreneur $e'$ can produce the same good with a different technology so as to be able to charge a lower price $p'$, he will capture not only the market segment of the first entrepreneur, but will in addition add that quantity demanded which was left unsatisfied because of the price $p$. As a consequence, the first entrepreneur $e$ will have to either reduce his price or leave the business to his competitor. In both cases, he suffers a financial loss as compared to the situation before. Either he has to apply his work more cheaply to the original technology, or he has to write off the technology and switch to the new method of production hit upon by entrepreneur $e'$. The financial loss thus incurred by the original entrepreneur may be large, but it is the intended result of a market economy. It is an external effect brought about by the second entrepreneur without any relationship between the two. It is, of course, possible to protect against such financial externalities. For example, through government regulation the original technology can be prescribed as being the only viable one. Typical examples can be found in building codes. Entrepreneurs can be licensed so as to bar others from entering the market. Prices can be fixed at the original level $p$. However, even in this case, the second entrepreneur would enter the market, as his technological advantage allows him to produce more cheaply.

A protection against such loss as a consequence of market competition is possible of course and has been practised for centuries and in many parts of the world. For example, the Middle Ages is known for the notion of the just price, a price that had been upheld as a matter of public order. Both prices and production methods used were set and new technologies such as a different plough or a different method of tanning required the permission of the feudal lord or the guild respectively. The reason for such arrangements was, of course, the very small extent of the market. This implied that division of labour could only be limited, and that economic life largely depended on uncontrollable vicissitudes such as the weather. In order to safeguard the production of necessities, tools and amenities, economic life had to be deeply regulated, typically by means of the church calendar. This system is mentioned here as a counter-example, in order to underscore the point that economic loss as a consequence of competition has to be regarded as the rule, and the protection against such loss should be seen as the exception. In turn, the exceptions have an economic rationale themselves, which can be illustrated with a simple diagram (see Figure 3.1). Let $p$ be the price of a particular good, where the supply curve is simply a production function with constant costs of production. The quantity sold results at the intersection of this production function as the supply curve and the demand curve QQ. We can accomplish a different price $p'$ by restricting market access to, for example, one supplier only, and a different quantity sold will result where $q'$ is smaller than $q$. The resulting triangle represents the classic welfare loss or Harberger triangle. The rectangle is economically more important, as it represents the economic rent derived from

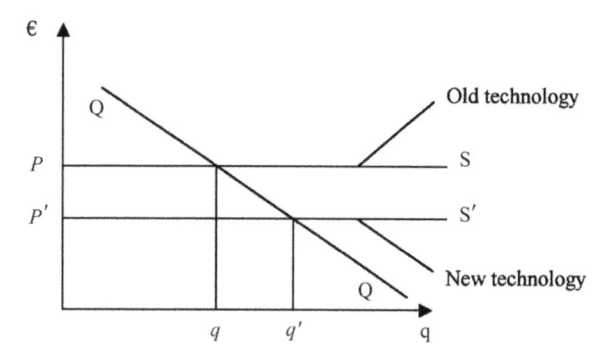

Figure 3.1: Pure economic loss due to technological change

the market restriction. The monopolist can appropriate this rent, and once we introduce market competition he suffers this amount as the economic loss. In general, as a principle of public policy, where such monopolies are detected, action will be taken in order to break them up by introducing competition. Obviously, no compensation requirement results. However, monopoly can be used as a device in order to foster technological change. Take the simple case of ethical drugs. Their production costs tend to be minimal, but the costs of research and development loom large. Pharmaceutical progress would be small if the costs of research and development could not be recaptured. In order to achieve this result, ethical drugs can be patented and licensed. Only once the patent expires can other producers enter the market and produce the drug generically. By that time, the research-based pharmaceutical producer will have to have earned back the investment made earlier into the research and development of the drug. With the advent of the generic producers, in order to maintain market share, the patent holder will have to reduce its price to almost the cost of production and the monopoly rent has disappeared. Of course, one could think of the expiration of the patent as an economic loss. But again, it is an intended one, as the original gain was an explicit and politically motivated incentive to produce knowledge that led to new products. Hence, the entire system of patents and trademarks, copyrights, special permits and licences describes a form of intended exemption from competition in order to foster specific intended results. To the extent that the intended specific result can be accomplished, appropriation of the rent is protected, and otherwise not.

In order to distinguish more sharply between those pure economic losses that need to be compensated and those that need not, we have

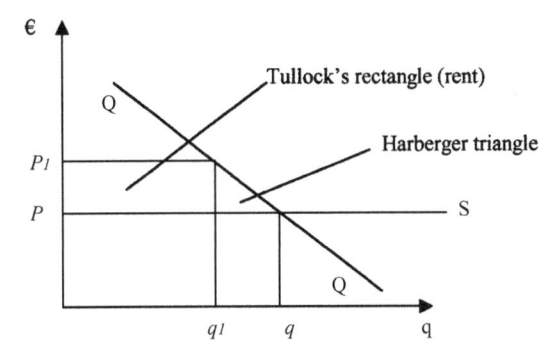

Figure 3.2: Rent seeking

to further introduce the concept of rent seeking. The rent (in Figure 3.2 the rectangle) is obviously the price worthy of many efforts. The effort to achieve a protected monopoly position is called rent seeking. It is then an effort to curtail competition. Such rent seeking or directly unproductive activities can impose enormous economic (but also welfare) losses on an economy and society. Often, rent-seeking activities can be accomplished through the use of legislatures and regulatory authorities. However, the rents can only be collected if the statutes or regulations thus created are enforceable. It is therefore important to consider the aspect of rent seeking as an argument in adjudication. Again, compensation for pure economic loss due to the removal of protection of a rent should be reduced to those few cases where the rent is granted in consideration of a socially useful prior or present activity.

Once we see externalities and economic rents in the dynamic context of market competition, that is, once we consider transaction costs, the extent of the market, the purpose of granting patents and privileges and the ubiquity of directly unproductive rent-seeking activities, we notice that economic loss can be the intended result of market dynamics. In particular, if market access and technological change are actively encouraged – this is currently, for example, the policy of the European Commission with respect to legal harmonization – every change in the regulatory and legal environment is likely to bring about economic consequences in areas which are not even directly addressed by the policymaking authority such as the European Commission. The larger the extent of the market, the more interrelated the different economic activities will be. In a system with a deep division of labour as a consequence of the large extent of the market, for example, in the common market of the European Union with its deep division of labour across the entire area of the EU, there is hardly any economically relevant activity which is not somehow related to another. This implies that any technological change introduced in any one economic activity will induce substitution effects in other economic activities, and these effects will in turn rip through the entire network of the economy. Hence any particular effect will spread over the entire economy as a consequence of market interaction, and in the total absence of contractual relations between the affected parties. It is very likely that many of these effects, some of which will be large and concentrated on very few, will be considered unfair by those who have to suffer the loss as a consequence of market activity which bring benefit to some. If an insulation material such as cork can be substituted more cheaply and the cork oak from which the cork used to be peeled is thereby rendered useless, the benefit from this new technology is spread over all those economic activities which require such insulation from shipping to building, the hotel and restaurant business and so forth. Yet the owners of the cork oak forests, whose trees have become obsolete, suffer the full burden of the economic change. With them suffer their labourers who used to peel the trees, as well as all those who used to be employed in the line of producing the cork-based insulation materials. However, the economic effect is intended and no compensation requirement can exist without endangering market dynamics.

## Looking at the cases

In illustrating the cases with the foregoing analysis, we can note for Case 1 ('Cable I – The Blackout') that there is neither an uninternalizable externality nor a specific rent involved. Transaction costs are low and therefore rectifications are easy. Compensation turns on fault and not on any responsible market activity. Cutting a cable is a risk inherent in any excavating activity. The operator is best positioned to reduce this risk and thereby optimize the cost inflicted on others. Insufficient care would externalize those costs of operation. The costs of damages caused by excavation can be reduced by hiring competent personnel, adequate supervision, adequate business routines and the firm's own interest in its professional record. With all these instruments at its disposal, the firm is finally best positioned to buy insurance for liability.

Case 2 ('Cable II – Factory Shutdown') is different. Since the damage imposed on Cato is considered an externality, the risk of power failure is a normal risk of business operations. Only the business operator himself can judge the costs and benefits of having a backup system such as a power generator in place. Although the two cases appear similar, they are not because the externality imposed on Cato is difficult to internalize. The transaction costs of internalizing would be prohibitively high, as the business opportunities foregone cannot be assessed with ease by a third party. Hence, these risks must remain where they fall.

Similarly, referring to Case 3 ('Cable III – The Day-to-Day Workers'), employment opportunities depend more generally on the environment in which employment opportunities can arise or temporarily disappear. This is a normal consequence of market activities. Where this result is not intended, different contractual forms can guarantee permanent employment. Depending on the skill level, a temporary worker can often command a higher wage than a permanently employed worker. This is because the temporary worker assumes the risk of unemployment and of contract discontinuation. Hence, the intended result is that no compensation be required.

In Case 4 ('Convalescing Employee'), as a matter of principle, no compensation requirement would arise. However, the legislature may intervene, as in Germany with the pay continuation statute (*Entgeltfortzahlungsgesetz*). The legislative solution may even have a transaction costs rationale. The employer is much better able and equipped to collect the damages from the tortfeasor than the injured worker. Hence, the continuation of pay and subrogation of claims can be considered a technique to reduce the secondary costs of accidents (the costs of displacement) in Calabresi's terms.[6]

Referring to Case 5 ('Requiem for an Italian All Star'), traffic accidents occur as people participate in traffic. The costs of such accidents depend on the accident and personal circumstances as in the case of Thomas the pivot. He himself is best able to judge the consequences of an injury for his team and the severity of the consequences of exposing himself to accident risk.

Case 6 ('The Infected Cow') is similar to the consequences of foot and mouth disease discussed earlier. In Britain, the cost of the incidence of the disease in early 2001 is already estimated to stand at £10 billion and continues to rise. Animals do escape as a consequence of normal herding operations, and the incidence of the disease is only very partly under the control of an individual farmer. The loss of access to public markets due to their closure is similar, from an economic point of view, to the

---

[6] See G. Calabresi, *The Costs of Accidents* (Yale University Press, New Haven, CT, 1971).

loss of power from the general provider. Alternative forms of marketing cattle are available.

Case 7 ('The Careless Architect') yields no specific new insights, and in Case 8 ('The Cancelled Cruise'), the collision of two ships is a standard tort case with the consequence of compensation requirements according to fault. No specific issues of transactions costs or protected economic rents arise.

As to Case 9 ('Fire in the Projection Booth'), the economic approach yields no additional consequences to the standard tort result. However, any reference to the causation link under the circumstances seems superfluous as the proximate cause cannot be adequately judged by the manufacturer, and the consequences are totally beyond his control. Again, the operator has an easy remedy in having backup equipment available.

In Case 10 ('The Dutiful Wife'), the notion of pure economic loss becomes apparent. The tortfeasor is responsible for the market value of the healthcare services, but not for the entire loss suffered by the wife who was looking after her husband and therefore was deprived of business income. This is the correct result from an economic point of view, as the couple faced the choice between hiring help and doing the care work themselves. The choice they made is their own responsibility, but the damage inflicted is the responsibility of the tortfeasor. Put differently, the choice of the couple reveals their expectation that the additional value in the spouse's care to both husband and wife exceeds the business income foregone. Had there not been an expected consumer surplus in non-market care, i.e. care by the spouse, the spouse would have continued her business activities and hired the respective help.

Case 11 ('A Maestro's Mistake') involves harm imposed on two parties. The artist suffers a loss in his reputation and his earning ability when skilful forgeries appear on the market and compete with the original work. Obviously, the artist has a claim against the forger, and so does the art buyer. But there is no connection through any sequence of choices made in the market between the artist and the art buyer in this case, and hence from an economic point of view, no compensation is required. The existence of forgeries so accomplished that they even fool the artist is a serious threat to the artist's ability to earn a living. He has therefore a strong interest in taking protective measures, such as marks of authenticity, working closely with experts or his main art dealer, keeping a register of the art and where it has been sold, etc. Such remedies are available, and they are useful for both the artist and the art buyer. Since these measures are incentive-compatible and likely to reduce the costs of transactions, notably the costs of information gathering and verifying, the issue of liability pales before alternative institutional enhancements of contract certainty.

In conclusion we note that in ten of the cases used here for illustration of the economic reasoning, the economic analysis correctly predicts the legal outcome unless there is special intervention on the part of either the legislature or the judiciary.

## Conclusion

This chapter offers an economic analysis of the concept of pure economic loss. The concept is explained in the context of market operation. Pure economic loss is the necessary outcome of market interaction. In order to show its role, first, this is discussed in the context of basic institutions of the market economy. Secondly, the dividing line between those forms of pure economic loss which are to be compensated and those which are not is found in the theory of externalities and in the theory of rent seeking amended by the concept of dynamic market operation. Where, in a Schumpeterian sense, market dynamics require creative destruction, the financial loss due to this destruction cannot be compensated. Otherwise, the creative destruction and thus the entrepreneurial activity would be hindered or even prevented.

### *A concise summary*

In the preceding analysis, we have identified constitutional guarantees with respect to basic rights on the one hand and procedural rules on the other. There are three basic rights, the guarantee of which has to be considered as central from an economic point of view. These guarantees protect the right of freedom of contract; the institution of liability (in the sense that those responsible for actions, or a lack thereof, can be held responsible for the effects of their activities or the lack thereof); and the institution of private property (in the sense that clearly specified and meaningful alternatives become available for economic agents to dispose of goods and services). These basic economic rights are supported by three ancillary economic rights guaranteeing a stable legal environment, a stable currency providing for a common language of contractual relationships and open markets which include the right to establish such markets in areas where they do not exist.

Procedural guarantees cover either the relationship between public bodies, or the relationship between public bodies and private citizens or other legal entities. The principle of due process requires in this context that citizens and legal persons have access to courts and bodies of appeal in meaningful ways, barring purely ceremonial procedures.

The economic analysis of constitutional rights obviously cannot substitute for constitutional jurisprudence. But economic analysis can substantially enhance the sharpness of jurisprudential analysis by spelling out the consequences of particular constitutional provisions (or the lack thereof), and the systematic interconnections between basic legal institutions such as property, contract and liability, as well as legal procedures. In this sense, the economic analysis can be integrated into jurisprudential analysis; by being embodied into the interpretation of constitutional provisions, economic analysis can become an integral part of constitutional scholarship.

## 3B Liability for pure financial loss: revisiting the economic foundations of a legal doctrine

FRANCESCO PARISI

As generally understood in the law and economics literature, the economic loss rule states that a plaintiff cannot recover damages for a pure financial loss. The comparative study of the pure economic loss rule reveals that the recognition and significance attributed to such rule, and to the notion of 'economic loss', varies considerably across Western legal systems. Bussani and Palmer analyse the results of an extensive case study on the issue of pure economic loss across all national legal systems of Europe and provide an interesting grouping of the approaches followed by national courts of Europe, describing them variously as 'liberal', 'pragmatic' or 'conservative'. The question has emerged in the European context in conjunction with the ongoing search for a common core of European private law and the consideration of a unified European civil code.[1] Comparative legal analysis reveals that the policies and rules governing tortious liability for pure economic loss in Europe are not governed by common principles.

Legal systems simply do not share a common approach to this issue. Even those that seek to preclude recoverability of pure financial loss use different definitions and follow different formulations of the problem. An interesting point recently brought to light by comparative legal analysis is that, unlike most other issues in the field of torts, the different approaches on the issue of pure economic loss do not follow the familiar common law/civil law divide.[2]

The comparative study unveils the existence of an area of law in which there is neither cross-national consensus, nor even always internal consistency in the recognition and application of the rule within

---
[1] See below M. Bussani and V. Palmer, Chapter 10.
[2] See below Bussani and Palmer, Chapter 8.

individual jurisdictions, due to the intellectual significance of divergent theoretical approaches.

Among different dogmatic constructs used by Western legal systems to address the issue of pure economic loss, a common element seems to characterize the jurisprudence of all modern legal systems, specifically, a tension between theoretical statements and practical solutions sought by fact-specific case law. Comparative legal scholars have struggled to find a way in which to compare different legal solutions within a consistent construct, but their efforts have often given way to historical explanations based on path dependence. That is, the explanations generally conclude that any jurisdiction's current application of the pure economic loss rule is eventually the result of mere historical accidents.[3] Similarly, other scholars have lamented the failure of tort scholarship to produce persuasive positive theories of liability for pure economic loss, and have gone so far as to recommend the abandonment of any effort to formulate any single general theory.[4] These individuals theorize that the economic loss problem is divisive, because it is simply non-unitary in character.[5] This chapter attempts to revisit the apparent contradictions brought to light by comparative legal scholars through the lens of economic analysis.

As is generally the case, comparative law is a valuable tool for revealing engaging issues for law and economics scholars.[6] This chapter reports on the recent findings of comparative law, revealing that legal notions of pure economic loss encompass several types of situations. In terms of economic analysis, these situations are easily distinguishable and have very different significance for social welfare analysis. What appear to be erratic judicial applications of a single economic loss rule are in fact justifiable and often valid applications of different underlying economic principles. From an economic perspective, it may in fact be necessary to have more than one dogmatic approach to the treatment

---

[3] R. L. Rabin, 'Tort Recovery for Negligently Inflicted Economic Loss: A Reassessment', (1985) 37 *Standard Law Review* 1513; Gary T. Schwartz, 'The Economic Loss Doctrine in American Tort Law: Assessing the Recent Experience', in E. K. Banakas (ed.), *Civil Liability for Pure Economic Loss* 103 (The Hague, Kluwer Law International, 1996); J. R. Gordley, 'The Rule Against Recovery in Negligence for Pure Economic Loss: An Historical Accident?', above, Chapter 2.

[4] W. Landes and R. Posner, *The Economic Structure of Tort Law* (Harvard University Press, Cambridge, MA, 1987).

[5] Schwartz, 'Economic Loss Doctrine'.

[6] U. Mattei and F. Cafaggi, 'Comparative Law and Economics', *New Palgrave Dictionary of Economics and the Law* (Macmillan, London, 1998).

of economic loss, given the substantial discrepancy between legal and economic categories. Consequentially, there is an inability of the legal notion of economic loss to easily capture and apply the many disparate economic situations that fall within any such iconoclastic rule.

The first section provides an economic redefinition of the concept of pure economic loss, distinguishing various situations. The second section briefly revisits the recent findings of comparative law scholars who are searching for comparable legal and economic categories. In conclusion, I suggest there is no single answer to the normative question of the liability for pure economic loss. In the final analysis, one must examine the general understanding of the economic function of civil liability, and the economic implications of alternative liability rules on individual incentives.

## The economics of pure economic loss

The law and economics literature suggests that, even where a rule of total liability is efficient, the victims should not necessarily be compensated to the full extent of their economic losses. In order to understand the logic that drives this result, it is necessary to proceed in two stages: first, analysing the notion of socially relevant economic loss, secondly, applying that concept to the design of optimal liability rules.

### Socially relevant externalities and the optimal scope of liability

From the perspective of law and economics, remedies in torts are necessary to specify and quantify externalities. As a general definition, an externality is a cost imposed on a third party outside the voluntary mechanisms of the market-place. In principle, liability in torts should ensure that the entire social cost of any particular activity is addressed by the responsible party or economic agent. The application of this principle necessitates focusing on the tortfeasor's expected *ex ante* liability, rather than on the victim's actual compensation.[7]

---

[7] This may occasionally require courts to set aside some other general principle of tort law. For example, the collateral-benefits rule, which may allow the victim to recover the full value of the loss without deducting the payments received from an insurance company for the same damage, is possibly quite efficient. First, because it creates efficient precaution incentives for the tortfeasor (liability should be linked to the true social loss occasioned by the accident, not the private uninsured loss of the victim). Secondly, because in most situations, the double payment from the insurance and the

As is well known in the economics literature, from the perspective of social welfare analysis, not every economic externality is socially relevant. The efficient design of liability rules should aim at addressing socially relevant externalities, thereby minimizing those external costs that reduce aggregate social welfare. However, some external costs have the peculiar effect of having only private effects: those private externalities do not induce direct or indirect social costs. I shall refer to this category of costs as socially irrelevant externalities. Given the administrative costs of the legal system, economic analysis suggests that socially irrelevant externalities can, and indeed should, generally be left uncompensated. From a policy standpoint, in the case of socially irrelevant externalities, the choice of alternative liability rules has no effects on the efficiency of individual conduct. The exclusion of liability in such cases is generally justified by the desire to minimize the total cost of accidents: liability would impose administrative and judicial costs on the legal system, while creating no beneficial incentives for the parties involved.

To maximize the net social benefit of an activity, one must also consider the aggregate adjudication costs. This requires a balancing and subsequent evaluation of all ascertainable externalities of the activity, both positive and negative. Some activities, while imposing private losses on some third parties, may create benefits for others. A legal system aiming at creating optimal incentives for potential tortfeasors should impose a dual system of liability: imposing (positive) liability for the negative externalities and, by the same token, recognizing (negative) liability for the positive externalities. From an efficiency point of view, the creation of a negative liability rule is as important a remedy as a positive liability rule in a standard tort situation.

## Pure economic loss as a social cost

As a policy matter, several legal limitations to the domain of compensable harm, including some variations of the economic loss rule, can

---

tortfeasor does not in fact amount to allowing the victim to recover double. As pointed out by Posner, and Landes and Posner, the insured plaintiff already paid for the insurance benefit under the form of insurance premium, rendering full liability necessary to make him whole. More generally, the risk of duplicate recovery should not necessarily be linked to one of overdeterrence, given the different relevance of the *ex ante* liability and *ex post* compensation on individual incentives. R. A. Posner, *Economic Analysis of Law* (3rd edn, Little Brown, Boston, 1986); Landes and Posner, *Economic Structure of Tort Law*.

be explained – or at least reinterpreted – as ways in which to confine liability to only socially relevant externalities.

The issue of pure economic loss poses a fascinating conundrum. This puzzle is best illustrated by contrasting a case of pure economic loss with a traditional situation of physical harm.

Generally in cases of physical harm, there is a correlation between an action and the extent of the private and social cost of the harm. That is to say, any loss suffered by an individual occasions a private cost to the victim, which in turn counts as a social cost for the community. In such cases, tortious behavior should be met with full liability and compensation for the victim's harm. Simply, efficient deterrence of activities that generate private harm is necessary to minimize the total social cost of accidents.

A different logic applies in the case of pure economic loss. For example, in the case of foregone profits or earnings there is no one-to-one relationship between the private loss of the victim and the resulting social loss. On the contrary, there is a strong tendency for the private and social costs to differ substantially from one another. Generally, the private loss exceeds the social loss, and the discrepancy between the two values may be large. This may lead to occasional paradoxes where the private and social cost have different results. For example, a social benefit may result from an act that causes private loss. In pure economic loss cases, we may have situations of wrongful behaviour that occasion an economic loss for one victim but which may impose no cost, or may even generate a net benefit, to society at large.

Whenever a wrongful behaviour creates a private loss, the magnitude of which differs from the resulting social loss, economic analysis indicates that the victim should not necessarily be compensated for the entire private economic loss.[8] Only the portion of the private loss (if any) which represents a social cost should be subject to liability.

Some of the policy dilemmas implicitly addressed by the economic loss rule concern wrongful behaviour which imposes a private economic loss on the victim, with no corresponding social loss. In the case considered

---

[8] J. Arlen, 'Tort Damages', in B. Bouckaert and G. De Geest (eds.), *Encyclopedia of Law and Economics*, vol. 2 682 (Edward Elgar, Challenham, 2000). As pointed out by Shavell, when a tort interrupts the production process of a manufacturing firm, the firm's lost profits are not necessarily social costs, given the possible presence of other firms who could enter the market or expand its production by making up the foregone output of the incumbent firm with the supply of perfect substitutes at comparable cost. S. Shavell, *Economic Analysis of Accident Law* (1987).

above, the private loss to the victim may be the source of a net gain for society at large.[9] In such cases, law and economics lead to the frequently paradoxical result that such wrongful behaviour should be encouraged and economically subsidized by the legal system. Put differently, liability rules should be put into effect according to their fundamental economic functions, providing both positive liability for negative externalities (i.e. losses to third parties) and negative liability for positive externalities (i.e. benefits to third parties). This dual function of liability rules would, in the abstract, consist of a combination of damage remedies paid to the victims and financial subsidies paid to the tortfeasor. For obvious pragmatic reasons, we rarely observe such combined operation of the liability system in the real world.

Beyond the irony of such theoretical considerations lies an important lesson. The core notion that seems to necessitate theoretical contradictions of the economic loss rule is the idea that the optimal scope of liability is determined by the impact of alternative liability rules on the total social cost of accidents. Activities that occasion a mere reallocation of costs and benefits, with no incremental social cost, as such cannot be considered socially harmful. If no other considerations of the parties' reliance and distributive justice enter into the policy considerations, the imposition of full liability would be unwarranted. If an individual occasions an unjustified transfer of wealth from one party to another and is made liable for the loss suffered by one victim, he should, by the same logic, be allowed to recover the value of the benefit from other third parties who received an unexpected benefit from his action. In case of wrongful behaviour which occasions a zero sum transfer of wealth, the amount of net liability imposed on the tortfeasor should also equal zero, given the offsetting effects of positive and negative liabilities when balancing harm to victims with potential benefits to unsuspecting third parties.

The important point here is to recognize that, according to several competing conceptions of justice, a zero net liability rule for the alleged tortfeasor does not necessarily justify a rule excluding liability altogether, denying compensation for those who suffered a private loss. Here lies one important element that drives the intellectual and dogmatic tension behind the economic loss rule. In the following section,

---

[9] On this point, Arlen observes that, if an incumbent monopolistic firm loses part of its market share to a competitor selling the same product at a lower price as a result of the tortious activity of the latter, the alleged tort, while occasioning the victim's lost profits, may actually be at the origin of a social welfare gain. Arlen, 'Tort Damages'.

I shall evaluate some elements of the traditional debate within the normative framework of law and economics.

## Pure economic loss: towards an economic restatement

From an economic perspective, the legal notion of pure economic loss is quite unfit to serve as a normative criterion of adjudication. As suggested above, the legal notion of economic loss is, in fact, a very imperfect proxy for the economic category of socially relevant cost, which ideally should guide the optimal design of liability rules.

The understanding of the relevant economic categories in this context may serve two valuable purposes: (1) as a positive criterion, to understand the many facets of the economic loss rule and to reconcile some of the apparent contradictions in the judicial implementation of such rule; and (2) as a normative criterion, to guide lawmakers and courts in the design and implementation of liability rules dealing with pure economic loss.

Contrary to the conclusions reached by several legal commentators on this issue, I suggest that the emergence and diffusion of the economic loss rule is more than a mere historical accident.[10] I suggest that such exclusion of liability is in many instances appropriate, and that several of the factual situations governed by the economic loss rule are correctly adjudicated. However, an economic analysis of the judicial applications of the economic loss rule in the various legal systems considered in this study, also unveils several mistaken applications of the rule.

### *In search of comparable categories: a hypothesis*

Legal systems utilize quite different constructs to define the boundaries of compensable harm for economic loss. We suggest that, to the extent that the economic loss rule may be understood as a way in which to restrict liability to only socially relevant externalities, it is appropriate to attempt a reformulation of the rule in terms that are consistent with its fundamental economic rationale.[11] A restatement of the exclusionary

---

[10] Schwartz, 'Economic Loss Doctrine'.
[11] For additional discussions of the issue of liability for economic losses from a law and economics perspective, see V. P. Goldberg, 'Recovery for Economic Loss Following the Exxon Valdez Oil Spill', (1994) 23 *Journal of Legal Studies* 1; Landes and Posner, *Economic Structure of Tort Law*, pp. 251–5; Rabin, 'Tort Recovery'; M. J. Rizzo, 'A Theory of Economic Loss in Torts', (1982) 11 *Journal of Legal Studies* 281; G. T. Schwartz, 'Economic Loss in American Tort Law: The Examples of J'Aire and of Products Liability', (1986) 23 *San Diego Land Review* 37; Schwartz, 'Economic Loss Doctrine'; Arlen, 'Tort Damages'.

rule consistent with the economic model of optimal liability would require distinguishing between different kinds of private loss. On the one hand, there are private losses that generate a corresponding social loss and on the other hand, there are private losses that generate a prejudice for certain individuals, yet also generate an offsetting benefit for other individuals, so as to result in no net social loss. Thus, the exclusionary rule would include the above economic qualification and would state that 'a plaintiff cannot recover damages for a purely *private* economic loss'.

The above restatement allows us to revisit some of the peculiar features of the existing version of the exclusionary rule verifying their consistency with the proposed economic reformulation. Most interestingly, we will examine whether the economic restatement explains some of the general features of the rule that could not satisfactorily be explained by the traditional rationales.

As a matter of ideal theory, lack of compensation for pure economic loss is inefficient to the extent that such uncompensated loss also involves social externalities. In such cases, full liability is both appropriate and necessary. In a fault-based system, liability for socially relevant externalities is desirable whenever the agent fails to adopt the optimal standard of behaviour, which we shall call $x^*$. In such case, the level of due compensation, $D$, is determined by the following rule:

(1) $\quad D = Ls(x) \quad \forall \quad x < x^*$

The rule states that damages $D$ should be paid in an amount equal to the social loss, $Ls$, every time the tortfeasor undertakes a level of precaution lower than the social optimum, $x^*$. As discussed in the previous section, the application of this liability rule in the context of pure economic loss is problematic for a variety of reasons.

First, the rule requires that the extent of liability be determined on the basis of the social loss, $Ls$, rather than the actual loss suffered by the victim, $Lp$. The decoupling of liability from the private loss is problematic since it may occasion undercompensation or overcompensation from the point of view of the victim.

(2) $\quad D < Lp \quad \forall \quad Lp < Ls$
$\quad\quad\, D > Lp \quad \forall \quad Lp > Ls$

In the presence of a discrepancy between the extent of a private loss, $Lp$, and the actual social loss, $Ls$, the damage award, $D$, will be linked to the social loss and would thus result as either undercompensatory or overcompensatory from the point of view of the victim. The damage award will be fully compensatory only in the limited case in which private and social loss coincide, $Lp = Ls$.

Secondly, the stylized liability rule in equation (1) may lead to some paradoxical applications. For example:

(3) $\quad D < 0 \quad \forall \quad Ls < 0$ (and for any value of $Lp$)

Negative liability (with the victim ironically made liable to compensate his tortfeasor) will result for all situations where the conduct generates a social benefit ($Ls < 0$), even when the victim suffered a private loss ($Lp > 0$). According to the application of the criterion of optimal liability, we may subsidize wrongful behavior whenever the private loss generates a social gain (e.g., a 'wrongful' action that leads to the breakdown of a monopoly, with a resulting social welfare gain).

These two practical difficulties may explain why the economic loss rule has evolved with such disparate contours in contemporary legal systems. In real life, we find the following additional constraints:

(4) $\quad D = Ls \quad \text{s.t.} \quad D > 0 \quad \text{and} \quad D \leq Lp$

That is, the additional limits imposed by modern legal systems on the stylized liability rule formulized in equation (1) are consistent with established legal dogmas, according to which the amount of liability for a private loss is non-negative (i.e., victims are never asked to compensate their tortfeasor, even if the private wrong is source of a social gain) (footnote) and where the amount of liability should not exceed the extent of the victim's loss (i.e., damages should not be overcompensatory, unless they are punitive in nature).

## Recasting the economic loss rule

As discussed above, desirability and extent of liability for pure economic loss depends on the critical relationship between private and social costs.

The above reconceptualization of the economic loss rule suggests that liability for economic losses should be excluded whenever a private economic loss is offset by gains enjoyed by other third parties, such that the wrongful behaviour does not generate any net social loss. In this context, the application of the economic loss rule should be quite attentive to its underlying economic rationale: the legal exclusion of liability should be based on the economic nature of the loss (i.e., private versus social externalities) rather than on the intrinsic nature of the loss (economic versus physical harm).

For example, several cases of economic loss often give origin to relevant social losses (e.g., imagine an accident that interferes with the manufacturing of goods with a resulting medium-term shortage in the market). With a downward-sloping demand curve, negative production shocks cause social deadweight losses, as shown by the fact that any shortage causes the goods (or their close substitutes) to be sold at a higher price with lower overall consumption. In such cases, the measure of the social loss is given by the difference between the variation in producer's surplus (if any) and the variation in consumer surplus. Such difference (i.e. the resulting deadweight loss triangle) constitutes an actual measure of social cost that should be included as a proper component of damages.

In adjudicating cases of economic loss, the purely economic nature of the harm suffered by the victim should not be dispositive and liability should be imposed on the tortfeasor, whenever the accident is the source of a socially relevant loss. In such cases, a pure economic loss – from a social welfare point of view – is indistinguishable from the social loss that follows from the destruction of a scarce physical resource.

It should be recognized clearly that on this subject there is a quite imperfect correlation between the legal and economic categories. As a consequence, it is not possible to formulate a general presumption as to whether economic loss should, or should not, be included in damage awards. Any general presumptive rule needs to be qualified with reference to the relevant economic categories: absent such reconceptualization, the application of the economic loss rule is likely to generate inaccurate levels of compensation with a resulting inefficient level of deterrence.

In applying the economic loss rule, courts and legislators should be aware that considerations of efficiency require an analysis of the level of social harm caused by the conduct. The optimal level of damages are those that create an *ex ante* level of expected liability equal to the expected social harm caused by the conduct. The quantification of the social harm should not necessarily include (but should not systematically exclude) the pure economic loss suffered by the victim, as currently intended in the legal discourse. In designing efficient liability rules, any reference to pure economic loss should be avoided, since such category quite rarely coincides with the appropriate notion of relevant social cost. Liability rules may exclude lost profits from the computation of damages only if they constitute a mere diminution of the victim's surplus to the benefit of other third parties, without any net impact on the aggregate well-being of society at large. Such an evaluation should include the potential benefits of other producers, sellers or consumers.

The above framework provides a viable hypothesis by which to explain the apparent exceptions and variations of the pure economic loss rule in modern and historical societies. Recasting the economic loss rule in such a fashion further assists the understanding of the appropriate scope of its application in real life cases. In turn, this allows us to sketch some presumptive normative guidelines for the adjudication of pure economic loss claims.

## Practical problems in the application of the economic loss rule

Several judicial applications of the economic loss rule place little or no emphasis at all on the economic loss aspect of the case, often relying on distinguishing criteria such as the directness of the loss. While such criteria of adjudication are often invoked as instrumental to specific functions of the liability rule, such as risk-spreading, they often reveal the courts' uneasiness with the practical implementation of the economic loss rule.

Practical problems in applying the rule emerge because, with rare exceptions, the measure of private economic loss does not coincide with the magnitude of the resulting social loss.[12]

In the more frequent case of competitive supply of substitutable goods, the amount of private economic loss generally constitutes an overestimate of the relevant social loss. Occasionally, however, the opposite may be true. For example, in the case of resources that are available with a perfectly inelastic supply (e.g. fixed-amount natural resources), the measure of private economic losses may represent an underestimate of the socially relevant losses. In the latter case, social losses exceed private economic losses, because true social losses result from the summation of the forgone producer surplus (i.e. the pure economic loss) and the lost

---

[12] Given the difficult quantification of private and social losses, it is often thought best to let the free contracting of the parties reveal private information through the bargaining process. This in many ways relates to the intrinsic limits of tort law versus contract law in dealing with private externalities. On the proper domain of the economic loss rule outside of the proper tort law scenario, see Schwartz, 'Economic Loss Doctrine'; Schwartz, 'Economic Loss in American Tort Law'. These works suggest that in products liability cases, contract law is the preferred legal framework within which to address claims concerning pure economic loss.

Table 3.1. *Applying the economic loss rule*

| | Private versus social loss | Relevance conditions | Remedy | Comments |
|---|---|---|---|---|
| 1 | $Lp = Ls$ | $Ls > 0$ | $D = Ls$ | Full recovery |
| 2 | $Lp > Ls$ | $Ls > 0$ | $D = Ls$ | Exclusionary rule should apply limiting liability to 'socially relevant' losses |
| 3 | $Lp > Ls$ | $Lp > 0$ $Ls \leq 0$ | $D = 0$ | No recovery (alternatives should be considered to subsidize positive social externalities) |
| 4 | $Lp < Ls$ | $Lp > 0$ | $D = Lp + T$ $T = Ls - Lp$ | Decoupling solution |
| 5 | $Lp < Ls$ | $Lp \leq 0$ $Ls > 0$ | $D = Ls$ or $Ls < D \leq 0$ | $D = Ls$ is efficient $Ls < D \leq 0$ can be adopted to reduce open-ended liability problems |

consumer surplus. Note here a practical problem in the conceptualization of liability. There is a component of the social loss that is not borne by the victim: in our example, there is an additional loss represented by the forgone consumers' surplus which is not borne by the producer of our example. From an economic point of view, such loss should enter as a proper component of damages (although the payment of such damages may appropriately be decoupled from the compensation of the victim and paid instead to consumers or other third parties).[13]

In order to organize ideas on a manageable template, it is desirable to map the relevant categories of economic loss and examine the appropriate legal solutions to the problem in each category.

Table 3.1 below shows the various combinations of private and social economic loss, defining the resulting levels of optimal liability of typical actions in torts.

Table 3.1 provides a summary presentation of the ideas discussed in the previous sections. The economic reformulation of the economic loss rule makes explicit reference to the critical relationship between the private and social components of the economic loss. Table 3.1 illustrates five situations, each characterized by a different qualitative balance between

---

[13] On the relationship between private economic loss and social loss, see W. Bishop, 'Economic Loss in Tort', (1982) 2 *Oxford Journal of Legal Studies* 1; Shavell, *Economic Analysis of Accident Law*, pp. 135–40; Arlen, 'Tort Damages'.

private and social costs. Each of the five scenarios outlines a different group of factual circumstances, which require different remedial solutions in order to create efficient outcomes.

The first category considers the limit case in which the extent of the private and social loss coincide. In this situation, absent other normative goals, there should be no application of the economic loss rule. Moreover, in the first scenario, full compensation for the private economic loss should be granted. The remaining four categories of cases consider a more general group of situations in which the private and social loss have different magnitudes. As a general criterion, in all such cases, the optimal level of liability should be linked to the extent of the social loss, $L_s$. But different practical and normative considerations are often in the way of a direct application of liability.

Proceeding in order, we can distinguish four general cases, based on the relative magnitude and sign of the private and social components of the loss.

In two situations, the economic loss rule serves a valuable purpose by excluding liability for a private economic loss for which there is no corresponding social loss, as in case 3, or by limiting liability to only the portion of the private economic loss that also reflects a positive social loss, as in case 2. These are the two situations most frequently discussed in the literature in conjunction with the economic loss rule. Case 3 is often illustrated by reference to economic loss due to forgone sales, when alternative sales at the same production cost can be made by the victim's competitors.[14] Case 2 could be illustrated along the same lines with reference to the more realistic situation of sales that are delayed or made by competitors at higher cost.

The two remaining cases are more complex. Case 4 represents a situation where the total social loss exceeds the private economic loss suffered by the victim. Along the lines of the previous example, this case can be illustrated by economic losses due to forgone sales, in the event that no alternative sales can be made by competitors or by the victim at a later time. In this event, the total social loss is likely to be greater than the private economic loss, due to the presence of forgone consumers' surplus. As discussed above, in order to maintain the efficient level of *ex ante* deterrence, the expected level of liability for the tortfeasor should equal the total social loss, $L_s$. However, if *ex post* liability is imposed in the measure of $D = L_s$, the victim would be overcompensated by the tort, since he would receive an amount of compensation higher than the loss

[14] Shavell, *Economic Analysis of Accident Law*, p. 136.

actually suffered (i.e. $D > Lp$). In several legal systems, longstanding principles of civil liability would rule out the application of full liability for the total social loss, given the general legal principle that compensation in torts should not exceed actual loss. In order to maintain efficient *ex ante* incentives, while avoiding victims' overcompensation, some unconventional solutions should be considered. One such approach might involve decoupling liability from compensation, so that the total expected liability faced by the tortfeasor could be linked to the expected social loss, $Ls$, while keeping the level of victim's compensation capped at the value of the private loss actually suffered, $Lp$.[15] The difference between the amount collected from the tortfeasor and the amount paid to the victim could be collected as a penalty or tax payable to the administration, or some other fund created for such purpose ($T = Ls - Lp$). Upon closer examination, it is possible to see that the combined effect of the liability for private damages and the additional penalty or tax for the social externality would yield the optimal level of *ex ante* deterrence (i.e. $D = Lp + T = Ls$). Such a decoupling solution represents only one way in which the optimal level of *ex ante* deterrence can be pursued.

The last group of cases include situations in which the tort generates a social loss, $Ls$, but which, paradoxically, generates a benefit for the immediate victim of the wrongful action (i.e. case 5). This is one of the hypothetical situations that, for the reasons explained below, falls outside the practical scope of application of the pure economic loss rule, but which I address briefly, for the sake of theoretical completeness. It is interesting to note that since $Lp \leq 0$, the immediate victim of the tort does not have any incentive to bring action against the tortfeasor. In this case, the third parties who bear the residual social cost, $Ls$, would have an interest to file suit against the tortfeasor. Here lies one of the difficult cases of pure economic loss. Any exclusion of liability would violate the *ex ante* efficient rule $D = Ls$, but any recognition of liability

---

[15] A few clarifications should be made at this point: (1) Not all economic losses should be compensable, only those economic losses that constitute a social loss, as extensively discussed above; (2) The payment of the additional damages for economic losses – if borne by a subject different from the immediate victim of the tort – should not necessarily be received by the immediate victim and could well be collected by an administrative fund or by the state. This will avoid the problem of overcompensation and moral hazard (i.e. adverse incentives for potential victims to suffer an economic loss, resulting in a potential gain). Obviously the complete decoupling of liability and compensation poses the practical problem of creating incentives for providing evidence of the extent of the actual harm, given the fact that the potential third-party victims would not receive any benefit from the proof of their loss.

would give rise to open-ended litigation and the creation of a 'balance deficit' in the liability of the tortfeasor.

The open-ended litigation would follow from the fact that third parties other than the immediate victims are, by construction, those who suffer the loss and who would require procedural standing for bringing suit. This would create the conditions for open-ended litigation, as will be discussed more extensively in the following section.

The balance deficit problem follows from the fact that, in order to avoid overdeterrence, liability in torts should be limited to the amount of $Ls$.

In situations illustrated by case 5, however, the wrongful action creates some positive benefit for the immediate victim of the tort. That is, there is a non-positive private loss $Lp \leq 0$, while simultaneously an actual loss on other individuals (i.e., $Ls > 0$). The total value of the loss imposed on the various subjects equals $Ls + \}Lp\}$, but as discussed above, only the net social loss, $Ls$, should be imposed under the form of liability on the tortfeasor. Thus we would have legal claims for compensation in torts that exceed in value the amount of optimal liability. Granting systematic compensation to all such claims would create inefficient overdeterrence. To avoid such overdeterrence, two alternative solutions could be examined: (1) allow the tortfeasor to recover the value of the benefit, $Lp$, from the immediate beneficiary of his wrongful action, allowing him to give full compensation to all those who suffered a loss; (2) devise some arbitrary criterion to curtail the number (and amount) of legal claims to the efficient level, $Ls$, allowing the third parties who benefited from the wrongful action to keep such benefit.

Any further speculation on this matter would fall outside the relevant scope of the present inquiry.

## The problem of foreseeability of pure economic losses

One of the common explanations of the economic loss rule relates to the composite dynamics of the economic consequences of a tort and the resulting complexity of the element of foreseeability of the harm. In US law, this rationale tends to surface as a common denominator of several limitations imposed on the extent of compensable harm, including cases of pure economic loss, emotional distress and loss of consortium.

Two objections to the foreseeability explanation should be considered at this point: one factual, the other theoretical. First, as a factual matter, it should be noted that the likelihood and extent of economic loss have a degree of foreseeability that does not differ qualitatively from the foresight of other non-economic consequences of a typical tort situation. Secondly, as a theoretical matter, from an efficiency standpoint, the optimal level of liability should include both foreseeable and unforeseeable consequences. To the extent that causality is satisfactorily established, efficiency requires that the tortfeasor be faced with all the consequences of his wrongful action, such that the *ex ante* level of expected liability coincides with the *ex ante* level of expected harm. Any departure from such criterion of liability would yield sub-optimal precaution incentives.

Both factually and theoretically, therefore, the rule cannot be justified by the alleged unforeseeability of pure economic losses. Many accidents produce a chain of costly economic consequences which can be statistically estimated and causally linked to the wrongful action on the basis of the *id quod plerumque accidit* principle, not unlike other effects of a tort. The presence or absence of foreseeability is a factual and legal matter that enters the equation of liability in the ways specified by the legal system, but no *a priori* distinction should be made between economic and non-economic consequences of a tort.

## *Problems of derivative and open-ended litigation*

Another frequently invoked explanation for the pure economic loss rule concerns the issues of open-ended liability and derivative litigation, i.e. the extension of liability *ad infinitum* for the consequences of a wrongful act.[16] In this context, arguments in favour of the economic loss rule have often invoked a variety of practical considerations, pointing out that in a complex economy, pure economic losses are likely to be serially linked to one another. The forgone production of a good often generates losses that affect several downstream individuals and firms who would have utilized the good as an input of their production activities, and so on. In such a world of economic networking, it becomes necessary to set reasonable limits to the extent to which remote economic effects of a tort should be made compensable. But the comparative study of tort law reveals that legal systems continue to struggle in their attempt to

---

[16] In the recent literature, scholars have pointed out that the judicial applications of the economic loss rule have been one aspect of a general attempt to limit tort liability. Schwartz, 'Economic Loss Doctrine'; Schwartz, 'Economic Loss in American Tort Law'. This goal is further evidenced by the fact that the economic loss rule is fundamentally at odds with the overall tendency to expand the scope of liability in other areas of tort law (e.g. personal injury and harm to property). Such opposite tendency is explained by the fact that the expansion of liability in those areas is rarely at the origin of problems of derivative and open-ended litigation.

identify the boundaries of compensable injury, with the implicit realization that there is no easy way to truncate the chain of liability without arbitrary solutions.

For the sake of methodological simplicity, in the preceding sections the discussion was confined to the incentives effects of the economic loss rule. In such context, I attempted to identify the optimal liability remedy in terms of creation of efficient incentives. We are now left with the task of analysing the issue of open-ended and derivative litigation, for the various categories of private and social economic loss discussed above.

Unlike the foreseeability argument, the concern for open-ended litigation is both factually and theoretically relevant. As discussed above, in many situations the economic loss rule is necessary in order to create efficient incentives for the parties. In such situations, the creation of efficient incentives justifies the application of the rule, even in the absence of any concern for open-ended litigation.

In other cases, we have seen that the economic loss rule cannot be justified in terms of optimal incentives. In these cases, considerations of open-ended liability may acquire relevance. However, concerns for open-ended liability cannot be regarded by themselves as dispositive of the normative solution and do not always justify the strict application of the economic loss rule.

When evaluating the alternative functions of the economic loss rule, it is important to note that it is not always possible to optimize the various policy objectives (i.e. the maintenance of optimal incentives and the avoidance of open-ended liability) with a single policy instrument (i.e. the economic loss rule). If the economic loss rule is used to prevent open-ended liability, it is important to realise that, absent decoupling of liability and compensation, the exclusion of liability for pure economic loss may have negative effects on the optimal *ex ante* incentives of the parties.

In a nutshell, the problem of open-ended litigation is an important one for the administration of justice. But, such an administrative problem cannot justify the choice of an inefficient substantive rule, which would create a sizeable bias in the quantification of damages and in the creation of incentives for efficient precaution. Other solutions, such as procedural standing rules, for example, can be utilized to pursue the same normative goal.[17] Put differently, if the true issue is one of open-ended liability, the appropriate solution should focus on correcting the

---

[17] For example, legal systems could limit active legitimation for an action in torts to the direct victims of a tort, regardless of the economic or physical nature of the harm. This would avoid the denounced problem of open-ended liability, barring downstream

derivative litigation problem, avoiding the creation of other problems on the front of individual incentives.

As a methodological matter, once the avoidance of open-ended liability is acknowledged as a driving rationale of the economic loss rule, such pragmatic concern should be addressed openly, avoiding the unnecessary and misleading use of other dogmatic constructs.

## Conclusion

In spite of its historical resilience, the judicial propensity to limit liability for various categories of pure economic loss still lacks a coherent theoretical formulation. The economic analysis of the pure economic loss rule raises some questions on the cogency and significance of the theoretical and dogmatic arguments often invoked by judges and academic writers to justify the rule. The corrective justice and risk-spreading justifications of the rule, for example, have little to do with the legal distinction between direct and indirect economic losses. Likewise, goals of economic efficiency have little to do with the dogmatic distinction between absolute and relative subjective rights, which is used to draw the boundary between compensable and non-compensable economic losses.

Behind the veil of rhetorical dogmatism, the analysis of actual cases of pure economic loss has revealed the judicial endorsement of sensible pragmatic goals. Due to the mixed use of dogmatic logic and judicial pragmatism, however, modern legal systems do not always draw the boundaries of the pure economic loss doctrines along coherent lines. As a result, some of the actual judicial applications are hardly defensible on economic grounds.

In this chapter, I have discussed the theoretical independence – as well as the occasional interrelationship – between the private and social components of the economic loss occasioned by a tort. Liability rules should be attentive to the competing goals of (1) maintaining optimal levels of expected liability and efficient *ex ante* incentives; (2) avoiding open-ended and derivative litigation; and (3) to the extent possible, respecting entrenched legal dogmas and general principles of civil liability.

creditors and other contracting parties of the victim from the exercise of remedies for the compensation of pure economic losses. The measure of damages, however, should be assessed by taking into account the entire social loss, without any *a priori* exclusion of pure economic losses.

As a matter of policy design, the adoption of the legal doctrine of pure economic loss for the purpose of confining litigation in torts is indefensible. The point for *ex ante* deterrence is not so much who obtains compensation, but how much should the tortfeasor pay, once a tort occurs. Some economic losses are as much a true social loss as other physical losses which are regularly treated as compensable harm. The doctrines of pure economic loss, while effective in avoiding open-ended litigation, occasionally create several problems on the front of *ex ante* efficiency. The question of whether the avoidance of open-ended liability is worth the distortion of *ex ante* incentives cannot be satisfactorily answered at this point. But, most importantly, the question may be properly avoided, once alternative solutions are taken into consideration.

This may require the theoretical reconceptualization of the rule. The economic loss rule is generally appreciated for its attempt to strike a practical balance between opposing needs to confine litigation while maintaining effective deterrence, within the dogmatic constraints imposed by modern legal systems. It should be possible in this way to evaluate the true pragmatic rationales of the rule in light of alternative legal solutions to the problem of pure economic losses.

# 4 American tort law and the (supposed) economic loss rule

GARY T. SCHWARTZ

## Introduction: the relative unimportance of an exclusionary rule in the United States

According to Chapter I of this volume, '[p]ure economic loss is one of the most discussed topics of European scholarship. Fascination with the subject...has developed into a wealth of literature about this frontier notion.' My introductory comment about the American situation is that such an assessment could not be fairly made about American tort scholarship, or about the American tort case law more generally. Instead, the doctrine that disallows recovery for economic losses in negligence cases is one that is rarely discussed by scholars and is indeed often ignored by courts. (The implications of this judicial neglect are discussed below.) However, there are one or two important exceptions to this generalization, which will be explained at some length below.

Let me now provide relevant background. The Restatement of Torts is a semi-official source of tort doctrine. The First Restatement was published, in relevant part, in 1939.[1] It included a section (§ 766) creating liability for the purposeful inducement to breach of contract and the purposeful interference with prospective economic advantage; but it said nothing at all about negligence liability. The Second Restatement was published, in relevant part, in 1979.[2] In §§ 766, 766B, and 767, it re-worked the rules on liability for purposeful or intentional interference. But in addition to that, the Second Restatement included a new provision (§ 766C) stating that 'one is not liable to another for pecuniary harm...if that harm results from the actor's negligently interfering with the other's performance of his contract or making the performance more expensive or burdensome', or if the harm results from 'interfering with

[1] 4 Restatement of Torts Vol. 3 (1939).   [2] 4 Restatement (Second) of Torts (1979).

the other's acquiring a contractual relation with a third person'. The Comment accompanying § 766C acknowledged that in denying liability, courts often fail to recognize explicitly the general rule of non-liability; rather, courts reason that the defendant's negligence was not the 'proximate cause' of the plaintiff's loss. The Comment proceeded to suggest that the real explanation for the denial of liability is the 'character' of the plaintiff's interest. 'Whatever the reason may be, there is as yet no general recognition of liability for negligent interference' with contractual opportunities. In explaining this lack of any 'general recognition of liability' – at least as yet – the Comment referred to the fear of excessive and unpredictable liability, and the difficulty (at least in some cases) in proving an adequate causal connection between the defendant's negligence and the plaintiff's economic loss. The Restatement then gave several 'illustrations' of non-liability. One illustration concerns a company that has insured property, and then has to make a payment on this insurance policy because the defendant's negligence has damaged the property. Another illustration relates to a plaintiff who has contracted to tow another party's barge from one port to another; that contract, with its profit opportunities, is then cancelled when the defendant negligently sinks the barge. A further illustration concerns an advertiser suing for lost profits when the negligence of the printer results in the advertiser's name and phone number being omitted from a telephone directory.

At the time of the Second Restatement, there was only one significant article dealing with the issue of negligence liability and economic loss. That had been published in 1972 by Fleming James Jr,[3] who had identified a 'pragmatic' objection to liability, an objection concerned with the prospect of a liability that would be unduly open-ended. The rule of non-liability recognized by the Restatement was largely absent from torts coursebooks on which law schools relied in the 1960s and 1970s.

However, in the very year in which the Second Restatement was published, things began to change. In 1979, the California Supreme Court issued an opinion (*J'Aire Corp.* v. *Gregory*)[4] which could be read as reversing the common law rule of non-liability and thereby recognizing a general doctrine favouring liability in economic loss cases. A somewhat similar opinion (*People Express Airlines* v. *Consolidated Rail Corp.*)[5] was

---

[3] F. James, Jr, 'Limitations on Liability for Economic Loss Caused by Negligence: A Pragmatic Appraisal' (1972) 25 *Vanderbilt Law Review* 43.
[4] 598 P 2d 60 (Cal. 1979).    [5] 495 A 2d 107 (NJ 1985).

handed down by the New Jersey Supreme Court six years later. Moreover, American scholars began to pay attention to the economic loss issue. In 1982, a law and economics scholar took notice of the rule of non-liability, and wrote an article attempting to provide the rule with an economics-oriented rationale.[6] In 1985, two articles were published in American law reviews on the economic loss problem, authored separately by Robert Rabin[7] and myself.[8] It can be noted, however, that the only reason Rabin and I chose to address the problem is that the two of us were invited to attend a conference – in England – on the topic of negligence law and economic loss, from a comparative perspective.[9] A few years later, another law and economics scholar, Victor Goldberg, focused on the economic loss problem, and published the first of what turned out to be a trio of valuable articles.[10] Yet for much of the 1990s the topic of tort law and economic loss fell again into general scholarly neglect. A treatise was prepared by Jay Feinman,[11] addressed to the general audience of lawyers; and of some possible interest is a book chapter that I wrote[12] – but I undertook that chapter only because I was (again) invited to a conference in England dealing with the economic loss problem from a comparative perspective. Overall, the problem remains a backwater within the discourse of American tort law.

## Products liability as an exception

There certainly is, however, at least one major exception to this generalization. In one major context the economic loss rule came dramatically to the attention of courts and academic commentators in the 1960s, and

---

[6] M. J. Rizzo, 'A Theory of Economic Loss in the Law of Torts', (1982) 11 *Journal of Legal Studies* 281.
[7] R. L. Rabin, 'Tort Recovery for Negligently Inflicted Economic Loss: A Reassessment', (1985) 37 *Stanford Law Review* 1513.
[8] G. T. Schwartz, 'Economic Loss in American Tort Law: The Examples of J'Aire and of Products Liability', (1986) 23 *San Diego Law Review* 37.
[9] The conference volume is, M. Furmston (ed.) *The Law of Tort: Policies and Trends in Liability for Damage to Property and Economic Loss* (1985).
[10] V. P. Goldberg, 'Accountable Accountants: Is Third-Party Liability Necessary?', (1988) 17 *Journal of Legal Studies* 295. See also V. P. Goldberg, 'Recovery for Pure Economic Loss in Tort: Another Look at *Robins Dry Dock v. Flint*', (1991) 20 *Journal of Legal Studies* 249; V. P. Goldberg, 'Recovery for Economic Loss Following the Exxon Valdez Oil Spill', (1994) 23 *Journal of Legal Studies* 1.
[11] J. M. Feinman, *Economic Negligence* (Boston, MA, 1995).
[12] G. T. Schwartz, 'The Economic Loss Doctrine in American Tort Law: Assessing the Recent Experience', in E. K. Banakas (ed.), *Civil Liability for Pure Economic Loss* (Kluwer Law International, The Hague, 1996), p. 103.

has remained within judicial attention ever since. This context involves claims against sellers of products (mainly manufacturers) for defects in products that lead to the product owners suffering various kinds of economic losses – mainly, the costs of repair and replacement, but also profits that are lost until repair or replacement can be arranged. It is exactly in the context of products liability claims that American courts have become accustomed to talking about the 'economic loss rule'. To assess this rule in the products context, it is necessary to sketch the background of the rules relating to manufacturer liability in tort for personal injury and property damage.

Early in the nineteenth century, American manufacturers became vulnerable to suit – under a negligence theory – by those who had suffered physical harm.[13] In the early 1960s, American jurisdictions (led by New Jersey[14] and California[15]) began innovating by creating (in cases involving physical harm) a strict liability right running against manufacturers and other product sellers. (Certainly, even the strict liability claim depends on the victim's proof of some 'defect' in the original product.) During the 1960s and 1970s, the strict liability doctrine became increasingly accepted by American jurisdictions.[16] As this happened, product owners began attempting to invoke the new strict liability doctrine in suing the manufacturer when a defect in its product brought about not physical harm, but rather economic losses. The first major opinion dealing with the economic loss issue was *Santor v. A & M Kargheusian, Inc.*,[17] from the New Jersey Supreme Court; moreover, the *Santor* court came to the conclusion that economic losses are indeed recoverable in a strict liability action. However, a few months later the California Supreme Court, in *Seely v. White Motor Co.*,[18] ruled that the strict liability doctrine does not cover economic loss claims. In the years that followed, almost all American jurisdictions aligned themselves with the California position rather than the New Jersey position: strict liability does not extend to claims of economic loss.[19] Moreover, in 1986 the Supreme Court decided *East River S.S. Co. v. Transamerica Delaval*,[20] a case involving admiralty law (which is federal law). In *East River*, the Supreme Court placed its own prestigious

---

[13] See *MacPherson v. Buick Motor Co.*, 111 NE 1050 (NY 1916).
[14] *Henningsen v. Bloomfield Motors, Inc.*, 161 A 2d 69 (NJ 1960).
[15] *Greenman v. Yuba Power Products, Inc.*, 377 P 2d 897 (Cal. 1963).
[16] Of great influence was the Restatement (Second) of Torts § 402A (1965).
[17] 207 A 2d 305 (NJ 1965).    [18] 403 P 2d 145 (Cal. 1965).
[19] This, for example, is the position taken in Restatement (Third) of Torts: Products Liability (1998) § 21.
[20] 476 US 858 (1986).

seal of approval on the result of no liability in tort for economic losses caused by product defects. Indeed, faced with a growing consensus nationwide, over the last fifteen years even the New Jersey Supreme Court has retreated from its original *Santor* position: in *Spring Motors Distributors v. Ford Motor Co.*,[21] it held that a commercial buyer of a product cannot claim in tort for economic losses. Then, in 1997, in *Alloway v. General Marine Industries, LP*,[22] the New Jersey Supreme Court extended *Spring Motors* so as to deny the tort claim of an ordinary consumer. However, the Court in *Alloway* did hedge its bet slightly. The product involved in *Alloway* was a luxury boat purchased by the plaintiff, which sank because of a defective seam. The Court noted that a 'luxury boat with a swimming platform' is not a 'necessity', and that there was no evidence that its purchaser was seriously lacking in 'substantially equal bargaining power'.[23] Accordingly, the Court left open what the right result would be in a case involving a 'necessary' product and an absence of 'equal bargaining power'. It will be interesting to find out how the New Jersey Supreme Court eventually handles this issue. The nationwide consensus – which that court otherwise took into account – has recognized no such distinction: the economic loss rule, rejecting strict liability in tort, applies to the full range of products that consumers and others might purchase.

As product owners became increasingly aware that they were unable to recover for economic losses in strict liability, they identified an obvious fallback: suing for economic losses under negligence law. After all, in rejecting economic loss claims brought under strict liability, courts did so in part because of their belief that the new strict liability doctrine was geared to the special problem of personal injury and physical harm; this judicial belief could be bypassed by suing for economic loss in traditional negligence rather than in novel strict liability. As of 1980, the judicial response to such negligence-based economic loss claims was divided. Certain courts agreed that the unavailability of strict liability was entirely consistent with allowing consumers to recover for economic losses under a negligence theory.[24] But other courts perceived that the exclusion of economic losses from strict liability called for the exclusion of those losses from the scope of negligence liability as well.[25] Courts in this latter group reasoned that strict liability had been rejected for

---

[21] 489 A 2d 660 (NJ 1985).    [22] 695 A 2d 264 (NJ 1997).    [23] Ibid. at 268, 269.
[24] See, e.g. *Berg v. General Motors Corp.*, 555 P 2d 818 (Wash. 1976).
[25] See, e.g. *Moorman Mfg. Co. v. National Tank Co.*, 435 NE 2d 443 (Ill. 1982).

economic loss because of the belief that contract and warranty provided the proper framework for resolving economic loss claims; and this point about the primacy of contract and warranty remains valid even when consumers sue under the more traditional tort theory of negligence. Interestingly, in most states the issue was a new one that courts needed to decide. Even though in personal injury cases manufacturers had been subject to negligence liability since early in the twentieth century, it appears that – until the modern post-1960 era of products liability – few, if any, product owners had ever attempted to recover from manufacturers for economic losses under negligence law. In any event, while the American cases may have been divided in their outcomes as of the early 1980s, by the end of the century a solid majority position could be identified to the effect that the economic loss rule in products liability applies to claims of negligence as well as claims of strict liability.[26] Courts who have contributed to this majority position include the United States Supreme Court, in *East River*, and the New Jersey Supreme Court, in *Alloway*.

In short, having begun by finding that strict liability does not apply in economic losses, courts have continued to largely reject the idea that the negligence doctrine can be invoked in such economic loss cases. Likewise, other limitations on the economic loss rule have been proposed and considered by the judiciary. Plainly, the rule applies if, for example, a new television set simply stops working because of a defect. On the other hand, if the television set catches fire because of a defect, and if that fire destroys the consumer's expensive carpet and (perhaps) the consumer's entire house, all of this is damage to the consumer's 'other property' that is clearly recoverable in an ordinary action in tort (including in strict liability). What is the result, however, if the television set catches fire because of the defect and merely damages itself? Does the fact that the owner's product is actually 'damaged' enable the property owner to sue in tort? American courts have almost uniformly answered this question in the negative.[27] As a functional matter, damage to the product imposes on the product owner merely the costs of repair and replacement, and possibly lost profits; and these are exactly the types of costs and losses that are covered by the economic loss rule.

---

[26] See, e.g. *Sunnyslope Grading Inc. v. Miller, Bradford and Risberg Inc.*, 437 NW 2d 213 (Wis. 1989) (reversing precedent).
[27] This is, for example, the position endorsed in the Restatement (Third) of Torts: Products Liability (1998) § 21 Comment d.

Consider, however, the situation in which the product, because of a defect, poses a danger to the safety of various parties (including the product owner). If a car's defective brakes makes the car dangerous to drive, does that danger enable the owner to recover in tort for the costs of their repair? The fact of danger makes the situation begin to look like a more traditional tort problem. Nevertheless, most courts have declined generally to find any exception to the economic loss rule that might cover products whose defectiveness renders them dangerous. Here too, courts have reasoned that the relevant costs facing the product owner are the costs of repair and replacement, and these are the costs that are routinely covered by the economic loss rule. But courts have not been unanimous on this: indeed, the recent New Jersey *Alloway* opinion leaves open the question of what the right result is when the product defect 'poses a serious risk to other property or persons', and hence needs to be repaired or replaced.[28]

What if the product, because of its defect, is involved in a dramatic event that could easily have resulted in personal injury – even though personal injury is fortunately avoided? Consider, for example, the product which brings about an explosion because of a defect; even though only the product itself is damaged in that explosion, the explosion could easily have injured innocent third parties. In the early 1980s, certain courts accepted the idea that when a product's defect brings about a 'sudden and calamitous event', this is a circumstance that justifies the product owner's suit in tort for economic losses.[29] What these courts in essence were saying was that 'it looks like a tort, it sounds like a tort, it must be a tort', even though the plaintiff's own losses are merely economic. Yet in more recent years the economic loss rule has reasserted itself; most courts now agree that even if the defect in the product brings about a potentially calamitous event, when the product owner merely incurs economic losses, and seeks to sue for those losses, the owner is not able to recover in tort.[30]

Recall, however, the example of tort liability given above: the defective television set that damages the consumer's 'other property'. With that example in mind, consider now the situation when I buy a new car from, say, Ford that contains a spark plug produced by a supplier, for example, Delco. Assume further that the Delco spark plug is defective,

---

[28] *Alloway v. General Marine Industries*, LP, 695 A 2d 264, 273 (NJ 1997).
[29] See, e.g. *Pennsylvania Glass Sand Corp. v. Caterpillar Tractor Co.*, 652 F 2d 1165 (3rd Cir. 1981).
[30] See, e.g. *Aloe Coal v. Clark Equip.*, 816 F 2d 110 (3rd Cir. 1987).

and causes a minor explosion within the car that damages other parts of the car – for example, its engine block. In these circumstances, can I sue Delco, and point to the damage in the remainder of my car by way of justifying my suit against the supplier of the component part? Most American courts now answer this question in the negative.[31] The consumer buys the entire car from the car dealer: what the consumer gets is an integrated product, and any damage to a part of that product is merely economic loss as far as the buyer of that product is concerned. Therefore the economic loss rule applies.

However, change the facts in an interesting way, and the result may be altered as well. Assume that I have owned my car for three years, and that its spark plug now needs replacing. I buy a new spark plug made by Delco from an auto parts store. The spark plug contains a defect which causes a minor explosion, which itself damages other parts of the car itself, including the engine block. In these circumstances, it cannot be said that I have bought an entire new car that happens to include a defective component. Rather, I already own a car – it is my 'other property' – at the time that I buy a component part to fit into the car. If, in these circumstances, the defective Delco explodes and causes damage to my 'other property', American courts would probably allow a tort recovery. It should be acknowledged, though, that there is an absence of cases that have actually affirmed this interesting point.

## Rationales of the rule

Having sketched the dimensions of the economic loss rule in products liability, I should now discuss its rationale. The reason given by American courts on behalf of the rule is that in products cases, contract law is the preferred framework within which to resolve claims of economic loss. Indeed, contract law has been elaborated on by the warranty provisions in the Uniform Commercial Code (UCC), which itself has been adopted in essentially every American jurisdiction. To allow tort recoveries, then, would undermine or circumvent the provisions of a statute – and generally judicial decisions are not allowed to bring about such a result. The preference for contract and for the UCC and its warranty opinions is, for example, what is expressed by the New Jersey Supreme Court in its recent opinion in *Alloway*. But in noting this judicial preference for

---

[31] This is the result endorsed in Restatement (Third) of Torts: Products Liability (1998) § 21 Comment e.

contract and warranty doctrines, it is worthwhile exploring what the extent of product owners' rights are under contract and UCC warranty. Under the UCC, there is an implied warranty of fitness for ordinary use that accompanies the sale of the product.[32] This implied warranty indeed makes the product seller liable – under a strict liability standard – when the product contains a defect that brings about economic losses. Under the UCC, the product owner's implied warranty right runs mainly against the retailer. Yet the UCC is not opposed to extending implied warranty to the manufacturer; rather, it leaves the issue open. In its opinion in *Spring Motors Distributors* v. *Ford Motor Co.*,[33] the New Jersey Supreme Court, even while rejecting the tort claims for economic loss of the commercial owner, agreed to interpret warranty law broadly and to recognize an implied warranty claim running directly against the manufacturer.

Still, implied warranty is disadvantageous to product owners in certain respects. First, the limitation period for an implied warranty claim under the UCC is four years from the time of sale.[34] By contrast, the statute of limitations in tort is in most jurisdictions two years from the time of harm. If a party has bought a product in 1993, and it contains a defect that manifests itself in 1998 and subjects the party to economic losses in that year, under the UCC the party's implied warranty rights have expired even before the party has actually suffered any loss. By contrast, if the tort law could be relied on as the source for economic loss claims, the owner would still have two years in which to sue. Indeed, it is limitation period considerations that explain why many plaintiffs have attempted to sue in tort rather than relying on their implied warranty rights. Notice, however, that this differential between tort and implied warranty is hardly necessary or organic. Rather, that differential may be happenstance: there would be nothing inherently uncontract-like were the UCC to adopt a limitation period that gives the product owner two years from the time of loss in which to bring a warranty claim.

Secondly, the implied warranty right conferred by the UCC can be disclaimed by clear and conspicuous language in the sales document.[35] By contrast, the general idea is that strict liability in tort cannot be disclaimed.[36] At first this seems like a major difference. However, the difference may be less than it appears. For one thing, as far as disclaimers

---

[32] UCC § 2-314(1) (1977).   [33] 489 A 2d 660 (NJ 1985).
[34] UCC § 2-725(1) (1977).   [35] Ibid. at § 2-316(2).
[36] This is the position taken in Restatement (Third) of Torts: Products Liability (1998) § 18.

are concerned, it is standard practice for American manufacturers to disclaim warranty in part – but only in part. If, for example, the consumer buys a new car, he is generally given a very broad express warranty that covers almost everything that might go wrong with the car for the course of a year (or longer). The express warranty then includes a provision disclaiming any warranties, including implied warranties, that might extend beyond the one-year period of the express warranty. Despite this disclaimer, during the original year of ownership the car owner is fully protected. Even less expensive ordinary household products such as toasters, television sets and refrigerators typically contain warranties that last for six months, a year or even longer.

Also, the hostility of tort law to disclaimers of liability should not be overstated. That hostility has been expressed mainly in cases involving ordinary consumers suffering personal injury. Assume now that a large company buys a product, and accepts a disclaimer on all tort liability. The product then catches fire, and damages 'other property' that the company owns. Because of this property damage, the company would have a tort claim against the manufacturer; this would not be a case of 'mere' economic loss. But in such a situation – involving mere property damage and also a product purchaser that seems capable of adequately bargaining in its own interest – many American courts would regard the disclaimer as valid after all.[37] Accordingly, even if courts were to recognize tort rights for economic loss, in this economic loss context those tort rights might well be held by courts to be disclaimable. Given such a judicial holding, the supposed advantage that tort might give to the plaintiff suing for economic loss would disappear. Furthermore, in economic loss cases, when the product purchaser is an ordinary consumer, certain jurisdictions have modified the UCC, and have prevented product sellers from disclaiming their implied warranty obligations.[38] Here too, the supposed distinction between (disclaimable) implied warranty rights and (non-disclaimable) tort rights does not hold up. It may be, then, that for purposes of disclaiming liability, the relevant line is not so much the line between tort and warranty, but rather a line between ordinary consumers (whose rights cannot be disclaimed under either tort or warranty) and institutional purchasers (for whom disclaimers are valid, whether the suit is brought in tort or in warranty).

---

[37] The issue is left open, ibid. at § 18 Comment d.
[38] E.g. *Ann. Laws of Mass.* ch. 106, § 2–316A (1984).

In any event, it is exactly in products liability cases that courts have most frequently discussed the 'economic loss rule', and in those cases it is a preference for contract (and the warranty doctrines that are part of contract) that explain why courts are reluctant to recognize liability in tort (whether in strict liability or in negligence). The California opinion in 1979 that seemingly broadened tort rights is *J'Aire Corp.* v. *Gregory*.[39] In *J'Aire*, the defendant was a contractor that had undertaken to renovate the property owner's building; the plaintiff was a restaurant that was a tenant in that building. Because of delays by the contractor in completing the renovations, the plaintiff was unable to reopen the restaurant at the expected time, and therefore suffered business losses. It is clear that the Second Restatement's rule would deny liability in a case such as this. Yet in *J'Aire*, the California court innovated by affirming the tenant's negligence claim against the contractor. The obvious objection to this innovation is that it is contract principles that ought to determine the scope of the various parties' rights and liabilities. The renovator has a contract with the building owner, who also has a contract with the restaurant. It can strongly be argued that this combination of contracts ought to determine the various parties' legal positions. Indeed, it is possible that the restaurant has a contract claim against the renovator. American tort law (unlike its English counterpart) includes a doctrine that renders 'intended third-party beneficiaries' of contracts appropriate parties to sue for contractual breach. In defining the scope of the restaurant tenant's tort rights, the California Supreme Court took into account that the contract between the renovator and the building owner was 'intended to affect' the tenant.[40] Yet the very finding of such an intention to affect the tenant could lead to a holding that the tenant can sue the renovator as an intended beneficiary for its own breach of contract. Overall, then, in *J'Aire* the contract alternative to the tort approach looms very large. Indeed, it is impossible to think about the renovator's negligence in *J'Aire* without taking its contract with the building owner into account. For example, it is only that contract that can identify what the target date is for the completion of the renovations. In this regard as well, the pertinence of contract makes it difficult to appreciate why tort rights should be recognized. In products liability cases, the applicability of contract explains why the economic loss rule is invoked; the pertinence of contract similarly suggests why the *J'Aire* court was wrong in declining to affirm the rule.

---

[39] 598 P 2d 60 (Cal. 1979).    [40] Ibid. at 63.

It can be noted, however, that in other suits for economic loss involving parties who are in a contract relationship with each other, contract and tort seem congruent, rather than incompatible. Consider the client who consults a professional, such as a lawyer or an accountant. It is well understood that professional malpractice is one branch of tort law that 'survives', despite the general acceptance of the economic loss rule of no tort liability.[41] However, in the contract between lawyer and client, courts find an implied promise that the professional will exercise reasonable care and provide reasonable services. Given the recognition of this implied promise, there is no conflict between tort and contract. Indeed, the client's malpractice claim against the lawyer is regarded as sounding simultaneously in tort and contract.[42] If, for example, the statute of limitations varies between tort and contract, the client can probably pick and choose as to whether to frame his claim in tort or in contract instead. Of course, insofar as contract is pertinent, one might assume that the lawyer in his contract with the client would be free to disclaim any liability for malpractice. However, there are rules of professional responsibility that make it improper for the lawyer to disclaim liability for malpractice.[43] So the combination of an obligation of reasonable care that is supported by both tort and contract and a prohibition (derived from the law of professional responsibility) against any disclaimers of that obligation render tort and contract compatible in terms of the liability obligations imposed on lawyers. Hence, for purposes of the client's claim against the lawyer, there is nothing in the norms of contract that militate against recognizing the client's tort rights. On the other hand, given the rights that are independently conferred on the client by contract, his tort claim is in a significant sense irrelevant or superfluous.

In other situations, the problem with recognizing tort liability for negligence that causes economic loss has nothing whatsoever to do with the primacy of contract. Consider the facts of *People Express Airlines, Inc. v. Consolidated Rail Corp.*,[44] a New Jersey case from 1985. Here the defendant was negligently responsible for a fire, which caused the temporary evacuation of a one-mile area surrounding the fire. Because of that evacuation, the plaintiff, an airline with facilities within the area, suffered a loss of business. There are a number of cases that comply with the structure of the problem in *People Express*: the defendant's negligence closes down

[41] *Collins v. Reynard*, 607 NE 2d 1185 (Ill. 1992).
[42] See, e.g. *Clark v. Rowe*, 701 NE 2d 624 (Mass. 1998).
[43] Restatement (Third): The Law Concerning Lawyers (2000) § 54(2).
[44] 495 A 2d 107 (NJ 1985).

a highway or a bridge, causing the plaintiff to suffer business-oriented economic losses.[45] Clearly, there is nothing in the law of contracts that in any way affects the liability issue in a case such as *People Express*. The defendant has no contractual relationship of any sort either with the local businesses or with the customers who might otherwise have patronized those businesses. According to the court's understanding in *People Express*, the traditional reason for opposing negligence liability in economic loss cases is the fear of a liability that would be unduly open-ended. To respond to this problem, the court affirmed the applicability of the negligence liability principle, but tied it to a requirement that the plaintiff (either individually or as part of a class) be 'particularly foreseeable' to the defendant at the time of its negligence; the doctrine of proximate cause should be given a 'sedulous' application, in order to keep liability within reasonable limits.[46]

The court in *People Express* was correct in understanding the concern expressed by many observers – that liability for economic loss might in many cases be disproportionate to the extent of the defendant's negligence.[47] For such observers, the solution developed in *People Express* – recognizing liability for economic loss, yet confining liability by way of a narrow doctrine of proximate cause – may well be quite satisfactory. However, the modern law and economics analysis of cases whose facts resemble *People Express* has identified a quite different rationale for the traditional practice of no liability.[48] Let us explain that rationale. In *People Express*, the plaintiff was an airline whose office was selling tickets for flights on particular routes. Assume that, because of the fire, travellers are unable to patronize that airline office. If so, those travellers will instead deal with another airline, and will buy tickets from that airline, rather than from People Express, for purposes of travelling (for example) from location A to location B. In these circumstances, the loss suffered by People Express is balanced by the gain experienced by the other airline (say, for example, United). From an economic perspective, the goal of tort law is to minimize 'social losses'. However, in the context

---

[45] See, e.g. *Stop & Shop Companies, Inc.* v. *Fisher*, 444 NE 2d 368 (Mass. 1983) (liability rejected under negligence law, but endorsed under the doctrine of public nuisance). Compare *532 Madison Avenue Gourmet Foods, Inc.* v. *Finlandia Center, Inc.*, 711 NYS 2d 391 (App. Div. 2000) (affirming liability) with *Goldberg, Weprin & Ustin, LLP* v. *Tishman Construction Corp.*, 713 NYS 2d 57 (App. Div. 2000) (rejecting liability).
[46] 495 A 2d 107 (NJ 1985) at 116–118.
[47] E.g. James, 'Limitations on Liability', at p. 3; Rabin, 'Tort Recovery', at p. 7.
[48] See W. Bishop, 'Economic Loss in Tort', (1982) 2 *Oxford Journal of Legal Studies* 1; Goldberg, 'Exxon Valdez Oil Spill'.

of *People Express*, while there may well be a 'private loss' incurred by the plaintiff, that private loss is offset by the private gain experienced by United. Though there is a private loss, there is no obvious social loss. Hence the deterrence advantage that economists associate with the rule of negligence liability is apparently inoperative.

All of this makes for an intriguing argument, and provides some support for the general intuition that economic losses are not 'real' in the same way that personal injury is real. However, as economists have themselves recognized, their argument is incomplete. If the consumers' original preference was to buy airline tickets from People Express rather than United, then consumers obviously regarded People Express as more advantageous than United. (Perhaps the times of the People Express flights are more convenient; their seats might be more comfortable; possibly the airfares they charge are lower.) In being induced by the defendant's negligence to shift from People Express to United, consumers do indeed suffer a private loss that is a 'social loss' in the sense of not being offset by any compensating private gains. Certainly, this social loss may well be considerably less than the private loss experienced by People Express itself; nevertheless, there is no reason to regard this social loss as insignificant. Accordingly, even though imposing full liability on the defendant for the People Express loss would be excessive from an economic perspective, subjecting the defendant to no liability would be inadequate in terms of providing the defendant with appropriate incentives. Accordingly from an economic perspective, the economic loss rule, by denying all liability, is unsatisfying in cases whose facts resemble *People Express*.

In such cases, there is another reason why that rule is unsatisfying. One can step away from the economic rationale for limiting liability and focus instead on arguments in favour of liability that are moral rather than economic in character. If the defendant by negligent conduct has caused the plaintiff to suffer harm (even economic harm), it can easily be argued that for the sake of fairness the defendant should be required to compensate the plaintiff for that harm. Of course, those who espouse an ethical approach to tort liability might favour the economic loss rule by stating that while a plaintiff has a 'right' to be free of physical injury and property damage, the plaintiff has no similar 'right' to be free of mere economic loss. Yet in cases whose facts resemble *People Express*, such an argument runs the risk of being somewhat circular. Plaintiffs have no 'right' to be free of economic losses caused by negligence, mainly because legal authorities (such as the Second Restatement) have concluded that such a right is absent.

## Contexts and cases

In short, the economic loss rule is most frequently invoked in two quite different sets of cases. In one, the plaintiff seeks to circumvent contract by suing under a negligence theory a party with whom it is in a contract-like relationship. In these cases, the rationale for denying liability in tort is quite strong. The other set of cases have nothing to do with contract. Rather, plaintiff's negligence claims raise the prospect of a liability that might be unduly open-ended or disproportionate to the extent of the defendant's negligence. In these cases, the rationale for denying liability is plausible, but not overwhelming. A number of recent cases dealing with negligence liability for economic loss can be looked at from the perspective of the economic loss rule and the policy considerations that may underlie it. Consider, for example, *Hakimoglo v. Trump Taj Mahal Associates*.[49] In this case a casino in Atlantic City, New Jersey (where casino gambling is lawful) had served alcoholic beverages to its patron, knowing that the patron was already intoxicated; the patron continued to gamble, and as a result suffered serious gambling losses. The patron then sued the casino, alleging that his economic losses were due to the casino's negligence. Is liability proper? The court majority answered this question in the negative, and in so doing relied on a variety of considerations, such as the problem of proving that the inebriation was indeed the cause of the gambling losses in question. Yet in reaching its result, the majority made no mention of the economic loss rule, nor did it acknowledge that this rule had been evidently rejected by the New Jersey Supreme Court many years before, in *People Express*. The dissent would have allowed liability, and the dissenting judge's opinion contained analysis that hints at the economic loss dimension of the problem:

> The most plausible objection to my position is that torts of negligence generally seek to deter and compensate for the destruction of wealth, while the tort in this case is arguably merely allocative. [In this case, on account of the defendant's alleged negligence,] society is no worse off; different parties just possess the wealth.[50]

This, of course, is a version of the distinction between social loss and mere private loss that has been discussed above as providing a possible rationale for the economic loss rule. But in finding that the distinction is an inadequate reason for rejecting liability, the dissent did not even see

---

[49] 70 F 3d 291 (3rd Cir. 1995).   [50] Ibid. at 298.

fit to explicitly mention the economic loss rule or its rejection in *People Express*, the relevant New Jersey precedent. In considering the contractual relationship between the casino and the patron in *Hakimoglo*, most of us would regard the patron's claim as weak. Our understanding is that the business of the casino is to provide both gambling and alcohol, while the natural interest of the patron lies in both gambling and drinking; it is the responsibility of the patron in the individual situation to determine the balance between the two activities.[51]

One recent and interesting case is *Register v. Oaklawn Jockey Club, Inc.*[52] Like *Hakimoglo*, this is a gambling case. A patron at a race track attempted to place a 'Classix wager' – in which the bettor needs to pick the winning horses in six consecutive races in order to win his bet. However, for reasons allegedly related to the defendant's negligence, the machine at the race track failed to issue a ticket that complied with the plaintiff's designated bet. Yet the plaintiff had picked the winning horses: had the ticket been properly supplied, he would have won a major share in the Classix. The Supreme Court of Arkansas ruled that the plaintiff could recover from the race track upon proof of the latter's negligence. In affirming this potential liability, the Court relied on general negligence reasoning, and made no mention of the economic loss exception to that reasoning. Interestingly, the plaintiff also asserted a contract claim against the race track. According to the Court, this claim might well have been valid; except for a state statute that required, as a condition for a valid race track betting contract, a regular ticket from an approved machine. The quite difficult question – which the Court's opinion fails to discuss – concerns whether the state statute, in blocking the plaintiff's contract claim, casts a shadow on his negligence claim as well.

Next, there have been recent suits against tobacco companies by union health insurance funds, which have incurred expenses in reimbursing their members for the costs of treating tobacco-related diseases, and by hospitals that have provided needed health services, often without reimbursement, for those suffering from such diseases. The suits against the tobacco companies have included claims of negligence, but have relied

---

[51] Consider the commercial bar that serves drinks to an already intoxicated customer. If that customer then drives drunk, and in doing so injures a pedestrian, most American states give the pedestrian a tort claim against the bar. But if the customer is involved in an auto accident that merely injures himself, the customer has no tort claim against the bar.
[52] 822 SW 2d 391 (Ark. 1992).

on a wide variety of other claims as well, including the companies' alleged violations of antitrust statutes and also their alleged violation of the federal racketeering statute (Racketeer-Influenced and Corrupt Organizations – RICO). Insofar as the cases raise negligence issues, the Second Restatement takes a position that is directly opposed to liability. Moreover, there is a contract analysis that supports this opposition. The contract between the insured and the insurer can easily be drafted so as to include a subrogation clause that enables the insurer to bring a suit in the name of the insured against any third party which injures the insured through its tortious behaviour. Such a subrogation clause, by lowering the insurer's eventual costs, should likewise lower the premium which the insurer charges the insured for the policy. If the insurer has failed to include such a clause in the insurance contract, then the insurer should not be able to claim in tort against the negligent third party. The result of non-liability can be explained in a related way. Assume the defendant, by negligence, injures a person who has a health insurance policy. That person pays a physician for his medical treatment, and then is reimbursed for this expense by his insurance company. The person then brings a tort suit against the negligent defendant. In light of what American law calls the 'collateral source rule', in that person's suit he can recover in full from the defendant for his medical expenses – even though he has already been reimbursed for those expenses by his own insurance company. If the company can also sue the defendant for its insurance payouts, the defendant would be subjected to an entirely inappropriate double liability.

In fact, the suits brought by the union health insurance trusts have been widely rejected by federal courts of appeal;[53] and the suits brought by hospitals have been generally rejected as well.[54] However, in turning away these suits, courts have shown almost no recognition of the fact that there is an economic loss rule that might explain the judicial outcomes. Rather, courts have generally relied on the idea that the defendants' alleged torts are not the 'proximate cause' of the economic losses about which the plaintiffs are complaining. Likewise, 'proximate cause' reasoning has been relied on by a distinguished federal district court judge, in rejecting a suit against tobacco companies by the Republic of

---

[53] See, e.g. *United Food & Commercial Workers Unions v. Philip Morris, Inc.*, 223 F 3d 1271, 1274 (11th Cir. 2000) (citing previous cases). But see *Blue Cross & Blue Shield of New Jersey, Inc. v. Philip Morris, Inc.*, 36 F Supp. 2d 560 (EDNY 1999) (a trial court opinion allowing an insurance company's claim to proceed under RICO).

[54] E.g. *Allegheny Gen. Hosp. v. Philip Morris, Inc.*, 228 F 3d 429 (3rd Cir. 2000).

Guatemala, on account of the costs the government incurred in treating its citizens' smoking-related illnesses.[55]

Whatever their reasoning, courts have in general rejected these suits seeking reimbursement for healthcare costs. However, let us now report the following. Just prior to the wave of recent judicial opinions, many American state governments had brought claims against tobacco companies, on account of healthcare costs borne by states in treating low-income citizens covered by various state-administered health plans. The tobacco industry, evidently fearful of the outcome of this litigation, agreed to settle, in 1998.[56] Moreover, the settlement was for an enormous amount – in excess of $200 billion. It should be made clear that there had been no major appellate opinions affirming the general propriety of such suits by the states. For that matter, there were not even any jury verdicts against the tobacco companies that appellate courts might have conveniently considered. The only case that went to trial before the settlement was in Minnesota; a state court jury was deliberating the case at the time when the industry agreed to settle the case (for a sum of $6.1 billion). One can acknowledge that the industry was facing a staggering economic risk in these cases: if the propriety of the suits had been eventually affirmed by the judiciary, the industry might have been confronted with an overwhelming liability. Nevertheless, the staggering price that the industry was willing to pay to avoid this risk of liability is remarkable – especially so in light of the subsequent pattern of judicial opinions rejecting similar claims brought by hospitals and union health funds. It can be noted that in many states there are indeed statutes that subrogate state governments to the tort claims that might be possessed by state citizens who receive healthcare services from the state. However, in their claims against the tobacco industry, the states made no effort to rely on statutory subrogation; their perception was that proving the validity of tort claims smoker-by-smoker would have been excessively costly. Rather, the states advanced the argument that the industry had behaved illegally and tortiously, and that this industry behaviour had increased the overall level of smoking within the state (and correspondingly, the rate of smoking-related diseases whose treatment the state was financing).

In short, in the recent tobacco cases the leading appellate opinions have vindicated the economic loss rule, on the one hand, though failing

---

[55] *In re Tobacco/Governmental Health Care Costs* litigation, 83 F Supp. 2d 125 (DDC 1999).
[56] See G. T. Schwartz, 'Tobacco, Liability, and *Viscusi*', (1999) 29 *Cumberland Law Review* 555.

to mention it by name. On the other hand, the tobacco industry's expensive settlement of the claims brought against it by state governments involves a major departure from that rule. Discussed below will be three other lines of recent cases that have considered the plaintiff's right to recover under negligence law for what amounts to economic loss. The lines of cases have reached diverging results. What is of immediate interest is that none of the cases have recognized the apparent relevance of the economic loss rule.

A large number of recent cases have concerned the situation of existing (or potential) employees who submit to drug tests or alcohol tests, as conducted by professional laboratories, under contract with employers. In the typical case the laboratory, because of its negligence, returns a 'false positive' to the effect that the testee is under the influence of alcohol or drugs; the testee is then denied a job offer or terminated from his existing job. The testee proceeds to bring a negligence claim against the laboratory. In recent years, many state courts have accepted such negligence claims,[57] while many others have rejected them.[58] In none of the judicial opinions has the issue been conceptualized in terms of economic loss and the economic loss rule. Rather, what the courts have focused on is the primary contract obligation which the lab owes to the employer, but not to the actual or prospective employee. Hence, while there is something of a contract problem that needs to be considered in these cases, it cannot be claimed that the testee is either evading or circumventing contract law by bringing a claim against the laboratory. The job applicant in particular has no contractual relationship with the lab, nor yet any contract with the employer itself. Nor do these cases raise any prospect of an open-ended liability: when the lab is negligent, there is one victim, and one alone. Accordingly, the court's failure to acknowledge the economic loss rule, while puzzling, is understandable.

Next, there are cases involving what is referred to as the 'negligent spoliation' of evidence. Assume, for example, that the plaintiff is injured while using a neighbour's power tool, and that the injury may well be due to a design defect in the power tool itself. In these circumstances, the plaintiff possibly has a tort claim against the product manufacturer. Assume, however, that the neighbour proceeds thoughtlessly to discard or throw away the damaged power tool, and thereby denies the plaintiff the evidence that he needs in order to bring a successful products

---

[57] E.g. *Duncan v. Afton, Inc.*, 991 P 2d 739 (Wyo. 1999).
[58] E.g. *Ney v. Axelrod*, 723 A 2d 719 (Pa. S Ct. 1999).

liability claim. Can the plaintiff sue the neighbour for negligent spoliation of the relevant evidence? Obviously, the claim the plaintiff would like to bring against the manufacturer concerns the plaintiff's personal injury. Nevertheless, what the plaintiff has lost because of the neighbour's alleged negligence is the opportunity to secure an economic asset – a court award of legal damages. In recent years, the issue of negligent spoliation has been frequently litigated, and courts have reached diverging results.[59] When courts have supported liability, they have relied on conventional negligence reasoning. When they have rejected liability, they have paid no attention to the economic loss rule. Instead, they have relied on a variety of practical and specific considerations, including the undesirability of encouraging so-called 'derivative' litigation, and all the problems that would be encountered in assessing what the result of the plaintiff's personal injury suit would have been, had the relevant evidence not been misplaced or lost. The judicial neglect of the economic loss rule may well be sensible: for these cases simply do not raise the issue of either an unduly open-ended liability or the circumvention of contract. However, there is one valuable point about contractual possibilities made by at least one court.[60] If the plaintiff wishes a third party to preserve the relevant evidence, the plaintiff should secure from the third party an agreement that it will do so; such a contractual agreement is then appropriate for judicial enforcement.

In another line of recent cases, adoption agencies have been sued by families who have adopted children, alleging the agencies' failure to disclose information about the physical or mental health problems of the adoptive children. The 'losses' suffered by these families seem largely economic: the costs the family bears in providing needed treatments or therapies to the child. Those losses may include an 'emotional' component as well – as the parents undergo the experience of coping with an adopted child who has serious health problems. However, classifying the loss as emotional does not make the problem of liability any easier: for just as there is a general rule denying liability for negligence that causes economic losses, so there is a nearly equal general rule denying the liability of the party whose negligence brings about mere emotional distress.[61] In these so-called 'wrongful adoption' cases, courts are divided

---

[59] Compare *Austin v. Consolidation Coal Co.*, 501 SE 2d 161 (Va. 1998) (rejecting negligent spoliation claim) with *Holmes v. Amerex Rent-A-Car*, 710 A 2d 846 (DC 1998) (accepting claim).
[60] *Coprich v. Superior Court*, 95 Cal. Rptr. 2d 884 (Ct. App. 2000).
[61] See Restatement (Second) of Torts (1965) § 436A.

in the results that they have reached, though the recent pattern has been favourable to liability.[62] When courts support liability, they are able to invoke the traditional tort of negligent misrepresentation, and to indicate that they are doing little more than 'extending' that tort.[63] Yet if, in deciding these cases, courts have neglected the economic loss rule, that neglect seems roughly sensible. The wrongful adoption cases do not raise any prospect of an open-ended liability; rather, there is merely one instance of liability for each instance of negligence. As far as honouring contract is concerned, the only contract-like issue relates to what the reasonable expectations are of a family in dealing with an adoption agency. In this regard, it seems appropriate to recognize an expectation that the agency will behave reasonably in communicating information to the prospective parents, when that information is obviously relevant to the decision that those prospective parents will be making.

To recap, there are several recent lines of cases in which the economic loss rule has been largely neglected; rather, courts have decided the cases by considering other factors. However, let us close this chapter by discussing a line of cases in which the economic loss rule, in its basic form, is now coming dramatically to the attention of American courts. These cases involve suits by homeowners against home builders and others for negligence in the construction of their homes – negligence that causes the homeowners to suffer economic losses, either in terms of the cost of repairing their homes or in terms of the depreciated value of the homes themselves. In California, the law relating to negligence claims was highly uncertain – until the California Supreme Court's recent decision in *Aas* v. *Superior Court*.[64] The *Aas* litigation involved one set of claims brought by original owners of homes, and another set of claims by those who had purchased houses from their original owners. The alleged negligence of the home builders related to defects in the homes that violated applicable local building codes. In considering tort doctrine, the California Supreme Court made clear that homeowners are able to recover in tort when the negligence of home builders results in personal injury or property damage. But the court's majority was unwilling to allow homeowners claims in negligence for mere

---

[62] E.g. *Jackson* v. *State*, 956 P 2d 35 (Mont. 1998); *McKinney* v. *State*, 950 P 2d 461 (Wash. 1998). But see *Richard P.* v. *Vista Del Mar Child Care Serv.*, 165 Cal. Rptr. 370 (Ct. App. 1980).
[63] See *Mallette* v. *Children's Friend & Service*, 661 A 2d 67 (RI 1995).
[64] 12 P 3d 1125 (Cal. 2000).

economic loss.[65] In considering this issue, the Supreme Court appreciated that it was required to choose between *Seely*,[66] which had applied the economic loss rule to bar tort claims against product manufacturers for economic loss, and *J'Aire*,[67] which affirmed the right to recover under negligence law for economic loss so long as the defendant's transaction was 'intended to affect' the plaintiff. (The court in *Aas* was quite willing to agree that the construction of homes is intended to affect both immediate and subsequent homeowners.) Faced with this choice, the *Aas* court supported the *Seely* line of analysis – with its rejection of negligence rights and its emphasis on contract and warranty as defining the rights between buyer and seller.

The court's holding in *Aas* is limited in certain respects. Because building codes are designed to prevent harm to life, health and property, the code violations in *Aas* evidently made the homes not only defective but also dangerous; even so, the *Aas* court relied on the point that the dangers in question seemed not especially serious. It is unclear what result the court would have reached if the defects had posed an immediate risk of serious personal injury. Likewise, although it denied liability for negligence that causes mere economic loss, the court endorsed a broad version of the rule that enables plaintiffs to recover under negligence law for damage to their 'other property'. Thus, according to the court's opinion, if one subcontractor performs negligently, and in so doing damages another portion of the structure, the homeowner has a negligence claim against that subcontractor, even though the homeowner has purchased an integrated product – the house – from the general contractor.

Despite these limitations, the holding in *Aas* which rejects negligence claims for economic loss is obviously important. Still, its overall impact should be placed in context. First, *Aas* is limited to California. American tort law is of course a federalism; every state court system makes up its own mind, and often does so in an independent way. In fact, the issue that was dealt with by the *Aas* court in California is one that has produced diverging responses nationwide.[68] In Florida, for example, a leading 1993 case had applied the economic loss rule so as to deny the

---

[65] A year before, the same court had rejected the claim by homeowners that they should be able to recover for the emotional distress they experienced because of defects they found in their new homes. See *Erlich v. Menezes*, 981 P 2d 974 (Cal. 1999).
[66] *Seely v. White Motor Co.*, 403 P 2d 145 (Cal. 1965).
[67] *J'Aire Corp. v. Gregory*, 598 P 2d 60 (Cal. 1979).
[68] For one good overview, see W. K. Jones, 'Economic Losses Caused Construction Deficiencies: The Competing Regimes of Contract and Tort', (1991) 59 *University of Cincinnati Law Review* 105.

homeowner's negligence claim against the home builder.[69] However, a subsequent Florida case, involving a complicated factual situation, casts some doubt on the continued validity of the court's earlier ruling.[70] In states such as North Carolina, courts have not only affirmed the negligence liability of the home builder, but have ruled that this liability extends to the person who buys the home from its original purchaser.[71]

As for the *Aas* case itself, it is also noteworthy that the claim was brought mainly against a general contractor. Assume a home buyer contracts with an architect to design a home, which a general contractor then constructs with the help of subcontractors. If there is negligence on the part of the architect in designing a home, then despite *Aas* the homeowner might have a winning claim. First of all, architects, like lawyers, are subject to a general obligation to provide reasonable professional services – an obligation that is regarded as implicit in the contract between the architect and the client.[72] Secondly, just as rules of professional ethics bar a lawyer from disclaiming his liability in his contract with the client, so it is possible that architects are not allowed to disclaim the negligence liability that is based in both tort and in contract. (By contrast, the general contractor, unlike the architect, is not regarded as a professional and hence is not subject to the variety of legal rules associated with professionalism.)

A further point is that while the court in *Aas* rejected the plaintiffs' negligence claim, the court was explicit that it was leaving open the plaintiffs' possible claims for breach of contract, breach of express warranty and breach of implied warranty. It is a weakness in the court's opinion that the opinion fails to discuss what particular rights the homeowners in question might have under contract and warranty law. With this weakness in mind, I have consulted the plaintiffs' lawyer in *Aas*, who has provided me with a copy of the sales contract. That contract included a page which warranted that the home is 'free of defective

---

[69] *Casa Clara Condominium Ass'n, Inc. v. Charley Toppino & Sons, Inc.*, 620 So. 2d 1244 (Fla. 1993).

[70] *Moransais v. Heathman*, 744 So. 2d 973 (Fla. 1999).

[71] *Oates v. Jag, Inc.*, 333 SE 2d 222 (NC 1985).

[72] For diverging views on the negligence liability of the professional in home construction cases, compare *Moransais v. Heathman*, 744 So. 2d 973 (Fla. 1999) (endorsing negligence liability) with *City Express, Inc. v. Express Partners*, 959 P 2d 836 (Haw. 1989) (rejecting negligence liability). My discussion in the text assumes that the home buyer is the client of the architect. If, instead, the architect is directly providing services only to the developer or the general contractor, the analysis of the home buyer's negligence claim against the architect obviously becomes more complicated.

materials or workmanship'. This concept of 'defect' was in turn defined to include 'failure to comply with building codes or to accepted standards of workmanship in the construction industry'. The contract then continued on with specific provisions that clarified the concept of defect in certain applications. While these provisions somewhat narrowed the express warranty, it still is clear enough that the defects involved in *Aas* fell within that warranty's scope. What made the express warranty unhelpful to the plaintiffs in *Aas* is that the warranty was limited to defects that are called to the attention of the home builder within a year of the time of sale. (Also, the express warranty stipulated that it could not be assigned to any subsequent purchaser.) The one-year duration of the express warranty obviously poses a problem for home buyers. However, that problem may be manageable. As a consequence of *Aas*, home inspectors in California are now offering their services to recent home buyers, and in making that offer are advising homeowners of the legal advantage of having a home inspection conducted within a year of the original purchase.

So much for the plaintiffs' express warranty claim. How about the implied warranty claims that may be available to them? In fact, in California, as in most states, the sale of new homes is accompanied by an implied warranty of habitability, and an implied warranty of good workmanship as well.[73] Certainly, these implied warranties can be disclaimed by clear and conspicuous language in the sales document. In *Aas*, however, the contract of sale contained no such disclaimer. To the contrary, the express warranty was clear that in giving you 'specific legal rights... you may also have other legal rights which may vary from state to state'. While the home builder's implied warranty extends only to the original purchasers of the house, at least this set of the *Aas* plaintiffs have implied warranty claims that seem quite relevant to their grievances. An implied warranty of good workmanship seems very close to a guarantee of non-negligence; and certainly implied warranties of habitability and good workmanship require compliance with applicable legal standards for home construction. Furthermore, the implied warranty recognized in California and elsewhere does not contain any one-year limit. In California, the only relevant time limitation is provided by the state's so-called 'statute of repose', which requires that all suits be brought

---

[73] For general treatment of these implied warranties, see G. Nelson and D. Whitman, *Real Estate Transfer, Finance, and Development* (5th edn 1998), pp. 171–94; Jones, 'Economic Losses'.

within ten years of the completion of construction.[74] Accordingly, even after the decision in *Aas*, those plaintiffs in the case who were original home buyers evidently had viable implied warranty claims against the home builder defendants.

In short, the *Aas* opinion, in rejecting plaintiffs' negligence claims, has the goal and effect of encouraging buyers of new homes to rely on their contract-based express warranty claims and their more general implied warranty claims. Moreover, if *Aas* itself is assumed to be a relevant example, then buyers' rights under express warranty and implied warranty are likely to be substantial rather than stingy. Subsequent purchasers of homes – those who buy the homes from their original owners – are likely to be beyond the reach of warranty law. Yet to recognize negligence claims by those purchasers against the home builder would be surprising. The surprise relates in part to the duration in time between the completion of construction and the resale of the home; it also relates to the way in which families buying existing homes generally arrange for their own inspection of the home, and then rely on their own inspector's report before finally committing themselves to the sales transaction. For that matter, in many states (including California), those persons offering existing homes for sale are required by law to make extensive disclosures as to defects in the home that have come to their attention during the period of their homeownership.

## Conclusion

The economic loss rule states that a plaintiff cannot recover for negligence that causes pure economic loss. The rule, which has been significant in products liability ever since the 1960s, has become even more significant in recent years, as courts have rejected possible exceptions to the rule. During recent years, the rule has also been invoked so as to bar negligence claims by home buyers against home builders. In these cases involving defective products and defective homes, courts have properly resorted to the rule in order to recognize the primacy of contract (and warranty). In other cases in which the rule has been applied, its rationale relates to a concern for protecting against an excessively open-ended liability. In such cases, American jurisdictions now apply the rule much of the time, but not all the time. In many cases in which the rule might be thought to apply, courts seem unaware of the rule's existence. Even so, in

---

[74] See California Code of Civil Procedure § 337.15 (West 1982).

certain cases courts implicitly acknowledge the rule and its rationales by denying liability under the heading of 'proximate cause' (hence healthcare providers have been denied claims against tobacco companies). In other cases in which the negligence of the defendant brings about the plaintiff's economic loss, neither the concern for contract nor the concern for an excessive liability seems germane. In such cases, in essence courts ignore the rule and decide the cases based on an assessment of the particular policy considerations that the cases raise.

Overall, then, there are at least four senses in which the economic loss rule can be called a 'supposed' rule. First, it is a 'supposed' rule in the sense that at least a limited number of leading modern opinions have professed to reject it. Second, in the sense that it breaks down into two distinct rules – one motivated by a concern for contract, the other motivated by a quite different concern; these two rules apply to quite different categories of cases. Third, in the sense that courts frequently fail explicitly to acknowledge the rule, even when they may be implicitly applying it. Finally, in the sense that courts ignore the rule altogether in many cases in which the various concerns that underlie the rule seem not to be pertinent. What all of this makes clear is that cases involving negligence and economic loss are multifarious in terms of the issues and problems they raise. Accordingly, no single rule can even begin to determine how all such cases should be decided.

# 5 The liability regimes of Europe – their façades and interiors

MAURO BUSSANI AND VERNON VALENTINE PALMER

Where would it all lead if everyone could be sued... An ill-advised statement, a rumor passed on, a false report, bad advice, a poor decision, a recommendation for an unfit serving maid by her former employer, information given at the request of a traveler about the way, the time, and so forth – in short, anything and everything would make one liable to compensate for the damage that ensued if there were gross negligence despite one's good faith...

*Rudolf von Ihering*[1]

Our system of civil responsibility founded on the *clausula generalis* – it could hardly be more *generalis* – of article 1382, has a knack of being everywhere at once [*le don de ubiquité*], which, to our somewhat prejudiced eyes, creates an incomparable advantage.

*Jean Carbonnier*[2]

In the area of tort liability, the strongest oppositions appear to be at the level of general definitions. The extreme positions are represented by general scholarly formulas and, a short distance behind, by overall legislative rules in France and Germany, whereas, moving toward 'midfield', we find more specific statutory formulations, the detailed scholarly solutions, and, finally, the operational rules applied by courts... The overall definitions generalize a rule instead of limiting its application... damage would seem to be always compensable, or liability to be always dependent on a right. The operative rules, in contrast, are more articulated.

*Rodolfo Sacco*[3]

## Introduction

The goals of this chapter are twofold. First, we wish to provide a theoretical matrix that situates the issue of pure economic loss within each

---

[1] *Jherings Jahrbücher für die Dogmatik des bürgerlichen Rechts*, vol. 4 (Jena, 1861), 12–13.
[2] J. Carbonnier, 'Le Silence et La Gloire', *Dalloz* 1951 Chron. 119.
[3] R. Sacco, 'Legal Formants: A Dynamic Approach to Comparative Law', (1991) 39 *American Journal of Comparative Law* 343, 369.

liability regime, and at the same time arranges these systems in some functional and explanatory way. This matrix will hopefully permit us to see how each country stands in relation to one another, what influences they have experienced, where their operational rules derive from, and possibly also to pave the way to an appreciation of the degree to which, if any, there is a common core of agreement on this subject at a European level. The second goal of this chapter is somewhat more practical. We wish to provide a clear framework which the reader can use to understand the country responses which follow in Part II of this book. These responses are highly condensed summaries reflecting individual national styles, particular code provisions, leading cases and doctrinal influences, and these would be somewhat incomprehensible without a general introduction to each country's liability regime. We hope in this chapter to build a conceptual bridge between the systems and the responses, a bridge that the reader can freely cross as many times as necessary.

## Two alternative formulas: from façades to operative rules

In modern legal systems we may at first sight observe two alternatives. There may be liability whenever a person causes damage to another; there may be liability only in certain typical situations. The former, known as the principle of *neminem laedere*, is the solution of the French Code Civil. The latter, enacted in the German Bürgerliches Gesetzbuch (BGB), was the solution traditionally associated with Roman law and common law. In both of these systems, there was a list of actions that a plaintiff could bring against the person who had injured him: in Roman law, actions for theft, robbery, insult and damage wrongfully done; in English law, for trespass, assault, libel and so forth. Every tort system in our study may be seen as a variant of these two alternatives, and each individual tort structure is at least the starting point for the analysis of the recoverability of pure economic loss. However, these imposing structures are not necessarily the most reliable means of viewing liability rules or of predicting outcomes; if we were to depend upon them as the exclusive criteria of classification, this would not present the systems in a helpful way. As we explain below, a functional and explanatory analysis must distinguish appearances from reality. It must take into account a wide variety of factors, traits and formants in order to arrive at the essential differences and similarities between the systems.

In situating the problem of pure economic loss within a comparative perspective, this introduction will cast a glance upon the liability regimes of Europe and compare the exterior architecture to the interior working of the system. In this respect we are often called upon to distinguish between the system's façade and its interior, namely operational rules that lie behind or within it. What we mean by 'the façade' is simply the exterior wrapper, the outer appearance, or even better, the initial and dominant perception received by the observer regarding the recoverability of pure economic loss. In a codified system this perception is usually conveyed by the blackletter words that the legislator has used; in an uncodified system it may be the words of judges hardened into precedents or the writings of old institutional writers. In either case the façade will be the objective set of public signals which *apparently* controls our issue. At first glance, a given system may seem committed to a wide principle of recovery; another system may seem committed to a general rule of no recovery, although a series of exceptions may be made. Or another system may seem resolutely opposed to all recovery because pure financial loss is regarded as an unprotected interest. These initial perceptions, we repeat, are due to the system's façade.

In resorting to the façade metaphor, we do not wish to imply that initial perceptions are always false and misleading. Obviously that would simply overstate the case. Nor can we say that all façades are mere camouflage for hidden forms of lawmaking. To the contrary, we have found that in a few systems the first impression given by the legislator or judge as lawgiver is also the lasting impression left by the jurisprudence and the doctrine. Even here, we think the word façade is appropriate and useful to indicate a genuine or authentic impression that in fact withstands further scrutiny. Nevertheless, it is also clear that for certain systems the deeper one delves into the doctrine, cases and operational rules, the more one is surprised by the contradictions and contrasts between outer appearance and inner reality. What began as a general clause may be administered as a scheme of protection focused upon absolute rights – i.e. what German jurists refer to as rights to life, body, health, freedom, property opposable to the world at large: *erga omnes*.[4] However, that may not be the end of the story. For what appears to be a scheme of absolute rights may be a decoy for an expansion of contractual actions which function much like tort remedies. It is for this reason that accepting

---

[4] Discussed above by J. Gordley in Chapter 2 at notes 47–70, and accompanying text.

façades at face value can be hazardous; they are very rarely a sufficient basis for a functional classification of these systems.

## General vs. specific characteristics

Conscious, therefore, that façades are sometimes *trompe l'œil* and that interior solutions are the principal interest of our study, we have attempted to organize the material into three functional and explanatory groupings which we call the liberal, pragmatic and conservative 'regimes' of tort. Before introducing these systems country-by-country, it will be useful to explain what we think are the distinguishing characteristics of these regimes. It is important to understand, however, that these may be subject-specific characteristics that have limited relevance outside of the context of pure economic loss. We emphasize this caveat for an obvious reason. Our purpose is not to describe the *general* characteristics of any of these systems: that would be a treatise in itself in each case, and would have nothing to do with the precise issue that we have selected. We must therefore confine our 'characteristics' to the subject at hand, without any pretension that they may be applied widely to other subjects not studied here.

## The liberal, pragmatic and conservative regimes of tort

Within the *liberal regimes* we group together five countries: Belgium, France, Greece, Italy and Spain. A leading characteristic of a liberal regime is the presence of a unitary general clause in the codified law which does not, *a priori*, screen out pure economic loss. Lacking a *numerus clausus* of protected interests imposed by the legislator, these regimes have no in-principle objection to allowing compensation for stand-alone economic harm. The unlawfulness of causing such a loss is not an antecedent abstract question but only an outcome dependent upon whether the normal elements of fault liability are satisfied. These systems are not simply liberal in appearance and approach but in their results as well. As compared to other regimes, they appear to yield the greatest number of successful actions in our hypothetical cases.

A second characteristic is that liberal regimes reach solutions to questions of purely pecuniary loss almost exclusively on the basis of extracontractual liability and not by crossing over to contract principles. The liberal regimes deal with pure economic loss autonomously in tort, unlike many conservative regimes where recourse to contractual and statutory solutions is a standard means of tempering the rigidity of the law of tort.

A final characteristic of this regime, but one that is difficult to discern and substantiate, is the possible use of surreptitious techniques to keep this liability issue under control. To the extent that judges in liberal regimes have any policy restraining recovery for pure economic loss, as some observers suspect they do,[5] they do not admit or deal with it openly. It would of course be possible to carry out such a policy covertly through subtle manipulation of the ordinary requirements of the general clause (particularly the causation requirement)[6] but judicial tendencies of this kind would be unavowed, uncertain and difficult to detect, concealed even from a fact-based method such as ours. The term pure economic loss and the debatable issues surrounding it therefore would remain generally unrecognized in the literature and jurisprudence of these countries.

The *pragmatic regimes* embrace England, Scotland and the Netherlands. Our choice of the term *pragmatic* relates to a shared approach to the problem and has little to do with how often a plaintiff succeeds. The judges in the Netherlands appear to be considerably more receptive to this form of loss than the judges in the United Kingdom, but it is the similarity in their reasoning, their technique and their candour which prompts us to group them with their English and Scottish counterparts.

These systems are characterized by a cautious case-by-case approach which carefully studies the concrete socio-economic implications of granting recovery for pure economic loss.[7] Results are not driven by the dictates of wide tort principle, nor by a checklist of absolute rights. The principal method of screening recoveries is through the 'duty of care' concept. The duty of care question is a matter of judicial policymaking that is overtly carried out by the judges. Each new situation requires an

---

[5] See, e.g. L. Khoury, 'The Liability of Auditors Beyond Their Clients: A Comparative Study', (2001) 46 *McGill Law Journal* 413; B. Markesinis, 'La politique jurisprudentielle et la réparation du préjudice économique en Angleterre: Une approche comparative', (1983) *Revue Internationale de Droit Comparé* 31, 44.

[6] In French law, for example, the requirements of causation are applied strictly insofar as the liability of a company accountant (*commissaire aux comptes*) toward the public is concerned. Consequently, compensation for pure economic loss is granted only rarely. See the French response, under Case 17 ('Auditor's Liability').

[7] It is important to note that the cases proceed on the basis of the *judge's* perception of the socio-economic consequences: there is no *evidence* of the economic effects of a finding of liability.

ad hoc determination that a 'duty' to guard against this harm should exist at all. Unless this issue is decided affirmatively, there is no reason to proceed further and consider whether the normal elements of tortious liability have been satisfied.

Thus there is an abstract prior question to be answered, but unlike the approach in the conservative regimes, the question has not been prejudged by a legislator, nor in our view, by a rigid conception of absolute rights. The judges themselves are expected to make a policy choice, and they exercise this function openly and discursively. And there seems to be no flight into contract law as relief against their own decisions which refuse liability in tort.[8] The tort scheme dominates the field.

Among the *conservative regimes* we have placed Austria, Finland, Germany, Portugal and Sweden. A striking characteristic of this regime is that pure economic loss does not figure among the so-called 'absolute rights' which receive protection under their tort law. Its exclusion from the enumeration in BGB § 823 (1) is well known and clear, but even in conservative systems where no enacted list is to be found, the same result has been achieved by other means. As developments in Austria and Portugal amply show, the judiciary's and/or the doctrine's readiness to import German doctrinal influence may result in a philosophy of absolute rights that is superimposed upon the general clause. The second characteristic is that the recoverability of pure economic loss is therefore an exception and any remedy must be found elsewhere in the system, either on the basis of more specific tort provisions or by an expansive application of contract principles. However, if we focus upon recoveries permitted by the tort law system and make that the point of comparison, the system is quite restrictive in its results. Answers to our questionnaire basically yielded far fewer successful actions than in the other regimes. This gives rise to a third characteristic: the recovery of pure economic loss in these systems often receives extensive lateral support from the law of contracts and/or certain statutory mechanisms, and when that lateral contribution is added to the overall picture, results in these systems are considerably liberalized. To the extent that these contractual actions have been stretched to function as tort remedies, the tort façade progressively becomes a misleading indicator.

Having considered these general characteristics rather abstractly, we turn to discuss each country's approach in greater detail.

---

[8] Of course, English contract law, which insists upon the requirement of consideration and rather restrictive notions of privity, makes recourse to contractual solutions theoretically very difficult.

## The liberal regimes of France, Belgium, Italy, Spain and Greece

*France – an enigmatic liberalism*

The general formula *neminem laedere*, 'injure no one', is the basis of article 1382 of the Code Napoléon, which reads: 'Any act whatever of man which causes damage to another [*tout fait quelconque de l'homme qui cause à autrui un dommage*] obliges him by whose fault it occurred to make reparation.' Article 1383 adds: 'Each one is liable for the damage which he causes not only by his own act but also by his negligence or imprudence.' Because of its encompassing reach as well as its indeterminate potential, this unitary principle does not screen out recovery for pure economic loss. It does not set forth a *numerus clausus* of protected interests; the legislator imposes no *a priori* check upon the judge's free sense of what constitutes recoverable harm.[9] Therefore the question whether causing pure economic loss is a source of tortious liability becomes a judicial question, a matter of jurisprudence and the advice of doctrine. Put another way, the protection of pure economic loss in France must be viewed as an oracular outcome, for there is no external, pre-existing concept of unlawfulness concerning this loss to determine or to exclude liability.

Nevertheless, the seamless quality of the general provision is not necessarily the determinant formant of a liberal or conservative approach to our subject. Behind virtually identical façades, national courts have been capable of reaching diametrically opposite results. On the one hand, judicial thought may become imbued with an 'implied' list of absolute rights, restrictively conceived in accordance with metalegal formants such as internal history, social policy and justice. In that event, despite a *façade de libéralisme*, the tort system may approach the question of pure economic loss little differently from systems in which the legislator has deliberately controlled recovery through crafted solutions.

Austria – which works with a French-style façade, yet arguably restricts the recovery of pure economic loss to a greater extent even than Germany – is a case in point. Here, metalegal considerations dominate judicial philosophy and it is this philosophy, not the permissive texts, which shape the approach. Given the inner reality, the Austrian code's façade is essentially *trompe l'œil*. French doctrine in the nineteenth

---

[9] Of all the European codes, writes von Bar, 'the French Code Civil gives the courts the least guidance', C. von Bar, *The Common European Law of Torts* (Oxford University Press, Oxford, 1998), no. 14, p. 22.

century had something in common with this approach. All French authors of the first half of the nineteenth century (and many thereafter) thought that articles 1382 and 1383 contained the kind of solution which the German BGB adopted later in §§ 823–826.[10]

In twentieth-century France, however, a new orientation emerged. The same text now sustains an expansive law of tort in which harm not only to absolute (*erga omnes*) rights but to almost any legal interest, including a purely economic interest, is unlawful and therefore recoverable.[11] Under the prevailing view, the prohibition on causing harm is the general rule, and the instances in which one is at liberty to cause harm are exceptions. Articles 1382 and 1383 have consistently been found not to contain any *a priori* limitations on the scope or nature of protected rights and interests, nor to contain an *a priori* class of protected persons. Thus, there has been no difficulty in admitting the economic loss of victims by ricochet, whether it be the expenses of a father forced to make repeated voyages to the bedside of his son who was injured in Greece through defendant's negligence,[12] or the expenses of an unmarried cohabiting partner of the injured victim.[13] The French general clause is considered hostile to the Aquilian relativity theory ('*relativité aquilienne*'), which explores the 'purpose' of legal rules to find the ambit of a defendant's liability to plaintiff, thus de-emphasizing the role of causation. But in

---

[10] The historical evolution of French delictual thought is lucidly traced by Rodolfo Sacco in 'Legal Formants', at 359 (Part Two). As Sacco indicates, the writings of Toullier and Huc show that the articles of the Code Civil were originally understood by the doctrine as applying to interference with 'absolute rights' of the victim, or to statutory standards of conduct protecting victims' rights. See also K.-S. Zachariae, *Droit civil français*, no. 444 (stating that harmful acts are not delicts unless they are '*illicite*', '*c'est à dire qu'il ait porté atteinte à un droit appartenant à autrui*.'); C. Aubry and C. Rau, *Le droit civil français*, vol. VI, nos. 117, 119, 120; F. Laurent, *Principes de droit civil*, vol. XX, no. 404. See further, von Bar, *Law of Torts*, I, at p. 33, note 76. This rights-based position is fundamentally restated by Planiol, who attempted to draw up 'a table' of legal obligations protected by art. 1382. He defined fault as the breach of a 'pre-existing obligation' and wrote that art. 1382 did not mean 'any act whatsoever' but only an act illegitimate in character. M. Planiol, *Traité élémentaire de droit civil*, no. 863, vol. II, pt. I (trans. Louisiana Law Institute, 1939).

[11] K. Zweigert and H. Kötz say that today in France, 'it is immaterial whether the harm complained of by the plaintiff is physical harm to person or property or not. Indeed the very idea of "purely economic loss" is not to be met with in judgements or books; liability under art. 1382 Code Civil attaches to a person even if his negligence affects nothing but the plaintiff's future income or business prospects', *Introduction to Comparative Law* (trans. T. Weir, 3rd edn, Oxford, 1998), p. 617.

[12] Cass. 1e Ch. 20 decembre 1960, D. 1961.141, note Esmein.

[13] See W. van Gerven, J. Lever and P. Larouche, Tort Law Scope of Protection (Hart, Oxford, 1998) at pp. 144–6; Y. Chartier, 'La Réparation du Préjudice', nos. 184–98 (Dalloz, Paris, 1983).

French law there is no relational 'duty' requirement as in English and Scots law, and the role of causation is not de-emphasized.[14] In this light, the concept of unlawfulness nearly becomes invisible: one could say it has been globally reassigned to the subsidiary determinations of fault, causation and damage.

While the unlawfulness question may have disappeared from view, it may possibly be operating at a different level, the level of judicial policy working tacitly within rather capacious notions. Obviously, the French judge retains at least some rough concept of unlawfulness, for there are still areas where a person is free to cause harm, including pure economic harm, without incurring liability under the Code Civil.[15] An entrepreneur may deliberately set up business next door to a business competitor and through fair competition drive him into bankruptcy.[16] However, these instances are exceptions that have been carved away from the general presumption in favour of actionability. They emerge from an inductive search of the case law. By developing justifications for non-liability based on the existence of particular factors, it has become possible to absolve a person who causes harm without abandoning the general principle that a person should make reparation for all the harm that he or she causes. However, the exercise of policy is more difficult to detect at the discrete level where the judge creates no exception, but simply attributes a negative result in the particular case to a tenuous causal link or perhaps to the indeterminateness of the plaintiff's loss. Here, unlawfulness is not a severable hurdle but simply the result of applying subsidiary elements of act, fault, causation and damage. Judgments denying relief at that level are not unknown in the jurisprudence. For example, a partnership could not recover for deals that failed to be concluded when the company president who was negotiating them was negligently injured.[17] A creditor whose borrower was negligently killed

---

[14] G. Viney, *Introduction à la responsabilité* (LGDJ, Paris, 1995), p. 566; G. Viney, 'Pour ou contre un principe général de responsabilité pour faute?', (2002) 49 *Osaka University Law Review* 31, 44; van Gerven et al. *Tort Law* (1998), at p. 32.

[15] For example, a doctor who negligently fails to terminate a woman's pregnancy incurs no liability to the parents for the extra expenditures of supporting a healthy but unwanted child. Civ. 1e, 25 juin 1991, D. 1991.566, note P. Le Tourneau. It has been held, however, by the Cour de Cassation en Assemblée Plénière (17.11.2000, JCP, 2000, n. 50, II.10438, pp. 2293 ff.), that an infant could claim damages resulting from being born with a handicap in circumstances where the negligence of his mother's doctor prevented her from exercising her choice to avoid giving birth to a handicapped child.

[16] See Viney, 'Introduction à la responsabilité', p. 375.

[17] Cass., 2e Civ. Ch., 12 juin 1987, JCP 1987.IV.286.

could not recover from the tortfeasor the sums which the decedent could not repay.[18] The reasoning in these cases seems unexceptional: the harm was not considered a 'certain' or 'direct' consequence of the negligent act. Obviously a latent concern with saddling excessive liability upon the tortfeasor may have influenced these pronouncements, but no one can be sure.[19]

A particularity of French law is the *non-cumul* of tort and contract actions. Unique in all of Europe,[20] this rule, in our view, probably propels French tort law in the direction of allowing reparation for pure economic loss. Like Molière's *Gentilhomme* who spoke prose or poetry and nothing in between, the French plaintiff discovers that they must sue in contract, if they have one with the defendant; if there is no contract,

---

[18] Cass. 2e Civ. Ch., 21 février 1979, JCP 1979.IV.145. On similar facts, see Cass. Civ. 2e. 25 juin 1975, Bull. Civ., II, no. 195. But see also, from the opposite perspective, Cass., 1e Civ. Ch., 13 février 2001, JCP 2002.II.10099, note C. Lisanti-Kalczynsky. B. Markesinis argues that the latter affords an excellent example of a concealed policy to place limits upon the recovery of pure economic loss via the manipulation of causal requirements, 'La politique jurisprudentielle et la réparation du prejudice économique en Angleterre: Une approche comparative', (1983) *Revue Internationale de Droit Comparé* 31, at 45–6. The plaintiff's debtor was killed in a car accident and the debtor's heirs refused to accept his succession. Accordingly the succession could not pay the debts of the deceased, including the debt owed to the plaintiff, so the plaintiff sought redress from the tortfeasor responsible for the car accident. However, the Court of Appeal ruled that the plaintiff's loss should not be viewed as the 'certain' result of the defendant's act and it was thus unrecoverable. In view of the length of time for repayment and the risks that the debtor might discontinue his work, the anticipated repayment was aleatory. However, the Cour de Cassation quashed this decision, ruling that repayment of a loan of money is never aleatory in a juridical sense, and returned the case to another court of appeal. The *Cour de renvoi* in turn ruled that while the loss was certain, it was not 'direct', since the refusal of the heirs to accept the debtor's succession broke the chain of causation with a *nova causa interveniens*. Bordeaux, 17 mai 1977, D., 1978 (observ. Larroumet), and this decision was confirmed by the Cour de Cassation. Cass. Civ. 2e, 21 février 1979, JCP 1979. IV. 145.

[19] There might be a relative lack of emotive appeal in pure economic loss as compared to the flesh and blood of physical damages. If cases of pure economic loss are intuitively less esteemed by French judges, as Lapoyade Deschamps suggests ('La réparation du prejudice pur in droit français', in E. K. Banakas, *Civil Liability for Pure Economic Loss* (Kluwer, London/Boston, 1996), at pp. 89–101), then perhaps one might expect cold detachment in the causal analysis that discourages recoveries.

[20] See G. Viney, 'La Responsabilité: Conditions', in J. Ghestin (ed.) *Traité de droit civil*, vol. IV no. 216–31, (1982); von Bar, *Law of Torts*, I, pp. 449 ff.; T. Weir, 'Complex Liabilities', in *International Encyclopedia of Comparative Law*, no. 52, vol. XI (1976); E. K. Banakas, 'Liability for Incorrect Financial Information: Theory and Practice in a General Clause System and in a Protected Interests System', (1999) 7 *European Review of Private Law* 261, 268.

they must sue the defendant in delict.[21] If plaintiff is refused relief in contract for pure economic loss, they cannot then sue in tort, for there is generally no concurrence of actions. The rule has been praised for bringing certainty of application to a system which, since its general delictual clause incorporates pure economic loss within its reach, would otherwise lack the theoretical means to prevent unrestrained concurrence or to exclude from its compass *dommage purement contractuel*.[22] We would argue that it has another important effect. In our view, this forced choice has encouraged the attitude that contract and tort should be broadly equivalent conduits for the recovery of pure economic loss. This is not to claim that the two actions operate in an identical manner. They do not. For example, the prescriptive period is usually shorter for most actions in contract,[23] and clauses limiting liability do not operate in delict.[24] Rather, our point is attitudinal. Having left the litigant without an option, French law can ill afford to discriminate on the sheer nature of the damage (as some 'conservative' systems do) against tort plaintiffs presenting pure economic loss cases. That would be so unfair to one class of litigants that we think the rule has, in the French context, the tendency to ease objections to this form of loss and to foster the expectation that tort law will achieve results in parallel with the law of contract.

To sum up, as the country report on France demonstrates, the expression 'pure economic loss' is almost unknown. The Gallic judges have faced the usual range of *Meroni*-like cases, cable cases, mistaken professional advice cases and such-like. But the French answers to the questionnaire show that this form of loss cannot be rejected on grounds of

---

[21] There are a few recognized exceptions to the rule (for details, see P. Malaurie and L. Aynès, *Droit civil: les obligations*, nos. 526–8 (1st edn, Cujas, Paris, 1985), pp. 370–3; Viney, 'Introduction à la responsabilité', at pp. 403, 411 ff.) but these are not germane to the discussion in the text.

[22] Von Bar, *Law of Torts*, at p. 452 ff.; P. Schlechtriem, 'The Borderland of Tort and Contract – Opening a New Frontier?', (1988) 21 *Cornell International Law Journal* 467.

[23] Contractual periods vary from one, two, five or ten years, depending on the type of contract, and contractual prescription begins to run from a relatively fixed date. See Code Civil arts. 2270, 2272–2277. However, prescription in delict is generally ten years after *manifestation* of the damage and thus the life of an action is liable to be much greater than in contract. Code Civil arts 2270–2271 (Law of 5 July 1985). Note, however, that tort actions based on defective products will prescribe in three years from the date of the victim's knowledge of his own damage and of the wrongdoer's identity (1386-17 CC) but in no event after the product has been in circulation ten years (1386-16 CC).

[24] For further differentiations, see Malaurie and Aynès, *Droit civil*, at nos. 517–20, pp. 360–2; see also Viney, 'Introduction à la responsabilité', pp. 305–7.

principle and damages might be granted in nearly every hypothetical situation.

From a comparative perspective France's accent on inclusiveness holds great interest. It presents an appearance of maximum permissiveness toward pure economic loss, as well as an appearance of maximum indifference to the strong policy arguments usually made elsewhere against its recovery.[25] Bernard Rudden draws attention to the paradox that 'the French seem to ignore almost all of Cardozo's warnings without suffering ill effects'.[26] Against all predictions that the sky will fall, the French judge is serene. To those who argue that the floodgates of liability must be firmly closed, the French experience must seem counter-intuitive, an empirical enigma awaiting an answer.

## In the Belgian looking glass

The tort provisions of the Belgian Civil Code are a mirror image of the Code Napoléon. Belgium possesses the same unitary principle found in France and has taken essentially a liberal position (though in our eyes not quite as liberal as France's) on reparation for pure economic loss.

Belgian jurists approach questions of tort liability by verifying the existence of the 'usual elements' of fault, causation and damage, rather than by preliminary reference to a *numerus clausus* of protected rights or interests. There is in consequence no material means by which recovery of this kind of loss can be peremptorily blocked before the tripartite elements are examined. In Belgium, as in France, articles 1382–1383 of the Civil Code have been consistently regarded as not containing any *a priori* limitations on the scope of protected interests, or on the classes of protected persons.[27] Since there is no limitation on the class of protected persons, there is no need to prove that a duty of care was owed to the

---

[25] There is hardly any specialized literature on this subject within France and almost no internal criticism of its liberal attitude. See, however, the strong remarks of Viney, 'Introduction à la responsabilité', pp. 56 ff.

[26] B. Rudden, 'Torticles', (1991–92) 6/7 *Tulane Civil Law Forum* 105, 107.

[27] Neither questions of 'fault' or 'damage' depend upon a showing that any right to receive revenues has been violated. The violation of plaintiff's 'legitimate interest in obtaining monetary support or payments is sufficient. Thus a concubine (whose claim for lost support could not be based upon a 'right' to be supported out of wedlock) was permitted to recover her 'pure' economic loss against a tortfeasor whose negligence caused the death of her partner. She qualified as a *victime par ricochet* (i.e. as a secondary victim) and the legitimacy of her interest in receiving support was recognized. See van Gerven et al., *Tort Law* (1998) p. 146.

plaintiff.[28] This suggests that, like their French counterparts, Belgian jurists made the same transition of thought from a rights-based to a legitimate interest-based interpretation of their general formula.

As stated earlier, Belgian law presents a favourable attitude towards liability for pure economic loss, but in our judgement it takes a slightly more guarded, less liberal view than France, despite the commonality of starting points.

The broad contractual principle, '*réparation intégrale du dommage*' (drawn from art. 1149 CC) has been extended to the law of tort by way of interpretation.[29] The principle of 'full' reparation strongly suggests that there should be no reason to exclude from the field of tort a form of damage so commonly recoverable in contract. The principle argues that a victim should be fully compensated, irrespective of the kind of loss that they have suffered.[30] Furthermore, the gapless coverage of the delictual principle of article 1382 suggests approaching this type of liability in terms which are no different from any other question of liability. Thus fault, causation and damage may be examined using standard rather than special rules. For example, pure economic loss should simply meet the same causal requirements that any other type of damage must satisfy with respect to proof of its existence or certainty.[31] To judge the causal link between defendant's act and plaintiff's damage, the courts normally apply the more factual causal theory called 'equivalence of conditions'.[32] This causal test is satisfied when the damage would not have occurred,

---

[28] The theory of Aquilian relativity has been formally condemned by the Belgian Cour de Cassation. Cass., 28 April 1972.

[29] R. O. Dalcq, *Traité de la responsabilité civile*, vol. II, *Le lien de causalité, le dommage et sa réparation* (Larcier, Bruxelles, 1962), p. 452, no. 3416; Cass., 13.4.1995, JT, 1995, p. 649; Cass., 23.12.1992, Pas., 1992, I, 1406.

[30] Belgium, however, does not fully follow the French rule of *non-cumul* and does not separate tort and contractual liability as rigidly. As a matter of principle Belgian law permits the plaintiff to opt between contractual and delictual actions (*concours des responsabilités*). See J. L. Fagnart, *Examen de la jurisprudence concernant la responsabilité civile, 1968–1975*, no. 2 (1976), p. 9 and cf. van Gerven et al., *Tort Law*, pp. 41 ff.

[31] The courts ease problems of proving the certainty of the loss (a problem frequently encountered in proving unrealized profits) by resort to estimating the value of the lost chance to the profit (*la perte d'une chance*). Dalcq, *Traité de la responsabilité civile*, p. 254, no. 2817; J. L. Fagnart, *La responsabilité civile. Chronique de jurisprudence 1985–1995* (Larcier, Brussels, 1997), no. 11 p. 23; R. O. Dalcq and G. Schamps, 'La responsabilité délictuelle et quasi-délictuelle, examen de jurisprudence (1987–1993)', (1995) RCJB 737.

[32] Cass., 12.1.1988, Pas., 1988, I, 563; Cass., 15.5.1990, Pas., 1990, I, 1054; Cass., 23.5.1990, Pas., 1990, I, 1079; Cass., 23.6.1990, Pas. 1990, I, 1126; Cass., 8.10.1992, Pas., 1992, I, 1124.

as it occurred, if the fault had not been committed. In principle this 'but for' test should leave little room for judicial policy to screen out pure economic loss at the causal level.

Despite this factual façade, however, the courts and a part of the doctrine have accepted until very recently a rule of causation, which on occasion 'interrupts' the causal link when plaintiff is said to have incurred the loss due to an 'autonomous' obligation. The theory clearly restricts the recovery of pure economic loss (although one cannot tell that it is directly aimed at this issue).[33] One may also detect occasions where apparently the same (restrictive) purpose has been achieved simply by applying a more demanding version of the theory of 'equivalence of conditions' to cases involving pure economic loss.[34]

While pure economic loss has not yet been studied by Belgian scholars or recognized by name in the courts, it may be that there is an unarticulated concern. To the extent that this may be true, the rules of causation serve as the vehicle which can place limits upon recovery.

## Italy's recent revolution

Rodolfo Sacco observes that in managing tort law issues, two different logical patterns can be detected.[35] According to the first, which works by subtraction, all injuries give rise to liability unless there is some defence. This is the pattern now established in France. According to the second, which works by addition, only injuries to an absolute right (plus all similar cases) result in liability. This is the pattern of the BGB. Yet in the case of Italy, Professor Sacco characterizes the situation as 'hybrid', at least from a textual perspective.[36] The legislator does not expressly require the violation of an absolute right for liability to be imposed,

---

[33] The Belgian report underscores that the Cour de Cassation finds the causal link 'interrupted' whenever plaintiff's damage results from an 'autonomous' obligation that would have forced plaintiff to incur the loss at all events, even when it is triggered by defendant's tortious act. A statutory or contractual obligation is autonomous when it requires an employer to pay his workers salaries regardless of the reason for a business interruption. In at least three cases (see Cases 3, 'Cable III – The Day-to-Day Workers', 6, 'The Infected Cow', 15, 'A Closed Motorway – The Value of Time'), liability would be excluded under this theory. It is notable that in the same cases, the French report finds no principled objection to the causal link.

[34] In a Belgian cable case, for example, the court used stricter than usual causal requirements to deny recovery to an enterprise that was deprived of electricity for several hours. The court called defendant's fault in damaging the cable 'the occasion' for plaintiff's loss but not necessarily the cause of it. Cass., 5 March 1974, Pas., 1, 692.

[35] Sacco, 'Legal Formants' at 366 (Part Two).   [36] Ibid. at 366.

but at the same time the judge is required to find that the injury was 'unjustified'. (art. 2043, CC: 'Any fraudulent, malicious, or negligent act that causes an unjustified injury [*danno ingiusto*] to another obliges the person who has committed the act to pay damages.') As a matter of principle it is evident that no textual distinction was made between physical damage and pure economic losses. Both could qualify as an unjustified type of injury. By failing to clarify the notion of an 'unjustified' injury, the legislator grants the Italian judge true discretionary power.

Until recently, the standard doctrine maintained that an injury is unjustified whenever there is an infringement of an absolute right of the victim, particularly the rights to property, liberty, life or reputation.[37] Only in such cases would the tortfeasor be bound to pay damages. However, the list of absolute rights has never been viewed as a limitation in the case of intentional torts, because it has always been recognized that any form of damage proceeding from an intention to harm should be recoverable.[38] From a comparative perspective, the standard doctrine was therefore quite similar to the German doctrine regarding tort liability under BGB §§ 823–826.[39]

In the 1960s a sustained scholarly effort made it possible to enlarge the scope of tort liability.[40] The old meaning given to 'unjustified injury' based upon the violation of a victim's absolute right gave way to recognition of various 'protected interests'.[41]

The turning point came in a Supreme Court (Corte di Cassazione) ruling nearly thirty years ago. In *Meroni*,[42] the Court held that a creditor

---

[37] See e.g. G. Brunetti, *Il delitto civile* (Firenze, 1906), pp. 215 ff.; G. Giorgi, *Teoria delle obbligazioni nel diritto moderno italiano*, vol. V, (7th edn, Firenze, 1909), p. 215; and cf. R. Sacco, 'L'ingiustizia del darno di cui all'art. 2043a', in *FP*, 1960, I, c. 1420 ff.

[38] For details see P. Cendon, *Il dolo nella responsabilità extracontrattuale* (UTET, Torino, 1976) *passim*, esp. pp. 21 ff., 250 ff.

[39] See J. Gordley, above Chapter 2.

[40] Cf. e.g. Sacco, 'L'ingiustizia', 1420; P. Schlesinger, *L'ingiustizia del danno nell'illecito civile*, Jus, 1960, p. 336; P. Trimarchi, *Rischio e responsabilità oggettiva* (Milano, 1961); F. D. Busnelli, *La lesione del credito da parte di terzi* (Milano, 1964); S. Rodotà, *Il problema della responsabilità civile* (Milano, 1967); P. Trimarchi, *Causalità e danno* (Milano, 1967).

[41] However, when a concurrent liability in tort and contract is at stake or when the judges deem it to be necessary, reference is still made to the concept of absolute right: see, e.g. the decisions cited in the Italian report sub Case 6, 'The Infected Cow'.

[42] *Torino Calcio SpA v. Romero*, Cass. civ., SU, 26.1.1971, no. 174, *GI*, 1971, I, 1, 681 noted by G. Visintini; *FI*, 1971, I, 342 noted by F. D. Busnelli. The case is known in Italy not by the name of the parties, but by the name of the famous soccer player fatally injured in the accident.

can recover damages for the pecuniary losses he suffered from an injury to his debtor. It was the case of a famous soccer player who was killed in a car accident. The soccer team, Torino Calcio SpA, sued for damages alleging an economic loss.[43] The creditor had only a relative right (a right *in personam*) derived from the contract. No absolute right of the plaintiff/creditor had been invaded by the tortfeasor. Nevertheless, the Supreme Court stated that – in principle – the team could recover damages: it was clear that the old doctrine had collapsed.

Besides the cases where an employee is injured, this 'Meroni' doctrine is now used whenever a right *in personam* is infringed, to the extent that 'the right to the integrity of one's assets' (*diritto all'integrità del proprio patrimonio*) has been violated.[44] Thus, in spite of the wide and longstanding debate about the meaning of *danno ingiusto*, current Italian operative rules do not now differ very much from the positions taken in liberal systems such as Spain and France. The general clauses in the Spanish and French codes are effectively the same as the old Italian code of 1865, before its renovation in 1942.

Hence, as a matter of principle, no distinction is made between physical harm and economic losses: both of them may represent an 'unjustified injury'; and as regards both of them the limiting factors for the recovery continue to rest upon causation,[45] remoteness of damage,[46] the need to show special blameworthiness in the conduct of the defendant,[47] and even the lack of infringement of an absolute right when causes of action in tort and contract may be brought simultaneously.[48]

## *The Spanish countercurrents*

Spain presents a codistic model very much akin to that of France. Article 1902 of the Spanish Civil Code reads: 'He who causes damage to another by action or omission, through fault or negligence, shall be obliged to repair the damage caused.' Within this general framework victims are allowed to sue for their economic losses even when they

---

[43] The Court held, on the basis of the principle stated above, but the team did not succeed in recovering damages because the evidence of an actual damage was not deemed satisfactory.

[44] See e.g. Cass. It. 24.5.1982, n. 2765, in *FI*, 1982, I, 2864, cited in the Italian report sub Case 11 ('A Maestro's Mistake').

[45] See Cases 6 ('The Infected Cow') and 7 ('The Careless Architect') in Part II of this volume.

[46] See Case 10 ('The Dutiful Wife'). [47] See Case 12 ('Double Sale').

[48] See Case 13 ('Subcontractor's Liability').

arise independently of physical harm.[49] The legislator imposes no *a priori* check upon the judges and whether pure economic loss is recoverable becomes a question for case law and the opinion of scholars. Under the prevailing view, the principle of *neminem laedere* appears to be the general rule, and the instances in which a person is at liberty to cause harm can be classified – as in the other liberal systems – as exceptions to the general rule. Thus many Spanish jurists approach questions of tort liability by verifying the existence of fault, causation and damage, rather than any preliminary reference to an *a priori* list of protected rights or interests.

Nevertheless, Spanish scholarship sometimes tends to oscillate between French and German patterns (sometimes finding a compromise in the Italian solutions, as happens with regard to the *culpa in contrahendo* principle: see Case 19, 'Breach of Promise'). This fluctuation is particularly evident when the right at stake is not an absolute one (see Cases 5, 'Requiem for an Italian All Star', and 17 'Auditor's Liability'). In these cases, the emphasis in discussion falls upon the existence of damage or the directness of the causal link (as the Spanish reporters wisely and clearly point out), and outcomes depend upon the interpretive view of scholars regarding the general clause contained in art. 1902 cc.

Case law in its turn appears more indulgent than scholars in awarding redress for losses in general and for pure economic loss in particular. Here too, however, the exercise of policy is difficult to detect at the discrete level where the judge creates no exception, but simply attributes a negative result in the particular case to a tenuous causal link or perhaps the uncertainty of the plaintiff's loss. In this perspective, the limits one can find to the recovery are the following: (1) the technical parameters of causation;[50] (2) policy considerations contained in the principle 'general risks of life';[51] (3) the judicial prerogative to reduce awards of damages whenever the defendant is liable for 'ordinary' negligence.[52]

The latter remark, coupled with the German-sounding reference to the 'general risk of life' (*allgemeines Lebensrisiko*), suggests that a balance

---

[49] See Case 3 ('Cable III – The Day-to-Day Workers') and cf. Cases 1 ('Cable I – The Blackout') and 2 ('Cable II – Factory Shutdown').
[50] See Case 15 ('A Closed Motorway – The Value of Time').
[51] As in Cases 6 ('The Infected Cow'), 15 ('A Closed Motorway – The Value of Time'), 16 ('Truck Blocking Entrance to Business Premises').
[52] If reliable figures could be collected, the exercise of the power to moderate damages is a datum whose weight, in assessing the actual impact of the operative rules, would deserve the highest consideration in studying every single tort law system.

has to be struck between Spain's liberal façade and actual interpretive outcomes. Certainly, this balance is most often arrived at through the technicalities of causation, but that is simply another way (and the most usual way in the systems so far examined) to allow judges and scholars to make critical choices.

## Greece's liberal credentials

The delictual framework in Greece begins with articles 914 and 919 of the Civil Code. They read respectively: 'A person who through his fault has caused in a manner contrary to the law prejudice to another shall be liable for compensation'; and 'A person who has intentionally caused prejudice to another in a manner contrary to morality shall be liable for damages.' The first provision states a broader principle than the second: liability under article 914 may include both *negligent* and *intentional* conduct which is contrary to 'law' in a broad sense, but liability under the second provision only arises for an *intentional* wrong contrary to *morality*.

As to the notion of unlawfulness, we see that the Greek legislator has not carved out a list of protected 'absolute' rights or interests,[53] but has simply cast the notion in the most general language: plaintiff's injury must be 'contrary to the law'. No attempt has been made to exclude pure economic loss, nor indeed any other type of damage from the purview of the notion 'prejudice to another'. Apparently the Greek system gives no *a priori* importance to the intrinsic nature of the damage. Thus it appears that whether plaintiff may receive compensation for pure economic loss requires an inquiry into defendant's violation of specific legal commands (special statutes, related code provisions and so forth),[54] or failing which, it may involve what has been called the issue of 'broadening the prerequisite of unlawfulness'.[55] According to the prevailing view, such a broadening process occurs principally by tying the standard of 'good faith' (arts. 281, 288) to the unlawfulness question: everyone should behave as good faith and business usages require. Greek jurisprudence

---

[53] Van Gerven et al., *Tort Law* (1998), p. 74.
[54] Unlawfulness under the Greek code will be shaped in diverse ways through the abuse of rights (art. 281), the duty to act in good faith (art. 288), harm to someone's body or health (art. 929), statutory violations, and even conduct which 'violates the spirit of the legal system', von Bar, *Law of Torts*, I, p. 28.
[55] K. Christodoulou, 'Introduction: (s. I, 2a) Greek Report on Pure Economic Loss' (on file with editors).

indicates that the breach of any duty of care imposed by good faith is unlawful.[56]

It is not surprising that fault and unlawfulness are interactive concepts that cannot always be kept apart. For example, unlawfulness may be considerably 'broadened' by the degree or manner of fault under article 914, on the argument that the negligence of the defendant *eo ipso* constitutes unlawful behaviour. According to our Greek reporter, the economic loss caused by the escape of the infected cow[57] illustrates this last kind of unlawfulness: it involves not only the violation of penal provisions applicable to animal custodians, but negligence which in and of itself would be unlawful.

Two other features add to Greece's liberal credentials. First, when a tortfeasor has damaged the property or person of another, the economic losses that ricochet to a secondary victim are recoverable, even though this secondary harm is purely financial. Greek law does not restrict the class of persons who are entitled to claim compensation for damages, though of course it will require proof of causal relation. As shown in Cable II – Factory Shutdown,[58] a Greek factory owner could recover for two days of lost production even though the only property loss (cut cables and damaged machinery) was sustained by other victims. Here, damage that in other systems meets scrutiny or even exclusion is in principle recoverable. Secondly, liability for pure economic loss has been recognized by incorporating the notion of *culpa in contrahendo* into the Civil Code (arts. 197, 198). Interestingly, it is treated as an extracontractual form of liability.

As in other liberal regimes, claims for pure economic loss may founder upon the shoals of causation. Greek writers and judges favour two standard tests of causation: (1) the defendant's act must be shown to be the *causa adequata* of the plaintiff's damage, meaning to Greek jurists that the damage must be *ex ante* foreseeable; (2) under the newly exploited theory of 'the protective purpose of the legal rule', the defendant's act must reach and infringe upon an interest thought to be protected by the purpose of the law. The limits of causation are thus the limits of the protected interests. Both means leave ample room for controlling the recovery of pure economic loss where it seems excessive.

---

[56] AP 640/1955 NoB 4, 491; AP 250/1956 NoB 4, 840; AP 510/1959 NoB 8, 251; AP 343/1968 NoB 16, 943; AP 854/1974 NoB 23, 479; AP 81/1991 NoB 40, 715; EfAth 7453/1988 EllDni 31, 848.
[57] See Case 6 ('The Infected Cow').   [58] Case 2 ('Cable II – Factory Shutdown').

## The pragmatic regimes of England, Scotland and the Netherlands

*England's cautious and pragmatic judges*

The dishevelled design of the English law of torts is due to the hand of history and the cumulative nature of common law growth. The disconnected structure, so different from the codified civil law, is the work of thousands of judicial architects and no central planners.[59] Ancient torts such as trespass stand side-by-side with modern torts such as negligence. Nominate torts such as trespass to land or to goods, defamation and conversion make up a lengthy table of wrongful actions, but each is just a snapshot freezing a precise scenario into invariable elements and predictable endings. Compartmentalization – the absence of general principles connecting the nominate torts – is a leading characteristic. The tort of intimidation has nothing to do with the tort of mayhem; slander of title cannot be compared to slander of women.

The English façade tends to make a continental lawyer think more of the criminal law (where all crimes are typically nominate) than the law of tort.[60] Most of these torts arose in defence of protecting a plaintiff's life, limb and property and are far removed from affording relief for pure economic loss. For sure, there are a series of intentional economic torts, notably actions for deceit, interference with trade, inducing breach of contract, passing off, misfeasance in public office,[61] intimidation and conspiracy, and if the defendant has intentionally caused such loss, the claim for pure economic loss may fit into one of these pigeonholes. If the loss was occasioned by negligence, however, these actions are unavailable. The plaintiff's chief recourse must therefore be to the tort of negligence.

[59] 'No other European country has as many statutes imposing liability as England, yet, as in Ireland and Scotland, its non-contractual liability law remains essentially judge-made', von Bar, *Law of Torts*, I, p. 267. As to the Irish tort law regime, which is substantially influenced by English patterns and rules, see, in comparative perspective, von Bar, *Law of Torts*, I, pp. 316 ff.

[60] C. von Bar, *Law of Torts*, I, at Rn. 254, p. 281. The language of the common law has always made a connection between civil and penal redress. 'We "commit" a tort as we "commit" an offence. We can be "guilty" of either or both; and all our crimes are nominate'. Rudden, 'Torticles', at 126.

[61] Cf. S. Arrowsmith, *Civil Liability and Public Authorities* (Earlsgate Press, Winteringham, 1992). See *David v. Abdul Cader* [1963] 1 WLR 834; [1963] 3 All ER 579 (PC); and, *obiter*, *X (some minors) v. Bedfordshire County Council* [1995] 2 AC 633, [1995] 3 WLR 152, [1995] 3 All ER 353 (HL); *Three Rivers DC and Others v. Governor and Company of the Bank of England* [2000] 2 WLR 1220 (HL).

The generic tort of negligence would appear, at first glance, to hold great promise for the recovery of pure economic loss. Animated by the 'neighbour principle' which *Donoghue* v. *Stevenson* announced in 1932, this tort has been compared to a general clause covering all forms of negligent behaviour. This is generally true within the realm of protection from physical harm (bodily injury or damage to property).[62] But according to a leading authority, *Murphy* v. *Brentwood DC*,[63] negligence is not primarily applicable to the compensation of pure economic loss. This means that the nature of the plaintiff's damage controls the existence of a duty to avoid causing it. Indeed, the common law as a matter of policy begins with the proposition that there is, as a rule, no duty of care to avoid causing pure economic loss. The occasions upon which such a duty is recognized are exceptional and must be kept so. This deep misgiving is based upon an instinctive fear of wide liability, customarily expressed by recourse to the floodgates metaphor or the 'nightmare scenario', but more fundamentally by a cautious case-by-case approach which studies the economic and social implications of each extension. The judges are willing to impose a 'duty of care' in the particular case brought before them only when satisfied on utilitarian grounds that it is socially and economically convenient to do so.

These exceptional cases are highly fact-sensitive and cover narrow fact situations. The exceptions began with *Hedley Byrne & Co. Ltd* v. *Heller & Partners*[64] and then multiplied. The general principle of no liability for pure economic loss survives, but with a number of exceptions that may be increased in the future if the courts find it 'fair, just and reasonable' to do so.[65] Thus far, the exceptions are limited to negligent misstatements made and relied upon (in a context of 'virtual' contract),[66]

---

[62] 1932 SC (HL) 31. Even here the principle has been overridden in certain exceptional situations where, for reasons of policy, it was inadvisable to impose a duty of care, though harm to plaintiff's property was the foreseeable result of defendant's negligence. See, for example, *The Nicholas H* [1995] 3 All ER 307.

[63] [1991] AC 398.   [64] [1964] AC 465.

[65] On the meaning of this phrase, which reserves judicial options for future development (in marked contrast to the more principled methodology announced in *Anns* v. *Merton London Borough Council* [1978] AC 278), see, e.g. *Caparo Industries Plc* v. *Dickman* [1990] 2 AC 605.

[66] *Hedley Byrne*, above [1964] AC 465. However, one should be aware that if, after a misrepresentation, the parties actually enter into a contract with each other, it is doubtful whether there is any practical need to resort to the rule of *Hedley Byrne*, since liability may end up being based on contract under s. 2(1) of the Misrepresentation Act 1967. The text provides that 'Where a person has entered into a contract after a misrepresentation has been made to it by another party thereto and as a result

negligent interference with the performance of a contract,[67] negligent defamation in the writing of a reference for a former employee,[68] professional negligence in the drawing up of a will[69] and breach of statutory duty.[70] What appears characteristic and consistent in these exceptions is the limited quantitative exposure of the defendant to a defined number of plaintiffs, or even better, a single plaintiff. The danger of unbounded financial repercussion is avoided. The total liability can be calculated in advance as not exceeding the value of a lost legacy, a lost job or lost investment. The plaintiff is a particular individual – the potential legatee of a will or a former employee – whose interests are very distinctly contemplated by the defendant at close range. But the presence of other factors which demonstrate a closer degree of proximity between the parties than mere foreseeability of economic harm may be insisted upon, such as defendant's 'assumption of responsibility' for the plaintiff's economic wellbeing coupled with the plaintiff's reliance upon it.[71] The class of claimants is thereby limited, as if an invisible privity paradigm structured the resulting bond in tort.[72] It may be noted that although actions may be brought concurrently, a contract action cannot be used in these circumstances for there is no 'consideration' and therefore no contract

---

thereof he has suffered loss, then, if the person making the misrepresentation would be liable to damages in respect thereof had the misrepresentation been made fraudulently, that person shall be so liable notwithstanding that the misrepresentation was not made fraudulently, unless he proves that he had reasonable ground to believe and did believe up to the time the contract was made that the facts represented were true.' Through this rule 'the tort of negligence became otiose' in this context: von Bar, *Law of Torts*, I, p. 449.

[67] *Junior Books* v. *Veitchi* [1983] 1 AC 520. This Scottish case, however, has been disapproved in almost every later English case. J. Stapleton, 'Duty of Care Factors: A Selection from the Judicial Menus', in P. Cane and J. Stapleton (eds.), *The Law of Obligations: Essays in Honour of J. Fleming* (1998), p. 59 and p. 80, fn. 82–3; J. M. Thomson, 'A Prophet Not Rejected in His Own Land', (1994) 110 *Law Quarterly Review* 361.

[68] *Spring* v. *Guardian Assurance PLC* [1993] 3 All ER 273 (CA).

[69] *White* v. *Jones* [1993] 3 All ER 481 (CA), [1995] 2 WLR 187 (HL).

[70] For relevant references, see von Bar, *Law of Torts*, I, pp. 328 ff.

[71] The phrase 'assumption of responsibility' originates in *Hedley Byrne*, [1964] AC 465, at 528 (Lord Devlin). It seems to make recourse to an underlying contract model to earmark occasions when it is appropriate to impose a duty of care: the assumption of responsibility and reliance upon it must be voluntary. See Lord Goff's speech in *Henderson* v. *Merrett Syndicate Ltd* [1995] 2 AC 145, [1994] 3 All ER 506, discussing the role played by voluntariness. See also Banakas, 'Liability for Incorrect Financial Information', 261, 270–2; J. M. Thomson *Delictual Liability* (Butterworths, London, 1994), p. 59.

[72] The opposite view is maintained in Germany. See below footnotes 98 ff. and accompanying text.

between plaintiff and defendant. Given its insistence on consideration, England's rigid contract law cannot protect legal strangers against such losses. Therefore, it was faced with the choice either to expand its tort law opportunistically or to deny these actions altogether.[73]

The English judges express their pragmatism in an open manner. Policy decisions are not cloaked behind a particular view of causation or of *culpa*, as we have already noticed in several continental systems. The unlawfulness issue is isolated as a preliminary policy decision. Thus, in English law the façade of judge-made tort law approaches the inner reality of the process. The use of legal policy, especially in tort cases involving patrimonial injury, is a distinct feature of internal common law culture.[74] Our national reporter cautions, however, that English legal policy should not be confused with continental concepts such as French notions of *ordre public* or the German concept of *Treu und Glauben*. He writes:

> Unlike these Continental concepts, the English concept of legal policy does not assume a legal rule, for which it is, then, judicially used as a limit of its application, but creates one for the case under trial and for the future. A rule that will moreover, change, every time legal policy is invoked again.[75]

The English judges refuse to be driven by the logical implications of the neighbourhood principle into recognition of a wide theory of fault. Besides proximity and foreseeability, something else is required in order to summon forth a 'duty of care' in the field of patrimonial loss. The English judge wishes to remain architect of this common law development.

### Scotland: an ambiguous pragmatism

Despite an official Roman and civil law façade, Scotland takes essentially the same pragmatic approach to the recovery of pure economic loss that we have just described in the case of England. There is a similar caution in screening new 'duty situations' on a case-by-case basis, and judges

---

[73] B. Markesinis, 'An Expanding Tort Law – The Price of a Rigid Contract Law', (1987) 103 *Law Quarterly Review* 354.

[74] Note, however, that an attempt was made in *Henderson v. Merrett Syndicate Ltd* [1995] 2 AC 145, [1994] 3 All ER 506, to lay down general criteria for the existence of a duty of care to protect pure economic loss without resort to a policy argument. According to J. M. Thomson, the importance of this case has not been sufficiently recognized. *Delictual Liability* (2nd edn, Butterworths, London, pp. 85 ff., 1999). See also Banakas, 'Liability for Incorrect Financial Information', 261, 271, 277 ff.

[75] Introductory comments, on file with editors.

carefully study the concrete socio-economic implications of extending the recovery of pure economic loss. Clearly, there is no general duty of care in Scotland to avoid causing mere financial injury. Leaving aside the case of intentionally caused economic harm, liability for economic loss based on negligence will generally coincide with the exceptional areas also recognized in England. A comparison of the two country reports is striking: the Scottish and English answers are remarkably similar to one another.[76] From the comparative point of view, this seems to be an unsurprising case of insular convergence.

Scotland is the oldest 'mixed jurisdiction' in the world (its mixity dating from the Treaty of Union with England in 1707, and arguably well before that event) and the only jurisdiction of its kind within the European Union. It is characteristic of mixed jurisdictions to retain private civil law within a surrounding system of Anglo-American public law; it is also characteristic to find in such systems that the law of delict, which obviously lies within the retained civil law sphere, constitutes an area particularly open to common law fertilization and the reception of common law cases and doctrine.[77] Scotland's law of delict is not an exception to that process, though the nature and degree of integration and convergence may well be subject to differences of opinion. The sources of the law of delict in Scotland reflect the layered complexity of this field. According to D. M. Walker, the sources of Scottish law in general include 'Roman law, indigenous custom, juristic interpretation, judicial modification, the influence of common law, and modern legislation'.[78]

In presenting the Roman and civil law façade to the reader, the Scottish writers take pride in stating that the law of delict has Roman roots and was elaborated by the *usus modernus pandectarum*. They studiously avoid the expression 'law of torts',[79] carefully employ civilian terminology, and place emphasis upon the differences with English law.[80] Perhaps the most notable of these differences, according to Walker, is

---

[76] This is quite apparent from our comparisons in Part III of this volume. The Scottish report records results, particularly the negative results, nearly identical to the English report. See Table 8.1, in Part III of this volume.

[77] V. Palmer (ed.), *Mixed Jurisdictions Worldwide: The Third Legal Family* (Cambridge University Press, Cambridge, 2001).

[78] D. M. Walker, *The Law of Delict in Scotland*, vol. I (Green, 1966), p. 17.

[79] Thus Walker's *Law of Delict in Scotland*, vols. I, II; Thomson, *Delictual Liability* (1999); W. J. Stewart, *Delict and Related Obligations* (2nd edn, Green, 1993).

[80] Von Bar mentions some of the specific characteristics of the Scots law of delict: the less exalted role of trespass; the missing distinction between private and public nuisance; the absence of torts actionable *per se*; absence of the distinction between libel and slander; the rejection of punitive damages; and the non-adoption of *Rylands* v. *Fletcher*. Von Bar, *Law of Torts*, I, at Rn. 299, pp. 319–20.

that Scottish law bases its law of delict on a general principle for wrongful conduct, not on a system of nominate torts.

The nomenclature of the English nominate torts, such as trespass, defamation and passing off, is well known and frequently used in Scotland, but Walker argues that in reality these names are 'no more than convenient titles for sets of circumstances giving rise to liability under one or other of the general principles of delictual liability accepted in Scots law'.[81] He stresses that while negligence is an independent nominate tort in England, in Scotland this is not so; when the term negligence is used it simply means damages for harm caused negligently.[82] Zweigert and Kötz, who seem to accept the claim that civilian principle plays a dominant role in the Scottish law of delict, state that: 'Scotland operates with only a few high-level principles and concepts, thereby demonstrating that inner economy which "civilian" thought regards as a virtue.'[83] Despite this assurance, however, outsiders may wonder whether Scotland's commitment to a wide civilian principle has had any measurable effect of expanding the scope of unlawfulness to include pure economic loss.[84] That principle appears to be basically limited by judicial interpretation to a set of protected rights and interests which largely excludes pure patrimonial loss. Interestingly, though Scotland has neither the English requirement of consideration nor a rigid law of contract, it has not seen fit to make lateral recourse to expanded contract remedies in these instances.

In our view, the Scottish law of delict is essentially arranged around a fixed set of protected rights and interests.[85] Norrie writes that '[t]he civil wrong of negligence [is] founded...on a moral imperative not to cause harm to others through carelessness', and that much work of the judges in the twentieth century 'has been devoted to the development of a unifying general principle (or at least a set of principles) governing negligence, explaining why some neglects are culpable and others are

---

[81] Walker, *Law of Delict in Scotland*, vol. II at p. 487.   [82] Ibid, vol. I, pp. 44–5.

[83] K. Zweigert and H. Kötz, *Introduction to Comparative Law* (2nd edn, Clarendon, Oxford, 1987), p. 210.

[84] Indeed one Scots jurist who is a specialist in this subject is sceptical of claims that a single principle really controls this issue in Scotland: 'The question whether the defender owes a duty of care to the pursuer to prevent him sustaining "pure economic loss" is one which, even in Scots law, it appears cannot be answered by the application of a simple general principle of liability', J. M. Thomson 'Delictual Liability for Pure Economic Loss: Recent Developments', 1995 SLT (News) 139.

[85] Thus Walker, who calls 'breach of duty' the fundamental concept of the modern Scottish law of delict, divides all breaches of duty into two categories: infringements of personality and damage to property, *Law of Delict in Scotland*, at pp. 31–2.

not, and limiting liability for neglect of duty within rational and acceptable bounds. This can be seen particularly through the concept of the "duty of care".[86] For Norrie: 'Liability would be uncontrollable if the law permitted recovery for all immediate and consequential damage caused carelessly, and the concept of duty was adopted as a useful – indeed essential – means of limiting liability within acceptable bounds.'[87]

The historic case of *Donoghue* v. *Stevenson* was a Scottish case instrumental in the coming together of the two systems. As noted earlier, subsequent interpretation revealed for both Scotland and England that the generality of the 'neighbourhood' principle was restricted to the recovery of physical damage. Every attempt to extend the principle beyond physical damage into the field of pure economic loss is subjected to the same preliminary 'duty of care' determination made under the English tort of negligence.[88] In this light, it is difficult to disagree with von Bar's conclusion that 'exactly where today's law of delict differs from the common law of torts is unclear. The two have converged in this century to the extent that differences, other than those from statute, are of secondary importance.'[89]

## A middle path in the Netherlands

The 1992 Civil Code of the Netherlands treads a middle ground between the liberal and conservative models of tort. On the one hand, the sweep of art. 6:162(1) reminds one of France's general clause:

1. A person who commits an unlawful act vis-à-vis another person, which can be imputed to him, is obliged to repair the damage suffered by the other person as a consequence of the act.

However, the next paragraph of the same provision, sets forth a list of 'unlawful' acts in a manner somewhat reminiscent of the BGB:

2. Save grounds for justification, the following acts are deemed to be unlawful: the infringement of a subjective right, an act or omission violating a statutory duty, or conduct contrary to the standard of conduct acceptable in society.[90]

---

[86] *Stair Memorial Encyclopaedia, The Laws of Scotland*, vol. 15, (Law Society of Scotland, Edinburgh), p. 129 paras. 217–8 (written by K. McK. Norrie).
[87] Norrie, *Stair Memorial Encyclopaedia*, at para. 257, p. 155.
[88] See, for example, Thomson, *Delictual Liability*, chs. 3 and 4.
[89] Von Bar, *Law of Torts*, I, at Rn. 299, p. 319.
[90] Moreover, the third paragraph significantly reads: 'An unlawful act can be imputed to its author if it results from his fault or from a cause for which he is answerable according to law or common opinion.'

The effect of this provision is that the Dutch legislator has taken a moderate, noncommittal stance toward the recovery of pure economic loss. It seems to be partially but not entirely precluded. Recovery would seem foreclosed in terms of the first type of unlawfulness (infringement of subjective right), but if defendant's actions violated a statute[91] or was deemed socially unacceptable behaviour, the economic loss might be considered unlawful under the second or third types. Indeed, the third type appears to be the most viable of the three and will likely be the centre of attention in most cases of pure economic loss.

Another provision gives further evidence of the middle path taken by the Dutch legislator. Art. 6:109(1)[92] permits the judge to reduce damage awards that he considers excessive, and this feature may alleviate in part one of the principal fears associated with the recovery of pure economic loss – the spectre of staggering liability.

Moderation and pragmatism characterize the jurisprudence as well. While Dutch codal provisions are imbued with traditional and sophisticated concepts,[93] the operative tort law seems to be less sensitive than other systems to the battle of slogans or, to put it another way, Dutch tort law is less inclined to live on the split between declamations and operative rules. This probably explains why the Dutch report is the most factually nuanced amongst the civilian contributions.

First, Dutch judges use the duty of care concept to help them resolve the unlawfulness issue; this is reminiscent of the way in which English judges begin with the need to establish the 'duty situation'.[94] This allows Dutch solutions to avoid the categorical 'yes or no' approach associated with German and Austrian law.[95] Secondly, since the system approaches

---

[91] Recoveries for statutory violations will be analysed in terms of the *Schutznorm* theory (*relativiteitsleer*) to which the Dutch Supreme Court has adhered since 1928. This theory is now expressed in art. 6:163 CC: 'No obligation to repair damages arises whenever the violated norm does not purport to protect from damage such as suffered by the injured.'

[92] Art. 6:109(1) provides: 'The judge may reduce the obligation to repair damage if awarding full reparation would lead to clearly unacceptable results in the given circumstances, including the nature of the liability, the legal relationship between the parties, and their respective financial capacities.'

[93] See e.g. art. 6:162 (which opens Title 3 'Unlawful Act'), above.

[94] As in Cases 1 ('Cable I – The Blackout'), 2 ('Cable II – Factory Shutdown'), 14 ('Poor Legal Services'), 16 ('Truck Blocking Entrance to Business Premises'), 17 ('Auditor's Liability').

[95] In the words of Willem van Boom, the Dutch reporter, 'The field of pure economic loss is very much like a labyrinth: turn a corner and an entirely new perspective awaits you. Dutch tort law is currently very much an open-ended collection of written

tort law issues primarily in terms of duty and not in terms of selected interests to protect, the search for limits to the extension of civil liability loses an important and useful landmark, but at the same time it profits from neater, more transparent arguments.[96]

The issue of making the tort liability boundaries socially and technically acceptable appears to be tackled in the Netherlands as follows. A possible ground to deny redress is simply to resort to policy reasons (just as common lawyers usually do, and as Dutch law does in cases such as the one presented in Case 15, 'A Closed Motorway – The Value of Time'). Another tool to restrict recoverability is the reference to statutory limits – for example, the limitation that ricochet damages under Dutch law can be claimed by third parties but only so far as the injured party could have claimed them had he himself suffered these losses (cf. Cases 5, 'Requiem for an Italian All Star', and 10, 'The Dutiful Wife').

Furthermore, Dutch lawyers make frequent resort to the technical devices upon which tort law has traditionally been built. Along with the duty criterion, causation has most often served as the divide between liability and non-liability in Dutch law. This is shown clearly by the range of possible solutions that the Dutch reporter presents to the hypotheticals dealing with the 'Day-to-Day Workers' (Case 3) and the fault-based liability of the manufacturer (Case 9, 'Fire in the Projection Booth'). But the crucial role of causation becomes striking as soon as one compares the general provision of the new Dutch civil code on causal relation[97] with the illuminating remarks made by the Dutch contributor in the introduction to his report:

> and, more importantly, unwritten duties and obligations. Apart from the obvious advantage of expeditious judicial law-making that can respond to societal developments, there are important drawbacks to this open-endedness. If a case has not yet been decided by the Supreme Court, one can only state the factors and circumstances that should be taken into account in deciding the case at hand. The exact outcome, however, remains uncertain. The most obvious cases have yet to be decided. This shows that Dutch (tort) law has a long way to go before a solid line of reasoning on pure economic loss will emerge.' Author's conclusion, on file with the editors.

[96] Lacking this technical cover, pragmatic systems are compelled to be more forthright in avowing whether the denial of compensation for pure economic loss is grounded on a policy reason.

[97] 'Compensation can only be claimed insofar as the damage is related to the event giving rise to liability in such a fashion that the damage, also taking into account its nature and that of the liability, can be imputed to the debtor as a result of this event.' Art. 6:98.

As far as the nature of the damage suffered is concerned, both case law and doctrinal writing are inclined to stretch the limits of causal connection *very far* whenever bodily harm is involved, somewhat *less far* when damage to property is involved, and the *least* in the case of loss related to neither of the former two categories (i.e. pure economic loss).[98]

Obviously, causal limits fluctuate not in accordance with different causal rules but because a hierarchical policy has been superimposed upon the same rule.

## The conservative regimes of Germany, Austria, Portugal, Sweden and Finland

*Germany: narrow in tort but wide in contract*

As we have seen, in spite of their conspicuous theoretical and actual differences, liberal and pragmatic regimes sometimes end up screening and refining the pure economic loss issue through the inner technicalities of tort law. To the contrary, the German legal system seems to deny even preliminary access to this kind of damages. Indeed, this prophylactic role is vested in a text that envisions liability only for injuries to certain enumerated rights. According to § 823 of the BGB, individuals are liable if they wilfully or negligently injure 'the life, body, health, freedom, property or other right' of the victim. Deliberately excluded in this list of so-called 'absolute rights' is any reference to injuries of a purely financial kind. It is therefore undisputed that, as a basic rule, pure economic loss is not recoverable in tort. Compensation may be obtained in tort in some exceptional situations, but the plaintiff must find a cause of action in some provision other than § 823 BGB.[99]

On the surface, German tort law rules have changed little since their enactment more than a century ago. The real change has been accomplished through case law. The judges' contribution has reached the point that our German contributor finds, in 'predicting the outcome

---

[98] Emphasis in original: on file with the authors.
[99] For example, under § 824 BGB, which provides that a person who declares or publishes, contrary to the truth, a statement which is likely to endanger the credit earnings or prosperity of another is liable for 'any damage' arising therefrom, even if he does not know of its untruth but should know of it. Here the protection against pure economic loss is the crux of the rule, but its scope is narrowed by the privilege granted in § 824 (2), (on this subject, and for further references see, in English, van Gerven et al., *Tort Law*, pp. 65 ff., 189). This provision has some relevance to the resolution of Cases 18 ('Wrongful Job Reference') and 20 ('An Anonymous Telephone Call').

of disputes, this case law is much more important than the academic literature'. While this is certainly not a phenomenon peculiar to German law,[100] nevertheless it is worth stressing if we are to understand a system that attempted a rigid legislative solution.

For example, German law requires the violation of a right (an 'absolute' one) but new rights have been added to the traditional set through interpretation. In this way, German law developed the so-called 'right of the established and ongoing commercial enterprise'. Something similar happened to § 823 (2) BGB, where wording about the infringement of 'a statute intended for the protection of others' became a vehicle to compensate pure financial losses arising out of such infringement, provided that the type of loss can be included within the sphere of the statutory aim.[101]

But this is not all. § 826 BGB provides that a person is liable if they intentionally cause harm to another in a manner contrary to public policy. To understand the subjective requirements of this provision, it is not deemed necessary that 'the defendant actually intended to cause harm'; it will be enough 'if he was conscious of the possibility that harm might occur and acquiesced in its doing so'.[102] The role this rule plays with regard to our issue can be appreciated if one looks at the factual situations to which it has mainly been applied. These are, for example, participating as a third person in a breach of contract committed by a contracting party, delaying someone's bankruptcy in order to obtain personal benefit at the expense of other creditors, giving false information or omitting to supply information in circumstances where there is a duty to give it.[103]

---

[100] Towards the end of the last century, French courts developed case law imposing liability for making a void contract, for seduction, for misleading information, for unfair competition, and so forth – all pursuant to a code that left open the meaning of 'dommage' and the interests to be protected. The courts in Germany, at the same time, felt the need to impose liability in the same types of cases, so that the legislator, in drafting the code, was able to enumerate the cases in which liability would be imposed: Sacco, 'Legal Formants', inst. II. See also J. Gordley, above, Chapter 2.

[101] Von Bar, *Law of Torts*, I, pp. 45 ff., 49.

[102] Zweigert and Kötz, *Introduction to Comparative Law*, at p. 463; B. Markesinis, *The German Law of Obligations*, vol. II, *The Law of Torts* (3rd edn, Oxford University Press, Oxford, 1997), at p. 895.

[103] K. Larenz and C. W. Canaris, *Lehrbuch des Schuldrechts* (13th edn, Beck, München, 1994), p. 276. See other references in C. von Bar, 'Liability for Information and Opinions Causing Pure Economic Loss to Third Parties: A Comparison of English and German Case Law', in B. Markesinis, *The Gradual Convergence* (Oxford University Press, Oxford, 1994), pp. 104 ff.

The flight to contract

In solving questions of pure economic loss, contract remedies are more widely employed in Germany than in other countries. The reason for the enlarged role of contract is probably twofold: on the one hand, apart from rules permitting the concurrence of tort and contract actions, tort law is considered too weak and narrow to safeguard all financial interests that merit legal protection. On the other hand, contract claims may seem to be the relatively safer path to those who dread unleashing the floodgates of tort, since there is certainly less danger of boundless damages occurring in a breach of contract situation. For whatever reason, courts and scholars certainly expanded the sphere of contractual liability beyond the limits marked by the BGB. This was accomplished through the exploitation of various devices, including the much longer prescriptive period in contract (thirty years, as opposed to three), the greater ease of establishing breach of contract rather than fault (§ 282 BGB) and the stronger regime of vicarious liability in contract (§ 278 BGB). The range of contractual duties was stretched to include 'implied' duties of care so that liability might arise, not only from the violation of the parties' express obligations, but also from the breach of a host of judicially imposed duties of care. Likewise, German interpreters extended these duties over time, so that in some cases they precede the conclusion of a contract (*culpa in contrahendo*)[104] and survive the termination or the performance of the contract itself.

The most important innovation of all, however, was that courts and commentators lowered the privity barrier in contract and applied these duties in favour of those who were not parties to any contract. The principal instrument in this regard is the 'contract with protective effects for third parties' (*Vertrag mit Schutzwirkung für Dritter*), which brings strangers to a contract under its umbrella and permits them to sue a promisor for breach of one of the contract's secondary obligations, notably (for our subject) some breach causing purely financial harm to the plaintiff. This institution would allow recovery in several cases in the questionnaire.[105] The function of the contract with protective effects is

---

[104] See its application to Case 19 ('Breach of Promise'). Under this doctrine, contractual duties may arise as soon as the parties set up a pre-contractual 'contact', thus well before any contract is concluded and even when none is ever in fact concluded. See Markesinis, *German Law of Obligations*, pp. 688 ff.

[105] See the German reporter's answers to Cases 13 ('Subcontractor's Liability') and 17 ('Auditor's Liability').

arguably tort-like in that the protected third party need not stand in a close personal relationship to the promisor, nor be specifically identified in advance. At the same time, it is operationally free of the 'absolute rights' requirement of German tort law and permits recovery of purely financial harm.[106]

Other kinds of economic losses may also be handled by contract law. This will include the multi-purpose device of pre-contractual liability (*culpa in contrahendo*) and the extended application of the joint and several liability rules to redress the loss incurred by the contractor (cf. Case 6, 'The Infected Cow').

All these rules are firmly established today to the extent that most of them have been included in the reform of the law of obligations recently adopted[107] and, as a result, many cases that an English, American or Italian lawyer would consider solely a matter of tort law are actionable in Germany in contract.

---

[106] It is not the only possibility under German law. Another institution of possible application in this field (but not relevant to our cases) is *Drittschadensliquidation*, which Markesinis describes as a quasi-contractual judge-made doctrine that allows a creditor to a contract to claim in contract for loss resulting from its breach, even though the loss falls not upon him but upon a third party, B. Markesinis, *The German Law of Torts* (2nd edn, Clarendon, Oxford, 1990), pp. 47–9. In England a similar concept has been described as 'transferred loss'.

[107] Indeed, the Act on the Modernization of the Law of Obligations 2001 (*Gesetz zur Modernisierung des Schuldrechts*, in BGBl, 29 November 2001, I, Nr. 61, pp. 3138 ff., which came into force on 1 January 2002) has deeply affected the legal landscape. It establishes, for example, new terms for the prescription of tort (up to 30 years) and contract (up to 10 years) actions, and codifies both the principles of *culpa in contrahendo* (see § 311 (2) and (3) as well as § 241 (1) BGB) and of the 'contract with protective effects for third parties' (see § 311, s. 3 BGB). For a general discussion of the reform, see H.-P. Mansel, 'Die Neuregelung des Verjährungsrecht', (2002) 55 NJW 89; W. Däubler, 'Neues Schuldrecht – ein erster Überblick', (2001) 54 NJW 3729; M. Schwab, 'Das neue Schuldrecht im Überblick', (2002) 1 JuS 11. See also R. Zimmermann, 'Breach of Contract and Remedies under the New German Law of Obligations', in Centro di studi e ricerche di diritto comparato e straniero (ed.), 48 *Saggi, conferenze e seminari* (2002); C.-W. Canaris (ed.), *Schuldrechtsmodernisierung* (2002); B. Dauner-Lieb, T. Heidel, M. Lepa and G. Ring (eds.), *Das neue Schuldrecht – ein Lehrbuch* (2002); S. Lorenz and T. Riehm, *Lehrbuch zum neuen Schuldrecht* (2002); P. Huber and F. Faust, *Schuldrechtsmodernisierung: Einführung in das neue Recht* (2002); G. Wagner, 'Das Zweite Schadensersatzrechtsänderungsgesetz', (2002) 55 NJW 2049; D. Zimmer, 'Das neue Recht der Leistungsstörungen, (2002) 55 NJW 1; H. Otto, 'Die Grundstrukturen des neuen Leistungsstörungsrecht', (2002) Jura 1; R. Schwarze, 'Unmöglichkeit, Unvermögen und änliche Leistungshindernisse im neuen Leistungsstörungsrecht', (2002) Jura 73; S. Meier, 'Neues Leistungsstörungsrecht', (2002) Jura 118. For a rule-by-rule commentary, see B. Dauner-Lieb, T. Heidel, M. Lepa and G. Ring (eds.), *Anwaltkommentar Schuldrecht, Erläuterungen der Neuregelungen zum Verjährungsrecht, Schuldrecht, Schadensersatzrecht und Mietrecht* (2002).

## Austria: a massive interior transplant

Austrian code provisions on delict bear the same natural law imprint which inspired French codistic rules. The scope of protection is seemingly not limited by the typecast actions of German law. Article 1295 of the *Allgemeines Bürgerliches Gesetzbuch* (ABGB) provides:

> A person is entitled to demand indemnification for the damage from a person causing an injury by his fault; the damage may have been caused either by the violation of a contractual duty or without regard to a contract.

Yet paradoxically, as far as operative rules and outcomes are concerned, Austrian law follows the intellectual lead of German thought[108] and must be classified among the conservative tort regimes of Europe. Thus, as a general rule, pure economic loss is unrecoverable in tort. There are a few tort provisions which permit compensation but on an exceptional basis. As in Germany, therefore, this has prompted an expansion of contractual actions to redress somewhat the deficit in tort. We will look first at available tort actions and then turn to contract.

### The transformed general clause

Rather than a change of façade, Austrian courts and scholars have redecorated the interior of this provision. They have restricted the class of persons entitled to damages: 'a person', as mentioned in article 1295 ABGB, is not any person. Likewise 'a damage' is not any kind of damage, but is limited to the *direct* infringement of life, body, health and property.[109] In this manner, Austrian judges and scholars crafted an approach to pure economic loss along German lines despite an utterly different legislative prescription, although the so-called 'Three Partial Amendments' to the Austrian code in 1916 borrowed heavily from the BGB of 1900 and thereafter the influence of German law never disappeared.

Interestingly, the subject of pure economic loss (*reiner Vermögensschaden*) did not attract much juristic interest in Austria until thirty years ago, when the concept itself was taken from German law together with its policy justifications. So successfully did the transplant take root that Willibold Posch and Bernd Schilcher believe that in some

---

[108] For a short and useful historical survey of cultural factors which led Austrian jurists, from the second half of the nineteenth century, to fall back on German legal thought see K. Zweigert and H. Kötz, *Introduction to Comparative Law* (trans T. Weir, 3rd edn, Clarendon, Oxford, 1998), pp. 160 ff.

[109] W. Posch and B. Schilcher, 'Introduction' to Austrian Report, on file with editors.

respects Austrian court practice exceeds the restrictive levels reached in Germany.[110]

The interior of the Austrian general clause was apparently transformed on the basis of three general arguments: (1) a policy rationale rooted in the perceived need to control the risk of a 'boundless inflation of claims for liability for damage';[111] (2) heavy reliance upon the use of simple causal labels to close the floodgates; Austrian judges and scholars systematically control recovery by characterizing the causal connection to pure economic loss as 'indirect' as opposed to direct;[112] (3) recourse to the same unlawfulness criteria found in German law, with the result that purely financial loss does not qualify as infringement of an 'absolute right'. Certainly, this kind of reasoning was or is actually shared by other legal models,[113] but the stark contrast between the code's French façade and its German interior is more remarkable than elsewhere[114] and once again illustrates the need to consider all legal formants and metalegal factors in describing and articulating liability rules.

Turning our attention from the general clause, we find other code provisions which are more favourable to the recovery of pure economic loss, but these cover somewhat exceptional situations. One is article 1295(2), which states: 'A person who intentionally injures another in a manner in violation of public morals, is liable therefor...' This provision protects against purely financial damage, but only when the tortfeasor commits a 'truly grave, abominable wrong'.[115] This provision did not form the basis for compensation in any of the cases in our study.

---

[110] This is convincingly shown by the answer to Case 1 ('Cable I – The Blackout') where Austria, using its restrictive causal formula, would deny recovery not only for pure economic loss but for property damage as well.

[111] See Posch and Schilcher, 'Introduction' to Austrian Report (on file with the editors).

[112] Thus in cable cases, *Meroni*-like cases and others, it seems that the Austrian courts dogmatically label the financial loss as 'indirect' as a matter of policy in order to limit liability, not because of a careful application of the principles of causation. See the reasoning in the answers to Cases 1 ('Cable I – The Blackout'), 2 ('Cable II – Factory Shutdown'), 3 ('Cable III – The Day-to-Day Workers') and 5 ('Requiem for an Italian All Star').

[113] Leaving aside the role vested in causation throughout all tort law systems, it suffices to advert to the historical prominence of the notion of *illicéité* within French tort law debate, or of the overt reference to policy factors in scholarly and judicial opinions within the common law systems – reference which seems to have a more cryptic, but no less incisive role in German law.

[114] This disparity has not been immune to criticism. See Rudolf Reischauer, in P. Rummel, *Kommentar zum ABGB*, vol. II, (2nd edn, Vienna 1992), § 1294, no. 16, observing that 'continuous squinting at the German BGB has obscured the view'.

[115] Posch and Schilcher, 'Introduction'.

Another exceptional basis in tort relates to the infringement of a statute which is intended for the protection of others. Again, damages for pure economic loss can be obtained, whether the protective statutory rule was broken negligently or intentionally: however, it must be clear that the statute was intended to protect against this type of loss.[116]

### The resort to contractual actions

Having veered widely from the danger of 'boundless' claims in tort, Austrian interpreters called upon contractual actions to bring greater balance into the system. In the 1960s, courts and scholars accepted from Germany the notion of contractual liability for the breach of pre-contractual duties (the theory of *culpa in contrahendo*)[117] and they also readily imported the concept of 'contracts with protective effects' for third parties.[118] The doctrine of 'positive violation of contract' is another import from Germany that permits wider contractual liability. A positive violation is assumed in the case of the breach of an implied duty of care and protection, and such constructive duties may include the duty to respect a contracting party's financial interests (see Case 19, 'Breach of Promise'). As a consequence, these contractual actions were expanded well beyond their original limits. Nevertheless, it would appear that the Austrian Supreme Court is somewhat more hesitant than German courts to accept recoverability of pure economic loss whenever a pre-contractual duty or a duty vis à vis a third party who is within the protective effect of a contract is broken.[119]

### *Portugal's continuous resort to German sources*

Tort law in Portugal shows the deep influence of German legal thought and its negative approach to the recovery of pure economic loss. The evidence in support of this is quite clear.

---

[116] See art. 1330. Another ground for recovery arises for negligent advice or statements given by experts and others with specialized knowledge: arts. 1299, 1300. This last provision states: 'An expert is liable when he negligently gives, for a consideration, bad advice in matters of his art or science. In other cases, a person giving advice is liable only for damage which he has knowingly caused to another by giving the advice.'

[117] See W. Posch, 'Austria' in E. H. Hondius (ed.) *Precontractual Liability, Reports to the XIIIth Congress of Comparative Law* (Deventer/Boston, 1991).

[118] Posch and Schilcher, 'Introduction'. Cf. Bydlinski, 'Vertragliche Sorgfaltspflichten zugunsten Dritter', JBl 1960, 359.

[119] Posch and Schilcher, 'Introduction'.

Among the provisions devoted by the Civil Code to the *Responsabilidade civil*, the opening section (art. 483.1) reads:

Whoever, whether by wilful misconduct or by negligence, unlawfully infringes the rights of another person or any legal provision intended to safeguard the interests of others must compensate the injured party for damage arising from such violation.

Although lacking the *numerus clausus* list of protected rights, this norm is not interpreted in Portugal as a French-like general clause. Rather, article 483/1 is a somewhat misleading façade whose actual interior resembles § 823 (1) BGB. Portuguese courts and scholars recognize that in using the word 'unlawfully', Vaz Serra, the author of the 1966 code, intended to protect only 'absolute rights' and this 'legislative' intent is generally read into the provision. Accordingly, the Portuguese wrongdoer is liable, (1) when they violate an absolute right (purely financial loss is thus excluded); or (2) when the damage falls within the scope and aim of a protective statute: while the violation of a protective statute may give rise to compensation for pure economic loss, this is an exception to the general rule of no recovery. Portugal is therefore decidedly hostile to damages for this type of loss.[120]

The subjective rights doctrine in Portugal has the same scope as the absolute rights limitation in Germany. That is to say, Portuguese scholars and judges do not work out the notion of unlawfulness in an open-ended perspective. They usually handle the problem of recoverability by reference to those discrete provisions, scattered throughout the legal system, which are construed as safeguarding the particular right or interest in issue. For example, a plaintiff can recover losses stemming from the infringement of rights to personality or to business reputation, inasmuch as these rights are established by particular provisions of the Civil Code (arts. 70ff. and art. 484).[121] Or recourse could be made to article 485, which decrees liability when the defendant has 'assumed' liability for information negligently given.

Certainly, the attempt to fashion a general clause of civil liability out of article 334 (sanctioning the *Abuso do direito* along the lines of

---

[120] Consistent with the above, one can find the case law springing from art. 493/1 – imposing liability for risks arising from dangerous property real and personal – where the courts usually ground liability on specific statutory duties to prevent the given risk. See von Bar, *Law of Torts*, I, p. 35.

[121] On the right to repose (*direito ao repouso essencial à existência*), tranquillity and recovery (*à tranquillidade e ao sossego*), see the references in von Bar, *Law of Torts*, I, pp. 37, 607.

§ 826 BGB) has so far obtained only a little scholarly support;[122] and it is equally true that the scope and the nature of *culpa in contrahendo* cause of action is still disputed.[123] Nevertheless, all these imported concepts testify to the strong and long-lasting influence of German legal science in Portugal. Thus, it is hardly surprising that infringements of pure economic interests are generally not reparable unless a specific provision addresses the question, or plaintiff benefits from the existence of a pertinent protective law. Nor is it any wonder that many of the answers to the questionnaire turn out to be identical to the German solutions,[124] and that all of this is consonant with the attitude of Portuguese scholars who continually resort to German sources and concepts (including the 'contract with protective effect of third parties'[125] and the *allgemeines Lebensrisiko* argument[126]).

## Sweden and Finland: nulla injuria sine lege?

For historical reasons, the Swedish and Finnish tort façades were built upon a narrow criminal law base that sharply restrains compensation for pure economic loss. Today, the general principles are contained in the Tort Liability Act 1972 (Sweden) and in the Tort Liability Act 1974 (Finland). Until the enactment of these statutes, Swedish and Finnish private law did not have statutory rules establishing general principles of civil liability. Civil liability rested upon criminal law statutes which were applied by analogy to civil wrongs. The judiciary was very reluctant to find civil liability where a violation of criminal law was absent and furthermore, in the absence of a crime, compensation was allowed only in those cases where there was a physical damage to persons or things. Therefore, the rules of the two Tort Liability Acts regarding pure economic loss reflect the restrictive attitudes developed within the context of this historical development.

---

[122] See especially J. F. Sinde Monteiro, *Responsabilidade por conselhos, recomendações ou Informações* (Almedina, Coimbra, 1989), pp. 545–82.

[123] See the Portuguese answers under Cases 8 ('The Cancelled Cruise'), 18 ('Wrongful Job Reference'), 19 ('Breach of Promise').

[124] The few which are different are grounded either on different statutory rules (Cases 12, 'The Double Sale' – here the watershed is the German *Abstraktioprinzip*; 14, 'Poor Legal Services'; 17, 'Auditor's Liability') or on a different construction of the case by the reporter (Case 9, 'Fire in the Projection Booth', concerning a 'parasitic economic loss').

[125] See, e.g the discussion under Case 7 ('The Careless Architect').

[126] See under Case 15 ('A Closed Motorway – The Value of Time').

Chapter 2: 1 of the Swedish Tort Liability Act 1972 states the general rule of tort liability: 'Whoever causes personal injury or property damage intentionally or negligently must make reparation, unless otherwise provided herein...' This *culpa* rule restricts reparation to bodily injuries and property damage, which suggests that liability rules in Sweden and Finland are really closer to the approach of § 823 BGB than to the general clauses of the liberal regimes. However, the Tort Liability Acts go on to define pure economic loss (*ren förmögenhetsskada*) as follows: 'By pure economic loss in the Act is to be understood economic loss arising without connection to anyone's bodily injury or property damage'; and then provide a general restriction on its recovery: 'Whoever causes pure economic loss through a crime shall compensate that injury according to what is prescribed with respect to injury to the person and to property...' (*Skadeståndslag* (SKL) 2: 4).[127]

Accordingly, this form of loss ends up as an exception to the general rule. Recoverability depends upon the commission of a punishable act.[128] Only victims of a crime may, in principle, demand civil reparation for pure economic loss.[129] Nevertheless, there may still be some flexibility left in the liability system. The legislature did not intend the above provision to be treated as entirely definitive or exhaustive. There is an explanatory memorandum to the Swedish Tort Liability Act 1972 expressly stating that the wording is not intended to deter the courts from imposing liability for pure economic loss in an appropriate case, even when there is no punishable act. The aim was to give a general orientation, and not completely to forbid courts from recognizing new instances of liability.

---

[127] There is usually no recovery for third persons under these provisions since Swedish and Finnish courts have a rigid view of causation which makes a third party's economic loss seem completely disconnected from physical injury of the primary victim. See our comparative comments to Case 2 ('Cable II – Factory Shutdown').

[128] However, particular legislation in environment law, copyright law and computer law, *inter alia*, imposes such liability in special cases. See B. Bengtsson, in H. Tiberg, F. Sterzel and P. Cronhult (eds.), *Swedish Law: A Survey* (Juristförlaget, Stockholm, 1994), pp. 157–8.

[129] This 'criminal law' restriction does not apply under Danish law, and therefore difficult cases can be treated with greater flexibility than in Sweden and Finland. Of course if economic loss arises out of a crime in Denmark (e.g. fraud by a bank employee against a bank customer) nothing prevents its recovery, but Danish jurisprudence has also recognized recovery for pure economic loss in non-criminal instances, such as negligently severed power cables and incorrect information furnished by non-contracting third parties. For details, see von Bar, *Law of Torts*, I, pp. 272–4.

Landmark cases decided by the Swedish courts in 1987 and 1990 show the judiciary to be moving in this direction.[130] Accordingly, it may now be the position that compensation under the Tort Liability Act 1972 is *at the outset* available only when the economic loss is caused by a crime; however, the judge is not necessarily prevented from awarding compensation outside of the Tort Liability Act 1972 in exceptionally important situations. Beginning from the far right of the liability spectrum, the Swedish and Finnish systems seem to be moving, albeit slowly and incrementally, towards the middle.

## Conclusion

In our chapter on the liability regimes of Europe, we have attempted to set forth a coherent way of describing the various approaches of the legal systems to the issue of pure economic loss. What is then the answer to the question posed in the introduction to this chapter? The answer is that a common theoretical matrix of pure economic loss does not exist in Europe.

The ways of approaching the problem are multifarious. We find the issue absorbed within the mainstream of the general clause in the liberal regimes and, in some others, we find it driven by the fear of 'liability in an indeterminate amount for an indeterminate time to an indeterminate class'.[131] This fear is managed of course through technical devices. These are, basically, the duty of care element in the pragmatic

---

[130] See NJA 1987, p. 692; NJA 1990, p. 24. In the 1987 decision (see discussion in von Bar, *Law of Torts*, I, p. 246), a real estate valuator issued a certificate to an estate agent which negligently assessed certain property to be five times higher in value than it in fact was. (The property was valued at 4.3 million krona, but its true value was only 80,000 krona). On the strength of the certificate, the estate agent obtained a bank loan of 1 million krona, partially secured by a mortgage up to 800,000 krona. The loan proved to be unrecoverable due to the eventual bankruptcy of the borrower and the inadequacy of the security which had been given, so the bank sued the valuer for negligence and was awarded compensation. The court recognized that a third party who provides information to a contracting party, knowing that the information will be relied upon by someone else, may be liable in tort for pure economic loss sustained by the relying party, despite the fact that carelessly providing false information does not amount to a crime. From the wording of the official commentary to the *Skadeståndslag* it was clear that the Act was not intended to hinder appropriate development of liability for pure economic loss beyond the context of criminal law.

[131] *Ultramares Corp'n v. Touche* 255 NY 170 (1931) at p. 179, *per* Cardozo CJ.

regimes and the unlawfulness requirement in the conservative systems – although some of these conservative regimes seek intense 'lateral' support to the recoverability of pure economic loss through contract law rules.

However, comparative analysis of European regimes makes clear a further point. Our classification of the systems into liberal, pragmatic and conservative regimes is designed to provide a framework that the reader may use to understand how jurists of a particular country reason their way to solutions. However, these are only façades, starting points, not the end of the journey. Here, our cautionary distinction between exterior appearances and operational interiors plays a capital role. We have seen that the façades are frequently deceptive edifices that conceal a complex theoretical substructure. Indeed, the usual way of approaching legal systems' notions and rules is strongly affected by what we can call the 'façade effect', that is to say, by a (covert or explicit)[132] set of assumptions which sometimes drive the observer far away from the actual rules and rationales that one finds at work in the given legal system.

Therefore, without an in-depth factual analysis many of the actual questions raised by the pure economic loss issue are bound to receive either no answer, or only a misleading one.

[132] See Sacco, 'Legal Formants', at 21–7.

# PART II · THE COMPARATIVE EVIDENCE CASE RESPONSES AND EDITORS' COMPARATIVE COMMENTS

# 6 Preliminary remarks on methodology

MAURO BUSSANI AND VERNON VALENTINE PALMER

## Aim and method of the study

The general purpose of this study is to inquire to what extent, if any, there exists a common core of principles and rules concerning compensation for pure economic loss within European tort law.

Being a research branch of the 'Common Core Project', our study shares with the latter its basic aims and methodology. For this reason the collective inquiry has been carried out on the basis of a factual approach and the most important tool of the research has been a fact-based questionnaire. In 1995, at a general meeting of the Common Core Project in Trento, Italy, the editors worked with a group of tort scholars from various parts of Europe to devise a questionnaire consisting of twenty fact situations, each to be solved or answered under the laws, codes and doctrines of one country. A team of national reporters was then assembled and began work on the project. It was our intent that every country in the European Union would be covered; however, as it proved impossible to obtain reporters for Denmark, Luxembourg and Ireland, the current study covers eleven national systems plus England and Scotland.

To make clear how the general methodological framework of the project has been exploited and adapted to the needs of our research, we first discuss: (1) the advantages and efficiencies of the 'Common Core' approach; (2) the reasons for adopting a three-level response.

## The common core approach

Stating it in very simple terms, we are seeking to unearth what is already common, if anything, in the tort law of EU Member States as to compensation for pure economic loss. Such a common core seems to us worth revealing in order to obtain at least the main outlines of a reliable geographical map of that specific field in the law of Europe.

Indeed, for the transnational lawyer the present European situation is as that of a traveller compelled to use a number of different local maps, and each one could contain misleading information. We wish to eliminate this misleading information. We do not wish to force an actually diverse legal reality into one single map simply for the sake of uniformity.

Our specific enterprise, like the general project from which it stems, seeks to find the common features of the 'pure economic loss' law in European national systems, but the goal is not to impose new rules and categories. Echoing the declaratory theory fashionable among common lawyers since Blackstone, 'the emphasis is not so much to create uniform rules as to find similar solutions and rules in the existing laws (and if they cannot be found, to state the differences) and to analyze and compare the legal reasoning behind them...'[1]

It is true that through the use of the comparative method many common features that remained obscure in traditional legal analysis of the field may be unearthed. But this is because the instruments and techniques provide more accurate and correct analysis, not because they force convergence where this does not exist. It is also true that a 'common core' research may be a useful instrument for legal harmonization, in the sense that it provides reliable data to be used in devising new common solutions that may prove workable in practice. But this has nothing to do with the common core research in itself, which is simply devoted to producing reliable information.

This strongly differentiates our project from any Restatement-like enterprise.[2] The latter involves the pursuit of rationality, harmony and

---

[1] W. van Gerven, 'Casebooks for the Common Law of Europe: Presentation of the Project', (1996) 4 *European Review of Private Law* 67, 69.

[2] There are other projects underway in Europe as well. One worth mentioning is the notable project called 'Study Group on a European Civil Code' directed by Professor von Bar. This is an initiative that was set up by European scholars in the aftermath of the 1997 Scheveningen Conference, 'Towards a European Civil Code'. The aim of the group is 'to abstract, through highly detailed analysis covering all jurisdictions in the European Union, fundamental rules for the European patrimonial law. The intention is not to create a draft for a European Civil Code; not only because the project is only concerned with a part of the subject matter which would be covered by a Civil Code, but also because the creation of a Civil Code is a political goal...The work is aimed at providing the basic research on principles necessary to lay the groundwork for the drawing up of a European Civil Code.' As to the structure, at present three working groups consisting of young researchers from all or most of the EU Member States have been created, under the direction of Professors Drobnig and Basedow (Hamburg), von

reform ideals, and this task implies the selection of the legal rules and materials that are best suited for the task. What does not fit in the Restatement-like framework is discarded. This is anathema from an analytical perspective such as ours. The very fact that rules and materials exist in a legal system requires that they be taken into consideration in the analysis and become part of the final 'map'.

All of the above allows us also to stress the differences between our study and other research projects, such as the ongoing efforts to create a series of European Law casebooks. The authors of the casebook project indicate that they wish

> to uncover common general principles which are already present in the living law of the European countries... [and] rather than setting up a European law school, teaching materials are developed which can be used in such a law school, and in the curricula of *other* law schools as well, and by courts looking for rules and principles to decide a case, throughout Europe.[3]

This description of the casebook project indicates that there are important similarities with our project, in the sense that they are both analytical, not openly prescriptive, and intend to consider the common features of private law in European national systems. However, what differentiates the two studies lies in their target and their method. Our project is aimed at scholars while the casebook project is aimed at students.[4] Producing suitable materials for didactic purposes implies that an accurate choice must be made of materials that will provide students with the elements needed to understand legal systems different from their

---

Bar (Osnabrück), Hondius, Barendrecht and Hesselink (Utrecht/Tilburg/Amsterdam). The Hamburg group is working on secured transactions (personal securities, securities in movables and account receivables, reservation of title) and insurance; the Osnabrück group on 'non-contractual' obligations (tort law, restitution, *negotiorum gestio*) and the Utrecht/Tilburg/Amsterdam group on contract law (sale and services). See A. Hartkamp, 'Perspective for the Development of a European Civil Code', in M. Bussani and U. Mattei (eds.), *Making European Law: Essays on the 'Common Core' Project* (Quaderni del Dipartimento di Scienze Giuridiche, Trento, 2000) at pp. 39, 52 ff. The 'Study Group' itself maintains a close connection with an analogous initiative, directed by Professors Spier and Koziol, which is in the process of elaborating the 'Principles of European Tort Law'. See J. Spier (ed.), *The Limits of Liability: Keeping the Floodgates Shut* (Kluwer, The Hague, 1996); J. Spier (ed.), *The Limits of Expanding Liability: Eight Fundamental Cases in a Comparative Perspective* (Kluwer, The Hague, 1998); H. Koziol (ed.), *Unification of Tort Law: Wrongfulness* (Kluwer, The Hague, 1998); U. Magnus (ed.), *Unification of Tort Law: Damages* (Kluwer, The Hague, 2001).

[3] W. van Gerven, 'Casebooks', 67, 68.
[4] Professor van Gerven, in a private communication to the authors, stresses that 'the target group has never been university students in the strict sense of the word but all "students of the law" in the broad sense that is including teachers, judges, practitioners and all those who... study the law continuously'.

own. Making this selection is the province of academics. In fact, the idea of these scholars is not only to collect cases but other materials as well, including legislation and scholarly writings, particularly short notes situating the other legal materials in their context.[5] Ultimately, the goal is to provide students with a grasp of foreign law while educating them as common European lawyers.

Our project may also provide some useful materials for teaching purposes, but this is not its primary task. It investigates a more specific area, delving in depth into technical problems. Hence, it may facilitate understanding and communication between professional lawyers already grounded in their own legal tradition, as opposed to prospective common European lawyers. Furthermore, our project focuses equally on all the European systems under review and, unlike the casebook project, places no emphasis on systems that are, or could be, considered to be leading or paradigmatic systems.

## The three-level response

The preliminary problem we had to resolve was how to obtain comparable answers to the questions that we wished to pose about different legal systems. The answers had to refer to identical questions interpreted as

---

[5] This project was first proposed at a conference organized at the University of Maastricht in 1991 on 'The Common Law of Europe and the Future of Legal Education'. Among the members of the steering committee are W. van Gerven, B. De Witte, T. Koopmans, and H. Kötz. The example of the United States has inspired the enterprise. In spite of the many marked differences among the laws of individual states, US legal education is based on a single national model which produces lawyers able to move from state to state without insurmountable difficulties. See, e.g. L. M. Friedman and G. Teubner, 'Legal Education and Legal Integration: European Hopes and American Experience', in M. Cappelletti, M. Seccombe and J. Weiler (eds.), *Integration Through Law: Europe and the American Federal Experience* (De Gruyter, Berlin, 1986), pp. 345, 351. See also P. Larouche, '*Ius Commune* Casebooks for the Common Law of Europe: Presentation, Progress, Rationale', (2000) 8 *European Review of Private Law* 101. The first books produced with this method are W. van Gerven, J. Lever and P. Larouche et al. (eds.), *Tort Law: Scope of Protection* (Hart, Oxford, 1998); W. van Gerven, J. Lever and P. Larouche (eds.) *Tort Law* (Hart, Oxford, 2000). The group has selected a number of subjects suitable for the study of common core principles: constitutional and administrative law, contracts, torts, conflict of laws, company and economic law, criminal law and social law. Though the casebooks aim also to show the impact of supranational law, both EC/EU law and ECHR law, on the national legal systems – and in that sense wish to help to find, as art. 288 (ex 215) para. 2 EC Treaty requires the ECJ to do, 'general principles common to the laws of the Member States' (see particularly chapter 9 of van Gerven et al., *Tort Law* (2000) at pp. 889 ff.) – the casebooks themselves will mainly concentrate on the English, French and German systems, including materials from other European systems only if they provide original solutions.

identically as possible by all the respondents. Besides, the answers had to be self-sufficient in two ways. First, they had to be complete answers: additional explanations should not be required. The level of specificity to be expected, therefore, was to be on a par with the most detailed rules. Secondly, they had to be authoritative answers which could be accepted at 'face value'. The editors would therefore refrain from superimposing their own views upon the scenario depicted by the national contributors.

To obtain consistency, after lengthy discussions within the working group, each hypothetical case was formulated with the view of taking account of any relevant circumstance occurring in any of the legal systems under consideration, so that these circumstances would be considered in – and therefore become comparable with – the analysis of every other system.

In this way another important objective was achieved. Often, the circumstances that operate explicitly and officially in one system are officially ignored and considered to be irrelevant in another system and yet, in that other system, they operate secretly, slipping in silently between the formulation of the rule and its application by the courts. Thus, one of the special features of our work is that it has made jurists think explicitly about the circumstances that matter, by forcing them to answer identically formulated questions, and asking them about the results that would be reached in particular cases, not about a doctrinal system. As a result, the responses may have given a picture of the law which is substantially different from the one usually found in the monographs, handbooks or casebooks circulating in their own country.

Indeed, what we learned from the methodology of Rudolf Schlesinger and Rodolfo Sacco is that, in order to have complete knowledge of a country's law, we cannot trust entirely what the jurists say, for there may be wide gaps between operative rules and the rules commonly stated.

A list, even an exhaustive one, of all the reasons given for the decisions made by the courts is not the entire law. The statutes are not the entire law. Neither are the definitions given by scholarly writings. In order to know what the law is, it is necessary to analyse the entire complex relationship between the so-called 'legal formants' of a system, i.e. all those formative elements that make any given rule of law amidst statutes, general propositions, particular definitions, reasons, holdings, and so forth.[6] All of these formative elements are not necessarily coherent with each

---

[6] See R. Sacco, 'Legal Formants: A Dynamic Approach to Comparative Law', (1991) 39 *American Journal of Comparative Law* 1.

other within each system, even though domestic jurists usually assume such coherence. On the contrary, legal formants are normally in conflict and can be pictured in a competitive relationship with one another.

However, all this may still be insufficient to understand the law in a given system. Statutes or code provisions in a national system can overlap with the provisions enacted in other systems, and yet be applied differently (compare, for example, the opposite results reached under art. 1382 of the French Code Civil with those reached under mirror-image language in art. 1295, s. 1 of the Austrian ABGB).[7] The reverse may also be true. Provisions or general definitions in two systems can differ but operative rules still reach the same results. In this respect, the Austrian and German codes, so textually dissonant yet operationally equivalent, afford a good example.[8]

A full understanding of what the legal formants are and how they relate to each other allows us to ascertain the factors that affect solutions, making clear the weight that interpretative practices (grounded on scholarly writings, on legal debate aroused by previous judicial decision, etc.) have in moulding the actual outcomes. Hence, the notion of legal formant is more than an esoteric neologism for the traditional distinction between 'loi', 'jurisprudence' and 'doctrine', i.e. between enacted law, case law and scholarly writings. Within a given legal system, the legal rule is not uniform, not only because one rule may be given by case law, one by scholars and one by statutes. Within each of these sources there are also formants competing with one another. For example, the rule described in the headnotes of a case can be inconsistent with the actual rationale of the decision, or the definition in a code can be inconsistent with the detailed rules contained in the code itself.[9] This complex dynamic may change considerably from one legal system to another, as well as from one area of the law to another. In particular, in each legal system certain legal formants are clearly leading in a different way – the differences in formants' leadership are particularly clear in the (traditional) distinction between common law and civil law.[10]

Given the factual methodology that we have adopted, it should be clear why our research cannot be regarded as a mere collection of

---

[7] See above, Part I, Chapter 5 and the French and Austrian answers to the questionnaire.
[8] See above, Part I, Chapter 5 and the Austrian and German answers to the questionnaire.
[9] See Sacco, 'Legal Formants', 1, at 21–7.
[10] As regards this topic, the state-of-art is delineated by U. Mattei, *Comparative Law and Economics* (University of Michigan Press, Ann Arbor, 1997), p. 69 ff.

decided cases. The data highlight differences as well as similarities in the national laws yet remain neutral as to the research uses to which it may be put.

As a general guideline, we have drafted our questionnaire with a sufficient degree of specificity so as to require the reporter's answers to address all the factors in his or her system which have practical impact on the operative rules. This is our best guarantee that rules formulated in an identical way (by an identical code provision, for example), but which may produce different applications, or even different doctrinal rhetoric, were not regarded as identical. This has also allowed us to expose the elements that play an official and declared role in one system, versus those that play a more cryptic, unsystematic and unofficial role in another system – the role of such cryptic elements being crucial of course when drafting the map of the applied law.[11] As previously mentioned, these considerations were particularly important because the systems within our study belong to the common law as well as to the civil law tradition. The structure of the judicial process and the 'style' of the legal system (in the broad sense described by Zweigert and Kötz and John Merryman)[12] could not be neglected if we were to obtain correct results. It is indeed in the structure of the legal process, which municipal lawyers take as given, that most of the differences can be detected, understood and possibly explained.[13]

All this hopefully leads one to understand why we asked every contributor to set up her or his answers on three levels, labelled I.'Operative Rules', II.'Descriptive Formants' and III.'Metalegal Formants'. In the interest of readability we have taken these working titles out of the responses; nevertheless we have left intact the inner structure of each response. Thus the three levels are maintained and are now simply indicated by the division of the responses into paragraphs marked I, II and III.

The level dealing with 'Operative Rules' is designed to be a concise summary. The reporters were asked to summarize the basic applicable rules and to state the outcome of the case that would be reached under national law. Reporters were also asked to indicate whether the

---

[11] See R. Sacco, 'Comparazione giuridica e conoscenza del dato giuridico positivo', in R. Sacco (ed.), *L'apporto della comparazione alla scienza giuridica* (1980), p. 241 .
[12] K. Zweigert and H. Kötz, *Introduction to Comparative Law* (3rd edn, trans. T. Weir, Clarendon, Oxford, 1998), pp. 63 ff.; J. H. Merryman, *The Civil Law Tradition: An Introduction to the Legal Systems of Western Europe and Latin America* (2nd edn, 1985).
[13] The participants in our project are comparativists, and were asked to deal with the questionnaires as comparativists.

reasoning and outcome would be considered clear and undisputed or only doubtful and problematic.

The level called 'Descriptive Formants' has a twofold goal. On the one hand, the aim is to reveal the reasons which lawyers feel obliged to give in support of the 'operative rules', and the extent to which the various solutions are consistent either with specific and general legislative provisions, or with general principles (traditional as well as emerging ones). Therefore, the reporter was obliged to investigate how the hypothetical case has been solved by case law in the given legal system; whether this is or is not the solution given by the other legal formants; whether all these formants are concordant, both from an internal point of view (the source of disaccord may be minority doctrines, including dissenting opinions in leading cases, opposite opinions in scholarly writings, etc.) and from a diachronic point of view whether the various solutions are recent achievements or were identical in the past; whether the solution is considered to be a question of fact or a question of law. The latter factor may determine not only the degree to which the solution can be enforced by supreme courts against lower courts, but also the impact of judicial precedent on the solution. On the other hand, the goal at this level is to understand whether the solution depends on legal rules and/or institutions outside private law, such as procedural rules (including rules of evidence), administrative or constitutional provisions.

Finally, the level 'Metalegal Formants' asks for a clear picture of the other elements affecting the operative and descriptive levels, such as policy considerations, economic factors, social context and values, as well as the structure of the legal process (organization of courts, administrative structure, etc.): this kind of data the researcher can never leave out whenever the aim is to understand what the law is.[14]

The following case studies cannot be dissociated then from the techniques by which our information and insights have been produced.

---

[14] As sometimes happens in collective enterprises such as this one, not each and every national reporter has perfectly abided by the guidelines that we established at the outset of the project. Nevertheless, there is, we believe, broad enough compliance in most cases to produce the advantages for which we had hoped.

# 7 The case studies

## National Reporters and the Editors

*Austria:* Willibald Posch and Bernd Schilcher
*Belgium:* Jean-Marc Trigaux
*England:* Estathios Banakas
*France:* Vernon Valentine Palmer and Christel de Noblet
*Germany:* Mathias Reimann
*Greece:* Kostas Christodoulou
*Italy:* Pier Giuseppe Monateri and Alberto Musy
*Portugal:* Jorge Sinde Monteiro
*Scotland:* Joseph Thomson and Lloyd Embleton
*Spain:* Pedro del Olmo and Fernando Pantaleón
*Sweden and Finland:* Alessandro Simoni
*The Netherlands:* Willem van Boom

## Comparative Commentary

Mauro Bussani and Vernon Valentine Palmer

## Case 1: cable I – the blackout

### Case

While manoeuvring his mechanical excavator, an employee of the Acme road works company cut the cable belonging to the public utility which delivers electricity to the Beta factory. The unexpected blackout caused damage to the machinery and the loss of two days of production. The factory owner is claiming compensation from the excavator not only for the damage of machinery but also for the damage caused by the loss of production.

## France

I. In French law, the factory owner would recover his property loss and his pure economic loss from Acme's employee or Acme itself, under articles 1382–1384.

Since there is no privity of contract between Beta and Acme, French courts would consider this a tort action and apply articles 1382 to 1384 CC. According to those articles, the factory, Beta, will be able to sue either the employee of Acme who cut the cable (under arts. 1382–1383) or the employer itself, Acme (under art. 1384 alinea 5).

II. In the case of suit brought against the employer or employee, the court will ask plaintiff to prove three factors: a fault on the part of the employee, the damage sustained by plaintiff and a causal link between the two. Recovery of pure economic loss in a very similar situation was confirmed by the Cour de Cassation in 1970. A bulldozer operated by an entrepreneur's worker broke a methane gas line which provided energy to the plaintiff's factory. Plaintiff's business sustained production losses due to the interruption of its activities. The Cour d'Appel ruled that plaintiff's case was well founded under article 1382 (fault liability) and article 1384 (strict liability) and held that plaintiff's economic loss was a 'direct consequence' of the ruptured gas line. The Cour de Cassation confirmed that this decision was well grounded.[1] The above case clearly indicates that French courts do award pure economic loss and not simply economic damage which is ancillarily derived from other physical loss.

The court may find the requisite fault on the part of the employee if there is a substandard behaviour (here the negligent cutting of the cable). The causal link between the fault and the injury must also be proved, and this may be the very part of the analysis where the pure economic loss issue is tested. Furthermore, French courts have permitted recovery of this type of damage claim where there was privity of contract between the parties, granting recovery where the cut-off of electrical power caused damage to plaintiff's computer database and thereby entailed a loss of production.[2] From a causal standpoint, the damage sought by Beta factory would not seem to become tenuous or remotely connected just because recovery is sought in tort. Indeed, to the contrary, doctrine supports the argument that tort law encompasses wider causation than contract law.

---

[1] Civ. 2e, 8 mai 1970, Bull. Civ. II 1970, no. 160.
[2] Trib. Com. Paris, 23 octobre 1989, JCP 1990.II.21573, note Plaisant.

III. The loss of production and damage to machinery both fall indifferently under the category of *dommages matériels*. There is no question that these damages are real and legitimate. Perhaps the real question is whether the loss of production is sufficiently direct and whether the causal link is considered *adéquat*. It has to be remembered that the *juges de fond* have not received clear rules about causation from the Cour de Cassation and they appear to have room for manoeuvre and vacillation upon the causal determination. Furthermore the Cour de Cassation has no control over the quantification of damages (*appréciation souveraine des juges du fond*). This finds illustration in the case of a strike that caused economic loss to a factory. The lower courts decided that the conditions for art. 1382 were fulfilled, but they merely awarded nominal damages. The plaintiff appealed to the Cour de Cassation which answered that it could not review the amount of the damages discretionarily set by the first judges.[3]

## Belgium

I. The Beta factory can recover both for damage to its machinery and for the loss of two days of production.

II. Liability: according to article 27 of the Belgian Law of 10 March 1925 on Distribution of Electric Energy, one who by lack of precaution has destroyed devices for the production, transformation, distribution and use of electric energy, or has prevented the transport of such energy, will be punished under article 563 of the Belgian Criminal Code.[4]

The negligence of the Acme employee is therefore a criminal offence.

According to article 1382 CC, Acme's employee shall therefore normally be liable towards the Beta Factory for the damage caused to its machinery and for the loss of two days of production.

However, according to article 18 of the Belgian Law of 3 July 1978 on Employment Contracts,

in case of damage caused by the employee to the employer or to third parties during the course of the performance of the employment contract, the employee will only be liable if he committed a gross fault or an intentional fault. He will be liable for his negligence only if this negligence is usual instead of accidental.

Whether the fault of the Acme's employee be intentional, gross or negligence, the Acme company will be liable for the damage caused to

---

[3] Soc., 16 juin 1993, arrêt no. 2286, pourvoi no. 91.15.292, Lexis.
[4] Trib. Civ. Louvain, 16 mars 1995, p. 394 and note P. Bauwens.

the machinery of the Beta company and for the loss of the two days of production by application of article 1384, al. 3 CC.

Each one is liable not only for the damage which he caused by his own act, but also for that which is caused by the act of persons for whom he is responsible, or by things which he has in his keeping.
[…]
Masters and principals are liable for damage caused by their domestics and employees in the function for which they have been employed.
[…]

Damage to machinery: if the damage to the machinery would not have occurred if the cable which delivered electricity had not been cut by the Acme employee, the Beta factory will be allowed to recover the damage to the machinery.

If the machinery can be repaired, the recoverable damage will be equivalent to the costs for repairing. However, if these costs are superior to the costs for replacing the machinery and if such replaced machinery is normally available, the recoverable damage will be limited to the costs for replacing the machinery.

Loss of two days of production: if the Beta factory can prove that it would not have lost two days of production if the cable which delivered electricity had not been cut by the Acme employee and that the profit resulting from these two days of production was certain, it shall recover this loss of profit.

## Italy

I. The Beta factory can recover both the damage to its machinery and the loss of two days of production.

II. First, we have to point out that excavation is considered as a dangerous activity under prevalent case law.[5]

Dangerous activity falls under article 2050 cc which renders a person liable who cannot show that they adopted all measures to avoid the damage which occurred:

*Article 2050: Liability for dangerous activities*

Whoever causes injury to another in the performance of an activity dangerous by its nature or by reason of the instrumentalities employed, is liable for damages, unless he proves that he has taken all suitable measures to avoid the injury.

According to article 1223 cc, the compensation of damages includes both the consequential damage (*damnum emergens*) and lost profits

[5] Cass. 12 dicembre 1988, no. 6739, *MGC*, 1988; Cass. 24.11.1971, no. 3415, *MGC* 1971.

(*lucrum cessans*), when these are direct and immediate consequences of the non-performance of an obligation:

*Article 1223: Measures of damages*

The measure of damages arising from non-performance or delay shall include the loss sustained by the creditor and the lost profits insofar as they are a direct and immediate consequence of the non-performance or delay.

However, the compensation cannot include damages that the creditor could have avoided through ordinary diligence.

The requirement of direct and immediate consequence is a feature of the general principle of causation. It is justified by the need to impose a limit upon remote and indirect consequences, thereby avoiding the danger that 'through a series of causality links, the final compensation can assume excessive and, therefore, unjust proportions'.[6]

We have to establish in this factual situation to what extent the physical damage to the machinery is a direct consequence of the breach of obligation. In order to receive compensation, damage must be certain and concrete. Certainty means that damage must not have an hypothetical existence, even if some degree of uncertainty may exist as far as its final qualification is concerned. Concrete existence implies that the damage has to be connected to the injury of a legal right claimed by the creditor. Case law subsequent to the *Meroni* decision permits recovery of damages for violation of contractual obligations and considers the creditor as possessing a legal right.

Loss of production caused by the interruption of the electricity supply is then easily recoverable under the flexible interpretation which doctrine and case law gives to article 1223 cc. The damage to the machinery is a typical case of injury to property that is recoverable even under the traditional and rigid interpretation of article 2043 cc.

Courts have considered compensation for loss of profits in the following contexts: interference with the use of an asset, interference with specific contractual relationships and the loss of professional reputation.

The case at hand is covered by *Puddu*[7] and *Enel* v. *Ditta Giampaoli*[8] which are the oldest cases matching these facts. Ditta Giampaoli cut a cable delivering energy to a factory while operating an excavator. The court held that Enel (the state-owned Italian electricity producer) was not

---

[6] Cass. 21.10.1969, no. 3438, *FI*, 1970, I, 501; Cass., 2.1.1968, no. 253, *FI*, 1968, I, 2628.
[7] Cass. 24.6.1972, no. 2135, *FI*, 1973, I, 99.
[8] App. Ancona, 23.11.1982, RGEnel, 1982, 747; for a similar case see the recent decision by Cass. 15.5.1999, in *DR*, 2000, 2, 167, noted by A. M. Musy, 'Taglio di cavi elettrici: il danno meramente patrimoniale'.

liable for breach of contract and that Giampaoli was liable for negligence in tort for all the economic losses due to the factory's blackout. This ruling was based on the broad principle of articles 2043 and 2050 cc, as commonly interpreted after *Meroni*.

In a Turin First Instance case – *Enel* v. *Borio* – the court held an excavator liable, for he did not inquire about the underground cable configuration before beginning excavation activity.[9]

III. Judicial interpretation given to the dangerous activity provision (art. 2050 cc) is now under critique for imposing an excessively broad liability on excavation activity. The burden of proof is so heavy that authors speak of quasi-strict liability.[10]

Using law and economic tools, some scholars are now focusing their attention on the problem of inefficiency in a system where the damaged party does not have enough incentive to invest in precautionary measures. An analysis which favours application of comparative negligence to these situations may lead to some adjustment in the present case law. What if the damaged party did not give enough information about the location of the subsoil wires?[11]

## Spain

I. In Spanish law the Beta factory can recover the total amount of damages. This result is quite clear.

II. In Spanish case law, many claims have arisen in which a cable or other type of underground conduit is cut during the execution of works. Most of these cases are not applicable to the present issue, however, because the plaintiff is the company who owns the cable or conduit.[12] It should be pointed out, however, that in the outcome of these cases the plaintiff is compensated both for damage to the cable as well as lost profits derived from the cut. (For example, it is very common for the telephone company to receive compensation for conference calls

---

[9] Trib. Torino, 31.5.1978, RGEnel, 1979, 379.
[10] S. Mannina, 'La responsabilità civile dell'esercente un'attività di escavazione in caso di danni a cavi sotterranei', note under App. Roma, 12.7.1995, *T Romana*, 1996, 643. Trib. Torino, 31.5.1978, RGEnel, 1979, 379.
[11] The point has been raised in a recent decision *Vecchio* v. *Telecom Italia SpA:* Cass. 23.8.1999, no. 8838, DR, 2000, 512. The note to the decision wonders about the inefficient effect that such a decision will have on the allocation of damages, see A. M. Musy, L. Zambelli, ' "Cable cutting" all'italiana. Ipotesi di concorso di colpa del danneggiato per omissione di informativa'.
[12] Supreme Court decisions delivered by the First Chamber, of 7.10.66, 25.1.68, 9.11.73, 29.3.82, 10.2.84, 16.5.84, 20.6.84, 3.7.84, 16.7.84, amongst many others.

that could not be made during the time the damaged cable was being repaired).

The Supreme Court decisions of 4 May 1982 and 18 September 1984 (both delivered by the First Chamber) offer more information on the problems of this case. In the first decision, the plaintiff was left without electricity when a high voltage cable was severed during an excavation project to construct an oil duct. The contracting and planning company, as well as the construction company, were held jointly and severally liable for damages suffered by the plaintiff, including interruption of factory production. The Supreme Court thus imposes liability upon those in charge of the excavation for the damage suffered by the factory. However, the Supreme Court granted the factory owner a lump sum, without breaking down the categories of damage, leaving it unclear as to what extent lost profits due to the halt in production were taken into account.

The Supreme Court decision of 18 September 1984 is not as interesting because the party, who in fact suffered loss of production due to a lack of electrical supply (an industrial company), also owned the cable which was cut. Furthermore, the company which caused the break in the cable during the street surfacing works was found not to be liable because it had been diligent in obtaining previous information on the location of the cable, but the cable was not laid on the spot indicated in the plans.

Legal scholars have not commented on these decisions. However, in the present case, problems will arise when setting the amount of compensation because of the Supreme Court's requirement that the damage be certain, as well as its reluctance to grant compensation for lost profits, especially in its oldest decisions.[13]

## Greece

I. Beta has the right to be fully compensated directly against Acme and its employee.

II. Since his negligence is proved,[14] the Acme employee has committed a tort, because the law prohibits any damage to the property of another

---

[13] See, for example, the Supreme Court decision 22.6.67. On the requirement that lost profits be 'certain', see, for example, J. Puig Brutau, *Fundamentos de derecho civil*, vol. II (3rd edn, Bosch, Barcelona, 1983), p. 183.

[14] The burden of proof of the fault of the wrongdoer is borne by the plaintiff, according to the general procedural rule that the burden of proof lies with the plaintiff. However, we can assume the following: it is most probable that the employee had no intention of harming the cables (as there was no reason for him to do so). So the damage is probably due to his negligence. Negligence is defined by art. 330 CC as the

person (such as the cables of a public utility belonging to the state or the city).

Therefore the employee is liable to compensate Beta, according to article 914 CC. It does not matter that Beta is a third party, not the one initially harmed. Greek law does not restrict the parties who are entitled to claim compensation for damages. It suffices that there is causal relation between the damage and the tort (the cutting of the cables). Causation is certain in view of both criteria proposed for testing it, either the foreseeability of the particular damage,[15] or whether the damage is part of the interests protected by the legal rule that the wrongdoer infringed.[16] Actually, we can easily presume that the purpose of the rule protecting real property is mainly to defend the owner's interests, as well as the ones usually (i.e. foreseeably) related to them. Thus, in view of both these criteria, the damage to electric machinery as well as the economic loss from its uselessness are typical risks of destroying public utility cables. So this type of interest is protected by the legislative prohibition of harm to the public property (see art. 382a Penal Code).

Acme is also tortiously liable for its employee's act, because according to article 922 CC, everyone is liable for the unlawful behaviour of his servants.

Thus Beta has the right to be fully compensated by Acme, as well as by its employee. According to article 926 CC, they are co-debtors in a joint and several obligation owed to Beta.

III. In Greece, damage to public utility cables usually occurs because of negligence by the Greek Public Power Corporation (a monopoly), not

> non-exercise of care, which business practice requires. Here it is clear that business practice requires that the operator of an excavator should take all the necessary measures in order not to harm underground public property. Whether, of course, the particular employee actually took these measures is a matter of proof; however, as there were no exceptional circumstances under which the accident took place, it is most probable that it was the excavator's user who did not exercise the necessary care to avoid the damage. This kind of consideration is called a 'prima facie' proof of negligence.

[15] AP 692/1990 NoB 40, 67; AP 1063/90; AP 979/92 ElD 35, 1044; K. Triantaphyllopoulos, *Law of Obligations* (Athens, 1935), p. 184; G. Balis, *Law of Obligations, General Part* (3rd edn, 1960), p. 100; A. Ligeropoulos (gen. ed.), *Interpretation of the Civil Code (A Commentary)* (ErmAK) (1949–1978), arts. 297–300 CC, no. 39; G. Fourkiotis, *Greek Law of Obligations*, p. 318; G. Michaélidès-Nouaros, *General Part* (1964), p. 31, etc.

[16] 'Theory of the protective purpose of the legal rule', *Law of Obligations* (1959) A. Georgiades and M. Stathopoulos, *Civil Code, Article by Article Commentary*, vols. II–IV (1979–1982), Commentary by M. Stathopoulos arts. 297–298, no. 67, 60–5; P. Sourlas, *Adaequanztheorie und Normzwecklehre bei der Begruendung der Haftung nach § Abs 1. BGB* (1974), pp. 15 ff.

because of third parties. However, it is obvious that in any case the injured party may claim compensation, both for its initial material damage and for consequential loss of profits. This has been accepted by several court decisions (see AP 1/1997,[17] which orders the Greek Public Power Corporation to pay compensation even for the loss of profits caused by a fire).

### England

I. The Beta factory owner can recover the cost of repair of the damaged machinery, and for the loss of profit which it would have obtained from the use of the damaged machine in processing material which was actually damaged by the shutdown. However, Beta would not recover the profit it would have made had it been able to process undamaged material during the two-day period.

II. Damage to machinery: Beta's action will be in negligence. Liability under the tort of negligence depends on proof by the plaintiff of the following:

(1) that he suffered damage recognized as recoverable by the law of negligence; property damage is clearly so recognized: see the identical case of *Spartan Steel v. Martin*;[18]

(2) that the defendant owed him a duty of care (*Donoghue v. Stevenson*).[19] If the Acme employee knew, or ought to have reasonably foreseen, the presence of the cable, he owed a duty of care to all persons in the vicinity which he ought to foresee might be physically affected in their person or property, by the rupture of the cable and the ensuing power cut: see, again, *Spartan Steel v. Martin*;[20]

(3) that the defendant breached his duty on the facts: the Acme employee had breached his duty, if he had failed to take the care of a reasonable excavator in similar circumstances; and

(4) that there was a causal link between the breach of the duty and the plaintiff's damage: legal causation depends on foreseeability of the *kind* of harm actually suffered (*The Wagon Mound*[21]). Beta must show that a reasonable person in the position of the Acme employee was able to foresee physical damage to property as a likely consequence of the power cut.

Loss of two days of production: assuming that the loss of production was production lost during the shutdown of the machinery for necessary repairs, and it was not loss of materials being processed when the

[17] AP1/1994 NoB 46, 17.   [18] [1973] 1 QB 27 (CA).   [19] [1932] AC 562.
[20] [1973] 1 QB 27 (CA).   [21] [1961] AC 388 (PC).

machinery came to a halt, it is a loss of production not recoverable in negligence: *Spartan Steel* v. *Martin*.[22] Neither is there a duty of care to protect against such loss: again, *Spartan Steel* v. *Martin*.[23] On the other hand it is clear from *Spartan Steel* and *SCM (UK) Ltd* v. *W. J. Whittall & Son*[24] that if the shutdown actually damaged materials then being processed, Beta would be entitled to the profits to be made from these materials.

III. Both the issue of what damage is recognized as recoverable in the tort of negligence, and the issue of when there exists a duty of care not to cause harm, are now clearly issues to be decided on a case-by-case basis, on the grounds of what the courts consider to be 'just, fair and reasonable': *Murphy* v. *Brentwood DC*,[25] or, as Lord Denning put it in *Spartan Steel* v. *Martin*, on grounds of 'legal policy'. This creates uncertainty, but is thought to give the system the necessary flexibility to screen out economic loss claims that, in the opinion of the judiciary, make bad political, social and economic sense.[26] *Murphy* confirmed beyond doubt the ruling in *Spartan Steel* that the loss of production is, as a matter of policy, not recoverable.

### Scotland

I. The Beta factory owner is not able to recover damages for that element of the loss of production which has merely resulted from the loss of an electricity supply for two days. He is unlikely to be able to recover the cost of the damage to the machinery and any consequential loss of production which flowed from that physical damage.

II. The leading Scottish case in this area is *Dynamco Ltd* v. *Holland and Hannen and Cubitts (Scotland) Ltd*[27] which concerned a similar factual scenario but in which no physical damage occurred to any of the pursuer's property. In the later Outer House (of the Court of Session) case of *Coleridge* v. *Miller Construction Ltd*[28] Lord MacLean summarized the *Dynamco* judgment as follows:

The court, both in the Outer and Inner Houses [of the Court of Session], rejected the pursuers' claim on the ground that, according to the law of Scotland, no one could recover damages for financial loss which did not arise directly from damage to his own property.[29]

---

[22] [1973] 1 QB 27 (CA).   [23] Ibid.
[24] [1971] 1 QB 137, [1970] 3 All ER 245.   [25] [1991] 1 AC 398 (HL).
[26] Full discussion of the policy of English law in cases of pure economic loss in E. K. Banakas, *Civil Liability for Pure Economic Loss* (Kluwer, The Hague, 1996), chs. 1 and 2.
[27] 1972 SLT 38, 1971 SC 257.   [28] 1997 SLT 485.
[29] Ibid, at p. 487L. *Dynamco* will be considered also in the answer to Case 2 ('Cable II – Factory Shutdown') below.

In *Coleridge*, Lord MacLean was confronted with the Case 1 ('Cable I – The Blackout') scenario of loss through, and consequent upon, actual physical damage (though of a secondary nature) to the pursuer's property. He held that the loss was not recoverable, even though physical damage had occurred. Having adopted the approach of Lord Steyn in the *Marc Rich* case that it was 'settled law that the elements of foreseeability and proximity as well as considerations of fairness, justice and reasonableness are relevant to all cases whatever the nature of the harm sustained by the plaintiff',[30] he resisted the argument that in cases of physical damage to property, the only requirement was proof of reasonable foreseeability of harm. It followed that the pursuer failed on two grounds.

First, knowledge being relevant to the question of proximity and remoteness, there was no averment that the defenders knew the nature of the pursuer's business and that it was essential for him to receive a constant and uninterrupted supply of electricity. This is a question of fact and, as Lord Cameron observed in *Dynamco*,[31] it can be appreciated that different considerations would come into play if the defender were actually intending to carry out work on a cable rather than merely encountering one while engaged in some other operation. Lord MacLean observed that

what [was] signally absent in relation to both defenders is any averment that the defenders or either of them knew the nature of [the pursuer's] business as manufacturers of glass and that it was essential for the proper operation of its business that it received a constant and uninterrupted supply of electricity.[32]

Secondly, even if the judge had been wrong about that factual issue, this being a challenge as to the relevancy of the pursuer's averments, for policy considerations Lord MacLean '[i]n the whole matter [did] not consider that it [was] fair, just and reasonable that the law should impose a duty of care upon those in the position of both defenders in the circumstances of [the] case in relation to the consumers of electricity whose supplies were interrupted'.[33]

In adopting the above approach, Lord MacLean chose not to apply the ratio of the English case of *SCM (UK) Ltd v. W. J. Whittall & Son*,[34] even

---

[30] *Marc Rich & Co. AG and Others v. Bishop Rock Marine Co. Ltd and Others, The Nicholas H* [1996] AC 211 at p. 235.
[31] 1972 SLT 38 at p. 44.     [32] 1997 SLT 485 at p. 491L.
[33] Ibid. at p. 492G. At least one writer has considered this decision to be flawed with regard to the question of the existence of a duty of care and to that of breach; see Brodie, D., 'Jesuitical Distinctions', 1997 SLT (News) 84
[34] [1971] 1 QB 137, [1970] 3 All ER 245, [1970] 3 WLR 694, 6 ILR 8.

though he regarded it as directly analogous. He also reached a different conclusion from Lord Denning MR in *Spartan Steel & Alloys Ltd* v. *Martin & Co. (Contractors) Ltd*[35] who said that: 'If the defendant is guilty of negligence which cuts off the electricity supply and causes actual physical damage to personal property, the physical damage can be recovered.'[36] Lord MacLean's reasoning was that Lord Denning's observation had been dependent upon a valid distinction between physical damage and economic loss, and that there was now doubt on the highest authority as to whether that distinction continued to be acceptable. Lord MacLean observed that it seemed to be

artificial and without justification to make recovery of loss by those supplied in these circumstances turn upon whether the damage sustained was physical or purely economic. After all, in all these cases, loss is computed in money terms so far as the action for recovery of damages is concerned although loss, no doubt, is more readily identifiable in one case rather than the other.[37]

Lord MacLean was persuaded by the following observations of Lord Oliver of Aylmerton in *Murphy* v. *Brentwood District Council*:[38]

The critical question... is not the nature of the damage itself, whether physical or pecuniary, but whether the scope of the duty of care in the circumstances of the case is such as to embrace the damage of the kind which the plaintiff claims to have sustained... Nor is it self-evident logically where the line is to be drawn. Where, for instance, the defendant's careless conduct results in the interruption of the electricity supply to business premises adjoining the highway, it is not easy to discern the logic in holding that a sufficient relationship of proximity exists between him and a factory owner who has suffered loss because material in the course of manufacture is rendered useless but that none exists between him and the owner of, for instance, an adjoining restaurant who suffers the loss of profit on the meals which he is unable to prepare and sell. In both cases the real loss is pecuniary. The solution to such borderline cases has so far been achieved

---

[35] [1973] 1 QB 27.  [36] Ibid, at p. 39.
[37] 1997 SLT 485 at p. 491C; however, Lord MacLean is aware of the practical difficulties. He makes reference to Lord Denning in *Spartan Steel* [1973] QB 27 at pp. 38–9 where he observes that 'if claims for economic loss were permitted for this particular hazard, there would be no end of claims. Some might be genuine, but many may be inflated, or even false. A machine might not have been in use anyway, but it would be easy to put it down to a cut in supply. It would be well nigh impossible to check the claims. If there was economic loss one day, did the claimant do his best to mitigate it by working harder the next day? And so forth. Rather than expose claimants to such temptation and defendants to such hard labour – on comparatively small claims – it is better to disallow economic loss altogether, at any rate when it stands alone, independent of any physical damage.'
[38] [1991] 1 AC 398.

pragmatically (see *Spartan Steel*...) not by the application of logic but by the perceived necessity as a matter of policy to place some limits – perhaps arbitrary limits – to what would otherwise be an endless, cumulative causative chain bounded only by theoretical foreseeability. I frankly doubt whether, in searching for such limits, the categorisation of damage as 'material', 'physical', 'pecuniary' or 'economic' provides a particular useful contribution. Where it does, I think, serve a useful purpose is in identifying those cases in which it is necessary to search for and find something more than the mere reasonable foreseeability of damage which has occurred as providing the degree of 'proximity' necessary to support the action.[39]

III. It is clear that policy considerations play a major role in the determination of what is 'fair, just and reasonable'. Lord MacLean acknowledged that this case brought 'into play the kind of policy considerations which Lord Denning dealt with in *Spartan Steel* at p. 38E'.[40] Previously, in *Dynamco*, Lord Cameron had said that 'it is not all consequences of negligent acts and omissions which are to be taken into account as qualifying for an award of damages; they may be too remote and remoteness may be determined by considerations of practical expediency or even of public policy'.[41]

## The Netherlands

I. According to Dutch law, the excavator Acme has a duty to the owner of the facility and to the consumers of the electricity to excavate carefully.[42] Acme neglected this duty. Therefore, the Beta company can claim the damage to the machinery and the damage caused by the loss of production time.

II. The facts described in Case 1 ('Cable I – The Blackout') are in many ways similar to those of a case decided in 1977 by the Hoge Raad, the Dutch Supreme Court.[43] Although the case was decided under the 'old' 1838 Civil Code, the decision of the Supreme Court is still considered 'good law' under the new Civil Code, which came into force on 1 January 1992.

---

[39] Ibid. at pp. 485H–6H.   [40] 1997 SLT 485 at p. 492C.
[41] 1972 SLT 38 at p. 43, 1971 SC 257 at p. 272.
[42] See on the subject, J. Spier, in A. T. Bolt and J. Spier, *De uitdijende reikwijdte van de aansprakelijkheid uit onrechtmatige daad* (Handelingen NJV, 1996–I), (Zwolle, 1996), p. 311.
[43] HR 1.7.1977, NJ 1978, no. 84. See also HR 14.3.1958, NJ 1961, no. 570; R. A. Salomons, *Schadevergoeding: zaakschade* (Monografieën Nieuw BW no. B-38), (2nd edn, Deventer, 1993), pp. 52–3. For ample comparative law remarks, see R. J. P. Kottenhagen, 'Over bris de cables, Kabelbruchfälle en cable cases', (1992), *Bouwrecht* 653.

The facts of the 1977 case were as follows. Contrary to normal procedure, a dragline operator started excavations without properly consulting detailed maps of the area. As a result, he had no knowledge of the exact location of cables and pipes. During excavations, the operator damaged a gas main owned by a public utility. Consequently, a neighbouring brick factory had to halt production for lack of gas. The factory owner successfully claimed in tort, and the compensation amounted to five hours of loss of production.[44]

The Dutch Supreme Court ruled, *inter alia*, that the operator of a dragline has a duty to act cautiously[45] *vis-à-vis* all those dependent on the gas facility. The Supreme Court decided that this duty is not merely owed to the owner of the pipe, but also to those who have an obvious interest in an uninterrupted supply, i.e. those who use the gas facility.

It was submitted by the defendant that if the scope of the abovementioned duty was indeed extended to include consumers of the gas as well, this would open the door for numerous claims. The Court simply brushed this argument aside: the mere circumstance that those who are at fault and therefore liable are at risk of being confronted with an extensive number of claims does not alter the duty imposed upon them by law.

The defendant further claimed that the causal connection between the act of damaging the gas main and the interruption of production was not sufficient for legal imputation of the damage to the tortious act. The defendant's main argument was that this specific form of damage was unforeseeable, and that the damage was caused first and foremost by the factory's excessive dependence on the public gas facilities. In dismissing this argument, the Supreme Court gave an essential decision on the dogma of causation. It decided that foreseeability is a factor that may be taken into account in the process of ascertaining causal connection. However, other circumstances must be taken into consideration as well.

Finally, the Court dismissed the defendant's argument of excessive dependence. In the Court's opinion, this dependence clearly showed the closeness of the causal connection of cause and effect.[46]

---

[44] On the topic of calculation of loss of production, see HR 18.4.1986, NJ 1986, no. 567.

[45] Hereinafter, I will equate the concept of 'duty of care' to the Dutch concept of 'maatschappelijke zorgvuldigheid'. Article 6:162 ss. 2 of the Dutch Civil Code considers improper social conduct (conduct contrary to the standard of conduct acceptable in society) to be tortious, unless grounds for justification are present. Unless the act cannot be imputed to the actor, he is liable in tort.

[46] The Supreme Court was not requested to decide whether this excessive dependence did in any way constitute so-called *contributory negligence* (comparative negligence). The defendant did not raise this line of defence. According to art. 6:101 ss. 1 CC, there are

The Court concluded that there was a sufficient causal link and that possible far-reaching social side-effects such as an avalanche of claims are not decisive.

## Germany

I. The Beta factory can recover both for damage to its machinery and for the loss of two days of production. This is firmly established and essentially undisputed.[47]

II. Damage to machinery: since this is damage to property, § 823 s. 1 clearly applies. If Beta can show fault on behalf of the Acme employee, it can recover from him.[48]

The only issue worth debating is one of proximate cause, i.e. whether there is a sufficiently strong connection between the wrongful act and the harm. In a very similar case, the *Bundesgerichtshof* had no doubt that there was.

One is liable for damage to a person or to property according to § 823 (1) BGB regardless of whether the cause produces the damage directly or only after transmission through a chain of events. If a constant supply of power is necessary to preserve an object, then he who destroys it by cutting this supply also legally causes its loss.[49]

Loss of two days of production: since Beta's property was damaged, it has a claim for damages according to § 823 (1). This claim encompasses the financial loss incurred since such loss is not *purely* economic. According to § 252 BGB, lost profits are also included.

Both outcomes follow directly from the provisions of the BGB as they have been interpreted by courts and legal scholars. They are fully consistent with the fundamental principle of German tort law embodied in § 823 (1).

---

grounds for reduction of the amount allowed in damages whenever circumstances imputable to the injured party have contributed to the damage. See on this specific topic: J. M. Barendrecht, 'Pure economic loss in the Netherlands', in E. H. Hondius (ed.), *Netherlands Reports to the Fifteenth International Congress of Comparative Law* (Intersentia, Antwerpen, 1998), pp. 125–8.

[47] BGHZ 41, 123 ff. (1964); This is in contrast to cases without direct property damage, see: BGHZ 29, 65 (1958); BGH BB 1977, 1419–20 and below Case 2 ('Cable II – Factory Shutdown').

[48] Whether it can recover from Acme as the employer itself, is a different question because such a claim would have to be based on § 831 BGB which provides for only limited liability of an employer for the wrongs of his employee, see above, fn. 10 and corresponding text. The difficulties Beta might encounter here, however, have nothing to do with the issue of pure economic loss.

[49] BGHZ 41, 123, at 125–6 (1964).

## Austria

I. The Beta factory cannot recover any damage, neither the damage to its machinery, nor the loss of two days of production. This has been questioned by legal scholars but is an established position of the Supreme Court.

II. Whereas in its earlier decisions the Austrian Oberster Gerichtshof (OGH) made a distinction between damage to property and loss of production,[50] the Court has abstained from such differentiation in more recent decisions[51] and resorted to the position that all harm done to a person resulting from a broken cable belonging to somebody else – whether damage to property or loss of production – is not compensable because it did not occur 'in the direction of the assault' (*in der Richtung des Angriffes*), but was attributable to a side-effect which arose in a sphere of interest not protected by the provision prohibiting the assault (*infolge einer Seitenwirkung in einer Interessensphäre eingetreten, die nicht durch das Verbot des Angriffes geschützt ist*). The Court believes that if such losses were accepted as compensable a 'boundless, economically intolerable expansion of liability' (*eine uferlose, wirtschaftlich untragbare Ausweitung der Schadenshaftung*) would result. Thus, it is nothing but a clear policy consideration used in support of the doubtful position held by the Supreme Court.[52]

A 'legal' justification for this restriction is found in the absence of 'directness': Only the owner of the cable or at least one who has a right *in rem* in the cable would qualify as victim of 'direct damage'.

III. Austrian legal scholars now favour a distinction dependent upon whether the damage caused by the rupture of the cable occurred to the property of the victim, or resulted in a mere halt of production, since damage to property would indicate unlawfulness of the activity having caused such damage, whereas a production loss would not.[53]

If there were a close relationship between the location where the cable was cut and the location of the Beta Factory, it could be possible that the court might resort to the concept of 'contract implying the protection of a third party', classifying the contract between Acme road works and

---

[50] OGH JBl 1973, 581; JBl 1973, 579; see comments by W. Posch, 'Der ungeschützte Strombezieher als Fall des "mittelbaren Schadens" in der Rechtsprechung des OGH', JBl 1973, 564.
[51] OGH JBl 1976, 210; ZVR 1979/93.
[52] For a comprehensive discussion, see A. Bürge, 'Die Kabelbruchfälle', JBl 1981, 57.
[53] Cf. R. Welser, 'Der OGH und der Rechtswidrigkeitszusammenhang', ÖJZ 1975, 1, 37; on cable cases, 41 *et seq.*

its partner (e.g. the community, if there is such a contract) as having a protective effect in favour of Beta, which then could recover both types of damage, since the loss of production appears as consequential (not as pure) economic loss.

There is growing scepticism among Austrian scholars about an unreasonable expansion in the field of application of the theory of 'contracts with protective effects to third persons'. Indeed, such constructions are often used simply to make corrections of the all-too restrictive statutory rules of non-contractual liability, in particular in the field of vicarious liability and with regard to recovery of pure economic loss.[54] Under a codified system of private law the courts cannot arrogate the legislative role to themselves.

**Portugal**

I. If the employee of the Acme roadworks company acted negligently, the Beta factory has the right to seek compensation for the damage caused to its machinery (fault is only required of the employee; the liability of the principal is objective under article 500 CC).

However, if production loss resulted from the failure of the machinery, there would also be a right to seek reparation for the consequent economic loss.

II. The violation of property (damage to the machines) constitutes an unlawful action (article 483/1, first modality of unlawfulness).[55]

The judgment of fault (and thus the foreseeability of damage) relates to the constitutive fact of liability. As regards subsequent damage, it is only required that a relation of causality with the unlawful fact exists.[56] The economic damage causally associated with the violation of the property is thus fully recoverable, given that there is no doubt about the existence of a causality nexus (and its foreseeability is not required).

The burden of proof of fault, for which assessment an abstract criterion is used, lies with the injured party (article 487). However, given that

---

[54] For a recent sceptical statement, see F. Harrer in M. Schwimann (ed.), *ABGB*, vol. 7 (2nd edn, Vienna, 1997) § 1295 nos. 106, 107.
[55] Article 483/1 of the Portuguese Civil Code: 'whoever, whether by wilful misconduct [*dolus*] or by negligence unlawfully infringes the rights of another person or any legal provision intended to safeguard the interests of others must compensate the injured party for damage arising from such violation'.
[56] M. de Andrade, *Teoria Geral das Obrigações* (with R. de Alarcão, Coimbra, 1963), p. 363, sub-para. f.

the damage was caused by a 'thing' (a machine) and that the use of excavators on the roadworks is likely to cause damage, fault is presumed; that is, there is an inversion of the burden of proving negligence, based on article 493/1 (damage caused by things), or even on the basis of article 493/2 ('dangerous activity by virtue of the means used').[57]

The facts stated in the hypothesis also permit the interpretation that loss of production was not caused by the machinery breakdown (thus, if these could have been repaired during the two days of interruption to the power supply, the repairing would not have caused the drop in production). In this case, the damage resulting from the stoppage of work would have to be treated in the same way as our answer for Case 2 ('Cable II – Factory Shutdown': see below, sub II).

III. The situation described imediately above in the preceding paragraph shows that pure economic damage can co-exist with damage to things, though it is not a direct consequence of that violation.[58]

## Sweden and Finland

I. The Beta factory can recover damage to the machinery, while compensation for the loss of two days of production remains much in doubt.

II. As far as damage to machinery is concerned, the Beta factory can recover its losses by proving fault on the part of Acme's employee,[59] as an application of the general liability principle for 'property damages' contained in *SkadestL* 2:1 (Sweden) and *SkadestL* 2:1 plus 5:1 (Finland).

Although Swedish and Finnish law are rather strict as far as causal connection is concerned, a case such as the one at hand should not raise problems from this point of view.

The recovery of damage caused by loss of production could be barred instead by the general principle of the law of torts which limits compensation for economic loss to the loss consequent upon personal injury or

---

[57] Judgment of the Appeal Court of Coimbra of 9 February 1993, *Colectânea de Jurisprudência*, year XVIII, vol. 1 (1993), p. 41. The decision on appeal held that the presumption of fault established in article 493/1 was applicable; judgment at first instance held that the presumption in article 493/2 was applicable. The issue in this case concerned damage caused by a mechanical excavator to a car that was passing by.

[58] Emphasizing this point, G. Davis, 'The Need for Flexibility in Pure Economic Loss Recovery', (1983) 1 *Australian Business Law Journal* 246.

[59] In the Swedish and Finnish context, however, the claim would most probably be brought against Acme instead of its employee, since the former would be fully liable on the basis of the vicarious liability rule contained in SkadestL 3:1 (Sweden) and SkadestL 3:1 (Finland), while personal liability on the part of the employee is subject to the limits set by SkadestL 4:1 (Sweden) and SkadestL 4:1 (Finland).

property damages suffered by the same subject, while the economic loss suffered by those who are third parties *vis-à-vis* the original injury or damage shall remain without compensation.

In the last cable case decided by the Swedish Supreme Court,[60] indeed compensation was granted on this basis only for damage to machinery. The loss deriving from the plants being made idle was seen as a loss for which the factory was a third party, not being the owner of the severed cable which caused the blackout.

The state of Swedish law on the point is, however, rather uncertain. The limits to compensation of third-party losses in cable cases has been much criticized by scholars,[61] and the abovementioned decision presents a scattered landscape of dissenting opinions.

It is important to mention that in another cable case[62] decided about twenty years before, the Swedish Supreme Court declared that third party losses can be compensated when the plaintiff has 'a concrete and near interest' linked to the cable, which in the case at hand was represented by the cable being owned by a group also including the plaintiff company which therefore had a 'decisive influence' on the use of the cable.

In a 1994 cable case, the Finnish Supreme Court, although refusing compensation in the case at hand, affirmed that liability could be admitted to some extent when the use of the cables takes place in forms somewhat comparable to property rights.[63]

*Editors' comparative comments*

This case indicates that there is a broad split in Europe at two levels. First, and at the deepest level, certain countries have and do not have special rules preventing or limiting the recovery of pure economic loss. This split is deep but it is not along civil law/common law lines. It basically lies between the conservative–pragmatic regimes on the one hand, and the liberal regimes of Europe on the other. Secondly, within the ranks of those countries that have special rules restricting recovery, there is an important split over the scope of what constitutes 'pure economic loss'. As a result of having different approaches, certain systems treat the lost production in Cable I as a case of 'pure' economic loss, even

---

[60] NJA 1988, s. 62.
[61] See, e.g. H. Andersson, *Skyydsändamål och adekvans* (Uppsala, 1993), p. 567.
[62] NJA 1966, s. 210.
[63] HD 1994: 94, H. Saxén, *Adekvans och skada* (Åbo, 1962), p. 179.

though there was accompanying property loss. However, other systems regard the lost production as 'consequential' economic loss (hence recoverable), because it arose out of property loss. Still others, purporting to de-emphasize distinctions based on the inner nature of the damage, categorically deny recovery in any event.

In Belgium, France, Greece, Italy, Spain and the Netherlands, both 'pure' and 'consequential' economic loss will receive compensation. These systems do not recognize a *per se* distinction between the types of damage that Beta sustained. The damage to Beta's machinery and the loss of two days' production simply fall within the notion of *dommages matériels*. Since the nature of the damage plays no role in the analysis, there is no occasion to ask whether there is a relationship of cause and effect between the two forms of loss. Unsurprisingly, the notion of 'consequential economic loss' does not arise and is not discussed in any of the reports from these countries.

Under English law, the inner nature of the loss has a decisive effect upon the policies which drive the duty of care and causation analysis. Thus, an English court would rule that Beta may receive compensation for damage to its machinery, and it may recover lost profits on materials or goods that were in the process of manufacture and were damaged by the halt of production. But aside from this possibility, there will be no other compensation for loss of production by the damaged machines. Even though this lost production is connected to the property damage (it would be regarded as parasitic economic damage in Germany), the English courts are specially exigent with respect to the nature of that connection. In their analysis, the loss of production was not 'truly consequential'[64] and thus it should be regarded in these circumstances as 'pure' economic loss. It arose 'independently' of the damage to Beta's machinery, and thus there is no duty of care to avoid causing it. The reasoning in Scotland possibly leads to a different scope for the duty of care. As a result of placing more importance on the duty of care than the categorization of damage, the court might grant no compensation on these facts, even for the damage to machinery.

In Germany and Portugal, once plaintiff establishes that they have sustained property loss (damaged machinery), they may then recover for consequential economic loss as well. Such loss is not deemed 'purely'

---

[64] '*Truly* consequential loss' is regarded as a separate compartment of liability law. For details, see R. Bernstein, *Economic Loss* (2nd edn, Sweet & Maxwell, London, 1998), pp. 146–54.

economic, as in England, and courts do not appear to probe deeply into the causal linkage between the two forms of loss. Arguable shades of consequential loss seem readily compensable.[65] A different approach prevails in Sweden and Finland. Although these systems will compensate for Beta's machinery damage, they refuse recovery for the accompanying economic loss, since *in relation to it*, the plaintiff is a 'third party' to the defendant's tort. Austria closes the floodgates just as tightly. The Austrian courts have abandoned efforts to distinguish one type of loss from another; they now deny the entire claim (property loss included) when the plaintiff is a third person who was 'not in the direction of the assault'.

It is clear that pure economic loss and consequential economic loss are actually causal constructs that are not uniformly conceived or applied in Austria, England, Finland, Germany, Portugal, Scotland and Sweden. Within these systems we may observe different approaches to 'purity' which, in turn, lead to different levels of protection. In Cable I, Germany and Portugal apply the notion of consequential loss somewhat more liberally than England, but Austria, Finland and Sweden offer less protection than England because their rules ignore such distinctions where 'third parties' have been damaged. They then apply a test that excludes both pure and consequential loss without examining its nature.

---

[65] In Portugal, however, it appears that some economic loss might be viewed as only concurrent with property loss, and hence not recoverable.

## Case 2: cable II – the factory shutdown

### Case

Under the same facts as above, Cato, another factory owner, experienced no damage to his machinery, but his plant was rendered idle and he lost two days of production.

### France

I. Cato would seem in principle entitled to recover damages for lost production under articles 1382–1383 CC.

II. Theoretically, there is no distinction in French law, as stated in Case 1 ('Cable I – The Blackout'), between property loss and pure economic loss. Both fall within the capacious category of *dommages matériels*. In both cases the main inquiry will center upon the causal question.

### Belgium

I. If Cato's plant was rendered idle because the Acme employee cut the cable which delivered the electric energy, it can recover the lost profits resulting from the idleness.

II. Liability: according to article 27 of the Belgian Law of 10 March 1925 on Distribution of Electric Energy, one who, by lack of precaution, has destroyed devices for the production, transformation, distribution and use of electric energy, or has prevented the transport of such energy, will be punished as mentioned in article 563 of the Belgian Criminal Code.[66]

The negligence of the Acme employee is therefore a criminal offence.

According to article 1382 CC, therefore the employee should normally be liable towards Cato for the loss of two days of production.

However, according to article 18 of the Belgian Law of 3 July 1978 on Employment Contracts,

in case of damage caused by the employee to the employer or to third parties during the course of the performance of the employment contract, the employee will only be liable if he committed a gross fault or an intentional fault. He will be liable for his negligence only if this negligence is usual instead of accidental.

---

[66] Trib. Civ. Louvain, 16 mars 1995, p. 394 and note P. Bauwens.

Whether the fault of the employee be intentional, gross or negligent, the Acme company will be liable for the loss of the two days of production by application of article 1384, al. 3 CC:

Each one is liable not only for the damage which he caused by his own act, but also for that which is caused by the act of persons for whom he is responsible, or by things which he has in his keeping.
[…]
Masters and principals are liable for damage caused by their domestics and employees in the function for which they have been employed.
[…]

Loss of two days of production: the main issue will be to determine whether the two days of production would have been lost if the cable had not been cut. If the two days of production would have been lost anyway (because of another event, such as, for example, a strike), the damage is not recoverable. If the two days of production would not have been lost, the lost profit resulting is recoverable.

Unlike other legal systems, Belgian tort law does not establish as a precondition for recovering the deprived gain that there also be a claim for a damage caused to property. The issue will be, however, that it is more difficult for the injured party to prove the causal link between that lost gain and the fault.

**Italy**

I. Damage for loss of profits is recoverable as long as there is a strong chain of causation, and concrete and certain damage.

II. The meaning of these terms was previously discussed in Case 1 ('Cable I – The Blackout'). Again, as in the previous case, we also have to recall that excavation works fall under article 2050 cc which is interpreted as a strict liability provision.

Italian law does not make any generic distinction between physical damages and pure economic damages; so far we cannot see any difference between Cable I and Cable II. In both instances the factory does not have an absolute right to an electricity supply, but both case law and scholars recognize that compensation may be awarded for third-party interference with a contractual relation.[67]

---

[67] *Torino Calcio SpA v. Romero*, Cass., SU, 26.1.1971, no. 174, *GI*, 1971, I, 1, 681 noted by Visintini; *FI*, 1971, I, 342 noted by Busnelli.

Courts have considered compensation for loss of profits in the following contexts: interference with the use of an asset; interference with specific contractual relationships; and the loss of professional reputation.

The case at hand is covered by *Puddu*[68] and *Enel* v. *Ditta Giampaoli*[69] which are the oldest cases matching these facts. Ditta Giampaoli cut a cable delivering energy to a factory while operating an excavator. The court held that Enel (the state-owned Italian electricity producer) was not liable for breach of contract and that Giampaoli was liable for negligence in tort for all the economic losses due to the factory's blackout. This ruling was based on the broad principle of articles 2043 and 2050 cc, as commonly interpreted after *Meroni*.

In a Turin First Instance case – *Enel* v. *Borio* – the court held an excavator liable, for he did not inquire about the underground cable configuration before beginning excavation activity.[70]

III. Judicial interpretation given to the dangerous activity provision (art. 2050 cc) is now under critique for imposing an excessively broad liability on excavation activity. The burden of proof is so heavy that authors speak of quasi-strict liability.[71]

Using law and economic tools, some scholars are now focusing their attention on the problem of inefficiency in a system where the damaged party does not have enough incentive to invest in precautionary measures. An analysis which favours application of comparative negligence to these situations may lead to some adjustment in the present case law. What if the damaged party did not give enough information about the location of the subsoil wires?[72]

---

[68] Cass. 24.6.1972, no. 2135, *FI*, 1973, I, 99.
[69] App. Ancona, 23.11.1982, RGEnel, 1982, 747; for a similar case, see the recent decision by Cass. 15.5.1999, in *DR* 2000, 2, 167, noted by A. M. Musy, 'Taglio di cavi elettrici: il danno meramente patrimoniale'.
[70] Trib. Torino, 31.5.1978, RGEnel, 1979, 379.
[71] S. Mannina, 'La responsabilità civile dell'esercente un'attività di escavazione in caso di danni a cavi sotterranei', note under App. Roma, 12.7.1995, *T Romana*, 1996, 643. Trib. Torino, 31.5.1978, RGEnel, 1979, 379.
[72] The point has been raised in a recent decision *Vecchio* v. *Telecom Italia SpA*, Cass. 23.8.1999, no. 8838, *DR*, 2000, 512. The note to the decision wonders about the inefficient effect that such a decision will have on the allocation of damages, see A. M. Musy and L. Zambelli, ' "Cable cutting" all'italiana. Ipotesi di concorso di colpa del danneggiato per omissione di informativa'.

## Spain

I. Cato can claim damages for lost profits.

II. In Spanish law the result in this case is very similar to the result of Case 1 ('Cable I – The Blackout'). Unlike the solution of the German legal system, under the Spanish system of delictual responsibility all damages are initially recoverable, and it is not particularly relevant whether the damage affected actual goods belonging to the plaintiff (i.e. the factory machinery).[73]

However, Cato could have more problems than the Beta factory in obtaining compensation, due to the restrictive criteria followed by the Spanish Supreme Court in dealing with claims for lost profits and the requirement about certainty of damages.

## Greece

I. Cato has the right to be fully compensated by Acme and its employee.

II. As already stated (under Case 1, 'Cable I – The Blackout'), since his negligence is proved, the Acme employee has committed a tort.

Therefore the employee is liable to compensate Beta, according to article 914 CC. It does not matter that Beta is a third party and not the owner of the damaged property (cables). Neither, according to article 298 CC, does the inner nature of Beta's damage matter, i.e. whether it concerns corporeal or incorporeal interests. It suffices that here, *causal relation* exists between the damage and the cutting of the cables according to both criteria proposed for testing it: either the foreseeability of the particular damage, or its inclusion in the interests protected by the infringed legal rule. The causation exists, because the plant's idleness and the loss of two production days are obviously foreseeable (typical and avoidable) risks of destroying public utility cables.

Acme is also tortiously liable for the unlawful behaviour of its employee (article 922 CC: vicarious tortious liability).

Thus, Cato has the right to be fully compensated directly by Acme and its employee. They are, according to article 926 CC, co-debtors in a joint and several obligation owed to Cato.

III. As mentioned earlier, damage to public utility cables usually occurs because of negligence of the Greek Public Power Corporation

---

[73] F. Pantaleón 'Comentario al artículo 1902', in *Comentario del Código Civil*, vol. II (Ministerio de Justicia – Civitas, Madrid, 1991), pp. 1971–2003, pp. 1972 and 1994.

(a monopoly), not because of third parties. Thus, if electricity causes only pure economic loss, the latter is usually not indemnifiable because, according to the contract between the Greek Power Corporation and each consumer, 'the Greek Power Corporation is entitled to stop the supply of electric current at any time'. Nevertheless, the validity of such terms is doubted, especially in view of the Greek Consumer's Act 2251/1994. Usually in such cases the Greek Power Corporation usually comes to an extrajudicial compromise.

## England

I. Cato cannot recover his loss of two days of production.

II. A pure loss of production, without any physical damage to property, is a loss of production not recoverable in negligence: *Spartan Steel v. Martin*.[74]

Neither is there a duty of care to protect against such loss: again, *Spartan Steel v. Martin*.

III. *Murphy v. Brentwood DC*[75] is in harmony with the spirit of *Spartan Steel v. Martin* and confirms that the pure loss of production is, as a matter of legal policy, not recoverable.[76]

## Scotland

I. Cato is not able to recover in damages the loss of his two days of production which resulted from the interruption to the electricity supply.

II. This is an example of secondary economic loss. As a result of the damage to the property of the public utility company, Cato has suffered economic loss because the contract which Cato had with the public utility company for the supply of electricity, cannot be fulfilled. As referred to under Case 1 ('Cable I – The Blackout'), the leading case in this area is *Dynamco*.[77] At first instance, after discussion of the relevant authorities, Lord Kissen had concluded that

financial or economic loss from damage to property owned by another person is not a legally admissible claim against the negligent wrongdoer, whether or not there was a contractual or other relationship with the owner of the damaged

---

[74] [1973] 1 QB 27 (CA). [75] [1991] 1 AC 398 (HL).
[76] Full discussion of the policy of English law in cases of pure economic loss in E. K. Banakas, *Civil Liability for Pure Economic Loss* (Kluwer, The Hague, 1996), chs. 1 and 2.
[77] *Dynamco Ltd v. Holland and Hannen and Cubitts (Scotland) Ltd* 1972 SLT 38, 1971 SC 257.

property. A negligent wrongdoer is not to be held bound to have surmised purely financial or economic loss to persons other than the owners or possessors of damaged property.[78]

On appeal, Lord Migdale (with whom the Lord President (Lord Clyde) agreed) followed Lord Kissen and held that '[t]he law of Scotland has for over a hundred years refused to accept that a claim for financial loss which does not arise directly from damage to the claimant's property can give rise to a legal claim for damages founded on negligence'.[79] Lord Migdale rejected the pursuer's claim because no part of their property was damaged. In passing he opined that the pursuers could not recover for loss of profits 'unless that loss arises from damage to their plant and materials'.[80] This seemed to cover our Case 1 ('Cable I – The Blackout') situation. However, as we have seen, the later case of *Coleridge* demonstrated that the fact of physical damage was only one element necessary for a successful delictual claim in the case of secondary damage.

The third judge in *Dynamco*, Lord Cameron, acknowledged in common with the other two judges that the above assertion was firmly based upon three unchallenged Scottish authorities.[81] The earliest of these contains our classic statement upon remoteness of damages. Lord Kinloch in *Allan* v. *Barclay* held that '[t]he grand rule on the subject of damages is, that none can be claimed except such as naturally and directly arise out of the wrong done; and such, therefore, as may reasonably be supposed to have been in the view of the wrongdoer'.[82] For Lord Cameron, applying this test, 'the loss would be too remote and indirect to be relevant to found a good claim for reparation'.[83] From this we are able to conclude that either Acme would not be said to owe a duty of care to Cato or, if it did owe him a duty of care not to cause him loss, the nature of the loss – being secondary economic loss – was 'too remote and indirect' to be relevant.

For completeness, in *Nacap Ltd* v. *Moffat Plant Ltd*[84] the Inner House held that the pursuers in the case had no title to sue where the damage had occurred to a pipeline in their possession. They neither owned it, nor had a possessory right or title, but merely had physical possession for the limited purposes under the contract. In other words, consistent

---

[78] *Dynamco Ltd* v. *Holland and Hannen and Cubitts (Scotland) Ltd* 1971 SLT 150 at p. 153.
[79] 1972 SLT 38 at p. 39.   [80] Ibid. at p. 40.
[81] *Allan* v. *Barclay* (1864) 2 M 873, *Simpson & Co.* v. *Thomson and Others* (1877) 5 R 40 (HL) and *Reavis* v. *Clan Line Steamers* 1925 SC 725, 1925 SLT 538.
[82] (1864) 2 M 873 at p. 874.   [83] 1972 SLT 38 at p. 42.   [84] 1987 SLT 221.

with *Dynamco*, the pursuers had suffered secondary economic loss from damage to the property of another party and had no title to sue.

III. Lord Kissen placed importance upon the judicial observations in the relevant authorities concerning 'the multiplicity of litigations which could follow one act of negligence' and 'the practical necessity for limitations'.[85] On this aspect he referred to the House of Lords and quoted Lord Pearce in *Hedley* who stated:

> How wide the sphere of the duty of care in negligence is to be laid depends ultimately upon the court's assessment of the demands of society for protection from the carelessness of others. Economic protection has lagged behind protection in physical matters where there is injury to person and property. It may be that the size and the width of the possible claims has acted as a deterrent to extension of economic protection.[86]

As Lord Kissen observed, the 'startling' range of possible claims, concerning utilities such as electricity, water and telephone, clearly influenced his and the Inner House's judgments.

## The Netherlands

I. The excavator Acme owes a duty to the owner of the facility and to the consumers of the electricity to excavate carefully.[87] Acme neglected this duty. Thus, the Cato company can claim loss of production, in spite of the absence of physical infringement.

II. Although the limits of causation are 'stretched the least' when pure economic loss is involved, it must be admitted here that stretching the limits 'least far' is indeed far enough to allow for recovery of 'second-degree damage' as suffered by the Cato company – as is shown in a 1977 Supreme Court decision.[88] As far as the nature of the liability is concerned, the 1977 decision shows that even a slightly negligent act satisfies the causality test.

The facts of the 1977 case were as follows. Contrary to normal procedure, a dragline operator started excavations without properly

---

[85] 1971 SLT 150 at p. 154.
[86] *Hedley Byrne & Co. Ltd* v. *Heller & Partners Ltd* [1964] AC 465 at p. 536 [1963] 2 All ER 575 at p. 615.
[87] See on the subject, A. T. Bolt and J. Spier, *De uitdijende reikwijdte van de aansprakelijkheid uit onrechtmatige daad* (Handelingen NJV, 1996) at p. 311.
[88] See, for a critical analysis of the 1977 Supreme Court decision from a comparative law point of view, Bolt and Spier, *De uitdijende*, at pp. 315–6. Compare R. A. Salomons, *Schadevergoeding: zaakschade* (2nd edn, 1993) at pp. 53–5 and R. J. P. Kottenhagen, 'Buiten-contractuele aansprakelijkheid voor economische schade', (1991) *Bouwrecht* 345–7.

consulting detailed maps of the area. As a result, he had no knowledge of the exact location of cables and pipes. During excavations, the operator damaged a gas main owned by a public utility. Consequently, a neighbouring brick factory had to halt production for lack of gas. The factory owner successfully claimed in tort, and the compensation amounted to five hours of loss of production.[89]

The Dutch Supreme Court ruled, *inter alia*, that the operator of a dragline has a duty to act cautiously[90] *vis-à-vis* all those dependent on the gas facility. The Supreme Court decided that this duty is not merely owed to the owner of the pipe, but also to those who have an obvious interest in an uninterrupted supply, i.e. those who use the gas facility.

It was submitted by the defendant that if the scope of the abovementioned duty was indeed extended to include consumers of the gas as well, this would open the door for numerous claims. The Court simply brushed this argument aside: the mere circumstance that those who are at fault and therefore liable are at risk of being confronted with an extensive number of claims does not alter the duty imposed upon them by law.

The defendant further claimed that the causal connection between the act of damaging the gas main and the interruption of production was not sufficient for legal imputation of the damage to the tortious act. The defendant's main argument was that this specific form of damage was unforeseeable and that the damage was caused first and foremost by the factory's excessive dependence on the public gas facilities. In dismissing this argument, the Court gave an essential decision on the dogma of causation. It stated that foreseeability is a factor that can be taken into account in the process of ascertaining causal connection. However, other circumstances must be taken into consideration as well.

Finally, the Court dismissed the defendant's argument of excessive dependence. In the Court's opinion, this dependence clearly showed the closeness of the causal connection of cause and effect.[91]

---

[89] On the topic of calculation of loss of production, see HR 18.4.1986, NJ 1986, no. 567.
[90] Hereinafter, I will equate the concept of 'duty of care' to the Dutch concept of 'maatschappelijke zorgvuldigheid'. Article 6:162 ss. 2 of the Dutch Civil Code considers improper social conduct (conduct contrary to the standard of conduct acceptable in society) to be tortious, unless grounds for justification are present. Unless the act cannot be imputed to the actor, he is liable in tort. See below for the full text of art. 6:162 CC.
[91] The Supreme Court was not requested to decide whether this excessive dependence did in any way constitute so-called *contributory negligence*. The defendant did not raise this line of defence. According to the present art. 6:101 ss. 1 CC, there are grounds for reduction of the amount allowed in damages whenever circumstances imputable to the injured party have contributed to the damage.

The Court concluded that there was a sufficient causal link and that possible far-reaching social side-effects such as an avalanche of claims are not decisive.

## Germany

I. Cato cannot recover his damages incurred by the loss of production. Again, this result is generally accepted although the exact reasons for it are subject to some discussion in the academic literature.[92]

II. Tort claims: Recovery under § 823 (1). Since a claim requires the violation of an 'absolute right', and since Cato has not suffered any property damage, at first glance there seems to be no doubt that his claim must fail. Yet, the courts have long recognized a 'right of the established and ongoing commercial enterprise' (*Recht am eingerichteten und ausgeübten Gewerbebetrieb*) as 'another right' under § 823 (1).[93]

Business owners have sought to invoke this right in cases such as the present one. They have failed because the *Bundesderichtshof* has denied that the 'right of the established and ongoing commercial enterprise' is affected where damage to a (public) power cable leads to a loss of production.[94] In order to find a violation of this right, the court has consistently required that the defendant's act be specifically related to the enterprise as such (*betriebsbezogen*).[95] This would be the case, for example, if the act were directed against the enterprise or if there were an interference with matters particular to the business, such as its marketing activities.[96] It is not enough, however, that the defendant's act affects the enterprise as it affects other victims or their property, e.g. other households, consumers, etc.[97] For lack of a violation of any 'absolute right', Cato's loss thus remains purely economic and is not recoverable under § 823 (1).

Recovery under § 823 (2): Cato would have to show that the defendant violated a statute intended (at least *inter alia*) to protect him against the kind of damage suffered. In a similar situation, a German plaintiff invoked the provisions of the state building code which were allegedly violated. Yet, the *Bundesgerichtshof* has denied that the respective provisions in these codes intend to protect against loss of production through loss of power.[98]

---

[92] See below, III.
[93] See RGZ 58, 24, at 29 (1904); BGHZ 29, 65, at 72 (1958).
[94] BGHZ 29, 65 (1958); BGHZ 41, 123, at 126–7 (1964).
[95] BGH NJW 1977, 2208, at 2209; BGH NJW 1983, 812, at 813.
[96] BGH NJW 1985, 1620.    [97] BGH BB 1983, 464, at 465.    [98] BGHZ 66, 388 (1976).

Recovery under § 826: Cato could recover even pure economic loss if he could show that the defendant acted intentionally and maliciously, but the facts of the case do not indicate any such conduct.

Contract claim: Cato could claim that the contract between Acme and its partner gave rise to a duty of care, protecting Cato as a foreseeable third-party victim of Acme's negligence. Such a claim would be contractual in nature and would thus include pure economic loss. This is recognized in principle but would fail in this case. Third parties are protected only if they are so closely related to (at least) one of the contract partners that this partner feels responsible for their safety and wellbeing (e.g. among family members). After an accident identical to Case 2 ('Cable II – Factory Shutdown'), the *Bundesgerichtshof* decided that this requirement was not fulfilled.[99]

III. The 'right of the established and ongoing commercial enterprise' was created as 'another right' under § 823 (1) by the *Reichsgericht* (the German Supreme Court until 1945)[100] and expanded by the *Bundesgerichtshof* in order to protect businesses which suffered harm from tortious conduct (such as interference with their business and marketing activities) but could not show any damage to specific property.[101] Today, the existence of this right is generally accepted by all courts and among academic writers.

However, this recognition entailed the risk that businesses (unlike individuals) could almost routinely recover pure economic loss – a clear violation of the basic principle of § 823 (1). Thus, it is generally acknowledged today that the right must be restricted. Yet, there is some debate about how to impose meaningful limits. The formula of the *Bundesgerichtshof* that the wrongful act must be specifically related to the enterprise as such (*betriebsbezogen*) has met with criticism in the literature, mainly on the ground that it is too vague to be meaningful. More effective alternatives have yet to be found.[102]

Ultimately, the decision whether the 'right of the established and ongoing enterprise' has been violated depends on balancing the protection of businesses against the restrictions imposed by § 823 (1), and upon other (mostly unarticulated) policy considerations in individual cases.

---

[99] BGH NJW 1977, 2208, at 2209.   [100] See RGZ 28, 238, at 247–8 (1890).
[101] See BGHZ 69, 128, at 139 (1977).
[102] See G. Brüggemeier, *Deliktsrecht* (1st edn, 1986) Rd.-Nr. 332; J. Esser and H. L. Weyers, *Schuldrecht Band II, Besonderer Teil* (7th edn, 1990) s. 55 I 2 c; W. Fikentscher, *Lehrbuch des Schuldrechts* (9th edn, 1997) Rd.-Nr. 1222; K. Larenz and C. W. Canaris *Lehrbuch des Schuldrechts* (13th edn, 1994) s. 81 I 1, and following.

The decision will turn on how the court views the facts before it; but it is still one of law and thus fully reviewable on appeal. The loss-of-power cases are among the few scenarios in which the result is clear and generally accepted.

### Austria

I. Cato's claim for recovery of his damage will be unsuccessful. This solution is questioned by legal scholars, but it is based on the established practice of the Supreme Court.

II. Again, the Supreme Court would maintain that no recovery of damage to a factory resulting from a broken cable belonging to somebody else would be possible, because if such losses were accepted as compensable, a 'boundless, economically intolerable expansion of liability' would ensue.

The Court would argue that the damage did not occur 'in the direction of the assault, but was attributable to a side-effect which arose in a sphere of interest not protected by the provision prohibiting the assault'. It would express its belief that, if such losses were accepted as worthy of compensation, a 'boundless, economically intolerable expansion of liability' would result.

III. If Cato had been the owner of the cable which was cut and caused the halt of production, he would have been able to claim compensation for the entire damage because the ruptured cable would be a 'direct property damage' entailing consequential loss in production.

### Portugal

I. In principle, Cato cannot claim compensation for the loss of two days' production.

II. In accordance with the intent of the author of the preparatory work on the Civil Code,[103] as well as the doctrine[104] and prevailing jurisprudence, only the violation of a so-called 'absolute right' generates an obligation to compensate.

---

[103] A. Vaz Serra, 'Responsabilidade Civil (Requisitos)', *Boletim do Ministério da Justiça*, n. 92. 37 ff. (122, n. 13) and 'Responsabilidade de Terceiros no Não-Cumprimento das Obrigações', ( . . . ) 85 *Boletim do Ministério da Justiça* 345.

[104] P. De Lima and A. Varela, *Código Civil Anotado*, vol. I (4th edn, Coimbra Editora, Coimbra, 1997), Vol. I (4th edn, 1997), vol II, 4th edn, Coimbra Editora, Coimbra, 1998) annotation 5, sub-para. (a), to art. 483. Cf. F. Pessoa Jorge, *Ensaio sobre os Pressupostos da Responsabilidade Civil* (Lisbon, 1968), pp. 296 ff.

In accordance with this orientation, the case being examined here does not concern the violation of this kind of right; consequently, no unlawful act exists.

However, it should be noted that the letter of the law does leave some room for interpretation. It is certain that the unlawfulness (first modality) requires the violation of a 'subjective right'. But article 483/1 does not expressly require an 'absolute right' to be involved.

If the tribunal considers that compensation should be allowed, this 'hermeneutic space' could be used. That is to say, it could be considered that by cutting the electricity cable, Acme prevented the energy distribution company from fulfilling a contractual obligation to Beta, qualifying this violation or 'interference' in a third-party credit (which is a 'relative right') as an unlawful fact[105] (concerning the so-called external effect of obligations, see Case 5, 'Requiem for an Italian All Star', below).

On the other hand, the second modality of unlawfulness of article 483/1 (violation of a legal provision intended to protect the interests of third parties) also operates with a certain flexibility.[106] Although it seems to us that the regulations which were violated (concerning the way in which the work was carried out) do not have the aim of protecting individuals against pure economic damage, the court may decide differently.

Therefore, even though it is unlikely, it is not wholly impossible that the court would accept Cato's claim.

---

[105] This possibility is considered, but expressly rejected, in the judgment of the Court of Appeal in Porto on 10 March 1994, *Colectânea de Jurisprudência*. Tomo II, 197–200 (a car struck two posts, one electricity and one telephone, which resulted in a nearby company losing one day of production). Interestingly, while denying the plaintiff's claim for procedural reasons, the Court held that the action would have succeeded if art. 794 (*commodum subrogationis* in the domain of contractual liability) had been invoked instead of art. 483 (liability in tort), the plaintiff being replaced by the energy supply company on the claim by the third party for the damage arising from the temporary non-fulfilment of the contract to supply energy. But it seems that the judgment is flawed. Article 794 only allows the creditor to take the debtor's place as regards an obligation acquired by the debtor against the third party 'in substitution of the object of the loan'. Provisions similar to art. 794 of the Portuguese Civil Code are arts. 1303 of the French Civil Code, 1259 of the Italian Civil Code, 338 of the Greek Civil Code and § 281, sub-para. 1, BGB.

[106] See the Supreme Court judgment of 6 January 1988, (1988) 373 *Boletim do Ministério da Justiça* 499–505. This case dealt with assigning protection (the case concerned the procedural legitimacy of the plaintiff) to what the Court referred to as 'diffuse interests' (legitimacy of a private individual to oppose urbanization work with infringement of the rules of public law).

In Case 1 ('Cable I – The Blackout', sub II), the court would perhaps be more likely to allow compensation for pure economic loss, given the 'inconvenience' of treating differently two kinds of damage arising from the same facts, even though such differentiation is technically justified.

III. The protection of absolute rights under tort law is traditional in Portuguese law, having been established in the 1867 Civil Code. There was some influence from German law and doctrine in the preliminary work on the current 1966 Civil Code, which came into force in 1967, although the formulation of article 482/1 is considerably more open than the corresponding § 823 (1) BGB.[107]

As regards the principle of non-recoverability for pure economic loss, the preparatory work on the Portuguese and German codes suggests that the intention was to place limits upon the number of compensation claims, it being difficult to restrict the circle of persons having a right to compensation in any other way.[108] Rather than indicating lower esteem for this type of damage, the practical motivation was to control the overall scope of liability. In accordance with this principle, reparation for pure economic loss raises fewer objections the nearer it is to what might be referred to as a 'special relationship'.

## Sweden and Finland

I. Almost certainly in Sweden, and most probably also in Finland, Cato cannot recover the damages incurred by the loss of production. This depends on the same reasons which made compensation for loss of production doubtful in Case 1 ('Cable I – The Blackout'). The absence of damage to machinery makes the same arguments stronger.

II. As mentioned before, the problem for the compensation of loss of production arises from the classification of such a loss as a 'third party' loss, i.e. a loss not incurred by the same subject who has suffered the

---

[107] J. F. S. Monteiro, 'Manuel de Andrade und der Einfluss des BGB auf das Portugiesische Zivilgesetzbuch von 1966', in E. Jayme and P. Mansel (eds.), *Auf dem Wege zu einem gemeineuropäischen Privatrecht – 100 Jahre BGB und die lusophonen Länder*, Symposium in Heidelberg, 29–30, November 1996 (Nomos Verlaggesselschaft, Baden-Baden, 1997), p. 41; C. von Bar, *Gemeineuropäisches Deliktrecht, Band I* (Beck, München, 1996), pp. 28–32.

[108] See Vaz Serra, 'Responsabilidade Civil', 67–8; G. Herrmann, *Zum Nachteil des Vermogens, Eine (un)rechtsvergleichende Betrachtung des Common Law of Negligence und der deutschen Farlässigkeitshaftung für 'blosse' Vermogensschaden* (Karlsruhe, Heidelberg, 1978), and E. Picker, 'Positive Forderungsverletzung und culpa in contrahendo – Zur Problematik der Haftungen (zwischen) Vertrag und Delikt', (1983) *Archiv für die civilistische Praxis* 369–519.

property damage (in this case, the cutting of the cable). The argument which seems most useful in order to avoid such an obstacle is to identify some sort of property damage caused directly to the plaintiff, who could then claim compensation for the loss of production as an economic loss 'consequent upon' a property damage, according to *SkadestL* 5:7 (Sweden) and SkadestL 5:5 (Finland).[109] The absence of any damage to machinery makes it harder to find a way out. In Finnish law, a narrow space for compensation is left by a decision of the Supreme Court admitting the possibility of granting some compensation when the use of the cables takes place in forms 'comparable' to property rights.[110]

*Editors' comparative comments*

This variation on the theme presents a classic case of stand-alone economic loss due to negligent conduct. It goes to the heart of the issues surrounding its recovery in Europe. The defendant's conduct in cutting the cable has not harmed Cato's machinery (as in Cable I); it has only idled his factory and disrupted his production. Cato's claim essentially involves the loss of an expectation – his lost profits and nothing else. There is no claim of consequential economic loss.

The responses reveal the wealth of conceptual resources that European systems bring to bear upon the problem. Each tradition favours a distinct methodology capable of producing varying results. Indeed, the responses suggest that there are four principal methodologies that dominate the European scene. The compensation issue may be left to (1) flexible causal determinations; (2) preliminary judicial screening; (3) exclusionary causal theory; or (4) a scheme of absolute rights. A few countries may even combine two of these approaches, but generally each has chosen a single mechanism to deal with this issue. However, operating behind these divergent methods are a set of policies (metalegal considerations) which, when they receive clearest expression, emphasize the need to limit recoverability.

The methodology of flexible causal determinations is characteristic of the liberal regimes. In Belgium, France, Greece, Italy, Spain and (for these purposes) the Netherlands, Cato's lost production or lost profits will be compensated under the general clause, in spite of the absence of physical

---

[109] Both statutory texts include loss of income as a recoverable loss in the case of property damage (for Sweden, SkadestL 5:7; for Finland, SkadestL 5:5); the Swedish text also calls 'obstacle to economic activity' as a further form of recoverable loss.
[110] HD 1994: 94.

loss. In this grouping, no special rules have been developed to govern this particular compensation issue; instead the ordinary requirements of conduct, fault, damage and causation complete the liability equation. Nevertheless, it should be noted that in each of the responses there is more emphasis upon the role of causation than any other element. This strongly suggests that if there is an Achilles heel to the plaintiff's claim to compensation, the judge will find and express it in the language of causation, e.g. by arguing that the lost profit is not certain, or by questioning whether the same loss might have been incurred anyway, via a different means or for a different reason (such as a workers' strike). Of course, there is no indication that a negative causal determination is likely to occur in Cable II: each response states clearly that on the present facts recovery would be allowed. This level of confidence derives from both doctrinal and jurisprudential considerations, particularly on the basis of favourable holdings by national courts in similar 'cable' cases. Nevertheless, as signalled earlier, the great flexibility inherent in the ordinary rules of causation leaves space for a certain amount of tacit policymaking that will be problematic in later cases.

The methodology of preliminary judicial screening underlies the approach in England and Scotland. It is certain there will be no compensation in this particular fact situation. Cato's 'pure' loss of production (completely unconnected to damage to the property belonging to the claimant) due to carelessness is not recoverable in negligence because, as a matter of judicial policy, there is no duty of care to protect against such loss. This 'duty of care' screening passes upon each duty scenario as it arises and reduces the pressure for judicial policy to be expressed through causal analysis or fault analysis. However, as the English and Scottish precedents show, causal notions of 'remoteness' and 'directness' are not altogether abandoned. They are still a rather important part of the screening process (before *Donoghue*, remoteness was the primary means of keeping liability within acceptable bounds),[111] but they are now woven into the situational finding on duty of care. Thus the duty situation is quite fact-sensitive. Even though no compensation will be given in Cable II, a duty of care to protect against pure economic loss can be recognized, on an exceptional basis, in later cases.

Austria, Finland and Sweden control the compensation issue through the use of exclusionary causation. No recovery is possible in the case at

---

[111] See *Stair Memorial Encyclopaedia, The Laws of Scotland*, vol. 15 (Law Society of Scotland, Edinburgh, 1996) p. 255, para. 379 (written by K. McK. Norrie).

hand because, as the Austrian courts reason, the damage did not occur 'in the direction of the assault' but only as a side-effect to a third person. Similarly, in Sweden and Finland the loss of production is classified as an unrecoverable 'third party loss' because it is not suffered by the same person who suffered the property loss (the owner of the cut cable). This group of countries is in effect resorting to a policy-driven 'two-party concept' of direct causation, simply as a categorical means of ruling out the recovery of pure economic loss in tort. The technique lacks flexibility (all claims for negligent harm in tort are effectively precluded) but it produces certainty of outcome. The justification for this sharp limitation is expressed in the forceful terms which typically echo throughout the conservative and pragmatic regimes: in the words of the Austrian judges, it is necessary to avoid 'a boundless, economically intolerable expansion of liability'.

There is no recovery in Germany and Portugal because pure financial loss caused by careless behaviour does not fit within the scheme of 'absolute rights' protected in tort. It makes little difference that Portugal has not spelled out this scheme in its Civil Code. The claim is excluded because the original policies of the BGB drafters is highly persuasive and the influence of German legal science is continuing. The Portuguese code fathers and contemporary judges and writers simply superimpose this thinking upon the general clause of the Civil Code.

The rather categorical denial of recovery by seven out of the thirteen countries within this study would indicate that the Cable II case conjures up the classic 'nightmare scenario' that many jurists find disturbing. The parameters of the case, however, should be closely observed. A slight change in the facts might vary the outcome. Thus if the cable were cut intentionally or recklessly instead of negligently, or if severing the cable violated a statute whose intended purpose is to protect third parties against such loss, or if defendant's conduct breached a contract with 'protective effects' toward third persons, then Cato might receive compensation.

## Case 3: cable III – the day-to-day workers

### Case

Again, in the same case, the halt of production meant that Cato had to lay off a number of workers hired on a day-to-day basis. These workers are now claiming compensation from Acme for the loss of two days' pay.

### France

I. There is no specific case addressing this issue in French Law, but the workers will certainly recover their economic loss either from the state under the *Code du travail* (Labour Code), or in the alternative from Acme under the Civil Code.

II. The situation where a factory has to lay off its workers because of an event of *force majeure* is called *chômage technique*. Assuming a day-to-day worker is treated as a normal worker by the French Labour Code, and assuming also that the halt of production may be viewed as an act of *force majeure*, the French Labour Code allows workers on *chômage technique* to be indemnified by the state (art. L351–352 of the Labour Code). If the state pays the loss of two days' wages, then the employees will have no need to sue Acme, since they will have been fully compensated.

Moreover, according to decisions of the Chambre Sociale of the Cour de Cassation, if the state refuses idemnification, the employer himself is supposed to pay the loss of salaries to his employees, at least when the number of hours to be worked had been fixed by contract.[112] This is obviously not the case in this situation, since the workers are hired on a day-to-day basis, and the employer did not necessarily 'owe' them those two days of unemployment.

If the workers are not compensated by the state or their employer, the question is whether they can sue Acme or not. The answer lies in the application of article 1382 of the Civil Code.

The court may well find fault on the part of Acme's employee. It may consider that the cutting of the cable was careless behaviour in the circumstances. It may also determine that the cutting of the cable was the direct cause of the lay-off because it is hard to say that the idled factory sustained direct damage, but the idled workers suffered only 'indirect' loss. If the employer had been liable to pay the workers salaries because of a fixed-term contract, as we have noted above, surely this

---

[112] Soc. 26 novembre 1987 and Soc. 16 juin 1988, D. 1988, Som. 311.

loss by the employer would be direct and foreseeable. The nature of the contract, which he entered into with his workers, should not be a causal distinction. This will depend on a determination by the judge, but in our view the causal link is direct.

The main question mark in this fact pattern is perhaps the 'certainty' issue. The defendants (Acme) could argue that, as the workers were hired on a day-to-day basis, they could not prove with certainty that they would have been employed from one day to another. Cases involving day-to-day workers are very rare in France, and we have found no authority stating whether this defence would be effective or not. It is of course possible, though not necessarily probable, that they would have been terminated anyway even if there had been no cut-off of electricity, but here it might be appropriate to compensate them for the loss of the chance to work for their employer, especially since that chance might seem to have been quite high. The jurisprudence has already indemnified one who was physically injured for the loss of a chance to receive a professional promotion, even when that promotion seemed relatively uncertain.[113] The same approach could be used to grant compensation to the day-to-day workers in Case 3.

**Belgium**

I. The workers could have a claim against Acme or its employee. However, it will not be very easy to recover the loss of two days' pay since that damage results mainly from the employment contracts with Cato and Cato's decision to lay them off.

II. The workers have a contractual relationship with Cato based on their employment contracts. The loss of two days' pay is a damage resulting from these employment contracts. If the workers have suffered a damage resulting from a breach of contract, the claim shall be first directed towards the person with whom they have executed their contracts.

Therefore, the matter is first a case of contractual liability, more precisely, a matter regarding the breach of an employment contract.

Since there is no contract between the workers and Acme or its employee, the claim for damage initiated against them will rest on article 1382 and on article 1384 al. 3 CC.

---

[113] Civ. 2, 3 novembre 1971, D. 1972. 667. See also Crim., 7 juin 1990, Bull. Crim. no. 24 (horse raiser compensated for the loss of a chance to train a filly).

*Article 1382*
Any act of a man which causes damage to another obliges him by whose fault it occurred to make reparation.

*Article 1384*
Each one is liable not only for the damage which he caused by his own act, but also for that which is caused by the act of persons for whom he is responsible, or by things which he has in his keeping.
[…]
Masters and principals are liable for damage caused by their domestics and employees in the function for which they have been employed.
[…]

The present case raises three issues. First, is the damage claimed by the workers (loss of two days' pay) a recoverable damage? More precisely, is the damage claimed by the workers the violation of a legitimate interest?

It is obvious that in the present case, the workers had no legal right to be employed. At most, such a right could only be based on their employment contracts.

In Belgian tort law, however, the violation of a right is not required anymore. The violation of a legitimate interest is sufficient.[114]

If the workers can prove that they normally would have earned those two days' pay, they should be considered as having a legitimate interest.

Secondly, to be recoverable, the damage should not have been already indemnified. Therefore, the claim of the workers shall be rejected if the workers have been already indemnified by their employer (Cato). But in such case, the employer would be subrogated to the rights of the workers.

Finally, Acme or its employee will be liable for that damage if the workers can prove that the damage has a causal link with the fault of Acme's employee. In accordance with the case law of the Supreme Court, Acme and/or its employee will be liable only if the damage would not have occurred as it occurred if Acme's employee had not cut the cable.

In the present case, it is not obvious that the workers will be able to prove that they would have certainly earned their two days' pay if the electric cable had not been cut by Acme's employee.

---

[114] R. O. Dalcq and G. Schamps, 'La responsabilité délictuelle et quasi-délictuelle, examen de jurisprudence (1987–1993)', (1995) 150 RCJB, 738.

Moreover, the Supreme Court has on several occasions stated that the causal link is interrupted when the damage claimed results from another autonomous obligation, such as one resulting from a statute or from a contract.[115]

Since the damage claimed by the plaintiffs in the present case results from the employment contract executed with Cato, the claim of the plaintiffs should be normally rejected.

## Italy

I. The workers may have a slight possibility of recovering for their lost wages against Acme under article 2043 cc.

II. The loss of economic opportunity is one of the main categories in which pure economic damages are recoverable.

In *Baroncini* v. *Enel*, the Corte di Cassazione ruled that a worker may recover damages for the lost opportunity he incurred when he was barred from participating by an internal recruitment procedure.[116] According to the Court, opportunities are a new absolute right, a valuable asset actually belonging to the plaintiff and therefore protected by article 2043 cc.

In *Baroncini*, however, the judges deemed that the right might be protected only when opportunities are over 50 per cent; yet, in several later decisions the Court changed its mind and admitted recovery for slighter chances of success.[117]

Aside from the loss of chance analysis, Italian case law focuses on the factual chain of causation. Courts opt for a very narrow view of causation: damages are recoverable only when they spring from a direct and immediate source.[118] This interpretation, which is found in the doctrine and some court decisions,[119] offers a more flexible tool to assess indirect and non-consequential damages.

---

[115] Cass., 17 janvier 1938, Pas., I, 8 and 11; Cass., 28 avril 1978, RCJB, 1979, p. 261; Cass., 26 septembre 1979, RGAR, 1982, no. 10431; Cass., 9 mars 1984, RCJB, 1986, p. 651; Cass., 15 mars 1985, Pas., I, 1985, 978; Cass., 28 juin 1984, Pas., 1984, I, 618; Cass., 18 avril 1988, Pas., 1988, I, 943; Cass., 4 octobre 1988, Pas, 1989, I, 118, 15 novembre 1991, I, 282.

[116] Cass. 19.12.1985, no. 6506, FI, 1986, I, 383 note by Principalli.

[117] Cass. 29.4. 1993, no. 5026, in GI, 1993, I, 1, 2567, noted by A. M. Musy; Cass. 22.4.1993, no. 4725 in Dir. e Prat. Lav., 1993, 26, 1775; Cass. 13.6.1991, no. 6657 in MGC, 1991.

[118] See Cass. Civ., 21.10.1969, no. 3438, FI, 1970, I, 501; Cass. Civ., 2.1.1968, no. 253, FI, 1968, I, 2628.

[119] Cass. Civ. 10.10.1967, no. 239, FI, 1968, I, 1311.

III. As frequently happens, scholars were ahead of courts in pushing for the recovery of damages in the case of lost opportunities.[120] At present, a large majority of Italian legal scholarship is favourable to full recognition of these awards.[121] However, some authors are calling for a sharper distinction between legally protected opportunities and non-recoverable expectations.[122]

## Spain

I. The workers could possibly obtain compensation for their damages.

II. While accepting that in both Case 1 ('Cable I – The Blackout') and Case 2 ('Cable II – Factory Shutdown') the damaged factories could obtain compensation from the roadworks company who initially cut the cable, under the Spanish legal system problems of causation would arise as to the workers' lost wages.

The Supreme Court decision (First Chamber) of 30 May 1986 indicates that the injury suffered by Cato's workers is in fact recoverable. There, an explosion occurred in the boiler of company A. As a result of this explosion, neighbouring factory B suffered damage to the extent that it was forced to halt production and lay off several employees. These employees sued company A for the difference between what they received as unemployment benefits and the salaries they would have received, had they continued their usual work in factory B. The Supreme Court awarded this compensation.

It should be noted, however, that in this Supreme Court decision the argument focused on whether company A's fault in causing the accident could be proved or not. There is no doubt that once the boiler's explosion was proven technically foreseeable and avoidable (i.e. there was fault), A was liable to B's employees for lost wages. This Supreme Court decision is good evidence that our tort system recognizes the protection of credit rights (*in personam*) and not only absolute rights.[123]

---

[120] F. D. Busnelli, 'Perdita di una chance e risarcimento del danno risarcibile', *FI*, 1965, IV, 47; P. G. Monateri, Sintesi di informazione, *RDC*, 1986, II, 364.
[121] C. Salvi, *Il danno extracontrattuale* (Napoli, 1985); G. Visintini, 'Risarcimento del danno', *RDC*, 1983, I, 811; A. Di Majo, 'Il problema del danno al patrimonio', *RCDP*, 1984, 397.
[122] A. De Cupis, 'Aspettativa legittima e risarcimento del danno', *GC*, 1983, II, 104.
[123] F. Pantaleón 'Comentario al artículo 1902', in *Comentario del Código Civil*, vol. II (Ministero de Justicia–Civitas, Madrid, 1991) p. 1994.

## Greece

I. The workers have no claim against the excavating employee nor against Acme, but they could perhaps still claim their salary from Cato, because their lay-off is probably invalid.

II. Liability of Acme and its excavator's user: according to article 914 CC, Acme is not (even vicariously) liable to the workers, because there is no causal link between their loss and the cutting of the cable. This is certain, according to both criteria proposed for testing it (either foreseeability of the particular damage,[124] or its inclusion in the interests protected by the infringed legal rule).[125] Indeed, the lay-off of the workers hired on a day-to-day basis seems to be an unforeseeable effect of the destruction of a cable belonging to a third person. Thus, it is out of the protective purpose area of the legal rule that the tortfeasor has infringed by cutting the public cables. So it is not to be indemnified.

The same conclusion could be reached also *e contrario* from article 929 sub-para. 2 CC, which stipulates that in the case of bodily injury, compensation from the wrongdoer may also be sought (apart from the victim) only by persons entitled by the law (not by a contract) to claim services from the victim.[126] The explanation of such a provision is simple: benefits provided by the law are foreseeable, because the law is already known and stable; benefits provided by a contract can be foreseen only by the parties, usually not by everyone. Thus, the workers do not have any claim against the employee or Acme.

Liability of Cato: the workers could perhaps still claim their wages from Cato, their employer, because when he hired them in the first place, he intended to keep them employed in order to keep his factory functioning. This fact is easily established from Cato's own claim for compensation because of the stopping of his factory's operation, which means

---

[124] AP 692/1990 NoB 40, 67; AP 1063/90; AP 979/92 ElD 35, 1044; K. Triantaphyllopoulos, *Law of Obligations* (Athens, 1935), p. 184; G. Balis, *Law of Obligations, General Part* (3rd edn, 1960), p. 100; A. Ligeropoulos (gen. ed.), *Interpretation of the Civil Code (A Commentary) (ErmAK): Law of Obligations* vols. I–III (1949–1978), arts. 297–300 CC, no. 39; G. Fourkiotis, *Greek Law of Obligations, General Part* (1964), p. 318; G. Michaélidès-Nouaros *Law of Obligations* (University lectures no daté) p. 31 etc.

[125] Commentary by M. Stathopoulos in A. Georgiades and M. Stathopoulos, *Civil Code Article by Article Commentary*, vols. I–IV (1978–1982) arts. 297–298, no. 67, 60–5; P. Sourlas, *Adaequanztheorie und Normzwecklehre bei der Begruendung der Haftung nach § 823 Abs. 1 BGB* (1974) pp. 15 ff.

[126] See Commentry by Georgiades in A. Georgiades and Stathopoulos, *Civil Code*, art. 928, no. 6; EphAth 5411/1977 NoB 26, 737; EphAth 5773/1972 Arm 27, 171; EphAth 4117/1972 Arm 27, 91; EphAth 775/1960 NoB 8, 510.

that his intention was to continue operation. Consequently, the day-to-day contract was simulated and concealed within it another hiring contract, on this occasion without any time clause. The simulated contract is invalid according to article 138, paragraph 1 CC, but the latent contract between Cato and the workers is valid according to article 138, paragraph 2 CC[127] Thus, the workers cannot be laid off because of temporary damage, which prevented the employer from accepting their work (art. 656 CC).

## England

I. The workers cannot recover any wages from Acme.

II. The workers' action would have to lie in negligence, as there is no mention of any harmful intention of Acme against them.

The tort of interference with contractual relations is not available to them, as it clearly requires either an intention of such interference, or, at the very least, that the defendant's conduct is *directed* towards interfering with another's contractual relations (see *Millar v. Bassey*).[128] Neither of these two is disclosed by the facts.

Liability under the tort of negligence is also excluded since the workers will not be able to establish:

(1) that they suffered damage recognized as recoverable by the law of negligence; loss of pay not connected with personal injury or illness is a pure economic loss clearly not so recognized: see the case of *Burgess v. Florence Nightingale Hospital for Gentlewomen*;[129]
(2) that the defendant owed them a duty of care (*Donoghue v. Stevenson*).[130] No such duty is owed to third parties who, without being harmed in their person or physical property, suffer loss of earnings as a result of a negligent action: see, again, *Burgess v. Florence Nightingale Hospital for Gentlewomen*.

III. Both the issue of what damage is recognized as recoverable in the tort of negligence, and the issue of when there exists a duty of care not to cause harm, are now clearly issues to be decided on a case-by-case basis, on the grounds of what the courts consider to be 'just, fair and reasonable': *Caparo v. Dickman*,[131] or, as Lord Denning put it in *Spartan Steel v. Martin*[132] on grounds of legal policy. This creates uncertainty,

---

[127] The prevailing view in Greece bases this conclusion on the prohibition of contracts 'in fraudem legis' (see AP 344/1969, EED 28, 974; AP 48/1971 EED 36, 429.
[128] Unreported, *The Independent*, 26 August 1993.   [129] [1955] 1 QB 349 (CA).
[130] [1932] AC 562.   [131] [1990] 2 AC 605 (HL).   [132] [1973] 1 QB 27 (CA).

but is thought to give the system the necessary flexibility to screen out economic loss claims that, in the opinion of the judiciary, make bad political, social and economic sense.[133]

## Scotland

I. The workers would not be able to recover damages for their lost wages.

II. Again, we may refer to *Dynamco*[134] and the judgment of Lord Migdale who held that '[t]he law of Scotland has for over a hundred years refused to accept that a claim for financial loss which does not arise directly from damage to the claimant's property can give rise to a legal claim for damages founded on negligence'.[135] In this scenario, the workers are in the same situation as Cato and have suffered no damage to their property (or, indeed, their person). As a result, like him, they are unable to claim damages. The reasons for this are related to the question of proximity by way of remoteness and also policy. The attitude of the Scottish courts would be similar to that expressed by Lord Denning MR in *SCM (UK) Ltd*. He said:

In actions of negligence, when the plaintiff has suffered no damage to his person or property, but has only sustained economic loss, the law does not usually permit him to recover that loss. The reason lies in public policy. It was first stated by Blackburn J in *Cattle v. Stockton Waterworks Co*,[136] and has been repeated many times since. He gave this illustration: when a mine is flooded by negligence, thousands of men may be thrown out of work. None of them is injured, but each of them loses wages. Has each of them a cause of action? He thought not. So here I would ask: when an electric cable is damaged and many factories may be stopped from working, can each of them claim for its loss of profit? I think not. It is not sensible to saddle losses on this scale to one sole contractor. Very often such losses occur without anyone's fault. A mine may be flooded, or a power failure may occur by mischance as well as by negligence. Where it is only mischance, everyone grumbles but puts up with it. No one dreams of bringing an action for damages. So also when it occurs by negligence. The risk should

---

[133] Full discussion of the policy of English law in cases of pure economic loss in E. K. Banakas, *Civil Liability for Pure Economic Loss* (Kluwer, The Hague, 1996), chs. 1 and 2; for a discussion of arguments in favour of elevating earning capacity to a protected status similar to that accorded to real property interests see E. K. Banakas, *Tortious Liability for Pure Economic Loss: A Comparative Study*, (Hellenic Institute of International and Foreign Law, Athens, 1989), pp. 150 ff.
[134] *Dynamco Ltd v. Holland and Hannen and Cubitts (Scotland) Ltd* 1972 SLT 38, 1971 SC 257.
[135] 1972 SLT 38 at p. 39.
[136] (1875) LR 10 QB 453 at p. 457, [1874–80] All ER Rep 220 at p. 223.

be borne by the whole community rather than on one pair of shoulders, i.e. on one contractor who may, or may not, be insured against the risk. There is not much logic in this, but still it is the law.[137]

The workers are in a contractual relationship with Cato, either a contract of employment or a contract for the hire of services, which is interfered with, albeit unintentionally, in the sense of their being unable to work for the two days. However, before Acme could be liable for damages under the delict of wrongful interference with the performance of a contract, they would have had to have acted with the intention of interfering with the contract and with knowledge of its existence.[138] Neither factor is present here. Presumably there is an express term in the contract of employment between the men and Cato that the men may be laid off without pay; if not, they should bring an action against Cato. At common law an employer is in breach of contract if he lays off an employee without pay in the absence of an express term permitting this.[139] Given that it is said the workers are hired on a day-to-day basis, presumably it is a term of the contract that work will not always be available and that the workers will only be employed when it is. If this is the case, the reason why Cato is unable to provide work for the workers should be totally irrelevant and were the workers to bring an action against Acme they would presumably be found to have no title or interest to sue.

III. As a result of the damage to the public utility's property by Acme, the public utility is unable to fulfil its contract with Cato who suffers secondary economic loss by being forced to halt production. If Cato has a contractual obligation to provide work for the workers he cannot fulfil it, and the consequent loss could be described as 'tertiary' in relation to the negligent act. If, as a matter of policy, secondary economic loss is considered too remote or indirect then it can be understood that any loss even more remote or indirect will not be considered by the courts.

## The Netherlands

I. The most likely scenario is that the workmen's claim will be denied. Although this matter has not been decided yet by the Dutch Supreme

---

[137] [1971] 1 QB 337 at p. 344B.
[138] *Torquay Hotel Co. Ltd* v. *Cousins* [1969] 2 Ch 106, [1969] 1 All ER 522.
[139] *Warburton* v. *Taff Vale Railway Co.* (1902) 18 TLR 420, *Hanley* v. *Pease & Partners* [1915] 1 KB 698.

Court, most authors have expressed great reticence in allowing for such a 'third-degree' claim.[140]

II. Regarding this issue, the Civil Code leaves much open to debate. However, on the occasion of a related subject the Dutch legislature has shown some reservation, but has left possible further legal development open to debate in scholarly writing and judicial opinions.[141]

First, it is unlikely that Acme's duty to excavate carefully purports to protect the interest of uninterrupted employment. If this observation is correct, then damaging the pipe is not unlawful vis-à-vis the employees of Cato.

Secondly, if one were to say – for argument's sake – that the act itself was unlawful, then a similar obstacle would be found in the causality test. Supposing that employment by the day was common in Dutch society, consequently, it would have been foreseeable for the excavator that his negligence would result in the workers' (temporary) unemployment. One's inclination is to think that, in spite of the foreseeability of this loss, the Dutch judiciary would be most hesitant to allow for recovery, given the nature of the damage and the grounds for liability.

III. As mentioned earlier, most authors have expressed great reticence in allowing for such a 'third-degree' claim. Having said that, if one thinks about it rationally, the case for the workmen seems rather strong. If we consider that, as a regular employer, Cato would be able to claim the cost of wages ('second-degree' damage), it would seem unreasonable to deny the employees the same compensation ('third-degree' damage) for the sole reason of their being employed as day-labourers. This problem is similar to that of so-called *verplaatste schade* ('shifted damage'), or damage *par ricochet*: damage that would normally have been suffered by the injured party is sometimes in fact suffered by a third party because of a special relationship between the injured and the third party. As long as the total amount in damages awarded to Cato and its employees does not exceed the amount that Cato would have been able to claim, had the company been obliged to continue to pay wages, I would personally see no objection to allowing the employees to claim compensation.[142]

---

[140] See the authors mentioned by R. A. Salomons, *Schadevergoeding: zaakschade* (Monografieën Nieuw BW no. B-38) (2nd edn, Deventer, 1993) at pp. 52–5.

[141] See Explanatory Memorandum on the act implementing a strict liability for the use of hazardous and noxious substances, *Kamerstukken* II 21 202, no. 3, pp. 18–19, as quoted by A. T. Bolt and J. Spier, *De uitdijende reikwijdte van de aansprakelijkheid uit onrechtmatige daad* (Handelingen NJV 1996-1) (1996) at p. 102.

[142] In any case, the floodgates argument would not be valid, for the total amount owed to injured employee and employer would not be more than the amount that would be owed to the employee alone.

## Germany

I. The workers have no claim against Acme. None of their absolute rights listed in § 823 (1) has been violated. In particular, their employment is not an absolute right but only a relative one since it arises from, and is limited to, their contract with Cato. Nor is there any contractual relationship between the workers and Acme that could conceivably give rise to a claim. This result is clear and undisputed.

II. It is a fundamental principle of German tort law that only the persons whose absolute rights have been violated have tort claims under § 823 (1). Others, i.e. third parties whose 'absolute rights' have not been affected, suffer only pure economic loss which is not compensable under this provision.[143]

There are only three exceptions, all provided for by the Civil Code itself: first, in case of death, the wrongdoer has to pay funeral expenses to those in charge of the funeral (§ 844 (1)). Second, he must compensate third parties for loss of support to the extent the victim had a statutory duty to support them (§ 843 (2)). Third, the tortfeasor must compensate third parties for the loss of services that the victim was statutorily obliged to render (§ 845). These exceptions are final and conclusive.[144] Courts and scholars agree that they reflect the legislative intent to circumscribe third-party tort claims narrowly and have thus refused to recognize additional ones.[145]

III. The workers would still have claims *against Cato* if he had no right to terminate their employment. In that case, he would remain liable for their pay even though he had no use for their services (§§ 615, 293–296 BGB).[146] If, however, the termination was legal and valid, Cato would not owe them anything, though the workers may have a right to unemployment insurance benefits.

## Austria

I. The workers' claim for compensation would be unsuccessful under Austrian law. Negligent interference in obligations is generally no basis for compensation claims, since 'rights *in personam*' are not generally protected against infringements by third parties. There is no doubt that

---

[143] RGZ 64, 344, at 345 (1906); BGHZ 7, 30 (1952); BGH NJW 1996, 2662.
[144] BGHZ 7, 30, at 33–4 (1952).
[145] J. Esser and H. L. Weyers, *Schuldrecht Band II, Besonderer Teil* (7th edn, 1990) s. 63 II 4 b; K. Larenz and C. W. Canaris, *Lehrbuch des Schuldrechts* (13th edn, 1994) s. 81 I 2 c.
[146] See M. Löwisch, *Albeitsrecht*, Rd.-Nr. 1003–10.

the Supreme Court would resort to the 'indirect damage formula' in a similar case.

II. Even if the halt in production which entails the workers' dismissal is attributable to the gross negligence of the Acme employee, there is nonetheless no 'direct' violation of the worker's property for which Acme must answer. Therefore, the Austrian Supreme Court would rule that the damage did not occur 'in the direction of the assault, but was attributable to a side-effect which arose in a sphere of interest not protected by the provision aiming to prevent the assault'.

III. It may well be that under certain applicable rules of Austrian labour law, Cato may have the obligation to pay the salaries irrespective of whether he could actually employ the workers for the intended job. It would then be incumbent upon Cato to seek repayment by the tortfeasor.

His claim against Acme would have little chance of success, however, unless Cato was the owner of the cable (of which there is no indication in the facts) as well as the factory; or unless the contract between Acme and whoever commissioned the roadworks were to be classified as a 'contract with protective effects to third persons', and Cato would thus fall under that protective effect.

## Portugal

I. There are no grounds whatsoever for the workers laid off by Cato to make any claim for compensation against Acme.

II. The workers have merely had an 'expectation of fact' frustrated, because they had no contractual right to be employed continuously.

If the unlawful act had caused a lasting impediment to normal work, the hypothesis of an infringement of the right to work might be applicable as a manifestation of the general personality right (protected as an absolute right), which is openly recognized in Portuguese law (art. 70 CC). But this hypothesis is not consistent with our case.

## Sweden and Finland

I. The workers have absolutely no claim against Acme. They can in no way be seen as having personally suffered any property damage, and the 'third party rule' applies here strictly.

II. The difficulties encountered by Swedish law in providing compensation for loss of production in cable cases make it *a fortiori* unthinkable to admit a claim like this. A worker has no property right or other comparable right in the damaged object on which to base his claim, and a simple contractual relationship is unanimously considered insufficient to include the plaintiff under the protection of the law of torts. This position is undisputed.[147]

*Editors' comparative comments*

This cable case is a more complicated version of the first two. Here, damage to a cable leads not only to Cato's factory shutdown and loss of production, but gives rise to a claim by day labourers who had been working for Cato. Their lost wages is a further repercussion of Acme's negligent conduct. It lengthens the chain of events and expands the radius of pure economic loss. The causal link is not only stretched, but also the nature of the plaintiffs' damaged interest is not as strong. The workers have lost no property; instead, they have been deprived of an employment opportunity of uncertain duration. The nature of their day-to-day 'right' to work may appear somewhat more fragile than Cato's loss of production: their employment might have been ended at any time, for any reason, by Cato or themselves.

The results show that for almost all countries within the study, this claim is not actionable. From a comparative standpoint, it is interesting to observe how the systems reach these results using the four methods already discussed above in Cable II.

For countries applying flexible rules of causation, the causal link between Acme's conduct and the plaintiffs' lost wages is increasingly problematic. It becomes noticeably more difficult for the reporters to state with certainty how the case would be actually decided. Because of the precarious nature of their work contract, the workers would have difficulty establishing that their wages were lost solely because of the defendant's act. The causes of their termination may have been multiple. They might have lost their jobs for reasons other than the interruption of power to the factory. Cato had no obligation to continue to employ them. The Belgian judge may conclude that the 'at will' contract is an *autonomous* obligation that interrupts the chain of causation. In Greece compensation may be denied on the basis of the *unforeseeability* of the workers' contractual arrangements with their employer. On the other hand, in France a proportioned amount of compensation might

[147] J. Hellner, *Skadeståndsrätt* (5th edn, 1995), pp. 362 ff.

be granted for the loss of a 'chance' to earn the two days' salary. The Spanish report also suggested, with caution, that the causal conditions might be satisfied.

Plaintiffs' claim is clearly rejected in all countries that take an exclusionary view of causation. Thus recovery is denied in Scotland because the lost wages are 'tertiary economic loss,' in Austria because the plaintiffs were 'not in the direction of the assault;' in Sweden/Finland because the plaintiffs fall under the 'third party rule,' and finally in the Netherlands because they present a 'third-degree claim.' Since Cato too falls under this exclusion and cannot recover (see Cable II), the reporters make the *a fortiori* argument that surely the workers cannot recover for loss which is even more remote than Cato's.

In England and Scotland the workers will not receive compensation because Acme did not owe a 'duty of care' to the workers in negligence with respect to this kind of loss.

The claims fall in Germany and Portugal because the defendant's act has not infringed upon an absolute right of the workers. Their work and their opportunity to continue it have been interfered with, but these are not absolute rights. They are relative rights governed by contract with Cato. Accordingly, the Portuguese reporter notes that defendant's act may have merely frustrated an 'expectation of fact', but apparently this has no significance within a scheme of absolute rights.

While the responses are broadly negative, one might question whether they are in fact driven by the floodgates policy, or whether they are also the product of methodologies that have a conceptual life of their own. As the Dutch reporter well observes, it is difficult to see that recognition of the workers' claim to lost wages should be subject to the floodgates argument. Had they been ordinary employees on fixed-term contracts, Cato would have been able, in a number of jurisdictions, to claim the cost of paying their wages. (Case 4, 'Convalescing Employee', deals precisely with that situation.) It would seem fortuitous and unreasonable to deny the workers themselves the same compensation just because they happened to be employed as day-labourers. So long as the total amount of the defendant's liability does not exceed the amount that Cato would have been able to claim had he been obliged to continue to pay wages, the claim of the day-labourers really represents no enlargement of defendant's liability. This could suggest that the methods applied to this problem are not always neatly tailored to fit the scope of the policy concern which gave rise to them.

## Case 4: convalescing employee

### Case

A worker was hit by a car and was off work for three months. The law (or the work contract) requires the employer to pay the employee his entire salary for the entire period of sick leave. The employer claims compensation from the injurer for all expenses (pay, insurance, etc.) which he has disbursed without receiving the worker's services in return.

### France

I. The employer will be fully reimbursed by the car owner or driver for wages and expenditures paid to his injured worker. The employer is subrogated to the victim's own claims by virtue of a special strict liability law of July 5, 1985 (*Loi Badinter*).

II. The employer who paid the employee his entire salary for the period of sick leave is entitled to claim compensation from the injurer for the amount paid, by virtue of article 29 of the law of 5 July 1985. Under article 30 of the same law, the employer is in such case subrogated to the victim's right to pursue the injurer, with the exception, however, that he is not subrogated to the victim's right to mental distress (art. 31).

As for any social security instalments paid by the employer, they are also recoverable by the employer under article 32 of the law.

III. Before 1985, cases involving traffic accidents could be brought against the *gardien* of the vehicle under article 1384 of the Civil Code and the basis of recovery was called strict liability.[148] Nevertheless, three defences were open to the *gardien*: *force majeure*, the act of a third person and the fault of the victim. This last defence meant that the victim's contributory negligence could reduce his recovery. Closing this loophole somewhat, the Cour de Cassation ruled in the *Desmares* case[149] that the victim's fault was only a defence when it had the characteristics of *force majeure* (unforeseeable and unavoidable).

However, the interpretation of *Desmares* differed widely in the lower courts, and the law of 5 July 1985 brought order into the picture.

By enacting the law of 5 July 1985, the intention of the French government was to indemnify automatically all victims of car accidents

---

[148] An alternative action under arts. 1382–1383 CC was of course also possible provided that the victim could prove the driver's fault.
[149] Civ. 2e, 21 juillet 1982, D. 82, 449.

in order to avoid the situations where injurers escaped liability.[150] The adoption of article 29 (granting reimbursement to the employer of a worker injured in a car accident) was specially advocated by Professor André Tunc, who was the author of the first draft of the law as well as the book *Pour une loi sur les accidents de la circulation* (1981).

## Belgium

I. The employer can recover the payment made to the injured worker from the tortfeasor because he is subrogated to the rights of the worker.

II. Claim via subrogation. According to article 54, § 1 of the Belgian Law of 3 July 1978 on Employment Contracts, in case of full incapacity to work because of an accident at work, the employer must pay the worker his normal salary during the first seven days following the first day of his incapacity.

Over this period of seven days imposed by the law, in accordance with a collective agreement or with the employment contract, the employer can be forced to pay the full salary during a certain period of time. This period could be, as in the present case, three months.

According to article 54 § 4 of the Belgian law of 3 July 1978, the employer has a claim against the tortfeasor for reimbursement of the salary and social security allowances paid in accordance with the law, a collective agreement or an individual agreement.

Tort claim. An old case of the Cour de Cassation developed a theory according to which the plaintiff is not allowed to claim the reimbursement of money paid to the injured party, if the payment results from another autonomous obligation implied by law or resulting from a contract.[151] In such a case, the damage claimed is not recoverable because the causal link is interrupted.

More recently, the Cour de Cassation has limited this theory by stating that the damage remains recoverable if the obligation, whether implied by law or resulting from a contract on which the payment is based is only 'secondary' with regard to the tortfeasor's obligation to repair.[152]

In that case, the Cour de Cassation validated a court decision which accepted the claim of a city council that had paid the costs to clear away

---

[150] H. Mazeaud, L. Mazeaud, J. Mazeaud and F. Chabas, *Leçons de droit civil*, Tome II, Vol. I, *Obligations. Théorie générale*. (8th edn Montchrestien, Paris, 1991), p. 614.
[151] Cass., 17 janvier 1938, Pas., I, 8 and 11.
[152] Cass., 13 avril 1988, Pas., 1988, I, 943; JT, 1988, p. 649; (1989) RCJB 631, and note F. Glansdorff and C. Dalcq.

a street after bullets had fallen from a truck. The city services cleared away the street in execution of a legal obligation to keep the streets safe.

However, the Court decided that this legal obligation was only secondary with regard to the obligation of the truck owners to repair the damage resulting from its fault.

In application of that caselaw, the employer could therefore also base his claim on article 1382 CC:

> Any act whatever of man which causes damage to another obliges him by whose fault it occurred to make reparation.

Finally, if the accident occurred during work or on the way to work, it must be added that article 49 of the Belgian law of 10 April 1971 regarding accidents during worktime forces the employer to execute insurance contracts covering the risk of accident for their employees and workers during work, and on the way to their work.

However, the indemnification is made through a fixed amount and is normally directly paid to the employee or worker. In case a compensation is paid to them, article 47 of the law provides that the insurance company or the fund created by the law, who ever made the payment, is subrogated to the rights of the injured person to the extent of the payment made.[153]

## Italy

I. Since 1982[154] it has been possible for the employer[155] to recover from the tortfeasor all payments made to the injured worker as well as to recover them directly from the insurer.

This may be enforced under two different provisions: damages recoverable for the unjustified damage within article 2043 cc which can be expansively interpreted to protect the labour obligation creditor; and damages recoverable through legal subrogation, provided by article 2110 cc, of the employer to the employee.

---

[153] L. Van Gossum, *Les accidents du travail* (3rd edn, De Boeck, Brussels 1994), p. 135.

[154] *Soc. Tirrena v. Soc. Ecol. it*, Cass. 27.5.1982, no. 3284, *MGC* 1982, the same solution has been adopted in *Soc. Polenghi Lombardo v. Soc. Calcagno*, Cass. 30.10.1984, no. 5562, *FI*, 1985, I, 149, noted by Troiano.

[155] See Cass. 11.7.1978, no. 3507, *FI* 1978, I, 1621 where the court stated that 'the employer is the real victim, for she is obliged by law or contract to continue paying the salary to the employee, even though the latter cannot perform her work obligation'.

II. In the last twenty years there has been continuing evolution on the issue. A first series of decisions denied damages to the private employer because private enterprises can easily replace a worker – at that time, statutory law was less demanding in terms of substantial protection of an employee's right to keep their position in case of injuries or prolonged illness.[156]

The turning point is represented by the ruling in *Proda S.p.A. v. Arduini*[157] where the Supreme Court decided that an employer can claim compensation from a tortfeasor for all the payments which the former owed to the employee (the Supreme Court, by focusing on the statutory duties of the employer towards the employee, avoided investigation of the remoteness of this damage).

Another debated issue was the recoverability of the *oneri sociali* (i.e. the amount of money that the employer must pay to the state for welfare assistance and for the national pension system). At first the Supreme Court did not admit recovery of welfare and pension contribution, considering those amounts due by a statutory provision that applies independently of the actual performance of employee's obligations.[158] Yet, under the pressure of lower courts and of legal scholarship,[159] the Supreme Court changed its mind in *Soc. Cespa v. Soc. Assic. Italiana*[160] and since then the question can be seen as settled.[161]

## Spain

I. There is no clear outcome to this case in the Spanish legal system. The case law is divided on this issue, the outcome depending on whether the claim is in civil or criminal court. There are court decisions which

---

[156] Only public administrations were granted compensation for the loss of an officer: see *Comune di Cortona v. Lloyd Adriatico Ass.*, Cass. 8.11.1980, no. 6008, *MGLav.*, 1981, 28 note by Castronovo.

[157] Cass. 28.8.1985, no. 4550, see G. Visintini, *I fatti illeciti* (Padova, 1987), p. 110.

[158] Cass., 2.12.1986, no. 7117, *FI*, 1987, I, 436.

[159] G. Alpa and M. Bessone, 'I fatti illeciti' in *Trattato di diritto privato diretto da Rescigno* (2nd edn, UTET, Torino, 1995) at p. 169; F. D. Busnelli, 'La tutela aquiliana del credito: evoluzione giurisprudenziale e significato attuale del principio', *RCDP*, 1987, 688.

[160] Cass. SU 12.11.1988, no. 6132, *FI*, 1989, I, 742, noted by Pardolesi, Di Majo and Poletti; *AC*, 1989, 267; *CG*, 1989, 43, noted by Di Ruocco. See also Cass. 25.06.1993 no. 7063, *MGC* 1993, 1083, where it was held that the sum of money due as salary and social insurance fees determine the value of lost work performances, and the amount of money that the wrongdoer must pay to the employer, regardless for the substitution and loss of production evidence.

[161] Cf. C. Castronovo, 'In attuazione della prestazione di lavoro e responsabilità del terzo danneggiato, *MGLav.*, 1981, 370.

grant compensation to the employer and make the author of the accident liable, while other decisions refuse to grant it. However, most legal scholars think that the employer should be compensated and awarded damages.

II. In the Spanish legal system there are abundant decisions where a driver runs over and injures a traffic policeman. These cases are similar to the case at hand because the law requires the state to continue paying a salary to the injured policeman during his recovery. The solution given to these cases would be no different if the employer paying these salaries is a private entity instead of the State.[162]

As previously mentioned, in cases similar to this one the case law is clearly divided. The Second Chamber of the Supreme Court (the highest judicial authority in criminal matters) usually requires the author of the accident to pay damages to the state, consisting of the salary the latter paid to the injured policeman during his recovery.[163] On the other hand, in civil jurisdiction, the First Chamber of the Supreme Court usually refuses to award damages to the state, for similar cases. At first, the First Chamber of the Supreme Court seemed to lean towards the compensation system of the criminal court,[164] but the present tendency in civil cases clearly favours non-acknowledgement of the state's right to compensation for continuing to pay a salary to a policeman who is unable to carry out his duties due to accident injuries.[165]

Regarding the question of whether an employer may claim the salary paid to its injured employee during recovery, the debate centres on two points.

The line of argument adopted by the Second Chamber of the Supreme Court recognizes the protection of credit rights as well as absolute rights by means of non-contractual liability. For example, because the state continues paying the injured policeman's salary despite the fact it has not received the policeman's services, it suffers damages to be compensated by the author of the accident. In order to reach this solution, the Supreme Court relies on article 104 of the former Criminal Code:

---

[162] F. Pantaleón 'Comentario a la S.T.S de 25 de junio de 1983', in *Cuadernos Civitas de Jurisprudencia Civil*, no. 3 (1983) 789–99, at 795 and F. Pantaleón, 'La indemnización por causa de lesions o de muerte', in *Anuario de Derecho Civil*, April–June (1989), p. 637, J. Santos Briz, *La responsabilidad civil: derecho sustantivo y derecho procesal* (6th edn, 2 vols, Montecorvo, Madrid, 1991), p. 225.

[163] Supreme Court decisions, Second Chamber, 28.11.74, 13.5.75, 12.5.78, 20.9.82, 13.12.83, 12.6.89 and 10.5.90.

[164] Supreme Court decision, First Chamber, 25.4.79.

[165] Supreme Court decisions, First Chamber, 14.2.80, 14.4.81, 25.6.83 and 29.9.86.

'Compensation for material damages and pain and suffering shall not only include those caused to the injured party, but also those derived from the criminal activity and caused to his family or to a third party' (article 113 of the current Criminal Code reproduces this exact legal content).

The Civil Code does not contain a similar clause, but legal experts and the Supreme Court decision (First Chamber) of 25 April 1979, readily affirm that the same result may be obtained by employing a wide interpretation of article 1902 CC, provided its general requisites are fulfilled.[166]

The line of caselaw originating from the First Chamber of the Supreme Court (against granting compensation to the state for the injured policeman's salary) does not refuse protection of credit rights (rights *in personam*) through the law of torts. Instead, what is decisive is the argument that the state has not proved that it suffered harm. That the state continued paying the injured policeman's salary due to third-party fault is insufficient to prove that a recoverable damage has been suffered. What is required is proof that the state had to incur additional expenses to cover the absence of the injured policeman in order for this public service to remain intact.

This line of argument by the First Chamber of the Supreme Court is criticized by legal scholars.[167] Fernando Pantaleón's opinion is that the employee's services are a real asset (since they are 'bought' and 'sold' on the market), and deprivation of a real asset is in principle a damage to be compensated by the responsible party. According to Pantaleón, the First Chamber of the Supreme Court's requirement of additional coverage expenses or further economic loss as a result of the accident is absurd.

Relating to the issue at hand, there is debate as to whether the Spanish tort system recognizes a non-contractual protection of the credit (rights *in personam*). It has already been said that the caselaw and the latest legal opinions readily admit it.[168]

---

[166] See, F. Pantaleón 'Comentario a la S.T.S.', 798 and F. Pantaleón, 'Comentario al artículo 1902', in *Comentario del Código Civil*, II (1991), pp. 1972 and 1994, J. L. Lacruz, *Elementos de derecho civil*, II, 2 (3rd edn, Bosch, Barcelona, 1995), p. 483, Santos Briz, *La responsabilidad*, p. 231.

[167] F. Pantaleón, 'Comentario a la S.T.S.' 798–9, Lacruz, *Elementos*, p. 507, L. Díez-Picazo and A. Gullon, *Sistema de Derecho Civil* (7th edn, Technos, Madrid, 1995), p. 618.

[168] From this point of view one may add the following Supreme Court decisions to those already mentioned: 13.3.76, 28.2.83, 30.5.86 and 7.6.85, Fourth Chamber; amongst legal experts, e.g. Pantaleón, 'Comentario al artículo 1902', p. 1994, Lacruz, *Elementos*, p. 478, R. Valpuesta, *Derecho Civil: Derecho de obligaciones y contratos* (2nd edn, Tirant lo Blanch, Valencia, 1995), p. 211.

Apart from this standpoint, the ideas of older authors should be reproduced.[169] From this point of view one can say that, in order to apply article 1902 CC, damage to an absolute subjective right is required. So, if a third party damages a credit right through fault, the owner of this credit (the creditor) may not bring an action against the third party through actions to which he alone is entitled. In these cases, article 1186 CC would be applied: 'Having extinguished the obligation for loss of the asset, the creditor shall have access to all actions against third parties the debtor may be entitled to.'

By applying this article to our case (overcoming the hindrance, pointed out by Pantaleón, of article 1186 which refers to obligations consisting in an activity 'to give' – *dare* – and not literally in an activity 'to do' – *facere*), the employer would not have an action of his own against the author of the traffic accident which injured his employee. The employer would only be able to sue the author of the accident through the actions available to the injured employee against the author of the damage (subrogation). There is a basic twofold drawback in this interpretation of the facts.[170]

Article 1902 does not require the existence of damage to a subjective and absolute right since the Spanish legal system, like the French system, on which it is based, does not set forth a list of protected interests (cf. BGB and the Portuguese Code models).

If we accept that article 1186 is applicable to the present case, compensation received by the creditor from the third party who damaged the credit would not be equal to the damage suffered by the former, and would instead be compensation for the damage suffered by the debtor. It is clear that these two types of damage need not be the same.

III. In the Spanish legal system criminal courts have wide discretionary powers to decide on matters of civil liability derived from a criminal action. Furthermore, norms of torts are sometimes different in the Penal Code and the Civil Code. This has a simple historical explanation: because penal codification preceded civil codification, the criminal law draftsman regulated the matter. Therefore, when the Civil Code was passed the relevant legislation was cross-referenced to the Penal Code.

---

[169] Such as L. Roca-Sastre Muncunill, 'El perjuicio del derecho de crédito por acto de tercero', (1962) *Revista Jurídica de Cataluña* 571–601 at 588–96.

[170] Pantaleón, 'Comentario a la S.T.S.', 796–8 and Pantaleón, 'Comentario al artículo 1902', pp. 1972, 1988.

Despite strong criticism by legal scholars, the latest Penal Code (passed on 23 November 1995) again has maintained these two distinctive bodies of law.[171]

This situation – a divided jurisdiction between civil and criminal courts and the existence of two separate bodies of law – is worsened under the Spanish legal system by the fact it is not possible for the First and Second Chambers of the Supreme Court to meet together and unify their decision-making criteria.[172]

**Greece**

I. In principle, the employer cannot sue the injurer directly, only indirectly, and only in the amount of the value of the employee's lost work, not in the amount of his paid salary.

II. Direct tortious liability of the driver as against the employer: according to article 914 CC, the injurer is not liable to the employer, because there is no causal link between the latter's loss and the injurer's tort. This is certain, according to both criteria proposed for testing it (either foreseeability of the particular damage,[173] or its inclusion in the interests protected by the infringed legal rule).[174] Indeed, in view of both these criteria, it is to be noted that the purpose of the prohibition of any injury to one's body is mainly to protect the plaintiff's physical integrity, as well as the interests usually, i.e., foreseeably, related to it. Some people hire out their work, and others work on their own as free professionals. It is therefore unknown and unforeseeable whether the loss of ability to work causes economic loss to another person. This could also be presumed *e contrario* from article 929, sub-para. 2 CC, which stipulates that in the case of bodily injury, compensation from the culpable party may

---

[171] Pantaleón, 'Comentario a la S.T.S.', 794, 'Comentario al artículo 1902', p. 1973 and pp. 6–10, Lacruz, *Elementos*, p. 460, Valpuesta, *Derecho Civil*, p. 483.
[172] Pantaleón, 'Comentario a la S.T.S.', 795.
[173] AP 692/1990 NoB 40, 67; AP 1063/90; AP 979/92 EID 35, 1044; K. Triantaphyllopoulos, *Law of Obligations* (Athens, 1935), p. 184; G. Balis, *Law of Obligations, General Part* (3rd edn. 1969, p. 100; A. Ligeropoulos (gen. ed.) *Interpretation of the Civil Code* (A Commentary) (ErmaK) (1949–1978) arts. 297–300 CC, no. 39; G. Fourkiotis, *Greek Law of Obligations, General Part* (1964), p. 318; G. Michaélidès-Nouaros, *Law of Obligations* (1959), p. 31 etc.
[174] Commentary by M. Stathopoulos in A. Georgiades and M. Stathopoulos, *Civil Code Article by Article Commentary*, vols. I–IV (1978–1982) arts. 297–298, no. 67, 60–5, P. Sourlas, *Adaequanztheorie und Normzwecklehre bei der Begruendung der Haftung nach § 823 Abs. 2 BGB* (1974) pp. 15 ff.

also be sought (apart from the victim) only by persons entitled by law (not by a contract) to claim services from the victim.[175] The explanation of such a restriction is easy: benefits provided by the law are foreseeable, because the law is already known and stable; benefits provided by a contract can be foreseen only by the parties, not usually by everyone. Thus, the loss of an employee's services as 'damage to a third party' does not appear to be a foreseeable event causally related (in a legal sense) to his physical injury. According to this thinking, the loss of the employee's services is an unforeseeable effect of the harm to his health. Thus, in principle, the employer cannot sue the injurer.

Indirect liability of the driver as against the employer: of course, the employer may possibly sue the injurer as creditor of the injurer's creditor (i.e., the employee), by lodging against the wrongdoer an 'indirect action' according to article 72 of the Code of Civil Procedure (CCPr). This provision lays down that the creditor has the right to sue the debtor of his debtor and make him pay the latter, so that the first creditor's claim could be satisfiable.

'Recourse' between the employer and the injurer: after a long period of reasonable hesitations, the Greek courts have recently accepted in some cases the theory of 'quasi joint and several debt'.[176] According to this theory, when two persons owe the same performance to someone, they are debtors in a joint and several debt, regardless of whether each one's obligation has the same legal *causa* or not. In view of this theory, the employer might sue any injurer, by virtue of the right of recourse between co-debtors in a joint and several obligation, although each one's obligation has a different legal *causa* (i.e. contract and tort).

No liability for the salaries, but only for the lost work: however, in any case, the indemnifiable damage is the value of the lost work and not the value of the employer's obligation to pay the salary or the insurance premiums. This is reasonable, because the latter would exist in any case, even if there was no injury to the employee, so there is no causal relation between the injury and the salary obligation, even according to the 'conditio sine qua non' theory.[177]

---

[175] See Commentary by A. Georgiades in Georgiades and Stathopoulos, *Civil Code* art. 928, no. 26; EphAth 5411/1977 NoB 26, 737; EphAth 5773/1972 Arm 27, 171; EphAth 4117/1972 Arm 27, 91; EphAth 775/1960 NoB 8, 510.

[176] AP 81/1991, NoB 40, p. 715.

[177] This theory relies only on physical causation. Nowadays, the barely physical-logical criterion of this theory seems no longer satisfactory, but still remains a necessary minimum in any causal relation, a truly *sine qua non* criterion.

III. The theory of 'quasi joint and several debt' is not fully persuasive. Its main disadvantages are twofold (even when it does not speak about a 'quasi', but about a pure joint and several debt).

First, this view has no direct grounding in law, insofar as the obligations forming a joint and several debt do not derive from the same legal *causa*, so the legal regulation of joint and several debt is not directly implementable here, at least in principle.

Secondly, as is always the case in the framework of analogy, it is unclear which of the specific provisions regulating joint and several debt is applicable here. For example, when the creditor is in default against one quasi co-debtor, is he in default against the other one too, as article 485 CC stipulates?

## England

I. The employer cannot recover from the tortfeasor any sums disbursed to the injured worker.

II. Sick pay, whether statutory or contractual, is a deductible benefit under English law: see *Turner* v. *Ministry of Defence*[178] and *Pulfrey* v. *Greater London Council*.[179] The tortfeasor, and his insurer, can ask for it to be set off against the award of damages for personal injury.

In English law, in the case of a wrongful personal injury, the tortfeasor owes no duty of care to any third party that suffers economic loss either because he had a contract with the injured person (see *Simpson* v. *Thomson*,[180] affirmed in *Spartan Steel* v. *Martin*, above), or because they are obliged by law to hand over benefits to the injured person. Employers have, therefore, no personal claim against tortfeasors for sick pay or any other expenses in a case such as this one.

In equity, there was always the possibility of an action by *subrogation*. But today, this doctrine finds clear application only in the cases of indemnity insurance. No such subrogation takes place in policies against personal accidents and therefore its function does not fit the employers' loss in having to pay wages or sick pay to injured workers.[181]

## Scotland

I. The employer will be unable to recover damages from the driver for the economic loss he has suffered as a result of the worker's inability to work.

---

[178] (1969) 113 Sol Jo 585 (CA).
[179] [1985] I CR 437. See also Social Security Act 1992.
[180] (1887) 3 AC 279, 289 (HL).    [181] Social Security (Recovery of Benefits) Act 1992.

II. The worker can sue in delict for the personal injury provided that: (1) he has suffered economic loss or has endured pain and suffering; (2) this was caused by the defender; and (3) the conduct of the defender was either intentional or wrongful if unintentional. To be wrongful the driver must have owed the worker a duty of care, which drivers do to other road users generally, and the defender must have breached that duty in the eyes of the law in the particular circumstances of the case. From the point of view of the employer, once more we have an example of secondary economic loss. The driver has caused physical harm to the worker but not to the employer. The employer suffers economic loss owing to the inability of the worker to fulfil his obligations under his contract with the employer for three months.

In *Reavis* v. *Clan Line Steamers Ltd*, at first instance Lord Constable considered the question 'whether the law of Scotland recognises any right of action by an employer for the loss of services of an employee against a person who negligently causes the death or incapacity of the employee',[182] and opined that it did not. The Inner House adhered, confirming his judgment.[183] Finding support in observations in the judgments of Lord Kinloch in *Allan* v. *Barclay*[184] and Lord Penzance in *Simpson & Co. and others* v. *Thomson and others*,[185] the Lord President (Lord Clyde) held that

> In the law of Scotland there is no such thing as a right or interest, in the nature of property, in the services of another; and a person claiming reparation for injury by another person's fault cannot go beyond the effects of such injury to his own person, his own health, his own business or other capabilities, and his own property.[186]

He agreed with the observation of Lord Kinloch, as quoted above in Case 2 ('Cable II – Factory Shutdown') and as it continued, that '[t]he personal injuries of the individual himself will be properly held to have been in the contemplation of the wrongdoer; but [that] he cannot be bound to have surmised the secondary injuries done to all holding relations with the individual, whether that of a master, or any other'.[187]

III. In the case of secondary economic loss the courts have decided that such loss is not actionable as there is no duty of care. This general rule, though subject to exceptions to be met in cases below, owes its existence to warnings such as that given by Lord Penzance in *Simpson*,

---

[182] *Reavis* v. *Clan Line Steamers Ltd* 1925 SLT 386 at p. 388.
[183] 1925 SC 725 at p. 738.   [184] (1864) 2 M 873.
[185] (1877) 5 R (HL) 40 at p. 46.   [186] 1925 SC 725 at p. 740.
[187] Ibid. at pp. 740–741, quoting *Allan* v. *Barclay* (1864) 2 M 873 at p. 875.

who saw dangers in one of the arguments put by the respondent in that case and the principle which underlay it. He opined:

The principle involved seems to be this, that where damage is done by a wrongdoer to a chattel, not only the owner of that chattel, but all those who by contract with the owner have bound themselves to obligations which are rendered more onerous, or have secured to themselves advantages which are rendered less beneficial, by the damage done to the chattel, have a right of action against the wrongdoer, although they have no immediate or reversionary property in the chattel, and no possessory right by reason of any contract attaching to the chattel itself, such as by lien or by hypothecation. This, I say, is the principle involved in the respondent's contention. If it be a sound one, it would seem to follow that if by the negligence of a wrongdoer goods are destroyed which the owner of them had bound himself by contract to supply to a third person this person as well as the owner has a right of action for any loss inflicted on him by their destruction. But if this be true as to injuries done to chattels it would seem to be equally so as to injuries to the person.

After giving a few examples of the consequences, he continued:

Such instances might be indefinitely multiplied, giving rise to rights of action which in modern communities, where every complexity of mutual relation is daily created by contract might be numerous and novel.[188]

On policy grounds, given such considerations, the courts are reluctant to impose a duty of care for fear of subjecting the negligent party to 'liability in an indeterminate amount for an indeterminate time to an indeterminate class'.[189]

## The Netherlands

I. Whenever statute or contract obliges the employer to provide his employee with sick pay, the employer can claim this amount from the injurer, if, and to the extent that, the injurer is liable *vis-à-vis* the employee (art. 6:107a CC).

II. Recently, a new article 6:107a has been added to the Dutch Civil Code, enabling employers to have recourse for the cost of continued payment of wages.[190] This addition to the Civil Code is part of the extensive deconstruction of the Dutch social security system that has been taking place over the last six years. Since 1 March 1996, employers have the

---

[188] (1877) 5 R (HL) 40 at p. 46.
[189] *Ultramares Corpn* v. *Touche* 255 NY 170 (1931) at p. 179, *per* Cardozo CJ.
[190] Staatsblad 1995, 691.

statutory duty to provide their employees with sick pay for a maximum of 52 weeks.[191] The employer has recourse for the amount of this sick pay if the injurer is liable in tort *vis-à-vis* the injured employee.

Thus, recourse for sick pay is possible.

## Germany

I. The employer can recover the payment made to the injured worker from the tortfeasor, but only because the employer's claim is subrogated to the worker's own claim.

II. Tort claims: the employer has no claims under § 823 (1) because none of his absolute rights were violated. Nor do § 823 (2) or § 826 help him since there is no indication that the tortfeasor violated a statute protecting the employer, or that he acted intentionally and against public policy. Finally, the employer cannot make a claim for loss of services under § 845[192] because this provision applies only to services owed according to statute (e.g. among family members), not to services owed under a contract as in the present case. In short, an employer has no direct tort claim for the loss of the services of an employee injured by someone else.

Claims via subrogation: the employer must continue to pay the worker under article 3 of the Pay Continuation Statute 1994 (*Entgeltfortzahlungsgesetz*). In return, article 6 of the same statute provides that the employer is automatically subrogated to the worker's claim against the tortfeasor, to the extent that the employer has continued to pay the worker under the statute. The employer can therefore sue the wrongdoer by presenting the subrogated claim.

However, the statute provides only for up to six weeks of pay, not for three months. Beyond the six-week period, in most cases, the worker will continue to receive (possibly reduced) pay. If this pay comes from a public insurance fund, the fund is automatically subrogated to the worker's rights.[193] If the pay is received from the employer on other grounds (e.g. a collective bargaining agreement or the individual employment contract), under these agreements the employer is subrogated to the worker's rights.[194]

---

[191] Statute amending the Civil Code (art. 7A:1638c CC; currently: art. 7:629 CC), Stb. 1996, 134.
[192] See above. Case 3 ('Cable III – The Day-to-Day Workers').
[193] See Löwisch, Rd.-Nr. 1090.   [194] See BGHZ 7, 30, at 49, 52 (1952).

III. The statutory solution of the problem through automatic subrogation preserves the basic tort principle that one cannot claim damages resulting from the violation of someone else's absolute rights. Yet, it also avoids both unjust enrichment of the worker and undue loss to the employer. Where statutory subrogation rules do not apply, the courts will imply a duty in the employment contract for the employer to be subrogated to the worker's rights.

## Austria

I. It has recently become clear that the employer may recover the salary he is bound to pay to the injured worker under the theory of 'liquidation of transferred loss' (*Liquidation des Drittschadens*).

II. The Supreme Court used to dismiss claims for compensation in cases of accidental injuries to employees, when the employer was bound to continue the payment of salaries pursuant to specific provisions of certain labour statutes,[195] if such claim for compensation was not expressly provided by statute.[196]

This obviously well-established practice was upheld for more than thirty-five years. However, only recently the Austrian Supreme Court significantly changed its practice. In two 1994 landmark decisions,[197] the Court ruled that statutory provisions imposing the duty on the employer of continuing payment of wages to the injured employee could not be interpreted as releasing the tortfeasor from his duty to compensate.

In the absence of an express subrogation provision, the loss of earnings resulting from an accident caused by a third person would fall upon the injured employee. The burden of bearing the loss an injured worker would otherwise suffer (from not being able to earn a salary) was shifted to the employer in order to help the victim. The tortfeasor should not benefit therefrom. Therefore, the employer should not be deprived of a cause of action against the actual tortfeasor.

The Supreme Court's change of opinion is based on an analogy to article 1358 ABGB[198] and article 67 VersVG[199] and appears to be irreversible

---

[195] Cf. in particular, § 8 AngG.  [196] Cf. OGH ZVR 1977/295 etc.
[197] OGH ZVR 1994/88, RdW 1994, 243; OGH ZVR 1995, 146.
[198] This provision reads: 'A person who pays the debt of another which he has assumed either personally or in regard to certain assets is subrogated to all the rights of the creditor and is entitled to demand the restitution of the amount paid by him from the debtor. For that purpose, the satisfied creditor shall deliver to the payor all pertinent documents and means of security.'
[199] *Versicherungsvertragsgesetz* (Statute on Insurance Contracts).

## Portugal

I. The employer's claim for compensation is successful only under special statutes and there is no other claim under general principles of civil liability.

II. If this is, simultaneously, an occupational accident and a road accident caused by a third party, the law allows the employer or insurer who has to pay compensation for the accident a right to claim against third parties, or their insurers.[200]

Nevertheless, this right to claim only covers damage in relation to which a causal nexus can be established. It seems that the insurance premiums, specifically those which would be paid even though no accident occurred, would not be included. If a bonus is lost, however, this can be claimed.[201]

If we are not dealing with an occupational accident, the issue is not directly concerned with the principles of civil liability.

Everything depends on the interpretation of the clause in the contract or the legal provision that imposes an obligation on the employer to pay the whole salary for the entire period of absence through illness.

If the clause or legal provision is held to attribute to the employee a benefit that is completely independent of the cause of the incapacity, the employer will not have any right against the third party.

If, as usually happens, the interpretation leads only to an additional guarantee for the employee, though we are not looking at a 'guarantee' in the technical sense, we feel the analogous or extensive application of article 592/1 would be reasonable. This provides that the payer is subrogated to the payee's rights when 'fulfilment is guaranteed' (legal subrogation or *ope legis*).[202]

---

[200] Article 18 of Decree-Law no. 522/85 of 31 December (compulsory insurance), in association with the base XXVII of Law no. 2127 of 3 August 1965 (occupational accidents). The new Law Concerning Occupational Accidents (Law no. 100/97 of 13 September) is not yet in force. However, art. 31 (nos. 1 and 4) provides for a regime identical to the previous one.

[201] Decision of the Court of Appeal of Coimbra, 21 September 1993 *Colectânea de Jurisprudência*, Tomo IV (point V in the summary), p. 37.

[202] Legal subrogation also applies when payment is made by whoever 'is directly interested in satisfying the credit'. Judgment no. 5/97 of the Supreme Court of Justice used this second way to justify the subrogation of the State in the rights of the injured party. But we feel the solution given in the text is more convincing.

In a case in which the employing entity itself assumes responsibilities that normally lie within the province of a social security institution, the Lisbon Court of Appeal (judgment of 16 October 1997) conferred on it a right of subrogation against the insurer of the individual who caused the road accident.[203]

Where the injured party is a civil servant and the accident is both an occupational and a road accident caused by a third party, the issue has been much discussed in the Portuguese courts. Following contradictory decisions handed down by the Supreme Court of Justice, judgment no. 5/97,[204] with the aim of making the court decisions uniform, held that the state has the right to be reimbursed, by way of legal subrogation, for the total amount defrayed in payments to one of its civil servants whose absence from work and incapacity to render reciprocal services is due to illness resulting from an accident caused by a third party that is simultaneously a road and an occupational accident.

A solution similar to that established by law thus prevails, quite clearly, in matters of occupational accidents. In cases of death or physical injury, article 495 establishes the legitimacy of certain third parties to seek compensation: 'those who render assistance to the injured party, as well as hospitals, doctors or other persons or entities who may have contributed to the treatment or assistance of the victim' (no. 2); and 'those who might claim from the injured party for alimonies or those to whom the injured party was paying them as a natural obligation' (no. 3).

In a case where the employer had a contractual obligation to bear the costs of hospitalization and medical assistance, the Porto Court of Appeal has held that the employer is entitled to claim *directly* against the insurer of the individual who caused the road accident, on the basis of article 495, no. 2.[205] It would not matter if the third party had acted while fulfilling a legal duty, for altruistic motives, by virtue of a legal transaction or for any other motive.

III. In the domain of social security, the general rule, enacted in article 16 of Law No. 28/84 of 14 August 1984 (Law of the Bases of Social Security) attributes a right of subrogation to the social security institution.[206]

---

[203] *Colectânea de Jurisprudência*, Tomo IV, pp. 116–17.
[204] Published in the *Diário da República*, I Serie – A, no. 73/97 of 27 March, pp. 1364 ff.
[205] Judgment of 8 June 1977, *Colectânea de Jurisprudência*, Tomo IV, p. 868.
[206] Case law had tended to enshrine some exceptions to this rule. Specifically the issue of death and funeral grants, which some decisions have considered (rightly, in our view) 'not reimbursable'. For more on this, see the judgment of the Porto Court of Appeal of 1.4.1998, *Colectânea de Jurisprudência*, Tomo II, p. 242.

As regards methods of resolving such 'case law conflicts', the traditional solution in Portuguese law, established in article 2 of the Civil Code, was that of *assentos* (rulings):[207] when the Supreme Court has resolved the same question of law in divergent ways, it is possible to resort to the Full Court (that is, the Supreme Court of Justice functioning with at least four-fifths of the judges from the different divisions), which besides deciding the concrete case, would pronounce a 'ground'. This would be published in the I Serie of the official journal (the *Diário da República*) having the binding force of law.

Nevertheless, this institution has come to be regarded as implying an invasion by the judicial authorities of an area reserved for the competence of the legislative authorities, and is therefore unconstitutional. 'Grounds' have thus been superseded and replaced by 'judgments conferring uniformity on case law', which are not binding.

**Sweden and Finland**

I. The employer cannot claim compensation from the injurer. Subrogation claims by the employer for the sums paid are admitted in Finland but no longer in Sweden.

II. Tort claims: the employer has no claim because of the application of the general principle which excludes compensation of the economic losses suffered by 'third parties', i.e. subjects different from those who have suffered personal injury or property damage. As far as personal injuries are concerned, the only statutory exceptions are provided by the Tort Liability Acts 1972 and 1974 and arise in the case of death for funeral expenses and lost maintenance allowances for survivors, on the basis of *SkadestL* 5:2 (Sweden) and *SkadestL* 5:3–4 (Finland). Among the albeit very limited exceptions developed in case law, none applies to this case.

Subrogation claims: in Finland, the employer can bring a subrogation claim against the tortfeasor for the sums paid to the worker.

In Sweden, subrogation as formerly admitted, is now excluded. Sums paid by the employer, by work insurance or social security because of the worker's sickness are not to be included in the calculation of damages, according to *SkadestL* 5:3.

III. Although allowed in principle, subrogation claims of this kind are fairly uncommon in Finland, as they were also in Sweden before

---

[207] A. Castanheira Neves, *O Instituto dos assentos e a Função Jurídica dos Supremos Tribunais* (Coimbra Editora, Coimbra 1983).

being explicitly excluded. The workers' losses are mostly covered by social insurance.

*Editors' comparative comments*

This problem brings to light the importance that legal subrogation may play in mediating the problem of pure economic loss. Liability regimes of all kinds rely to a great extent upon subrogation to solve and control the incidence of financial liability. In liberal regimes (Belgium, France, Italy) and conservative regimes (Finland, Germany, Portugal) the subrogation of the financially damaged employer to the claims of the physically injured employee operates as a means of recouping transferred losses. The device is clearly more crucial to the latter systems than the former. To see the role of subrogation in clear perspective, first let us look at the question as it presents itself in tort. Secondly, we will discuss the effects of subrogation upon the liability between the parties.

The claim of the employer to recoup from a tortfeasor the salary that he must continue to pay his injured employee is not generally actionable except in a few of the liberal regimes. As we have seen, in certain liberal systems the claim may be problematic on grounds of causation.[208] The causation issue resurfaces in the present case. In Greece it appears that the employer's loss would be regarded as 'unforeseeable' from a tortfeasor perspective and thus not actionable; in Belgium the causal link may be deemed interrupted by the 'autonomous' obligation of the employer to continue to pay wages, and again the claim may possibly fail. In the pragmatic and conservative regimes, a tort claim is clearly inadmissible. In England and Scotland, it is said the claim will fail because there is no duty of care to any third person who suffers economic loss due to their conventional or legal obligation to pay the injured person. Under German and Portuguese law there can be no recovery in tort since the tortfeasor violated no absolute right of the employer, and in Austria, Finland and Sweden, such claims are structurally excluded. Thus, without the assistance of the subrogation concept, the law of tort would generally refuse compensation, even though it may be questioned whether there is a strong policy reason for the denial in these circumstances.

---

[208] One should also note that if the employer's recourse is by way of subrogation (as it is not, for example, in France in respect of social security payments made by the employer during the sickness of the employee – art. 32, Law of 5 July 1985) the recovery will be reduced by the employee's contributory negligence.

In the present case the device of subrogation serves to bridge many of the obstacles thrown up by these liability approaches. It places the financially damaged employer in direct relation with the wrongdoer, as if the latter had wronged him directly. From a policy perspective, there is now far less danger of an indeterminate number of claimants since the right of subrogation often arises specially in a discrete context and the number of subrogated beneficiaries is controlled. Thus the employer's subrogated claim arises exceptionally in France under the 1985 automobile law (*Loi Badinter*), in Belgium under a 1978 employment law, in Italy under article 2100 CC, in the Netherlands under article 6:107a CC and in Germany under the Pay Continuation Statute. There is also less concern about the indeterminate size of claims or perhaps their excessive disproportion to the degree of defendant's fault. If an employer's recourse is by way of subrogation, the recovery may be reduced by the employee's contributory negligence. Lost wages are already generally recoverable by the worker's own claim, and thus allowing the employer to recoup wages that the law or his contract obliges him to pay does not increase the overall liability of the tortfeasor. Indeed, if the employer's claim were viewed as unrecoverable it would reduce the tortfeasor's normal liability, and this is the motive for Austria's decision to develop the doctrine of 'liquidation of transferred loss' (*Liquidation des Drittschadens*) which functions in a manner similar to subrogation.

For liberal regimes, the effect of introducing subrogation into the picture is to recognize that two claims exist concurrently in the employer, one that arises directly, in their own right under the general clause, and another that arises as a subrogated tort claim. The latter action may be the more reliable of the two, for it obviates most questions about the causal link between the actor's negligence and the third person's financial loss. For purposes of causation, the employer enjoys the position of the injured car accident victim. Since generally an action in tort is precluded in the conservative regimes, a subrogated claim may provide the only avenue of relief. Theoretically, it overcomes the inability of the employer to show a violation of his absolute rights. The employer steps into the shoes of an injured employee whose absolute rights were violated. And for conservative regimes that resort to structural exclusion of third-party claims, the subrogated employer is no longer a third party.

## Case 5: requiem for an Italian all star

### Case

Thomas is a pivot in the All-Stars basketball team. A few days before the end of the championship, Thomas is hit by a car and unable to play for three months. In the absence of its best player, the team (until then at the top of the league standings) drops to fourth place. This results in considerable losses for the team owners. Can the All-Stars sue the car driver?

### France

I. According to a similar case decided in 1955, the All-Stars should be able to sue the car driver and recover at least some pecuniary loss under articles 1382–1383.

II. In the *Football Club de Metz* v. *Wiroth* case,[209] the Cour d'Appel (Court of Appeal) held that any person, even a *personne morale*, who suffers a pecuniary loss, is entitled to recover damages from the injurer under article 1382 CC. In this case, a famous professional player was killed in a car accident. The Court held that the club was entitled to recover the pure financial loss since the loss was the direct result of the injurer's negligence.

Interestingly, the Court of First Instance denied recovery on the ground that there was lack of certainty to the club's damage: the player was only bound by a contract at will and therefore he might not have continued to play for the football club even if he had not been injured in any accident.

However, the Cour d'Appel viewed the club's loss as the loss of a chance (*perte d'une chance*) to maintain the player's services. The Court reasoned that if the accident had not occurred, this player (who was in excellent health) would have probably signed another year's contract (thus helping to make the club profitable), or he might have demanded a transfer to another club, in which case the acquiring club would have had to pay a sum (transfer indemnity) to the transferring club. Either way the Football Club de Metz lost a chance to realise an advantage from a patrimonial asset. Therefore, the Cour d'Appel returned the case to the Court of First Instance to arrive at the estimated value of the lost chance. The Cour

---

[209] Colmar, Ch. dét. à Metz, 20 avril 1955; *Football Club de Metz* v. *Wiroth*, JCP 1955.II.8741.

d'Appel expressly refused an award on the basis of the club's declining revenues at the box office, since these losses did not seem well proven.

As in *Football Club de Metz*, so in Case 5, the team's claim for its own economic loss would probably be reasoned in terms of delictual liability under article 1382.[210] The major question to be anticipated might not involve the proof of fault on the part of the cab driver, or of a direct causal link to the team's sporting success, but rather the question of proving that the alleged economic loss has certainly occurred. Yet even if the All-Stars' damages seem somewhat hypothetical (and even if their best player remained uninjured, who knows whether they would have remained in first place?), a French court might use the *perte d'une chance* concept in order to award at least some compensation, but would probably not award an amount designed to fully compensate the All-Stars for their drop in league standings.

## Belgium

I. The All-Stars have no claim against the driver for the damage resulting from the drop from the first place to the fourth place of the championship.

II. Since there is no contract between the All-Stars and the driver, the potential claim will rest necessarily on article 1382 CC:

Any act whatever of man which causes damage to another obliges him by whose fault it occurred to make reparation.

To hold the driver liable, the All-Stars will have to prove the fault of the driver, a damage and a causal link between the damage and the fault. In the present case, it will not be easy for the All-Stars to prove the existence of these conditions.

First, it will be very difficult for the All-Stars not only to calculate the amount of the damage resulting from the drop to fourth place, but also to prove that they would have become champions.

To be recoverable, the damage must be 'certain'.[211] In the present case, the All-Stars will not be able to prove that they would normally have

---

[210] For his own physical injuries from the car accident, Thomas would proceed against the owner/driver under the special law of 5 July 1985 (*Loi Badinter*).

[211] R. O. Dalcq and G. Schamps, 'La responsabilité délictuelle et quasi-délictuelle, examen de jurisprudence (1987–1993)', (1995) 149 RCJB, 737; J. L. Fagnart, *La responsabilité civile – Chronique de jurisprudence 1985–1995* (Larcier, Brussels, 1997), p. 23, no. 11.

been champion. They can only claim that they lost a real opportunity to be champion.

The loss of an opportunity is also recoverable if the opportunity was real and not merely hypothetical.[212]

In the present case, and considering the uncertainty of sport, the possibility that the All-Stars would have become champions seems very speculative and hypothetical. Therefore, the damage appears to be speculative or hypothetical and is not recoverable.[213]

Secondly, to hold the driver liable for the damage suffered from the losses resulting from the drop to fourth place, the All-Stars would have to prove that this damage has a causal link with the fault committed by the driver.

In order to appreciate if there is a causal link between the fault and the damage, the Belgian Supreme Court uses a theory known as *l'équivalence des conditions*. According to that theory, the fault is causally linked with the damage if the plaintiff can prove that the damage would not have occurred, as it occurred, if the faulty act had not been committed.[214]

Since the All-Stars will not be able to prove that if Thomas was not hit by the driver, they would have been champion, the Belgian courts will most certainly reject the claim.

## Italy

I. Damages can be awarded under article 2043 cc since all conditions provided by the Italian tort liability systems are met.

II. The player was injured by a wrongful event and harm was inflicted upon a legally enforceable interest. Indeed, following the rationale of the famous *Meroni* case,[215] the All-Stars club can claim a legal right to

---

[212] Cass., 19 octobre 1937, Pas., 1937, I, p. 298; Cass., 8 décembre 1958, Pas., 1959, I, p. 354; Cass., 15 octobre 1962, Pas, 1963; I, 195; Cass., 15 septembre 1972, RGAR, 1973; no. 9121; Cass., 4 mars 1975, Pas., 1975, I, 682; Cass., 19 juin 1987, RW, 1987–1988, p. 709.

[213] R. O. Dalcq, *Traité de la responsabilité civile, Tome II, Le lien de causalité, le dommage et sa réparation* (Larcier, Bruxelles, 1962), p. 254, no. 2817; J. L. Fagnart, *La responsabilité civile*, p. 23, no. 11.

[214] Cass., 12 janvier 1988, Pas., 1988, I, 563; Cass., 15 mai 1990, Pas, 1990, I, 1054; Cass., 23 mai 1990, Pas., 1990, I, 1079; Cass. 23 juin 1990, Pas, 1990, I, 1126; Cass., 8 octobre 1992, Pas., 1992, I, 1124.

[215] *Torino Calcio SpA v. Romero*, Cass., SU, 26.1.1971, no. 174, *GI*, 1971, I, 1, 681 noted by Visintini; *FI*, 1971, I, 342 noted by Busnelli. The case is actually known in Italy not by the name of the parties, but by the name of the famous soccer player involved and fatally wounded in the accident.

the pivot's obligation to play and recover damages from the defendant whose negligence prevented the athlete from playing the final games of the season.

The real problem, from an operational point of view, will be to demonstrate that this event had direct consequences on the All-Stars team.

III. The case recalls one of the most relevant changes in the interpretation of the main provision in Italian tort law:

*Article 2043 Compensation for unlawful acts*

Any fraudulent, malicious, or negligent act that causes an unjustified injury to another obliges the person who has committed the act to pay damages.

The formula is very similar to the famous article 1382 of the *Code Napoléon* (c. Nap.).[216] At the beginning the system was self-restrained, and the old interpretation followed a German-inspired doctrine.[217] According to that doctrine, there was an unjustified injury whenever there was an offence against an 'absolute right' of the victim, such as the right to property, liberty, life or reputation (reducing the *neminem laedere* formula to a solution close to § 823 BGB). Only in such protected areas should the tortfeasor be bound to pay damages, otherwise the victim cannot recover, except when the tort was intentional.

However, the works of Schlesinger, Sacco, Rodotà, Trimarchi and Busnelli were moving towards a broader conception of unjustified injury (*ingiustizia del danno*) mentioned in article 2043 cc.[218]

In the *Meroni* case[219] the judges eventually accepted the interpretation offered by the above-mentioned scholars. The soccer team, Torino Calcio SpA, sued for damages alleging an economic loss.[220] *Meroni*'s doctrine is now followed whenever an employee is injured or killed in an accident. In these cases, the employer who is bound by statutes to pay wages or

---

[216] *The Italian Civil Code and Complementary Legislation* (trans. M. Beltramo, G. E. Longo and J. H. Merryman, Oceana, Dobsferry, NY, 1993).

[217] In other words, standard doctrine interpreted a transplanted French normative solution quite similarly to German tort liability code provisions (§§ 823–826 BGB).

[218] R. Sacco, 'L'ingiustizia di cui all'art. 2043 cc, *FP*, 1960, I, 1420; P. Schlesinger, *La ingiustizia del danno nell'illecito civile* Jus, 1960, 336; P. Trimarchi, *Rischio e responsabilità oggettiva* (Giuffrè, Milano, 1961); F. D. Busnelli, *La lesione del credito da parte di terzi* (Milano, 1964). S. Rodotà, *Il problema della responsabilità civile* (Giuffrè, Milano, 1967); P. Trimarchi, *Causalità e danno* (Giuffrè, Milano, 1967).

[219] Torino Calcio SpA v. Romero, Cass. civ., SU, 26.1.1971, no. 174, *GI*, 1971, I, 1, 681 noted by Visintini; *FI*, 1971, I, 342 noted by Busnelli.

[220] The Court held to the principle stated above, but the team did not succeed in recovering damages because the evidence of an actual damage was not deemed satisfactory.

other sums to the employee or his family is allowed to recover those damages from the tortfeasor.

Although it is quite evident that the origin of the employer's economic loss is a physical damage to the employee, Italian courts interpreted this precedent in a very liberal way.[221]

## Spain

I. This issue does not have a clear solution in the case law. Legal writers have different opinions about the result to be obtained in cases such as this.

II. The usual tendency of the Spanish courts in the case of serious injury is to acknowledge the legal right of the victim's relatives and close friends.[222]

The position of legal doctrine is equally unclear. First, there are authors who do not express an opinion on the matter and simply mention it.[223] There are also authors with conflicting points of view. Second, Santos Briz asserts that the damage should in fact be repaired.[224] This damage would consist of services which were impossible for the victim to render as a result of the accident. He is backed up by the Supreme Court decisions mentioned in our response to Case 4 ('Convalescing Employee'). The author also points out that in such cases it will be difficult and problematic to prove damages, but that the fungible nature of the services due by the injured party is irrelevant for compensation purposes.

Third, Díez-Picazo asserted that this type of damage is indirect and should not be recoverable. He described a hypothetical case similar to the present case where a theatre manager was forced to cancel a show as a result of a singer's injuries. The author asserted that the damage from cancelling the show should not be recoverable because it was merely an indirect damage.[225] The author points out that these types of cases present difficult problems of causation. However, in any case there would

---

[221] G. Alpa and M. Bessone, 'I fatti illeciti', *Trattato di diritto privato diretto da Rescigno* (1st edn, UTET, Turin, 1982; 2nd edn, 1995).
[222] More information on this can be seen in our reply to Case 10 ('The Dutiful Wife').
[223] J. Lacruz, *Elementos de derecho civil*, II-2 (3rd edn, Bosch, Barcelona, 1995).
[224] J. Santos Briz, *La responsabilidad civil: derecho sustantivo y derecho procesal* (6th edn, 2 vols, 1991), p. 352.
[225] L. Díez-Picazo, 4th edn, *Fundamentos de derecho civil patrimonial*, II (Civitas, Madrid, 1993) p. 605; along the same lines see R. Valpuesta, *Derecho de obligaciones y contratos* (2nd edn, Tirant lo Blanch, Valencia, 1995), pp. 211–12.

indeed be an obligation to compensate the manager if the tortfeasor had acted in bad faith.

Relevant case law includes a Supreme Court decision of 25 April 1986 (Fourth Chamber, administrative jurisdiction) which refused to compensate a manager suing a third party who had injured his employee. In that case, a policeman's gunshots injured an employee and the employer sought compensation from the public authorities. However, this decision should not be automatically applied in civil cases, given that it was (1) an administrative case; and (2) decided on the standard of strict liability (without fault) for the state. Consequently, according to Pantaleón, the problems regarding the link of causation are usually more strictly interpreted since causation will automatically indicate liability.[226]

We think that if a case similar to the above were brought before the civil courts it is very likely that the manager would be compensated, since from a causation standpoint the author of the accident should be liable. But it is also very likely that the courts, while awarding damages to the manager, would make use of the discretionary powers of article 1103 CC in order not to make an exorbitant award.

## Greece

I. In principle, the All-Stars cannot sue the injurer directly, but only indirectly and only in the amount of the value of Thomas's lost work, but not for the salary paid to him, nor for the team's decline in the standings.

II. According to article 914 CC, the injurer is not liable to the employer, because there is no causal link between the latter's loss and the injurer's act. This is certain, according to both criteria proposed for testing it (either the foreseeability of the particular damage,[227] or its inclusion in the interests protected by the infringed legal rule.)[228] Indeed, in view of

---

[226] F. Pantaleón, 'La indemnización por causa de lesiones o de muerte', in *Anuario de Derecho Civil*, April–June (1989), p. 639.

[227] AP 692/1990 NoB 40, 67; AP 1063/90; AP 979/92 ElD 35, 104; K. Triantaphyllopoulos, *Law of Obligations* (Athens, 1935), p. 184; G. Balis, *Law of Obligations, General Part* (3rd edn, 1960), p. 100; A. Ligeropoulos (gen. ed.); *Interpretation of the Civil Code (A Commentary.) (ErmAK)* (1949–1978) arts. 297–300 CC, no. 39; G. Fourkiotis, *Greek Law of Obligations, General Part* (1964) p. 318; G. Michaélidès-Nouaros, *Law of Obligations* (1959), p. 31 etc.

[228] A. Georgiades and M. Stathopoulos, *Civil Code, Article by Article Commentary*, vols. II–IV (1979–1982), see Commentary by M. Stathopoulos, arts. 297–298, no. 67, 60–5; P. Sourlas, *Adaequanztheorie und Normzwecklehre bei der Begründung der Haftung nach § 823 Abs. 1 BGB* (1974), pp. 15 ff.

both these criteria, it is to be noted that the purpose of the prohibition of any injury to one's body is mainly to protect the plaintiff's physical integrity, as well as the interests usually, i.e. foreseeably, related to it. Some people hire out their work and some others work on their own as free professionals. It is therefore unknown and unforeseeable whether the loss of the working ability causes economic loss for another person. This could also be presumed *e contrario* from article 929, sub-para. 2 CC, which stipulates that, in the case of bodily injury, compensation from the tortfeasor may also be sought (apart from the victim) only by persons entitled by law (not by a contract) to claim services from the victim.[229] The explanation of such a restriction is easy: benefits provided by the law are foreseeable, because the law is already known and stable; benefits provided by a contract can be foreseen only by the parties, usually not by everyone. Thus the loss of Thomas's services as 'damage to a third party' does not appear to be a foreseeable event, causally related (in a legal sense) to his physical injury.

According to this line of thought, the loss of Thomas's services is an unforeseeable effect of the harm to his health. Thus, in principle, the All-Stars team cannot sue the injurer.

In any case, the decline of the basketball team seems an even more distant event, unrelated (i.e. unforeseeably connected) to the harm to his health, at least if we are not speaking about a basketball player famous all over the country, playing with obviously inferior teammates. By way of conclusion, the progress of one's basketball team is not included in the sphere of interests protected by the legislative prohibition on injury to another human being. Thus no compensation for the decline of the All-Stars can be claimed from the driver.

III. In Greece, professional sport was only recently statutorily recognized. Thus, no one tries to solve such problems judicially. In any event, the economic losses of a basketball team would be judged as unforeseeable, so that the Greek courts would deny indemnification.

## England

I. The All-Stars cannot sue the car driver.

II. In English law, in the case of a wrongful personal injury, the tortfeasor owes no duty of care to any third party that suffers economic

---

[229] See Georgiades and Stathopoulos, *Civil Code*, Commentary by A. Georgiades, art. 928, no. 26; EphAth 5411/1977 NoB 26, 737; EphAth 5773/1972 Arm 27, 171; EphAth 4117/1972 Arm 27, 91; EphAth 775/1960 NoB 8, 510.

loss because he had a contract with the injured person: *Spartan Steel* v. *Martin*[230] is in agreement with the approach of the House of Lords in *Simpson* v. *Thomson*.[231]

III. The policy of the law in third-party economic loss cases is that such losses ought to lie where they fall, except in very exceptional cases, such as loss of support suffered by dependants from a wrongful death or medical care expenses disbursed for an injured member of the family.[232]

## Scotland

I. The All-Stars cannot sue the car driver.

II. For the reasons discussed in Case 4 ('Convalescing Employee') above, Thomas could bring an action against the driver but his employer, the All-Stars, cannot. This is a good example of where the damages, in Lord Kinloch's words, are not 'as may reasonably be supposed to have been in the view of the wrongdoer'. We also have the additional factor of causation. Under Scots law the loss must be caused by the wrongous conduct. This is expressed in the maxim *damnum injuria datum*. With respect to factual causation, applying the 'but for' test, we cannot say for certain that but for the absence of their star player the All-Stars would have been in a better position than fourth and hence better off financially. Though factual causation need only be established on the balance of probabilities, this may be beyond the All-Stars. Even with their star player the All-Stars may still have suffered a slump, and so we cannot say that 'but for' the driver's negligence the All-Stars would not have suffered harm. Even if factual causation could be established, with respect to legal causation we encounter similar problems. Could we say that the driver's negligence was, in a selection of the legal terms used, the direct, proximate, dominant or effective cause of the All-Stars' loss when so many imponderables contribute to a team's sporting success? One would be hard pressed to argue that it was reasonably foreseeable that if the driver did not exercise due care on the roads, a basketball franchise would lose money from losing games it might otherwise have won. There are too many subsequent links in the chain of events.

III. Given the degree of chance involved in the success or otherwise of the team it would be exceedingly harsh to make the driver liable

---

[230] [1973] 1 QB 27 CA.   [231] (1887) 3 AC 279, 289 (HL).
[232] See details in E. K. Banakas, *Tortious Liability for Pure Economic Loss: A Comparative Study* (Hellenic Institute of International and Foreign Law, Athens, 1989), pp. 223; also, Case 10 ('The Dutiful Wife'), below.

when he has not acted deliberately, but merely unintentionally, albeit negligently. The courts seek to limit the liability of the driver to what he might reasonably have had in contemplation if he had set his mind to it. From the point of view of the team this is just another misfortune that it must live with, such as injuries to its players or mistakes made in a game.

## The Netherlands

I. A claim for loss of profit by the employer as a result of personal injury is blocked by article 6: 107 CC.

II. Whenever personal injury is involved, one must beware of the limitations imposed by the Civil Code on claims by third parties for damage that was suffered as a consequence of the injury. In case of personal injury, Dutch law, as a rule, only allows for a claim by the injured person himself. Third-party claims are considered blocked by article 6: 107 CC, which states:

> If a person suffers physical or mental injury as a result of an event for which another person is liable, that other person is not only obliged to repair the damage of the injured person himself, but also to indemnify a third person for costs [...] incurred for the benefit of the injured, which the latter, had he incurred them himself, would have been able to claim from that other person.

The article was basically meant to be a restatement of article 1407 of the 1838 Civil Code and, according to constant case law, the latter article only allowed for recovery by the injured party, and only for damages suffered by that person.[233] The only novelty introduced by article 6: 107 CC is that so-called damage *par ricochet* can now be claimed by third parties, but only insofar as the injured could have claimed them himself, had he himself suffered this damage. As far as a claim based on article 107 is concerned, it is sufficient that the injurer acted unlawfully *vis-à-vis* the injured party. It is irrelevant whether a duty of care existed *vis-à-vis* the third party.

When introducing article 107, the legislature explicitly intended – from a socio-economic point of view – not to augment the total financial burden of those responsible for injury and their insurers in comparison to the legal situation that existed under the 'old' Civil Code. Thus, it is assumed that conseqential damages, suffered by employers as a result of

---

[233] See H. A. Bouman and G. M. Tilanus-van Wassenaer, *Schadevergoeding: personenschade* (Monografieën Nieuw BW no. B-37) (Deventer, 1998), pp. 23 ff.

physical injury of their employees, cannot be claimed in any way. Even if the unlawful act that led to the injury, was also unlawful *vis-à-vis* the employer, any claim of the employer is blocked by article 6: 107 CC.

**Germany**

I. The All-Stars have no claim against the driver. Only Thomas's 'absolute rights', i.e. his body and health, have been injured, not the team's. Thus the All-Stars cannot rely on § 823 (1). Other tort provisions do not apply either and there is no contractual relationship between the team and the wrongdoer.

II. Tort claims: the employer has no claims under § 823 (1) because none of his absolute rights were violated. Nor do § 823 (2) or § 826 help him since there is no indication that the tortfeasor violated a statute protecting the employer, or that he acted intentionally and against public policy. Finally, the employer cannot make a claim for loss of services under § 845[234] because this provision applies only to services owed according to statute (e.g. among family members), not to services owed under a contract as in the present case. In short, an employer has no direct tort claim for the loss of the services of an employee injured by someone else.

Claims via subrogation: the employer must continue to pay the worker under article 3 of the Pay Continuation Statute (*Entgeltfortzahlungsgesetz*). In return, article 6 of the same statute provides that the employer is automatically subrogated to the worker's claim against the tortfeasor to the extent that the employer has continued to pay the worker under the statute. The employer can therefore sue the wrongdoer by presenting the subrogated claim.

However, the statute provides only for up to six weeks of pay, not for three months. Beyond the six-week period, the worker will, in most cases, continue to receive (possibly reduced) pay. If this pay comes from a public insurance fund, the worker's rights are automatically subrogated to the fund.[235] If the pay is received from the employer on other grounds (e.g. a collective bargaining agreement or the individual employment contract), the worker must subrogate his rights to the employer under these agreements.[236]

III. There seem to be no German cases of athletic clubs suing for damages suffered by the loss of a player's services, probably because it is clear that a claim would fail for the reasons stated.

---

[234] See above, Case 3 ('Cable III – The Day-to-Day Workers'), Sub II.
[235] See Löwisch, Rd.-Nr. 1090.   [236] See BGHZ 7, 30, at 49 (1952).

## Austria

I. The All-Stars team cannot expect to have any success in bringing a claim for compensation for lost profits against the owner of the car or his third-party liability insurance.

II. The Supreme Court would find the damage to be 'indirect', and would apply its 'indirect damage formula' to the facts, holding that the damage did not occur 'in the direction of the assault, but was attributable to a side-effect which arose in a sphere of interest not protected by the provision aiming to prevent the assault'.

III. It is obvious that a judgment similar to that issued by the Corte di Cassazione in the famous *Meroni* case[237] is actually beyond the power of the courts in Austria. It is not foreseeable that the OGH will change its practice and side with the plaintiff in the future.

A case which resulted in comparable 'indirect' damages occurred in Austria in 1976, when on 1 August one of the bridges crossing the Danube river in Vienna suddenly collapsed and caused an interruption to ship traffic for several weeks. Property damage and personal injury were rather insignificant.

Whereas compensation was awarded to the owners of two ships having been towed underneath the bridge, no information has surfaced as to the success of claims eventually brought to cover the financial losses caused by the interruption of the shipping route. Obviously, they have either been withdrawn or settled amicably.

## Portugal

I. The All-Stars basketball team has no basis on which to sue the car driver.[238]

Although differences do exist in relation to the question of the so-called 'external effect of obligations', in this particular case the doctrine is unanimous in excluding compensation.[239]

---

[237] *FI* 1971, I, 342, 1285.
[238] Portuguese law enshrines objective responsibility in the domain of road accidents (arts. 503 ff.). However, the intention there is to protect against the risks of road traffic themselves, and this kind of damage does not fall within the scope of protection.
[239] A. Menezes Cordeiro, *Direito das Obrigações* vol. I (2 vols., AAFDL, Lisbon, 1980), p. 281, while in favour of the external effect, considers that there is no causality link in this hypothesis. Cf., for German law, H. Kötz, *Deliktsrecht* (7th edn, Luchterhand, 1996), pp. 32–3, and for Italian law, G. Visintini, 'Il Caso Meroni: Un precedente giudiziale?', *NGCC* 1977, Parte seconda, 33–6.

The solution might be different if the car driver had injured Thomas wilfully, with the intention of causing harm to the All-Stars basketball team. The unlawful nature of the act would then be certain.

II. The question of whether a third party, who interferes with a contractual relationship, prevents the debtor's fulfilment and thereby causes damage to the creditor, should compensate the latter (external effect), has been much disputed in both doctrine and in case law.

The violation of the credit right by a third party may occur in several ways, namely:

(1) attack on a substratum of the credit, such as (a) the actual object of the rendering or something that may be indispensable to the fulfilment of the obligation (e.g. damaging an electricity cable and preventing fulfilment of a contract to supply energy); or further, (b) on the very person of the debtor (e.g. injuring him physically, preventing him from fulfilling an employment contract);
(2) a direct attack on the credit itself.

In the second type of situation, there has been much discussion of the case where the third party, being aware of the existence of the credit right (usually a contract), colludes with the debtor in the non-fulfilment, principally when this leads to failure of the contract.

It seems possible to say that the prevailing doctrine and caselaw continue to oppose the external effect.[240] In accordance with this orientation, in the case of inducing the failure of the contract, there is no unlawful act as such,[241] but the third party might be called upon to respond if the act were deemed very censurable and might be considered an abuse of right.[242]

---

[240] M. Henrique Mesquita, *Obrigações Reais e Onus Reais* (Coimbra, Almedina, 1990), pp. 53, 66 ff.

[241] Cf. H. Koziol, 'Wrongfulness under Austrian Law', in H. Koziol (ed.), *Unification of Tort Law: Wrongfulness* (Kluwer, The Hague, 1988), II f. 19 (case 2).

[242] M. de Andrade, *Teoria Geral das Obrigações* (Coimbra, 1963) (n. 13), pp. 51 ff.; J. Antunes Varela, *Das Obrigações em Geral*, vol. I (9th edn, 1996), pp. 552 and 644; Rui de Alarcão, *Direito das Obrigações* (Coimbra, 1983) pp. 82 ff.; J. F. Sinde Monteiro, *Deliktsrecht in Europa, Landesbericht Portugal* (Almedina, Coimbra, 1994), pp. 181 ff. According to A. Ferrer-Correia, 'Da responsabilidade do terceiro que coopera com o devedor na violação de um pacto de preferência', (1998) *Revista de Legislação e Jurisprudência* 355–60 and 369–74, in the hypothesis of co-operation of a third party in the infringement of a preferential agreement there would be, in principle, an abuse of the right. In case law, decisions in favour of the external effect have been handed down by the Supreme Court of Justice on 16 July 1964 (1998), *Revista de Legislação e Jurisprudência*, ano 19 ff. (with critical annotations by Vaz Serra, pp. 25 ff.) and on 25 October 1993, *Colectânea de Jurisprudência*. Tomo III, 86 (*Boletim do Ministério da Justiça* no. 430, 455);

III. If the infringement of credit rights by a third party were considered illicit, this would mean attributing greater weight to the interests of the creditor over those of the third party, because illicitness always implies an added value at the level of weighing values or interests.[243]

But, the interests of the creditor and third party are presented at the outset as being of equal value: 'to the interest of the creditor in the maintenance of his/her pretension to the rendering corresponds an interest, of at least equal value, of the third party in not having his/her economic activity harmed by alien contractual relations'.[244]

In Portuguese law, there is no rule in the chapter concerning civil liability that declares the malicious causation of damage by means of an act contrary to *boni mores* to be unlawful. But the general part of the Civil Code contains a general prohibition of the abuse of the right, in the following terms: 'the exercise of a right is illegitimate when its holder manifestly exceeds the limits imposed by good faith, by good practice or by the social or economic end of such right' (article 334).[245] This rule is adequate to handle cases where the failure of a contract may have been induced.

## Sweden and Finland

I. The All-Stars cannot claim compensation from the driver (or better, the insurance company). This is firmly established and is beyond discussion.

II. Here again, the employer has no claim because of the application of the general principle which excludes the compensation of economic losses suffered by subjects different from those who have directly suffered personal injury or property damage. As far as personal injuries are concerned, the only statutory exceptions are provided by the Tort Liability Acts 1972 and 1974 and arise in case of death for funeral expenses and lost maintenance allowances for survivors, on the basis of *SkadestL* 5:2 (Sweden) and *SkadestL* 5:3–4 (Finland). Among the – albeit very limited – exceptions developed in case law, none applies to this case.

---

against, judgments on 17 June 1969, *Boletim do Ministéro da Justiça* no. 188, 146, and on 27 January 1993, *Colectânea de Jurisprudência*, Tomo I, 84, as well as that already cited, judgement of the Porto Court of Appeal on 10 March 1994 (above fn. 105).

[243] A. De Cupis, *Il Danno*, vol. I (3rd edn, Milano 1979), p. 11.

[244] A. Georgiades, 'Standpunkt und Entwicklung der griechischen Deliktsrechts', in *Festschrift Larenz zum 80. Geburtstag*, 175 ff., 187.

[245] The wording of this article is the same as that of art. 281 of the Greek Civil Code.

*Editors' comparative comments*

The instant case bears a strong analogy to the famous *Meroni* decision which heralded Italy's 'recent revolution' (above chapter 5) on the recoverability of pure economic loss. The financial losses of a sports club resulting from the death of its star player throw into relief the complexity of this subject. The great majority of countries would not award compensation on these facts. True, the claim for compensation is not necessarily excluded in principle in Belgium, France, Greece, Italy and Spain, yet it is clear there is little chance of an award since the alleged damages of the club will probably be regarded as too speculative or hypothetical. However, in France, it might be possible to use the *perte d'une chance* concept in order to award at least partial compensation, though this amount would not be designed to fully compensate the All-Stars for their drop in league standings.

The causal link will certainly be difficult to prove, not only in *Meroni*'s native land, but in Scotland as well. The Scottish reporter argues that the All-Stars may well fail to establish even a 'but for' causal relationship between the tortious act and the alleged financial damage, since no one can be certain that but for the absence of the star player, the team would have been in a better position than fourth place and hence better off financially. *A fortiori* he would fail, using the standards of 'legal' causation, to show the negligence was the direct, proximate or dominant cause of the loss, considering all the imponderables of the game.

In the rest of Europe, the forecast is even clearer. The claim will be rejected in principle in Germany and Portugal because the infringement of the club's contractual relationship with its star is not regarded as an invasion of a protected 'absolute right'. The team's contract with him has no 'external effect', the Portuguese reporter explains, because a contract is only a relative right and negligent 'interference' with such a right is not 'unlawful'. The same outcome is also predicted in Finland, Sweden and Austria, simply because of exclusionary causal doctrines, already discussed in the earlier cases, which preclude compensating injured third parties.

## Case 6: the infected cow

### Case

A cattle raiser allowed an infected animal to escape from his premises. The escape of the infected animal obliged the authorities to close the cattle and meat market for ten days. The cattle raiser is being sued by:

(1) other cattle raisers who for ten days have not been able to sell their cattle;
(2) the market traders who have lost their supplies; and
(3) the butchers who during this time have not been able to conduct their business.

### France

I. In principle, the three groups of plaintiffs may recover their economic losses against defendant, perhaps in a claim grounded upon article 1382, or more likely in a claim grounded upon article 1385.

II. The ground for these claims might be under the general tort articles (1382–83 CC) or under the more specific liability of the *gardien* of an animal causing injury (art. 1385 CC).

As it is implied that the authorities had no choice but to close the cattle and meat market for ten days, there is probably a direct causation between the escape of the animal and the damage suffered by the victims. There does not seem to be much question as to the certainty or reality of that damage under the facts given.

The three groups of plaintiffs are composed of people with the same professional interests, and they apparently suffered the same kind of pure economic loss. Each of them is entitled to sue the defendant separately and recover damages for the pecuniary loss, or following the American 'class action' model recently adopted in French law,[246] these groups might elect that:

(1) one person can sue on behalf of all the others;
(2) they can form an association that would represent and defend everyone's interests.

One should keep in mind the difference which exists between the claim under article 1382 and that under article 1385 CC. As far as article 1382 is

[246] Soc., 11 oct. 1994, Bull. 1994, V, no. 266; JCP 1994, éd. G.IV.2463.

concerned, the affected groups will have to show that the defendant was at fault in allowing the infected animal to escape, the damage suffered and the link between the two. As for article 1385, they will have to prove only that the defendant was the *gardien* who had custody of the infected animal, the certain existence of the damage, and the direct causal link with the animal's escape. Under article 1385, the *gardien* is liable without proof of fault. This liability is based upon the notion of *garde* and if the *garde* is transferred, so is the liability, since the *garde* is based upon the direction, usage and control of the thing.

## Belgium

I. There are few chances that the claimants under (1), (2), or (3) could recover their damage against the cattle raiser since the damage claimed is the consequence of the authorities' decision to close the cattle and meat market.

II. The tortfeasor is liable according to article 1382 CC for the damage resulting from its fault:

> Any act whatever of man which causes damage to another obliges him by whose fault it occurred to make reparation.

To hold the cattle raiser liable, the claimants will have to prove the fault of the cattle raiser, a damage and a causal link between the damage and the fault.

In the present case, it might not be easy to prove the fault of the cattle raiser. Did he violate a legal obligation? Did he act differently in comparison with the behaviour that the *bonus pater familias* would have had in the same circumstances?

The plaintiffs could therefore prefer to base their claims on article 1385 CC:

> The owner of an animal or he who avails himself of it while it is being put to his use is liable for the damage which the animal causes, whether the animal was in his keeping or whether it had strayed or escaped.

If the owner of the animal is presumed to have committed a fault because the damage resulted from the animal's act, the claimants will still have to prove the existence of the causal link.

In order to appreciate if there is a causal link between the fault and the damage, the Belgian Supreme Court uses a theory known as *l'équivalence des conditions*. According to that theory, the fault is in a causal link with the damage if the plaintiff can prove that the damage would not have occurred, as it occurred, if the fault had not been committed.[247]

To recover the damage, the claimants will have to prove therefore that their damage would not have occurred as it occurred if the cattle raiser had not allowed the infected animal to escape.

At first glance, it seems that they could prove it. However, the Supreme Court has on several occasions stated that the causal link is interrupted when the damage claimed results from another autonomous obligation, such as one resulting from a statute or from a contract.[248]

Since the damage claimed by the plaintiffs in the present case results from the authorities' decision to close the cattle and meat market, the plaintiff's claim will be most certainly rejected.

**Italy**

I. There are no cases matching the facts, but we do think that the answer to the problems raised here can be found in some financial cases where courts restricted the domain of liability for economic losses.

The answer to sub-question (1) might be positive, i.e. the other cattle raisers appear to have an action against the defendant, for an absolute right to their property (the cattle) has been infringed.

The answers to sub-questions (2) and (3) are negative, because there is no direct relation between the infection and the market collapse. The closing of the market is due to the intervention of a public authority and this shifts the individual's recourse into the administrative courts (i.e. from private to public law grounds). No civil court has the power to force the administrative authority to do or not do something.

II. Although the rule of Italian case law is the *conditio sine qua non* rule,[249] courts often use the 'too remote causation nexus'[250] argument

---

[247] Cass., 12 janvier 1988, Pas., 1988, I, 563; Cass., 15 mai 1990, Pas, 1990, I, 1054; Cass., 23 mai 1990, Pas., 1990, I, 1079; Cass. 23 juin 1990, Pas, 1990, I, 1126; Cass., 8 octobre 1992, Pas., 1992, I, 1124.
[248] Cass., 17 janvier 1938, Pas., I, 8 and 11; Cass., 28 avril 1978, RCJB, 1979, p. 261; Cass., 26 septembre 1979; RGAR, 1982, no. 10431; Cass., 9 mars 1984, RCJB, 1986, p. 651; Cass., 15 mars 1985, Pas., I, 1985, 978; Cass., 28 juin 1984, Pas., 1984, I, 618; Cass., 18 avril 1988, Pas., 1988, I, 943; Cass., 4 octobre 1988, Pas, 1989, I, 118, 15 novembre 1991, I, 282.
[249] Cass. 3.12.1983, no. 7237, FI, 1984, I, 60; Cass. 10.2.1981, no. 826, MGC, 1981; Cass. 8.1981, no. 170, MGC, 1981; Cass. 6.1.1981, no. 73, MGC, 1981; Cass. 4.7.1981, no. 6716, MGC, 1981; Cass. 24.3.1980, no. 1949, MGC, 1980.
[250] See, for this critique, P. G. Monateri, *La responsabilità civile* (Turin, 1998), pp. 165 ff.

to deny liability in certain factual situations, where equitable considerations suggest that liability would otherwise be too broad. This may result in contradictory holdings, but it has been used several times under the label of 'unforeseeable consequences' (*conseguenze imprevedibili*).[251]

The cattle raiser case might be one in which the court could resort to this argument. It could rule that the market traders' and butchers' economic losses – even if deriving from the escape of the infected cattle and falling under the *conditio sine qua non* rule – may not be recovered for they represent an unforeseeable consequence.

## Spain

I. There is not a clear outcome of cases similar to this one since there is no pertinent decision in Spanish case law.

II. In Spanish law, as is the case in the French Code, there are special norms regulating damage caused by animals, i.e. articles 1905 and 1906 CC (the latter is applicable to hunting animals and is thus not relevant for the present purposes).[252]

Article 1905 establishes the strict liability of the animal's keeper (not necessarily its owner), following a constant stream of Supreme Court decisions. It is therefore not a *iuris tantum* presumption of fault, but rather one of strict liability with only two exemptions: fault of the victim or *force majeure*.[253]

This said, it should be pointed out that the problem posed in this case is not resolved in Spanish case law and there are no doctrinal studies directly covering it. In order to attempt to solve this case, we would be faced with two types of problems.

The first one would be one of causation. The large majority of cases solved by the Supreme Court in application of article 1905 refer to damages caused by the animal's material action (e.g. an animal kicking a person, darting into a road and causing a traffic accident, etc.) which presents more general issues of causation.

The only Supreme Court decision which contemplates damage caused by infection is the First Chamber's decision of 10 February 1959, which

---

[251] *Safac v. Ministero Giustizia*, Cass. 20.1.1983, no. 567, *FI*, 1983, I, 1264.
[252] C. Rogel Vide, *La responsabilidad civil extracontractual en el derecho español* (Civitas, Madrid, 1977), p. 168.
[253] For all, see Rogel Vide, *La responsabilidad*, pp. 168 and 170, J. Santos Briz, *La responsabilidad civil: derecho sustantivo y derecho procesal* (6th edn, 2 vols, 1991), p. 961, and R. de Ángel, *Tratado de responsabilidad civil* (3rd edn, Civitas, Madrid, 1993), p. 562.

is somewhat exceptional[254] and criticized by legal scholars.[255] In that case, a worker had helped to collect the corpse of a dead animal which happened to have an infectious disease. Under doctor's suggestions, the worker took an anti-rabies vaccine and reacted so badly he was eventually left with serious after-effects (the court decision declared that there was no fault incurred by the doctors who applied the treatment). The worker brought legal action against the owner of the animal (not his employer) and the Supreme Court finally awarded damages.

Returning to our case, it should be said that Spanish law – despite the above Supreme Court decision – would probably not accept a legal action for the injured parties in the present case against the cattle-owner. The above damage would not be objectively imputable (*imputatio facti* or the German *objektive Zurechnung*) to the cattle-owner's doing: i.e. this would be excluded by the principle of 'general risks of life' (*allgemeine Lebensrisiko*).[256] Things would be different if the cattle-owner had acted in bad faith. If that were the case, the link of causation would be interpreted more freely and there would be no problem in attributing the damage caused to the cattle-owners's bad faith.[257]

The second problem would be to calculate the amount of damages that the various plaintiffs could have claimed. Each case raises an issue of lost profits, which legal scholars warn is problematic because in general, the Supreme Court is reluctant to admit compensation for lost profits, particularly as shown in the earliest Supreme Court decisions.[258] Also, a Spanish court possibly might apply article 1103 CC to adjust the award of damages if it were deemed excessive.

## Greece

I. The other cattle raisers, market traders and butchers can probably be compensated for their damages, except for their loss of unforeseeable profits.

---

[254] It is exceptional in Díez-Picazo's opinion; see L. Díez-Picazo, *Estudios sobre la jurisprudencia civil*, vol. I (2nd edn, Technos, Madrid, 1973), p. 264.
[255] Rogel Vide, *La responsabilidad*, p. 169, Santos Briz, *La responsabilidad*, pp. 962–3.
[256] See F. Pantaleón 'Comentario al artículo 1902', in *Comentario del Código Civil*, II (1991), p. 1985 and 'Causalidad e imputación objetiva: criterios de imputación', *Centenario del Código Civil*, II (1990), pp. 1566–8; this principle is also supported by De Ángel, *Tratado*, p. 787 and J. L. Lacruz, *Elementos de derecho civil*, vol. II (3rd edn, Bosch, Barcelona, 1994), p. 485.
[257] Lacruz, *Elementos*, p. 489, De Ángel, *Tratado*, p. 810.
[258] Rogel Vide, *La responsabilidad*, pp. 61–3, J. Puig Brutau, *Fundamentos de derecho civil*, vol. II (3rd edn, Bosch, Barcelona, 1983), pp. 183–4, Lacruz, *Elementos*, p. 505, Santos Briz, *La responsabilidad*, p. 286.

II. Since his negligence is proved, the cattle raiser has committed a tort according to article 914 CC, because the law prohibits putting the public health at risk (because even the attempt is prohibited, art. 42, 308 (284) Penal Code, or art. 284, 57 CC), even without wilful conduct. The unlawfulness is even more obvious, if we consider here as legal grounds for the cattle raiser's liability not only the assault on public health, but also his negligence, this time not regarded as simple fault but as unlawful behaviour, because the events mentioned in the case are typical risks of bad cattle husbandry. This negligence is considered to be a breach of the duty of care imposed by good faith.[259] This view is grounded in articles 914, 281 and 288 CC, which ordain that everyone should behave as business usages require.

Therefore, the culpable cattle raiser is liable to compensate the other cattlemen, market traders and butchers, since their losses are causally related to his tort. Indeed, these events are foreseeable[260] effects of the prohibited threat to the health of the meat consumers. So they are causally related to it. Of course, the unforeseeable earnings of the plaintiffs are not indemnifiable.

III. The Greek courts have not yet faced such a case. Nevertheless in such an instance they would probably use the theory of broadening the unlawfulness, according to which negligence itself already constitutes *eo ipso* an unlawful behaviour, prohibited by articles 281 and 288 CC. According to this point of view, the cattle raiser's negligence in failing to control his premises would possibly be considered as an unlawful act too, and he would be probably judged liable.

### England

I. All claimants must fail in their claims, both in negligence, and under the rule of *Rylands* v. *Fletcher*;[261] it is also likely they will not succeed under the tort of public nuisance.

---

[259] AP 640/1955 NoB 4, 491; AP 250/1956 NoB 4, 840; AP 510/1959 NoB 8, 251; AP 343/1968 NoB 16, 943; AP 854/1974 NoB 23, 479; AP 81/1991 NoB 40, 715; EfAth 7453/1988 EllDni 31, 848; AP 678/1998 NoB 47, 1416; MprThes 9830/1997 Arm 53, 77. On the contrary see P. Papanikolaou, *The Liability of the Bank as Underwriter* (ed. A. Sakkoulas, 1998), pp. 174 ff. On the function of the good faith principle see also M. Stathopoulos, 'The Liability of the Bank because of Immoral Prejudice', NoB 40, 498.

[260] About the foreseeability as causation's criterion see, e.g. AP 692/1990 NoB 40, 67; AP 1063/90; AP 979/92 ElD 35; K. Triantaphyllopoulos, *Law of Obligations* (Athens, 1935), p. 184; G. Balis, *Law of Obligations, General Part* (3rd edn, 1960), p. 100; A. Ligeropoulos (gen. ed.), *Interpretation of the Civil Code (A Commentary)* (ErmAK) (1949–1978), arts. 297–300 CC, no. 39; G. Fourkiotis, *Greek Law of Obligations, General Part* (1964), p. 318, G. Michaélidès-Nouaros, *Law of Obligations* (1959), p. 31 etc.

[261] (1866) LR 1 Ex 265, affirmed (1868) LR 3 HL 330 (HL).

II. The case is very similar to the English case *Weller & Co. v. Foot & Mouth Research Institute*:²⁶² the escape of a virus from the research laboratory led to the local authority closing down the cattle market, causing economic loss to auctioneers who would have sold cattle on commission.

Negligence: the English Court of Appeal held that there was no liability in negligence on the grounds that the loss was too remote a consequence of the escape, and therefore, the claim fell on lack of causal link.

The rule of *Rylands v. Fletcher*: there was also no liability under the rule in *Rylands v. Fletcher* in *Weller*, as recovery under this rule presupposes loss linked with interest in land.

In the present case, even if the infected animal had escaped on *land* on which the plaintiff raised his cattle, the position might not have been different, following the recent decision of the House of Lords in *Cambridge Water Co. v. Eastern Counties Leather Plc*,²⁶³ requiring now that the loss was reasonably foreseeable to the defendant at the time of the escape, in conjunction with the older *Liesbosch Dredger v. Edison SS (Owners)*,²⁶⁴ postulating that the necessary foresight in cases of economic loss must include not only the *nature* of the harm (as is the case with physical harm), but, also, the *extent* of the harm and the *way* in which the harm was inflicted.

Public nuisance: civil liability may arise in English law from the crime of public nuisance, i.e. action or omission 'which obstructs or causes inconvenience or damage to the public in the exercise of rights common to all Her Majesty's subjects', and when as a result, an individual has suffered particular damage over and above the inconvenience or damage to the public at large.²⁶⁵ Economic loss is clearly recoverable under this tort.²⁶⁶ The crime of public nuisance is a common law offence, and the plaintiffs in the present case would need to establish that the escape of the infected animal amounts to a public nuisance; this is unlikely, in the absence of evidence that the public at large is inconvenienced by it.

III. As Lord Denning observed in *Spartan Steel v. Martin*,²⁶⁷ economic loss is often held to be 'too remote' a consequence of a tort to be compensated not on pragmatic, but on *policy* grounds. The case is a good illustration of the 'nightmare scenario', which is responsible for the greatest objection to liability for economic loss, i.e. that it can be so

---

[262] [1966] 1 QB 569.   [263] [1994] 2 AC 264 (HL).   [264] [1933] AC 449.
[265] See the review of authorities by Scholl J in *Walsh v. Ervin* [1952] WLR 361.
[266] See *Tate & Lyle Indus. v. GLC* [1983] 1 All ER 1159 (HL).   [267] [1973] 1 QB 27 (CA).

widespread in amount that no defendant ought to be asked to carry the risk of compensating it.[268]

## Scotland

I. It is highly unlikely that any of the above will be able to succeed in an action against the cattle raiser.

II. We are again in the area of duty of care as a limiting factor when all that is suffered is pure economic loss. There is no decided Scottish case in point on similar facts. The case of *Robertson v. Connolly*,[269] which involved negligent behaviour with an infected horse, was concerned not with pure economic loss but with actual physical damage to horses belonging to another party through the subsequent transmission of that infection to them. Even in that case the judges were alert to the risk of subjecting the negligent party to a potentially wide-ranging claim. The defender's counsel had pointed out that the losses might extend *ad infinitum* if the horses in question had been taken to other stables rather than back to their owner's. It must be observed, however, that we have more knowledge and awareness about the transmission of disease today and mechanisms for its control than they did in 1851. Hence the type of proactive intervention by the authorities here in this case. The Lord President (Boyle) held:

> [T]he loss of these three horses is a direct consequence of the defender's misconduct in putting the unsound pony into the field; for, when the pursuer found his horse to be in bad health, where would he take it so naturally as to his own stable? It would be a very different case if these other horses had been sold, and had carried the disease to other stables. That damage might be very remote. But here we must look to the fact that damage was done in the first stable into which the horse was put, that being the stable to which he would naturally be sent.[270]

Lord MacKenzie was of the same opinion, and added that although '[i]t may be possible with a little ingenuity to figure alarming consequences from this decision... this case does not go far, and [he] wish[ed] it to be understood that [he gave] no opinion beyond the case before us'.[271]

The Lord President speaks of the hypothesized damage in his judgment being 'very remote'. This is significant since, as Norrie observes, '[r]emoteness was originally the primary means adopted by the law for

---

[268] More in E. K. Banakas, *Tortious Liability for Pure Economic Loss* (Hellenic Institute of International and Foreign Law, Athens, 1989), p. 36.
[269] (1851) 13 D 779.   [270] Ibid. at p. 781.   [271] Ibid. at p. 781.

keeping liability within acceptable bounds, but at least since *Donoghue* v. *Stevenson* that role has been played by the concept of the duty of care.'[272] In our case there has been no physical damage, and we have seen from *Dynamco* as discussed above that when all that is suffered is pure economic loss, the courts have held that no duty of care exists except for limited exceptions which will be encountered in the cases to be considered below.

In the English case of *Weller & Co. and Another* v. *Foot and Mouth Disease Research Institute*[273] Widgery J held that auctioneers who had suffered pure economic loss were not within the scope of the defendant research institute's duty of care, since

> the defendant's duty of care to avoid the escape of the virus was due to the foreseeable fact that the virus might infect cattle in the neighbourhood and cause them to die. The duty of care [was] accordingly owed to owners of cattle in the neighbourhood [and] the plaintiffs [were] not owners of cattle and [had] no proprietary interest in anything which might conceivably be damaged by the virus if it escaped.[274]

It is thought that the Scottish courts would follow a similar line and that the market traders and butchers would have no action, since no duty of care was owed to them. And, even though the cattle raiser owed a duty of care to his fellow cattle raisers to avoid their animals becoming infected, the economic loss from being unable to sell their cattle would probably also be seen to be outside the duty of care.

III. Once again we see public policy at work in a situation in which, in the words of Lord Denning MR in *SCM (UK) Ltd*,[275] '[t]he risk should be borne by the whole community rather than on one pair of shoulders...'[276] If any animals were actually infected then an action would lie against the cattle raiser, and that is the risk they run from their negligence. To extend this to the other consequences would appear to run counter to the policy of the courts hitherto laid down.

### The Netherlands

I. Dutch law does not provide a clear-cut answer.

II. In this case, no immediate infection occurs, but as a result of the intervention of the authorities, other cattle raisers, market traders and

---

[272] *Stair Memorial Encyclopaedia, The Laws of Scotland*, vol. 15 (Law Society of Scotland, Edinburgh, 1996), p. 255, para. 379 (written by K. McK. Norrie) (footnotes omitted).
[273] [1966] 1 QB 569.   [274] Ibid. at p. 587F.
[275] [1971] 1 QB 337.   [276] Ibid. at p. 344D.

butchers suffer pure economic loss. Strict liability of the cattle raiser for damage caused by the infected animal does not apply.[277] Nonetheless, there seems to be grounds for fault-based liability. It can safely be said that in a densely populated country such as the Netherlands, farmers have the duty to prevent their infected livestock from escaping. As soon as the farmer has (constructive) knowledge of the infection, he has the duty to prevent stock from escaping. Having said that, the next question is, of course, exactly to whom this duty is owed. No case law on the subject exists, but it seems safe to assume this duty is owed at the very least to the owners of animals that are at risk of being infected. The main aim of the duty is to protect other animals from the obvious danger of infection. But it cannot be ruled out that the duty purports to protect others and their financial interests as well.

In this case, no immediate infection occurs, but as a result of the intervention of the authorities, a strict economic loss for other cattle raisers does occur. It can be concluded from existing caselaw on related subjects that several factors should be taken into account. Case-law indicates that *foreseeability* is a factor of considerable weight: was it foreseeable that the authorities would intervene (do they normally do so in cases like these?);[278] and was it foreseeable that this specific damage would arise as a result?[279]

But even if it can be foreseen that the authorities will act upon the escape of the infected animal, and their closing down the market is totally justified in the interest of the general public, must a single person, because of their (slightly) negligent act, bear the immense burden of the financial loss of so many? I personally would hesitate to open these 'floodgates'. However, it must be admitted that the leading case on the subject, the 1977 Supreme Court decision on the damaged gas main (see above, Cases 1, 'Cable I – The Blackout', and 2, 'Cable II – Factory Shutdown'), seems to advocate the cattle raiser's liability for foreseeable damage. The question, then, is whether the interests of other cattle raisers are obvious and foreseeable interests that should have been

---

[277] See art. 6:179 CC, which reads: 'The possessor of an animal is liable for the damage caused by the animal, unless, pursuant to the preceding section, there would have been no liability if the possessor would have had control over the behaviour of the animal by which the damage was caused.' In 1984, the Dutch Supreme Court decided that this article, in principle does not apply whenever an animal merely spreads an infectious disease. See HR 24.2.1984, NJ 1984, no. 415.

[278] Given recent events surrounding an epidemic of swine fever in the Netherlands, the answer must be affirmative.

[279] See, e.g., HR 13.11.1987, NJ 1988, no. 210, HR 25.5.1990, NJ 1990, no. 577.

anticipated by the injurer. Again I am reluctant to respond. Before answering, it would be necessary to know more about the dangers of the infection, the procedure that is normally followed by reasonable cattle raisers in general and the cost of preventing escape. In the end, the facts of the case will be decisive.

Although damage is suffered from loss of tangible property (the meat supplies have been lost), there is no closer causal connection between the escape and the loss than between the escape and the sales restriction. As before, it is difficult to judge.

Butchers are dependent on the business of the meat market. This 'second-' or even 'third-degree' damage would have to be filed under ordinary business risks. In all our dealings we are dependent on others, directly or indirectly. It seems to me that it would be stretching the limits of tort law too far to say that cattle raisers owe a duty to butchers of cattle to prevent their infected stock from escaping. But again, every case should be decided on its own merits; the factors stated above should be taken into consideration.

As far as 'second-degree' damage is concerned, mention must be made of a decision of the Amsterdam *Gerechtshof* (Amsterdam Court of Appeal).[280] The facts in this case were as follows. A shopkeeper contended that the City of Amsterdam was liable in tort for the negligent manner in which the city had cleared a building of squatters. For two weeks after the eviction, there were riots in the vicinity of the building. As a result, the shopkeeper lost a substantial number of customers during these and subsequent weeks. The Amsterdam Court of Appeal was reluctant in assigning liability; the Court decided that even if a duty was owed to the shopkeeper to vacate the building most cautiously in order to avoid riots, and even if this duty had been neglected, the loss that had occurred could not reasonably be imputed to the city. The Court decided that the nature of the damage (pure economic) required a closer cause-and-effect connection than would be the case had the damage consisted of personal injury or damage to property.[281]

---

[280] Hof Amsterdam 27.5.1986, NJ 1987, no. 712.
[281] Note, however, that in a similar case the District Court of Dordrecht (24.12.1986, BR 1987, pp. 835 ff.) decided that the municipality of Dordrecht was liable in tort for loss of customers of a shopkeeper. In that case, the shopkeeper experienced an unexpected loss of customers as a result of contamination of the soil of the entire neighbourhood where nearly all his customers lived. As the customers were evacuated from their homes, the shopkeeper lost his clientele. The Court considered the municipality in principle to be liable. See R. J. P. Kottenhagen, 'Buiten-contractuele aansprakelijkheid voor economische schade', (1991) *Bouwrecht* 343–4.

## Germany

I. None of the claimants under (1), (2), or (3) have a right to recover against the cattle raiser. They suffer pure economic loss which is not compensable under these circumstances. However, this outcome is debatable to some extent.

II. § 823 (1) probably provides no basis for the plaintiffs' actions. Certainly, none of their absolute rights specifically listed in this provision have been violated. Yet, they could try to claim that the cattle raiser's negligence amounts to an infringement of their 'right of the established and ongoing commercial enterprise'.[282] This would require demonstration that the defendant's act was directed at, or specifically related to, their businesses as such.[283] While there seems to be no case exactly in point, the case law and academic commentary on this requirement suggest that it should not be fulfilled here. The cattle raiser's act (or omission) was not directed against, nor immediately related to, the plaintiffs' businesses. Instead, it was negligence *vis-à-vis* the public as a whole and affected the meat industry only indirectly.[284]

§ 823 (2). The plaintiffs could also invoke § 823 (2), claiming that the defendant violated a statute intended to protect them. There is indeed an Animal Diseases Law of 20 December 1995, and it is conceivable that the cattle raiser violated one or more of its provisions. This law may be a protective statute in the sense of § 823 (2) BGB, e.g. in cases where other animals or humans are infected, but it is highly unlikely that the courts would construe it to protect the meat industry against financial loss as well.

§ 833. Finally, one could think of § 833 BGB as a basis for liability: if a person is killed, or the body or health of a person is injured, or a thing is damaged, by an animal, the person who keeps the animal is bound to compensate the injured party for any damage arising therefrom.

Yet, reading this article immediately shows that it applies only in case of injury to the human body, health or property. Since the plaintiffs suffered none of this, claims under this provision will fail as well.

III. Admittedly, there is room to debate whether the defendant's negligence did or did not amount to a violation of the plaintiffs' 'right to an established and ongoing concern'. The requirement that the act (or omission) be immediately related to the business (*betriebsbezogen*)

---

[282] See above Case 2 ('Cable II – Factory Shutdown').
[283] See ibid. [284] But see below III.

is rather vague and allows for different applications. It would not be clearly unreasonable to argue that, in the present case, there is indeed a specific relationship between the escape of an infected animal raised for meat, and the loss suffered by the meat industry. Yet, there is also reason to believe that the courts would still reject the claim. The *Bundesgerichtshof* has repeatedly cautioned against an undue expansion of liability to affected businesses.[285] If an infringement of the 'right of the established and ongoing business' were found in the present case, the cattle owner could be liable to a large number of plaintiffs for enormous losses. Even in other cases, the *Bundesgerichtshof* has refused to compensate the members of the whole chain of distribution, expressly saving defendants from the crushing liability that they would otherwise suffer.[286]

## Austria

I. No damages will be awarded in any of the variations of the case. Obviously, the cattle raiser is only to blame for simple negligence. None of the damages resulting from his mishap are such as to indicate unlawfulness stemming from the violation of protected rights.

II. There is a provision on the liability for damage caused by animals in the Austrian Civil Code: namely, article 1320 ABGB.[287] Notwithstanding its wide scope, this provision is not a basis for liability in this case since it aims at liability for the realization of the typical danger caused by a certain category of animals, and does not extend to pure financial losses.

In cases such as the one under consideration, a claim for recovery fails due to the absence of an element indicating unlawfulness. Rather, such damage lies within the typical risk of cattle raisers, meat traders and butchers. They can only expect to have a claim if a protective statute has been violated by the defendant. Such statutory provisions could eventually be contained in national statutes and international conventions on epizootic diseases. Whether the cattle raiser is to blame for a violation of such a statute to protect others from injury is not clear from the facts.

---

[285] E.g. BGHZ 29, 65, at 73 (1958).   [286] See BGHZ 40, 91, at 99–107 (1963).
[287] It reads: 'If a person is injured by an animal, the person is liable therefor who has incited or irritated the animal thereto or who has neglected to keep it well guarded. The possessor of the animal is liable if he does not prove that he took precautions to ensure that the animal was properly guarded and kept.'

III. Cases of this kind appear to support the horrific vision of a 'boundless, economically intolerable expansion of liability' to which the Austrian Supreme Court tends to resort in much less crucial cases. It is not probable, therefore, that the practice will change in the near future.

## Portugal

I. None of these categories of victims can seek compensation from a cattle raiser who has allowed an infected animal to escape.

II. Indeed, even if we acknowledge the existence of fault, we are not facing an unlawful act, as required by article 483/1 CC. In every case business activities have been interfered with, but no subjective right has been violated.

The law establishes liability for presumed fault for damage caused by animals, a presumption which falls on anyone in possession of an animal with a duty to watch over it (art. 493/1 CC). However, unlawfulness is a requisite independent of fault, though sometimes, especially in the domain of contractual liability, it is difficult to disentangle the two.

On the other hand, for damage caused by animals, an objective responsibility is also established. This lies with whoever uses the animal in their own interests, 'once the damage results from the special danger involved in their utilisation' (art. 502). But it does not appear that pure economic loss is covered by the protective scope of the rule.

III. A comparison between the damage in this case and the preceding case raises the issue whether, as a matter of legislative policy, interference with a non-contractual expectation (as in the present case) is more deserving of protection than interference with a contractual relationship (the preceding case). We do not think it is settled that this would be so.[288]

## Sweden and Finland

I. All three groups of claimants will find it rather difficult to bring a claim against the wrongdoer, although no definitive answer eitherway can be given.

II. We are here confronted with 'pure economic loss' in the Swedish–Finnish meaning of the term, i.e. an economic loss not arising

---

[288] Cf. P. S. Atiyah, *The Rise and Fall of Freedom of Contract* (Clarendon, Oxford, 1979), pp. 762–4, and 'Economic Loss in the United States', (1985) 5 *Oxford Journal of Legal Studies* 485, 486–7.

in connection with anybody suffering bodily injury or property damage. According to the Tort Liability Acts, 1972 and 1974, pure economic loss is in principle compensated when it is caused by a crime (*SkadestL* 4:2 for Sweden; *SkadestL* 5:1 for Finland), although the text (in Finland) and the preparatory works (in Sweden) of the Tort Liability Acts 1972 and 1974 do not bar compensation if the courts find strong reasons for it. However, courts have been very restrictive in using such discretionary power. In this case, it must be noted that in both Sweden and Finland there are some statutes on protection against animal diseases containing provisions which could in some circumstances apply a criminal sanction to the conduct of the cattle raiser.[289]

III. Cases such as this are unlikely to occur, because the abovementioned Swedish and Finnish acts on protection against animal diseases contain an extensive system of compensation by the state for the economic losses suffered by cattle raisers, in case of the intervention of public authorities which aims to avoid the spread of animal diseases. Therefore, litigation against a private defendant is not financially attractive.

*Editors' comparative comments*

This case introduces the hitherto untreated question whether the owner/custodian of an infected animal that poses a threat to public health and occasions vast financial losses may be held liable. Whether it is a claim based on negligence or upon strict liability, the issues are complex. The chain of causation may fail in a number of countries on either grounds. Furthermore, the large number of plaintiffs (there are three classes) and the potentially huge financial losses once again create the nightmare scenario. If it seems disproportionate to impose this potentially crushing burden upon a single individual because of their negligent act or omission, it may seem particularly unfair to hold defendant liable for such sums even when they have not been negligent at all. In the following comments we restrict ourselves to the strict liability aspects of this case.

In a number of code countries the liability of the *gardien* or custodian of an animal in his keeping rests upon the footing of strict liability. The code provisions in Austria, Belgium, France, Italy, Portugal, Spain, and the Netherlands do not differentiate between different types of animals.

[289] Epizootilag (1980: 369) (Sweden); Lag om djursjukdomar 18.1.1980/55 (Finland).

Whether the animal is considered a domestic, farm or luxury animal is immaterial. In our case, therefore, no-fault liability should apply to the case of the custodian of an escaped cow. In Germany and Greece, however, only the keeping of a 'luxury' animal engages the keeper's strict liability. Liability for losses occasioned by domestic animals such as cows and cattle would require proof of the custodian's fault.[290] Thus, the defendant in our case would be judged by stricter standards in some countries than in others.

However, this differing treatment may not make that much difference with regard to the outcome of our case. In the 'no-fault' countries such as France the troublesome issue remains, as we have seen before, whether the financial damage is sufficiently certain and not too remote; in Belgium the authorities' decision to close the markets might be viewed as an interruption of causation due to an 'autonomous obligation'. In 'fault' countries such as Germany, the scheme of absolute rights applies to this domain as well. The BGB (§ 833) only protects against *personal injury* and *property damage* 'caused' by animals. Therefore, pure economic loss cannot be recovered. A similar scheme of protected subjective rights will exclude liability in Portugal, although the code provision itself is unrestrictively formulated and calls for strict liability. The Austrian code provision, notwithstanding its wide formulation, will not extend to this case because causing pure economic loss is not among the typical dangers associated with the keeping of animals.

---

[290] Cf. C. von Bar, *The Common European Law of Torts*, vol. I (Oxford University Press, Oxford, 1998), p. 230.

## Case 7: the careless architect

### Case

An owner hires a contractor to build a house. The owner also hires an architect to supervise the construction. Because of poor supervision by the architect, the contractor has to do the same work twice. Can the contractor sue the architect for his loss if the owner does not have to pay for the additional work?

### France

I. A court would probably hold that the contractor is able to recover his pure economic loss from the architect.

II. The courts have held that the contractor has a tort action against the architect under article 1382 CC for damages sustained because of the architect's poor supervision.[291] This was the case, for example, when a balcony with three workers on it collapsed and caused their injury. The contractor who had been held totally liable sued the architect to contribute half of the liability. The court held that the architect was liable for his failure to correctly supervise the works.[292] The Cour de Cassation would expressly refuse to recognize a contract action between the contractor and the architect under the theory of *groupe de contrats*. It obviously believes that the architect and contractor's rights are protected well enough by the law of torts.[293] However, the case of the balcony addresses personal and property loss. There is no case of this kind precisely dealing with pure economic loss, but we do not think this should make any difference to a judge provided that the prejudice is considered direct and certain. Both property and pure economic loss are in the same category of *dommage matériel*, and the economic prejudice in Case 7 seems to be a direct result of the architect's carelessness (a clearly foreseeable result from the architect's perspective); so one is left with no doubt as to the existence or the quantification of the prejudice.

III. France's insistence on the strict bifurcation of contract and delict regimes has given rise to the criticism that perhaps in areas involving professional liability there ought to be a third regime. It has been noted that the application of these two regimes depends upon pure chance

---

[291] Civ. 1, 7 nov. 1962, D.1963, S, 61; Civ. 3, 1 mars 1983, Gaz. Pal. 1984. I. 119.
[292] Civ. 1, 7 novembre 1962.
[293] Civ. 3, 1 mars 1983, Bull., III, no. 57; Civ. 1, 16 février 1994, Bull., I, no. 72.

(i.e. who causes the loss and whether that person is a co-contractor or a third person), whereas the regimes differ entirely in terms of length of prescriptive periods, clauses limiting responsibility, and the nature of the act producing liability (*fait générateur de la responsabilité*).[294]

**Belgium**

I. The contractor has a claim against the architect, the outcome of which depends on circumstances to be evaluated by the judge.

II. The relationship between owner and architect is based on a contract which includes the obligation for the architect to supervise the work done by the contractor.

According to the Belgian law of 20 February 1939 on the protection of the profession of the architects, control over the work is an exclusive mission of the architect. This obligation stems from the law.

Therefore, a third party, such as the contractor in the present case, could normally sue the architect and claim the damage resulting from poor supervision.

However, the issue raised by the present case is whether the damage claimed by the contractor results from the architect's poor supervision or whether it results from the fault of the contractor himself.

According to the contract executed between himself and the owner, the contractor has the contractual obligation to build the house in accordance with the owner's directives and with those of its agent, namely the architect.

If the contractor did the same work twice because the first time he did not do it correctly, and because the architect did not see immediately that the work had not been correctly done, the judge will rule certainly that the damage suffered by the contractor resulted exclusively from the contractor's fault. Even if the architect had supervised correctly, the work would have had to be done a second time anyway. In such a case, the damage will not be recoverable by the contractor.

On the other hand, if the contractor has done the same work twice because the first work was done because of poor supervision or wrong directives by the architect, the judge will rule probably that the damage suffered by the contractor resulted from the architect's fault. In such a case, the contractor's damage will be recoverable. However, if the

[294] G. Viney, *Introduction à la responsabilité*, *Traité de droit civil* (1995), nos. 243–4.

contractor was concurrently at fault, the judge might limit the recovery and apportion the damage between the parties.[295]

## Italy

I. As a matter of principle there should be tort liability of professionals toward third parties. The constructor might use article 2043 cc, the general clause of the code, in order to recover his damages from the architect.

II. There are no cases about professional supervision of a constructor's work, but in general Italian law recognizes the special status of intellectual professions[296] and provides a special regime for professional liability. This is grounded on the qualification of the professionals' obligations as obligations of means,[297] and therefore the performance of these obligations is evaluated in the light of the general clause on the standard of care,[298] article 1176 cc:

*Article 1176: Diligence in performance*

In performing the obligation the debtor shall observe the diligence of a good *pater familias*.
In the performance of an obligation inherent in the exercise of professional activity, diligence shall be evaluated with respect to the nature of that activity.

Recently, however, judges have been treating professional liability more strictly, deeming professionals bound by an obligation of result when the kind of activity they are offering might be considered a routine job.[299]

---

[295] Cass., 29 juin 1995, Dr. Circ., 1996, p. 12; Cass., 6 janvier 1993, Pas., 1993, I, 11.
[296] Civil Code – Libro V *'Del lavoro'*, *Titolo II 'Del lavoro autonomo'*, Chapter II.
[297] Cass., 28.4.1961, no. 961, *MGC*, 1961; Cass., 18.6.1975, no. 2439, *MGC*, 1975; Cass., 18.4.1978, no. 1845, *MGC*, 1978; Cass., 21.12.1978, no. 6141, *MGC*, 1978; Cass. 21.6.1983, no. 4245, *MGC*, 1983.
[298] Cass., 6.4.1983 no. 2404, *MGC*, 1983; Cass., 15.4.1982, no. 2274, *MGC*, 1982; Cass., 13.7.1998, no. 6812, *MGC* 1998.
[299] When events occur within the normal course of the exercise of profession, more and more often have the courts made recourse to the *res ipsa loquitur* rule: the victim has to give evidence of the existence of a causal link between the professional's act and the specific damage; the professional will escape liability only if he is able to show that he acted with due care: Cass. 22.2. 1988, no. 1847, in *Arch. civ.*, 1988, 684; see also Cass., 27.2.1996, no. 1530, *MGC* 1996; Cass., 21.3.1997, no. 2540, *MGC*, 1997; Cass., 28.1.1995, no. 1040, *MGC* 1995; Cass., 7.5.1988, no. 3389, *MGC*, 1988; Cass., 13.11.1973, no. 2998, *MGC* 1973. On this subject the bibliography is endless; see e.g. G. Cattaneo,

Moreover, when the obligation to be performed is characterized by 'a special difficulty', according to article 2236 cc[300] the harm caused by the professional can be compensated only if the plaintiff can prove gross negligence in the conduct of the professionals. This solution is supported by legal scholarship, where the predominant view is in favour of an enlargement of professional duties of care, information and, eventually, of professional liability itself.[301]

Spain

I. If the owner were to obtain a judgment against the architect and the contractor, the latter could direct an action against the architect since the defects are exclusively attributable to the architect's fault. This result is clear and undisputed.

If the dispute arose when the works were in progress, however, most likely the contractor could not obtain compensation. This outcome is quite debatable though.

II. It should be noted that, once the house is completed and handed over, if the owner of the works were to obtain a judgment for joint responsibility against the architect and contractor for defects in construction, it would be possible for the contractor later to direct a claim for reimbursement against the architect, given that in this case the defects in construction would only be attributable to poor supervision of the works.[302] If the plaintiff could prove that the defects were exclusively due

---

La responsabilità del professionista (Giuffrè, Milano, 1958); and more recently for a critical analysis of case law and doctrine trends, G. Visintini, I fatti illeciti. II. L'imputabilità e la colpa in rapporto agli altri criteri di imputazione della responsabilità (2nd edn, Cedam, Padua, 1998), pp. 183 ff.; G. Alpa, M. Bessone and V. Zeno-Zencovich, 'I fatti illeciti', in Trattato di diritto privato diretto da Rescigno (2nd edn, UTET, Turin, 1995), pp. 84 ff.

[300] Art. 2236 ('if the professional services involve the solution of technical problems of particular difficulty, the person who renders such services is not liable for damages, except in case of fraud, malice, or gross negligence') had proven to be troublesome for case law. However, courts have ended up establishing that the provision concerns only the services involving special professional skill: see Corte cost. 28 Novembre 1973, no. 166, in FI, 974, I, 19, and subsequently Cass. 21 Dicembre 1978, no. 6141, in GI, 1979, I, 1, 953 (as to the broader issue regarding the role of subjective superior skills and features as factors affecting tort liability, see, under the comparative law perspective, M. Bussani, La colpa soggettiva. Modelli di valutazione della condotta nella responsabilità extracontrattuale (Cedam, Padua, 1991), at pp. 17, 43, 75, 215 ff.).

[301] P. G. Monateri, La responsabilità civile (1998), at pp. 541 ff., F. Cafaggi, 'La responsabilità dei professionisti', entry Dig. It. IV Discipline Privatistiche, (Utet, Turin, 1998).

[302] J. M. Fernández Hierro, La responsabilidad por vicios de construcción (Universidad de Densto, Bilbao, 1976), p. 133, C. Gómez de la Escalera, La responsabilidad civil de los

to technical mismanagement attributable to the architect, most likely only the architect would be liable.[303] In any case, it would have to involve mistakes in technical management which the contractor could not recognize as such, since otherwise he would incur liability for not having warned his client.[304]

This case presents the facts in a somewhat different light because it appears that the dispute arose during construction of the house. No solution may be found in Spanish case law for similar situations and its legal doctrine does not appear to have gone any further. Still, it is a common assumption that the Civil Code norms regulating building construction are incomplete and out of date.[305] Under these circumstances, the most likely solution in the Spanish legal system for the above dispute could be the following:

(1) if technical mismanagement by the architect was evident to the contractor, his obligation is not to construct inadequately; if the architect refuses to correct his instructions, the contractor may continue with the job, expressly exempting himself from liability towards the owner of the works;[306]

(2) if the architect's instructions appear correct, but later the construction defect is discovered and the instructions are found to be incorrect, the contractor's obligation is to refuse to redo the job and to notify the owner of the works (who could retain part of the fees owed to the architect).[307] In the present case, if the contractor redoes the job without notifying the owner of the works, he could not later direct a claim against the architect using an action for tortious liability. In this case the contractor should not complain: the damage suffered (doing the same job over again without being able to receive double payment) by the contractor is due to his own conduct.

It is possible for a Spanish legal scholar to reach another solution: the contractor could in fact direct a claim against the architect in this case,

---

*promotores, constructores y técnicos por los defectos de la construcción* (Bosch, Barcelona, 1990), p. 123, Supreme Court decisions, First Chamber, 14.7.88 and 8.5.91, amongst many others.

[303] Supreme Court decisions, First Chamber, 7.6.86, 12.6.87, 20.6.89.
[304] Supreme Court decision, 19.4.79, First Chamber.
[305] For all, see Roca Trias, 'Naturaleza de la relación entre el arquitecto y los clientes. Responsabilidad extracontractual de los arquitectos', (1975) *Revista de Derecho Privado* 783–97.
[306] L. López Mora and F. De La Cámara Mingo, *Tratado práctico del derecho referente a la construcción y a la arquitectura* (1964), p. 594.
[307] M. A. Del Arco and M. Pons, *Derecho de la construcción* (Hespenia, Jaéns, 1980), pp. 53 and 90.

given that this standpoint has been defended in other neighbouring countries with a similar legal system.[308]

## Greece

I. No direct claim can be raised by the contractor against the architect. However, the contractor can sue the architect indirectly, and make him pay the owner.

II. In this case a 'trilateral legal relation' occurs. More accurately, there are two contracts: one between the architect and the owner, and one between the owner and the contractor. As the principle of privity of contract (art. 361 CC) stipulates, the contractor owes performance only to the owner by virtue of their contract, and the architect owes supervision of the work only to the owner (not to the contractor) by virtue of their own contract. In this framework there are two possible scenarios:

Possible (direct) claims of the contractor against the architect: the contractor has no contractual claim against the architect (as he was contractually related only to the owner), nor was the architect's behaviour unlawful. Certainly the architect was negligent, but this has to do only with his contract with the owner. Nevertheless, according to the jurisprudence,[309] when two persons owe the same performance to someone, they are debtors in a joint and several debt, regardless of whether each one's obligation has the same legal *causa* or not. In view of this, the contractor might sue the architect directly, by virtue of the right of recourse between co-debtors in a joint and several obligation, since they both owe him compensation for the same thing (i.e. the value of the work), although each one's obligation has a different legal *causa* (i.e. a different contract).

Indirect claims of the contractor against the architect through the owner: according to art. 72 CCPr., the contractor might sue the architect in order to make him pay the money to the owner (if they have not already done so) and make satisfiable their own (the contractor's) claim against the architect ('indirect action').

III. The theory of 'quasi joint and several debt' is not fully persuasive. Indeed, since the obligations forming a joint and several debt do not derive from the same legal *causa*, e.g. the same contract or tort, so the

---

[308] E.g. G. Bricmont, *La responsabilité des architecte et entrepreneur* (3rd edn, Larcies, Bruxelles, 1991), p. 198.

[309] See, for example, AP 81/1991, NoB 40, p. 715.

legal regulation of joint and several debt is not directly implementable here, at least not in its entirety. So, as is always the case in the framework of analogy, it is unclear which of the specific provisions regulating joint and several debt can be also applicable here. For example, when the creditor is in default towards the one quasi co-debtor, is he in default towards the other too, as article 485 CC stipulates?

**England**

I. It is probable that the contractor can sue the architect in negligence under the principle of *Hedley Byrne* v. *Heller*,[310] for negligent advice.

II. *Hedley Byrne* is a case which still serves as authority for allowing claims for economic harm due to negligent advice or information, provided such claims are capable of subjection to its rule.[311] The rule states that a person reasonably relying on the advice or information of another, who possesses (or claims to possess) the necessary skills, can recover economic loss caused by such advice or information being negligently wrong or inaccurate. The House of Lords has recently confirmed and somewhat extended *Hedley Byrne* in *White* v. *Jones*.[312] The special conditions of liability in English law, for economic loss caused by negligent advice or information, now appear to be as follows.

(1) The duty of care is founded on the existence of 'close proximity' between plaintiff and defendant, a concept that seems to mean that the defendant knew, or ought to have known, that the plaintiff, as an individual identified to him and not merely as a member of a class of persons, would rely on his advice or information. Some cases demand that the defendant *intended* the plaintiff to rely on his advice or information;[313] there is in this writer's opinion no doubt that this close proximity exists in cases such as the present, where the defendant is employed, albeit by a third party, solely to advise the plaintiff, without having a contractual relationship with him.[314]

(2) 'Reasonable reliance' of the plaintiff on the defendant's advice. This is, again, evident in cases such as the present, where the defendant is a professional applying his skills to supervise the plaintiff: see *White* v. *Jones*.[315]

[310] [1964] AC 465.
[311] See T. Weir, *A Casebook on Tort* (9th edn, Sweet and Maxwell, London, 2000), p. 67.
[312] [1995] 2 AC 207 (HL).
[313] See *Galoo Ltd* v. *Bright Grahame Murray* [1995] 1 All ER 16 (CA).
[314] See, for a survey of the professions, Weir, *Casebook*, pp. 84 ff.
[315] [1995] 2 AC 207 (HL).

III. Liability for negligent advice or information has developed in the English law of negligence rather differently from that for acts or omissions. The main reason is that in a great number of cases of wrongful advice or information the parties are so close, working in a business relationship, and but for the absence of either consideration or privity, there would have been a claim in contract. In such cases of close relationship and reliance, the courts do not wish the risk of professional fault to be carried by the innocent party. But the limits of this liability are narrowly defined and closely policed by the courts, who have repeatedly denied recovery of losses suffered by more than one individual, not in personal contact with the defendant.[316]

## Scotland

I. It is thought that the contractor could succeed in an action against the architect for the economic loss that he suffered owing to the architect's negligent performance of his contract with the owner. He may alternately have a remedy under the *ius quaesitum tertio*.

II. The question is whether the courts would impose a duty of care upon the architect in these circumstances. Up to now we have had examples of pure economic loss where the courts have held that no duty of care exists. Although Lord Atkin in *Donoghue* v. *Stevenson* stated that '[y]ou must take reasonable care to avoid acts or omissions which you can reasonably foresee would be likely to injure your neighbour',[317] in the case of pure economic loss the courts have required additional factors before a duty of care is imposed. There must be a sufficient degree of proximity between the parties for a duty of care to be present. This has been found to be possible in a number of situations and the current case is likely to be another of them.

In *Hedley Byrne & Co.* v. *Heller & Partners*,[318] which concerned a negligent misrepresentation, the loss was purely economic but a duty of care was held to exist. Lord Morris of Borth-Y-Gest stated that

> it should now be regarded as settled that if someone possessed of a special skill undertakes, quite irrespective of contract, to apply that skill for the assistance of another person who relies on such skill, a duty of care will arise. The fact that the service is to be given by means of, or by the instrumentality of, words can make no difference.[319]

---

[316] More in E. K. Banakas, *Civil Liability for Pure Economic Loss* (Kluwer, The Hague, 1996), chs. 1 and 2.
[317] 1932 SC (HL) 31 at p. 44.   [318] [1964] AC 465.   [319] Ibid. at pp. 502–503.

Lord Pearce stated that

if persons holding themselves out in a calling or situation or profession take on a task within that calling or situation or profession they have a duty of skill and care. In terms of proximity one might say that they are in particularly close proximity to those who, as they know, are relying on their skill and care, although the proximity is not contractual.[320]

In *Henderson and Others* v. *Merrett Syndicates Ltd and Others*,[321] Lord Goff referred to 'the principle established in *Hedley Byrne* itself, from which it follows that an assumption of responsibility coupled with the concomitant reliance may give rise to a tortious duty of care irrespective of whether there is a contractual relationship between the parties'.[322]

In *Caparo Industries plc* v. *Dickman and Others*[323] Lord Bridge of Harwich set out three criteria for a duty of care. He stated:

[I]n addition to the foreseeability of damage, necessary ingredients in any situation giving rise to a duty of care are that there should exist between the party owing the duty and the party to whom it is owed a relationship characterised by the law as one of 'proximity' or 'neighbourhood' and that the situation should be one in which the court considers it fair, just and reasonable that the court should impose a duty of a given scope on the one party for the benefit of the other. But it is implicit in the passages referred to that the concepts of proximity and fairness embodied in these additional ingredients are not susceptible of any such precise definition as would be necessary to give them utility as practical tests, but amount in effect to little more than convenient labels to attach to the features of different specific situations which, on a detailed examination of all the circumstances, the law recognises pragmatically of giving rise to a duty of care of a given scope.[324]

The House of Lords in *Caparo* adopted the dictum of Brennan J in the High Court of Australia. He said:

It is preferable in my view, that the law should develop novel categories of negligence incrementally and by analogy with existing categories, rather than by a massive extension of a prima facie duty of care restrained only by indefinable 'considerations which ought to negative, or to reduce or limit the scope of the duty or class of person to whom it is owed'.[325]

This incremental approach by analogy was applied subsequently by Lord Browne-Wilkinson and Lord Nolan in *White and Another* v. *Jones and*

---

[320] Ibid. at p. 538.  [321] [1995] 2 AC 145.  [322] Ibid. at p. 194.
[323] [1990] 2 AC 605.  [324] Ibid. at pp. 617–618.
[325] *Sutherland Shire Council* v. *Heyman* (1985) 60 ALR 1 at pp. 43–4.

*Others*[326] and Lord Steyn in *Marc Rich*.[327] Although *Hedley Byrne* was an English case, its principle has been accepted as a part of Scots law.[328] Looking to the facts of this case it is arguable that both an assumption of responsibility, in the architect contracting to supervise, and concomitant reliance by the builder upon that supervision, are present. There is proximity in the relationship, though it is not contractual, in that the contractor is relying directly and specifically upon the skill and care of the architect. It is as a direct consequence of a failure of supervision that the contractor is caused economic loss and this was reasonably foreseeable.

As to whether it is fair, just and reasonable to impose a duty of care, one is left to look to the analogous situations where a duty of care has been held to exist. As with the bankers, underwriting agents, solicitors, accountants, surveyors and valuers who have been found to owe a duty of care, the architects belong to the same professional or quasi-professional class of person and cannot plead that they are being made liable to an indeterminate class. They are being paid to oversee the contractor and in that they have been negligent resulting in an economic loss to the contractor. It is likely that the courts would not permit the architect to escape the consequences of his negligence and would allow the contractor a delictual remedy.

We have applied the *Caparo* criteria here but equally one might have applied the *Henderson* v. *Merrett* criteria which is discussed in detail under Case 11 ('A Maestro's Mistake') below. If it meets the latter criteria, then duty arises without having to meet the former; in which case, according to Lord Goff of Chieveley in *Henderson* v. *Merrett*, it would be strictly unnecessary to consider whether it was fair, just and reasonable to impose a duty of care.[329]

In the absence of a contractual relationship with the architect, a delictual action is not the only remedy open to the contractor. Scots law recognizes the *ius quaesitum tertio* giving title to sue to third parties. In contrast to English law, Scots law 'does not regard "consideration" as the badge of a valid informal contract, and thus has not been restricted to the same extent by the doctrine of "privity of contract" which prevented

---

[326] [1995] 2 AC 207.
[327] *Marc Rich & Co. AG and Others* v. *Bishop Rock Marine Co. Ltd and Others, the Nicholas H* [1996] 1 AC 211, [1995] 3 All ER 307, [1995] 2 WLR 227, [1995] 2 Lloyd's Rep 299.
[328] *John Kenway* v. *Orcantic Ltd* 1979 SC 422, 1980 SLT 46, OH; *Eastern Marine Services (and Supplies) Ltd* v. *Dickson Motors Ltd* 1981 SC 355, OH.
[329] [1995] 2 AC 145 at p. 181.

the English common law from recognizing the *ius quaesitum tertio*'.[330] Therefore 'the rule that the contracting parties alone have the right to enforce their contract suffers exception in cases where it is shown that the object or intention was to advance the interests of a third party'.[331] The court looks to the intention of both the contracting parties. There are a number of things to be established by the builder if he is to be successful.

One may argue that the owner has hired the architect for their own benefit, to ensure the house is soundly and cost-effectively constructed. At the same time it is to provide guidance for the builder and hence is to his benefit that he might better properly and cost-effectively fulfil his contractual obligations to the owner. Gloag wrote that 'if two parties enter into a contract to secure their own purposes, the mere fact that a third party is interested in the fulfilment of the obligations undertaken by one of them will not give any title to sue. A *ius quaesitum tertio* is the exception, not the rule'.[332] The fact that the owner is entering the contract to secure their own purposes does not necessarily prevent the builder from establishing a *ius quaesitum tertio*. In *Mercedes-Benz Finance Ltd* v. *Clydesdale Bank plc*, Lord Penrose made the following observations:

Superficially the passage in Gloag and Henderson, para 11.6 provides some support for the defenders: 'Without any express provision a *jus quaesitum tertio* may be inferred in cases where the one party who has any substantial interest in the fulfilment of the contract is a *tertius*.' I have no doubt that is correct as far as it goes. It reflects the view of Professor Gloag. But for the defenders to succeed at this stage they require to establish more. They require to establish that the only case in which a *jus quaesitum tertio* may be inferred is where the *tertius* and he alone has any substantial interest in the fulfilment of the obligation. In my opinion that would be going beyond any of the authorities to which I was referred.[333]

One further problem which may confront the builder is that 'there are several *obiter dicta* which indicate that although a third party may sue for non-performance of the contract he cannot sue for damages for defective performance thereof'.[334] However, in the Outer House case of

---

[330] T. B. Smith, '*Jus Quaesitum Tertio*: Remedies of the *Tertius* in Scottish Law', in T. B. Smith (ed.) *Studies Critical and Comparative* (Green, Edinburgh, 1962), p. 183.
[331] Gloag and Henderson, *The Law of Scotland* (10th edn, Green, Edinburgh, 1995), p. 140.
[332] W. M. Gloag, *The Law of Contract – A Treatise on the Principles of Contract in the Law of Scotland* (2nd edn, Green, Edinburgh, 1929, reprinted 1985), p. 237.
[333] 1997 SLT 905 at p. 913F.    [334] Gloag and Henderson, *Law of Scotland* (1995), at p. 142.

*Scott Lithgow Ltd* v. *GEC Electrical Projects Ltd*, Lord Clyde expressed the following opinion:

> In general I can see no reason why a third party should not be entitled to sue for damages for negligent performance of a contract under the principle of *jus quaesitum tertio*, but whether he is so entitled must be a matter of the intention of the contracting parties. That has to be ascertained from the terms of the contract. I see nothing to prevent the parties expressly agreeing such a provision and if they did so, no reason why it should not be effective. If done expressly, then it could be clearly agreed how far any limits or exclusions which might operate in relation to a claim by the contracting party should extend to a third party. I see no reason why it should not be possible to infer such a provision from the terms of a contract although I would accept that it may well be difficult to do so.[335]

There are other aspects of the *ius quaesitum tertio* upon which the builder may stumble, but one would need more information to comment meaningfully upon these.

III. As we have seen, when an act has been negligent there is generally no duty of care to avoid causing pure economic loss. However, there are a number of exceptions to what was accepted as a general rule at the time of *Dynamco*, and these date from the first inroad into the rule in *Hedley Byrne* which was decided several years earlier. Norrie has written that *Hedley Byrne*

> can either be regarded as having reversed the general rule of no liability for pure economic loss, or as simply having created an exception thereto...Later developments have made it plain that an incremental approach to the development of the law is appropriate rather than a wholesale expansion of liability, and the current position seems to be that there remains a general duty excluding liability for pure economic loss but that the exceptions thereto can be added to from time to time when the facts presented to the court make it fair, just and reasonable to do so.[336]

Thomson believes that

> where the courts are being asked to extend delictual liability into hitherto uncharted waters, the courts, under the guise of determining whether or not there is a sufficient degree of proximity for the imposition of a duty of care, are undoubtedly influenced by policy considerations. In doing so the courts are

---

[335] 1992 SLT 244 at p. 260K.
[336] *Stair Memorial Encyclopaedia, The Laws of Scotland*, vol. 15 (1996), p. 170, para. 274 (written by K. McK. Norrie) (footnote omitted – the 'later developments' he refers to are covered in detail at p. 160, para. 264).

governed by their concept of a fair distribution of risk in contemporary society – allowing the loss to be compensated in some areas, letting the risk lie where it has fallen in others.[337]

## The Netherlands

I. The contractor possibly has a claim for contribution; a claim in tort is not likely to succeed.

II. If we assume that the contractor has to bear the cost of rebuilding,[338] he can try to claim from the architect. Such a claim can be founded in tort or in the rules on the contribution of concurrently liable persons, which state that whenever two persons are obliged to repair the same damage, they are *hoofdelijk* (jointly and severally) liable. Whenever one of them has paid, he has a right of recourse against the other; the extent of this right is decided by their respective share in the causation of the damage (art. 6:102 CC). Although no hard-and-fast rules are available, it seems safe to say that the contractor had the greater share in causing the damage. Therefore, it seems unlikely the architect will have to bear much – if any – of the costs of reconstruction.

The first possibility, the possibility of a claim in tort, might also prove to be unsuccessful. The traditional view is that the architect owes his duty to supervise to the owner and not to the contractor.[339] In the event of poor supervision, the architect is liable in contract and not in tort, or so it seems. This implies that the contractor cannot claim on the basis that the architect has neglected a duty owed to him. However, it cannot be ruled out that such a duty does indeed exist. In their respective dealings with the owner, both contractor and architect have entered into a special relationship. Though there is no contractual relationship between them, their obligations *vis-à-vis* the owner purport to establish the same result, i.e. the delivery of a building that is fit for its purpose. In their dealings with each other, they will have to co-operate in order to fulfil their respective obligations.

---

[337] J. M. Thomson, *Delictual Liability* (Butterworths, Edinburgh, 1999), pp. 59–60 (footnote omitted).

[338] According to Dutch construction law, the architect's poor supervision would most probably be imputed to the owner as contributory negligence. The contractor would not be forced to bear the cost of reconstruction, or at least not entirely. See generally M. A. M. C. van den Berg, *Ondanks nauwlettend toezicht* (Tilburg inaugural lecture, 1993).

[339] See, e.g., M. A. M. C. van den Berg, *Samenwerkingsvormen in de bouw* (PhD thesis, University of Tilburg, 1990) (Deventer 1990), p. 71.

This relationship, aimed at achieving one and the same result,[340] might indeed lead to the existence of a special duty for the architect not to disregard the (financial) interests of the contractor.[341] The duty not to disregard another's (financial) interests – as it has been developed in case law – is considered to be an application of 'the standard of conduct acceptable in society', as laid down in article 6:162 ss. 2 CC. Although this duty is considered to be one of the cornerstones of Dutch tort law, its exact content and tenor remain unclear.

III. It must be noted that the architect will, in my opinion, undoubtedly be liable *vis-à-vis* the contractor if he acted with intent to inflict the loss on the contractor. Indeed, it seems safe to say that article 6:162 CC as a rule does not allow unnecessary intentional infliction of loss.

### Germany

I. The contractor has a claim against the architect. This claim is of a somewhat curious nature because it has nothing do with tort law. Instead, it is a claim for contribution (here amounting to full indemnification) between partners jointly liable in contract.

II. Tort claims: tort law avails the contractor nothing because the architect's conduct neither violated any of the rights enumerated in § 823 (1) nor triggered any of the special tort provisions in the code.

Contract claims: contract law does not seem to help the contractor either for lack of a contractual relationship between him and the architect.

Contribution and indemnification: However, the *Bundesgerichtshof* has allowed an action for contribution under § 426 (1) BGB which provides that 'as among themselves, joint debtors are liable in equal shares unless it is otherwise provided...'. Thus, this article allows the debtor held liable by the claimant to recover from his co-debtor. Such recovery can be full (i.e. amount to full indemnification) if the co-debtor is solely at fault for the loss, as seems to be the case here.

---

[340] The Germans would consider this to be a *Zweckgemeinschaft*, leading to *Gesamtschuld* (joint liability) of contractor and architect; see O. Palandt *Bürgerliches Gesetzbuch*, § 421, no. 4.

[341] This duty was first mentioned in a Supreme Court decision on the liability of a Bank vis-à-vis the creditors of the bank's client; it was held possible to sue a bank in tort for sustaining the appearance of credit-worthiness of the client. Under certain conditions, the bank can be held liable for the loss when the client turns insolvent. See HR 28.6.1957, NJ 1957, no. 514, HR 25.9.1981, NJ 1982, no. 443 and HR 19.2.1988, NJ 1988, no. 487.

While this provision is clear enough, it is not beyond cavil that the contractor and the architect are indeed 'joint debtors'. Under § 421 BGB, this requires that 'several persons owe *one* performance' (emphasis added). This is normally interpreted to mean 'the same kind of performance', which is far from obvious here because the architect owes supervision while the contractor owes building.[342] Yet, the *Bundesgerichtshof* has interpreted § 421 BGB liberally, arguing that under the German law on contracts for work (*Werkvertrag*, §§ 631–651, especially § 633–635 BGB), the contractor's and architect's duties are closely intertwined. The Court has also pointed to § 840 (1) BGB which provides for joint liability of co-tortfeasors. Certainly, the provision does not apply directly, but the Court considered its underlying principle applicable in other cases as well.[343]

There is widespread agreement that this result is correct, although the Court's precise reasoning has met with some criticism from scholars who have suggested alternative tests for establishing joint debtorship.[344]

III. The *Bundesgerichtshof's* decision is result-oriented. The Court takes the contract route in connection with general principles of joint liability in order to support a result that it considers just. Without stretching § 421 BGB (and thus without an action under § 426 BGB), the contractor would be without remedy, as would the architect if the owner were to sue him instead in a reverse scenario. But there is no good reason to let the loss lie where the owner (freely) decides to put it. Instead, it should be shifted, in part or in whole, as the parties' fault requires.

## Austria

I. The contractor may have a claim against the architect based on the concept of a contract with protective effect to a third party.

II. The architect is responsible pursuant to article 1299 ABGB. This means that the owner would be to blame for contributory negligence if he knew, or ought to have known, about the inexperience of the architect.

---

[342] Persons may also be joint debtors in contract if they 'bind themselves jointly to effect a divisible performance', § 427 BGB, but this is surely not true in the present case.

[343] BGHZ 43, 227, at 233–4 (1965); BGHZ 51, 275, at 278 (1968).

[344] See H. Brox, *Allgemeines Schuldrecht* (21st edn, 1996), Rd.-Nr. 429; Larenz *Lehrbuch*, s. 37 I; D. Medicus, *Bürgerliches Recht* (18th edn, C. Heyman, Köln, 1999) s. 35 II 1 b; K. Rebmann and F. J. Säcker (eds.), *Münchener Kommentar zum Bürgerlichen Gesetzbuch* (7 vols., 2nd edn, Beck, Munich, 1984–1990; 3rd edn, 1992– ) s. 421 BGB Rd.-Nr. 8; O. Palandt, *Bürgerliches Gesetzbuch* (Beck, Munich, 2000) s. 421 BGB, Rd.-Nr. 7.

The architect is contractually bound to carefully supervise the construction. He has to provide a standard of care that corresponds with the care of an experienced member of the profession. If the architect failed to live up to this higher standard of care, he may be held liable even for the pure financial losses of the person who hired him.

However, it is not the owner who claims compensation but the contractor. Since the contract between the owner and the architect may be classified as having protective effects to the financial interests of the contractor, the contractor may have a chance of recovering some of his financial losses stemming from unexpectedly high expenses.

It is also clear from the facts that, being an expert himself, he will have to bear a significant part of the loss because he may be considered contributorily negligent under article 1304 ABGB.

III. It is doubtful whether the courts would resort to the solution indicated by assuming that the contract between the owner and the architect provides protection for the contractor's financial interests. It is also contestable whether this approach is legally sound. However, it would comply with the trend of Austrian courts and some influential scholars who have suggested that the concept of 'contracts with protective effects to third persons' ought to be expanded.[345]

## Portugal

I. The contractor may possibly have a claim for compensation under the theory of third-party beneficiary contract, or under a contract with protective effects, or on the basis of abuse of right, or even – though more unlikely – under an obligation to give correct information.

II. If the owner had made a contract with the architect 'in favour of a third party', requiring the architect to give the builder the information and advice needed for the proper execution of the work, then the builder would have grounds for a claim. Portuguese law, in an exception to the principle of relativity of contracts,[346] allows this contractual modality with some degree of breadth (articles 443 cc ff.).

However, to be able to talk about a contract in favour of a third party, the agreement must embody an intention to grant to the third party a right to the performance. If this is not the case, the position of the builder is more problematic.

---

[345] See below, remarks to Case 12 ('The Double Sale').
[346] M. J. de Almeida Costa, *Direito das Obrigações* (7th edn, Almedina, Coimbra, 1998), p. 297.

Though there are no precedents, Portuguese doctrine supports accepting 'contracts with the effect of protecting third parties'.[347]

The case description enables us to acknowledge that we have a situation which justifies recourse to this institution. That is, it is one in which the builder could reasonably rely on the competence and diligence of the architect who, for his part, was aware that the fulfilment or non-fulfilment of the contractual duties assumed with the owner would have direct repercussions on the builder's performance. In these circumstances, it is not impossible that, if these grounds were invoked (as we have said, there is not a legal tradition for this), the court would uphold the builder's position.

Another possible hypothesis is that the architect had behaved in an extremely censurable manner, knowing and being indifferent to the damage caused to the builder, and seriously violating principles of professional ethics. In these circumstances, censure for abuse of right is justified, and this affects acts as much as omissions, when the duty to act (here, to inform or advise) is imposed so flagrantly that the omission could be said to go against *boni mores*.[348]

In Portuguese law there is a special provision concerning responsibility for advice, recommendation or information (article 485 cc). We believe that a proper interpretation of this provision does not prejudice the application of the general principles of the law of obligations. However, to impose responsibility it is essential to find a special ground (as we have attempted above), since the general rule is the non-existence of an obligation to compensate the damage resulting from following advice or information (or from its omission), even when this is negligent: 'mere advice, recommendation or information do not confer liability on whoever gives it, even though there may be negligence on their part' (article 485/1).

Under the terms of article 485/2, 'the obligations to compensate exist, however, when the responsibility for damage has been assumed, when there is a legal duty to give advice, recommendation or information and this has been done with negligence or intent to harm, or when the behaviour of the agent constitutes a punishable act'.

---

[347] As to this concept, see J. Sinde Monteiro, 'Responsabilidade por Informações Face a Terceiros', (1997) LXXIII *Boletim da Faculdade de Direito da Universidade de Coimbra*, 35. (also in (1998) 7 *Direito, Revista Jurídica da Universidade de Santiago de Compostela* 1, 203).

[348] A. P. S. Vaz Serra, 'O Abuso do Direito (em Matéria de Responsabilidade Civil)', *Boletim do Ministério da Justiça* no. 85, 243, 324–5.

An earlier wording of this precept stated that the obligation to compensate exists when there was a legal duty to give advice 'or to proceed with diligence in giving advice'. A small alteration in the wording has changed the meaning completely. But, on pain of irremediable contradictions, it has to be admitted that this legal provision does not prejudice the application of the general principles of pre-contractual, contractual and aquilian responsibility, as clearly resulted from the project.[349]

III. Looking at Austrian law, we see that it is written that §§ 1299 and 1300 of the General Civil Code 'raise more problems than they resolve', and that the response to these questions cannot be found in a solitary consideration, rather 'these paragraphs have to be examined against the background of the law on damage as a whole, of the law of contract and the theory of legal transactions'.[350]

For its part, § 675 of the BGB is frankly remissive in character. It thus seems that the 'special provisions' of the European civil codes relative to responsibility for information are substantially less 'special' than a formal consideration leads one to believe.[351]

Finally, it is clear that the admission (proposed by the doctrine) of the 'contracts with the effect of protecting third parties' aims to fill some gaps in the law of tort. Its regime should never be purely contractual or purely tort.

## Sweden and Finland

I. The contractor has no basis for a claim against the architect.

II. The contractor has absolutely no claim in tort against the architect, since this is a 'pure economic loss' in the Swedish-Finnish meaning of the term, i.e. an economic loss not arising in connection with anybody suffering bodily injury or property damage. According to the Tort Liability Acts 1972 and 1974, pure economic loss is in principle compensated when it is caused by a crime (*SkadestL* 4:2 for Sweden; *SkadestL* 5:1 for Finland), although the text and the preparatory works of the Tort

---

[349] Besides Sinde Monteiro, *Responsabilidade*, 449–54, see J. Baptista Machado, 'A Cláusula do Razoável', (1986) 119 *Revista de Legislação e Jurisprudência*, 65, and (1987) 120, 164.

[350] R. Welser, *Die Haftung für Rat, Auskunft und Gutachten* (Manzsche Verlags- und Universitätsbuchhandlung, Wien, 1983), p. 6.

[351] V. F. D. Busnelli, 'Itinerari europei nella "terra di nessuno tra contratto e fatto illecito": la responsabilità da informazioni inesatte', (1991) 2 *Contratto e impresa*, 539; de lege ferenda, see C. von Bar, 'Deliktsrecht', in *Gutachten und Vorschläge zur Überarbeitung des Schuldrechts*, Band II (Bundesanzeiger, 1981), p. 1681, § 828/1 (p. 1761).

Liability Acts 1972 and 1974 do not completely bar compensation should the courts find strong reasons for it. However, courts have been very restrictive in using their discretion, and there is no basis for suggesting that an exception would be admitted in a case such as this. The lack of a contractual relationship seems to make it impossible to bring a contract claim either.

*Editors' comparative comments*

This case strongly suggests that the line between tort and contract solutions becomes at times a blurry frontier. In this grey zone we find recourse being made to an array of contractual ideas that function as an alternative to the law of tort, and the use of these paracontractual actions notably expands the limits on the protection of pure economic loss.

As a matter of first impression, the question raised in this case would seem to fall squarely within the domain of tort law. The negligent architect has no contract with the contractor who has suffered economic loss. These two parties have separate contracts with a third (the owner), and they are close collaborators on the same construction project, but strictly there is no contractual link between them. Thus, it might appear at first glance that the recoverability of the loss sustained by the contractor would be resolved according to the individual rules and methods of the various tort regimes. This conclusion is indeed correct in terms of French and English law. The path must be in delict because, in the case of French law, the Cour de Cassation expressly refuses to recognize a contract action between the contractor and the architect under the theory of *groupe de contrats*; while in the case of English law the doctrine of consideration, which defines the notion of contract restrictively, is a fundamental barrier to recourse in contract.

In other European countries, however, the rules of tort do not tell the whole story. The closer the parties are situated with respect to each other within a network of contracts, the greater the possibility that their rights and duties will be resolved by paracontractual ideas that provide an alternative means of compensation for pure economic loss. Thus, although a tort claim might be denied in Germany, Greece and the Netherlands, a claim for *contribution between co-debtors* would succeed. The 'co-debts' which this claim adjusts are related contractual debts owed to the owner of the project under separate contracts with him. This rule of contribution – which is neither clearly contractual nor delictual in nature – redistributes an economic loss in accordance with the proportion of fault attributed to each party. It may make the architect either partially or entirely liable to the contractor for compensation. In Austria and Portugal a tort action would not succeed, but compensation could be awarded on the basis of a contract with protective effects for a third person.

# Case 8: the cancelled cruise

## Case

A collision prevented a passenger liner from sailing for a month. The Shipwreck Company, which has leased the ship, was forced to cancel two cruises in the Caribbean. Shipwreck sued those responsible for the collision, claiming compensation for its expenses uselessly incurred prior to the collision, and for its loss of earnings due to cancellation of the two cruises.

## France

I. The ship lessee should recover for its economic losses from the owner of the boat responsible for the collision pursuant to a special maritime statute allocating liability on the basis of fault, and completed by Civil Code rules dealing with the nature and extent of the damages which are recoverable.

II. Collisions between boats are governed by special rules edicted by the law of 7 July 1967.[352] Thus we do not apply the Civil Code dispositions here. Neither article 1382 CC nor the custodial liability under article 1384 al. 1, directly applies.[353]

The statute of 7 July 1967 governs collisions between two sea vessels (*navires de mer*), or between a sea vessel and an inland vessel (*navires de mer et bateaux de navigation intérieure*), and allocates losses upon the basis of the fault principle. Article 3 of the law stipulates that: 'If the collision is caused by the fault of one of the boats, the damage must be repaired by whoever committed the fault' ('*Si l'abordage est causé par la faute de l'un des navires, la réparation des dommages incombe à celui qui l'a commise*'). This article states the same principle which previously existed in the 1910 Convention de Bruxelles (art. 3). The same principle also appeared in the Commercial Code of 1807 (art. 407, al. 2), and in the Ordinance of 1681 (L.III, T.VII, art. 11).

Given our facts, one may assume that there has been a collision entirely due to the fault of the other vessel.[354] Thus, the Shipwreck Company has to sue the owner of the other vessel and show that those

---

[352] Cf. Commercial code 1995–6, *Dalloz*, p. 538.
[353] Civ. Cass. 12 Juin 1945, DMF 1949, 53; Civ. 19 décembre 1966, DMF 1967, 208.
[354] If we were to suppose contrariwise and to assume that the collision occurred fortuitously and without fault on any side, there would be no recovery by the ship lessee. Under art. 2 of the statute, such losses would remain where they lie.

in control acted wrongfully, and that Shipwreck's losses are the direct result of this wrongful act. Indeed, in a collision case, the person responsible is not the crew, but the owner of the boat as stated in article 3 of the law of 1967. The defendant owner will be vicariously liable for the crew's mistakes under the fault principle. The Shipwreck Company must establish causation, and its losses must be certain and direct.

The law of 7 July 1967, however, does not provide any rules regarding the damages that can be awarded, and thus the *droit commun*, i.e. the general rules on French civil responsibility, will apply. The damages that the Shipwreck Company is able to recover consist of *damnum emergens* and *lucrum cessans* (*perte subie et gain manqué*) as described in article 1149 CC. Its claim for 'expenses uselessly incurred prior to the collision' fall under the category of *damnum emergens*, while the demand for 'loss of earnings due to cancellation' of future cruises fall under *lucrum cessans*. Therefore the facts give rise to a claim for pure economic loss on the part of the lessee of a damaged boat who has suffered neither property damage nor personal injury. The lessee's loss seems to result directly from the tortfeasor's act because the latter must easily foresee, given the pervasive system of vessel leasing around the world, that his careless action may invade a lessee's interests. The French courts have recognized the lessor's claim to lost rents in similar circumstances. The Caen Court of Appeal decided that where a ship was damaged in a collision, the company leasing out the ship could recover the rents that it could have collected had the ship not been damaged.[355] The injury is arguably no less direct to the lessee who has been denied the exploitation of the vessel as a cruise ship. Of course, it may be objected that the lessee's proof of lost profits from cancelled cruises is somewhat indefinite. If the court doubts the certainty of the lost profits, it may have recourse to calculating the *perte d'une chance*.

## Belgium

I. The Shipwreck Company can recover the loss of earnings due to the cancellation of the two cruises, but not the expenses uselessly incurred prior to the collision.

II. In the present case, there is a lease agreement between the Shipwreck Company and the owner of the passenger liner. Because of the collision, the owner was unable to give to the Shipwreck Company

---

[355] Caen, 31 mars 1909, Autran XXII, 82.

the use of the liner. However, there is no contractual liability of the owner of the liner since the collision can be considered as an act of God (*force majeure*).

Since there is no contract between those responsible for the collision and the owner of the liner on the one hand, and no contract between them and the Shipwreck Company on the other hand, the Shipwreck Company can sue them and claim the damages arising from the collision.

The claim will be based on article 1382 CC:

Any act whatever of man which causes damage to another obliges him by whose fault it occurred to make reparation.

A basic rule about the recovery of damage in Belgian tort law is that damage shall be fully indemnified,[356] but also that reparation shall not exceed the amount of the damage.

In order to calculate the damage, one must compare the situation created by the fault with the situation which would have existed if the circumstances rendering the tortfeasor liable had not occurred.[357]

Moreover, it is difficult to prove the existence of a causal link between the fault and these prior expenses, because such costs were incurred before the fault was committed.

Therefore, the costs that would have been suffered anyway are not recoverable.

If the Shipwreck Company can prove that the earnings were certain (not hypothetical) and that they would have been earned if the collision had not occurred, the loss of these earnings will be recoverable.

Of course, the Shipwreck Company is not allowed to recover for the damage caused to the liner – such damage can only be claimed by the owner. The Shipwreck Company is only allowed to recover the damage, which is a result of the loss of his use of the ship.

It may be added that plaintiff must take reasonable steps to reduce or mitigate his loss of earnings; for example, if his losses could have been reduced by easily replacing the damaged liner and if a reasonable company in Shipwreck's situation would have replaced the liner.[358]

---

[356] Cass., 13 avril 1995, JT, 1995, p. 649; Dr. Circ. 1995, p. 308; Cass., 23 décembre 1992, Pas., 1992, I, 1406; RW, 1993-94, 1455; Bull. Ass., 1993, p. 255.
[357] R. O. Dalcq, *Traité de la responsabilité civile, Tome II: Le lien de causalité, le dommage et sa réparation* (Larcier, Bruxelles, 1962), at p. 338, no. 3080.
[358] R. Kruithof, 'L'obligation de la partie liée de restreindre le dommage', RCJB, 1989, p. 12.

## Italy

I. Shipwreck can recover for pure economic loss under article 2043 cc, but it must provide evidence of future earnings. Such evidence is liberally accepted and evaluated by the courts under article 1226 cc which allows for judicial 'equitable' discretion in the evaluation of future losses:[359]

*Article 1226: Equitable measure of damages*

If damages cannot be proven in their exact amount, they are equitably liquidated by the court.

II. Even if there are special rules on navigation, general principles on tort liability are held to cover the issue of this case.[360] The case resembles other cases where business losses caused by defective ships have arisen in Italian case law.[361] In the first case, a defective ship caused damages to the business of the plaintiff, a professional fisherman. In the second, a defective ship caused a loss of profit to a ship renter. The court ruled in both cases against the plaintiff, stating that the damages occurred because of an infringement of a relative right (a right of credit), and still adopting the traditional doctrine before *Meroni*. Today the answer would unquestionably be in favour of the plaintiffs, since *Meroni*'s doctrine is now broadly accepted.

## Spain

I. In this case the plaintiff could indeed claim damages for lost profits.

II. Legal scholars who have studied liability in collision cases agree that the special norms on the matter contained in the Commerce Code are a mere derivation of the general rules on non-contractual liability contained in the Civil Code.[362] Consequently, the principle of full compensation for the damage caused prevails, covering both consequential damages and lost profits.[363]

---

[359] See *Ditta Panichi v. Moscia*, Trib. Pisa, 13.8.1990, *ACirc.*, 1991, 325.
[360] See *Lo Negro v. Giuliano*, Cass., 18.7.1989, no. 3358, *MGC*, 1989.
[361] Trib. Firenze, 23.5.1980, *GI*, 1981, I, 2, 656 and Trib. Firenze, 29.4.1980, *RFL*, 1981, 374, strongly criticized by Alpa, 'Costruzione di nave e responsabilità del fabbricante', *RGCirc.*, 1981, 528.
[362] I. Arroyo, *Estudios de derecho marítimo*, I (Bosch, Barcelona, 1985), p. 351, G. J. Calero, *Derecho de las averías y de los accidentes marítimos* (Pons, Madrid, 1992), pp. 54 and 59, L. E. Echevarria Rivera, *El transporte marítimo* (Aranzadi, Pamplona, 1973), p. 105, F. Mayo Jáimez, *Abordajes y varadas* (Naval, Madrid, 1989), p. 195.
[363] Arroyo, *Estudios*, p. 359, Calero, *Derecho*, p. 77, Mayo Jáimez, *Abordajes*, p. 201.

There are a few decisions in the case law which award damages for lost profits due to a traffic accident resulting in the unproductivity of a truck or taxi.[364] In the Supreme Court case (First Chamber) of 5 October 1992 the Court awarded damages for profits lost by the owner of a ship involved in a collision with some concrete blocks negligently left unmarked by the company in charge of renovations in a port. Because of the accident, the ship could not take part in a campaign for oceanographical research and consequently suffered lost profits which the Supreme Court eventually awarded.

In this court decision the plaintiff was the shipowner and not a person who had entered into an agreement with the owner for the use of the ship. Nevertheless, in a tort system such as the Spanish one, which operates according to a general liability clause – article 1902 CC – and not according to a classified system such as the German one, the fact that the plaintiff does not own the property damaged in the accident should not present any obstacle for his compensation.

To end this commentary, it is not superfluous to remember the restrictive criteria followed by our courts dealing with lost profits and the possibility of using article 1103 CC to adjust the amount of compensation if it were deemed excessive.

### Greece

I. The company has the right to claim from the persons responsible the indemnification of its loss of earnings, but not its expenses uselessly incurred prior to the collision.

II. The person responsible for the collision is liable to compensate Shipwreck according to article 914 CC, because its loss is causally related to the tort committed. Indeed, the purpose of property law is mainly to protect the owner's interests, as well as those usually, i.e., foreseeably,[365] related to them, such as those of the persons who have received the possession of the thing from the owner (here, the lessee). The economic

---

[364] Supreme Court decisions, Second Chamber, 21.1.74, 5.10.82; J. Santos Briz is in agreement, *La responsabilidad civil: derecho sustantivo y derecho procesal* (6th edn, 2 vols, 1991).

[365] About foreseeability as causation's criterion see, e.g. AP 692/1990 NoB 40, 67; AP 1063/90; AP 979/92 ElD 35; K. Triantaphyllopoulos *Law of Obligations* (Athens, 1935), p. 184; G. Balis, *Law of Obligations, General Part* (3rd edn, 1960), p. 100; A. Ligeropoulos (gen. ed.), *Interpretation of the Civil Code (A Commentary) (ErmAK)* (1949–1978), arts. 297–300 CC, no. 39; G. Fourkiotis, *Greek Law of Obligations, General Part* (1964), p. 318; Michaèlidès-Nouaros, *Law of Obligations* (1959), p. 31, etc.

loss due to its uselessness is a typical (foreseeable) risk of the collision. So this sort of interest is protected by the legislative prohibition of the harm to property. If this is true, the company's loss of earnings is a damage causally related to the collision, so that the company has the right to claim its indemnification by the persons responsible.

On the other hand, the indemnifiable damage does not include the company's expenses uselessly incurred prior to the collision, because those would have occurred in any case, even if there had been no collision, so there is no causal relation between the collision and these, even according to the *condicio sine qua non* theory.

III. According to Greek law and jurisprudence,[366] not only are the asset owner's losses supposed to constitute indemnifiable damages, but also the losses of its lessee, although he has no real right in the asset. Thus the losses of the lessee of the ship may also be indemnifiable.

**England**

I. Shipwreck Company can recover neither for expenses incurred prior to the collision, nor for its loss of earnings due to the cancellation of the two cruises from those responsible for the collision; this would also be the case had the Shipwreck Company chartered the vessel on a charter party agreement.

II. In *The Mineral Transporter*,[367] the Privy Council put it beyond any doubt, also for English law, that the charterer who pays for the use of a ship has no claim for financial loss arising from damage to it. This case follows the rationale of *Spartan Steel* v. *Martin*,[368] which is now generally held as authority for the proposition that when property is negligently damaged, only persons with a proprietary or possessory interest in that property may bring an action for economic loss.[369] According to *The Mineral Transporter*, maritime contracts for the exclusive use of a vessel do not confer a possessory interest strong enough for the purposes of a claim in tort.

III. The position of English law is explained by a judicial policy to favour placing the cost of insurance of vessels on persons with financial interests in the use of the vessel. In the case of a charter party contract,

---

[366] EfAth 1448/1958 NoB 6, 940; EfAth 836/1961 NoB 10, 655; EfAth 373/1970 NoB 18, 836.
[367] [1985] 2 All ER 935 (PC); note by T. Weir in [1986] CLJ 13.
[368] [1973] 1 QB 27 (CA).
[369] More in E. K. Banakas, 'Negligence and Property Rights in the Common and the Civil Law', 40–41 *Revue Hellénique de Droit International* 41–99.

the charterer has stronger possession rights in law than the owner, during the period of the time-charter; it is thought preferable by the courts that the charterer, not the owner, should carry the risk of loss of the use of the vessel, and therefore insure against it.

## Scotland

I. The Shipwreck Company will not be able to sue those responsible for the collision. As they are neither the owners of, nor have a possessory title to, the passenger liner but merely enjoy a contractual right of possession, the court would find that they had no title to sue in the action.

II. The obvious starting point is *Dynamco*, the judgment which we noted in Case 1 ('Cable I – The Blackout'). Lord MacLean summarized as follows: 'The court, both in the Outer and Inner Houses, rejected the pursuers' claim on the ground that, according to the law of Scotland, no one could recover damages for financial loss which did not arise directly from damage to his own property.'[370] As to what constitutes 'his own property' in this particular context, the principal case in point is *Nacap Ltd v. Moffat Plant Ltd*,[371] discussed above under Case 2 ('Cable II – Factory Shutdown'), where the Inner House approved and elaborated upon certain dicta of Lord Brandon of Oakbrook in *Leigh and Sillavan Ltd v. Aliakmon Shipping Co. Ltd 'The Aliakmon'*.[372] He stated:

> My Lords, there is a long line of authority for a principle of law that, in order to enable a person to claim in negligence for loss caused to him by reason of loss of or damage to property, he must have had either the legal ownership of or a possessory title to the property concerned at the time when the loss or damage occurred, and it is not enough for him to have only had contractual rights in relation to such property which have been adversely affected by the loss or damage to it.[373]

In *Nacap*, the Inner House focused upon what it meant to have a possessory right or title after observing the different forms in which this had been expressed in a number of cases. The Inner House held that 'in the context in which these expressions appear, it is clear that the distinction which is being drawn is between ownership or a right of possession similar to that of an owner on the one hand and, on the other

---

[370] 1997 SLT 485 at p. 487L.   [371] 1987 SLT 221.   [372] [1986] AC 785.
[373] Ibid. at p. 809; two of the lines of authority were *Cattle v. Stockton Waterworks Co* which we considered under Case 3 ('Cable III – The Day-to-Day Workers') and *Simpson & Co. and Others v. Thomson and Others* which we considered under Case 4 ('Convalescing Employee').

hand, mere contractual rights to have the use or services of the chattel for certain limited purposes'.[374]

In the case considered here, the Shipwreck Company merely have a contractual right to the use of the ship and not possession similar to that of an owner. It is thought that a similar approach would be adopted to that of the Privy Council in *Candlewood Navigation Corp Ltd v. Mitsui OSK Lines Ltd and Another [The Mineral Transporter, The Ikbari Maru]*.[375] The judgment of the Board, delivered by Lord Fraser of Tullybelton, stated:

> There is a long line of authority in the United Kingdom for the proposition that a time charterer is not entitled to recover for pecuniary loss caused by damage by a third party to the chartered vessel. The reason for this is that a time charterer has no proprietary or possessory right in the chartered vessel; his only right in relation to the vessel is contractual...The proposition in relation to a time charterer is thus only one example of the more general principle stated by Scrutton LJ in *Elliot Steam Tug Co Ltd v. Shipping Controller* [1922] 1 KB 127 at 139–140 in these words: 'At common law there is no doubt about the position. In case of a wrong done to a chattel the common law does not recognise a person whose only rights are a contractual right to have the use of services of the chattel for purposes of making profits or gains without possession of or property in a chattel. Such a person cannot claim for injury done to his contractual right'.[376]

Their Lordships accepted the principle of Scrutton LJ as the common law limitation.

The position is slightly complicated in Scots law by the fact that 'the concept of a possessory title does not fit easily into the Scots law classification of rights as real or personal'.[377] In *North Scottish Helicopters Ltd v. United Technologies Corp Inc.*[378] Lord Davidson in the Outer House interpreted one aspect of the *Nacap* formulation, i.e. 'a right of possession similar to that of an owner', to cover the first pursuer's possession of a helicopter damaged by fire under an onerous lease and the second pursuer's physical possession of the same derived from the first pursuer in accordance with an arrangement approved by the lessors. He opined:

> I am, however, of the opinion that the *Nacap* formulation creates no difficulty for either of the pursuers in this action...one effect of the lease was to put the second pursuers in the position of being owners of the helicopter in substance if not in legal title...[it] was analogous to that of a charterer of a vessel by demise...on the day that the first pursuers possessed the helicopter by virtue

---

[374] 1987 SLT 221 at p. 223A.   [375] [1986] 1 AC 1.   [376] Ibid. at p. 15.
[377] Gloag and Henderson, *The Law of Scotland* (10th edn, Green, Edinburgh, 1995), at p. 515 (fn. 56).
[378] 1988 SLT 77.

of precarium, they too had the advantage of the terms of the lease, which did not presume to limit the first pursuer's enjoyment of possession. It appears that in *Nacap* the court was not impressed by the quality of the possession which the pursuer had of the site and what was on it. In that case the pursuer was given possession, not to enable him to enjoy the broad right of possession, but for the sole purpose of carrying out contractual obligations, including the laying of pipes. Assuming that it is necessary to take into account the quality of the possession, I consider that both pursuers in the present action are in a strong position, because they enjoyed, or were entitled to enjoy, a broad right of possession, Scamba [the owners] imposing no limitation on the purpose for which the helicopter could be used.[379]

Thus Lord Davidson considered the pursuers had far more than mere lawful possession and that this entitled them to sue.

III. The reason for the general approach by the courts is set out clearly by the Privy Council in *Candlewood*. Lord Fraser of Tullybelton, expressing the conclusion of the Board, stated:

Their Lordships consider that some limit or control mechanism has to be imposed on the liability of a wrongdoer towards those who have suffered economic damage in consequence of his negligence. The need for such a limit has been repeatedly asserted in the cases, from *Cattle's* case to *Caltex [Caltex Oil (Australia) Pty Ltd v. Dredge Willemstad* (1976) 136 CLR 529, Aust HC], and their Lordships are not aware that a view to the contrary has ever been judicially expressed. The policy of imposing such a limit is consistent with the policy of limiting the liability of ships and aircraft in maritime and aviation law by statute and by international agreement. The common law limitation which has generally been accepted is that stated by Scrutton LJ in *Elliot*...which has already been mentioned. Not only has that rule been generally accepted in many countries...but it has the merit of drawing a definite and readily ascertainable line. It should enable legal practitioners to advise their clients as to their rights with reasonable certainty, and their Lordships are not aware of any widespread dissatisfaction with that rule.[380]

In Scots law, in the light of the decision in *North Scottish Helicopters*, it is not quite so clear what will be considered mere contractual rights and what will amount to possessory rights. Nevertheless, it is submitted that an action here will not lie in delict. The charterer's remedy lies in contract against the owner. Alternatively, in Scots law, the owner can agree to assign its right to sue in delict to the Shipwreck Company.

---

[379] Ibid. at p. 81.   [380] [1986] 1 AC 1 at p. 25.

## The Netherlands

I. The Shipwreck Company can claim in tort.

II. The key to the answer lies in a 1977 Dutch Supreme Court landmark decision.[381] The facts of the 1977 case were as follows. Contrary to normal procedure, a dragline operator started excavations without properly consulting detailed maps of the area. As a result, he had no knowledge of the exact location of cables and pipes. During excavations, the operator damaged a gas main owned by a public utility. Consequently, a neighbouring brick factory had to halt production for lack of gas. The factory owner successfully claimed in tort, and the compensation amounted to five hours of loss of production.[382]

The Dutch Supreme Court ruled, *inter alia*, that the operator of a dragline has a duty to act cautiously[383] *vis-à-vis* all those dependent on the gas facility. The Supreme Court decided that this duty is not merely owed to the owner of the pipe, but also to those who have an obvious interest in an uninterrupted supply, i.e. those who use the gas facility.

Furthermore, the Court gave an essential decision on the dogma of causation. The Court stated that foreseeability is a factor that can be taken into account in the process of ascertaining causal connection. However, other circumstances must be taken into consideration as well.

This decision can be applied *per analogiam* to the facts of this case. Furthermore, it should be borne in mind that the damage suffered by the lessee of the cruise ship could easily, at least *in abstracto*, have been suffered by the ship's owner if the owner had operated the cruise business himself. It is accepted that the owner of a damaged vessel can claim not only the cost of repairs, but also the loss of profits and other costs incurred. The owner can make a claim within the boundaries set by the general rules on damages.[384] In my view, the damage suffered as a result

---

[381] HR 1.7.1977, NJ 1978, no. 84.
[382] On the topic of calculation of loss of production, see HR 18.4.1986, NJ 1986, no. 567.
[383] Hereinafter, I will equate the concept of 'duty of care' to the Dutch concept of *maatschappelijke zorgvuldigheid*. Article 6:162 ss. 2 of the Dutch Civil Code considers improper social conduct (conduct contrary to the standard of conduct acceptable in society) to be tortious, unless grounds for justification are present. Unless the act cannot be imputed to the actor, he is liable in tort. See below for the full text of art. 6:162 CC.
[384] See M. H. Claringbould, *Boek 8 – Verkeersmiddelen en vervoer* (Parlementaire Geschiedenis van het Nieuwe Burgerlijk Wetboek) (Deventer, 1992), pp. 573–4.
See also HR 27.6.1941, NJ 1942, no. 188. Compare S. Mankabady, *The Law of Collision at Sea* (Amsterdam, 1987), pp. 312 ff.

of the forced cancellation could be imputed to the ship that caused the collision.

Therefore, from an abstract point of view, allowing the Shipwreck Company a claim in tort does not open any floodgates. Thus arguing, one might say that the duty to prevent collisions from happening does not only purport to protect the (pure economic) interests of shipowners, but also to protect the *derivative* interests of lessees (or charterers) who have, as it were, 'taken over' a part of the owner's rights of exploitation. The damage caused here is most foreseeable; therefore nothing would stand in the way of liability for this damage.

**Germany**

I. The Shipwreck Company has a tort claim for the lost earnings against those responsible for the collision, but only if Shipwreck already had possession of the vessel.

II. Cause of action: for lack of any contractual relationship with the wrongdoers, Shipwreck's claim can only rest in tort. Here, the only provision arguably applicable is, again, § 823 (1) BGB. Thus, Shipwreck has to show that one of its absolute rights has been violated.

Ownership is out of the question since Shipwreck does not own the vessel.

The right to use the ship under the lease is not an absolute right protected under § 823 (1) BGB. Under German law, the lessee has no property right. Instead, his right is purely contractual and thus merely 'relative', i.e. effective against the lessor. It is not itself protected *vis-à-vis* third parties.

Yet, lawful possession is generally recognized as an absolute right (i.e. as 'another right') protected under § 823 (1) BGB.[385] Of course, the possessor cannot recover for the physical damage to the object – such damage is a violation of the owner's property right so that the claim normally belongs to the owner itself.[386] But if the possessor has a right to use the object and damage results in the loss of its use, this is a violation of possession for which the possessor can recover.[387]

---

[385] BGH WM 1976, 583, at 584; O. Jauernig, *Kommentar zum Bürgerlichen Gesetzbuch Unerlaubte Handlungen* (9th edn, Beck, Munich, 1999), art. 823 BGB A 5 d dd; K. Larenz and C. W. Canaris, *Lehrbuch des Schuldrechts* (13th edn, Beck, Munich 1994), s. 72 I a; O. Palandt, *Bürgerliches Gesetzbuch* (59th edn, Beck, Munich, 2000), art. 823 BGB Rd.-Nr. 13.
[386] There are exceptions, e.g. OLG Frankfurt, NJW-RR 1994, 23.
[387] NJW-RR 1994, 23.

As a result, Shipwreck can recover, but only if it already had possession of the vessel. If the damage occurred before Shipwreck took over the cruise liner, only a contractual right would be affected. This would be pure economic loss and no claim would lie under the circumstances of this case.

Scope of damages: Shipwreck can recover only for its lost earnings, not for the expenses uselessly incurred prior to the collision. The basic provision on damages in the Civil Code, § 249 BGB, provides in s. 1 that the plaintiff must be put into the 'situation which would have existed if the circumstance rendering [the defendant] liable had not occurred'. Thus damages are determined by measuring the difference between the plaintiff's financial situation with and without the damaging event.[388] Without the damaging event, Shipwreck would have made earnings which are therefore recoverable (including lost profit, § 252 BGB). But Shipwreck would still have incurred the expenses prior to the collision so they are not covered.

III. There seems to be a growing trend in Germany, at least among the courts, to protect possession almost like ownership. In 1993, the German Constitutional Court (*Bundesverfassungsgericht*) held that the tenant's possession of an apartment is 'property' in the constitutional sense and therefore protected under article 14 of the German Constitution (*Grundgesetz*).[389] This affects the (private) law of landlord and tenant as well but it applies only to leases of apartments for private habitation.

### Austria

I. The Shipwreck Company has a claim against the person responsible for the collision.

II. Until recently, the lessee of a car could not resort to a claim in tort for compensation when the leased car was damaged by a third person. Only the lessor was entitled to sue in tort. However, the lessor had, as a rule, suffered no loss because of contractual provisions which shifted the burden of risk of any damage to, or loss of, the vehicle to the lessee.[390] Finally, in 1992 the Supreme Court held that the lessee himself could sue for compensation on the grounds of the rule of 'transferred loss'.[391]

---

[388] See Jauernig, *Kommentar*, under art. 249 BGB II 3; D. Medicus, *Bürgerliches Recht* (18th edn, 1999), Rd.-Nr. 287; Palandt, *Bürgerliches*, for art. 249 BGB Rd.-Nr. 8.
[389] BVerfGE 89, 1 (1993).   [390] Cf. OGH JBl 1985, 231; SZ 52/93; WBl 1989, 319 etc.
[391] OGH JBl 27.5.1992, 1993, 43.

The arguments of the Court were that damage to cars normally affects their owners. If, as usual, there is a special clause in the leasing contract imposing the risk of loss on the lessee, it is the rule of transferred loss which entitles the lessee to bring an action sounding in tort against the tortfeasor.

These rules apply to the case of a ship company that leases a vessel. However, only the lost earnings may be recovered as a result of the shipwreck; the expenses incurred prior to the collision do not appear to have a causal connection with the tortious act.

III. Prior to the 1992 breakthrough decision, the Supreme Court refused to employ the transferred loss rule in leasing cases, arguing that the damage to the lessee was merely indirect, namely, a harm which did not occur 'in the line of the assault', but surfaced as a 'a side-effect, not protected by law'.[392]

As mentioned earlier, the policy behind this broad argument is the fear of a flood of claims and boundless recoveries.

## Portugal

I. Assuming that the collision was negligent,[393] the chance of the Shipwreck Company being compensated (on the amount, see below) would be improved if the ship was in its possession at the time of the collision.

If, despite the conclusion of the lease contract,[394] the Shipwreck Company had not yet used the ship, the case would probably be regarded as a common situation of a credit violation. In principle, there would be no place for compensation.

If the Shipwreck Company was already using the ship, the court would probably allow compensation for the violation of its 'personal right to enjoyment' (*direito pessoal de gozo*). However, the costs incurred prior to the collision would probably not be included in the compensation.

---

[392] See F. Bydlinski in H. Klang (ed.), *Kommentar zum allgemeinen bürgerlichen Gesetzbuch*, IV/2, 180 (2nd edn, 1978); H. Koziol, *Österreichisches Haftpflichtrecht*, vol. II (2nd edn, Vienna, 1984), 90; OGH EvBl 1976/168, JBl 1977, 146.

[393] There is no objective liability (Commercial Code arts. 664–675, particularly art. 669; Brussels International Convention on Collision, of 23 September 1910, arts. 2 and 3) except in the case of accidents caused by leisure craft (Decree-Law no. 329/95 of 9 December, Pleasure Boats Act art. 43).

[394] J. M. P. Vasconcelos Esteves, *Contratos de Utilização do Navio* (Livraria Petrony, Lisboa, 1988).

II. The opinions given above are in accordance with the most recent study on this topic in the Portuguese literature.[395]

The Civil Code refers more than once to the category of the personal right to enjoyment (especially in art. 407), that is, generally speaking, a 'personal right' to the enjoyment of something belonging to another. The best example is that of a contract for lease. On occasion, these rights have been treated in the doctrine as credit rights; at other times as *in rem* rights. In the study in question this kind of subjective right is regarded as a *tertium genus*.[396] Nevertheless, the particularities of the personal right to enjoyment compared with the credit rights only manifest themselves when there is 'immediacy' between the holder and the thing (sometimes there may be an initial, purely credit-related phase). In these circumstances (where there is 'immediacy'), the personal right to enjoyment seems to merit aquilian protection under article 483.[397]

Regarding costs incurred prior to the collision, the point can be made that the theory of adequate causality has the theory of *condicio sine qua non* as its basis. Therefore, as regards prior expenditure, this nexus of conditionality would not be confirmed.[398]

### Sweden and Finland

I. For both expenses and loss of earnings, it is unclear whether Shipwreck would get compensation. While there is no case law which can give a clear basis for compensation, scholars tend to admit a claim of this kind.

II. According to the basic principle which excludes compensation of 'third party losses', i.e. economic losses incurred by subjects different from those who have directly suffered personal injury or property damage, Shipwreck should not get compensation since it has no property right on the ship, but merely a contractual right to make use of it.

Scholars try to lessen the rigidity of the 'third party rule' also on the basis of a statement of the Swedish Supreme Court in the first cable case of 1966, in which indemnification of a third party was admitted when he had a 'concrete and near interest' linked to the damaged object, and a case from the Finnish Supreme Court admitting the possibility

---

[395] J. M. Andrade Mesquita, *Direitos Pessoais de Gozo* (Coimbra, 1998). Cf. A. Menezes Cordeiro, *Direitos Reais* (Lex, Lisboa, 1993), nos. 164–6.

[396] Andrade Mesquita, *Direitos*, pp. 191 ff.   [397] Ibid, pp. 226 and 330.

[398] Expenses incurred before the reasonable expectation has been generated in the other party that the contract is going to be performed are entirely at the risk of whoever incurs them (judgment of the Lisbon Court of Appeal on 18 January 1990, *Colectânea de Jurisprudência*, Tomo I, p. 144).

of granting some compensation when the use of cables takes place in forms 'comparable' to property rights.[399]

To admit compensation in a case such as the one at hand, scholars require that the contractual relation between the third party and the owner directly concerns the use of the damaged property, and that the right to make use of the object that the plaintiff draws from such a relationship is personal and exclusive to him.[400]

*Editors' comparative comments*

This case involves claims for two quite different kinds of damages: the prior expenses that were incurred in preparation for a cruise that had to be cancelled, and also the lost profits that the charterer expected to make from the cancelled voyage. All of the legal systems agree, however, that if compensation for the charterer's lost profits were to be granted, then that party should not be also entitled to be reimbursed for any prior expenses they might have incurred, since those kinds of losses were causally unrelated to the defendant's negligence. It is rightly reasoned that those expenses would have been incurred anyway, even if there had been no accidental collision putting the ship out of service, and thus to award expenditures in addition to lost profits would in effect overcompensate the plaintiff.

As to the charterer's claim for lost profits, this question indicates how important underlying conceptions of private law are to the analysis of pure economic loss. The underlying conceptions in this instance relate to the kinds of property interests and contractual interests which the delictual law will protect. Has the party at fault in a maritime collision interfered with a recognized property interest of the boat charterer, or has the tortfeasor simply interfered with the charterer's contractual rights to exclusive possession of the boat for the term of the lease? European systems are divided as to the nature and ranking of these 'interests', and some may even not understand the pertinence of this question. As to pertinence, it is interesting to observe that in Belgium, France, Greece, Italy, Spain and the Netherlands, the nature of Shipwreck's affected interest plays little or no part in the resolution of the problem. Even if Shipwreck's interest in the liner is described as no more than a mere contractual right to possess it for the duration of the charter, it may receive the profits of which it has been deprived, provided

---

[399] HD 1994: 94.   [400] See H. Andersson, *Skyydsändamål och adekvans* (Uppsala, 1993).

that the amount of the loss can be proved with some certainty. For these countries, a tortfeasor's negligent interference with a simple credit right (also called 'relative' right) may serve as a starting point for aquilian liability.

In England and Scotland, however, we see that this type of interest is regarded as an insufficient foundation for an action in negligence. Maritime contracts may confer a possessory interest on the plaintiff, but this is not as significant as a possessory 'title' to the use of the boat.[401] Hence Shipwreck's loss of profits does not flow from an antecedent proprietary interest that the law of tort recognizes and protects, and consequently this is unrecoverable pure economic loss.

Plaintiff's possessory interest receives somewhat higher protection under the law of tort in Germany and Portugal. German lawyers do not suggest that the lessee's contractual right should be protected as a 'property right' but nonetheless they have considered it to be 'another right' under BGB § 823 (1) and have accordingly accommodated it within the scheme of absolute rights. However, for this purpose they distinguish between damage to the plaintiff's actual possession (in which there is immediacy between the holder and the thing) and damage to his mere right to possess it. Only the first type qualifies for aquilian protection. It follows that if Shipwreck was in physical possession at the time of the collision, both German and Portuguese law would award compensation for the charterer's lost profits. We would note that, in distinguishing the different gradations of this possessory right, these systems seem to be giving legal recognition to a hybrid genus which falls somewhere between property and contract.[402] Attention to similar considerations seems to explain Austria's recent change of position on this question. The Austrian courts now recognize that a lessee may sue for lost profits when the risk of physical losses has been 'transferred' to the lessee under the contract. Thus, if Shipwreck bears the risk of the owner's property loss under the charter party (which is unclear in this hypothetical, though likely to be the case in practice) it may recover its financial loss,

---

[401] As the Scots reporter properly cautions, however, there is no assurance that the notion of a 'possessory title' will fit comfortably into the Scottish property framework.

[402] For example, a new Portuguese study by José Mesquita, *Direitos*, regards this personal right of enjoyment of a thing as a *tertium genus*. See also C. von Bar, *The Common European Law of Torts* vol. II (Clarendon Press, Oxford, 2000), p. 55. For a comparative survey and in-depth analysis of possessory issues, see R. Sacco and R. Caterina, 'Il possesso', in L. Mengoni (ed.), *Trattato di diritto civile e commeriale, Cicu-Messineo* (2nd edn, Giuffrè, Milano, 2000), *passim*; J. Gordley and U. Mattei, 'Protecting Possession', (1996) 44 *American Journal of Comparative Law*, 293.

apparently because it has something more than a mere credit right, though something less than a real right in the vessel.

The response of the reporter for Sweden and Finland cautiously indicates that these countries might deny Shipwreck's claim under the basic principle of no compensation for third-party losses. Yet the reporter also notes if an exception were to be made from this position, it would perhaps be allowed by the courts in circumstances in which a third party, such as Shipwreck, had a 'concrete and near' interest to the damaged object. We submit that this characterization should be seen also as an attempt to articulate a hybrid notion using the grammar of proprietary and contractual conceptions.

The ability of three conservative regimes to develop internal reasoning leading to results consistent with the outcomes reached by the liberal regimes may perhaps be explained by the confined scope of the economic loss in this problem. It is believed that there is no persuasive floodgates argument against allowing compensation for Shipwreck's lost profits. In our taxonomy, the case is one of 'transferred loss' rather than of ricochet loss. The same economic loss suffered by Shipwreck would have been suffered by the owner of the passenger liner if they had operated a cruise business. Therefore, allowing this action does not effectively enlarge the defendant's potential liability, nor should it induce dark fears of a sea of claims.

## Case 9: fire in the projection booth

### Case

One evening, during the screening of a motion picture at the Fine Arts Theatre, the film projector briefly caught fire due to a manufacturing defect in the electrical wiring. The fire was quickly extinguished and there were no personal injuries nor any property damage other than to the projector itself, which was a total loss. The Fine Arts Theatre was forced to close for five days until another projector could be located and installed. The theatre owner claims damages for the loss of clientele and profits during the closure against Italian Optics, the manufacturer of the projector. The local retailer from whom the theatre purchased the projector has declared bankruptcy.

### France

I. Tort rules will not apply to this case. The Fine Arts Theatre will have a contractual action against the manufacturer and should recover, in principle, the price of the projector and its lost operating profits.

II. First, it may be noticed that there would be no action available to Fine Arts under the recent product liability legislation in France (Law of 19 May 1998 which adapted French law to the EC Product Liability Directive of 25 July 1985) since the new provisions of the Civil Code (see arts. 1386-1 to 1386-18 CC) provide an action only for injuries to plaintiff's person or to their property *other than the defective product itself* (art. 1386-2 CC).[403] The only physical damage in this case was to the defective projector itself, and thus Fine Arts could not predicate a claim for that loss or the ensuing economic losses on the new code provisions.[404] Theoretically it might be supposed that an action in tort

---

[403] In a recent judgment of 25 April 2002 (*EC v. French Republic*, Case 52/00) the European Court of Justice condemned France for failing to properly transpose the Product Liability Directive into national law. The Court noted that the French legislation was out of line in several respects: 'The Directive contains no provision expressly authorising the Member States to adopt or to maintain more stringent provisions in matters in respect of which it makes provision, in order to secure a higher level of consumer protection.'

[404] An additional reason why the new French legislation implementing the Directive has no application here is that only property 'for private use or consumption' falls under the EC Directive (see art. 9 b(i–ii)), whereas in Case 9 ('Fire in the Projection Booth') the damaged property is clearly commercial. Admittedly, the French provisions do not seem to differentiate between consumer and commercial property, but query whether they should do so.

might still be brought under articles 1382–1383 CC, but in these circumstances, French law regards the plaintiff's action to lie exclusively in contract.

As conceived by French jurisprudence, this case raises a question of the seller's warranty against hidden defects (*vices cachés*) in the thing sold. This warranty arises in contract under the sales provisions of the Civil Code beginning with article 1641. The Fine Arts Theatre should have the same right against Italian Optics as it has against the local retailer. Article 1648, which states that an action involving 'hidden defects' (*vices rédhibitoires*) should be introduced within a short period of time (*brefs délais*), no longer applies to products posing a danger to personal security, according to the decision of 12 July 1991.[405]

French courts take the position that, in case of successive contracts dealing with the same object (*chaîne de contrats*), a direct action may be brought by the second buyer (*sous-acquéreur*) against the original seller (*fabricant*). The particularity of such an action is that it is based on the initial contractual relationship that existed between the original seller and its immediate buyer, although no contract existed between the original seller and the final buyer.

The Cour de Cassation expressly adopted this contractual approach in a case decided in 1979: 'The action that the second buyer can introduce against the manufacturer or the first buyer to recover for the hidden defects of the good is necessarily by nature a contractual action' ('*l'action directe dont dispose le sous-acquéreur contre le fabricant ou un vendeur intermédiaire, pour la garantie du vice caché affectant la chose vendue, est nécessairement de nature contractuelle*').[406]

However, the Cour de Cassation restricted this direct contractual action when it added the qualification that it would run against the original seller only when there has been a successive transfer of property (*transfert de propriété*). The Assemblée Plénière held that 'the new owner of the property has exactly the same rights and actions attached hereto as the original buyer'.

The theory that the action is necessarily contractual has become *jurisprudence constante* since the 1979 case.[407]

In 1977, the Cour de Cassation also declared that in addition to rescission of the sale and restitution of the price paid, the buyer could also

---

[405] Ass. Plén., 12 juillet 1991, D. 1991, 549; JCP 1991.II.21743.
[406] Civ. 1, 9 octobre 1979, Bull. 1979, I, no. 241 p. 192.
[407] Civ. 1, 3 mai 1984, Bull., I, 1954, no. 149, p. 126; Aix-en-Provence, 17e Ch. Civ., 1 mars 1993, JCP 1993.II.2564.

claim its loss of profits.[408] In a similar manner the Fine Arts Theatre could bring a direct action against the manufacturer to recover the price paid for the projector and the profits lost during its closure (subject to proof that such profits were certain to accrue).

III. By enabling the final buyer to sue the original seller on the ground of the contractual relationship that existed only between the original seller and its proximate buyer, the Cour de Cassation satisfied the majority of doctrinal opinion which favoured recognition of a direct action in contract.[409] This rule presents several advantages: it simplifies the legal procedure (only one suit instead of two), and increases the legitimate expectation of the parties (all is written in the contract existing between the original seller, and its proximate buyer). The rule generalizes the effects of the original contract of sale (between manufacturer and the first buyer) for all other parties contractually involved in the *chaîne de contrat*.

Of course the rule of *non-cumul* is at work in such circumstances. This prevents the plaintiff from attempting to convert the action onto the more favourable terrain of tort where prescriptive periods are different and contractual limitations on warranty do not apply. Nevertheless, the effect of casting a case (which other systems might regard as a tort action) in contract makes the pure economic loss question appear simple and to make the French system's approach to pure economic loss appear liberal.

### Belgium

I. The Fine Arts Theatre can recover the loss of profits but can probably not recover the loss of clientele.

II. Under article 1 of the Belgian Product Liability Law of 25 February 1991 (modelled after the EC Product Liability Directive of 25 July 1985), the manufacturer is strictly liable for the damage caused by its defective product.[410]

However, this law does not apply because article 11 of the law limits the recoverable damages.

---

[408] Com. 14 mars 1977, D. 1977, 284: *la cour d'appel était en droit de condamner le concessionnaire à rembourser le prix contre remise du véhicule et à payer des dommages-intérêts en réparation de la privation de jouissance et de l'immobilisation de capitaux que l'acquéreur avait dû supporter*

[409] Malinvaud, D. 1984 Chron. p. 41.

[410] M. Fallon, 'La loi du 25 février 1991 relative à la responsabilité du fait des produits défectueux', JT, 1991, p. 465.

According to article 11 §1, the reparation, which can be obtained in accordance with the law, covers the damages caused to the person (resulting from a physical harm or a death), including damages for mental distress.

According to article 11 §2, the damages caused to property are only recoverable if they regard assets which are of a type normally used or consumed for private reason, and if they have been used by the injured party mainly for private reasons. Moreover, the damage caused to the product itself is never indemnified.

Since the film projector was used for professional reasons, this law is not applicable.

Neither does the Fine Arts Theatre have a contract claim against Italian Optics since there was no contract between them.

The Fine Arts Theatre's claim can therefore only be based on article 1382 CC:

Any act whatever of man which causes damage to another obliges him by whose fault it occurred to make reparation.

To hold the manufacturer liable, the Fine Arts Theatre will have to prove the fault of the manufacturer, the damage caused and the causal link between the fault and the damage.

The issue in the present case is to determine whether the loss of clientele and the loss of profits suffered by the Fine Arts Theatre is a damage which can be qualified as certain and not as hypothetical. The court's appreciation is sovereign in that matter. The loss of clientele will most probably be regarded as hypothetical and therefore not taken into account.

On the contrary, the loss of profits – even if its amount might not be very easy to evaluate – will probably be accepted by the courts.

## Italy

I. The standard principle of article 2043 cc applies in this case. The theatre owner may recover for the profits lost during the closure, provided there is sufficient proof of the anticipated profits.

II. According to the typical rulings, the theatre owner must present strong evidence of their economic losses and must also establish the nexus of causation between those losses and the manufacturer's fault. This case is not covered by the Product Liability Act 1988 (d.p.r. 224/1988, adapting the EC Product Liability Directive of 25 July 1985) since the plaintiff is not a consumer but a business person.

## Spain

I. Following the Civil Code general norms, the plaintiff could obtain compensation from the projector manufacturer.

II. In order to study this case we must first exclude it from the scope of the Civil Liability for Damage Caused to Defective Products Act No. 22 of 6 July 1994 (this Act adapted the Spanish legal system to the EC Product Liability Directive of 25 July 1985, regarding the harmonization of legal, regulatory and administrative norms of Member States on damage caused by defective products).

According to article 10 of the 1994 Act, this case would be excluded because damages caused to the defective item itself are excluded from the scope of the statute.[411] Damages to items of professional use (not private use[412]), other than the defective goods, are also excluded.

However, article 10 of the 1994 Act states that damages beyond its scope, including pain and suffering, may be recovered under general civil law. Damages similar to those described in this case could therefore be recovered under the general principles of liability in the Civil Code.[413] Spanish legal scholars who have conducted a general study on manufacturer's liability favour the application of delictual responsibility.[414] This opinion has been backed up by abundant Supreme Court decisions, some of which are quoted below.

---

[411] Strict contractual liability is considered sufficient to adequately cover these kind of damages; see M. A. Parra Lucán 'Notas a la Ley 22/94, de 6 Julio, de responsabilidad civil por los daños causados por productos defectuosos', Actualidad Civil, 1995-IV, p. 752.

[412] On this see G. Alcover Garau, *La responsabilidad civil del fabricante* (Civitas, Madrid, (1990)), p. 81.

[413] Lucán, 'Notas a la Ley', 729–30.

[414] J. Santos Briz 'La responsabilidad del fabricante frente a terceros en el derecho moderno', in *Estudios de Derecho Civil en Honor del Prof. Castán* (1969), p. 546; E. R. A. Rojo, *La responsabilidad civil del fabricante* (1974), pp. 178-1; Parra Lucan (90) p. 242, Alcover Garau, *La responsabilidad*, p. 22; and R. Mullerat Balmaña, (1979) 1 *Revista Jurídica de Cataluña* 9–63, at 11. From the Spanish point of view, it should be pointed out that in this case the theatre owner cannot direct a contractual claim against the manufacturer of the projector. In the Spanish legal system, both case law and scholars uphold the non-contractual path to reach the manufacturer. They do not assume the (French) idea that, in this case, the theatre owner can use (because he had 'purchased' them) the contractual remedies that the local retailer would have had against Italian Optics.

In this light, it seems that the Spanish courts' response to the issue in this case would be that the injured party would have a claim against the manufacturer for the damages arising from the closing of the premises while the projector was replaced. In order to reach this conclusion, we assume that there will be no problem proving that the product was defective or that the manufacturer was at fault. Regarding the latter issue, legal scholars point out that under case law the requirement of the manufacturer's fault in this matter is becoming less essential.[415]

In the Supreme Court decision of 3 October 1991 (First Chamber) a farmer directed a claim against the manufacturer of a chemical product, the label of which said that a certain lemon tree plague could be avoided by its use. The product had been purchased from a local supplier who helped the farmer to spray the lemon trees with the product, ensuring that this activity was carried out following the strict conditions established by the manufacturer (amounts used, application method, pumping systems, etc.). However, the product turned out to be ineffective in preventing the specific plague that the farmer was trying to avoid on his plantation. This resulted in crop damage by the plague. Given these facts, the Supreme Court stated that all requirements were met to ascertain the non-contractual liability of the product manufacturer. First, there was bad faith or negligence in launching a product on the market which was ineffective as advertised. Second, the user of the product suffered damages consisting of loss of the crop. Finally, the causal link was established between the use of the ineffective product and the damage caused to the crop by the plague. The Supreme Court awarded damages to the plaintiff farmer for the following items:

(1) Damages for lost profits due to the plague (not including the costs necessary to obtain a normal crop). When estimating these lost profits, the Supreme Court took into account the fact that during that year there were harsh frosts which reduced the normal yield of the lemon trees in the area.
(2) Damages were also awarded for the costs incurred as a result of ineffective fumigation (staff salaries, tractors used, etc.).

Together with this Supreme Court decision, the decisions of 2 May 1961, 13 April 1964, 20 October 1983, 14 November 1984 and 25 March 1991 (all of which were also delivered by the First Chamber of the

---

[415] E.g. M. C. Gómez and S. Díaz Alabart, 'Responsabilidad civil por los daños causados por productos defectuosos', *Actualidad Civil* 1995–IV, 532; for greater depth and detail see Parra Lucán (90) pp. 295–296.

Supreme Court) may be mentioned. The Spanish legal experts who have studied these decisions generally uphold the Court's judgments regarding this issue.[416]

It must be noted, however, that there would be a heavy burden of proof on the plaintiff when calculating lost profits due to the defective projector.

## Greece

I. The Fine Arts Theatre may claim compensation for its damages against Italian Optics in the framework of contractual liability. This solution has almost absolutely prevailed in Greek doctrine, but not yet in Greek court decisions.

II. Non-contractual liability of the producer: tortious liability of the retailer or the manufacturer cannot be established at first glance, because neither of them acted statutorily unlawfully, there is no infringement of any particular legislative rule, e.g., as it would be in case of harm to the physical integrity of the human body, or the theatre's property, etc. Nevertheless, the Greek courts do regard the producer as possibly liable in tort.[417] This occurs not only when the defect in the product causes material damages, but also when it causes pure economic loss. In the first case it is obvious that a tort has occurred; in the second case the Greek courts broaden the notion of unlawfulness by including any breach of the duties of care imposed by good faith.[418] According to this view (theory of 'objective defectiveness'), producers are tortiously liable for any defect of their products, since this will probably be caused by a breach of the duty of care.

The so-called 'liability of the producer' cannot be founded on the modern special legislation, because article 9 of the EC Product Liability Directive of 1985, as well as the Greek adaptation, Act 2251/1994, stipulate that physical harm to the human body or to things is the only indemnifiable damage in this case.[419]

The contractual liability of the producer to Fine Arts: many Greek scholars[420] assume that privity of contract between the buyer and the

---

[416] J. G. Storch De Gracia 'Daños causados por los productos elaborados', (1985) 1 *La Ley* 615–25 at 619, Parra Lucán (90) pp. 297 and 299, R. De Ángel, *Algunas previsiones sobre el futuro de la responsabilidad civil* (Civitas, Madrid, 1995), p. 650.
[417] EphAth 1039/1979 NoB 27, 985; EphThes 1259/1977.
[418] AP 81/1991 NoB 40, 715; EfAth 7453/1988 EllDni 31, 848.
[419] See J. Karakostas, *Producer's Liability for Defective Products* (1993), pp. 180, 233.
[420] M. Stathopoulos, *Law of Obligations, General Part*, I (p. 92; M. Maggivas, *The Liability of the Producer of Standardised Goods* (1978), p. 73.

local retailer should yield to the principle of good faith (art. 288 CC). Thus, this view considers the contract between producer and retailer as a 'contract with protective effects in favour of a third party', i.e. the final buyer, because the object of the performance (i.e. the product) is not destined to be used by the retailer but by the buyer. Therefore the producer is liable for any defect in the product as against the buyer. Thus the producer and the buyer are bound by a sort of *lato sensu* obligation, by way of contrast to the relation between the producer and the retailer, which of course, is a *stricto sensu* obligation. According to this view, the Fine Arts Theatre may claim compensation for its damages against Italian Optics.

A more traditional/conservative, but nevertheless effective grounding of the producer's contractual liability to Fine Arts could also be developed in the framework of indirect liability through the following line of thought: the buyer has against the retailer the right to be compensated for the defects of the product sold, because the fault of the latter as to his failure duly to fulfil the performance is legally presumed (rebuttable presumption of the debtor's fault in any case of breach of the contract according to arts. 336, 342, 363 CC). On the other hand the retailer's obligation constitutes a damage he suffers owing to a producer's fault, so that the former has in his turn the right to be compensated by the latter for the same value. Thus the producer is the buyer's debtor's debtor, so that the buyer can sue the producer by lodging against him the 'indirect action' established by article 72 CCPr., which lays down that the creditor has the right to sue the debtor of his debtor, in order to satisfy his own right.

III. The theory of 'contracts with protective effects in favour of a third party' has not been confirmed by the Greek court decisions, although not rejected. This means that contractual liability based on the legal construction of the contract with protective effects in favour of a third party (i.e. the consumer) would usually occur here only concurrently (with tortious liability). Consequently, there is no particular need to use such a legal construction, except only in order to make the producer bear the burden of proving that he is not at fault (because particularly in the framework of contractual liability, the fault is presumed).

This is certainly already a very relevant feature for the case, but not, however, in the eyes of the Greek judge. The explanation of this paradox is that Greek judges always avoid solving a case by using the consequences of the burden of proof, because faults in implementing the rules which regulate the burden of proof constitute legal reasons for the revision of a decision by the Supreme Court according to article 559, paragraph 1. No. 13 CCPr. This means that in such a case, the legal knowledge of the judge may be examined by his superiors. On the other hand, no possibility of such an examination arises if the judge has no need to implement the rules of burden of proof, namely, where the judge has been fully convinced of every disputed fact, because factual views of the judge are beyond the Supreme Court's control.

The above constitutes one more reason for Greek judges to try to fully detect the truth of the arguments of the parties, so that there is practically no decision resting on disputed facts, e.g. the fault of the defendant. As far as this is true, it is clear that there is no particular need for the judge to search for one more legal basis to ground the liability of the producer.

### England

I. The Fine Arts Theatre will fail in its claim in tort against Italian Optics for loss of clientele and profits.

II. It is, at present, a well-settled rule of English law that where only economic loss is suffered by a distant consumer, the producer of a defective product has no duty of care and is not liable in negligence, even if it is established that the defect was caused by his fault: *Muirhead* v. *Industrial Tank Specialities*.[421] The strict liability of the producer under the Consumer Protection Act 1987 also is expressly excluded by the Act in case of a pure economic loss. This non-liability rule was also endorsed by the general thread of the Law Lords' speeches in *Murphy* v. *Brentwood DC*.[422] The position does not appear to be different in cases where the defect lies in a separable component of a 'complex structure' product, manufactured by a different manufacturer, which causes the whole product to be damaged after its purchase by the consumer, although in such a case it could be argued that the consumer is also suffering a *property damage*.[423] Lord Bridge's dicta on 'complex structures or complex chattels' in *D & F Estates Ltd* v. *Church Commissioners*[424] are generally thought[425] as having not survived *Murphy* v. *Brentwood DC*, where he himself seems reluctant to pursue them.

---

[421] [1985] 3 All ER 705 (CA).   [422] [1991] 1 AC 398.
[423] See analysis of English and German Law in this connection in E. K. Banakas, *Tortious Liability for Pure Economic Loss: A Comparative Study* (Hellenic Institute of International and Foreign Law, Athens, 1989), pp. 173 f.
[424] [1989] AC 177 (HL).
[425] See W. V. H. Rogers, *Winfield and Jolowicz on Tort* (14th edn), pp. 249–50.

III. The clear policy of English law in cases of economic loss caused to a distant consumer by defective products is that it should not be recoverable, because imposing such liability on manufacturers is most unrealistic and harmful to market operations. But a possible exception lies in cases where the defective product exposes the consumer to legal liability to a third party: see the cases of *The Greystoke Castle*,[426] *The Esso Bernicia*[427] and *Lambert v. Lewis*.[428]

## Scotland

I. The Fine Arts Theatre is unable to sue Italian Optics in delict since the only property damaged is the defective projector itself. Fine Arts' remedy lies in contract against the local retailer who sold him the defective goods. Since he is bankrupt, Fine Arts could seek to obtain an assignation of the rights that the local retailer had under his contract with Italian Optics from the permanent trustee in sequestration; however, as an unsecured creditor, they would have little practical chance of obtaining such an assignation.

II. The starting point here is *Donoghue v. Stevenson*[429] which is the origin of the principle covering the extent of delictual liability of manufacturers to consumers for defective products that cause loss. It has become authority for the

general principle that a manufacturer of any product owes a duty of care to the ultimate consumer not to cause injury to his person or property as a result of a latent defect in a product which could not be discovered by inspection before use and was intended by the manufacturer to be used by the ultimate consumer in the same condition as it left the manufacturer. If, by his careless conduct, the manufacturer breaches his duty causing injury to the ultimate consumer's person or property, then he is liable in delict to make reparation for the damage suffered by the consumer.[430]

Two limitations are that the defect must be latent and the duty is to prevent injury to the person or property of the consumer. Hence, damage to the product itself, being considered by the courts to constitute pure economic loss, is not recoverable in delict. Where a defect is discovered and repaired before any damage occurs, or if the defect causes damage and repairs are then effected, or if the defect does not require repairs

---

[426] [1947] AC 265 (HL).   [427] [1989] 1 All ER 37 (HL).
[428] [1982] AC 225 (HL).   [429] 1932 SC (HL) 31.
[430] J. M. Thomson, *Delictual Liability* (Butterworths, Edinburgh, 1999), p. 56.

but merely renders the product of less value to the consumer, it is easy to see these as pure economic loss equal to the repair cost or the loss in value. Where, as here, the defect results in the complete destruction of the product then it is thought the loss is still pure economic loss but to the extent of the full cost of the product itself.

One Scottish decision appears to stand against this proposition: *North Scottish Helicopters Ltd v. United Technologies Corp Inc. (No. 2)*.[431] The proof which followed the preliminary proof referred to above under Case 8 ('The Cancelled Cruise'), saw damages being awarded for the loss of a helicopter which had merely destroyed itself owing to a manufacturing defect. Lord Davidson allowed items of consequential loss, including expenses incurred as a result of the helicopter being out of operation, in addition to the largest single item of loss which was the repair to the helicopter itself.

In light of the judgment of the House of Lords in *Murphy v. Brentwood District Council*[432] it is thought that this decision would be unlikely to be followed.[433] Their Lordships' view is adequately summed up in the speech of Lord Bridge of Harwich, who stated:

If a manufacturer negligently puts into circulation a chattel containing a latent defect which renders it dangerous to persons or property, the manufacturer, on the well-known principles established by *Donoghue v. Stevenson*...will be liable in tort for injury to persons or damage to property which the chattel causes. But if a manufacturer produces and sells a chattel which is merely defective in quality, even to the extent that it is valueless for the purpose for which it was intended, the manufacturer's liability at common law arises only under and by reference to the terms of any contract to which he is a party in relation to the chattel; the common law does not impose on him any liability in tort to persons to whom he owes no duty in contract but who, having acquired the chattel, suffer economic loss because the chattel is defective in quality. If a dangerous defect in a chattel is discovered before it causes any personal injury or damage to property, because the danger is now known and the chattel cannot be safely used unless the defect is repaired, the defect becomes merely a defect in quality. The chattel is either capable of repair at economic cost or it is worthless and must be scrapped. In either case the loss sustained by the owner or hirer of the chattel is purely economic. It is recoverable against any party who owes the loser

---

[431] 1988 SLT (Notes) 788, (1987) Outer House cases (full transcript on Lexis).
[432] [1991] 1 AC 398, [1990] 2 All ER 908, [1990] 3 WLR 414, [1990] 2 Lloyd's Rep 467, 50 BLR 1, 22 HLR 502, 21 Con LR 1.
[433] See J. M. Thomson, 'Delictual Liability for Pure Economic Loss: Recent Developments', 1995 SLT News 139 at 141.

a relevant contractual duty. But it is not recoverable in tort in the absence of a special relationship of proximity imposing on the tortfeasor a duty of care to safeguard the plaintiff from economic loss.[434]

As to the *North Scottish* case, it is not clear from the report whether the fact that this was a manufacturing defect causing damage to the product itself was clearly argued, even though it was a very expensive product. Rather than being viewed as economic loss, the loss is described as being 'consequential' and appears to be accepted as such.[435] Lord Davidson, at the proof stated:

Counsel for the first defenders also submitted that the first pursuers were not entitled to recover the items of loss claimed by them. Since this submission was based substantially upon arguments about title to sue which I repelled after the preliminary proof...I merely record that this argument was renewed. In any event evidence and argument adduced since the preliminary proof have not altered my opinion on this point. There was no suggestion that there was any duplication in the items of loss which are claimed...in practical terms the various items claimed represented losses incurred by the pursuers who respectively had paid for them.[436]

In fact at the preliminary proof the question of title to sue related to the pursuers not being owners and did not appear to focus on the heads of damages. The court seemed to have concerned itself with whether the losses were established or not, and totally missed consideration of whether they were consequential or purely economic. After *Murphy* it is unlikely that such an omission would occur again.

Here, the projector is worthless owing to the defect and it must be scrapped. The loss is pure economic loss and not recoverable in delict. The 'complex structure theory', propounded as a possibility of explaining the decision in *Anns v. Merton London Borough*,[437] if it could be argued in this case, would be of no use as one would only recover the cost of the projector, it being the extent of the property damaged by the faulty wiring. As this has been supplied as an integral part of the projector by Italian Optics, there is little possibility of the projector being considered a complex structure and the faulty wiring a separate source of the damage. If a bulb supplied by a different manufacturer had exploded and taken the projector with it, then the complex structure theory may

---

[434] [1991] 1 AC 398 at p. 475.  [435] 1988 SLT 77 at p. 79C–D.
[436] 1988 SLT (Notes) 778, (1987) Outer House cases (from full transcript on Lexis).
[437] [1978] AC 728, [1977] 2 All ER 492, [1997] 2 WLR 1024; a seven-judge bench in *Murphy* overruled *Anns*.

have some application. But again, one would only recover the cost of the projector so this would be of no assistance to Fine Arts.

Finally, for completeness, there would be no liability under the Consumer Protection Act 1987, Part I. Under s. 5(2), there is no liability under the Act if the only loss is the defective product itself. Under s. 5(3), only loss or damage to property intended by the person suffering the loss or damage mainly for his own private use, occupation or consumption will be relevant liability under the Act. The projector is non-consumer property.

III. The Scots law approach to defective property is explained by Norrie, who writes:

> [T]he costs of putting right the defect, or the diminution in value of the property because it has a defect, cannot be recovered because the loss was purely economic. The somewhat anomalous distinction between liability, lies in when the defect or damage was caused. If the property falls into the pursuer's ownership whole and is then affected by the defender's careless acts or omissions, the economic loss caused by the damage is recoverable. If the property falls into the pursuer's ownership already damaged by the defender's carelessness, then the property is said to have a defect, which may well be latent, and the economic loss this constitutes is not recoverable. There are sound policy reasons why there should not be a duty of care to avoid diminishing the value of another's property in this way. A manufacturer or seller of defective property ought not to be held liable for the pursuer's economic loss since otherwise the manufacture or sale of property would always carry with it a non-contractual warranty of its worth to the whole world. If there is loss, that should fall on the property owner who must be taken to have had an opportunity to inspect the property before acquiring it. A purchaser who discovers goods are worth less than he paid for them cannot recover the difference in an action for negligence because there is no duty on a seller to ensure that the purchaser does not pay over the odds.[438]

However, the purchaser may well have a remedy for breach of contract against the seller who sold him defective goods. This is, of course, subject to any valid exception clauses in the contract which operate to protect the seller.

## The Netherlands

I. Although Dutch (case) law does not provide a clear-cut answer to this problem, I am inclined to believe the manufacturer is liable for this damage that was caused by their negligence.

---

[438] *Stair Memorial Encyclopaedia, The Laws of Scotland*, vol. 15 (Law Society of Scotland, Edinburgh, 1996), p. 172, para. 276 (written by K. McK. Norrie).

II. One must be cautious in evaluating this case, since the Dutch Supreme Court has seldom been confronted with product liability cases. However, the two leading Supreme Court decisions on the subject suggest that manufacturers must observe utmost care to avoid the physical injury of consumers.[439] Whether a similarly high standard of conduct applies when loss of profit of professional users is concerned is unknown. In cases such as this, where loss of profit is suffered as a result of a defective product, the question is whether the manufacturer acted negligently vis-à-vis the theatre. A number of factors are decisive, most important of which seems to be whether it was foreseeable to the manufacturer that this kind of damage might occur if the product turned out to be defective, and whether – given this foreseeability – he was under the obligation to prevent this damage from occurring.[440] It is interesting – but somewhat confusing – to see that 'foreseeability' is one of the factors that, on the one hand, determine the impropriety of the act itself, and on the other, sets the limits of causal connection. Once it has been established that the damage was foreseeable, and that the manufacturer owed a duty vis-à-vis the theatre, the damage at hand can be imputed to the negligence of the manufacturer.

In my view, the manufacturer of professional film projectors must reckon with the possibility of this kind of damage. It is not an improbable category of damage, quite the opposite. Furthermore, the manufacturer owes a duty to the theatre to take all reasonable precautions to avoid this foreseeable loss. I would be inclined to conclude that the manufacturer is liable for the loss of profits during the closure if negligence in the process of production caused the defect.

In the case, there is no mention of any possible contributory negligence on the part of the theatre. I will therefore not touch upon the subject, but it goes without saying that the theatre is under obligation to avoid increasing the loss (e.g. by calling for replacement of the projector). One might even suggest that the theatre is obliged to have a spare projector.

### Germany

I. The Fine Arts Theatre has a claim against Italian Optics for the loss of clientele and profits (as well as for the projector itself). This claim is based on § 823 (1) BGB, i.e. on a violation of the plaintiff's property right.

---

[439] HR 2.2.1973, NJ 1973, no. 315, HR 30.6.1989, NJ 1990, no. 652.
[440] On foreseeability in products liability, see HR 25.3.1966, NJ 1966, no. 325.

II. Contract claims: the Fine Arts Theatre has no contract claims against Italian Optics. Under German law, the manufacturer of a defective product is not liable towards third parties (i.e. everybody except the first buyer) in contract, but only in tort.[441]

Tort claims: at first glance, it might seem as if there was no tort liability for the loss of clientele and profits because this loss is purely financial. Yet, under German tort law, even financial loss is recoverable *if* it follows proximately from the violation of an absolute right. In other words, once such a violation (e.g. of property) under § 823 (1) BGB has been established, all damages proximately following from it are recoverable.

The crucial issue in this case is therefore whether Italian Optics has violated the Fine Arts Theatre's property right.

Perhaps somewhat surprisingly, this is a serious issue. The basic rule is that the manufacture (or sale) of a defective product is, in and of itself, not a violation of the buyer's property right in that same product. The buyer did not suffer damage to a once non-defective chattel, but simply obtained a product that was defective from the very beginning. Thus, he may have a warranty claim against the seller under the law of sales,[442] but he has no tort claim against the manufacturer.[443]

The courts have made an exception from this rule. The exception concerns cases in which the defect is originally limited to a relatively small and functionally separate part of the product, such as a safety switch in a machine, or the accelerator cable in a car. The defective part then causes damage to, or the destruction of, the whole product. In such cases, the courts hold that the owner has suffered damage to his property which, as a whole, had been previously intact.[444] This exception applies in the present scenario since the defective wiring ultimately destroyed the whole projector. While Italian Optic's liability is still based on fault under § 823 (1) BGB, German courts have long reversed the burden of proof regarding fault in product liability cases.[445] Since Italian Optics has apparently not exonerated itself (a task well-nigh impossible under the standards set by the courts), it is liable to the Fine Arts Theatre under this article.

---

[441] This has been firmly established since the leading case BGHZ 51, 91 (1968) (*Hühnerpest* case).
[442] But see below, III.    [443] See BGHZ 39, 366 (1963); BGH NJW 1978, 1051.
[444] BGHZ 67, 359 (1976); BGHZ 86, 256, at 257–63 (1983); BGH NJW 1978, 2241, at 2242–3; see also BGH NJW 1983, 812, at 813 (claim denied); see also W. Fikentscher, *Lehrbuch des Schuldrechts* (8th edn, 1992), Rd.-Nr. 1210.
[445] BGHZ 51, 91 (1968).

As explained above, once liability for property damage is established, the Fine Arts Theatre's claim includes recovery for the loss of clientele and profits as well.

Liability under special legislation: under § 1 (1) of the German Product Liability Law (modelled after the EC Product Liability Directive of 25 July 1985), the manufacturer of a defective product is strictly liable to the ultimate user or consumer. In the present case, however, this law does not apply because § 1 (1) excludes damage to commercially used products.[446]

III. The exception explained above under tort claims is needed lest most buyers in similar situations – i.e. where a small component part destroys the whole product – be without remedy. They would have no tort claim against the manufacturer for lack of a property violation.

**Austria**

I. The Fine Arts Theatre has a claim against Italian Optics for the loss of the projector and for the loss of clientele and profits. The claim can be based on articles 1295, 1331, 1332 ABGB (violation of the plantiff's property right), as well as on the contract between Italian Optics and the local retailer which has 'protective effects to a third party', i.e. the Fine Arts Theatre.

II. Contract claims: under Austrian law, the contract between the manufacturer of a defective product and the retailer establishes 'protective effects' on the consumer for whose purpose the product was finally manufactured.

This complies with the theory of liability for pure economic loss: if it is obvious that the contractual performance is in the interest of the consumer, his pure economic loss is recoverable.

In the present case, however, it is not a question of infringement of economic interests since a property right, namely the projector, was damaged.

Under Austrian law the entire damage is recoverable including financial loss if such loss arises – as in the present case – from the violation of an absolute right e.g. a property right[447] (consequential loss).

---

[446] It also expressly excludes liability for damage to the product itself, although it is arguable this clause does not forbid the exception explained above, see K. Larenz and C. W. Canaris, *Lehrbuch des Schuldrechts* (13th edn, Beck, Munich, 1994), § 84 VI 1 c; D. Medicus, *Bürgerliches Recht* (18th edn, 1999), Rd.-Nr. 650.

[447] See H. Koziol, *Österreichisches Haftpflichtrecht*, vol. II (2nd edn, Vienna, 1984), p. 88; OGH SZ 60/91; JBl 1991, 522.

Tort claims: if a defective part causes damage to the buyer of the product because a defect materializes in this product, such damage may be recoverable provided that the claimant can prove the manufacturer's fault, or that the employee responsible for the defective manufacture was unfit for the job.[448]

Italian Optics, if liable for damage to the projector, is also responsible for the loss of clientele and profits.

Liability under special legislation: under articles 1(1) and (2) of the Austrian Product Liability Act[449] the manufacturer of a defective product is strictly liable to the ultimate user or consumer.

Article 1(1) explicitly excludes liability for damage to the product itself. The Supreme Court has held[450] that, where a defective part causes damage to the non-defective portion of the purchased goods, no claim is available under the product liability statute.

Article 2(1) excludes damage to products which were predominantly used or consumed within the professional activities of the plaintiff. Therefore, in the present case there is no claim for damages under the Austrian Product Liability Act.

III. In cases such as the one at issue, one could resort to the theory of contracts with protective effects to a third party, in which case (contrary to tort law) pure financial loss is recoverable.

## Portugal

I. This damage is not recoverable under the special legislation on producers' objective liability (Decree-Law No. 383/89 of 6 November 1989, article 8, no. 1).

Recovery is problematical under general tort principles; the requisite of unlawfulness seems to be lacking.

II. Under the terms of article 8, n. 1 of Decree-Law no. 383/89, of 6 November 1989 (transposition of the EC Product Liability Directive of 25 July 1985), 'damage resulting in death or physical injury and damage *in rem* different from the defective product are recoverable, where it is normally intended for private use or consumption and the injured party had principally attributed this end to it'.

---

[448] See H. Koziol and R. Welser *Grundriss bürgerlichen Rechts*, vol. II (12th edn, Vienna, 2001), p. 353; OGH ecolex 1994, 384.
[449] BGBl 1988/99 as amended by BGBl I 2001/98.
[450] OGH SZ 67/22, JBl 1994, 477, EvBl 1994/159.

When a final product is damaged by virtue of a fault in one of its components supplied by a different producer, it is a matter for argument whether the issue concerns damage in a thing that is different from the defective article or damage in the article itself, with this latter interpretation seeming to be the more correct one.[451]

As regards the application of the general principles of tort liability, despite it being uncertain that a Portuguese court would resolve the question along the lines suggested in paragraph I, mainly for lack of specialized doctrinal support,[452] it appears that the spirit of the system could be invoked in its favour, drawing on 'parallel situations'.

In the domain of contract, the Civil Code expressly removes the validity of those clauses by which the creditor foregoes in advance the rights that the law allows in the event of non-fulfilment on the part of the debtor (art. 809),[453] showing thereby that an idea of lack of liability is repugnant to it, even if it results from an agreement. Therefore, outside the domain of contract, it seems inconsistent with this idea to accept that the author of the negligent act does not respond in relation to the damage that his conduct typically produces, and that it could even appear to be the sole damage.

Situations of this kind could be within the letter, but they are not, we believe, within the spirit of article 483. If the law had foreseen cases such as these, it would surely have proposed a different solution.

III. The *raison d'être* of non-recoverability for pure economic loss does not seem to us to be valid for this kind of situation. The intention is to prevent an indiscriminate expansion of the number of people with the right to compensation, not to impede compensation when the pure economic loss could well be the sole consequence of a negligent act, as with the case in question.

We doubt whether a Portuguese court would reject the action once the projector manufacturer was shown to be at fault. Technically, it could be said that the delivery of a defective article that causes its destruction is a violation of the right of ownership of the article from which an economic loss arises. We personally feel that it is better to support an interpretation of article 483, no. 1 which, based on its *ratio legis*, permits recovery of pure economic loss when it is the sole and direct

---

[451] João Calvão Da Silva, *Responsabilidade Civil do Produtor* (Almedina, Coimbra, 1990), pp. 702–6.
[452] Cf. Calvão Da Silva, *Responsabilidade* no. 2, p. 706, pp. 706–8.
[453] A. J. M. Pinto Monteiro, *Cláusulas limitativas e de exclusão da responsabilidade civil* (Coimbra, 1985).

consequence of an injurious act executed negligently. If the degree of fault is disproportionately slight in relation to the damage, the law allows the judge to set compensation at an amount that is less than the damage.[454]

### Sweden and Finland

I. Strict liability according to the Product Liability Acts based on the EC directive cannot of course be applied, since the Fine Arts Theatre is not a consumer but a professional. Fine Arts will get compensation if it can bring evidence of fault on the part of Italian Optics.

II. A line of decisions of the Swedish Supreme Court[455] has affirmed liability for the fault of the manufacturer toward the final buyer, as a simple application of the *culpa* rule. The lack of a direct relation between manufacturer and final purchaser has never been seen as a problem by the Swedish Supreme Court. It must be noted that strict liability in such a case is certainly doubtful but cannot be totally excluded. Some decisions[456] tend to affirm a strict liability for the manufacturer based upon a fictional warranty theory. Scholars usually do nothing more than quote the existence of such case law without trying to draw from it a general principle.

Once liability for property damages is affirmed on the above-mentioned basis, the losses of the Fine Arts Theatre are compensated as a 'loss of profit' and 'obstacle to economic activity' according to *SkadestL* 5:7 (Sweden) and *SkadestL* 5:5 (Finland).

### *Editors' comparative comments*

This case is essentially a products liability case and its outcome depends upon the intricacies of what may be called the 'products liability law' of each system. Whether the self-destruction of a film projector is classified as the buyer's property loss, or is instead treated as 'pure economic loss', will depend upon the workings of these general rules of liability

---

[454] Art. 494: 'If the liability is based upon negligence compensation may be equitably settled at a lesser amount so as to correspond to the damage caused, as long as the degree of culpability of the agent, his financial conditions and those of the injured party and other circumstances justify it.'

[455] NJA 1949 s. 460, NJA 1961 s. 94, NJA 1977 s. 538, NJA 1977 s. 788, NJA 1982 s. 421, NJA 1987 s. 417.

[456] See, for example, NJA 1983 s. 118.

which are essentially tort and contract rules applied to defective products, and not upon special legislation that has been passed throughout Europe in response to the EC Product Liability Directive of 25 July 1985. Neither that Directive, nor the legislation at the national level which implemented it, applies to the kind of damage in this case.

As we saw earlier in Cable I, the conservative and pragmatic regimes of Europe are not unanimous about the meaning and scope of pure economic loss. In the present hypothetical, their differences bear directly upon the viability of Fine Arts' tort claims. For England and Scotland which, as we have seen, adhere to a strict conception of pure economic loss, compensation is refused. The self-destruction of the projector is not considered a property loss for the Fine Arts Theatre. From the outset it owned a product with a defect, and defendant's negligent manufacture of a defective product is not, in and of itself, a violation of the buyer's property right in that same product. Thus, the loss of the projector is a form of pure economic loss that is unrecoverable in negligence. It follows that any consequential loss of clientele or box office revenues cannot be regarded as parasitic upon property loss, and thus will be unrecoverable as well.

On the other hand, Germany, Sweden and Finland and possibly Austria and Portugal regard the destruction of the projector as a property violation, and thus Fine Arts' ensuing financial losses are parasitic and may be recovered in tort. Comparatively speaking, their conception of 'consequential loss' is considerably less technical than that in England and Scotland. It is interesting to observe that, in particular, Germany has created an exception to its general rule, accepting that when one part of a product is defective and causes the loss of the whole product, there has been a violation of the owner's property under BGB § 823 (1).

## Case 10: the dutiful wife

### Case

A man was seriously injured and confined to bed for two months, during which time he was entirely unable to look after himself. His wife, who owns and runs a small shop, was forced to close her business while she looked after her husband. She is now suing the perpetrator of the accident for loss of earnings during the period of her enforced idleness.

### France

I. The wife will likely recover her loss of earnings against the tortfeasor under articles 1382–83 CC.

II. The wife's claim for economic loss will be treated as a normal case of tort liability under articles 1382–83 CC. Therefore, she will have to establish the normal elements (fault, damage and causal link) in such a claim.

The Cour de Cassation has decided under article 212 CC (which requires spouses to give mutual fidelity, help and assistance), that the increased workload imposed upon a wife due to the incapacitated state of her husband after injuries in a car accident is a prejudice for which the author of the accident must be responsible.[457]

It might be noted, though, that the couple in Case 10 could have hired a nurse, whose cost would probably have been reimbursed by the social security system, thus mitigating the damages incurred by the wife. However, the principle of mitigation of damages does not clearly exist in France.[458] The attribution of damages being a question of fact lies within the *appréciation souveraine des juges du fond*, which means the French judges could practically take this argument into account without saying so, and reduce the wife's damages.

### Belgium

I. The wife can recover against the tortfeasor the loss of earnings she suffered during the period of her enforced idleness. However, the loss of earnings will be limited to the market value of her services and will

---

[457] Civ. 2e, 18 mars 1981, Bull. 1981, II, no. 70.
[458] M. Ravanel, 'Pour une application de la "Mitigation of Damages" en droit français' (Mémoire pour le Diplôme de DEA en droit comparé, 1996, unpublished paper, on file with the editors).

be indemnified subject to the husband not having been indemnified for the same damage.

II. The husband's claim: it is clear that the husband has a claim under article 1382 CC:

Any act whatever of man which causes damage to another obliges him by whose fault it occurred to make reparation.

The recoverable damage within such claim will include the costs that he suffered but also the income he might have lost. The costs of necessary services during the period of recuperation are normally part of the recoverable damages if the need of such services is proven.

Case law was initially reluctant to take into account this last part of the damage when the plaintiff has not paid anything for it. However, this rule has been disputed, especially in cases of serious injury such as for people suffering serious burns.[459] The majority of present case law accepts therefore that the need for assistance calls for indemnification even if the services are actually performed by the wife without remuneration.[460]

The wife's claim: since there is no contract between the wife and the tortfeasor, the claim of the wife can only be based on article 1382 of the Belgian Civil Code.

The first issue raised by a claim for loss of earnings will be the causal link, since the loss of earnings results also from the wife's decision to stop working.[461]

Therefore, this claim will only be accepted if the loss of earnings is inferior to the costs that the husband would have incurred if he had hired another person to take care of him (corresponding to the market value of the services).

This outcome can also be based on the rule according to which the injured party is obliged to mitigate the damage.[462]

The second issue is that in some circumstances, the case law has accepted to indemnify the injured party himself for services during the period that he is unable to look after himself, even if the injured party

---

[459] R. O. Dalcq and G. Schamps, 'La responsabilité civile délictuelle et quasi-délictuelle, examen de jurisprudence (1987–1993)', RCJB 1995, pp. 737–8 at p. 770, no. 191.
[460] Cass., 30 novembre 1977, Pas., 1978, I, 351; Liège, 25 juin 1991, RGAR, 1992, no. 11.930; Liège, 11 mars 1988, RGAR, 1990, no. 11.737; Anvers, 29 avril 1988, BA, 991, p. 141; Corr. Tournai, 22 avril 1991, BA, 1991, p. 930.
[461] See R. O. Dalcq, Traité de la responsabilité civile, Tome II, Le lien de causalité, le dommage et sa réparation (1962) at p. 296, no. 2947.
[462] R. Kruithof, 'L'obligation de la partie liée de restreindre le dommage', RCJB, 1989, p. 12.

has not paid anything. For example, when his wife has performed the services.

In such a case, the wife's claim will be rejected, at least for the portion of the damage that has already been repaired.

## Italy

I. The case may be brought under article 2043 cc. Whereas the husband can recover from the tortfeasor and/or the insurer what he has expended for his own care (such as by hiring a nurse), courts might deny recovery of the wife's economic losses by pointing to the remoteness of the damage.

II. The Supreme Court, in *Dall'Olio v. Comp. Lavoro e Sicurtà*,[463] found the tortfeasor not liable towards the relatives of the victim. In that case, a husband had to stop work to look after his wife, who had been badly injured in a car accident. He sued the tortfeasor's insurance company for his lost earnings. The Supreme Court held that the damages were too remote. The argument was supported by the consideration that damages for personal injury claimed by the wife were intended to cover not only physical injuries but also all other expenses, including those incurred to hire a person to attend to her needs.

## Spain

I. In this case, the answer provided by the Spanish legal system definitely would be affirmative: the wife – *iure proprio* – can recover from the perpetrator of the accident.

II. As explained by legal scholars, anyone who can prove the existence of an actual injury resulting from a damaging activity may claim recovery.[464] In other words, each injured party may make a claim for the injuries that he has suffered, although he may not be immediately affected by the damaging activity.[465]

These ideas have been reproduced in the case law. There are many decisions of the Supreme Court which recognize a right of the injured

---

[463] Cass., 7.1.1991, no. 60, *GI*, 1991, I, 1, 1193, noted by Tedeschi; A. Baldassarri, 'La responsabilità civile', in P. Cendon (ed.) *Il diritto privato nella giurisprudenza* (Torino, 1998), p. 30.

[464] F. Pantaleón 'Comentario al artículo 1902', in *Comentario del Código Civil*, I (1991), p. 1994.

[465] J. Santos Briz, *La responsabilidad civil: derecho sustantivo y derecho procesal* (6th edn, 2 vols., 1991), pp. 212 and 221–6, R. De Ángel, *Algunas previsiones sobre el futuro de la responsabilidad civil* (Civitas, Madrid, 1995), p. 891.

party's relatives to direct a claim, in their own name, against the author of the accident. Thus, in the Supreme Court decision (First Chamber) of 9 February 1988, damages were awarded to the wife of a bricklayer who suffered an accident at work. Compensation was based on the fact that the couple's life together was affected, since the wife underwent pain and suffering by being permanently deprived of a normal relationship with her husband.

In the Supreme Court decision (First Chamber) of 30 July 1991, the husband of a woman suffering serious brain damage as a result of the negligent administration of anaesthesia in a surgical operation brought a suit in his own name. The Supreme Court recognized the husband's right of action and compensated him for the damages involved in dedicating time and money to care for his wife, being deprived of her company, and for his pain and suffering in contemplating her condition.[466]

Furthermore, two judgments delivered by the Fifth Chamber (administrative jurisdiction) of the Supreme Court are worth mentioning. In a decision of 23 February 1988, damages were awarded to the parents of a young boy injured by a policeman's gunshot. This decision is important because the Court expressly acknowledged the right of the plaintiffs to be compensated for costs incurred in travelling to their son's hospital, and for lost profits incurred as a result of the necessary personal assistance required by his serious condition.

The second decision of the Fifth Chamber to be mentioned is that of 25 April 1989. Here, the Supreme Court accepted an award of damages in favour of the parents of a child who was injured in an accident due to the negligent surveillance of a public swimming pool. The child suffered permanent neurological after-effects. This decision took account of the parents' pain and suffering and considered their future expenditures to care for the child who, as a consequence of the accident, required continuous assistance from other people to perform even life's most basic functions.

### Greece

I. The wife can claim compensation directly from the tortfeasor by virtue of article 929 CC, but only for an amount equalling half of the needs of an average household of that kind.

---

[466] For similar cases in which the victim's relatives and close friends are awarded damages, see Supreme Court decisions delivered by the First Chamber of 26.1.72, 2.2.73 and 23.4.92; Second Chamber, Supreme Court decision of 10.2.72, 17.5.73, etc.

II. In view of both criteria of causation (either foreseeability or inclusion of the interests protected by the rule infringed), we can readily conclude that the purpose of the prohibition on injury to one's body is mainly to protect the plaintiff's physical integrity, as well as the interests usually (i.e. foreseeably) related to it. Whether the plaintiff owns a business or not cannot be certain. Some people hire out their work and others work on their own as free professionals. Therefore, it is unknown and unforeseeable whether the victim's loss of ability to work causes economic loss to another person (his wife). Thus, the wife's lost earnings are not causally related to the tort committed and therefore her earnings are not indemnifiable.

Nevertheless, the wife may claim from the tortfeasor whatever her husband owed to her as his contribution to the common needs of their household, in accordance with his ability to do so, as articles 1390 CC and 1389 stipulate. This solution is based on article 929, sub-para.2 CC, which stipulates that compensation from the wrongdoer may also be sought by persons (apart from the victim) entitled *by the law* (not by a contract) to claim services or maintenance from the victim (the wife was entitled to ask her husband to contribute to the needs of the household).[467] Indeed the Greek courts directly implement in such cases article 929 sub-para.2 CC, in order to cover the part of the wife's loss that is equivalent to the value of the husband's contribution to the common needs.[468] It is self-evident that this liability lasts only while they remain married and do not divorce.[469]

III. Art. 929 sub-para.2 simply clarifies *ad hoc* the general clause of article 914 CC. Indeed damages provided by the law are foreseeable, because the law is already known and stable (by way of contrast, obligations provided by a contract can be foreseen only by the parties, usually not by everyone). This means that the additional expenses, which the wife incurred owing to her husband's inability to fulfil his legal obligation to contribute to the household, are damages provided by the law, thus foreseeable damages; therefore these damages are causally related to the victim's injury, i.e. indemnifiable damages.

---

[467] See, *ad hoc*, AP 172/1969; AP 583/1967; EphAth 730/1967 NoB 16, 1169; EphAth 553/1966 NoB 14, 443; EphAth 787/1991 NoB 19, 1161; A. Georgiades and M. Stathopoulos, *Civil Code Article by Article Commentary*, vols. II–IV (1979–1982), see article 928 and Commentary by A. Georgiades no. 27.
[468] AP 1433/1979; EfAth 10917/1979 NoB 28, 836.
[469] See, by analogy, EfAth 3311/1977 NoB 26, 236.

## England

I. The wife cannot recover her loss of earnings, but the husband can recover, and must hold in trust for her, an amount representing the cost of reasonable health care services that he might have hired in the absence of his wife's offer of voluntary care.

II. Loss of earnings resulting from the personal injury of another person is not recoverable in English law, even if the claimant is a close relative of the injured person, i.e. a husband or wife: see *Burgess v. Florence Nightingale Hospital for Gentlewomen*.[470] A reasonable amount can be recovered, however, *by the victim of the personal injury himself*, representing the probable commercial rate of hiring the care services of a professional health worker, to compensate a spouse or other close relative who offers voluntary care to the victim of a personal injury at the expense of earning his or her own livelihood. The measure of recovery is laid down in *Housecroft v. Burnet*.[471] That the money is held on trust for the caregiver is laid down by the House of Lords in *Hunt v. Severs*.[472] Equally recoverable are expenses disbursed in buying medicines or special equipment for the injured. The helping spouse has no legal right to this money against the injured person recovering it in their own name; but he or she is expected to turn the money into the family budget, holding it 'on trust' for the family: the loss of earnings of the spouse is, therefore, regarded as a 'family', rather than personal loss.

However, under no circumstances can the caring spouse recover loss of earnings not directly caused by the need of taking care of the injured: *Burgess v. Florence Nightingale Hospital for Gentlewomen*.[473]

III. I have discussed elsewhere arguments in favour of elevating earning capacity to a protected status in tort law similar to that accorded to real property interests.[474] Unfortunately, this is not yet the position of English law, and the exceptional recovery of family care losses is still a long way away from recognizing in principle the importance of earning capacity as an independent protected interest.

## Scotland

I. The wife cannot sue for the loss of earnings. Nor can the husband sue for the loss of earnings that she has suffered. However, he can sue

---

[470] [1955] 1 QB 349.   [471] [1986] 1 All ER 332, 342–3.
[472] [1994] 2 All ER 385.   [473] [1955] 1 QB 349.
[474] See E. K. Banakas, *Tortious Liability for Pure Economic Loss: A Comparative Study* (Hellenic Institute of International and Foreign Law, Athens, 1989), pp. 150 f.

to recover in damages an amount which equates to a reasonable remuneration for the necessary services which the wife has rendered to him. This amount he must then account for to his wife.

II. It was established in *Robertson* v. *Turnbull*[475] that 'where a person was injured, the defender did not owe a threshold duty of care to the victim's spouse or relatives who had suffered economic loss as a result of the injuries sustained'.[476] This is yet another example of irrecoverable secondary economic loss. Lord Fraser of Tullybelton stated the matter as follows:

> [T]his appeal raises the question whether a wrongdoer, whose negligence has caused physical injuries, but not death, to another person, can thereby incur liability in damages to any one other than the injured himself.[477]

In the case of death arising as a result of personal injuries sustained through the fault of a third party, Scots law allows a limited class of near relatives a right of action against the wrongdoer for *solatium* and loss of support. Their Lordships decided that this was not based upon any principle but was an exception, first established in *Eisten* v. *North British Railway Co.*,[478] from the general rule excluding such actions. Lord Fraser agreed with Lord Keith of Kinkel who, in *Jack* v. *Alex McDougall & Co.*, said that in his opinion 'it [was] clear that the right of action available in the case of the death of the spouse, or the parent or child, of the pursuer arises from breach of duty owed by the defender to the deceased, not of any breach of duty owed to the pursuer.'[479] Lord Fraser stated:

> With regard to principle, any extension of the right of action by relatives to cases where the victim had suffered non-fatal injuries would open the door to a wide range of claims by other persons... if these heads of claim [i.e. *solatium* and loss of support] were admitted, it is not easy to see any principle on which the right to claim for loss caused by non-fatal injury to another person should be restricted to his relatives... I do not think the restriction could be based on foreseeability, for surely it is not substantially more foreseeable that an adult will have obligations to his dependants than that he will have obligations to many other people who will suffer loss if he is disabled – for example, partners, employees, employers, creditors and others with whom he is in contractual relations. Yet claims by such persons are precluded, rightly in my opinion, as being too remote. That was decided long ago in *Allan* v. *Barclay*...'[480]

---

[475] 1982 SC (HL) 1, 1982 SLT 96 (HL).
[476] J. M. Thomson, *Delictual Liability* (Butterworths, Edinburgh, 1999), p. 191.
[477] 1982 SC (HL) 1 at p. 7.   [478] (1870) 8 M 980.   [479] 1973 SLT 88 at p. 90.
[480] 1982 SC (HL) 1 at p. 11.

He gave as a modern example *Reavis*.

It had already been established in *Edgar v. Lord Advocate*[481] that the pursuer himself was unable to recover damages for economic loss suffered by a relative as a result of the pursuer's injuries. The Lord President (Clyde), discussing the possible meaning of the averments in the case, said:

> This averment does not make it clear what exactly is the basis of this item of claim...it may mean that the pursuer is claiming against the defender for his wife's loss of wages [while looking after him]...[this] is irrelevant. The loss in question would be a loss sustained, not by the pursuer, but by his wife, and she is not a party to this action. The pursuer had no title to present his wife's claim.[482]

Thus, while the husband could sue for his own loss of earnings, that being of the nature of a derivative economic loss, i.e. deriving from his personal injuries and recoverable, he could not sue for his wife's loss of earnings. Lord Clyde continued:

> It would have been another matter altogether if the pursuer had actually paid some third party, or had entered into a contract to pay some third party for this domestic assistance...[it] could then have formed a relevant item in his claim for damages...It would be contrary to principle in our law that a pursuer should not only obtain domestic assistance for nothing without any obligation to pay for it, but at the same time to secure for himself payment for these services from the defender. Damages are payable only on proof of loss...Our law does not approach the ascertainment of a pursuer's damages by considering whether the wrongdoer is to be benefited or penalised, but by considering what loss the pursuer has sustained.[483]

The reason why the operative rule allows a sum to be recovered which is of the nature of a secondary economic loss is that the common law in some respects has been superseded by statute. As a result of s. 8 of the Administration of Justice Act 1982 (as amended by the Law Reform (Miscellaneous Provisions) (Scotland) Act 1990, s. 69) an injured person now has the right to recover reasonable remuneration for necessary services rendered or to be rendered in future, by a relative, as well as reasonable expenses incurred in connection therewith. The legislation emphasizes that it is the injured person and not the relative who has the title to sue with a corresponding duty to account to the relative for any damages recovered, though not explicitly for that part referable to future services.

---

[481] 1965 SC 67.   [482] Ibid. at p. 71.   [483] Ibid.

The decision to be made by the wife here is an economic as well as an emotional one. Presumably it would be better for the injured person to arrange for a healthcare provider if the amount of income forgone by the wife would be greater than would be paid to the healthcare provider and vice versa. At least if the wife feels that she could not leave it to another to care for her loved one, some of her losses will be offset.

III. Many of their Lordships involved in the *Robertson* v. *Turnbull* case had expressed the opinion that the position under the common law might not be ideal. For example, Lord Maxwell in the Outer House said that he appreciated 'on grounds of humanity there may be good arguments for giving a claim to close relatives of a person seriously injured but not killed',[484] while Lord Wilberforce felt the appellants' claim merited sympathy, and Lord Fraser considered that the law was harsh. All agreed, however, that it was for the legislature to alter the law.

The amendments in the Administration of Justice Act 1982 were similar to those in a draft Damages (Scotland) Bill proposed by the Scottish Law Commission (SLC) (Scot. Law Com. No. 51 (1978)). The work of the SLC involves recommending ways in which Scots law might be improved, and this is an example of their influence at work. Some initiatives come from the SLC themselves; in other instances the SLC is approached by others to come up with solutions to problems or inadequacies perceived to exist within the Scots legal system. Not all their recommendations are adopted by Parliament. Here, a decision was taken by the legislature to vary the common law rule in certain respects.

## The Netherlands

I. The spouse can claim insofar as the injured man could have claimed himself, had he availed himself of a private nurse.

II. This case, at least according to Dutch law, is considered to be a matter of damage *par ricochet*, and the Civil Code legislator explicitly intended for this claim to be subjected to the limits set out in article 6:107 CC, which states:

> If a person suffers physical or mental injury as a result of an event for which another person is liable, that other person is not only obliged to repair the damage of the injured person himself, but also to indemnify a third person for costs [...] incurred for the benefit of the injured, which the latter, had he incurred them himself, would have been able to claim from that other person.

---

[484] 1980 SC 108 at p. 116.

Article 6:107 CC allows this claim of damage *par ricochet*, but only insofar as the injured could have claimed them himself, had he himself suffered the damage. In the event of excess costs, the spouse cannot claim the excess.

As far as a claim based on article 6:107 is concerned, it is sufficient that an unlawful act has been committed vis-à-vis the physically injured party. It is irrelevant whether a duty of care existed *vis-à-vis* the third party. More than that, it is assumed that consequential damages suffered by the spouse as a result of physical injury to her husband cannot be claimed in any way. Even if the unlawful act that led to the injury was also unlawful *vis-à-vis* the spouse, any independant claim of hers in tort is blocked by article 6:107 CC.

Furthermore, it must be noted that the claim for 'shifted damage' is conditional on the existence and extent of a claim of the injured party himself. The liable party can raise the same defences that he would have had against the injured party. Consequently, if the injuries were partly caused by the husband's contributory negligence, this defence can be raised against the wife's claim as well.[485] If such a defence is raised successfully, an apportionment of the 'shifted damage' is made between the injurer and the spouse.[486]

III. When introducing article 6:107 CC, the legislature explicitly intended – from a socio-economic point of view – not to augment the total financial burden of those responsible for injury and their insurers in comparison to the legal situation that existed under the 'old' Civil Code.

Although substantive opposition to the limited number of claims and claimants exists in doctrinal writing, this example in particular shows that the limitation can be justified from a 'law and economics' perspective: if the spouse were allowed to claim her loss of income, even if it amounted to a substantially higher claim than the amount of loss that would have accrued to the injured himself, the law of damages would encourage economically inefficient behaviour. On the other hand, from the proposition that the outcome of article 6:107 CC in this particular

---

[485] See art. 6:107 ss. 2 CC, which reads: 'He who has been held responsible by the third party pursuant to the preceding paragraph can raise the same defences as he would have had against the injured person.'

[486] See art. 6:101 CC, which reads: 'Where circumstances which can be imputed to the injured have contributed to the damage, the obligation to repair is reduced by apportioning the damage between the injured and the injurer in proportion to the degree in which the circumstances which can be imputed to each of them, have contributed to the damage.'

example is justified, it cannot be deduced that it will always lead to a just and reasonable outcome.

## Germany

I. The wife herself cannot recover, but her husband has a claim against the tortfeasor in the amount of the market value of her services.

II. The wife's claim: the wife has no claim because none of her absolute rights as listed in § 823 (1) BGB was violated. Thus her loss is purely economic. In case of injury or death of one party, another party can recover financial loss only in the three cases expressly provided for in the civil code, i.e. funeral expenses (§ 844), loss of support (§ 844), or loss of services (§ 845). None of these exceptions apply (the husband has not lost her services, quite to the contrary), and courts and commentators have consistently refused to create new ones.[487] Nor is there any other basis for recovery in either tort or contract.

The husband's claim: it is clear that the husband has a claim under § 823 s. 1 BGB because of injury to his body and health. It is also clear that the cost of necessary services during the period of recuperation are part of the recoverable damages.[488]

The only question is whether this is also true if the services are being rendered gratuitously by a family member, e.g. because of the legal obligation of support between husband and wife (§ 1360 BGB). In case of a *permanent* need for services, § 843 (4) BGB expressly supports the claim. The *Bundesgerichtshof* has held that the same rule applies in case of temporary services. As a result, the injured person, i.e. the husband, has a claim against the tortfeasor in the amount of the fair market value of the services of his wife.[489] This may be less or more than her lost income.

III. The *Bundesgerichtshof* has honoured the letter of the rule that (non-injured) family members cannot recover their economic loss except in the cases listed in the code. Yet, it seems that allowing the injured person to recover the value of a family member's services violates the spirit of the rule. This is because allowing such recovery makes sense only if the money ultimately goes to the family member rendering the services. This is particularly true where the Court has allowed an injured child

---

[487] BGHZ 7, 30, at 33–4 (1952); BGH NJW 1979, 598; see also above Case 3 ('Cable III – The Day-to-Day Workers').
[488] In case of permanent need for services, this is expressly provided for in § 843 (1).
[489] BGH VersR 1978, 149, at 150.

to recover the costs that her parents incurred by visiting the child in the hospital.[490]

A careful reading of the respective opinions suggests, however, that the decisions are not driven only by the desire to compensate the victim or his family. The *Bundesgerichtshof* also wishes to honour a principle of German law which is closely akin to the common law collateral source rule: the wrongdoer must not benefit from the fact that the victim is entitled to gratuitous services from someone else (normally a family member).[491] Since it is impossible under German law to give the non-injured kin themselves a right against the tortfeasor, the Court allows the victim to claim the value of the services as part of his own damages.

Curiously enough, it is far from clear whether the family member rendering the services has any legal (as opposed to moral) claim to the money against the victim. It would be interesting to see what happens if the victim wished to keep the money for himself and was sued by his or her spouse (or parents, as the case may be).

## Austria

I. Under Austrian law, both the wife and the injured husband are entitled to sue for compensation. Both claims can be based on articles 1295(2) and 1325 ABGB.

II. The wife's claim: the wife can sue under the rule of transferred loss. Third parties who take care of the injured person, or pay for such services without wanting to release the tortfeasor from his duty to compensate, are entitled to compensation.[492] In such a case the loss typically affects a third person.[493]

The husband's claim: the husband has a claim under articles 1295(1) and 1325 ABGB because of the physical injuries and damage to his health. The average costs of necessary nursing care during the period of recuperation are part of the recoverable damages, even if these services were rendered gratuitously by family members.[494]

---

[490] BGH NJW 1985, 2757, at 2758; limited in BGH NJW 1991, 2340-2. See also concerning the claim of one spouse for costs incurred by the injury of the other spouse, BGH NJW 1979, 598.
[491] See BGH VersR 1978, 149, at 150. The Court cites § 843 (4) BGB which expresses exactly this principle.
[492] See OGH RZ 1976/84, ZVR 1976/23, SZ 48/199.
[493] See OGH RZ 1984/12, EfSlg 43.525; ZVR 1987/9 R. Reischauer, in P. Rummel (ed.), *Commentary on the General Civil Code*, vol. 2 (2nd edn, Vienna, 1992), § 1325 nos. 12, 17.
[494] See OGH SZ 25/318, JBl 1953, 547; SZ 62/71, ZVR 1990/48, JBl 1989/587.

III. The first policy behind the rule of transferred loss bears a close resemblance to the common law collateral source rule: the wrongdoer must not benefit from the fact that the victim can demand gratuitous services from family members.

A second consideration is that expenses for nursing care normally have to be borne by the injured party himself. Under certain exceptional statutory provisions, however, third persons are charged with these costs (e.g. as a result of duties emerging from marital consortium) and these persons are entitled to bring an action in their own name.

## Portugal

I. Following precedents, a Portuguese court would uphold the wife's claim for compensation for the loss of earnings arising from having to close her shop to look after her husband for the period (two months) when he was unable to look after himself.

II. There is no doubt that if the injured party needs the help of a third person, he himself could claim compensation for this damage. The peculiarity is only that the spouse is claiming compensation.

To give a positive response to a claim of this nature, the courts seek support in the rules of family law, which impose a 'duty of mutual succour and assistance' (art. 1674 CC) on spouses[495] or on parents the duty of 'watching over the safety and health of children' (art. 1878, no. 1).[496]

Acting in fulfilment of a legal duty, the spouse or children would have the right to be compensated, averting the argument that there was no nexus of causality.

In one decision, article 495, no. 2 of the Civil Code[497] was also invoked as a ground.[498]

III. The solution appears to be just and reasonable, giving due emphasis to moral and family aspects.

The aim of article 495, no. 2, conferring a right to compensation on some third parties, is to encourage the rendering of assistance to victims.

---

[495] Judgment of the Porto Court of Appeal of 4 April 1991, *Colectânea de Jurisprudência*, Tomo II, p. 254.
[496] Judgment of the Supreme Court of Justice of 16 December 1993, *Colectânea de Jurisprudência*, Tomo III, p. 181.
[497] Ibid, at 183.
[498] Compare our answer to Case 4 ('Convalescing Employee'), sub II.

**Sweden and Finland**

I. The state of the law is rather uncertain. While the wife has no claim if court practice is taken into consideration, in insurance practice the loss of earnings of a spouse tend to be compensated not in full but to the extent corresponding to what would have been the cost of professional assistance.

II. In principle, the wife should have no claim since the only kind of economic losses to be recovered by third parties in case of personal injuries are funeral expenses and loss of support (*SkadestL* 5:2 in Sweden, *SkadestL* 5:3-4 in Finland). Until now, no open exceptions to the statutory rule have been admitted[499] in case law that could build a basis for the wife's claim.

However, it is true that the strength of the 'third party rule' seems to be increasingly uncertain, as is shown by several decisions admitting with different artifices the recovery of some costs incurred, for example, by parents assisting injured children and so on.

In Sweden, the recently published final report of a government commission, which studied the problem of the amount of compensation for personal injury, proposed that compensation should include, besides the costs incurred by the injured person, also those incurred by persons who are 'specially close to him'. Such compensation to third parties would be limited to what is 'reasonable'.[500] A government report on the reform of the rules on the amount of compensation is also under preparation in Finland.

III. The uncertainty about the state of the law also depends on the fact that litigation in court about the amount of compensation for personal injury takes place in a relatively low number of cases, while the real source of law consists of the practice of the dispute resolution bodies within the insurance sector.

*Editors' comparative comments*

Case 10 ('The Dutiful Wife') presents a question of pure economic loss that arises in the context of the obligations of succour and support between husband and wife. The duties of family members to render support and assistance to one another are generally fixed by law. Thus, we

---

[499] In NJA 1982 s. 668 travel costs – but not loss of income – were granted to the son who travelled from Australia while his father was dying following a traffic accident.
[500] See SOU 1995: 33 Ersättning för ideel skada vid personskada, p. 41.

find a typical provision in French Civil Code article 212 declaring that *Les époux se doivent mutuellement fidélité, secours, assistance*. All the countries in this study agree that a husband who receives physical injuries may, in his own action against the tortfeasor, seek compensation not only for his injuries but *inter alia* for the reasonable cost of healthcare services that he has incurred in hiring someone to care for him during convalescence. A similar claim may also succeed, however, even when the husband did not need to hire or pay a nurse or other professional, but received the ministrations of a dutiful spouse. When the husband submits a claim for the reasonable value of her services as part of his overall recovery, it does not present a question of pure economic loss. But when the wife presents her own claim for compensation, as in our hypothetical case, it offers a clear example of our subject. Two preliminary comments may be made. First, the responses show that a majority of the countries permit the action, but the configuration is somewhat interesting, since Austria and Portugal join with the liberal countries on this question. Under our taxonomy this is a case of 'transferred loss', in that an award of compensation to the wife is not really an enlargement of the defendant's usual liability toward her husband. The fact that there is liability neutrality from a tortfeasor point of view undoubtedly allays fears of indeterminate and excessive liability. Secondly whether the action is brought by the husband or alternatively by his wife, the level of compensation will be reduced in either case to the reasonable value of the wife's services. It will not be measured by the revenues or profits that she would have earned at her store.

In Austria, Belgium, France, Greece, Portugal, Spain and the Netherlands, the wife's separate action for compensation would be recognized in tort. The loss might be variously described in France and Belgium as damage *par ricochet* or, in the case of Austria, as the 'liquidation of transferred loss'. As noted earlier, however, these systems would not base compensation upon the lost revenues brought about by closing down her store. As a matter of causation, the loss of these revenues is either not foreseeable, too remote, or not directly arising. Her claim would probably be restricted to the reasonable value or market value of her services. Put another way, she may claim to the extent that the husband could have claimed himself, had he hired a private nurse.

It is clear in England, Germany and Scotland that the claim for the reasonable cost of services can only be brought by the husband. According to the English and Scottish cases, an independent action fails because there is no threshold duty of care to prevent this type of loss to the dutiful wife; whereas in Germany she cannot show that any of her absolute rights have been infringed.

It will be observed that all of the systems would seem obliged to deal with a logical difficulty in this fact situation: if the wife cares for her husband without demanding or expecting compensation, then it may be objected that he has not experienced any loss since he has had no expense, and she has not been deprived of any gain since she had no such expectation. How can the action of either party succeed if there has been a donation of healthcare services? The Austrian and German answers allude to the probable reason. The policy behind these recoveries is based upon considerations similar to the 'collateral source' rule at common law. The wrongdoer should not benefit from the fact that the victim is entitled to gratuitous services from family members.

## Case 11: a maestro's mistake

### Case

Giorgio was about to buy a painting of considerable value by the famous artist Quirinalis from Franco. Before paying for the picture, however, Giorgio visited Quirinalis who (in the course of conversation) assured him that the work was authentic. Relying on this expertise, Giorgio then bought the picture. Sometime later, expert examination established without a shadow of doubt that the painting was skilled forgery. Unable to contact Franco, Giorgio has decided to sue Quirinalis.

### France

I. Giorgio will probably be able to recover his pure economic loss under article 1382 of the Civil Code if he can prove Quirinalis's fault in failing to detect the forgery of his own work.

II. Many cases and an abundant doctrine address the hypothesis of a disappointed buyer or seller of a picture suing the other party to the contract, but none deal with the tort law situation of a disappointed buyer suing a third-party expert, much less an artist consulted as an expert on his own *oeuvre*.

Giorgio can sue Quirinalis under article 1382, and will succeed if he proves Quirinalis's fault, the damage Giorgio himself incurred, and the causal link between the two. At first glance it may be thought that Quirinalis obviously committed a fault, whether intentional or not, in not recognizing that the painting was a fake. He caused Giorgio to buy the painting at a price certainly higher than the price of a fake. Giorgio's damage is thus the difference between the value of the forgery he owns and the price he paid for the supposed Quirinalis's painting. Giorgio has also to prove how Quirinalis's assertion of authenticity really induced him to buy the painting, and that he had not already made up his mind before talking to Quirinalis. As always, the amount of proof to be brought and the final amount of damages all lie in the discretion of the *juge du fond*.

Nevertheless, on second thought the question of Quirinalis's fault in this case is troubling and may not be so self-evident. Perhaps an artist (like any other person for that matter) is not a good judge in his own case. His realm may be the creative and he does not necessarily possess the analytical and technical skills for judging the provenance of art. Since Quirinalis may have had no training or experience in detecting skilful forgeries, he may not be held to the standards of an art expert and might not be considered at fault in these circumstances.

French judges would probably rely on a court-appointed expert from the art world to give an opinion as to the relative ease or difficulty for an artist to discern the authenticity of his own work.

III. In French tort law the distinction between intentional and non-intentional fault is not officially relevant to the scope of the damage award. The various degrees of fault are treated the same way for purposes of triggering the *réparation intégrale* to which the injured party is entitled. The rule is that all forms of fault oblige their author to repair entirely the damage he has caused. It may be true (though it seems impossible to verify it) that the judges tend to proportion the amount of the damages to the gravity of the fault, but it is certainly true they could not admit it without opening their judgment to being quashed by the Cour de Cassation. Accordingly, the question of fault is apparently the question of its existence, not its gradations, and this has an all-or-nothing effect upon the claim against Quirinalis for pure economic loss.

## Belgium

I. Giorgio has no claim against Quirinalis unless he intentionally misled Giorgio or he should have known that in acting as he did, he would cause him a loss.

II. Contract claim: Giorgio will normally have a contract claim against Franco, the seller with whom he had a contract. Subject to certain conditions, Giorgio could obtain the nullity of the contract based on mistake or on fraud (if Quirinalis acted on Franco's request) or he might obtain an indemnity covering the damage suffered.

Tort claim: since there is no contract between Giorgio and Quirinalis, the basis for a claim against Quirinalis will be article 1382 CC:

Any act whatever of man which causes damage to another obliges him by whose fault it occurred to make reparation.

Quirinalis will only be liable if Giorgio can prove fault, his damage and the causal link between the fault and damage.

The first issue is to prove the fault of Quirinalis. According to Belgian tort law, a fault in the sense of article 1382 CC is a violation of law or is a type of behaviour that the '*bonus pater familias*' would not have engaged in under the circumstances.[501]

---

[501] J. L. Fagnart and M. Denève, 'La responsabilité civile (1976–1984)', JT, 1986, no. 41, p. 297.

When the behaviour deviates from that of 'a normal person', it constitutes a fault, provided the damage was foreseeable.[502] If, in the course of conversation, Quirinalis assured Giorgio that the work was authentic without knowing that Giorgio was about to buy the painting, it would be very difficult to prove Quirinalis's fault.

The second issue concerns the question of causation. It may be difficult to prove that Giorgio bought the painting because Quirinalis assured him it was authentic. If Giorgio would have bought the painting anyway, there is no causal link.

The last issue for Giorgio to prove is that he suffered damage. This would not be the case if Franco had refused to guarantee the painting's authenticity in their sale agreement.

The only possibility for Giorgio to obtain reparation from Quirinalis is to prove that Quirinalis knew that the painting was not authentic and deliberately lied to Giorgio in order to induce him to buy it from Franco.

## Italy

I. Giorgio can sue Quirinalis and recover damages on the basis of article 2043 cc.

II. Here, the false information given by Quirinalis caused a loss in Giorgio's '*patrimonio*', which is the set of all assets and properties belonging to an individual. According to the Supreme Court decision in *Failla* v. *Paskwer (ved. De Chirico)*,[503] everybody should have a 'right to the integrity of the personal asset (*patrimonio*)'. Failla's right was violated because he wasted his money in purchasing a mere copy rather than the authentic artwork he wished to obtain. The Supreme Court also stated that Failla had a right to freely decide to buy or not, and that the misinformation he received from De Chirico violated his right to a free choice.

III. Under Italian law, a third party in good faith who 'interferes' with another party's contract is not considered liable *per se*. This is the basic rule, governing interference with contractual relations,[504] which was applied also by the Supreme Court in *Failla*. In this ruling, though, the liability threshold has been overcome by the finding of a gross negligence

---

[502] R. O. Dalcq and G. Schamps, 'La responsabilité civile délictuelle et quasi-délictuelle, examen de jurisprudence (1987–1993)', (1995), RCJB 536, no. 6.

[503] Cass., 24.5.1982, no. 2765, *FI*, 1982, I, 2864; in *GC* 1982, I, 1745, noted by A. Di Majo, 'Ingiustizia del danno e diritti non nominati', A. Di Majo, 'Il problema del danno al patrimonio', RDC, 1986, 298.

[504] Trib. Monza, 15.2.1996; Trib. Trieste, 13.7.1994.

in the conduct of the third party (the painter De Chirico) who was aware of the existence of the agreement between the plaintiff and the other party.

Legal scholarship[505] endorses the same solution, sponsoring plaintiff's extra-contractual remedy for those cases of third parties' tortious interference in contractual relations where third party's conduct is proved to be, at least, grossly negligent.

## Spain

I. There is neither case law nor specific doctrinal comments on this matter.

II. We believe that the most likely solution given by a Spanish court would be to deny that Quirinalis's behaviour could give rise to an action against him in favour of Giorgio: it seems clear that in the course of an informal conversation there is no duty of care. The idea of a 'duty of care' is not used in Spanish case law, nor by Spanish legal scholars.[506] Consequently, the most likely outcome would be to say that Quirinalis's behaviour was not negligent because he was only obligated to give an honest opinion. It goes without saying that the solution to the question raised in this case would be a definite yes if Quirinalis had acted in bad faith.

## Greece

I. In principle Giorgio has no chance of recovering against Quirinalis, unless the latter could be considered as contractually bound to examine the authenticity of the picture or unless he acted deliberately for an immoral purpose, which seems rather improbable.

II. As article 729 CC lays down, if a person has given advice or made a recommendation, he will not be liable for any loss resulting from it, unless he assumed responsibility by contract or acted fraudulently. It is thus *e contrario* clear that, if Quirinalis had already realised that the picture was a forgery, he would be liable as against Giorgio (according

---

[505] See Monateri, *La responsabilità*, p. 628; F. Ziccardi, *L'induzione all'inadempimento* (Milano, 1979), p. 58; G. Visintini, *I fatti illeciti*, I, *L'ingiustizia del danno* (Padova, 1987); G. Ponzanelli, 'Il Tort of interference nei rapporti contrattuali: le esperienze nordamericana e italiana a confronto' (1989), 6 Q 69.

[506] F. Pantaleón, *La responsabilidad civil de los auditores: extensión, limitación, prescripción* (1996), pp. 114–16, has recently attempted to introduce it.

to art. 919 CC as well, insofar as he acted deliberately and against good morals). Nevertheless, it is Giorgio who has the burden of proving Quirinalis's *wilful conduct*, otherwise, he has no chance of success in suing Quirinalis.[507] The reason is that a possible error on Quirinalis's part constitutes neither an unlawful act, nor a breach of contract: in the course of a simple conversation with Giorgio, he did not have an intention of creating legal relations, i.e. *the intention of binding himself*.[508] The Greek Civil Supreme Court is very careful in upholding an advisor's liability under article 729 CC. According to its decisions,[509] liability for advice or opinion without wilful conduct may only be imposed if the opinion is given as a counter-performance or if the advice serves the advisor's own financial interests. In such a case, the Supreme Court confirms an intention to bind oneself. Consequently the answer given by the Greek courts here would probably be negative.

A different solution could be proposed only by virtue of good faith and only very exceptionally. More particularly: Quirinalis might be considered as contractually bound, even without his own intention, if his declaration to Giorgio had objectively the meaning that he bound himself contractually, as for example, in case the opinion was given as counter-performance (see above). In this case Quirinalis would, of course, be in error as to his declaration according to article 140 CC, but nevertheless according to article 144, no. 2, he might not invoke his error in order to cause the annulment of the contract, as far as this would be in conflict with good faith.

Quirinalis might be liable only if his negligence in detecting the forgery was not considered this time simply as a fault, but as unlawful behaviour. This latter view of negligence (i.e., as an unlawful behaviour)[510] is grounded on articles 281 and 288 CC, which ordain that everyone should behave as the business customs require.

III. The line between contractual undertakings and gentlemen's agreements remain unclear. Civil law theories (e.g. the theory of *de facto* contractual relations), as well as methodology, general theory and philosophy of law, struggle to solve adequately the famous general problem of the limitation of 'area-free-of-law' (*Rechtsfreierraum*), where no liability may arise.

---

[507] See Karassis in Georgiades Stathopoulos, Civil Code art. 729 no. 5.
[508] Ibid., no. 2.
[509] AP55/1968 NoB 17, 161.
[510] See this view in M. Stathopoulos, *Contract Law in Hellas* (1995), no. 256. AP 81/1991 NoB 40, 715; EfAth 7453/1988 EllDni 31, 848.

**England**

I. Giorgio has a valid claim in tort against Quirinalis, provided it is established that both were aware of the seriousness of their exchanges concerning the painting, i.e. that Quirinalis knew that the reason for Giorgio's request of information was the purchase of the painting.

II. Giorgio will be able to sue Quirinalis under the principle of *Hedley Byrne* v. *Heller*,[511] for negligent advice.[512]

*Hedley Byrne* is generally considered as capable of allowing claims for economic harm due to negligent advice or information, provided such claims are capable of submission to its rule.[513] The rule states that a person reasonably relying on the advice or information of another who possesses, or claims to possess, the necessary skills, can recover economic loss caused by such advice or information being negligently wrong or inaccurate. The House of Lords has recently confirmed and somewhat extended *Hedley Byrne* in *White* v. *Jones*.[514] The special conditions of liability in English law for economic loss caused by negligent advice or information seem now to be as follows.

The duty of care is founded on the existence of 'close proximity' between plaintiff and defendant, a concept that seems to mean that the defendant knew, or ought to have known, that the plaintiff, as an individual identified to him and not merely as a member of a class of persons, would rely on his advice or information. Some cases demand that the defendant *intended* the plaintiff to rely on his advice or information;[515] there is in this writer's opinion no doubt that this close proximity exists in cases such as the present, where the defendant is the painter whose style was faked in the forged painting, choosing freely to advise the plaintiff, albeit without entering into a contractual relationship with him.[516]

'Reasonable reliance' of the plaintiff on the defendant's advice: this is, again, probable in cases such as the present, where the defendant should clearly be seen as being in a position to offer an expert opinion on a painting alleged to be one of his own. The only reservation could be: was, on the facts, the defendant aware of the purpose for which advice was sought?[517]

---

[511] [1964] AC 465.   [512] See also above, Case 7 ('The Careless Architect').
[513] See T. Weir, *A Casebook on Tort* (9th edn, Sweet & Maxwell, London, 2000), p. 67.
[514] [1995] 2 AC 207 (HL).
[515] See *Galoo Ltd* v. *Bright Grahame Murray* [1995] 1 All ER 16 (CA).
[516] See for a survey of the professions Weir, *Casebook*, pp. 84 ff.
[517] *Galoo Ltd* v. *Bright Grahame Murray* [1995] 1 All ER 16 (CA).

III. Liability for negligent advice or information has developed in the English law of negligence differently from that for acts or omissions. The main reason is that in a great number of cases of wrongful advice or information, the parties are so close, working in a business relationship and, but for the absence of either consideration or privity, there would have been a claim in contract. The courts do not wish (in such cases of close relationship and reliance) the risk of professional fault to be carried by the innocent party. But the limits of this liability are narrowly defined and closely policed by the courts, who have repeatedly denied recovery of losses suffered by more than one individual, not in personal contact with the defendant.[518]

## Scotland

I. Giorgio should at least be able to bring an action but whether he is successful depends very much on the particular facts of the case, the mere summary of which is given here. As such, it is not enough for one to say with greater certainty what the outcome would be. He does have an arguable case.

II. We are dealing here with negligent advice given, or a careless misrepresentation made, by Quirinalis as to the provenance of a work which, uniquely among men, he should have been in a position to establish. We are once more dealing with pure economic loss but, in an exception to the general rule, it was established in *Hedley Byrne* v. *Heller*[519] that in particular circumstances a duty of care exists not to make negligent statements which might be relied upon by others causing them pure economic loss. Rather than a duty of care being limited to fiduciary relationships, Lord Reid stated the following:

> I can see no logical stopping place short of all those relationships where it is plain that the party seeking information or advice was trusting the other to exercise such a degree of care as the circumstances required, where it was reasonable for him to do that, and where the other gave the information or advice where he knew or ought to have known that the enquirer was relying on him...A reasonable man, knowing that he was being trusted or that his skill and judgment were being relied on, would, I think, have three courses open to him. He could keep silent or decline to give the information or advice sought: or he could give an answer with a clear qualification that he accepted

---

[518] More in E. K. Banakas, *Civil Liability for Pure Economic Loss: A Comparative Study* (Hellenic Institute for International and Foreign Law, Athens, 1989), chs. 1 and 2.

[519] [1963] 2 All ER 575; discussed in Case 7 ('The Careless Architect') above.

no responsibility for it or that it was given without that reflection or enquiry which a careful answer would require: or he could simply answer without any such qualification. If he chooses to adopt the last course he must, I think, be held to have accepted some responsibility for his answer being given carefully, or to have accepted a relationship with the enquirer which requires him to exercise such care as the circumstances require.[520]

The leading case is now *Henderson and Others* v. *Merrett Syndicates Ltd and Others*,[521] and the leading speech that of Lord Goff of Chieveley. After considering a number of statements in *Hedley Byrne* and their application in the case, he stated:

[W]e can derive some understanding of the breadth of the principle underlying the case...it rests upon a relationship between the parties, which may be general or specific to the particular transaction, and which may or may not be contractual in nature. All their Lordships spoke of one party having assumed or undertaken responsibility towards the other...Further, Lord Morris spoke of that party being possessed of a 'special skill' which he undertakes to 'apply for the assistance of another who relies upon such skill'. But the facts of *Hedley Byrne* itself...show that the concept of a 'special skill' must be understood broadly, certainly broadly enough to include special knowledge. Again, though *Hedley Byrne* was concerned with the provision of information and advice...the principle extends beyond the provision of information and advice to include the performance of other services. It follows, of course, that although, in the case of the provision of information and advice, reliance upon it by the other party will be necessary to establish a cause of action (because otherwise the negligence would have no causative effect), nevertheless there may be other circumstances in which there will be the necessary reliance to give rise to the application of the principle...In seeking to contain that category of persons [to whom the maker of a statement owes a duty of care] within reasonable grounds, there has been some tendency on the part of the courts to criticise the concept of 'assumption of responsibility' as being 'unlikely to be helpful or realistic in most cases'... However, at least in cases such as the present, in which the same problem does not arise, there seems to be no reason why recourse should not be had to the concept, which appears after all to have been adopted, in one form or another, by all of their Lordships in *Hedley Byrne*...Furthermore, especially in a context concerned with a liability which may arise under a contract or in a situation 'equivalent to contract', it must be expected that an objective test will be applied when asking the question whether, in a particular case, responsibility should be held to have been assumed by the defendant to the plaintiff...In addition, the concept provides its own explanation why there is no problem in cases of this kind about liability for pure economic loss; for if a person assumes responsibility to another in respect of certain services, there is no reason why he should

---

[520] Ibid. at p. 486.   [521] [1995] 2 AC 145.

not be liable in damages for that other in respect of economic loss which flows from the negligent performance of those services. It follows that, once the case is identified as falling within the *Hedley Byrne* principle, there should be no need to embark upon any further inquiry whether it is 'fair, just and reasonable' to impose liability for economic loss...[522]

To begin to understand Lord Goff's reasoning, and the extent to which he sees his principle applying, it is necessary to have given a fairly full quotation. Later in the speech, however, Lord Goff expresses his view more succinctly by stating:

[I]n the present case liability can, and in my opinion should, be founded squarely on the principle established in *Hedley Byrne* itself, from which it follows that an assumption of responsibility coupled with the concomitant reliance may give rise to a tortious duty of care irrespective of whether there is a contractual relationship between the parties...[523]

If we look at the facts in this case and relate them to the various requirements that Lord Goff sets out, we can see that they may or may not be satisfied. None of the requirements is actually missing but not all may satisfy the court as being adequately present. Objectively, has Quirinalis voluntarily assumed responsibility for Giorgio's economic interests? One would have to know in what context, and with what knowledge of the situation, did Quirinalis assure Giorgio that the work was authentic. Was he assuring him that the actual work referred to was his, or merely that he had painted a particular work and assumed the one that Giorgio was referring to was it rather than a mere copy? As to the 'special skill', he would be expected to know what he had himself painted from a description but not necessarily, without actual inspection, whether a particular painting was his work or a copy of his work. Was his work regularly copied; was this the first example; were works often represented as being by him because the style was similar, even though he had never painted the particular subject matter; was this the first example, etc.? Without knowing this we cannot know whether Giorgio was relying upon Quirinalis's special skills or whether Quirinalis was applying those skills for the assistance of Giorgio. Likewise, we cannot know whether Quirinalis was aware that Giorgio would rely on his expertise in making his decision to purchase the picture. Was Giorgio a friend or a stranger to Quirinalis? What was the purpose of the visit to Quirinalis? Unlike professionals such as surveyors, solicitors and insurance agents,

---

[522] Ibid. at pp. 180–181.   [523] Ibid. at p. 194.

the artist was not being paid for his expertise, but then neither are employers giving references for former employees or banks answering enquiries about customers. As Lord Reid observed in *Hedley*, he could have kept silent or, at least, qualified his observations to protect himself. Despite all the variables, what is without doubt is that if an artist assures a person that a work is his in circumstances where he is in a position to give an authoritative assessment, then any apprehensions one might have in spending a vast sum purchasing a painting on grounds of a questionable provenance would be overcome. In the right circumstances the court may be convinced that this is another case suitable for the type of incremental development by analogy now favoured by the courts, and hold that Quirinalis had a duty of care to Giorgio which was breached.

III. Lord Pearce in *Hedley Byrne* stated the following:

> How wide the sphere of the duty of care in negligence is to be laid depends ultimately on the courts' assessment of the demands of society for protection from the carelessness of others. Economic protection has lagged behind protection in physical matters where there is injury to person and property. It may be that the size and the width of the range of possible claims has acted as a deterrent to extension of economic protection.[524]

Considerations such as these would determine whether Quirinalis would be found liable.

**The Netherlands**

I. Giorgio and Quirinalis do not have a contractual relationship; Giorgio's claim in tort will not succeed.

II. The reassuring information given by the artist led the buyer to believe that the painting was genuine. As far as liability for inaccurate information is concerned, Dutch case law has found that two tests are decisive.[525] First, it must be ascertained whether the person giving the information had (constructive) knowledge of the purpose for which the information would be used. This first test has been used in liability cases involving accountants, banks and notaries *vis-à-vis* third parties (i.e. other than their direct clients).[526]

---

[524] [1964] AC 465 at pp. 536–537.
[525] See, e.g., J. M. Smits, 'Aansprakelijkheid voor aan derden verschafte informatie; enige dogmatische en praktische kanttekeningen bij derden-aansprakelijkheid', in: R. P. J. L. Tjittes and M. A. Blom, *Bank & aansprakelijkheid* (Zwolle, 1996), p. 91 ff.
[526] See, e.g., HR 10.12.1993, NJ 1994, no. 667. Compare Smits 'Aansprakelijkheid', at p. 98.

Secondly, it must be established whether a reasonable person in similar circumstances would have acted upon the information, i.e. whether he would have taken the information seriously and would have justifiably relied on it. This second test is commonly used in cases on misrepresentation and the reliance on statements made in the course of closing contracts. It can be used in tort law as well.

In my view, a third factor must also be taken into consideration: whether there was a special relationship between the artist and the buyer, obliging the artist *to verify* the information. Of course, this third factor is of eminent importance. Does an artist being interviewed by a prospective buyer have a duty to this buyer to verify, to the best of his ability, the authenticity of a certain painting? If the assumption is correct that the artist had reason to think the painting real, and there were no counter-indications compelling him to question its authenticity, I do not believe he has a duty to the buyer to submit the painting to a (thorough) examination.

This duty might well arise if the buyer explicitly asks for the expert opinion of the artist. In that case, the artist might be under the obligation to verify his beliefs. However, this was not the actual situation; the buyer asked about the painting at odd moments in the course of normal conversation.

### Germany

I. Giorgio's chance of success is small. He probably has no claim against Quirinalis, neither in tort nor in contract. But this result is not free from doubt.

II. Tort claims: Giorgio has no claim under § 823 (1) BGB because Quirinalis did not violate any of his absolute rights. Instead, Giorgio's loss is purely economic.

Quirinalis would be liable in tort nonetheless if he acted wilfully and caused 'damage in a manner contrary to public policy' (§ 826 BGB). In that case, Giorgio could recover even pure economic loss.

Contract claims:

Quirinalis may be liable to Giorgio because he breached pre-contractual duties, arising from *culpa in contrahendo*, which he may have had even as a third party. In 2002, the BGB was amended and now codifies the principle of *culpa in contrahendo*, including the liability of third parties for violation of pre-contractual duties. In particular § 311 (2) and (3) now provide:

(2) An obligational relationship imposing duties according to § 241 (2)[527] also arises from:

1. the initiation of contract negotiations,
2. [not applicable]
3. similar business contacts.

(3) An obligational relationship imposing duties according to § 241 (2) can also be created vis-à-vis persons who are not intended themselves to become parties to the contract. Such an obligational relationship is created particularly if the third party claims a special degree of trust and thus considerably influences the negotiations or the conclusion of the contract.[528]

Thus, the question then becomes who exactly may be liable for *culpa in contrahendo*. It is generally recognized today that besides the prospective partners in contract themselves, an agent may be liable as well if he has a particular economic interest in the contract, or if he claims particular expertise and trust.[529] The reason is that in such a situation, the other party will be influenced by, and rely on, the agent rather than the principal. Thus, had Quirinalis been Franco's agent there would be little doubt – in light of Quirinalis's special expertise – about his liability to Giorgio.

The problem is that Quirinalis was not Franco's agent. Yet, the *Bundesgerichtshof* has occasionally held third parties liable for *culpa in contrahendo* even though they were not agents. The basis for their liability was the special trust that they enjoyed, the particular expertise they proffered, or the strong influence on the making or execution of the contract they exercised.[530] These cases come perilously close to the present one although they are distinguishable on various grounds, the explanation of which would require a dissertation in its own right. Suffice it to say that the defendants who were not agents of one party but still held liable to the other for *culpa in contrahendo* either had an economic interest in the contract, or were somehow closely involved in its making or execution.

---

[527] § 241 (2) provides: 'An obligational relationship may, according to its content, impose a duty on either party to be considerate of the rights and interests of the other party.'
[528] The basic liability provision for breach of any duties arising within obligational relationships is now § 280 (1) BGB.
[529] The agent is then known as a *Sachwalter* which roughly means attorney (though obviously not attorney-at-law); see BGHZ 14, 313, at 318 (1954); BGH NJW-RR 1989, 110, at 111–12; D. Medicus, *Bürgerliches Recht* (18th edn, 1999) Rd.-Nr. 200–200a; O. Palandt, *Bürgerliches Gesetzbuch* (Beck, Munich, 2000), 675 BGB Rd.-Nr. 6 and § 276 BGB Rd.-Nr. 97.
[530] BGHZ 56, 81–82 (1971); BGHZ 70, 337 (1977).

In the present case, however, it seems that Quirinalis had neither an economic interest nor anything at all to do with the contract between Franco and Giorgio. Thus, Quirinalis would be held liable based *solely* on his particular expertise. There is no support in either case law or literature for such a result. It seems that it would also violate § 675 (2) BGB and simply go too far.[531]

III. The ultimate question is whether Quirinalis should be considered to be within the purview of the contractual relationship between Franco and Giorgio – in which case he may be liable to Giorgio for *culpa in contrahendo* – or completely outside of it, in which case his liability could only rest in tort.

Ultimately, it is not entirely clear exactly where the limits of third-party liability for *culpa in contrahendo* are located. The *Bundesgerichtshof* has been criticized for having pushed these limits too far already.[532]

If Quirinalis acted wilfully, he would be liable in tort in any event, and if he was merely negligent, holding him liable for giving a gratuitous opinion without apparent economic interest would be questionable. German courts are not likely to make this argument openly, but they are sure to be influenced by it nonetheless.

### Austria

I. Giorgio has a claim against Quirinalis under article 1300 ABGB.

II. The question is whether the claim is based on contract or *culpa in contrahendo*. Article 1300 ABGB holds an expert liable 'when he gives, for a consideration, negligently bad advice in matters of his art or science'. It is not clear what the notion 'for a consideration' really means.

In a recent decision, the Austrian OGH held an investment consultant liable for the financial advice that he gave to a woman who thereupon invested her money into an account opened by the main defendant. This defendant went bankrupt. Although the investment consultant – the second defendant in the case – had not charged a fee for his recommendation, the OGH obliged him to pay for the loss the woman had suffered because he 'expected a commission from the first defendant'.[533] Today,

---

[531] See W. Fikentscher, *Lehrbuch des Schuldrechts* (9th edn, Walter de Gruyter, Berlin, New York, 1977) ss. 320–1 (Rd.-Nr. 523) § 675 (2), reads as follows: 'A person who gives advice or a recommendation to another is not bound to compensate for any damage arising from following the advice or the recommendation, without prejudice to his responsibility resulting from contract, delict, or other statutory provisions.'

[532] D. Medicus, *Bürgerliches Recht* (1999), Rd.-Nr. 200b.

[533] See OGH JBl 1985, 38.

the formula 'for a consideration' is understood by the courts as meaning 'not solely for altruistic motives'.[534]

In a much older case, the OGH awarded compensation for false information given by a travel agent about the flight connections between Reval and Helsingfors. The plaintiff was entitled to sue the travel agent for loss of earnings on the ground of breach of 'precontractual obligations'.[535]

According to courts and learned scholars, a 'business contact' is also sufficient ground for the assumption of a quasi-contractual relationship. The same is true with cases where the defendant ought to have been aware that the injured party would make his decision dependent on his advice.

In the present case, Quirinalis may expect to gain personal advantage from the sale of the picture. Additionally, his professional advice creates special trust. Together, these two aspects may have sufficient weight to justify the imposition of liability on him. If it had been obvious to Quirinalis that Giorgio solely relied on his expertise, he would without any doubt be liable.

III. Article 1300 ABGB is of outstanding importance in cases of pure economic loss. Pursuant to this provision, two categories are to be distinguished: if the expert consciously gives bad advice, he will be liable in tort. If his wrongful advice is due to mere negligence, some additional aspects must be given for a quasi-contractual liability to be created.

## Portugal

I. Giorgio's chances of succeeding in an action against Quirinalis depend on the demonstration that the painter realised he intended to buy a painting and that the guarantee of authenticity, supplied by the author himself, was a crucial element in the decision to make the contract.

Given these presuppositions, it would be hard for Quirinalis to escape censure for his particularly blameworthy conduct, which would be an abuse of the law (art. 334). Non-liability would be the equivalent of accepting a *venire contra factum proprium*.

In any case, the unlawfulness presupposes an especially qualified fault here. It would be necessary to examine the circumstances of the case to see if this exists.

II. It is not impossible that a contract was concluded between Giorgio and Quirinalis, namely, a 'contract of guarantee'. One of the exceptions to

[534] Cf. OGH ecolex 1992, 84.   [535] OGH SZ 17/98.

the rule of non-liability for information (established in no. 1, art. 485 CC), even for negligence as established in article 485 no. 2, would have to be confirmed.

But, to judge from the experience of everyday life, this is not usually the intention of the parties. With respect to contracts, Portuguese law expressly requires the so-called 'awareness of declaration'.[536] With this, the possibility of resolving problems of liability for statements by accepting the existence of contracts for advice or information concluded by tacit declaration (as happens in Germany) is removed.

As there is no unlawful act under the terms of article 483, no. 1, there remains recourse to the theory of abuse of the law. On this level, we do not feel that its application in this case would raise major questions on the part of either doctrine or case law.

III. As stated in Case 5 ('Requiem for an Italian All Star'), section III, there is no specific provision concerning the abuse of law in matters of tort. This is why we are arguing that there should be recourse to the provision contained in the general part of the Civil Code,[537] which is restricted to requiring a 'manifest abuse' of the limits imposed by the 'good faith' or '*boni mores*' (or by the 'economic or social goal' of the right).

Whenever we are faced with an act that is contrary to *boni mores*, if the agent has foreseen the possibility of damage and accepts it accordingly (*dolus eventualis*), it seems that an abuse of law should be affirmed for the purposes of civil liability. But the letter of the law lets us go further, when this is justified, foregoing the proof of malicious damage: that is, serious or gross negligence would be enough.[538]

---

[536] Article 246: 'The declaration is without any effect if the declarant is unaware that he is making a transactional declaration or was coerced by physical force to issue it; but, if lack of awareness of the declaration was through fault, the declarant is obliged to compensate the declaree' (*declaratário*).

[537] Some authors do not think there should be recourse to the theory of abuse of law in the case where the issue is a simple one of generic freedom to act: the 'abuse' would presume the existence of a law that was abused: e.g. M. A. Carneiro Da Frada, *Uma 'Terceira Via' no Direito da Responsabilidade Civil?* (Almedina, Coimbra, 1997), pp. 61–3. But then the existence of an unwritten principle of law of 'generic prohibition of injurious conduct contrary to good practice' (at p. 63) is unnecessary when we have a provision which can give direct support; nor does that viewpoint harmonize with the perspective of the author of the preparatory work: A. Vaz Serra, 'O Abuso do Direito (em Matéria de Responsabilidade Civil)', *Boletim do Ministério da Justiça*, 85, 243, n. 41.

[538] J. Sinde Monteiro, *Responsabilidade por Conselhos, Recomendações ou Informações* (Almedina, Coimbra, 1990), pp. 545 f.

For the case in the questionnaire, it could be discussed whether an appeal to good faith or *boni mores* should be made. This is because good faith presupposes, in principle, a special relationship[539] and in the case under discussion there seems to exist only a qualified social contact.[540]

## Sweden and Finland

I. It should be possible, but far from certain, for Giorgio to obtain compensation.

II. We are here facing another very good example of 'pure economic loss' in the Swedish/Finnish meaning, i.e. an economic loss arising without connection with anybody suffering personal injury or damage to things. According to the statutory rule in *SkadestL* 4:2 (Sweden) and *SkadestL* 5:1 (Finland), this is in principle to be compensated when it is consequent upon a criminal behaviour, although the text and the preparatory works of the Tort Liability Acts 1972 and 1974 do not completely bar compensation should the courts find strong reasons for it. Courts have been very restrictive in granting exceptions to the general principle.

In a case such as this, it is possible to draw an analogy with one of the leading cases concerning liability for pure economic loss in the absence of a crime, i.e. NJA 1987 s. 693, where the Supreme Court affirmed the liability of a real estate evaluator who negligently stated the value of a real estate for the losses caused to a bank which, on the basis of the certificate, gave a loan to the real estate owner, who later went bankrupt.

Some scholars advocate the possibility of according compensation if the wrongful information is due to gross negligence (and *a fortiori* if it is intentional, although still outside the limits of criminal law). They criticize the fact that information and advice, even on commercial matters, provided within a relation pertaining to private life enjoy what has been called a 'torts law immunity'.[541] However, the idea that such immunity could be set aside when the wrong information is provided intentionally or with gross negligence has never been tested in court.

The same is true for the theory specially advanced by the leading scholar in the field of pure economic loss, who wants to weigh the existence of factors which induced plaintiff to strongly rely on the

---

[539] A. Menezes Cordeiro, *Da Boa Fé no Direito Civil*, vol. II (Coimbra, 1984), p. 1223.
[540] Cf. Fikentscher, *Schuldrechts*, § 27 I, and D. Medicus, *Schuldrecht I, Allgemeine Teil* (9th edn, Beck, Munchen, 1996), § 16 II.
[541] J. Kleineman, *Ren förmögenhetsskada* (1987), p. 513.

information (in this case, for example, Quirinalis was assumed to be the original painter and thus the person most qualified to discover a forgery).[542]

*Editors' comparative comments*

Analysis of the answers to this case confirms the crucial role played by the notion of pure economic loss in revealing operative, as opposed to theoretical, borderlines among the classic fields of private law.

Perusal shows that in the particular circumstances of the case, most of the European countries examined (excepting the Dutch, Swedish and Finnish fact-driven positions) allow the recoverability of the plaintiff's loss whenever the defendant's conduct is particularly blameworthy, although Austria, Germany and Greece tend to achieve the same result by means of rules other than tort law rules.

Again, from a technical point of view, one notes that England and Scotland, at least in principle, bridge the gap between their pragmatic regimes and the liberal ones by admitting recoverability through reference to 'close, almost physical, proximity' and the criterion of 'reasonable reliance' as set forth in *Hedley Byrne*. A partial turnabout from current comparative standpoints occurs, on the other hand, in those civil law countries which rely on a rule of liability (contractual in Greece and Germany, quasi-contractual in Austria) implemented when a consideration has been given to the defendant – the provider of the bad advice.

In the circumstances of this case, it comes as no surprise to find that, contrary to what happens when the result is channelled through straightforward rules (or attitudes), the endeavour to strike a balance between the interests of the giver and recipient of the 'bad advice' makes each contributor carefully weigh every single aspect of the cause of action, no matter on what the latter is grounded – be it common tort law, common contract law, general principles such as 'abuse of the law', statutory or codistic rules. Nor is it surprising to find that in many legal systems (Belgium, Germany, Greece, Italy, Portugal, Spain and the Netherlands) liability depends on proof of a high degree of fault upon Quirinalis – which appears to be the key factor in deciding whether to leave the loss as it stands or to shift it to the painter. Both these orientations simply answer a general need that transcends the legal solution to be given to a particular case.

[542] Kleineman, *passim*.

Needless to say, one cannot take seriously a view which either regards tort liability as a system of independent modules, or attributes a role unaffected by the specific circumstances of the case to each element of the cause of action. Remarks such as 'some interests are protected against certain types of conduct, others against other types of conduct',[543] or *la diligence requise à l'égard des biens garantis est beaucoup plus grande que celle requise à l'égard des intérêts purement économiques*,[544] are nothing but the 'nutshell' outcomes of a longstanding scientific tradition[545] that should be taken for granted by every tort specialist, regardless of whether he or she is a civil or common lawyer.

---

[543] J. S. Colyer, *A Modern View of the Law of Torts* (Pergamon Press, Oxford, 1966), p. 30. See also, e.g. H. T. Terry, 'Proximate Consequences in the Law of Torts' (1914) 28 *Harvard Law Review* 10, at 15, 26; D. Payne, 'Foresight and Remoteness in Negligence' (1962) 25 *Modern Law Review* 16; W. L. Prosser and W. P. Keeton, *On the Law of Torts* (5th edn, St. Paul, 1984), pp. 205 ff., 296 ff.; E. Deutsch, *Fahrlässigkeit und erforderliche Sorgfalt* (Köln, 1963), pp. 62 ff., 157 ff., 171.

[544] J. Delyannis, *La notion d'acte illicite considéré en sa qualité d'élément de la faute délictuelle* (Paris, 1952), p. 119. See also C. Aubry and C. F. Rau, *Cours de droit civil français* (6th edn, ed. P. Esmein, Paris, 1956), (Eng. trans., St. Paul, 1969), § 444 bis, 445): 'certain interests are not protected, either because they are counterbalanced by interests judged to be more important for society, such as the case of damage caused by lawful competition, or because they cannot be fully safeguarded, and because anyone suffering an injury to them has the advantage of being able to inflict the same inconvenience upon others, as in the case of reasonable disturbances of neighbourhood.'

[545] See a short survey in C. von Bar, *The Common European Law of Torts*, vol. II (Oxford University Press: Oxford, 2000), pp. 249–71; M. Bussani, 'Perfiles comparativos sobre la responsabilidad civil: La culpa al servicio de los débiles', in J. F. Palomino Manchego and R. Velasquez Ramirez (eds.), *Modernas tendencias del derecho en America Latina*. Actas de la I Convención Latinoamericana de Derecho (Grijley, Lima, 1997), pp. 393 ff.; M. Bussani, *La colpa soggettiva. Modelli di valutazione della condotta nella responsabilità extracontrattuale* (Cedam, Padova, 1991); M. Bussani, *As peculiaridades da noção de culpa: um estudo de direito comparado* (Livraria do Advogado, Porto Alegre, Brazil, 2000). Some further examples in R. Demogue, *Traité des obligations in général*, 1, III (Paris, 1923), p. 378; J. B. Ames (1905) 18 *Harvard Law Review* 411, 412; W. A. Seavey, 'Negligence – Subjective or Objective?' (1927) 41 *Harvard Law Review* 1, at 13; Restatement of the Law, Torts, 2d, § 298 d; H. De Page, *Traité élémentaire de droit civil belge*, II (2nd edn, Bruxelles, 1948), pp. 1012 ff.; A. Sourdat, *Traité général de la responsabilité ou de l'action en dommages-intérêts en dehors des contrats* I, 2 (Paris, 1872), pp. 614 ff.; J. J. Honorat, *L'idée d'acceptation des risques dans la responsabilité civile* (Paris, 1969), *passim*, esp. pp. 28 ff., 89, 230; G. Viney and P. Jourdain, *Les conditions de la responsabilité* (2nd edn, Paris, 1998), pp. 491 ff.; P. Cane, *Atiyah's Accidents, Compensation and the Law* (5th edn, London, 1993), pp. 5, 95; H. L. A. Hart and A. Honoré, *Causation in the Law* (2nd edn, Oxford, 1985), pp. 40, 77, 149 ff., 482 ff.; F. Chabas, *L'influence de la pluralité de causes sur le droit à réparation* (Paris, 1967), p. 92.

# Case 12: double sale

## Case

Antonio sold his flat to Betty, and then to Cinzia who (1) knew or (2) did not know about the prior sale. Immediately afterwards, Antonio left the country with the money. Cinzia was able to complete the formalities relative to the sale of the property more rapidly than Betty. Will Betty be able to obtain compensation from Cinzia for the economic damage she has incurred?

Would the answer be the same in the case of a computer that was first sold to Betty but then resold and delivered to Cinzia?

## France

I. If Cinzia did not know that the flat or computer had been previously sold to Betty, Betty has no action in tort against her under article 1382 CC. However, where Cinzia knew of the prior sales and intentionally interfered, Betty has a good action in tort, not to recover her economic loss but rather to rescind the second sale (either of flat or computer) and have her ownership in the property recognized.

II. The sale of the flat: the principle observed in French sales law is consensualism. When property is sold, the right of ownership is transferred even before delivery has been made, as soon as there is a meeting of the minds. However, the consensualism principle encounters certain limits, especially when immovable property is to be transferred. In that instance, the new owner must properly register the property so as to be able to assert good title against third parties. If a seller sells the same property twice, the 'second' buyer will be considered to be the real owner if she was the first to register, *unless* she was aware of the prior sale.[546]

So, in our case:

(1) Cinzia knew about the prior sale of the flat. Betty can sue Cinzia in tort under article 1382 CC. If she shows that Cinzia was aware of the prior sale, i.e. that Cinzia was acting in bad faith, Betty will be able to have, as a matter of tort law, the remedy of *réparation en nature*. The contract of sale between Cinzia and Antonio will be rescinded since she

---

[546] G. Cornu, *Droit civil, Introduction: les personnes et les biens* (7th edn, Montchrestien, 1994) p. 366.

must be considered as the real owner of the flat.[547] Indeed, this is what French law calls the tort of intentional interference with contractual relations, an action which French judges recognize as wrongful under article 1382.[548] In this case, however, there would be no recovery of economic loss but instead direct recognition of Betty's right of ownership.

Cinzia did not know about the prior sale of the flat: assuming Cinzia acted in good faith, Betty will not be able to recover against her in tort, nor have the sale rescinded. Rather, and very theoretically, she would have only the right to be compensated by Antonio because of his breach of contract, but since Antonio left the country with her money, she suffers an economic loss for which she has no practical remedy.

The sale of the computer: where movables (*meubles corporels*) such as a computer are concerned, there must be delivery for the sale to be effective against third parties. The buyer who gains possession of the good is considered to be the real owner. Article 1141 CC solves the conflict that may arise between two successive buyers by giving the preference to the one who first obtained possession, *unless* this party knew about the prior sale.

Article 1141 is confirmed by article 2279 which states: 'In matters affecting movables, possession is equivalent to title' (*En fait de meubles, la possession vaut titre*).

Cinzia knew about the prior sale of the computer: Betty can sue Cinzia under article 1382 CC and have the sale rescinded as in the case of the flat. This again is the tort of intentional interference with contractual relations. There will be, however, no economic loss to recover in this case since Betty can claim the thing itself.

Cinzia did not know about the prior sale: if Cinzia acted in good faith, she is protected by articles 1141 and 2279. Betty cannot have the sale rescinded, and as in the case of the flat, she suffers an economic loss for which she has no practical remedy.

## Belgium

I. If Cinzia knew about the prior sale, Betty can recover her damages from Cinzia. If Cinzia did not know about the sale, Betty has no claim

---

[547] Civ. 3, 22 mars 1968, D. 1968, 412, note Mazeaud. See G. Viney, 'Introduction à la responsabilité', in J. Ghestin (ed.), *Traité de droit civil* (1995), no. 205.
[548] See V. Palmer, 'A Comparative Study (From a Common Law Perspective) of the French Action for Wrongful Interference with Contract', (1992) 40 *American Journal of Comparative Law* 297.

against her. This is true whether the object of the sale is a flat or a computer. The answer is clear and undisputed.

II. Since there is no contract between Betty and Cinzia, the claim for damages against Cinzia will be based on article 1382 CC:

Any act whatever of man which causes damage to another obliges him by whose fault it occurred to make reparation.

In the present case, article 1382 CC will be the basis of a specific action. According to a theory, *la tierce complicité*, a third party to a contract (Cinzia) can be held liable for the breach of a contract (the sale agreement between Antonio and Betty) if he participates in the breach of that contract.

However, the third party will be liable only if the plaintiff can prove not simply that the defendant knew of the existence of the contract (and the obligations resulting from it), but also knew that in acting as he did, he participated in the breach of the contract.[549]

This theory does not make any distinction between movable and immovable assets.

The answer is therefore identical whether the object of the sale is a flat or a computer.

## Italy

I. Betty can successfully sue Cinzia only if the latter is proved to have been in bad faith at the time when the contract (between Cinzia and Antonio) was made.

II. The flat: the first purchaser not registering her contract in the immovable assets records cannot sue the second purchaser in bad faith using the contractual action under art. 1483 cc. The immovable assets records (*trascrizione immobiliare*), arts. 2643 ff. cc, and especially art. 2644(2), reads: Effects of transcription: "After first transcription, any successive transcription or registration of: titles against the author cannot be enforced, even if the title had been acquired at a prior date."

---

[549] Cass., 22 avril 1983, RW, 1983–1984, p. 427; RCJB, 1984, p. 359; Liège, 13 mai 1991, JT, 1992, p. 38; Bxl., 21 février 1996, JLMB, 1996, p. 1214; Mons 11 janvier 1995, RDC, 1996, p. 732; J. L. Fagnart, 'La tierce complicité et les usages honnêtes en matière commerciale', RDC, 1989, p. 469; C. Parmentier, 'Un nouveau cas de tierce complicité', RDC, 1993, p. 284.

*Article 1483: Total eviction from thing*

If the buyer suffers total eviction from the thing as a result of rights enforced in it by a third person, the seller is bound to compensate him for damage according to Article 1479 but using the general tort action provided by art. 2043.[550]

The solution enforced by courts until 1982 was that the second purchaser who completed the formalities before the first purchaser is not liable – even if he had notice of the first sale.[551]

In *Magli* v. *Vetrugno*,[552] the Supreme Court changed its mind and stated that the second purchaser is bound to pay damages in tort (art. 2043 cc), but specific performance is not allowed, so the second can retain the immovable property. Thus, as Cinzia knows about the sale, Betty can recover damages in tort against Cinzia.

Computer: if a movable, the computer, has been sold to a person and then delivered to another, article 1153 cc applies:

*Article 1153: Effect of acquisition of possession*:

He to whom movable property is conveyed by one who is not the owner, acquires full ownership by means of possession, provided that he be in good faith at the moment of consignment and there be an instrument or transaction capable of transferring ownership.

Ownership is acquired free of rights of others in the thing, if they do not appear in the instrument of transaction and the acquirer is in good faith.

If Cinzia was in bad faith and knew about the prior sale to Betty, she will be obliged to return the computer and compensate Betty's losses. Otherwise, if she was in good faith the computer is hers and no claim can be made by Betty.

III. The Supreme Court in *Magli* v. *Vetrugno*[553] reached a solution sponsored by Sacco[554] in the early 1960s.

## Spain

I. If Cinzia acted in good faith, she would keep the flat (or the computer) and Betty could not obtain compensation from her. If Betty can

---

[550] An example is offered by Gazzoni, *Manuale di diritto privato*, VI (6th edn, Napoli, 1996), p. 676.
[551] Cass. 1.6.1976, no. 1983, *GC* 1976, I, 167.
[552] Cass. 8.1.1982, no. 76, *FI* 1982, I, 1, 1548 note by Pardolesi; *GI*, 1982, I, 1,1548, noted by Cirillo; *GC*, 1982, I, 607; *RCP*, 1982, 174, noted by Benacchio.
[553] But see also *Troebinger* v. *Urthaler*: Cass., 22.11.1984, no. 6006, *MGC* 1984.
[554] R. Sacco, 'L'ingiustizia del danno di cui all'art. 2043 cc, *FP*, 1960, 1, XV, 1420 ff, at p. 98.

prove that Cinzia acted in bad faith, Betty would have a right to gain possession of the flat (or the computer) so she would have no claim for compensation against Cinzia.

II. In theory, the problems presented in Case 12 would never arise in Spain due to the infrastructure of our legal system. The conveyancing system currently existing in Spanish law requires both a valid contract in order to transfer ownership and the delivery of the thing (art. 609 CC). The thing in question may be delivered, basically, both by material means as well as by executing a certain type of document (public deed).

In the event that neither of the two sales executed by Antonio was completely performed (i.e. neither Betty nor Cinzia obtained possession of the flat), article 1473 CC, which regulates what is known as a double sale, would apply. This provision determines which of the two purchasers is given preference and therefore ownership of the flat.

Article 1473 establishes several preferential criteria (registration at the Land Registry, date of the contract), but in every case the existence of good faith is essential:[555] unless there is good faith (unawareness at the time of agreement that the property had already been sold),[556] Cinzia may not acquire ownership of the flat. This good faith requirement is justified on the basis that the party who co-operates with the seller (by carrying out the second sale) in order to deceive the first purchaser, deserves no protection. There is abundant case law and expert legal opinion supporting this premise.[557]

Therefore, if by applying article 1473 CC Cinzia turns out to be preferred, that would imply that she would have acted in good faith (or at least that Betty could not prove Cinzia's bad faith), and thus, Betty would have no claim against her. Betty would have to fall back upon her contractual claims against Antonio.[558]

Let us imagine for a moment that Antonio sells the flat to Betty and delivers it. From that moment onwards Betty would be the owner of

---

[555] Article 1473 does not require the existence of good faith literally in all its norms; nevertheless, both the case law and the scholars have introduced this good faith element in all the art. 1473 preferential criteria.

[556] Supreme Court decisions delivered by the First Chamber, of 30.1.60 and 3.10.63.

[557] See Supreme Court decisions delivered by the First Chamber of 31.12.61, 17.12.84 and 30.6.86; amongst the legal experts, e.g. L. Díez-Picazo and A. Gullón, *Sistema de Derecho Civil*, II (7th edn, 1995), p. 313, García Cantero, 'Comentario al artículo 1473', in *Comentario del Código Civil*, II (1991), p. 932, J. Lacruz, *Elementos de derecho civil* (3rd edn, 1994), p. 45 and A. Molina García, *La doble venta a través de la jurisprudencia* (1975), p. 285.

[558] García Cantero, 'Comentario', p. 933.

the flat and Antonio's subsequent sale to Cinzia would not be a 'double sale', but a 'sale of another person's property' (therefore art. 1473 would not be applicable). Under these circumstances, theoretically it would be possible for Cinzia to make recourse to the law regulating acquisition *a non domino*. However, since the norms regulating acquisition *a non domino* in Spanish law require the purchaser's good faith, the solution would be the same.

These conclusions do not vary in the case of the double sale of a movable. There, good faith is also an essential requisite to be fulfilled by the purchaser who is eventually protected (art. 1473). In our case (a computer sold and delivered to Cinzia), the solution would consist in Cinzia asserting her ownership if she acted in good faith (and Betty would have no claim against her); if Cinzia acted in bad faith, Betty would be given preference and could demand that the computer be returned.

**Greece**

I. Betty has in principle no rights against Cinzia, because of privity of contract between Betty and Antonio.

II. By the contract of sale the purchaser, i.e. Betty, acquires from the vendor, i.e. Antonio, only the right to seek the transfer of the flat or the computer to her; she does not acquire ownership of the flat or the computer. The ownership of the computer or the flat may be transferred by another agreement between the parties (possibly made at the same time as the sale). Nevertheless, the legal effects of this last agreement take place only after the transcription of the immovable, i.e. registration of the flat's transfer in the public records (according to art. 1033 CC) or after the delivery of the movable, i.e. placing Betty, the new owner, in possession (art. 1034 CC). Thus we must divide the legal solution to this case into two parts.

As to the sale of the flat: (1) the principle. If Cinzia registered that the flat was transferred to her before Betty registered her own agreement, then Cinzia (not Betty) would acquire ownership of the flat. At that point the fulfilment of Antonio's performance to Betty is already legally impossible, owing to his wilful misconduct. Antonio is no longer the owner of the flat, so that he can no longer transfer the flat to Betty (*nemo plus juris ad alium transferre potest quam ipse habet*; art. 239 CC *e contrario*). As article 335 CC provides in such a case, the creditor of the obligation, i.e. Betty, would have the right to be compensated by Antonio for the value of his flat. Betty has in principle no rights against Cinzia, because the contract between Betty and Antonio does not bind Cinzia as *res inter alios acta*. Furthermore, Cinzia owed no contractual obligation to Betty (as she was contractually related only to Antonio), nor was her behaviour unlawful (sale is a lawful and valid legal act).

(2) The exception: if Cinzia knew of the prior sale of the flat, however, her behaviour might – under specific circumstances – perhaps be considered immoral. In this case, Betty can sue her directly for compensation equal to the flat's value according to article 919 CC, which lays down that anyone who wilfully and immorally causes prejudice to someone else is obliged to compensate him.[559] Nevertheless, Greek courts are especially careful when implementing article 919 CC, in order not to put the stability of contracts at risk. In view of this, the Greek courts do not consider any breach of contract in favour of a third party *eo ipso* as tort.[560] This happens only exceptionally, with specific prerequisites, among which are the following circumstances:

(1) the tortfeasor has pre-planned the breach before concluding the contract;[561]
(2) the tortfeasor is a third party inciting the breach of the contract, and he is not a competitor of the injured party acting with legitimate motivation.[562]

As to the sale of the computer: the same solutions will be reached if Cinzia has already taken delivery of the computer, because in this way (as already mentioned, by virtue of art. 1034 CC) she became its owner, so that the fulfilment of Antonio's performance to Betty is already legally impossible, owing to his wilful misconduct, exactly as above.

### England

I. Sale of the flat: Betty will not be able to obtain compensation from Cinzia, whether or not the latter knew of the prior 'sale'.

Sale of the computer: Betty will be able to obtain compensation from Cinzia, and/or ask for the computer to be handed to her, only if Cinzia knew of the prior sale.

---

[559] Even more so, if because of the specific circumstances of the contract between Antonio and Cinzia, the latter is in conflict with good morals, this latter contract is null according to art. 178 CC, so that Cinzia is not yet owner of the flat and Betty can of course claim its transfer directly from Antonio, as if nothing had happened up to now.
[560] EfAth 2896/1977 NoB 26, 223; 4734/1978 EDP 1979, 133.
[561] AP 317/1968; EfThes 187/1964.   [562] EfThes 2169/1958 NoB 7, 195.

II. Sale of the flat: the case is, unfortunately, not very hard to imagine as likely to occur,[563] in the light of current conveyancing rules and practices in England and Wales. We should assume that 'completing the formalities' means that Cinzia has exchanged contracts, completed the transfer of possession and registered title in her name, before Betty was able to do any of these things. There is, indeed, no 'sale' of real property in English law before these formalities are completed; an agreement to sell is not binding on the parties (it is always understood as made 'subject to contract', meaning 'subject to the completion of formalities'). That being the case, Cinzia is the only rightful owner/possessor of the flat. The facts disclose no evidence of any other kind of possessory right (e.g. tenancy) vested in Betty by virtue of her prior 'agreement' with Antonio. Therefore, Betty has no rights whatsoever as far as the flat itself is concerned, against its new rightful owner/possessor, Cinzia. Of course, she might have an action *against Antonio*, for *deceit*.[564] However, such an action is not available to her against Cinzia for the economic damage, even if Cinzia knew of the prior 'sale', as there is no evidence that Cinzia herself did or said anything to deceive Betty into acting in a way financially detrimental to herself. Cinzia's knowledge of the prior 'sale' is, alone, not able to amount to deceitful conduct. To quote a leading English tort lawyer: 'England has not yet quite evolved a general principle comparable to that of § 826 BGB, but it may be...that it is actionable to cause *intentional harm* to another by *wrongful means*'.[565] The facts in the present case disclose neither intention to harm nor use of wrongful means.

Sale of the computer: the rule of English law is that a buyer of goods can sue a third party for conversion if he has ownership of the goods, even though he has not yet possession of them.[566] However, here Cinzia may be entitled to keep the computer since she has obtained possession of it by a disposition of a seller (Antonio) who, although no longer owner (ownership having passed to Betty), remained in possession of it. This

---

[563] The practice of completing with a person other than the one to whom the seller originally agreed to sell is known as 'gazumping'; the new British administration has announced a review of the law of property to eliminate it from England and Wales (Scotland has different rules that do not allow such a practice to occur).

[564] See *Derry v. Peek* (1889) 14 AC 337 (HL).

[565] T. Weir, *A Casebook on Tort* (9th edn, Sweet & Maxwell, 2000), p. 567 (emphasis in original text).

[566] See, e.g. *North West Securities Ltd v. Alexander Breckon Ltd* [1981] RTR 518. English law does not have a rule of *traditio*, as many other European legal systems do, that follow Roman law in this respect.

exception to the principle *nemo dat quod non habet* is laid down in the Sale of Goods Act 1979, s. 24. But this is so only if Cinzia is in good faith. If she were aware of the prior contract, she will be liable in conversion and also for inducing breach of contract. Although conversion as a tort normally leads to an award of monetary damages, the court has power to order the restitution of the chattel (Torts (Interference with Goods) Act 1977, s. 3).

III. In the case of the double 'sale' of real property, English law finds it hard to provide at the moment a remedy to a person in Betty's position as, in the absence of a legally binding agreement if contracts have not been exchanged, third parties who complete first can be liable neither for inducing breach of contract, nor for intentional harm using wrongful means. In the case of the double sale of goods, English law provides adequate protection to the first lawful buyer who acquires ownership, if the second buyer is not buying in good faith.[567]

## Scotland

I. As to the flat, if Cinzia did not know of the prior sale, Betty would have no remedy against her. Even if she knew of the prior sale, although not impossible, it is highly unlikely that Betty will be able to obtain compensation from Cinzia in delict for the flat. Cinzia has not committed a fraud in her own right as she has not deceived Betty. One way is if she knew of the prior sale, and the court could be convinced that she was liable in delict for conspiracy to injure Betty in league with Antonio by unlawful means. However, this would be a novel use of the delict fraught with difficulties. Perhaps a more straightforward way, which may have success, would be the intentional economic delict of inducement of breach of contract. Under conveyancing law, however, if Cinzia knew of the prior sale, Betty could have her title reduced and her own substituted resulting in Cinzia incurring the loss instead of herself.

As to the computer, Betty will be able to recover the computer from Cinzia if property in the computer had passed to Betty at the time of the original sale, even though delivery of it to her had not occurred – but only if Cinzia did know about the previous sale. If Cinzia did not know, or if the property had not passed to Betty, then Betty could not

---

[567] Although the relevant tort rules are by no means clear and rational: see Weir, *Casebook*, pp. 491–6.

recover possession. If property had not passed to Betty at the time of the original sale, but Cinzia did know about it, then Betty would probably have a delictual action against Cinzia on general principles of *culpa* (i.e. loss caused by wrongful conduct). The most likely form of this would again be inducement of breach of contract. Betty would also have an action in restitution against Cinzia.

II. First, we shall consider the heritable property, the flat. This is an example of fraud and also involves Scots conveyancing law. The usual consequence of fraud is pure economic loss, as has occurred here. Where fraud is established, the courts in Scotland allow recovery of damages even though the loss is purely economic. This is in contrast to the situation with unintentional conduct. One obvious reason for this is that with intentional delicts 'there is a built-in limitation on the range of potential pursuers'.[568] The fraud has been perpetrated by Antonio, and against him Betty has both a contractual and a delictual remedy. Antonio has breached his contract since the title deed will contain a Clause of Warrandice, if not express then implied, which guarantees that Antonio will pass a good title – and he has not owing to his subsequent action. He has put himself into the position where the property is no longer registered in his name because he provided the means whereby Cinzia could (and did) win a race to the register (i.e. the Land Register of Scotland where it applies, or the Register of Sasines where it does not as yet). Until registration a right is personal (*ius in personam*), which gives one rights merely against the granter of the deed; upon registration it is real (*ius ad rem*), which gives one rights against the world at large. Betty could recover the price that she has paid as well as other expenditures, as the court would seek to return her to the position she was in before the contract was formed. Betty has no contract with Cinzia and therefore has no contractual remedy against her.

As to the delict of fraud in Scots law, Erskine has defined it as 'a machination or contrivance to deceive'.[569] The first thing to say is that if Cinzia knew nothing about the prior sale then she could not be liable in intentional delict in any shape or form. She may have been so reckless as to whether there was a prior sale in circumstances when she should have been put on notice and made inquiries, but it would be hard to establish such a thing and such speculation leads us nowhere. Let us assume that

---

[568] *Stair Memorial Encyclopaedia, The Laws of Scotland* (Law Society of Scotland, Edinburgh, 1996), vol. 15, p. 388, para. 586 (written by J. M. Thomson).
[569] Erskine, *Institute* III.1.16

she either knew about the contract or she did not. Lord Herschell LC in *Derry* v. *Peek* describes fraud as 'a false representation made by the defendant knowingly, or without belief in its truth, or recklessly, careless whether it be true or false, with the intention that the plaintiff should act in reliance upon the representation, which causes damage to the plaintiff in consequence of his reliance upon it'.[570] By inducing Betty to contract with him for the sale of the flat, accepting the price, and then intentionally disposing of the subject matter of the contract in direct contravention of one of the undertakings that he made in contracting with the result that Betty incurs a loss, Antonio will be liable for fraud in delict.

The practical problem is his absence, and hence Betty looks to Cinzia. With respect to Cinzia, the delict of fraud could not be established since the central requirement of the delict, i.e. a misrepresentation, is missing. Betty has not been deceived in any way by Cinzia because Cinzia has made no representation to Betty. Betty has been deceived by Antonio. The reality of this is not affected in any way by Cinzia either knowing or not knowing of the prior sale. Cinzia would not be liable in delict for fraud to Betty. It is assumed that there is no delict of conspiracy to commit fraud in Scots law because there is one other alternative, the conspiracy to injure, which would seem to encompass such a thing. Again, as with fraud, as we are dealing with intentional conduct we do not have the problem of the general rule against allowing damages where the loss is only economic. Though there are no cases, it is possible that if Cinzia knew of the prior sale then she could be found liable in delict for conspiracy to injure Betty. Walker states:

> Conspiracy has been defined as consisting of an agreement of two or more to do an unlawful act or to do a lawful act by unlawful means; to be actionable actual damage must have resulted. Most of the cases have dealt with trade rivalry, but the principle is not limited thereto...The wrong consists in the agreement or combination of two or more persons to use unlawful means or to do an unlawful act, calculated to, and actually causing, damage to the pursuer's interests. Bare agreement is not civilly actionable and the wrong is committed only if the combination is put into effect and damage to the pursuer results.[571]

The House of Lords in the case of *Quinn* v. *Leatham* had held that 'if A and B combine together with the intention to harm C, then A and B are liable in delict for harm caused to C as a result of their combination or

---

[570] (1889) 14 AC 337 at p. 374.
[571] D. M. Walker, *The Law of Delict in Scotland* (2nd edn, 1981), pp. 927–8 (footnote omitted).

conspiracy against him'.⁵⁷² The problem would be in establishing that there was actual agreement between Antonio and Cinzia. Also, although in the case of an unlawful means conspiracy the pursuer need only establish that the conspirators had an intention to harm the pursuer,⁵⁷³ this may be difficult to establish. It is unlikely that Betty would take this route as it is fraught with complications.

A more fruitful alternative, if Cinzia knew of the prior sale, would be the delict of inducement of breach of contract. Again, as this is an intentional delict we do not have a problem with the fact that the loss is purely economic. In *British Motor Trade Association* v. *Gray*, Lord Russell approved the following description of the delict:

[B]y the law of Scotland an actionable wrong is committed by one who intentionally and without lawful justification induces or procures someone to break a contract made by him with another, if damage has resulted to that other, provided the contract creates contractual relations recognised by law.⁵⁷⁴

According to Walker, the 'justification for this is that a violation of a legal right (including a contractual right) committed knowingly is a cause of action'.⁵⁷⁵ This principle, first applied in contracts of service, has been applied subsequently in other contractual situations. It is probable that it would be applied in a contractual situation such as in the present case. Thomson focuses upon the necessity for the party inducing the breach to intend harm to the party suffering loss.⁵⁷⁶ Arguably, Cinzia's intention is not to harm Betty but to obtain the flat for herself. At the same time, it is apparent that she is not concerned that she harms Betty in the process. Is this an intention to harm? Walker, looking to the requisite intention, writes:

It does not, however, matter whether the defender had a malicious motive, i.e. acted from ill-will or malevolence. Nor need the intention have been to cause any damage by the breach, still less to have caused the precise kind or extent of harm which in fact ensued. It may even be that a defender is liable if, in the knowledge of the existence of a contract, he does something, which has as its direct consequence the breach of that contract.⁵⁷⁷

Upon this interpretation of the delict it would appear that Cinzia would find herself liable.

---

⁵⁷² [1901] AC 495 (HL). J. M. Thomson, *Delictual Liability* (Butterworths, Edinburgh, 1999), p. 41.
⁵⁷³ *Lonrho plc* v. *Fayed* [1992] 1 AC 448.    ⁵⁷⁴ 1951 SC 586 at p. 603.
⁵⁷⁵ Walker, *Law of Delict in Scotland*, p. 919.    ⁵⁷⁶ Thomson, *Delictual Liability*, pp. 33–4.
⁵⁷⁷ Walker, *Law of Delict*, at pp. 920–1 (footnotes omitted).

Betty has a more straightforward alternative. If she is able to establish that Cinzia knew about the prior sale, then under Scots conveyancing law she would be able to bring an action to obtain a decree of reduction of Cinzia's contract with Antonio on the ground that Cinzia was not in the circumstances in *bona fide*, being aware of the prior contract.[578] Once the decree had been registered in the Register of Sasines, then the title would revert to Antonio and she would be able to register her own title. The situation is slightly complicated if the title is registered in the Land Register, since that is intended to provide a guarantee of title rather than just a record of title as is the case with the Register of Sasines. A decree of reduction cannot be recorded in the Land Register. Under s. 9 of the Land Registration (Scotland) Act 1979, rectification of the register by the Keeper is permitted where 'the inaccuracy has been caused wholly or substantially by the fraud or carelessness of the proprietor in possession'.[579] Thus Betty must establish fraud on the part of Cinzia in her argument to obtain an order for rectification of the register. It is possible that for this particular purpose the courts may accept a rather broad definition of fraud, allowing her to satisfy the requirements of the 1979 Act. Once rectified, Betty's own title would be registered. If Cinzia were in ignorance of the prior sale and thus acting in *bona fide* then, having won the race to the register, she would have a good title and Betty would be unable to obtain a reduction of her title having no grounds upon which to seek it.

As to the computer, in Scotland under the common law it used to be the case that a contract to sell goods had no effect on the transfer of ownership of the goods and the real right in them remained with the seller until delivery to the buyer had occurred. All the buyer had was a *jus in personam*. This has been changed by statute. Under the Sale of Goods Act 1979, where the goods are specific or ascertained, the property passes in them to the buyer at such time as the parties intend it to pass.[580] This is determined by the terms of the contract, the conduct of the parties and the circumstances. If no different intention appears then a number of rules are set out for ascertaining the intention.[581] So, even though the computer has not been delivered, it is possible that property in it has passed to Betty. In Scotland, the general rule is that the purchaser of goods obtains no better title to them than the seller possessed.[582] It is immaterial in Scots law that the sale may have taken place in a market overt.[583] So, if property has passed to Betty then Cinzia will only

---

[578] *Rodger (Builders) Ltd v. Fawdry* 1950 SC 483.  [579] Section 9(3)(iii).
[580] Sale of Goods Act 1979, s. 17.  [581] Section 18.  [582] Section 21.
[583] Gloag and Henderson, *The Law of Scotland* (10th edn, Green, Edinburgh, 1995), at p. 231.

have a *jus in personam* against Antonio. Therefore, if Cinzia knows that the computer has already been sold then she will have no better title than Antonio had when he sold it to her. However, if Cinzia was unaware of the prior sale then she will obtain property in the computer, leaving Betty with a remedy against Antonio only. The reason for this relates to provisions in the 1979 Act concerning sales by ostensible owners which aim to protect those who purchase from them. In particular, it provides:

> Where a person having sold goods continues or is in possession of the goods, or of the documents of title to the goods, the delivery or transfer by that person, or by a mercantile agent acting for him, of the goods or documents of title under any sale, pledge, or other disposition thereof, to any person receiving the same in good faith and without notice of the previous sale, has the same effect as if the person making the delivery or transfer were expressly authorised by the owners of the goods to make the same.[584]

What matters is continuity of possession regardless of the alteration of the legal title under which possession is held.[585] This would fit the situation where Antonio continued to hold the computer after the sale to Betty. So if Cinzia is unaware of the prior sale she will be able to keep the computer. Betty will be left pursuing Antonio.

Where delict may play a role is if property had not passed to Betty at the time of the original sale and Cinzia did know about the sale, then Betty would probably have a delictual action against Cinzia on general principles of *culpa* (i.e. loss caused by wrongous conduct). Though the court would have to view Cinzia's conduct as wrongous, they most probably would. Again, we are looking at inducement of breach of contract which we have discussed above.

III. This is an example where the pursuer's remedy would appear to lie more appropriately in other areas of the law. Complications arise in trying to do justice to parties who purchase in good faith, which results in complications for those who have been the victims of prior fraudulent behaviour.

## The Netherlands

I. A claim in tort against Cinzia can only be successful if she had knowledge of the prior sale. However, actual knowledge of the prior sale in itself does not render Cinzia's behaviour unlawful.

---

[584] Section 24.  [585] Gloag and Henderson, *Law of Scotland*, at p. 232.

II. According to Dutch law, the sale of real estate does not coincide with transfer of legal ownership. The sale of a flat will almost always be concluded prior to transfer of ownership. A deed, drafted by a notary public, and public registration of this deed are compulsory for successful transfer of ownership (art. 3:89 CC). So, it must be assumed that Cinzia has acquired legal ownership and Betty has not. Betty can sue debtor Antonio for damages (art. 6:74 CC also art. 7:22 CC).

Suing Cinzia for damages is not possible if Cinzia had no knowledge of the prior sale. According to Dutch law, Cinzia could not have known of the prior sale by checking the public registries. A mere sales agreement cannot be registered;[586] therefore, Cinzia cannot be blamed for not checking the public registries.

If Cinzia actually knew of the prior sale, Betty's claim in tort might be more successful. Actual knowledge of the prior sale *per se* does not render Cinzia's behaviour unlawful.[587] More than just having knowledge of the sale, Cinzia must consciously have taken *advantage* of Antonio's breach of contract. The Dutch Supreme Court has chosen, on the basis of art. 6: 162 CC, a case-by-case approach in this area: the circumstances of the case at hand decide the unlawfulness.[588] Among the circumstances mentioned in case law are knowledge of the severe damage that the prior buyer would suffer, the special position of trust that the second buyer enjoys with the seller and the resulting influence on the seller.

If Cinzia acted unlawfully *vis-à-vis* Betty, she could be forced to transfer ownership to Betty. This would indemnify Betty by other means than payment of damages.[589]

The answer would be the same if a computer had been sold instead of a flat. The only difference might be that ownership had already passed on to Betty, since no formalities but the transfer of (constructive) possession of the computer would have to be fulfilled (art. 3:90, also 3: 114, 115 CC). In that case, the question would not be whether Cinzia was liable for damages, but whether Betty or Cinzia had acquired legal ownership. In general, the buyer who has acquired real rather than

---

[586] HR 17.5.1985, NJ 1986, no. 760. A bill presently pending before the Dutch Parliament (Bill no. 23 095) will, eventually, introduce the possibility of registration of sales agreements, prior to legal transfer of ownership.

[587] See HR 3.1.1964, NJ 1965, no. 16, HR 17.11.1967, NJ 1968, no. 42, HR 18.6.1971, NJ 1971, no. 408, HR 27.1.1989, NJ 1990, no. 89.

[588] See A. S. Hartkamp, *Verbintenissenrecht; deel III – De Verbintenis uit de wet* (Mr. C. Asser's handleiding tot de beoefening van het Nederlands Burgerlijk recht) (10th edn, Zwolle, 1998), no. 51b.

[589] See HR 17.11.1967, NJ 1968, no. 42.

constructive possession, in good faith and for value, is considered to have acquired legal ownership. If the computer has indeed been delivered to Cinzia, the question is whether the computer was delivered (i.e. *constituto possessorio*) to Betty first. If so, then Cinzia acquires ownership if she acquired it in good faith and for value. Otherwise, she will have to give the computer to Betty. If the computer had not been delivered to Betty first, then Cinzia might have acquired legal ownership. But if she had knowingly taken advantage of Antonio's breach of contract (see above), she might be forced to transfer ownership to Betty. Legal cause for this compulsory transfer would be the tort committed by Cinzia *vis-à-vis* Betty.[590]

**Germany**

I. Betty has no claim against Cinzia. This is true regardless of Cinzia's knowledge, and for flats and computers alike.

II. Sale of the flat: Betty has no contractual relationship with Cinzia, so a claim for damages would have to rest in tort. Cinzia has not violated any of Betty's absolute rights, thus no claim under § 823 (1) BGB arises. A contractual right, such as Betty's against Antonio, is merely a 'relative' one not protected under this provision.

As in the previous case, the only conceivable basis for a tort claim is § 826 BGB which does allow recovery for pure economic loss, but requires that Cinzia acted wilfully and against public policy. If Cinzia did not know of the previous sale to Betty, she did not act wilfully to begin with. But even if she did know, she would not be liable because intentional interference with someone else's contractual rights does not, in and of itself, violate public policy. There is no obligation to surrender one's own interest to the contractual rights of another.[591]

In order to hold Cinzia liable under § 826 BGB, Betty would thus have to show special circumstances which made the interference with her contractual rights particularly reprehensible, such as a conspiracy between Antonio and Cinzia or the employment of improper means.[592] The violation of public policy is a question to be answered in light of the totality of circumstances in the individual case, and the requirements are rather strict. In the present scenario, there is no indication that

---

[590] See HR 17.11.1967, NJ 1968, no. 42.
[591] See BGHZ 12, 308, at 317–18 (1954); BGH NJW 1979, 1704, at 1705.
[592] See BGH NJW 1981, 2184, at 2185.

Cinzia did anything but to pursue her own, legitimate interest and beat Betty to the finish. This is clearly not enough to violate public policy.

Sale of a computer: the result would be exactly the same. This result will surprise lawyers from many, if not most, other countries. They will reckon that Betty has acquired a property interest in the computer through the contract of sale so that she can claim violation of an absolute right under § 823 (1) BGB. Under German law, however, this is not the case. A contract of sale has no effect whatsoever on the parties' property rights. Instead, with immovable as with movable property, transfer of title requires additional action by the parties. Without such action (i.e. without transfer of possession and an agreement that title shall pass, §§ 929-931 BGB), Betty had no property right in the computer and thus no tort claim under § 823 (1) BGB.

III. Liability under § 826 BGB is an exception which is by and large narrowly construed. To hold someone in Cinzia's position liable would essentially elevate merely contractual claims to the status of an absolute right and protect it generally in tort, i.e. even in the absence of special circumstances. This would violate the very principles on which German tort law rests.

### Austria

I. Whether Cinzia knew or did not know about the sale basically makes no difference: in both cases Betty does not have a claim against Cinzia. The same is true in the case of the sale of a computer first to Betty and then to Cinzia. However, an action by Betty against Cinzia either in the case of the flat or the computer sale is available if Betty in fact occupied the flat (the computer) and Cinzia knew or should have known about this occupation.

II. Cinzia knew or should have known about the prior sale of the flat to Betty.

In either case there is generally no action for Betty against Cinzia. Under Austrian law, Betty only owns a right *in personam* (a claim based on obligation) against Antonio and no property right (claim *in rem*) against any tortfeasor.

Rights *in personam* are generally not protected against infringements by third parties, even when this party was aware of the prior sale. Article 1295(2) ABGB demands wilful action against good faith in order to compensate such losses. In Betty's case she would have to prove, for example, a conspiracy between Antonio and Cinzia or the use of improper means.

However, Betty's legal position changes when she had already moved into the flat and Antonio afterwards sold it for a second time to Cinzia, who knew or negligently failed to learn of Betty's occupation. Then Betty might sue for restitution of her property on the ground of article 1323 ABGB, irrespective of Cinzia's ownership.[593] The infringement of an occupier's right, under the Austrian case law in tort, leads to equal treatment with cases of real property rights. Courts and scholars expressively speak of a 'right *in personam* manifested by occupation'.

If restitution is impossible or impractical, or if Betty does not want the restitution of the flat, she is entitled to receive compensation for her pure economic loss. This result complies with the rule that even pure financial losses are recoverable in tort law if the protected right is tangible and evident.[594]

Betty's claim against Cinzia when Betty did not move into the flat: if a right *in personam* is not manifested by possession, the only basis of a tort claim – as stated above – is article 1295(2) ABGB. Betty has to prove a conspiracy between Antonio and Cinzia or the use of improper means.[595]

Sale of a computer: the results are exactly the same for the reasons indicated above. If Betty had taken possession of the computer and Cinzia had only been granted 'constructive possession' based on agreement with Antonio,[596] Betty would have been entitled to sue under the provision of articles 1295(1) and 1323 ABGB if Cinzia had been negligent.

There is no claim for Betty against Cinzia if she had not obtained possession of the computer, except the specific case of article 1295(2) ABGB.

III. The fact that a discernible right *in personam* should be granted the same protection as an absolute right appears to be an advance in legal protection. The same is true with discernible financial losses. Whether simple knowledge of a right *in personam* forms sufficient ground for granting the same protection is open to dispute. After all, one has to

---

[593] See B. Schilcher and W. Holzer, 'Der schadenersatzrechtliche Schutz des Traditionserwerbers bei Doppelveräußerung von Liegenschaften', JBl 1974, 445, 512; and in compliance therewith OGH EvBl 1976/176; JBl 1977/257; JBl 1981/535; most recently the Supreme Court granted a claim based on tort to a tenant: OGH JBl 1990, 648.
[594] For greater details, see B. Schilcher and W. Posch, 'Civil Liability for Pure Economic Loss: An Austrian Perspective', in E. K. Banakas (ed.), *Civil Liability for Pure Economic Loss* (London, 1996), pp. 149, 176.
[595] See OGH JBl 1981, 535 – 'inducement of breach of contract' ('Verleitung zum Vertragsbruch').
[596] Cf. art. 428 ABGB.

take into account that, according to article 1300 ABGB, knowledge is sufficient cause.

**Portugal**

I. Double sale of an apartment: the sale of real estate has to take place through a public deed of conveyance (art. 875 CC) and it must be registered. If it is not registered the sale is valid *inter partes*, but has no legal effect in relation to third parties (arts. 4 and 5 of the Code of Land Registration, Decree Law No. 224/84 of 6 July 1984).

If Cinzia knew about the earlier sale, the traditional position (still defended by Coimbra's legal school) is that possible knowledge of the earlier sale is irrelevant[597] (good faith) from the standpoint of the second buyer's acquisition of the property (*a non domino*). The Supreme Court recently gave a majority ruling if only in *obiter dicta* on this point.[598]

However, a large part of the doctrine argues that the second purchaser (Cinzia) only acquires the property if there was good faith.[599]

If this second position is the case, Betty would keep the apartment. A claim for compensation would then be of little interest to her. If the traditional position is the case it would be more plausible, for some, for Betty to seek compensation from Cinzia. This issue has not been debated in Portuguese doctrine.

Although the question concerns a claim for compensation by the first purchaser against the second for damage arising from the deliberate 'attack' on her contractual position, this is not a pure problem of external effect, given the implications for rights *in rem* and registration law.

We are inclined to think that, in normal circumstances, this claim would be rejected by a Portuguese court.

---

[597] C. A. Mota Pinto, *Teoria Geral do Direito Civil* (3rd edn, Coimbra, 1985), pp. 367–9; Antunes Varela and Henrique Mesquita, 'Annotation to Judgement of the STJ of 3 June 1992', (1994) 126 *Revista de Legislação e Jurisprudência* 3837, 374, and (1994) 127, 3838, 19; O. De Carvalho, 'Terceiros para Efeitos de Registo', (1994) *Boletim da Faculdade de Direito* 97–106.

[598] STJ, ruling of 20 May 1997 (on the concept of 'third parties for the purposes of registration'), in the *Diário da República* (I-A) of 4 July 1997 467 *Boletim do Ministério da Justiça* 88, 92.

[599] J. Oliveira Ascensão, *Direito Civil – Reais* (5th edn, Coimbra Editora, Coimbra, 1993), pp. 376–9; A. Menezes Cordeiro, *Direitos Reais* (Lex, Lisboa, 1993), pp. 275–80; A. Carvalho Fernandes, *Lições de Direitos Reais* (2nd edn, Lisboa, 1997), pp. 125–30; H. E. Hörster, *Zum Erwerb vom Nichtberechtigten im System des Portugiesischen Bürgerlichen Gesetzbuchs* (Coimbra, 1988), pp. 43 ff.

If Cinzia did not know of the earlier sale (there is good faith) or at any rate, if it is not proved that she did,[600] she would become the owner of the apartment, and we cannot discover any grounds for Betty to receive compensation from Cinzia.

Nevertheless, it is not impossible that, in the light of the circumstances of the case, the conclusion of the second contract would be contrary to *boni mores*, which implies its invalidity (art. 281) and upholding the right of the first purchaser.

Inasmuch as the damage is not wholly recoverable by this route, there could still be claim based on abuse of law.

Double sale of a computer: in the event of the double sale of a movable that is not subject to registration, it does not matter if the second buyer knew about the first contract or not (good faith), since in either case, the property always belongs to the first buyer, with or without delivery (*traditio*) of the thing (unless there is acquisition by *usucapio*).

Betty could thus exercise her inherent rights of ownership to reclaim the property (art. 1311).

II. To understand the explanation given in section I above, it is worth considering some ideas.

In Portuguese law, the *princípio da consensualidade* operates, by which the constitution or transfer of rights *in rem* over a determined thing takes place simply on the basis of the agreement (*solus consensus*), independently of the delivery (*traditio*) of the thing or other formalities (article 408, no. 1, cf. also art. 879, sub-para. a).

On the other hand, the principle 'possession is equivalent to title' established, for example, in article 2279 of the French Civil Code (*en fait de meubles, la possession vaut titre*) does not operate in Portuguese law.

However, the law does give special protection to the buyer in good faith in the case of a purchase from a seller who deals in a good of the same or similar type. The party seeking the return of the thing is then 'obliged to reimburse the price that the acquirer has given for it, but has the right of recourse against whoever negligently caused the harm' (art. 1301).[601]

---

[600] Cf. art. 7° of the Código do Registo Predial (Code of Land Registration). We are grateful to Paulo Videira Henriques for allowing us to read part of an as yet unpublished study on land registration, which we found very useful.

[601] Concerning real estate and movables requiring registration, third parties acting in good faith who acquire by onerous title are protected insofar as the avoidance or annulment of a previous transmissible contract cannot be opposed against them if

III. In accordance with what has been said, one of the conclusions drawn by Rodolfo Sacco in his comparative study on the transfer of the ownership of goods does not apply in Portugal. The learned author states that 'if a person, after selling a good to a first buyer, sells it to a second and delivers this good to the latter, the second buyer, if he has purchased in good faith, becomes the owner of the good...'.[602] This regime does not operate in Portuguese law.[603]

The principle of transfer of property merely on the basis of a contract was already enshrined in the Civil Code in 1867 under the influence of the *Code Napoléon*.

## Sweden and Finland

I. Betty has no claim against Cinzia unless she proves that the participation of the latter in the transaction was a crime (from this perspective, Cinzia's knowledge would thus be a relevant element).

II. This case involves 'pure economic loss' in the Swedish/Finnish meaning of the term, i.e. an economic loss arising without connection to anybody suffering personal injury or damage to things. According to the statutory rule in *SkadestL* 4:2 (Sweden) and *SkadestL* 5:1 (Finland) it can be compensated when it is consequent upon a criminal behaviour, although the text and the preparatory works of the Tort Liability Acts 1972 and 1974 do not completely bar compensation if the courts find strong reasons for it. Courts have been very restrictive in making exceptions to the general principle.

However, a pure torts law perspective must be integrated here with the property rights aspect. It must indeed be taken into consideration that a second acquirer in bad faith could not get ownership to the real estate or the movables. That is to say, Betty does not incur any loss if Cinzia knew about Betty being the first buyer. If Cinzia is in good faith, that is to say she was unaware of Betty being the first buyer, she may become the owner of the property if she gets possession of the property or is registered as the owner of the real estate before Betty can register. In such a case Betty has no claim against Cinzia, but only towards Antonio.

the registration of the acquisition was prior to the registration of the claim of voiding or annulment and took place three years after that contract (art. 291; for annulment of registration, see art. 17, no. 2 of the Land Registration Code).

[602] 'Le transfert de la propriété des choses mobilières déterminées par acte entre vifs en droit comparé', *Rivista di Diritto Civile*, 1979, Parte Prima, 442 f., 447.
[603] J. M. V. Gomes, *O Conceito de Enriquecimento O Enriquecimento Forçado e Os Vários Paradigmas do Enriquecimento Sem Causa* (1998), 24.

## Editors' comparative comments

Here again is a hypothetical which shows that pure economic loss lies at the intersection of many legal concepts. When the case is approached in terms of the line between contract and tort, one realises that the usual way of framing the issue as 'wrongful interference with contractual relationship',[604] at the very least fails to consider the variable nature of the contract (e.g., sale or contract for services)[605] and the different subject matter (e.g., movable or immovable) which may be involved.

The point is that all the national answers hinge directly or indirectly on the law governing transfer of title. Indeed, the need to protect the consistency and trustworthiness of transfer of title induces legal systems either to disregard the interests of the deluded first buyer, or to select a particular state of mind (perhaps associated with some discrete form of blameworthy behaviour) of the second buyer as the minimum threshold above which the latter becomes liable.

Thus, Spain and Portugal (with regard to the sale of the computer) and England (with regard to the sale of the flat) treat the legal question of wrongful interference as pointless, because its occurrence is precluded by the specific rules on transfer of ownership.

The legal systems in which the issue may arise require more than carelessness on the part of the second buyer before liability will be imposed on her. The relevant prerequisite of liability lies at some point along a scale ranging from simple knowledge (Belgium, France, Scotland and the Netherlands) to bad faith (Greece, Italy and, as regards the computer, England), to immoral behaviour (Germany, Portugal and, requiring the perpetration of a crime, Sweden and Finland).

Finally, even the notion of 'transfer of ownership' may be deceptive if we take it to be the label for a clear-cut and single content. The notion can only have a simple meaning if all the attributes of ownership are simultaneously transferred from one party to the other. But, as the national contributions have demonstrated – and as other scholars have already pointed out[606] – the rules of a system are distorted when we seek to subsume them under a general proposition which states that all the

---

[604] See e.g. W. van Gerven, J. Lever and P. Larouche, *Tort Law* (Hart, Oxford, 2000), pp. 238, 247.

[605] See, in fact, below, sub Cases 14 ('Poor Legal Services'), 17 ('Auditor's Liability') and 20 ('An Anonymous Telephone Call').

[606] See e.g. R. Sacco, 'Legal Formants: A Dynamic Approach to Comparative Law' (1991) 39 *American Journal of Comparative Law* 349, 370, 381; L. P. W. van Vliet, *Transfer of movables* (Ars Aequi Libri, Nijmegen, 2000), *passim*.

attributes of ownership are transferred at this or that moment. In the systems examined, general formulas are often coupled with, and counterbalanced by, rules which divert the actual outcome from the goal that the general principle should secure. General formulas tend toward solutions that are unitary or monistic: 'ownership is transferred at the moment of consent', or 'ownership is transferred at the moment of delivery'. The operative rules that each particular system actually enforces find intermediate solutions between two extremes.

# Case 13: subcontractor's liability

## Case

Laura hired the Cronos Company to refurbish her flat. Cronos called in Giovanni, an independent contractor, to lay the floors. However, the work was done badly and Laura was forced to hire another workman to replace the floors entirely. Laura now learns that the Cronos Company has gone bankrupt which means that she cannot sue it for damages. Can Laura recover her economic loss from Giovanni?

## France

I. Laura may recover for her economic loss from Giovanni under articles 1382–83 CC.

Laura will have to prove Giovanni's professional fault, the loss she suffered hiring another workman to replace the floors, and the causal link existing between these last two elements to be able to recover her economic loss from Giovanni.

II. This is necessarily a tort action.[607] Since Laura (the *maître de l'ouvrage*) is not contractually linked to Giovanni (the *sous-traitant*), the action of the former against the latter must be grounded on article 1382 CC.

This first point regarding the nature of the action was decided in 1991 by the Assemblée Plénière of the Cour de Cassation.[608] The decision ended the controversial stance formerly taken by a single chamber of the Court which held the view that the action between the owner and subcontractor who had priority of contract was 'necessarily contractual'.[609] The basis for the Assemblée Plénière's view was the literal interpretation of article 1165 CC (*Les conventions n'ont d'effet qu'entre les parties contractantes; elles ne nuisent point aux tiers, et elles ne lui profitent que dans le cas prévu par l'article 1121 (stipulation pour autrui)*).

Since this action is delictual, Laura will have to prove three elements in order to recover her loss from Giovanni under articles 1382–83: Giovanni's professional fault, the loss she suffered hiring another worker to replace the floors and the causal link existing between these elements.

---

[607] P. Malaurie and L. Aynès, *Droit civil, les obligations* (edn. Editions Cujas 1995/96), p. 401, especially p. 408, no. 700. P. Malaurie and L. Aynès, *Droit civil, les contrats spéciaux* (Editions Cujas 1993/94), p. 414.
[608] Ass. Plén., 12 juillet 1991, D. 1991, 549; JCP 1991.II.21743.
[609] See Civ. 1, mars 1988, JCP 1988.II.2107.

The first two elements seem concededly satisfied by the facts given in Case 13. The third element, causation, may not be problematical either. The resulting damages do not have a hypothetical, speculative or uncertain character and they occur directly to Laura.

## Belgium

I. Laura has no claim against Giovanni.

II. Laura has executed a contract with the Cronos Company. This company has called in Giovanni to perform part of its obligations.

If Giovanni did not do his work properly, the contract is not performed as it should have been and Laura will have a contractual claim against her co-contractor (Cronos).[610]

Since there is no contract between Giovanni and Laura, the only claim of Laura rests on article 1382 CC:

Any act whatever of man which causes damage to another obliges him by whose fault it occurred to make reparation.

However, in a leading case,[611] the Cour de Cassation has decided that a party to a contract has a claim towards the subcontractor if, and only if:

(1) the breach of the contract is also a fault in the sense of article 1382 CC (a violation of law or a behaviour different from the one the '*bonus pater familias*' would have had in the same circumstances);
(2) the damage claimed is not a damage resulting merely from the non-performance of the contract;

This rule has been confirmed thereafter.[612]

The case law of the Cour de Cassation has been disputed often by legal scholars.[613] This rule is however still applied by the courts.

In the present case, the second condition is absolutely not fulfilled. The damage claimed by Laura is a direct consequence of the breach of her contract with Cronos. She cannot therefore recover her loss from Giovanni.

III. The case law of the Cour de Cassation is based on the idea that the contractual claim against the co-contractor is preferable to a tort claim against the subcontractor.

---

[610] Cass., 21 juin 1979, JT, 1979, p 675  [611] Cass., 7 décembre 1973, Pas., 1974, I, 376.
[612] Cass., 3 décembre 1976, RCJB, 1971, p. 423; Cass., 8 avril 1983, RW, 1983–84, p. 163.
[613] See R. O. Dalcq, 'Restriction à l'immunité de responsabilité de l'agent d'exécution', RCJB, 1992, p. 503 and ibid., further references.

## Italy

I. Laura can successfully sue Giovanni on a tort basis under either article 2043 or article 1669 cc.

II. Even if there is no contract between Laura and Giovanni, the latter has the duty to perform his obligation properly and according to the average standard. The damage caused to Laura's property in consequence of the breach of this duty can be seen as an unjustified damage covered by article 2043 or by article 1669 cc. The latter provision reads:

*Article 1669: Destruction and defects of immovables*

In the case of buildings or other immovables intended by their nature to last for a long period of time, if within ten years from completion the work is totally or partially destroyed by reason of defects in the soil or in construction, or if such work appears to be in evident danger of destruction or reveals serious deficiencies, the contractor is liable with respect to the customer and his successors in interest, provided notice of said destruction or defects has been given within one year of their discovery.

The right of the customer is prescribed in one year from the notice.

The rule is seen as establishing an extracontractual liability not only on contractors, but also upon subcontractors and professionals.[614] Actually, most often the architect and the contractor have been charged with a joint and several liability to the plaintiff.[615]

## Spain

I. The answer to this case is clearly found in the case law: in effect, the owner of the works may bring an action against the subcontractor.

II. In the Supreme Court decision (First Chamber) of 23 November 1985, the contractor and subcontractor were held jointly and severally liable for the damage caused to some flat owners who had suffered damages when moisture filtered through the roof of the building defectively

---

[614] See esp. Cass. 7.1.2000, *GI*, 2000, 977; Cass., 8.1.1985, no. 5463, *MGI*, 1985, 1021; Cass., 27.8.1994, no. 7550; *GI*, 1995, I, 1, 375; Cass., 21.3.1989, no. 1406, *MGI*, 1989, 207. As to legal scholars, see M. Bianca, *Inadempimento delle obbligazioni* (Commentario Scialoja-Branca, Roma Bologna, 1967), p. 120; G. Cattaneo, *La responsabilità del professionista* (Milano, 1958); C. Maiorca, 'Colpa civile (teoria gen.)', in *Enciclopedia del diritto*, vol. VII (Milano, 1960), p. 534; L. Mengoni, 'Obbligazioni di risultato e obbligazioni di mezzi', *RDComm.* 1954, I, 185; P. G. Monateri, *Il cumulo di responsabilità contrattuale ed extracontrattuale* (1989) at p. 75.

[615] Cass. 5.2.2000, no. 1290, *MGC*, 2000, 246; Cass. 25.8.1997, no. 7992, *FP*, 1999, I, 6; Cass. 23.9.1996, no. 8395, *FI*, 1997, I, 1217; *DR*, 1997, 250.

constructed by the subcontractor. The subcontractor attempted a privity of contract defence, alleging that he was only contractually bound to the constructor. The Supreme Court declared that this non-existing bond could not prevent the existence of joint and several liability of the constructor – of a non-contractual nature – taking into account that the plaintiffs had suffered damages attributable to an undeterminable extent to the subcontractor: article 1902 CC is applied.[616]

The Supreme Court decision (First Chamber) of 22 June 1990 handled a case similar to the above and reached the same result. One must recognize that the plaintiff could choose between a claim against the constructor, a direct claim against the subcontractor or a claim against both.[617]

Apart from construction cases, similar ideas regarding non-contractual responsibility of the subcontractor may be found. In the Supreme Court decision (First Chamber) of 18 June 1979, the injured party brought his claim for non-contractual responsibility directly against the subcontractor (which in this case was a company of dock stevedores) and was compensated for the damages caused to some merchandise. The Supreme Court decision (First Chamber) of 10 May 1984 reflects the joint and several liability of the carrier and the subcontractor for damages caused to the carried merchandise. The subcontractor's liability again is of a non-contractual nature.[618]

Salvador Coderch points out that, in spite of the clear position in case law, the majority opinion actually denies that the owner of the works may bring a direct claim against the subcontractor.[619] In cases such as the present, contractual bonds should be taken into account in such a way that the client may only bring his claim against the contractor and not against the subcontractor, notwithstanding the fact that the contractor could later bring a claim for reimbursement against the latter.[620]

---

[616] Along these lines, see Supreme Court decisions 14.11.88 and 6.3.90.
[617] This same idea is expressed in the Supreme Court decisions of 1.3.84 and 22.3.86.
[618] F. Pantaleón 'Comentario a la S.T.S. de 10 de mayo de 1984', (1984) 5 *Cuadernos Civitas de Jurisprudencia Civil*, at 1645 ff. and R. De Ángel, *Tratado de responsabilidad civil* (3rd edn, 1993), p. 376 are in agreement with this decision.
[619] P. Salvador Coderch, 'Comentario a los articulos 1588–1600', in *Comentario del Código Civil*, II (1991), pp. 1175 ff.
[620] E.g. L. López Mora and F. De La Cámara Mingo, *Tratado práctico del derecho referente a la construcción y a la arquitectura*, IV (1964), p. 672 or O. V. Torralba Soriano, 'La responsabilidad por los auxiliares en el cumplimiento de las obligaciones', *Anuario de Derecho Civil*, II (1971), 1143–66, at p. 1166; the contrary position is

Perhaps it should be pointed out that, while accepting the majority opinion that the client has no direct claim against the subcontractor, the owner of the works would still have another means of action. In effect, in Case 13 Laura could exercise what is known as the *acción subrogatoria* (action in subrogation) contained in article 1111 CC. In this way, given Cronos's insolvency, accepting that Laura could not bring a direct claim against Giovanni and assuming that Cronos would maintain a passive attitude towards Giovanni's breach of contract, Laura could bring a claim against the latter by exercising Cronos's contractual claims ensuing from Giovanni's breach of contract. The main disadvantage of this indirect method of reaching the subcontractor is that Laura could only claim the damages that Cronos could have claimed.[621]

**Greece**

I. Giovanni is personally liable for his acts according to article 914 CC, only if he can be deemed having (unlawfully) physically harmed Laura's flat by his fault.

II. According to articles 334 and 922 CC[622] Cronos is vicariously liable for the behaviour of its agent (the so-called 'auxiliary performer',)[623] i.e. Giovanni. Cronos will be liable whenever Giovanni's conduct can be seen as breach of a contractual duty owed by Cronos to Laura. Only Cronos can be contractually liable, because only the latter is contractually bound to Laura (principle of privity of the contract). In his turn, according to article 914 CC., Giovanni is tortiously liable insofar as his behaviour is unlawful: this could possibly happen only in the case that Giovanni

---

exclusively upheld by J. M. Fernández Hierro, *La responsabilidad por vicios de construcción* (Universidad de Deusto, Bilbao, 1976), p. 134, J. Herrera Catena, *Responsabilidades en la construcción*, I-2° (1977) and C. Gomez De La Escalera, *La responsabilidad civil de los promotores, constructores y técnicos por los defectos de la construcción* (1990), p. 173.

[621] J. Sirvent, *La acción subrogatoria* (1996), pp. 151 and 188; F. Pantaleón, 'Comentario al artículo 1902', in *Comentario del Código Civil II, 1971–2003* (1991), p. 1972.

[622] See M. Stathopoulos, *Law of Obligations, General Part* I (1979–1983), p. 220. Nevertheless the Greek courts deny the implementability of art. 922 CC in the case of an independent contractor (see, e.g. AP 300/1980 EEN 47, 581; EphThes 1430/1982 Arm 38, 24; EphAth 590/1983 Arm 38, 455).

[623] See A. Gazis, 'About the Legal Sense of "Auxiliary Performer"' in *Eranion* [Festschrift] *for G. Maridakis*, II (1963), p. 300, no. 23; Stathopoulos, *Law of Obligations, General Part* I, p. 224.

damaged Laura's flat by his own fault and thus harmed her ownership, because such behaviour is prohibited by law.

Thus, only if Giovanni harmed Laura's property, i.e. her flat, (unlawfully) physically and by his fault, is he personally liable for his acts according to article 914 CC; but these facts are to be proved by Laura. Nevertheless, even if there is no unlawful physical harm to property, the Greek courts could possibly confirm the worker's liability by using the theory of broadening the unlawfulness. According to this theory negligence itself already constitutes *eo ipso* an unlawful behaviour, prohibited by articles 281 and 288 CC. In fact, what court decisions consider unlawful is the breach of any duty of care imposed by good faith.[624]

## England

I. It is somewhat doubtful that Laura has a claim in tort against Giovanni.

II. The facts here are almost identical to those in the case of *Junior Books v. Veitchi Co. Ltd*,[625] a case described as 'now largely fallen from favour but the effects of which may not be wholly spent'.[626] Whether this case is still regarded as authority (even on identical facts) is not clear. In *D & F Estates Ltd and Others v. Church Commissioners for England and Others*,[627] the House of Lords in effect confined *Junior Books* to its facts and refused just such a claim. Furthermore, Laura's claim is perhaps factually different in that, far from having nominated Giovanni as subcontractor, she appears not to know him at all. This leaves it unclear whether an English court would grant her relief.

## Scotland

I. It is possible that Laura could recover her economic loss from Giovanni, but she would have to establish that, what has become known as a *Junior Books* duty of care was owed to her and was breached causing her loss. This may not be easy and is very much dependent upon the particular facts of the case.

---

[624] AP 640/1955 NoB 4, 491; AP 250/1956 NoB 4, 840; AP 510/1959 NoB 8, 251; AP 343/1968 NoB 16, 943; AP 854/1974 NoB 23, 479; AP 81/1991 NoB 40, 715; EfAth 7453/1988 EllDni 31, 848; AP 678/1998 NoB 47, 1416; MprThes 9830/1997 Arm 53, 77.
[625] [1983] 1 AC 520.
[626] W. V. H. Rogers, *Winfield and Jolowicz on Tort* (15th edn, Sweet & Maxwell, 1998), at p. 98.
[627] [1988] 2 All ER 992.

II. As we have seen, in light of the decision in *Henderson*, a defender owes a general duty of care to prevent a pursuer from sustaining relational economic loss [i.e. pure economic loss in the context of interference in the pursuer's contractual relationships] when the defender has voluntarily assumed responsibility for the pursuer's economic interests with the knowledge that the pursuer will rely on the defender's expertise.[628]

Where the defender intentionally interferes with the performance of a contract he may be found liable in damages for wrongful interference with performance of a contract.[629] However, when the interference is unintentional, in general the courts have held, for various reasons, that the pursuer is unable to sue the defender in delict for his relational loss owing to the unintentionally defective performance of the defender's contract. We have seen this in *Reavis*, *Dynamco* and *Nacap*. These factual situations can be seen as not meeting the requirements laid down in *Henderson*.

One situation where the courts found a duty of care to exist when the performance was merely negligent was in *Junior Books Ltd* v. *Veitchi Co. Ltd*.[630] This case involved a relationship between the owner of property and a nominated subcontractor working on that property. Though this decision predated *Henderson*, and was based upon the two-test approach of Lord Wilberforce in the now overruled *Anns*, it has not itself been overruled although it is usually distinguished and considered to be restricted to its particular facts. *Junior Books* has proved especially controversial in England. It was distinguished in *Muirhead* v. *Industrial Tank Specialities Ltd*[631] where Goff LJ (as he then was) stated that he thought it was 'safest for this court to treat *Junior Books* as a case in which, on its particular facts, there was considered to be such a very close relationship between the parties that the defenders could, if the facts as pleaded were proved, be held liable to the pursuers'.[632] It was not followed in *D & F Estates Ltd and Others* v. *Church Commissioners for England and Others*[633] where Lord Bridge of Harwich stated that

[t]he consensus of judicial opinion, with which I concur, seems to be that the decision of the majority is so far dependent on the unique, albeit non-contractual,

---

[628] *Stair Memorial Encyclopaedia, The Laws of Scotland*, vol. 15 (Law Society of Scotland, Edinburgh, 1996), p. 391, para. 588 (written by J. M. Thomson).
[629] The seminal case is *Torquay Hotel Co. Ltd* v. *Cousins* [1969] 2 Ch 106, [1969] 1 All ER 522 (CA).
[630] 1982 SC (HL) 244, 1982 SLT 492.   [631] [1986] 1 QB 507.
[632] Ibid. at p. 528.   [633] [1979] AC 177.

relationship between the pursuer and the defender in that case and the unique scope of the duty of care owed by the defender to the pursuer arising from that relationship that the decision cannot be regarded as laying down any principle of general application in the law of delict or tort.[634]

Thomson has argued that *Junior Books* is an important and principled decision, and believes that

> the reason for this scepticism is that *Junior Books* has not been regarded as a case which is only concerned with wrongful interference with the pursuer's existing contracts. Instead, it has been read as laying down potential liability for economic loss arising from the careless manufacture of a defective product, which is not dangerous, in the sense of causing injury to the pursuer or damage to property. If this were the case, then there would, indeed, be cause for concern. But if analysed as above, *Junior Books* liability does not have this potential. Within its narrow sphere, *Junior Books* is both an important and principled decision.[635]

Arguably, it meets all the *Henderson* criteria and this can be seen in the following observations. In asking whether there was the requisite degree of proximity to give rise to the relevant duty of care, Lord Roskill stated:

> I regard the following facts as of crucial importance in requiring an affirmative answer to that question. (1) The appellants were nominated subcontractors. (2) The appellants were specialists in flooring. (3) The appellants knew what products were required by the respondents and their main contractors and specialised in the production of those products. (4) The appellants alone were responsible for the composition and construction of the flooring. (5) The respondents relied upon the appellant's skill and experience. (6) The appellants as nominated subcontractors must have known that the respondents relied on their skill and experience. (7) The relationship between the parties was as close as it could be short of actual privity of contract. (8) The appellants must be taken to have known that if they did the work negligently... the resulting defects would at some time require remedying by the respondents expending money upon the remedial measures as a consequence of which the respondents would suffer financial or economic loss... all the conditions existed which give rise to the relevant duty of care... turn[ing] to Lord Wilberforce's second proposition... I see nothing whatsoever to restrict the duty of care arising from the proximity of which I have spoken... in the present case the only suggested reason for limiting the damage... recoverable for the breach of duty of care just enunciated is that hitherto the law has not allowed such recovery and therefore ought not in future to do so... I do not think that this development, if development it

---

[634] Ibid. at p. 202.
[635] J. M. Thomson, *Delictual Liability* (Butterworths, Edinburgh, 1999), p. 81.

be, will lead to untoward consequences. The concept of proximity must always involve, at least in most cases, some degree of reliance...[636]

The facts in that case equate well with those in our fictional case here. As with Laura, Cronos and Giovanni, the parties (A, B and C) were connected by a series of contracts. Giovanni (like C) breaks his contract with Cronos (B) by his careless conduct in laying the floors, resulting in Cronos delivering a defective performance to Laura (A) causing her economic loss. Although the case concerned the recovery of pure economic loss, the House of Lords by a majority found a duty of care to exist owing to the existence of sufficient proximity between the parties.

What we may term the '*Junior Books* duty of care' would appear to have a number of limiting factors and it would be necessary for the facts here to meet all of these before Laura can recover her loss from Giovanni; in other words, for sufficient proximity to exist. The first is satisfied in that there is an existing contractual nexus at the time of the careless act. Secondly, there must be reasonable foreseeability of loss resulting from the careless act which, again, was satisfied on similar facts in *Junior Books*. Thirdly, the defender must have known of the pursuer's identity. On the facts we do not know whether that was the case here. What degree of knowledge of identity will be sufficient is not clear from the facts of *Junior Books*. In subsequent cases, it was emphasized how close the relationship was. In *Junior Books* itself, Lord Fraser of Tullybelton had stated that '[t]he proximity between the parties is extremely close, falling only just short of a direct contractual relationship'.[637] This led Lord Bridge in *D & F Estates*, as we have seen above, to characterize the relationship in *Junior Books* as 'unique', probably in an effort to limit its applicability to other similar but not identical factual situations. However, by way of comparison, in *Scott Lithgow* v. *GEC Electrical Products Ltd*,[638] Lord Clyde made the following observation:

Furthermore it is not easy to see that the circumstances of it [*Junior Books*] were necessarily unusual or unique. A building contract involving a nominated subcontractor who is a specialist in his particular trade is by no means unusual. I find it hard to believe that there could not be other cases in which the subcontractor knows that he is relied upon and a comparably close relationship be found to exist...If a duty of care can exist in the circumstances of the *Junior Books* case there seems no reason why in other circumstances where a correspondingly close proximity of relationship can be found a duty of care should

[636] 1982 SC (HL) 244 at p. 277.   [637] Ibid. at p. 265.   [638] 1992 SLT 244.

not also be affirmed. If, as appears to be the position, the essential is the discovery of a sufficiently proximate relationship then the question must be one to be resolved in the light of the circumstances.[639]

So, the question is whether Giovanni knew of Laura. If he was a nominated subcontractor, that would appear to satisfy the *Junior Books* test. Fourthly, it is clear from *Henderson* that where a contractual nexus exists, the terms of the contract, such as exemption or indemnity clauses, may preclude the pursuer from pursuing a remedy in delict.[640] We are not given such information here. Finally, 'the defender must anticipate loss to the particular pursuer as a result of the defender's defective performance'.[641] In *Simaan General Contracting Co. v. Pilkington Glass*,[642] Dillon LJ held:

It is clear...that foreseeability of harm or loss does not of itself and automatically lead to a duty of care. Foreseeability of harm is a necessary ingredient of a relationship in which a duty of care will arise, but not the only ingredient...the duty in a *Hedley Byrne* type case must depend on the voluntary assumption of responsibility towards a particular party giving rise to a special relationship...[643]

Again, we are not given the information necessary to determine whether this had occurred.

III. It is the first and third limiting factors which convince Thomson that *Junior Books* liability will be kept within fairly defined limits.[644] Quite often, as was the case in *D & F Estates*, there will be no existing contractual nexus when the careless act takes place. More importantly, since the defender is required to know the identity of the pursuer, the apparent concern of the English courts that *Junior Books* lays down 'potential liability for economic loss arising from the careless manufacture of a defective product, which is not dangerous, in the sense of causing injury to the pursuer or damage to property',[645] would seem unfounded. Even if there is a contractual nexus when a manufacturer carelessly produces a defective product which is incorporated by another in his product and then supplied to other parties, the original manufacturer will rarely, if ever, know the identity of the ultimate consumer – rendering a *Junior Books* duty of care almost impossible to establish. What matters is the voluntary assumption of responsibility and the concomitant reliance.

---

[639] Ibid. at p. 250B.   [640] [1995] 2 AC 145 at pp. 184 ff. *per* Lord Goff of Chieveley.
[641] Thomson, *Delictual Liability*, p. 80.   [642] [1988] 1 QB 758.   [643] Ibid. at p. 784F.
[644] See the discussion in J. M. Thomson, 'A Prophet Not Rejected in his Own Land', (1994) 110 LQR 361.
[645] Thomson, *Delictual Liability*, p. 81.

That would be the exception rather than the norm in the case of mass produced goods. This reality is reflected in the Court of Appeal judgment in *Muirhead*, where a very close proximity of relationship was not found to arise in that case between the ultimate purchaser and the manufacturer of goods supplied under a chain of ordinary contracts of sale.[646]

### The Netherlands

I. Laura's claim is successful if Cronos was her undisclosed agent. Otherwise, a claim in tort might be successful.

II. Independent subcontractor Giovanni has not entered into a contractual relationship with the owner Laura. There seem to be two solutions to this dilemma. First, Laura might try to sue Giovanni in tort. Secondly, Laura might try to have the contractual rights of Cronos transferred to her.[647]

This second foundation for Laura's claim is based on the agency-like relationship that Laura and Cronos maintain. Article 7:420 ss. 2 CC (*jo.* art. 7:424 CC) allows a principal to transfer to himself the contractual rights that his agent has *vis-à-vis* a third party, even if the agent acted for an unknown *middellijk vertegenwoordigde achterman*, i.e., for an 'undisclosed principal'. This 'self-help'-like transfer is permitted if the third party does not fulfil his contractual obligation to the agent.

The first foundation of Laura's claim offers an array of questions and factors that are similar to the questions and factors that came up for discussion in Case 7 (architect/contractor). If a subcontractor takes it upon himself to bring about a result (i.e. to lay floors), he should be held responsible for not performing. It should not make any difference whether the claim of the damaged party be in tort or in contract: it was clear from the outset that the benefits of Giovanni's performance would accrue to Laura. Therefore, it was quite foreseeable that the substantive damage resulting from non-fulfilment of the contract would primarily burden Laura and not Cronos.

Apart from that, the total amount due by Giovanni (the cost of replacing the floor) is not altered by the fact that the damaged party is not his partner in contract, but a (foreseeable) third party. One might look

---

[646] [1986] 1 QB 507 at pp. 528–9, *per* Robert Goff LJ.
[647] If Cronos acted as a *onmiddellijk vertegenwoordiger*, as a disclosed agent for Laura, there would have been a direct contractual relationship between Laura and Giovanni. See art. 3:66 CC. However, this does not seem to be the case.

upon Laura's case as a matter of *actieve legitimatie* ('active legitimation'): it is clear that *someone* has (or at least should have) the right to claim for the financial consequences of Giovanni's non-fulfilment.[648] If the contractor does not sue (for whatever reason), then Laura should be allowed to sue in tort.[649] Though the basis would be tort, the extent of her claim would – in my view – be confined to a claim in a (hypothetical) contract.

### Germany

I. Laura can probably recover her loss from Giovanni, but only in contract, not in tort. This result is not entirely free from doubt.

II. Tort claim: Laura has no tort claim against Giovanni. In order to recover under § 823 (1) BGB, she would have to show that Giovanni's poor workmanship amounted to an infringement of her property right (provided that she owns the house or apartment). As a basic rule, substandard construction work in and of itself does not constitute such an infringement. The customer simply never owned a proper work product which the contractor could possibly have damaged.[650] Thus Laura cannot recover in tort for the cost of replacing the work. Her damages are pure economic loss.

Yet, the customer's property right is violated to the extent that the bad work has affected property other than the work product, i.e. the floor itself.[651] If Laura has suffered damage to her house or apartment – e.g. because the foundation of the floor was ruined – Giovanni is liable for the cost of repair.

Contract claim: it is true that Laura has no contract with Giovanni himself, only with Cronos. But she is likely to be protected under the contract between Cronos and Giovanni as a third party. As mentioned, a contract between two parties can have 'protective effect' (*Drittschutzwirkung*) for third parties. In such a case, the third party can sue for breach and recover pure economic loss as well.

---

[648] On the subject of *samenloop* ('concurrency') of contract- and tort-based claims accruing in different estates, see, e.g., I. P. Michiels van Kessenich-Hoogendam, *Beroepsfouten* (Zwolle, 1995), pp. 14–17.

[649] If one would agree with me that the contractual relationship of Laura and Cronos might – under circumstances – be classified as an agency-like relationship, then Cronos is allowed to claim for damages suffered by his undisclosed principal Laura. Art. 7:419 CC also 7:424 CC states: 'If an agent has, in his own name, contracted with a party that does not fulfil his contractual obligations, then this party is also obliged [...] to repair the damage suffered by the principal.'

[650] BGHZ 39, 366, at 367 (1963).

[651] BGHZ 55, 392, at 394–5 (1970); BGHZ 96, 221, at 228 (1985).

The crucial issue is whether the contract between Cronos and Giovanni had 'protective effect' for Laura. Four conditions must be met.[652]

First, the third party must be in close proximity to the object or performance of the contract so that the breach of a contractual duty is likely to affect her.[653] This is clearly true in the present case because the work was done in Laura's home, and bad work was sure to affect her (in fact, she was likely to be the primary victim).

Second, one of the actual parties to the contract must have a legitimate interest in the wellbeing of the third party. Originally, this meant that there had to be some kind of personal relationship, such as among family members or between employer and employee.[654] Today, this requirement is construed more broadly. It is sufficient that the third party was intended to come into contact with the performance or the object of the contract, and that there is at least a potential interest of a party to protect her.[655] In the present case, courts and commentators would probably decide that this requirement is fulfilled because Cronos had good reason to wish to protect Laura. Cronos was hired by Laura and the company knew that it would be liable if one of its subcontractors did bad work. Nonetheless, this conclusion is open to debate.

Third, the party held liable must have been able to understand that the first two requirements were fulfilled. In other words, he must have been able to recognize the risk of harm to the third party as well as his partner's interest in protecting her.[656] This seems to be no problem in the present case.

Finally, the third party must be in need of protection. This is not true if she already has a claim for breach of contract against someone else.[657] In the present case, this is arguably a problem because strictly speaking, Laura already has a claim for breach of contract against Cronos (Cronos being liable for the performance of its subcontractor). Nonetheless, courts and commentators are likely to consider her in need of protection vis-à-vis Giovanni, because her claim against Cronos is worthless after the company's bankruptcy. Yet, again, there is room to differ about this issue.

---

[652] See H. Brox, *Allgemeines Schuldrecht* (25th edn, 1998), Rd.-Nr. 378; D. Medicus, *Bürgerliches Recht* (18th edn, 1999), Rd.-Nr. 844; W. Fikentscher, *Lehrbuch des Schuldrechts* (9th edn, 1997), Rd.-Nr. 261.
[653] See BGHZ 70, 327, at 329 (1977).   [654] BGHZ 56, 273 (1971).
[655] BGHZ 69, 82, at 86 (1977); BGH NJW 1984, 355, at 356.
[656] BGHZ 75, 321, at 323 (1979); BGH NJW 1985, 2411.
[657] BGHZ 70, 327, at 330 (1977).

If all requirements are fulfilled, Laura can sue Giovanni for breach of contract, and thus for pure economic loss, as a third party protected under the contract between Cronos and Giovanni.

III. The protection of third parties under a contract was developed in co-operation between scholars and courts and is firmly established today. The only question open to debate is where the line should be drawn between parties protected by the contract and those outside of its sphere. This line-drawing is difficult in large part because the *Bundesgerichtshof* continues to give mixed signals. On the one hand, the Court keeps reiterating that, in principle, only parties in privity with each other are protected and that the protective effect for third parties must not be carried too far. On the other hand, the Court has constantly expanded this protection to include ever more parties and situations.[658] Reading the opinions, one receives the impression that the decisions often turn on the merits of the individual case and on considerations of fairness and equity.[659] However, this makes it difficult to predict outcomes in scenarios that are somewhat novel or unusual.

### Austria

I. Laura has a claim against Giovanni based on a contract with protective effects to a third party.

II. The contract with protective effect to a third party: Laura has a contract with Cronos, which has gone bankrupt. She has no contract with Giovanni, the independent contractor. However, she is deemed to be protected by the contract between Cronos and Giovanni.

The acknowledgement of such contractual protective effect to a third party is the result of Austrian scholars' borrowing from German developments and their influence on the Austrian Supreme Court. There are three conditions that must be met:[660]

First, the third party must be in higher need for protection because the breach of a contractual duty is likely to affect it.

Second, one of the partners in the contract must have a legitimate interest in the wellbeing of the third party e.g. in the same way as a father vis à vis his children or an employer *vis-à-vis* his employees.

---

[658] See BGHZ 69, 82, at 86 (1977); BGH NJW 1984, 355–6.

[659] See, e.g. BGHZ 51, 91, at 96 (1968); BGH NJW 1970, 38, at 40; BGH NJW 1975, 867, at 868.

[660] See F. Bydlinski, 'Vertragliche Sorgfaltspflichten zugunsten Dritter', JBl 1960, 359; H. Koziol, *Österreichisches Haftpflichtrecht*, vol. II (2nd edn, Vienna, 1984), p. 86; OGH 47/72, JBl 1974/573; JBl 1982, 601; SZ 53/169.

Third, the third party's contact with the performance must potentially be foreseeable.

All three requirements are fulfilled in the present case because the work was done in Laura's home and thus she was likely to be the primary victim. Cronos had a legitimate interest in seeing that Laura was protected. Finally Cronos, and potentially Giovanni, were in a position to foresee Laura's proximity to the performance of the contract.

The need for protection: whereas in Germany the third party can only rely on the protective effect of a contract if it does not have a proper claim for breach of contract, the Austrian Supreme Court does not emphasize this aspect. So far there is only one case in which non-availability of a contract claim was made a requirement.[661] On the other side, the OGH issued verdicts for the plaintiffs in several cases where the defendant, causing the damage through his fault, was employed by the person having a contract with the victim.[662]

But even if the contract with protective effects to a third party would only be accepted by exception as a secondary measure by the courts, Laura's need of protection *vis-à-vis* Giovanni appears to be evident because after the company's bankruptcy her claim against Cronos is worthless.

III. Thus, the device of a contract with protective effects to a third party proves to be helpful in many cases where compensation of economic loss seems to be just and equitable. It is, however, virtually impossible to predict which group of third parties would be accepted as falling within the protective effect of a given contract by the OGH. Whereas postmen tumbling down defectively constructed staircases were denied access to the protected class, a visitor to a hospital was accepted. The definite positions the Supreme Court may take in a given case are not foreseeable.

## Portugal

I. We start from the assumption that the requirements for the liability of the Cronos Company *vis-à-vis* Laura are fulfilled (on this, see Section II

---

[661] See OGH JBl 1980/39, EvBl 1979/101, SZ 51/176: a towing service had commissioned a subcontractor to carry out a complicated salvage which failed, however. The OGH denied that the victim could base his claim against the subcontractor on the protective effects of the contract of the subcontractor and the towing service: the latter was responsible for breach of contract for the failure of a servant, namely the subcontractor.

[662] See e.g. OGH HdBW V/11.

below), concerning ourselves only with the relationship between Laura and Giovanni.

The subcontract (here, *subempreitada* – art. 1213) does not establish a true legal relationship between the first contracting party in the main contract and the subcontracting party. Thus, in principle the solution is that Laura cannot claim compensation from Giovanni for the defective performance of the subcontract.

However, this is only the solution in principle. Bearing in mind the particular circumstances of the case and some support in the doctrine, it is not impossible that the court would uphold Laura's action against Giovanni, allowing her a direct action.

At any rate, Laura could launch a subrogation action (art. 606), exercising against Giovanni the rights not exercised by her debtor (Cronos Company; cf., however, below, II).

II. There are no precedents enabling us to state that a Portuguese court would decide according to the solution in principle.[663] Notwithstanding, besides the principle of relativity of contracts being viewed today with more *souplesse*, and some important modifications in the field of legislation,[664] we can see some measure of support for that line of thinking in the modern specialized literature.[665]

It is not lawful for the owner of the job to correct the defects[666] him/herself or to proceed with new building work (or entrust this to a third party) at the expense of the contractor. This is only possible by an executive claim, always assuming the prior condemnation of the contractor.[667]

Under the terms of article 609, 'subrogation exercised by one of the creditors profits all the others'.

---

[663] Cf. judgment of the Supreme Court of Justice of 28 May 1981, *Boletim do Ministério da Justiça* no. 307, 266, and P. de Lima and A. Varela, *Código Civil Anotado*, vol. I (4th edn, Coimbra Editora, Coimbra, 1997), vol. II (4th edn, Coimbra Editora, Coimbra, 1998), annotations 1 and 4 to art. 1213.

[664] In the matter of credit for consumption, in the case of a sale financed by a third party, if he has the monopoly on concession of credit, the purchaser can sue not only the seller, but also the assignor of credit (art. 12, no. 2, of Decree-Law no. 359/91 of 21 September 1991).

[665] P. Romano Martinez, *Contrato de Empreitada* (Almedina, Coimbra, 1994), p. 129.

[666] Except in the event of 'manifest urgency', in terms of being able to speak of a *status necessitatis* (judgment of Coimbra Court of Appeal of 10 December 1996, *Boletim do Ministério da Justiça* no. 462, 499).

[667] See the Portuguese report in J. Sinde Monteiro, *La responsabilité des constructeurs, Travaux de l'Association Henri Capitant*, Tome XLII (1991) (Litec, Paris, 1993), pp. 197–202.

III. The existence of an economic link between the two separate contracts seems to justify relaxing the strictness of the principle of relativity of contracts.

## Sweden and Finland

I. Laura's chances of obtaining compensation are rather poor, because of the lack of a direct contractual relationship. Direct action in contract exists in case Giovanni has provided misleading information about the character of his work or otherwise provided some sort of warranty of its outcome.

II. The possibility of a direct action in contract against the independent contractor who provided misleading information, or issued a warranty of the quality of his product or service, is accorded in Sweden by § 33 of the Consumer Services Act 1985[668] and in Finland by § 10, chapter 5, of the Consumer Protection Act 1978.[669] Otherwise, the possibility of a contract claim seems to be barred in both jurisdictions by the absence of a contractual relationship between Laura and Giovanni. An action in tort on the basis of evidence of Giovanni's negligence should be possible, assuming that a court is ready to classify the badly done floor as a 'property damage'. In this case, Laura could claim that Giovanni is jointly liable in tort with Cronos Company.

*Editors' comparative comments*

Under the circumstances of this case, the plaintiff's losses do not go uncompensated. Recovery can be afforded either through tort law – by considering the additional costs incurred by the owner of the flat as a 'pure' or 'parasitic' economic loss – or by means of an array of contractual and paracontractual devices which provide alternative protection for the economic interests at stake.[670] At first sight, the issue raised by this case apparently falls squarely within the domain of tort law. The negligent subcontractor has no contract with the owner who has suffered economic loss. These two parties have separate contracts with a third (the contractor), but strictly speaking there is no contractual link between them. Thus it might appear that the recoverability of the loss sustained by the contractor can be determined according to the individual rules

---

[668] Konsumenttjänstlag (1985: 716).    [669] Konsumentskyddslag 20.1.1978/38.
[670] See our comments on Case 7 ('The Careless Architect').

and methods of the various tort regimes. This conclusion is correct as regards French, Italian and Spanish law, as well as the law in England and Scotland, where the doctrine of privity – which defines the notion of contract restrictively – is a fundamental barrier against recourse in contract. In other European countries, however, the rules of tort law do not afford the same protection to the plaintiff.

We find that the closer the parties are situated to each other within a network of contracts, the more likely it becomes that their rights and duties will be resolved by paracontractual ideas which provide an alternative means of compensation for pure economic loss. This explains why, under the present circumstances, the Dutch solution is much more favourable to the plaintiff than it was in Case 7 ('The Careless Architect'); why in Austria and Germany, compensation may be awarded quite liberally on the basis of the category of 'contract with protective effects for a third person'; why in Portugal and Spain, recourse can be made to subrogation;[671] and why in Sweden, Finland and again in Portugal and the Netherlands, a possible remedy available to the owner is the so-called 'direct action' – i.e. the direct claim that a creditor can bring against the person indebted to his debtor.[672] It should be noted, however, that from a policy perspective, 'contract with protective effects for a third person', 'subrogation' and 'direct action' pose little danger that an indeterminate number of claimants will arise, because these legal devices are used in a specific context where the number of beneficiaries is usually controlled *ex ante*.

A further device used by some countries concerns extension of the proprietary approach to the legal construction of the loss suffered by the owner (so that the flat's floor is viewed as the damaged item). This accounts for the possible success of a tort claim against the subcontractor in Greece, under article 911 CC, and in Germany, under § 823 BGB.

This last solution confirms two basic assumptions to which we have already referred:[673] (1) parasitic economic loss is, in principle, recoverable anywhere in Europe – even under conservative regimes; (2) parasitic loss and 'pure' economic loss do not differ in kind or in principle; they are distinguishable only by virtue of the circumstances in which they originate and the technical constraints imposed upon their recoverability.

---

[671] See also our comments to Case 4 ('Convalescing Employee')
[672] E.g., H. Koetz and A. Flessner, *European Contract Law*, I (trans. T. Weir, Oxford University Press, Oxford, 1997), pp. 242, 254.
[673] Above, Part I, and see our comments to Case 1 ('Cable I – The Blackout').

# Case 14: poor legal services

## Case

Grandfather Roberto wanted Giacomo to inherit most of his estate. However, his wish was frustrated by a number of errors committed by the notary drawing up his will. What chances does Giacomo have of receiving compensation from the notary for the damage incurred?

### France

I. Giacomo will very certainly recover the loss caused by the notary, either from the notary's insurance, or from a guarantee fund, or lastly from the notary's personal assets.

II. Traditionally, notaries are subject to liability for their errors and omissions under article 1382 CC. Thus any person who could prove the notary's fault (or negligence), a prejudice to themselves and a causal link could successfully sue. It is a fault for a notary to issue an act containing errors of law or errors of pure form. Giacomo has obviously incurred damage, since he cannot inherit the estate that his grandfather intended to leave him. The mistakes of the notary have obviously caused pure economic loss and Giacomo will very probably receive compensation.

However, today this compensation will not come primarily from the notary himself, but rather from his insurance company, since all notaries have the obligation to be insured for their civil liability.[674] Only 10 per cent of the damages remain the personal charge of the notary. A further question thus arises when the notary has no personal fortune and cannot even pay his 10 per cent share of the damages. This explains why the same decree established a 'collective guarantee fund'. The legislator wanted the whole profession to be responsible for the acts of its members. The fund receives annual contributions from notaries and provides indemnification to the clients in cases not covered by insurance. These essentially fall into three categories: where the notary has committed an intentional fault, or where the damages exceed the amount for which he is insured, or where the notary cannot pay his 10 per cent share of the damages.

Hence, a person suing a notary will, if the latter is held liable by the court, very certainly recover his or her damages, either from the insurance company, or the guarantee fund.

---

[674] Décrêt no. 55–604 du 20 mai 1955, *Dalloz* 1955, 260, art 13.

## Belgium

I. Giacomo could normally recover the damage from the notary if he can prove the violation of his professional duties.

II. The Belgian notary holds a public office regulated by an old law of Ventose 25, an XI. The office of a notary is required in several acts which the law deems very important, such as a donation, a mortgage or a public will.

When a party requires the services of a notary, the notary is not only liable for the form of the act but also has a duty to inform his client completely on the conditions and the consequences of the act suggested.

In the case of a will, the notary is directly liable for the damage resulting from the cancellation of the will because the forms required by law have not been correctly executed. In such a case, the claim can be based on article 68 of the law of Ventose 25, an XI regarding the notary.[675]

Applying these rules, in 1959 the Tribunal of Nivelles held a notary liable for the damage resulting from the cancellation of a public will because he did not check the legal capacity of the witnesses. More recently, the Tribunal of Tongres admitted the possibility of holding a notary liable for the damage resulting from the cancellation of a public will because one of the witnesses was related to the testator. It ruled however in that case that it was not proven that the notary committed a fault since he had completely informed and questioned the witnesses.[676]

Regarding the other conditions and the consequences of the act, the notary has a duty to completely inform his client.[677] Therefore, the notary will only be liable if the client or a third party, such as Giacomo, can prove that the notary's duty to inform his client has not been performed.

If the claim is initiated by the client, it will be based on contractual liability. If it is initiated by a third party, it will rest on article 1382 CC.

In order to hold the notary liable, Giacomo will also have to prove the damage he suffered and the causal link between the errors of the notary and the damage.

In the present case, Giacomo will have to prove that, if the notary had not committed the errors, he would have inherited more assets than he did.

---

[675] Gand, 15 mars 1994, RNB, 1995, p. 253.
[676] Civ. Tongres, 3 mars 1995, RGDC, 1995, p. 504.
[677] Mons, 2 mai 1991, RNB, 1992, p. 141; Civ. Gand, 8 mai 1990, TGR, 1990, p. 84; R. Bourdseau, 'Le devoir du conseil du notaire', J.L.M.B.-centenaire, 1988, p. 21; J. F. Taymans, 'Devoir de conseil et offre de service', in *Congrès notarial 1994, l'Europe des consommateurs et le Notariat* (Verviers-Eupen), p. 109.

III. The notary's liability is increasingly based on the duty to inform. Since the law regulates the office of a notary, liability exists not only towards his clients but also to third parties. When a notary participates in an act, due to its importance and the legal function given by the law to the notary, it is clear that a third party shall have the right to rely on its validity.[678]

## Italy

I. Giacomo may successfully sue the notary under article 2043 cc.

II. According to both scholars[679] and case law,[680] the notary as a professional, besides the contractual duties owed to his client, is under a duty not to infringe the interest of those parties who can directly suffer losses from the misperformance of his services.

## Spain

I. In Spanish law, without a doubt, Giacomo could sue the notary and demand compensation equivalent to the net profits he was unable to obtain due to the errors committed by the notary in drawing up the will.

II. This solution is clear and categorical in Supreme Court case law and the opinion of legal experts.[681]

The matter is particularly clear-cut if the notary's errors render the will null-and-void for nonfulfilment of any of the legal requirements for executing a will. In this case article 705 CC would be directly applicable, rendering the notary liable. Although article 705 is usually interpreted in such a way as to require the existence of fault or gross negligence on the part of the notary, legal experts point out that it would be hard to imagine an error committed by the notary in the formalities of a will which involved ordinary negligence.[682]

---

[678] See C. Vanhalewijn, *La responsabilité civile professionnelle du notaire, dix années de jurisprudence belge: 1980–1989* (Averbode, Altoria, 1991).

[679] V. Roppo and G. Benedetti, 'La responsabilità professionale del notaio', DR 2000, 8–9, 801; F. Angeloni, *La responsabilità civile del notaio* (Cedam, Padova, 1990).

[680] *Albano v. Benedetti*: Cass., 25.5.1981, no. 3433, MGC 1981; Cass., 13.7.1998, no. 6812, MGC 1998.

[681] See Supreme Court decisions delivered by the First Chamber of 3.7.65, 11.6.88 and 9.5.90. See the very clearly stated opinion by J. Santos Briz, *La responsabilidad civil: derecho sustantivo y derecho procesal* (6th edn, 2 vols, 1991), p. 808.

[682] R. Blanquer Uberos, 'Comentario al artículo 705', in *Comentario del Código Civil*, I (1991), pp. 1789 and 1791.

If the notary's breach cannot be redirected to article 705, the notary would still be held non-contractually liable to Giacomo according to article 1902 CC.[683]

Whether by applying article 705 CC or article 1902, it is clear that the person whose succession rights are thwarted due to errors committed by the notary may claim damages for the net value of what he would have inherited if the will were correctly drafted.[684]

### Greece

I. The notary is in principle tortiously liable against Giacomo, but not in the amount of Roberto's whole property.

II. The notary is according to Greek law a public functionary, obliged by the law to write down declarations. In this case he falsified a public document. This is prohibited and punished by article 242 PC.[685] Thus the notary unlawfully caused damage to Giacomo. Whether he is liable to compensate him according to article 914 CC depends on whether Giacomo could prove the notary's fault.

Here, the indemnifiable damage is the result of comparing the present value of the plaintiff's property with the value that his property would have foreseeably had, if the unlawful act had not happened (i.e. the act which led to the present invalid will). In view of this, it must be mentioned that if the present public document had never been drawn, it remains uncertain whether Roberto would still have wanted to make another will at all, or even another will in favour of Giacomo; furthermore, it is also uncertain that this will would not have later been revoked. Indeed, anyone is free to dispose of his estate as he chooses. Thus it is not foreseeable that, if the notary's tort had never taken place, Giacomo would have inherited most of Roberto's estate. So, in this case the only certain foreseeable and consequently indemnifiable damage could be, for example, Giacomo's expenses for writing the will (lawyer's or notary's fee, etc.).

III. Every document written by a notary is a public document. Thus what a notary confirms is irrebuttably presumed to be true according

---

[683] Santos Briz, *La responsabilidad*, p. 808, M. Albaladejo, *Comentarios al Código Civil y compilaciones forales* (arts. 705 ff.), x–1 (1987), p. 101, J. M. González Porras, *Comentarios al Código Civil y Compilaciones Forales* (arts. 694–705), IX–1–B (1987), p. 297.

[684] González Porras, *Comentarios* (1987), p. 299, Albaladejo, *Comentarios*, p. 102 and Blanquer Uberos, 'Comentario', p. 1791.

[685] *Ad hoc*, AP 246/1980 Pin Chr 30, 467.

to article 455 CCPr, unless the contrary is proved by a separate judicial decision, usually a penal one. This means that the main problem in this case is not the indemnifiable nature of one more kind of pure economic loss, but rather a matter of proof: it is to be discovered whether the notary issued a false document.

### England

I. Giacomo will be able to recover from the negligent notary the monies that Roberto intended him to inherit with his will.

II. Following the decision of the House of Lords in *White v. Jones*,[686] solicitors drawing up wills for clients are liable to identified beneficiaries in the will, for errors resulting in the beneficiaries' rights under the will being frustrated.

III. *White v. Jones* has been criticized for adopting the way of a tort remedy to redress a situation of obvious injustice, instead of leaving it to the legislator to provide for a statutory remedy rectifying erroneously drafted wills to allow benefits to be conferred according to the testator's wishes. Be that as it may, the case is an authority for the exceptional recovery of the economic loss of beneficiaries resulting from a defective will.

### Scotland

I. It is thought that Giacomo would have a good chance of receiving compensation from the notary who drew up the will.

II. We are dealing here with an example of what is generally referred to as the disappointed beneficiary. The loss suffered is pure economic loss. The question whether the disappointed beneficiary has a remedy has been decisively answered in England as a result of the case of *White and Another v. Jones and Others*.[687] In that case Lord Goff of Chieveley stated:

> In my opinion, therefore, your Lordship's House should in cases such as these extend to the intended beneficiary a remedy under the *Hedley Byrne* principle by holding that the assumption of responsibility by the solicitor towards his client should be held in law to extend to the intended beneficiary who (as the solicitor can reasonably foresee) may, as a result of the solicitor's negligence, be deprived of his intended legacy in circumstances in which neither the testator nor his estate will have a remedy against the solicitor.[688]

---

[686] [1995] 2 AC 207.   [687] [1995] 2 AC 207.   [688] Ibid. at p. 268.

In Scotland the difficulty for pursuers in Giacomo's position is the House of Lords' decision in the Scottish case of *Robertson* v. *Fleming*.[689] A number of dicta in that case appeared to establish a general principle limiting the scope of a solicitor's duty of care. A clear example of this is found in the statement of Lord Wensleydale, who said:

> It is said, however, that by the law of Scotland, quite independent of the question who the contracting parties are, whenever an attorney or agent is employed by anyone to do an act which when done will be beneficial to a third person, and that act is negligently done, an action for negligence may be maintained by the third person against the attorney or agent. I cannot think that any such proposition is made out to be part of the law of Scotland.[690]

There were earlier Scottish cases where potential liability in such a situation was recognized. In *Goldie* v. *MacDonald*,[691] an action was successful against a negligent factor and in *Webster* v. *Young*,[692] the Inner House, though doubtful that what was alleged could be proved, allowed as relevant an action against a law agent. In *Webster*, the Lord Justice-Clerk (Hope) said: 'The defender did not dispute the principle that a beneficiary under an incomplete deed may have a good action against the agent through whose neglect it remains uncompleted.'[693] Similarly, Lord Moncrieff said that 'the averments are such, as, if proved, would infer the defender's liability'.[694]

One possible interpretation is that in *Robertson*, the House of Lords overruled the judgment of the Inner House in *Webster*. This was the view accepted by Lord Weir in *Weir* v. *J. M. Hodge & Son*.[695] Having been referred to *Goldie* v. *MacDonald*, *Goldie* v. *Goldie's and Threshie's Representatives*[696] and *Webster* v. *Young*, Lord Weir held:

> It is not evident that any proposition of general application is discoverable from a study of these cases and in any event any expressions of opinion to the contrary must yield to the authoritative decision of the House of Lords in *Robertson* v. *Fleming*...I am inclined to the view that the decision...is binding upon me and that is conclusive of the present case.[697]

It had been argued to Lord Weir that the dicta in *Robertson* being *obiter*, he was free to ignore them. However, Lord Weir felt that the observations of Lord Campbell LC, Lord Cranworth and Lord Wensleydale were illustrative of the *ratio* of the case. An argument which had more

---

[689] (1861) 4 Macq. 167.   [690] Ibid. at pp. 199–200.   [691] (1757) Mor 3527.
[692] (1851) 13 D 752.   [693] Ibid. at p. 754.   [694] Ibid. at p. 755.   [695] 1990 SLT 266.
[696] (1842) 4 D 1489.   [697] 1990 SLT 266 at p. 269F.

success with Lord Weir was that developments in the law of negligence from *Donoghue* to *Hedley Byrne* had superseded *Robertson*. He accepted that 'the decision in *Robertson* v. *Fleming* is to be regarded as out of sympathy with the modern law of negligence',[698] but felt that as a Lord Ordinary he was bound by the decision.

In *MacDougall* v. *MacDougall's Executors*,[699] Lord Cameron of Lochbroom said:

Like Lord Weir...I am compelled to the view that that decision is still binding upon me though it is proper to note that since that case was decided *Ross* v. *Caunters* has been cited, for instance, in *Caparo* and *Murphy* without disapproval...Even if I had been persuaded to the opposite effect and felt able to follow the reasoning in *Ross* v. *Caunters*, namely that in the circumstances a duty of care arose not only to the client...but also to the beneficiary named by him in his will...I would not have been persuaded that the ambit of that duty of care extended to the pursuer who was not a beneficiary under the will.[700]

Norrie has argued strongly that Lord Weir was wrong to reject the argument that the relevant dicta in *Robertson* were *obiter*.[701] He focuses upon the fact that the Lord Chancellor is rejecting an argument which he describes as 'unnecessarily' contended for, and argues that 'if a proposition is unnecessary for the decision in a case, it *cannot* be the *ratio* of that case'.[702]

Judicial support for this position is to be found in *White* v. *Jones* where Lord Goff of Chieveley stated:

Statements such as these [in *Robertson* v. *Fleming*] no doubt represented the law as understood in this country over a century ago...Nowadays questions such as that in the present case have to be considered anew, and statements of the law, such as that of Lord Campbell LC, cannot be allowed to foreclose the argument of the plaintiffs in the present case; indeed, although they demonstrate the importance attached to the doctrine of privity of contract in 1861, nevertheless they did not form part of the *ratio decidendi* of the case, in which the question in issue in the present case did not fall to be decided. It follows that, although the views expressed on the point in *Robertson* v. *Fleming* are still entitled to great respect, your Lordships are in my opinion free to depart from them without having recourse to *Practice Note* [1966] 3 All ER 77, [1966] 1 WLR 1234 for that purpose.[703]

Although two Lords Ordinary have held that they considered themselves bound by *Robertson*, it is obvious that their sympathies lay

[698] Ibid. at p. 270A.   [699] 1994 SLT 1178.   [700] Ibid. at p. 1184C.
[701] K. McK. Norrie, '"Binding" precedent and disappointed beneficiaries', 1990 JR 107.
[702] Ibid. p. 109.   [703] [1995] 2 AC 207 at p. 259.

elsewhere if they had not been so bound. The statement made subsequent to those decisions made by Lord Goff of Chieveley may mean that a future pursuer such as Giacomo would probably be more successful. This was confirmed by the Inner House in the unreported decision of *Robertson* v. *Watt & Co.* The opinion of the court delivered by the Lord Justice-Clerk (Ross) contained the following passage:

> It is clear from the sheriff's note that he sustained the defender's second plea-in-law insofar as it related to the defender's [a firm of solicitors] alleged breach of duty to the pursuer prior to her husband's death because he felt bound by the decision in *Robertson* v. *Fleming* (1861) 4 Macq 167. Here again the sheriff's decision has been overtaken by events and in particular by a subsequent decision in the House of Lords. In *White* v. *Jones* the majority of the House of Lords held that the law had moved on from the time of *Robertson* v. *Fleming* and that the court was free to depart from the views expressed in *Robertson* v. *Fleming*... In *White* v. *Jones* it was observed that that dictum [of the Lord Chancellor in *Robertson*] was *obiter* and did not form part of the *ratio decidendi*... Having regard to these views expressed in *White* v. *Jones* we have come to the conclusion that the sheriff was not well founded in sustaining the defender's second plea-in-law to this extent. Whether or not the pursuer is entitled to a remedy in terms of the principle enunciated by the majority of the House of Lords in *White* v. *Jones* will depend upon the circumstances and, until the circumstances have been established in evidence, it is not possible to say whether the pursuer will be held to be entitled to a remedy against the defenders.[704]

According to Norrie the present Scottish situation is as follows:

> The contentious statement from *Robertson* v. *Fleming* is merely, and expressly, *obiter*. As such, *Webster* v. *Young* remains good law and *Weir* v. *J. M. Hodge & Son* is incorrectly decided. As in England, therefore, a solicitor can be liable in Scotland to a disappointed beneficiary, so long as there is a relationship of proximity between the pursuer and the solicitor, which relationship is established by showing that the latter assumed responsibility to the former not to cause economic loss. Cases are likely to be difficult to prove, but in principle liability is open in Scotland as it is elsewhere.[705]

So Giacomo's problem would be one of proving that the notary had assumed responsibility not to cause him (Giacomo) economic loss. Ultimately, solicitors are not a special class apart from other professional

---

[704] Extract printed as a note to the judgment of *Strathford East Kilbride Ltd* v. *HLM Design Ltd and Another* 1997 SCLR 877; not in SCLR but on Lexis the legal database. *Strathford* was treated as authoritative by the Lord Ordinary (Kingarth) in *Holmes* v. *Bank of Scotland* 2002 SLT 544.

[705] *Stair Memorial Encyclopaedia, The Laws of Scotland*, vol. 15 (Law Society of Scotland, Edinburgh, 1996), p. 180, para. 283 (footnotes omitted).

classes when it comes to liability for negligence, as *Robertson* might have seemed to imply.

III. In *Ross* v. *Caunters* Sir Robert Megarry V-C stated the following in the course of finding the solicitor's liability established:

> I find it difficult to envisage a fair and reasonable man, seeking to do what is fair and reasonable, who would reach the conclusion that it was right to hold that solicitors whose carelessness deprives an intended beneficiary of a share of a testator's estate that was destined for the beneficiary should be immune from any action by that beneficiary, and should have no liability save for nominal damages due to the testator's estate.[706]

Many conceptual problems arise in the case of a solicitor acting for his client. These are too complex and numerous to consider here. However, Lord Goff of Chieveley in *White* v. *Jones* felt that owing to these, and its failure to address them, the approach of Megarry V-C in *Ross* was inappropriate. In particular, Lord Goff observed that Megarry V-C, in holding 'liability could properly be imposed in negligence for pure economic loss... [had used as a preferred basis]... direct application of *Donoghue* v. *Stevenson* [1932] itself'.[707] Despite the conceptual problems, Lord Goff stated:

> Even so, it seems to me that it is open to your Lordship's House... to fashion a remedy to fill a lacuna in the law and so prevent the injustice which would otherwise occur on the facts of cases such as the present... I only wish to add that, with the benefit of experience during the 15 years in which *Ross* v. *Caunters* has been regularly applied, we can say with some confidence that a direct remedy by the intended beneficiary against the solicitor appears to create no problems in practice.[708]

Ultimately, as we have seen above, Lord Goff preferred a remedy under the *Hedley Byrne* principle. In conclusion he observed the following:

> Let me emphasise that I can see no injustice in imposing liability upon a negligent solicitor in a case such as the present where, in the absence of a remedy in this form, neither the testator's estate nor the disappointed beneficiary will have a claim for the loss caused by his negligence. This is the injustice which, in my opinion, the judges of this country should address by recognising that cases such as these call for an appropriate remedy, and that common law is not so sterile as to be incapable of supplying that remedy when it is required.[709]

---

[706] [1980] ch. 297 at pp. 311–312.
[707] [1995] 2 AC 207 at p. 261; see also the criticisms in K. McK., Norrie, 'Liability of solicitors to third parties', 1988 SLT (News) 309 and 317 at 317.
[708] Ibid. at p. 268.    [709] Ibid. at p. 269.

## The Netherlands

I. The notary is liable in tort for the damage incurred.

II. In a recent landmark decision, the Dutch Supreme Court ruled that the role of the notary public in Dutch society compels him, under specific circumstances, to consider not only the interests of his clients, but also those of third parties who might be involved in the official acts which his clients requested him to perform.[710] The Court held that it was feasible for a notary to be liable *vis-à-vis* the creditors of an insolvent bank if the notary knowingly rendered his services to moneylending operations that would leave the bank without sufficient mortgage coverage for their loans. The notary would be liable if he knew, or should have contemplated, the likely possibility that the bank would face insolvency as a result of these operations.

This example of one of the gravest of duties of care sets the standard for the case at hand. Assuming that the deed drafted by the notary is null as a result of the notary public's negligence, liability is inferred.[711] In all his dealings, a notary must exercise the utmost care in order to avoid nullity of the deed and consequential damages. This duty purports to protect not only the client, but also those upon whom the benefits of the will were supposed to be conferred.[712] Although the Supreme Court has not yet been asked to decide a case such as the one at hand, there is no doubt in my mind that the notary public is liable for avoidable nullities *vis-à-vis* a third party who justifiably expected to inherit. Even if this third party had no knowledge of the contents of the will, he lost a profit nonetheless. This, in my view, is sufficient grounds for damages.

According to Dutch law, a notarial deed is generally compulsory for a will to be legally binding. The interests of a third party who will benefit from the will must be taken to heart by the notary. This third party may sue in tort whenever the notary fails to perform his primary duty, i.e. to draft a legally sound deed.

---

[710] HR 15.9.1995, NJ 1996, no. 629.

[711] See for a recent example: HR 4.10.1996, NJ 1997, no. 594. In this case, the Supreme Court held a notary liable for failure to secure the consent of a surety's spouse; this failure resulted in nullification of the surety. The notary was held liable for the consequential damage.

[712] See Amsterdam Court of Appeal 19.1.1984, 31.1.1985, NJ 1985, no. 740. Compare, on the subject of liability of banks vis-à-vis third parties, J. M. Smits, 'Aansprakelijkheid voor aan derden verscrafte informatie; enige dogmatische en praktische kanttekeningen bij derden-aansprakelijkheid', in R. P. J. L Tjittes and M. A. Blom (eds.), *Bank & aansprakelijkheid* (1996), at p. 91.

## Germany

I. The result is straightforward: § 19 (1) of the Federal Notary Law of 24 February 1961 (as amended on 27 April 2002 – *Bundesnotarordnung*) provides that a notary is liable for all damages (including pure economic loss) proximately caused by the violation of a professional duty.

II. § 19 (1) of the Federal Notary Law clearly applies because it is settled that a notary has a professional duty of care towards third parties who would take under the will the notary is hired to draft.[713]

III. A German notary is statutorily liable for damages caused by a violation of his professional duties mainly because he holds a public office (although he is paid by his clients).[714] Certainly, this liability is based on negligence, but the professional standards are so high that committing errors in drawing a will is a sure indication of fault.

Even if the defendant were not a notary at all but merely an attorney-at-law, the result would be the same. In that case, however, liability would not be statutory. Instead, Giacomo would have to sue as a third party protected under the contract between Roberto and the notary.[715] In the present case, such a liability would not be in doubt.[716]

## Austria

I. Giacomo has a good chance of receiving compensation from the notary for his damages on the ground of a contract with protective effects to a third party.

II. The contract between the notary and the testator appears to protect the heir. Notaries are experts according to article 1299 ABGB. Therefore they owe a significantly higher standard of care.

The breach of a notary's duty of care which follows from a contract passed before the notary or under his supervision, or a notary's error in the formulation of a last will, as a rule entails nothing more than pure financial loss. In the case of a faulty testament, it is impossible

---

[713] See K. Seybold, H. Schippel and U. Bracker, *Bundesnotarordnung Kommentar* (6th edn, 1995), art. 19 Rd.-Nr. 34 (with further references and citations to case law).
[714] In some German states, a notary may also practise law as an attorney, in other states this is not allowed.
[715] See above, Case 13 ('Subcontractor's Liability'), section III.
[716] See BGH NJW 1965, 1955; the case is almost exactly identical with the present scenario. The only differences are that the defendant was not a notary but only an attorney-at-law, and that the defendant completely failed to draw up the will although he had a contract with the deceased to render this service.

that the testator could personally bring a claim. Therefore the Supreme Court has always decided in favour of the heirs: the notary is liable for the damage he negligently caused.[717] This practice is unanimously supported by scholars.[718]

III. The reason for the notary's liability *vis-à-vis* a third person with whom no contractual tie exists is not simply attributable to the fact that he holds a public office. Attorneys are similarly liable for an heir's financial loss caused by the attorney's negligent performance of a contract with the testator. The explanation for this well-established rule can be found in the fact that it is quite obvious to everybody that the heir shall be the beneficiary and should take the place of the deceased testator.

## Portugal

I. Although there are no precedents with circumstances quite the same as in the case described, it does not appear that there is anything to prevent Giacomo seeking reparation for the damage that he suffered.

II. There are two different legal systems governing the liability of the state and its organs, depending on whether private or public administration is involved.[719] As notaries are civil servants in Portugal[720] and there can be no doubt that, when they draw up a will or a deed, they are engaged in an act of public administration,[721] the public law system is applicable, as contained essentially in Decree-Law no. 48051 of 21 November 1967.[722] The suit will be heard in the administrative court.

However, the conditions of liability are similar to those in private law.[723] Protection should embrace not only those who request the

---

[717] See OGH GlUNF 330/1898; NZ 1987, 129, SZ 59/106.
[718] See e.g. R. Reischauer, in P. Rummel (ed.), *Commentary on the General Civil Code*, vol. 2 (2nd edn, Vienna, 1992), ABGB II2 § 1299 no. 17; K. Wagner and G. Knechtel, *Notariatsordnung* (5th edn, Vienna, 2000), § 39 no. 9, etc.
[719] P. De Lima and A. Varela, *Código Civil Anotado*, vol. I (4th edn, 1987), annotation to art. 501.
[720] Art. 25° of the Lei Orgânica dos Serviços do Registo e do Notariado (Organic Law on Registration and Conveyancing Services) (Decree-Law no. 519-F2/79 of 29 December 1979).
[721] S. F. Taveira Machado, 'Pressupostos da responsabilidade civil dos notários', (1986) 7 *Revista do Notariado* 25, 345, 348–9.
[722] The Notarization Code contains no specific provisions on liability. Article 184 presupposes its existence by establishing that 'the revalidation or ratification of notarial acts does not exempt officials from responsibility for the damage that they may cause'; and the same is said of art. 71 of the Organic Law, as we mention in the text.
[723] See M. Cortez, *Responsabilidade Civil da Administração par Actos Administrativos Ilegais e Concurso de Omissão Culposa do Lesado* (Coimbra Editora, Coimbra, 2000), pp. 47 ff. In

services but also third parties such as the (frustrated) beneficiary of a will voided because of an error on the part of a notary.[724]

The Organic Law, Decree Law no. 519/F2 of 29 December 1979,[725] establishes that 'The Safe (*Cofre*) of Conservators, Notaries and Justice Officials assume joint responsibility on behalf of the State for the damage that officials in the Registration and notarisation services may cause...'

According to Decree-Law no. 48051, the official (here, the notary) is not directly liable *vis-à-vis* the injured party, except where he has acted with malice or 'exceeded the limits of his functions' (art. 3, no. 1). Otherwise, the official is only open to recourse by the state or public body (legal person) if he had 'proceeded with manifestly less diligence and zeal than would be compelled by reason of his duty'.[726]

Nevertheless, some authors and legal decisions have felt that this regime is incompatible with article 22 of the Constitution, which would impose a regime of direct responsibility of the agent or official (jointly with the state or other public body).[727] This is still an open question.

With regard to the grounds for liability, this lies exclusively within the province of tort. It is very likely concerned with, among other things, the tradition of a notary being solely a civil servant (neither a counsellor nor an attorney).[728]

III. Some similar cases that occur in comparative law, but dealing with lawyers (especially in England and Germany),[729] would have a different and more problematical framing.

---

general, see F. Quadros (ed.), *Responsabilidade Civil Extracontractual da Administração Pública* (Almedina, Coimbra, 1995).

[724] Taveira Machado', 'Pressupostos', no. 77, 357, with reference to the hypothesis that the will is void through absence of witnesses.

[725] Above, fn. 620, at art. 71, no. 1.

[726] Article 2, no. 2 of Decree-Law no. 48051. According to art. 71, no. 2 of the Organic Law cited, this right of appeal is exercised through the Safe (*Cofre*).

[727] See J. F. Sinde Monteiro, 'Aspectos particulares da responsabilidade médica', in O. Ascensão, N. de Roche, M. Raposo, J. Sinde Monteiro, S. Correia, S. Martines, F. do Amaral, P. Lobato de Faria and J.-M. Andy (eds.), *Direito da Saúde e Bioética* (Lex (AAVV), Lisboa, 1991), pp. 133–52, 138–45, and Cortez, *Responsabilidade*, 23–8, with bibliographical references. Regarding judicial decisions, judgments of the STJ of 6 May 1986, *BMJ* 357, 392, and (as *obiter*) of 8 July 1987, CJ II, 153, 154. Finally, concerning art. 22 of the Constitution, J. Gomes Canotilho and V. Moreira, *Constituição da República Portuguesa Anotada* (3rd edn, Coimbra Editora, Coimbra, 1993), annotation to article 22.

[728] J. C. Gouveia Rocha, 'Deveres dos Notários. Sua Responsabilidade', (1983) 6 *Revista do Notariado* 29–39.

[729] W. Lorenz, 'Anwaltshaftung wegen Untätigkeit bei der Errichtung letztwilliger Verfügungen, Eine vergleichende Betrachtung des deutschen und des englischen Rechts', (1995) 50 *Juristen Zeitung*, 317–24.

As liability in tort does not exist (through absence of unlawfulness), the route to try would be that of 'contracts with the effect of protecting third parties'.

At the level of legislative policy, the Ministry of Justice has stated its intention to make profound changes in the notary profession, which will move into the private sector.

## Sweden and Finland

I. This example is explicitly quoted in the classical Swedish textbook on torts as one of 'uncertain solution'.[730] Compensation is likely to be accorded, but this is far from sure.

II. A prima facie interpretation of the tort legislation would exclude compensation because this is a 'pure economic loss', i.e. an economic loss arising without connection to anybody suffering personal injury or damage to things. According to the statutory rule in *SkadestL* 4:2 (Sweden) and *SkadestL* 5:1 (Finland), this is in principle to be compensated when it is consequent upon criminal behaviour, although the text and the preparatory works of the Tort Liability Acts 1972 and 1974 do not completely bar compensation should the courts find strong reasons for it. As mentioned in the introduction, courts have been very restrictive in granting exceptions to the general principle.

There is no case law concerning cases such as this, apart from a Swedish case of 1939[731] which affirmed the responsibility of a lawyer who committed a mistake in the procedure for enforcing a will. The facts of the case were, however, such that a sort of contractual relation between the lawyer and the beneficiary was possible to identify. In scholarly writings[732] an extension is proposed of the lawyer's liability in cases such as the one at hand, quoting German and Anglo-American case law as models to follow.

As in Case 11 ('A Maestro's Mistake'), it is possible to draw an analogy with one of the leading cases concerning liability for pure economic loss in the absence of a crime, i.e. NJA 1987 s. 692, where the Supreme Court affirmed the liability of a real estate evaluator who negligently stated the value of a real estate for the losses caused to a bank which, on the basis of the certificate, gave a loan to the real estate

---

[730] J. Hellner *Skadeståndsrätt* (5th edn, 1995), p. 79.
[731] NJA 1939 s. 374.
[732] See, for example, J. Kleineman *Ren förmögenhetsskada* (1987), pp. 555 ff.

owner who later went bankrupt. One can indeed argue that the lawyer acted negligently, being aware that his actions would most probably affect the heirs, thus building a base for compensation along the lines of the 1987 case. However, such possibility has not yet been tested in court.

III. The case must in the Swedish/Finnish context be understood as making reference to a lawyer (*advokat*) and not to a notary, since the latter does not exist in its continental form in the Nordic countries.

A leading Swedish scholar[733] observes that there is no evident reason for the absence in Sweden of litigation of the kind described here, something which must probably be ascribed to the recourse to extrajudicial settlements.

*Editors' comparative comments*

This case is based on circumstances which show that: (1) there is no direct contact between the wrongdoer and the plaintiff; until the will comes to light the grandson may not even know that his grandfather sought legal advice; (2) the economic loss at issue is not even parasitic. Consequently, no possible role can be played in the solution by any 'reliance' put by the plaintiff on the defendant's conduct.

However, none of these factors prevents the large majority of legal systems (a problematic approach is taken only by Sweden and Finland) from awarding damages to the plaintiff. Moreover, most of the countries examined make recovery possible under tort law rules, some of which are special statutes (Austria, which makes recourse to the 'contract with protective effects for a third person', is the exception).[734]

The ultimate and proper reason for this attitude is probably the need to maintain the highest possible public confidence in a certain standard of legal services. The overall outcome is nevertheless relevant to our purposes, because it enables plaintiffs to recover pure economic losses caused by those legal professionals regardless of the general features and traditions upon which the given tort law system is built.[735]

---

[733] Ibid. p. 552, note 82.
[734] Germany would make recourse to the same concept if an attorney, rather than a notary, had been involved in this case. See above, the German answer, C. von Bar, *The Common European Law of Torts* (Clarendon Press, Oxford, 1998), p. 521 and fn. 560.
[735] See our comments on Cases 17 ('Auditor's Liability') and 20 ('An Anonymous Telephone Call').

## Case 15: a closed motorway – the value of time

### Case

Due to the fault of a driver, Ned, a truck loaded with chemicals overturned on the motorway at a moment when traffic was particularly heavy. No other vehicle was involved or physically damaged in the accident. However, the authorities were forced to close the motorway for twelve hours. Certain vehicles were trapped in the consequent traffic jam, while many other drivers were warned in time and diverted to side roads. What will be the outcome of a claim brought by truck owner Mario who, because he was blocked on the motorway for five hours, arrived late at his destination and could not make another delivery on the same day? And what are the chances of a claim for compensation by another lorry driver who had to make a detour of some hundreds of kilometres because the motorway was closed, consuming a great deal of petrol and wasting considerable time?

### France

I. The truck drivers cannot recover their pure economic loss from Ned under the statutory liability scheme for car accidents, established by the Law no. 85-677 of 5 July 1985.[736] They may, however, assert a claim for the loss under articles 1382–83 CC.

II. The statutory liability scheme for car accidents was established because it was thought that the general tort provisions of the Civil Code were not adapted to the massive litigation caused by car accidents.

Within its domain, the new law is exclusive: every time the conditions for its application are fulfilled, it must be applied, instead of the general tort regime of the Civil Code.[737] Even when the new law applies, however, it does not necessarily control every question that arises. The general law of tort applies for all matters not covered by the special regime, for example for the evaluation of damages.

The conditions for application of the law require:

- a motor vehicle (car, truck, etc);
- an accident on a road;
- the implication of this vehicle in the damages sustained by the victims; and
- a damage.

[736] Law no. 85–677, 5 juillet 1985.
[737] Civ. 2, 4 mai 1987, Bull. 1987, II, no. 87; D. 1987, 187, note Groutel.

The two first conditions (a motor vehicle involved in a road accident) are obviously fulfilled in our case. Even if only one vehicle is involved and no collision has occurred, the law still applies. The Cour de Cassation has so held in a case[738] where a truck's dumpster detached from the truck cabin and caused damages to the motorway, though not hitting any other vehicle.

However, it is not so clear under the Law of 5 July 1985 that Ned's vehicle was implicated in the losses sustained by other road users. The purpose of the Law of 5 July 1985 is to allow the victims of a car accident to recover their losses. In Case 15, however, the drivers are not themselves victims of a road accident. They suffer from the consequences of a road accident, but they have not been involved at all in the accident. Furthermore, the fourth requirement of the statute – damage – is not satisfied. The Law of 5 July 1985 distinguishes two kinds of damages: personal damages (*atteintes à la personne*) and property damages (*dommages aux biens*).

Under article 3 of the Law, personal damages are defined as physical injuries. The Cour de Cassation has given a broad interpretation to the meaning of physical damages. It has held that the costs incurred by the family of an accident victim in organizing his funeral were 'damages' resulting from harm to the person.[739] It also allows the recovery of economic loss (*manque à gagner*) as a consequence of physical injuries under article 3 of the Law. But in each of these cases, the economic loss is preceded by a personal injury to a victim, whereas there is no preceding personal injury to the delayed truckers.

Under article 5 of the Law, property damages are defined as the property lost in a road accident such as vehicles, clothes, personal property, animals and goods.[740] It has been clearly stated by the Cour de Cassation that property damage under article 5 does not include any economic loss which may arise from personal injuries. Article 5 is confined to material damage to things.[741] Consequently, pure economic loss neither seems to fit under article 3 nor article 5 of the Law.

Moreover, article 6 of the Law compensates for the prejudice suffered by a third party because of an injury sustained by the primary victim. The theory of the *victime par ricochet* does not apply to the drivers blocked on the motorway.

---

[738] C. Cass, 22 janvier 1992, arrêt no. NC 76, pourvoi no. NC. 90.17.385 (Lexis).
[739] Crim., 20 juin 1989, Dame Laurent, Resp. Ass. 1989, no. 337.
[740] J.O. déb. Ass. Nat. 22 mai 1985.   [741] Cass. Civ. 2e, 24 janvier 1990, note J.-F. Barbiéri.

The general conclusion, therefore, is that the statute is inapplicable to the facts of Case 15. Professor Viney agrees with this conclusion.[742]

Though this case falls outside the scope of the Law of 5 July 1985, it would be possible to recover pure economic loss under the general provision, article 1382 CC. In a somewhat analogous case, the City of Marseille was awarded the losses that it sustained when its buses were immobilized in a traffic jam caused by a car accident. The traffic delay diminished the revenues of the city, a loss which the Tribunal de Première Instance (Court of First Instance) considered neither hypothetical nor indirect. Refusing to quash, the Cour de Cassation declared that the lower court had legally justified its decision.[743]

III. Whether recovery for pure economic loss in these circumstances will be awarded is very difficult to say. As Esmein observed in his note to the above-cited case, French judges have maximum discretion to award or not to award pure economic loss without serious fear of being overruled by the Cour de Cassation. While the *juges du fond* may declare the damage is 'direct', Esmein warns that 'this affirmation is without significance because the judges declare damages to be direct or indirect in accordance with their desire to award, or not to award, an indemnity'.

## Belgium

I. Neither Mario nor the driver who has to make the detour have a claim against Ned since their damages result from the decision of the authorities to close the motorway.

II. The tortfeasor is liable for the damage resulting from its fault. The plaintiff must therefore prove that the damage is the consequence of the defendant's fault.

In order to appreciate if there is a causal link between the fault and the damage, the Belgian Supreme Court uses a theory known as *l'équivalence des conditions*. According to this theory, the fault is sufficiently linked to the damage if the plaintiff can prove that the damage would not have occurred, as it occurred, if there had been no fault.[744]

---

[742] See her remarks at p. 110 in J. Spier, *The Limits of Expanding Liability* (Kluwer, 1998).
[743] Civ. 2, 28 avril 1965, D. 1965, 777 note Esmein.
[744] Cass., 12 janvier 1988, Pas., 1988, I, 563; Cass., 15 mai 1990, Pas, 1990, I, 1054; Cass., 23 mai 1990, Pas., 1990, I, 1079; Cass. 23 juin 1990, Pas, 1990, I, 1126; Cass., 8 octobre 1992, Pas., 1992, I, 1124.

According to the Supreme Court, the causal link is interrupted, however, when the damage in question results from another autonomous obligation such as one imposed by a statute or a contract.[745]

Since the damage claimed by Mario and the driver who had to make a detour result from the authorities' decision to close the motorway, which is most certainly based on a regulatory obligation, the court will probably reject the claim because the causal link has been interrupted.

## Italy

I. Mario can recover damages for the economic loss only if he can provide strong evidence of the link between the fault and the losses. The driver forced to make a detour cannot claim for damages.

II. As to the question of Mario's recovery of damages, the same situation has been treated in *Pirolo*,[746] where a highway was closed due to a truck that overturned and caught fire because of the driver's negligence. The court held the truck driver liable because the damage caused to the plaintiff had been directly caused by the former's negligence.

The driver forced to make a detour cannot claim for damages because the closing of the motorway is due to an act of a public authority, and the Italian court would refuse to assess damages because of public authority intervention. Indeed, case law considers all provisions and acts taken by the public authorities as an occurrence which interrupts the causation link between the defendant's conduct and the harmful event.[747]

## Spain

I. Neither case law nor specific doctrinal studies provide a solution to this case. However, the most probable result is that none of the drivers could bring an action against Ned.

---

[745] Cass., 17 janvier 1938, Pas., I, 8 et 11; Cass., 28 avril 1978, RCJB, 1979, p. 261; Cass., 26 septembre 1979; RGAR, 1982, no. 10431; Cass., 9 mars 1984, RCJB, 1986, p. 651; Cass., 15 mars 1985, Pas., I, 1985, 978; Cass., 28 juin 1984, Pas., 1984, I, 618; Cass., 18 avril 1988, Pas., 1988, I, 943; Cass., 4 octobre 1988, Pas, 1989, I, 118, 15 novembre 1991, I, 282.

[746] Cass., 16.10.1991, CP 1992, 2, 29.

[747] Cass., 28 novembre 1998, no. 12093, DR 1999, 47; Trib. Monza, 21 maggio 1986, AC, 1987, 48.

II. Under Spanish law, the matter may be resolved by arguing that the action taken by the authorities breaks the chain of causation and that, consequently, the owner of the lorry involved in the accident could not be sued. From the point of view of the *imputatio facti*, damages would not be imputable if we exclude them under the principle of 'general risks of life' (*allgemeines Lebensrisiko*).

### Greece

I. The lorry driver's additional expenses could constitute indemnifiable damages, but this is not certain. On the other hand, Mario's loss of another current delivery cannot be compensated since it was unforeseeable.

II. Although not corresponding to a specific material or incorporeal property asset, common use of public things is protected by the law within the framework of the right to personality (art. 57 CC). This has been repeatedly confirmed by court decisions.[748] Thus, in principle, anyone hindering common use of the highway is liable, since he commits a tort. In view of this, Ned committed a tort, because the law lays down that roads are things in public use (art. 967 CC); and to prevent someone from using them is prohibited (art. 57 CC).[749] Thus, under article 914 CC Ned is liable to compensate Mario and the other lorry driver, provided that there is causal link (causation) between their damages and Ned's tort.

Two criteria have been proposed for testing causation: either the foreseeability of the particular damage,[750] or whether the damage relates to the interests protected by the legal rule that the tortfeasor infringed.[751] One can readily conclude that the purpose served by the prohibition

---

[748] See, for example, AP 684/1973 NoB 22, 175; AP 150/1976 EEN 43, 580; AP 31/1967 NoB 15, 653.

[749] AP 259/1971, NoB 19, 853; A. Georgiades, *General Principles of Civil Law* (2nd edn, 1996), p. 127.

[750] AP 692/1990 NoB 40, 67; AP 1063/90; AP 979/92 ElD 35, 1044; K. Triantaphyllopoulos, *Law of Obligations* (Athens, 1935), p. 184; G. Balis, *Law of Obligations, General Part* (3rd edn, 1960), p. 100; A. Ligeropoulos (gen. ed.), *Interpretation of the Civil Code (A Commentary) (ErmAK)* (1949–1978), arts. 297–300 CC, nr. 39; G. Fourkiotis, *Greek Law of Obligations, General Part* (1964), p. 318; G. Michaélidès-Nouaros, *Law of Obligations* (1959), p. 31, etc.

[751] A. Georgiades and M. Stathopoulos, *Civil Code, Article by Article Commentary*, vols. II–IV (1978–1982), Commentary by M. Stathopoulos, arts. 297–298, no. 67, 60–5; P. Sourlas, *Adaequanztheorie und Normzwecklehre bei der Begründung der Haftung nach § 823 Abs. 1 BGB* (1974), pp. 15 ff.

on interference with the use of public things is to protect the foreseeable interests of the people who use the road in one way or another (as passengers or consignees of goods).

Thus, avoiding unnecessary expense and wasted time is the easily presumed interest of somebody using a rapid transit motorway, so the lorry driver may seek compensation from Ned. Nevertheless, the foreseeability of any particular damage of this kind is still very doubtful. Indeed, for example, is it foreseeable to make a detour of additional kilometres, in order to arrive at the lorry's destination on this particular day? Is it foreseeable that, if the traffic jam had not taken place, the lorry driver might have needed to make a detour anyway, this time due to another jam caused by one of the thousands of accidents that happen every day on the Greek motorways? Furthermore, is it fair to compensate every driver in the case of even the slightest accident or traffic jam?

As to the claim of Mario who could not deliver a shipment on time, the occurrence of the loss and moreover the exact value of the delay of course cannot be easily foreseen. Mario's loss seems inadequately related to Ned's fault. His claim for compensation will not succeed.

## England

I. Neither Mario, nor any other driver, can recover any damages from Ned or the authorities for their economic losses.

II. Public nuisance: Ned's act is a common law offence, obstruction of the highway, and as such, also a public nuisance. As already analysed above,[752] civil liability may arise in English law from the crime of public nuisance, i.e. an action or omission 'which obstructs or causes inconvenience or damage to the public in the exercise of rights common to all Her Majesty's subjects', and when, as a result, an individual has suffered particular damage over and above the inconvenience or damage to the public at large.[753] Economic loss is clearly recoverable under this tort.[754] But neither Mario, nor any other driver involved in the upheaval in this case, can show such 'particular damage, over and above the inconvenience or damage to the public at large'.

Negligence: in the light of *Murphy* v. *Brentwood DC*,[755] confirming beyond doubt the Court of Appeal approach to negligent financial harm

---

[752] Case 6, 'The Infected Cow'.
[753] See the review of authorities by Scholl J in *Walsh* v. *Ervin* [1952] WLR 361.
[754] See *Tate & Lyle Indus.* v. *GLC* [1983] 1 All ER 1159 (HL).
[755] [1991] 1 AC 398 (HL).

in *Spartan Steel* v. *Martin*,⁷⁵⁶ there can be no duty of care in negligence owed to other road users not to cause pure economic loss to them by blocking the highway.

III. The case is another good illustration of the 'nightmare scenario', responsible for the greatest objection to liability for economic loss, i.e. that it can be so widespread in amount that no defendant ought to be asked to carry the risk of compensating it.⁷⁵⁷

## Scotland

I. Neither of the lorry drivers would have any chance of recovering damages from Ned for the economic loss that they have suffered.

II. The reasons for this have been clearly set out in various cases considered above. None of the parties has suffered any damage to their property. They are confronted by the general rule of non-liability for secondary economic loss as we have seen developed from *Allan* v. *Barclay*, through *Reavis* v. *Clan Line* and down to *Dynamco*. Briefly to reiterate, Lord Migdale in *Dynamco* held that '[t]he law of Scotland has for over a hundred years refused to accept that a claim for financial loss which does not arise directly from damage to the claimant's property can give rise to a legal claim for damages founded on negligence'.⁷⁵⁸ In particular circumstances there may be exceptions to the general rule. We have discussed *Hedley Byrne*, *Junior Books*, *Henderson & Merrett* and other cases. As we have seen, however, central to these exceptions are proximity of relationship, assumption of responsibility and concomitant reliance. None of these is present here. We also have the hurdle expounded by Lord Bridge of Harwich in *Caparo* that 'the situation should be one in which the court considers it fair, just and reasonable that the court should impose a duty [of care] of a given scope on the one party for the benefit of the other'.⁷⁵⁹ On grounds of public policy one could not imagine that the court would so find a duty of care was reasonable in the circumstances here. In such a case as the present, as Lord Denning MR observed in *SCM (UK) Ltd*, '[t]he risk should be borne by the whole community rather than on one pair of shoulders'.⁷⁶⁰

III. With intentional delicts the class of potential pursuers will be limited (unless one was dealing with the insane or terrorists); it extends

---

⁷⁵⁶ [1973] 1 QB 27 (CA).
⁷⁵⁷ More in E. K. Banakas, *Tortious Liability for Pure Economic Loss* (Hellenic Institute for International and Foreign Law, Athens, 1989), pp. 36 ff.
⁷⁵⁸ 1972 SLT 38 at p. 39.   ⁷⁵⁹ [1990] 2 AC 605 at p. 618.
⁷⁶⁰ [1971] 1 QB 337 at p. 344D.

to those whom the defender intended to harm. With unintentional but careless conduct the defender is, prima facie, liable to anyone who suffers harm as a result of his careless conduct. The duty of care is used in Scots law as a way to restrict the defender's potential liability in delict. To hold that Ned has a duty of care in circumstances such as these, short of physical damage, would be to open him up to (as Cardozo CJ so elegantly expressed it) 'liability in an indeterminate amount for an indeterminate time, to an indeterminate class'.[761] It is the policy of the Scottish courts not to open negligent parties up to such wide-ranging claims.

## The Netherlands

I. There is no relevant difference between the damage suffered by Mario and the damage suffered by the other truck driver. Having said that, it remains unclear whether either can claim in tort. Dutch law does not provide a clear-cut answer.

II. In a 1917 ruling, the Dutch Supreme Court favoured the following line of reasoning: blocking a public road constitutes a violation of a statutory duty (i.e. the duty laid down in the statutes on road traffic), and whenever someone is in violation of this rule, they can be held liable for subsequent damage.[762] However, this decision can no longer be considered to be good law.[763] Since 1928, the Dutch Supreme Court has adhered to the *relativiteitsleer* (better known as the *Schutznorm* theory),[764] which means that an unlawful act *as such* will not infer liability unless the violated statute or unwritten rule of conduct purports to protect against *such damage as was suffered by the injured*.[765]

Applying the *relativiteitsleer* to this case, one should ask whether the statutory duty to avoid a traffic jam purports to protect against damage caused by the delay and the detour respectively. In answering, one should look into parliamentary proceedings relative to the statute, or – if the parliamentary proceedings contain no mention of the issue – case law that clarifies the intentions of the legislature. The most obvious

---

[761] *Ultramares Corp'n v. Touche* 174 NE 441 (1931) at p. 444; 255 NY 170 (1931) at p. 179.
[762] HR 30.3.1917, NJ 1917, pp. 502 ff.
[763] See G. H. Lankhorst, *De relativiteit van de onrechtmatige daad* (Deventer, 1992), pp. 14 ff. Apparently, *contra*: Kottenhagen, at p. 342.
[764] HR 25.5.1928, NJ 1928, pp. 1688 ff.
[765] See currently art. 6:163 CC, which reads: 'No obligation to repair damages arises whenever the violated norm does not purport to protect from damage such as suffered by the injured'. Compare Spier, *Limits of Expanding Liability*, at p. 113.

aims of this statutory duty are to avoid collisions resulting in casualties and damage to vehicles. Even if the purpose of the statute is to avoid economic loss as a result of delay, it is not entirely clear whether the legislature envisioned civil liability arising from a violation of the statute.

If the statute in itself does not purport to infer civil liability *vis-à-vis* the hundreds or even thousands of people that suffered some sort of loss from the delay, it should be asked whether the lorry driver acted contrary to the standard of conduct acceptable in society (art. 6:162 ss. 2 CC). Does the driver of a motor vehicle have a duty of care to his fellow drivers to take all reasonable precautions in order to avoid accidents and subsequent traffic jams? The factors that determine the impropriety of the driver's behaviour do not really indicate only one right answer. Although it is *foreseeable* that a traffic jam will occur when a truck overturns and that the *chances* of loss occurring because of the delay are considerable, accidents will inevitably happen. So, in any case, the driver must be guilty of some sort of negligence in handling his truck or prior to departure – the cargo. Checking the other factors and circumstances will likewise prove to be indecisive. It all depends on exactly what caused the truck to overturn, the degree of blameworthiness of the driver, the cost of preventing the accident from happening, the relationship between those injured and the injurer, and finally, the nature of the damage. These two last factors do not favour liability in this case: there is no legal proximity, as the English would say; and the nature of the damage does not favour liability either – pure economic loss would lead to reticence in allowing for a claim in damages.

In my view, this reluctance to allow a claim against the truck driver stems from a well-founded fear of the unknown. If the Supreme Court were to allow recovery for loss by delay (be it because of Mario being stuck in the jam, or because of a forced detour by the other driver), it would certainly open floodgates for similar claims in similar cases. I myself would be most hesitant to allow either claim against driver Ned. But we cannot close our eyes to the fact that the Dutch Supreme Court in its 1977 gas main decision showed no fear of the unknown. In that case, it was decided that the excavator owed a duty to all of those who had an immediate and obvious interest in an uninterrupted gas supply.[766] It might well be argued that Ned has a duty to handle his truck and cargo properly to all of those who have an immediate and obvious interest in

---

[766] HR 1.7.1977, NJ 1978, no. 84.

the uninterrupted flow of traffic. If Ned can be blamed for the accident, then it could well follow that he is liable for the pure economic loss. Seen from this perspective, the 1977 Supreme Court decision is very much like a Pandora's box.

To conclude, I personally would hesitate to open these floodgates, but the Dutch Supreme Court seems less hesitant. This observation is more or less confirmed by another Supreme Court decision. In the *Rijksweg 12* decision,[767] the Court allowed a claim in tort for the cost of cleaning up a motorway incurred by the Dutch public authorities as a result of the overturning of a truck loaded with chemicals. Although the cost of cleaning up might not be filed under pure economic loss, the decision shows that the Court tends to draw the circumference of the driver's duty quite widely.

**Germany**

I. Mario's claim: Mario's claim against Ned will fail because none of Mario's absolute rights were violated.

Other truck driver's claim: a driver who has to make a detour has no claim against Ned either.

II. Mario's claim: Mario will not be able to show that any of the rights listed in § 823 (1) BGB were violated.

Mario will not be able to recover for an infringement of his freedom. It is true that common sense suggests that one who is locked in a traffic jam suffers such an infringement, but the standard interpretation of the term *Freiheit* in § 823 (1) BGB does not support this. While there is considerable debate about exactly what that term means, the prevailing opinion is that it includes solely the personal ability physically to change location, e.g. to leave a place. Since Mario could have left the scene (including his truck, of course), he still had his freedom in that narrow sense. The freedom to move by a particular means of transportation, such as a car, is not protected in § 823 (1) BGB.[768]

It is conceivable to think of the confinement of the truck as a violation of Mario's property right. The *Bundesgerichtshof* has held that the loss of the use of a ship amounted to such a violation where a barge was locked

---

[767] HR 19.10.1975, NJ 1976, no. 280; compare HR 26.5.1978, NJ 1978, no. 615.
[768] See E. Deutsch, *Unerlaubte Handlungen, Schadensersatz und Schmerzensgeld* (3rd edn, 1995), Rd.-Nr. 183; J. Eckert, 'Der Begriff der Freiheit im Recht der unerlaubten Handlungen', JuS 1994, 625–31. The 'freedom' of economic activity is not protected either, RGZ 100, 213, at 214 (1920).

into a canal for several months.⁷⁶⁹ Yet, the Court has also decided that the owner of land whose access by public road was blocked for a few hours has no claim for violation of property right.⁷⁷⁰ The present case is much closer to the second scenario than to the first. As a result, it is almost certain that the courts would reject a claim for violation of property rights.

Mario's right of the 'established and ongoing commercial enterprise' (if Mario's truck was his business) was not violated because the interference was not directed at, or specifically related to, the business as such.⁷⁷¹ Instead, the accident affected all users of the road alike.

The right to use public highways is not recognized as 'another right' protected by § 823 (1) BGB.⁷⁷²

There is no claim either under § 823 (2), i.e. because of the violation of protective statute. Even if Ned had violated traffic rules, these rules are not intended to protect other road users against delays caused by traffic jams.⁷⁷³

Other tort provisions in the Civil Code do not apply.

Mario could try to sue Ned under the Road Traffic Act 1952 (as amended 25 July 2002 – *Straßenverkehrsgesetz*) which provides for liability of the vehicle owner (art. 7: quasi-strict liability) and driver (liability for negligence with reversed burden of proof). Such a claim would fail as well because this liability covers only personal injury or death and physical harm to property.

Other truck driver's claim: there is no basis for the other truck driver's claim whatsoever. A violation of property or other rights is completely out of the question because the driver has not lost the use of the truck.⁷⁷⁴

III. The rejection of claims in cases such as the present is strongly motivated by the fear of an undue expansion of liability. It is not at all inconceivable to conclude that a person caught in a traffic jam with his vehicle suffers a loss of freedom, and that damages resulting from such a loss of freedom are covered by § 823 (1) BGB. But such a decision would lead to an almost boundless liability of everyone who causes an accident on Germany's crowded roads, and it would unleash a flood of lawsuits. Thus, the *Bundesgerichtshof* has indicated (although somewhat vaguely) that the loss of the use of public highways or a short-term blockage of

---

[769] BGHZ 55, 153, 159 (1970).    [770] BGH NJW 1977, 2264, at 2265–6.
[771] See Case 2 ('Cable II – Factory Shutdown'), Section II.
[772] BGHZ 55, 153, at 160, 162 (1970).    [773] BGH NJW 1977, 2264, at 2265.
[774] See BGHZ 55, 153, at 160–2 (1970).

access is part of the general risk that everyone must bear.[775] Similar arguments can be found in the academic literature.[776]

## Austria

I. Mario has no claim against Ned because there is no absolute right which Ned violated by his negligent behaviour.

Other lorry drivers do not have a claim against Ned for the same reasons.

II. Mario's claim: the infringement of Mario's right to personal freedom as acknowledged by articles 16 and 1329 ABGB is not strong enough to entitle him to sue Ned. Under Austrian law it makes a difference if Mario was intentionally blocked, or if he only became stuck in a negligently caused traffic jam. If Ned had intentionally interfered with Mario's right to personal freedom, e.g. by planning the traffic breakdown in order to prevent him from being elsewhere, such behaviour would probably be sufficient for the success of a claim against Ned.

Similar considerations will govern the question under articles 1331 and 1332 ABGB[777] as to whether Ned might be liable for the financial loss which Mario sustained when the use of his property became temporarily impossible. In the context of damages resulting from demonstrations, the OGH has remarked in *obiter dictum* that the mere fact that a person is impeded in the use of their property is not sufficient grounds for a compensation claim.[778]

There is no basis under Austrian law to apply the genuine German doctrine of 'violation of the right of the established and ongoing commercial enterprise' (assuming Mario's truck was his business).[779]

There is also no available claim based on article 1311 ABGB (violation of a protective statute). Statutory traffic rules may qualify as statutes to protect traffic victims against financial loss. It is generally accepted,

---

[775] BGH NJW 1977, 2264, at 2266.
[776] J. von Staudinger, *Kommentar zum Bürgerlichen Gesetzbuch* (12th edn, 1986), § 823 Rd.-Nr. 48.
[777] § 1331 ABGB: 'If a person's property is injured intentionally or by the gross negligence of another, he is entitled to demand any lost profits and, if the damage has been caused by an act forbidden by criminal law or by an act of wantonness and malice, the particular value of the property damaged.'
[778] Cf. OGH JBl 1995, 658 (blocked gateway); consenting note by Karollus-Brunner, JBl 1995, 662; see also P. Rummel, 'Wettbewerb durch Umweltschutz – Überlegungen zum Mißbrauch subjektiver öffentlicher Rechte', RZ 1993, 36.
[779] Cf. H. Koziol, *Österreichisches Haftpflichtrecht*, vol. II (2nd edn, Vienna, 1984), p. 39.

however, that these rules do not protect road users against delays caused by traffic jams.

Other lorry drivers' claims: as none of the drivers has lost his truck or the use of his truck, there is no violation of property or other absolute rights protected by tort rules.

III. If Ned's accident was not caused by his or anyone else's fault, the Statute on the Liability of Railways and Automobiles 1959,[780] which subjects railways and most motor traffic on roads to a regime of strict liability, may apply. However, this statute does not provide for compensation of pure economic loss.[781] This is considered to be a consequence of the theory that, under the rules of fault-based delictual liability, financial interests should not be protected to the same extent as they are under contract law. Proceeding on this basic assumption, the policy is even clearer that recoverability of pure economic loss should be denied whenever liability is based on a less convincing ground for liability, such as the mere fact that an activity creates a high danger that damage may occur. Moreover, the particular purpose and specific policy background of this statutory regime of strict liability do not suggest that pure financial losses are protected.

This hypothetical case shows that different types of invasions to an absolutely protected right such as property do not entail the same legal consequences. The mere impeding of the use of property is not the same as the direct violation of the property right. In particular, this is true when the impediment is shortlived: such inconveniences have to be borne as a rule by the owner.

The same is true with deprivation of liberty. However, a combination of the two may occur which proves sufficient to ground liability: if the interests for which protection is sought are of minor importance in a given case, the wrong must be more weighty to justify the imposition of liability on the person who caused the violation.

## Portugal

I. Neither the owner of the vehicle held up for five hours, nor the driver forced to make a lengthy diversion could seek compensation from the

---

[780] 'Eisenbahn-Kraftfahrzeug-Haftpflichtgesetz' (EKHG) BGBl 1959/48.

[781] See § 1 EKHG; the same is true with other strict liability statutes: cf. § 1a RHG, § 146 LFG, §§ 160, 163 MinRoG, § 10 RohrlG, § 47 ForstG.

driver (or the owner) of the transporter of chemicals that overturned on the motorway through the driver's fault, causing the motorway to be closed for twelve hours.[782]

II. Technically, the most direct way to justify refusing compensation consists of an argument that there has been no violation of subjective rights or of a legal provision intended to protect the particular type of interests affected (art. 483/1).

It may be a matter for discussion whether there has been violation of a right of ownership (of the owners of the vehicles that are prevented from circulating for a prolonged period), or of a personality right (freedom of movement).

The distinction between the violation of a right and a simple disturbance in the exercise of it is never clear and it should be acknowledged that, on occasion, it can constitute a kind of technical trick to achieve (or justify) the preferred *de iure condendo* solution.

With respect to the non-application of the provisions that establish a liability through risk (arts. 503 ff.), this is related to the fact that the damage in question does not fall within the protective purpose of the rule.

III. Independently of the legal grounds, we believe that the solution would be consensual in Portuguese law. In the final analysis, we are dealing with accepting the idea that the risk of losing time (or other inconveniences) owing to traffic conditions is inherent in modern society. Such risks must be borne by every citizen, even when its occurrence is due to the negligence of an individual, rather than an accidental circumstance.

## Sweden and Finland

I. None of the prospective claimants will get compensation.

II. Here, the main obstacle is again the general principle of the law of torts that limits compensation of economic losses to losses suffered by those subjects who have been the direct victims of a personal injury or property damage. 'Third parties' are in principle not entitled to compensation. Here indeed, strictly speaking, the only 'property damage' has been suffered by the defendant.

---

[782] This question is similar to hypothesis 3 of the Tilburg Group. See the Portuguese report and the comparative law report in Spier, *Limits of Expanding Liability*, at pp. 177 and 51 ff., respectively.

None of the arguments used (as in the cable cases) to soften the third-party rule seems to be applicable in a case such as this, especially since case law seems to be very sensitive to the 'floodgates' argument.[783]

III. The possibility of getting compensation seems especially remote since we are in the context of traffic accidents. Although the Swedish Traffic Damages Act 1975[784] and the Finnish Traffic Insurance Act 1959[785] are based on the same concepts of 'personal injury' and 'property damage' as general torts law, the actual determination of compensation is done in the great majority of cases by dispute resolution bodies different from the courts, and they are likely not to be very prone to extend liability beyond traditional standards.

*Editors' comparative comments*

This case casts the 'floodgates' argument in the brightest possible light, and it also evokes a corollary of the argument, namely, that some losses must be left where they lie because they are part of the general risk borne by everyone in their daily lives.

Except for the French liberal (in principle) position, all the legal systems considered here deny recovery under the circumstances of this case. In support of this denial, the national contributors refer to an array of technical explanations, at the very core of which, however, lies fear of the 'nightmare scenario' commonly depicted in Cardozo CJ's words as a 'liability in an indeterminate amount for an indeterminate time, to an indeterminate class'.[786]

The 'floodgates' argument is discussed in our introduction.[787] Here it will suffice to summarize its main points.

Obviously, no pocket is ever deep enough to compensate everyone. Certainly, economic loss poses causation issues stemming from uncontrolled spreading of the loss beyond the patrimony of the primary victim.

Nevertheless – and regardless of the position taken on the recoverability of pure economic loss in the circumstances of this case – the arguments normally adduced to deny liability, because its imposition might expose defendants to a large volume of claims, are ultimately unconvincing. Or at the very least, they are counterbalanced by the following:

---

[783] See J. Kleineman, *Ren förmögenhetsskada* (1987), chs. 5 and 6.
[784] Trafikskadelag (1975: 1410).    [785] Trafikförsäkringslag 26.6.1959/279.
[786] *Ultramares Corporation v. Touche* 174 NE 441 (1931) at p. 444; 255 NY 170 (1931) at p. 179.
[787] Above, Part I, Chapter 6.

(1) the law is usually content to impose liability when the potential plaintiff class is large;[788]
(2) it would be very odd if defendants could argue that they should not owe a duty because they would have too many victims;[789]
(3) the denial of liability for pure economic loss would be hard to reconcile with recovery for a potentially large economic loss resulting from negligently caused physical injuries;[790] and
(4) any possible grounding of the 'floodgates' argument on the wisdom of history – which would support and encourage an *a priori* limitation on the scope of tort law protection – should be read against the conclusions drawn by James Gordley at the end of his chapter in this volume.[791]

Gordley writes (with specific regard to the countries deemed to be 'stingiest' in allowing tort law recovery for the loss in question), that the denial of compensation for pure economic loss

---

[788] Besides mass torts (on which see, with special regard to our issue, J. van Dunné, 'Liability for Pure Economic Loss: Rule or Exception? "A Comparatist's View of the Civil Law–Common Law Split on Compensation of Non-physical Damage in Tort Law"', (1999) 4 *European Review of Private Law* 397, 426) one can note that e.g. in *AB v. South West Water Services* [1993] 1 All ER 609, an individual's single moment of carelessness gave rise to liability in negligence towards 182 plaintiffs – and this is a case which comes from a jurisdiction where the floodgates argument is a cornerstone of legal reasoning as to the recoverability of pure economic loss. See J. Stapleton, 'Duty of Care Factors: A Selection from the Judicial Menus', in P. Cane and J. Stapleton, *The Law of Obligations. Essays in Honour of J. Fleming* (1998), pp. 59 ff., p. 66 with fn. 27 and p. 68 with fns. 37 and 38; D. Howarth, 'The General Conditions of Unlawfulness', in A. Hartkamp, M. Hesselink, E. Hondius, C. Joustra and E. du Perron (eds.), *Towards a European Civil Code* (2nd edn, Ars Aequi Libri, Nijmegen, 1998), pp. 397, 424 ff.

[789] In the leading Australian case on economic loss, *Perre v. Apand Pty. Ltd.* (1999) 198 CLR 180, it was noted: 'it is not the size or number of claims that is decisive in determining whether potential liability is so indeterminate that no duty of care is owed. Liability is indeterminate only when it cannot be realistically calculated. (at 221)...Apand need only have knowledge of an ascertainable class, not a "defined and small class". The size of the class is irrelevant...Apand knew that there was an ascertainable class whose members were at risk of economic loss. Its numbers are not to the point. The principle of indeterminacy is designed to protect the defendant against indeterminate liability, not numerous plaintiffs' (at p. 233, *per* McHugh J). '[I]ndeterminate liability...means more than "extensive" or "large". The damage suffered by persons affected by the defendant's negligence may be very large; there may be many who are affected. But neither of those considerations means that the liability is indeterminate. What is meant by indeterminate in the present context is that the persons who may be affected cannot readily be identified' (p. 303, *per* Callinan J).

[790] R. Bernstein, 'Civil Liability for Pure Economic Loss Under American Tort Law', (1998) 46 *American Journal of Comparative Law* 111, 126; see also J. Stapleton, 'Tort, Insurance and Ideology', (1995) Mod. LR 820, 825.

[791] Above, Part I, Chapter 2.

was preserved by the deference of German judges to the Civil Code and of English judges to precedent. Just as the way in which it was adopted should encourage us to re-examine the rule, the way in which it was preserved should encourage us to re-examine our ideas about the authority of codes and precedents. It is one thing to say that they should have authority. It is another to say that courts should defer to a rule founded on academic ideas, now discredited, in the minds of drafters and treatise writers long dead. The courts could instead take a critical and historical approach to their authorities. Otherwise they may find themselves deferring to a fossilized error.[792]

[792] Above, 'conclusion' to Chapter 2.

## Case 16: truck blocking entrance to business premises

### Case

David parks his large truck across the entrance to Peter's garden centre. Due to inadequate maintenance of its engine, the truck cannot be started or removed for two days. As a result, Peter loses a large sum in lost sales because customers are unable to get to the garden centre.

### France

I. Peter will be able to recover from David for the economic loss he suffered under articles 1382–83 and article 1384, al.1 CC.

II. David could be liable under article 1382 for his faulty behaviour both in badly parking his truck in an area used as an entrance and in not maintaining the truck's engine which thereby made it impossible to remove the truck from the entrance. Peter will have little difficulty establishing David's fault, the economic loss, the damage he suffered and the close causal link between the two.

But David could also be liable under article 1384, al.1 since he was the *gardien* of the vehicle. As seen in Case 6, Article 1384, al.1 has been interpreted by the jurisprudence as stating a strict liability principle. The Chambres Réunies of the Cour de Cassation declared the meaning of the code provision in the following terms:

> The presumption of liability established by Article 1384, al.1, against the person who has the inanimate thing which has caused damage to another, in his *garde* cannot be destroyed except by proof of a fortuitous event or overwhelming force or of some external cause which cannot be imputed to him; it does not suffice to show that he has not committed any fault or that the cause of the injury remains unknown; the law, as far as the presumption which it decrees is concerned, does not distinguish whether the thing which caused the damage was or was not activated by the hand of men; it is unnecessary that the thing possess an inherent defect capable of causing the loss; Article 1384, al.1 attaches liability to the *garde* of the thing, not to the thing itself.[793]

There are a few decisions indicating that, in principle, article 1384, al.1 may lead to liability for pure economic loss.[794] The relative infrequency

---

[793] Author's free translation. Ch. Réunies, 13 février 1930, *Dalloz* 1930.I.57.
[794] See Cass. Civ., 2è, 19 mars 1980, JCP 1980.IV.216: dragline equipment which fell into water and was not retrieved created a 'zone of insecurity' and blocked the port, thus causing economic harm to plaintiff whose boat was unable to gain access and

of such recoveries, however, suggests that the main vocation of article 1384, al.1 has been the reparation of physical harm.

In this case, the presumption of liability which rests upon the *gardien* cannot be rebutted since there is no evidence of *cas fortuit, force majeure*, or *cause étrangère*.

### Belgium

I. Peter can recover his loss from David but it will not be very easy to evaluate the damage, which consists of the lost opportunity to make profits.

II. The first issue for Peter will be to convince the court that the damage he claims is certain.[795] In order to do so, Peter will have to prove that the sales were not hypothetical but certain.

However, the case law has softened this requirement in some circumstances by indemnifying the loss of an opportunity (*la perte d'une chance*) subject to the evidence that the opportunity was real or sufficiently certain.[796]

This theory is often used in connection with the professional liability of lawyers when the damage consists in the loss of an opportunity to make an appeal. Was the possible modification of the lower court's judgment by the Court of Appeal a real or only a hypothetical opportunity?[797]

When the opportunity is only hypothetical, the damage resulting from its loss is not recoverable.[798]

Because it can be difficult to evaluate the damage resulting from the loss of an opportunity, the damage is mostly calculated *ex aequo ac bono*, which means the award of a lump sum.[799]

---

discharge cargo; Cour d'Appel Paris, 5è ch., 23 avril 1979, Gaz. Pal. 1979.295 (note Rodière): *pacquebot* at anchor blocked the free circulation of boats through port and caused losses to plaintiff whose oil supertanker was forced to make a detour.

[795] R. O. Dalcq and G. Schamps, 'La responsabilité délictuelle et quasi-délictuelle, examen de jurisprudence (1987–1993)', RCJB, 1995, p. 737, no. 149; J. L. Fagnart, *La responsabilité civile – Chronique de jurisprudence 1985–1995* (Larcier, Brussels, 1997), p. 23, no. 11.

[796] Cass., 19 octobre 1937, Pas., 1937, I, p. 298; Cass., 8 décembre 1958, Pas., 1959, I, p. 354; Cass., 15 octobre 1962, Pas, 1963; I, 195; Cass., 15 septembre 1972, RGAR, 1973; no. 9121; Cass., 4 mars 1975, Pas., 1975, I, 682; Cass., 19 juin 1987, RW, 1987–88, p. 709.

[797] See for instance Civ. Bxl., 23 mai 1996, JLMB, 1997, p. 435 and note J. P. Buyle.

[798] See for instance: Civ. Marche, 11 février 1988, RGAR, 1990, no. 11.719 – damage claimed for the loss of the opportunity to make a career in the army.

[799] See for example: Mons, 6 mai 1996, JLMB, 1997, p. 432; Anvers, 1er janvier 1996, TDRB, 1995–6, p. 271 (damage resulting from the lost opportunity to re-implant a tooth).

## Italy

I. Peter can recover damages under article 2043 cc.

II. As a matter of principle, a plaintiff can always recover for loss of profits due to the negligence of the defendant whose conduct did not meet the standard of care implied in the normal course of business.[800] In such a case as the one under review, however, one should be aware of the plaintiff's need to meet the victim's duty of care test, as set forth by article 1227 cc, which reads:

> When negligent behaviour by plaintiff has contributed to determine the damage, compensation will be reduced according to the degree of negligence and the actual consequence suffered therefrom.

Under the circumstances, it will therefore be hard to prove that the blockade could not have been removed by means less costly than the amount of money lost during the two days' closing of the garden centre.

## Spain

I. There is no theoretical obstacle to Peter's claim for compensation. He would probably obtain compensation in a Spanish court, especially if he had signposted that parking in front of the entrance was prohibited.

II. We have not found any case decisions which involve a similar situation. The solution to this case can be reached as follows.

Since Spanish law has a general liability clause in article 1902 CC, in theory there is no problem with compensating Peter's pure economic loss. What would remain is the general problem of proving lost profits and the relatively strict attitude of the Spanish courts when calculating them.

The link of causation between David's behaviour and Peter's loss is quite clear. Nevertheless, a distinction must be made from the point of view of the *imputatio facti* (*objektive Zurechnung*). From this view (supported by Pantaleón and accepted by De Ángel and Lacruz et al.), the principle of responsibility based on the scope of protection intended by the infringed norm (*Schutzzweck der Norm*) would favour compensation for Peter, so long as a 'no parking' sign were established at the entrance to his business premises. The norm prohibiting parking in front of an entrance to business premises, signposted as a clearance, does in fact aim to allow easy

---

[800] *Orciani v. Donato*, Cass., 22.1.1991, no. 1908, *MGC* 1991; Giudice di Pace Perugia, 27.1.1999, *RG Umbra* 1999, 803.

access by customers. Thus, breach of these norms means that damages suffered are compensated.

The contrary solution (not compensating Peter) would be reached if Peter had not marked the entrance to his business premises as a clearance. This conclusion would be reached on the basis that the scope of protection intended by requiring proper maintenence of a lorry's engine would be insufficient to hold David liable for the damages suffered by Peter.

A Spanish court faced with such a case could have recourse to article 1103 CC in order to adjust compensation in the event the amount were deemed 'excessive'.[801]

Likewise, Peter would be subject to the general duty of the plaintiff to minimize damage.[802] Thus, Peter would be obligated to hire the services of a crane to withdraw the lorry and enable access by his customers, provided such an operation were feasible and reasonably simple. For the same reason, Peter would not be able to claim damages for not having customers for a whole month if it were reasonably simple to remove the lorry.

**Greece**

I. The indemnifiable damage in this case would be the average (i.e. the usual, the objectively foreseen) level of Peter's sales.

II. David was at fault ('inadequate maintenance of David's truck's engine'). Since it is prohibited to prevent someone from using things of public use (arts. 57 and 967 CC), he committed a tort.[803] This would be even clearer if David had parked inside Peter's private garden (since it is unlawful to prevent someone from using his own property).

Thus, David is liable to compensate Peter if his business losses are causally related to David's tort. Two criteria have been proposed for testing causation: either the foreseeability of the particular damage,[804] or whether it is part of the interests protected by the legal rule that the

---

[801] See, e.g. J. Lacruz, *Elementos de derecho civil* (3rd edn, Bosch, Barcelona, 1995), p. 502, S. Morales and S. Sancho, *Manual práctico de responsabilidad civil* (1993), p. 102, who quote numerous case decisions.

[802] De Ángel, *Tratado de responsabilidad civil* (3rd edn, Civitas, Madrid, 1993), p. 845, J. Santos Briz, *La responsabilidad civil: derecho sustantivo y derecho procesal* (6th edn, 2 vols, 1991), p. 116, Lacruz, *Elementos*, p. 504, amongst others.

[803] AP 259/1971, NoB 19, 853; A. Georgiades, *General Principles of Civil Law* (2nd edn, 1996), p. 127.

[804] AP 692/1990 NoB 40, 67; AP 1063/9; AP 979/92 ElD 35, 1044.

tortfeasor infringed.⁸⁰⁵ Under these criteria, we can readily conclude that the purpose of the prohibition against interference with the use of public things is to protect the foreseeable interests of the people who use them in one way or another (as passengers or consignees of goods). Even more clearly, the purpose of the prohibition against interfering with persons using their own property is to protect their own foreseeable interests. Thus when the entrance of a commercial centre is closed, it is to be foreseen that some business will be prevented. The average, (i.e. the usual, the objectively foreseen) level of sales at this time will be the compensable amount. Of course, this assumes that everybody would realise that the place where the truck was parked was a commercial garden centre.

III. Any owner may sue any possessor (or even holder) of their own property and claim compensation for its material deterioration or for any loss of profit that the owner suffered owing to the possessor's fault. The owner's claims are grounded in article 914 CC. In this case article 914 CC is implemented concurrently with articles 1094–1108 which regulate liability in *rei vindicatio*, as well as in *actio negatoria* with regard to the thing. This was accepted both by Greek doctrine[806] and Greek jurisprudence.[807] This theory is called 'theory of the concurrent implementation' of articles 1094–1108 with other liability rules such as article 914.

### England

I. David will be liable to compensate Peter for his loss of trade. Also, Peter can probably demand the issue of an injunction against David to prevent him from parking his truck in front of his entrance.

II. David cannot be liable in negligence: *Spartan Steel* v. *Martin*.[808] But by obstructing access to Peter's premises, he is likely to be creating a nuisance, and should be liable to Peter in private nuisance,[809] as well as in public nuisance, if his act also causes an obstruction of the highway.

---

[805] A. Georgiades and M. Stathopoulos, *Civil Code, Article by Article Commentary*, vols. II–IV (1978–1982), Commentary by M. Stathopoulos arts. 297–298, no. 67, 60–5; P. Sourlas, *Adaequanztheorie und Normzwecklehre bei der Begruendung der Haftung nach § 823 Abs. 1 BGB* (1974), pp. 15 ff.
[806] See, for example, A. Georgiades, *Real Law*, vol. I (1991), pp. 602–3.
[807] EfAth 2073/1987 NoB 35, 1066.    [808] [1973] 1 QB 27 (CA).
[809] See *Hubbard* v. *Pitt* [1976] QB 142 (CA) (obstruction of access by picketing on the highway); *A-G* v. *Gastonia Coaches Ltd* [1977] RTR 219 (motor coaches parked on the highway in front of the plaintiff's house held to be a nuisance).

In the latter case, Peter's loss of trade would have to qualify as 'special damage' over and above the general inconvenience suffered by any other members of the public.[810]

The temporary nature of the blockage will be taken into account, but it is likely that loss of trade will be seen by the court as a consequence serious enough to justify imposing liability, despite the temporary nature of David's interference with Peter's enjoyment of his land.[811] The short duration of the blockage will not prevent the award of damages for the loss of trade, but could lead to a denial of an injunction.

III. If the economic loss results from interference with the plaintiff's property interests in the enjoyment and use of his land, English law sees, in principle, no objection to its recovery.[812] Obviously, the arguments against liability unlimited in scope and extent do not apply.

## Scotland

I. Peter may be able to sue successfully, in nuisance, although this is not straightforward. Possibly, though less certainly, he may bring an action in delict on the basis of negligence even though his loss is purely economic. It would be a novel claim but he may succeed here also.

II. The category of nuisance has uncertain boundaries and in Scots law its scope is narrower than in English law. One should mention at the outset the fact that nuisance is a continuing wrong and, to be that, there must be more than one act. Would the two days of blocking the entrance to the garden centre be considered as one act of blockage, which if it were to be repeated at a later date would constitute a nuisance, or would it be considered a series of individual acts, say with each hour which passed, which added up to two days in total? It is possible that the court would opt for the former and so render the following discussion as to nuisance a moot one. Let us assume the blockage of the entrance is a continuing wrong.

---

[810] *Wilkes v. Hungerford Market Co.* (1835) 2 Bing. NC 281; *Harper v. Harden & Sons Ltd* [1933] Ch. 298, 306–7.

[811] *Iveson v. Moore* (1699) 1 Ld. Raym. 486: however, here the obstruction of the highway was much longer: a little less than a month. In *Wildtree Hotels v. Haroow London BC* [2000] 3 All ER 289, 301, Lord Hoffmann noted the relevance of the duration to the tort of nuisance: 'In the first place, a temporary obstruction of the highway (such as leaving a skip in the road for a few days) may not be a sufficiently serious interference with the public's right of passage to amount to a public nuisance at all...The time for which an obstruction has existed can also be relevant to whether the plaintiff can show that he has suffered special damage...'

[812] See more in P. Cane, *Tort Law and Economic Interests* (2nd edn, 1996), pp. 21 ff.

# CASE 16: TRUCK BLOCKING ENTRANCE TO BUSINESS PREMISES

With unintentional harm, 'in Scotland such cases have been almost invariably decided on principles of *culpa* or negligence without reference to nuisance'.[813] However, Bell's definition of nuisance is as follows:

Whatever obstructs the public means of commerce and intercourse whether in highways or navigable rivers; whatever is noxious, or unsafe, or renders life uncomfortable to the public generally or to the neighbourhood; whatever is intolerably offensive to individuals in their dwelling-houses, or inconsistent with the comfort of life, whether by stench, by noise or by indecency is a nuisance.[814]

Although the most common instances of nuisance are those referred to in the latter part of the definition, the first part would appear to cover the situation in this case. Although the usual remedy is interdict, 'damages may be sought by one who has suffered loss as the result of nuisance'.[815] The question is whether damages would be permitted when the loss was economic. There are examples of frontagers protecting free access to their property against obstruction of the highway but these have been by way of actions of interdict.[816] We can see that in a case such as this elements of private and public nuisance are combined. The public, Peter's customers, cannot get to the garden centre and the private individual on his property, Peter, cannot enjoy the use of his property commercially without those customers having free access. David has obstructed the public means of commerce affecting both the public and Peter. Thomson believes that 'only a person with a recognised interest in heritable property has title to sue in nuisance and that it is only damage to that property which is reparable'.[817] That would exclude the public having a claim in nuisance against David. As to the type of damage, it does not appear to be restricted to physical damage. In *Hunter* v. *Canary Wharf*,[818] where the House of Lords held that in an action for damages based on the tort of nuisance, only a person with a recognized interest in land has title to sue, that compensation was due only for damage to the property, and that damage was held to include diminution in its amenity value while the nuisance subsists.[819] Peter

---

[813] *Stair Memorial Encyclopaedia, The Laws of Scotland*, vol. 14 (Law Society of Scotland, Edinburgh, 1988), pp. 790–3, paras. 2017–21 (written by N. R. Whitty).
[814] C. J. Bell, *Principles of the Law of Scotland* (10th edn, reprint 1998), para. 974.
[815] Gloag and Henderson, *The Law of Scotland* (10th edn, 1995), at p. 505.
[816] For example *Central Motors (St Andrews) Ltd* v. *St Andrews Magistrates* 1961 SLT 290; *Pedie* v. *Swinton* (1839) MacL & R 1018; *Anderson Aberdeen Agricultural Hall Co.* (1879) 6 R 901; *Manson* v. *Forrest* (1887) 14 R 802; *Adam* v. *Alloa Police Commissioners* (1874) 2 R 143.
[817] J. M. Thomson, 'Damages for Nuisance', 1997 SLT News 177 at p. 178.
[818] [1997] 2 WLR 684; [1997] 2 All ER 426.
[819] Summary of decision taken from Thomson, 'Damages for Nuisance' at p. 178.

certainly has the necessary interest in land and, perhaps, the economic loss which Peter suffers while the truck blocks access to his garden centre can be characterized as a direct valuation of the diminution in its amenity value as a commercial premises.

Turning to the relationship between nuisance and negligence, recently the Inner House gave guidance on 'the difficult question as to what types of delictual conduct on the part of the defender, amounting to *culpa* or fault on his part, are actionable on the ground of nuisance and what types are actionable by reference to the ordinary principles of negligence'.[820] The Lord President (Hope), with whom Lord Kirkwood and Lord Murray agreed, held:

> [L]iability in damages for nuisance is a species of delictual liability. That is the foundation for the principle that liability in damages for nuisance is based on *culpa*. According to the law of Scotland liability in reparation for damages arises either *ex contractu* or *ex delicto*. There is no other basis on which a liability in reparation for damages can arise, according to our law...It arises where there is an invasion of a pursuer's interest in land to an extent which exceeds what is reasonably tolerable. The *plus quam tolerabile* test is peculiar to the liability in damages for nuisance. Where that test is satisfied and *culpa* is established, the requirements for the delictual liability are satisfied. Liability in damages for negligence, on the other hand, depends on a failure to take reasonable care where there is a foreseeable risk of injury. That is another species of delictual liability, the basis for which also depends on *culpa*...the usual categories of *culpa* or fault are malice, intent, recklessness and negligence. To that list may be added conduct causing a special risk of abnormal damage where it may be said that it is not necessary to prove a specific fault as fault is necessarily implied in the result.[821]

So does David's obstruction of Peter's entrance constitute an invasion of a Peter's interest in land to an extent which exceeds what is reasonably tolerable? It is suggested that it might.

Later in the same judgment, the Lord President made an observation which demonstrates the lack of clarity of the law in this area. He states that 'liability for nuisance did not arise merely *ex dominio* and without fault. The essential requirement is that fault or *culpa* must be established. That may be done by demonstrating negligence, in which case the law of negligence will provide an equivalent remedy'.[822] Thomson has written:

> The import of this passage is not clear. What Lord Hope could be arguing is that where the defender did not intend to harm the pursuer's property, but

---

[820] *Kennedy v. Glenbelle Ltd* 1996 SLT 1186 at 1188H.
[821] Ibid. at p. 1188J.   [822] Ibid. at p. 1189K.

was nevertheless careless, an action for damages must proceed on the basis of negligence not nuisance. If so, the pursuer must establish that the defender owed the pursuer a pre-existing duty of care which was broken by his careless conduct. In many situations such a duty will be readily found – but why should this be necessary given that the *plus quam tolerabile* test already provides a mechanism to limit the defender's potential liability? Surely to insist on the full panoply of the law of negligence is gilding the rose in this situation. Should it not be enough to establish *culpa* for the purpose of a claim for damages in nuisance that the defender's conduct simply fell below the standard of reasonable care?[823]

If the case were to be brought on the basis of negligence, Peter would have to establish a duty of care. Peter is confronted by the general rule of non-liability for secondary economic loss. We described in Case 7 ('The Careless Architect') the three rules suggested by Lord Bridge of Harwich in *Caparo* for establishing a duty of care in such a case, and the adoption of the observations of Brennan J in *Sutherland* by various Lords to the effect that 'the law should develop novel categories of negligence incrementally and by analogy with establish categories'.[824]

As to the duty of care, delivering the opinion of the court in *Weir* v. *National Westminster Bank Plc*,[825] the Lord President (Hope) said:

> Lord Bridge of Harwich pointed out in *Caparo*...the difficulties which have arisen from attempts to define a single general principle which may be applied to determine the existence of a duty of care. This led him to say at p. 618C that the law has now moved in the direction of attaching greater significance to what he described as the more traditional categorisation of distinct and recognisable situations as guides to the existence, the scope and the limits of the varied duties of care which the law imposes. This, it must be accepted, is a tradition more in keeping with that of the English common law, which prefers to develop the law on a case-by-case basis rather than by reference to a principle. But there can be no doubt that cases involving pure economic loss give rise to situations of particular difficulty, and that it is in this field especially that reliance on general principle may produce results which are unreasonable. As Lord Bridge went on to say at p. 618E–F: 'One of the most important distinctions always to be observed lies in the law's essentially different approach to the different kinds of damage which one party may have suffered in consequence of the acts or omissions of another. It is one thing to owe a duty of care to avoid causing injury to the person or property of others. It is quite another to avoid causing others to suffer purely economic loss.'[826]

---

[823] Thomson, 'Damages for Nuisance', at p. 178.
[824] *Sutherland Shine Council v. Heyman* (1985) 60 ACR 1.
[825] 1994 SLT 1251.   [826] Ibid. at p. 1258D.

The problem for Peter is that the facts here do not appear to fall within the categories of case where it has been held in the past that there is a special relationship between the parties such as to give rise to a duty of care not to cause pure economic loss. The categories are: (1) where there is a fiduciary relationship; and (2) where there has been voluntary assumption of responsibility along with concomitant reliance in a situation where the pursuer was relying on the skill of the defender. It is possible that a Scottish court may be less reluctant than an English court to ignore the lack of analogy to established categories, if the three-stage test of Lord Bridge of Harwich were satisfied.

An example of this is the Sheriff Court judgment in *Saeed v. Waheed and Another*.[827] This case concerned the unlawful occupation of shop premises which caused the true occupier a loss of profit. As to whether the unlawful occupier owed a duty of care to the pursuer, applying Lord Bridge of Harwich's three-part test, Sheriff Principal C. G. B. Nicholson, QC decided that the pursuer's claim in respect of economic loss was relevant and should go to a proof before answer. He held:

> [T]he present case does not, as I have earlier observed, readily fall within any of the categories where a duty of care in respect of economic loss has been recognised hitherto. Given what has been said in earlier cases, this has caused me some anxiety. At the end of the day, however, I have come to the conclusion that the very fact that nearly all the decided cases have, to a greater or lesser extent, been what might be described as 'reliance' cases, may in itself have led to things being said which were simply not foreseen as having bearing on circumstances of a totally different character. Given the circumstances of the present case, it seems to me that it would be remarkable if our law did not recognise a remedy in respect of economic loss; and, given also that, at least in my opinion, the present case amply satisfies the test propounded by Lord Bridge of Harwich in *Caparo*, I consider that on the basis of general principle I am entitled to say that the pursuer's claim in respect of economic loss is one which is fundamentally relevant and which is entitled to go to a proof before answer.[828]

This recent approach to what was a novel category, which Peter's claim would be in a Scottish court (albeit a Sheriff Court), is the best for which he could hope. However, in the recent Outer House case of *Strathford East Kilbride Ltd v. H. L. M. Design Ltd*, Lord MacLean was referred to *Saeed* and made the following observations:

---

[827] 1996 SLT (Sh Ct) 39, 1995 SCLR 504.   [828] Ibid. at pp. 44H–I, 45H–I, 45K–46A.

[W]hat the Sheriff Principal did in this case was to apply the *Hedley Byrne* principle in a way in which it has never been applied before. That principle had been applied, broadly, in well-recognised situations where those in professional positions were charged with or assumed responsibility for looking after other people's economic interests...[after giving examples, he continued]...The further consideration of whether it is 'fair, just and reasonable' to imply and impose the duty, which impressed the Sheriff Principal in *Saeed* and to which the Lord President referred in *Weir* (at p. 1258), is, I believe, simply a means of stating the policy which the court wishes to apply in the particular case...What the Sheriff Principal did in *Saeed* in relation to squatters went far beyond what, in my opinion, the law permitted. I do not think he was well founded nor do I think that the case was correctly decided. I would find it very hard to see where the line could sensibly be drawn in the application of the principle.[829]

It can be seen that David would have to surmount considerable hurdles in establishing a claim for negligence, although it is not impossible. Was the damage of the character claimed readily foreseeable by David? arguably, yes. Were they in a relationship of proximity or neighbourhood of a kind to give rise to a duty of care not to cause such damage? arguably, yes. David established that relationship by parking across Peter's entrance. He could have parked anywhere but chose to park across what was, presumably, clearly the entrance to commercial premises which would require daily access. Is it fair, just and reasonable? again arguably, yes. We do not have an unlimited or indeterminate liability. Parking across the entrance merely affected the owner of the garden centre and it exists only as long as the truck could not be removed. What would be important was whether he was aware that the truck was inadequately maintained. Presumably, since it is his truck he would have known this. Liability to the customers, even if they had somehow suffered economic loss by not being able to gain access to the garden centre, would be considered too remote on grounds of policy.

The problem presented here is a very good example of how Thomson's view would help a pursuer such as Peter. He would only have to establish that David's conduct fell below the standard of reasonable care, as opposed to the full panoply of the criteria for negligence, in order to sue for damages in nuisance. If Thomson's view is correct then Peter will win.

III. On the facts it would seem that Peter should have a remedy, but this area of the law appears less predictable than most. In his favour

---

[829] 1997 SCLR 877 at p. 891A.

## The Netherlands

I. Peter can probably claim from David on the basis that David acted negligently in parking his vehicle across the entrance, thus creating a specific risk that, unfortunately, materialized.

II. The question is (1) whether David acted unlawfully *vis-à-vis* Peter when inadequately maintaining his truck; or (2) whether David, as the owner of a truck, has the societal duty to bear the cost of its removal and/or bear any subsequent loss if removal is impossible.

It is undoubtedly true that the owner of a motor vehicle has a duty to maintain his vehicle properly in order to avoid personal accidents and damage to property.[830] It is clear that this duty is owed to fellow road users. But it is doubtful whether this duty purports to protect against pure economic loss, such as loss of profits because of blockage of the entrance. On the other hand, if there was no justification for parking the vehicle across the entrance in the first place, David's act will more likely be considered tortious. From case law, it can be derived that the owner of a motor vehicle has a special duty to ensure that his vehicle does not become a nuisance to others.[831] In the *Rijksweg 12* decision,[832] the Dutch Supreme Court allowed a claim in tort for the cost of cleaning up a motorway incurred by the Dutch public authorities as a result of the overturning of a truck loaded with chemicals. Although the cost of cleaning up might not be filed under pure economic loss, the decision shows that the Court tends to draw the circumference of the driver's duty quite widely.

Whether David can be blamed by Peter for not maintaining his truck is uncertain. However, it is certain that David has the societal duty to remove his truck upon first request. If he refuses, Peter is allowed to remove it. Peter can then claim the cost of removing the truck. This follows from two Supreme Court decisions on the subject of a tree that had fallen over on a neighbouring house and of a shipwreck that blocked fluvial traffic.[833]

---

[830] See, e.g., HR 16.4.1942, NJ 1942, no. 394.
[831] HR 19.10.1975, NJ 1976, no. 280. Compare HR 7.5.1982, NJ 1983, no. 478, and HR 14.10.1994, NJ 1995, no. 720.
[832] HR 19.10.1975, NJ 1976, no. 280; compare HR 26.5.1978, NJ 1978, no. 615.
[833] Cf. HR 7.5.1982, NJ 1983, no. 478, and HR 14.10.1994, NJ 1995, no. 720.

But is David also obliged to pay for consequential damage if the truck cannot be removed? From case law, it can be derived that the owner of a motor vehicle has a special duty to ensure that his vehicle does not become a nuisance to others.[834] David must take all reasonable steps necessary to remove the truck. In general, swift removal is possible. If not, then David will have performed his duty if he – although in vain – did his best to comply.

**Germany**

I. Peter can probably recover his loss from David but this answer is not free from doubt.

II. Everything depends on whether Peter can persuade the courts that the blockage of access to his garden centre amounted to a violation of one of his absolute rights under art. 823 (1) BGB. He has two options.

Violation of property rights: he can claim that the blockade violated his property rights. Whether this argument prevails depends primarily on how the court views two leading precedents. In the first case, the *Bundesgerichtshof* has held that the loss of the use of a ship amounted to such a violation where a barge was locked into a canal for several months.[835] In the other case, the Court decided that the owner of land whose access by public road was blocked for a few hours has no claim for violation of a property right.[836]

One could argue that the present scenario lies almost exactly in the middle. The interference lasted neither several months nor hours but two days. Here, the question is whether a blockage of two days is still 'short term' (*kurzfristig*) and merely 'temporary' (*vorübergehend*) and thus too insubstantial to count as a violation of a property right.[837]

Yet, Peter's case is really much stronger than the property owner's claim in the second decision by the *Bundesgerichtshof*. Where the Court denied the property owner's claim, the blockade was not only much shorter but also caused by police vehicles and fire trucks during a fire on nearby land. Arguably, every citizen must bear the risk of interference with his rights by public authorities responding to an emergency. In the present case, however, the blockage was caused by a private vehicle which was improperly maintained with no public interest involved. This

---

[834] See above, fn. 731.   [835] BGHZ 55, 153, 159 (1970).
[836] BGH NJW 1977, 2264, at 2265-6.   [837] BGH NJW 1977, 2264, at 2265.

is not a risk the property owner should have to bear but a wrongful act for which the truck owner should pay.[838]

Right of an established and ongoing commercial enterprise: Peter could also claim a violation of his 'right of an established and ongoing commercial enterprise'.[839] But such a claim is probably weaker than an action based on a violation of property rights. When the *Bundesgerichtshof* denied the property owner's claim in the case previously mentioned, it also rejected a claim for interference with the right of an established and ongoing commercial enterprise. The Court refused to allow an action for business owners where other citizens would have to bear the risk of blocked access themselves. One must also remember that a violation of this right requires that the defendant's act be directed against, or substantially related to, the business as such. This seems not to be the case here because David could just as well have blocked access to other, non-business property.

### Austria

I. Whether Peter is entitled to recover his loss from David on the ground of articles 1329 or 1331 and 1332 ABGB depends on additional information.

II. Peter can try to base his claim for compensation on David's violation of property rights pursuant to articles 1331 and 1332 ABGB. If it is proved that David was parking his truck in front of the entrance to a well-attended garden centre, thereby making customer visits impossible, Peter's loss of income appears to be easily foreseeable. This is primarily an objective aspect, however, that has a significant impact on the intensity of his fault. A truck driver who blocks the entrance to a busy place of business is not merely responsible for slight negligence.

The combination of increased objective foreseeability and of David's gross negligence makes recovery plausible. Moreover, in contrast to Case 15 ('A Closed Motorway – The Value of Time'), the damages involved in

---

[838] In an opinion, the *Bundesgerichtshof* referred to the liability of a construction company to a car owner where the company had illegally dug a ditch in front of the car owner's garage, rendering the car temporarily useless, see BGHZ 66, 203, at 206. Strangely enough, this reference is without citation, and I could not locate any such case actually decided. Perhaps the Court was just trying to give a general example. In that case, the example is not very helpful because it fails to provide information about a point which seems to be crucial in other cases, namely the duration of the interference.

[839] See above, Case 2 'Cable II – Factory Shutdown', sub II.

this case do not appear to be 'socially adequate'. Unlike the inconvenience caused by traffic jams on motorways, damage of the kind that Peter has had to suffer should not have to be tolerated. At the moment, however, a clear court practice does not exist.

The same is true with violations of the right to liberty (arts. 16 and 1329 ABGB).

III. In this case responsibility is based on the combination of 'grounds for imputation' (*Zurechnungsgründe*): where there is a high degree of objective foreseeability (danger) of damage together with gross negligence, and where there are no counter-arguments (socially adequate tolerance of damage), the impediment on the use of one's property is sufficient ground for the court to treat the case as if it were a direct infringement of the property right.

### Portugal

I. Peter's claim can be successful in principle, but this outcome depends on establishing that a right was infringed upon and that David was at fault.

II. For fault to be confirmed, David's negligence in not maintaining the lorry engine is not enough. David must have foreseen the violation of a right (previously admitting the existence of such) or, having foreseen it, he had no reason to rely on it not occurring.[840]

This judgment is based on elements of fact: e.g. if it was the first time that the engine had failed to start, if the mechanical knowledge of an average driver would be sufficient to permit him to foresee that outcome, etc.

If enough facts are found on which an ethical–legal judgment of censure can be based, particularly in the case of a fairly serious fault, we think that the court would hold the violation of Peter's property right as proved, despite this being a somewhat atypical case.[841]

It may be that David has disregarded a 'No Parking' sign. On the hypothesis that the purpose of the prohibition (to prevent blocked access to the specified place) is represented by the sign itself (then there is no doubt that the damaged interest lies within the protected sphere);[842]

---

[840] These two kinds of non-intentional fault or negligence are usually termed 'unconscious negligence' and 'conscious negligence'.

[841] Cf. J. M. Vieira Gomes, 'O Dano da Privação do Uso', (1986) XII *Revista de Direito e Economia* 169.

[842] The 'adequacy of the rule' is then confirmed ('Normadäquanz'): E. Deutsch, *Allgemeines Haftungsrecht* (2nd edn, Carl Heymanns, Köln, 1996), pp. 98–9.

the verification of the violation of this legal provision, independently of the verification of the physical result, could be a basis for liability.

It is not necessary to have material injury for there to be violation of a property right.

The Civil Code (article 1305) characterizes this right by resorting to *inter alia*, the concepts of use and enjoyment. Thus, it may be admitted that the enjoyment of a commercial establishment is impeded when public access to the site is blocked for a long period.

The differences relative to Case 2 ('Cable II – Factory Shutdown') are certainly slight and perhaps more formal than substantial in nature; but they do exist. In the earlier case, the agent damaged a good belonging to a third party, which indirectly resulted in the injured party being unable to work, and also resulted in inconvenience or damage to an undetermined number of persons; in this case, there has been a direct assault on the injured party or to a determinable number of persons.

There are precedents for a relatively broad interpretation of the concept of property, for the purposes of civil liability.[843]

In addition to the mere infringement of a legal protection provision leading to the presumption of fault,[844] it is likely that fault would have to relate to the violation of the legal protection itself, independently of (the predictability of) verifying an injurious outcome.[845]

III. The legal-technical framing of this question would be improved we feel if the 'right to enterprise' were to be made an independent subjective right, conceived as a personality economic right.[846] Instead of discussion on the violation of the property right, the conditions under

---

[843] Judgment of the Lisbon Court of Appeal of 30 September 1993, *Colectânea de Jurisprudência*, ano XVIII (1993), Tomo IV, pp. 116–17. The defective work carried out on the Estoril motor racing circuit caused the formation of a small 'lake', which led to 'the creation of stagnant pools of water [...] which resulted in swarms of mosquitoes congregating there and caused a nauseating stench which reached a nearby hotel, whose guests then complained, to the detriment of the hotel's image and prestige, affecting the use of it and its services'.

[844] Judgment of the Coimbra Court of Appeal of 21 September 1993, *Colectânea de Jurisprudência*, IV, 37 ff., 39, 1a col.

[845] J. F. Sinde Monteiro, *Responsabilidade por Conselhos, Recomendações ou Informações* (Almedina, Coimbra, 1990), pp. 239–40. Regarding the first kind of unlawfulness, there is a shortening of the point of reference of fault. That is different from the concept of negligence *per se* (J. G. Fleming, *The Law of Torts* (5th edn, Sydney/Melbourne/Brisbane/Perth, 1977), p. 123; see Deutsch, *Allgemeines Haftungsrecht* pp. 242, 243, citing Cardozo CJ in *Martin v. Herzog* 126 NE 815 (NY 1920).

[846] Cf. G. Brüggemeier, *Deliktsrecht* (Nomos Verlagsgesellschaft, Baden-Baden, 1986), pp. 220 ff.

which violation of this other right gives rise to a duty to compensate would be debated. But this route has no tradition in Portuguese law.

Sweden and Finland

I. Peter would probably recover his loss from David, but this is not completely certain, at least if David's behaviour is not to be considered, under the specific circumstances, as a criminal breach of traffic rules.

II. The uncertainty derives from the fact that such a loss is a good example of the borderline between, on the one hand, 'pure economic loss' in the Swedish/Finnish meaning, i.e. an economic loss arising without connection with anybody suffering personal injury or damage to things, and on the other hand, economic loss consequent upon property damage. The former can in principle be compensated when it is caused by a criminal action (see for Sweden SkadestL 4:2 and for Finland SkadestL 5:1), although the text and the preparatory works of the Tort Liability Acts 1972 and 1974 do not completely bar compensation should the courts find strong reasons for it. As mentioned before, courts have been very restrictive in granting exceptions to the general principle.

The preparatory works of the Swedish Tort Liability Act 1972 consider as property damages some situations (e.g. an object temporarily lost) in which there is no physical modification of the object, and Swedish scholars tend to extend the concept to the 'blocking cases'. The standard Finnish treatise (in Swedish)[847] takes the same position by quoting a Swedish case of 1959 where, however, the court did not classify the kind of loss, moreover stressing that the defendant was in that case liable to a criminal sanction.[848]

*Editors' comparative comments*

Under the circumstances of the case, it comes as no surprise to find that the liberal regimes might award compensation. As to the other legal systems, however, the case is noteworthy because it shows that the line between the recoverability and unrecoverability of pure economic loss is crossed when the infringement of a protected interest is found. Framing Peter's damage as a loss consequential upon the infringement of a property right opens the door to compensation in most of these regimes. This

[847] H. Saxén, *Skadeståndsrätt* (1975), p. 73.
[848] J. Kleineman, *Ren förmögenhetsskada* (1987), p. 171; H. Andersson, *Skyydsändamål och adekvans* (1993), p. 542.

is made clear by (1) the reasoning one finds in the Dutch, Finnish and Swedish contributions – even though the Netherlands alone takes a clear position; (2) by the Austrian, German and Portuguese solutions, which award compensation to the plaintiff provided that he can prove the infringement of a property right; (3) by the possible recourse, in England and Scotland, to the remedy labelled 'private nuisance', which is centrally concerned with interference with the enjoyment of the plaintiff's land.

From a different perspective, two further remarks are in order. First, considering the circumstances and the legal implications of this case, the usual argument against allowing compensation for economic loss due to the risk of an indeterminate liability toward an indefinite number of persons does not apply. This surely helps to explain why even Austria, England, Germany and Scotland – i.e. the legal systems most receptive to this argument – do not bar recovery in principle.

Secondly, to be noted is the framing of the legal arguments that may lead to compensation being awarded in Germany,[849] on the one hand, and in Scotland and England, on the other. In Germany, (1) the crucial factor is whether the plaintiff is able to persuade the court that the blocking of access to his garden centre amounted to a violation of his property rights; and (2) whether or not this argument will prevail depends, in turn, on how the court assesses the magnitude, in terms of duration, of that infringement. This argument places itself along the same lines that lead English and Scottish lawyers to evaluate the presence of the private nuisance, determination of which is necessary for liability to be established under the circumstances. Indeed, since the latter is a 'continuing wrong', the point can be summarized by our Scottish contributor's rhetorical question, and answer:

Would the two days blocking the entrance to the garden centre be considered one act of blockage, which if it were to be repeated at a later date would constitute a nuisance, or would it be considered a series of individual acts, say with each hour which passed, which added up to two days in total? It is possible that the court would opt for the former and so render the following discussion as to nuisance a moot one.[850]

---

[849] But see also the Portuguese contribution, under II.
[850] See, above, Scottish response (s. II) to Case 16.

# Case 17: auditor's liability

## Case

Donna audits the accounts of Caterpillar, Inc. inaccurately. Paul relies on these published accounts to launch a takeover bid. This is successful, but Paul then discovers that the accounts overestimated the value of the company and that the price Paul paid per share was twice its actual value.

## France

I. Upon showing fault and that the inaccurate audit was the cause of his loss, Paul may recover against Donna if she is the statutory auditor of the company, but he may be denied recovery if she is a specially hired contract auditor.

II. Donna's liability has a different basis and scope, depending on her status. If she is the statutorily required auditor of Caterpillar (*commissaire-aux-comptes*) she has wider civil and penal responsibility, including liability towards third persons such as Paul. If she is instead a specially hired auditor under contract for a particular purpose, her responsibility is essentially governed by her contract and her liability toward third persons in delict is restricted. Case 17 does not specify Donna's status and therefore both possibilities will be dealt with.

Donna is the statutorily-required auditor of Caterpillar: the *commissaire-aux-comptes*'s essential mission is to certify that the annual accounts of a French company present 'a faithful picture' of the company's operations. The *commissaire-aux-comptes*'s obligation is not one of result but one of means, that is, an obligation to be diligent and prudent.[851] The *commissaire-aux-comptes*'s civil liability rests upon the fault principle for this is the basis articulated in the special law of 24 July 1966 (Law no. 66-537). Article 234 of that law declares:

> The Commissioner of accounts (*commissaire-aux-comptes*) is responsible both toward the company as well as toward third persons for the harmful consequences of the fault or negligence which they have committed in the exercise of their functions.[852]

The *commissaire-aux-comptes* is seen as fulfilling a public institutional role to present accurate accounts. The *commissaire-aux-comptes*'s duties are

---

[851] Petites Affiches, p. 4. [852] Author's translation.

not only to keep the company and its shareholders properly informed, but to keep company workers, creditors and third persons properly informed as well. If the *commissaire-aux-comptes* deliberately misstates financial information, he may incur penal responsibility by way of a fine or prison term.[853]

Coming back to civil liability toward Paul, the latter would have to establish fault, causation and damage. In terms of fault, Donna's liability may first depend upon whether the company accounts were certified 'with reserve' or 'without reserve', or perhaps with 'observations' that may qualify or explain the financial information's meaning or warn the reader to be on guard as to its reliability. Assuming, however, that Donna's certification was 'without reserve' or that no qualifications or reserves were issued, her fault may be established by showing serious inaccuracies which a competent auditor should have discovered.[854] Given the enormity of the valuation error in Caterpillar's case, it may well be that serious professional mistakes were made. Nevertheless, the auditor is not a guarantor of the authenticity of the information he compiles. It has been held by the Tribunal de Commerce de Paris that where incomplete and disordered documents were submitted, which included a fraudulent invoice that had no suspicious appearance, fault was not shown because such matters could escape a normally vigilant auditor's attention.[855] On the other hand, the *commissaire-aux-comptes* has been found liable in circumstances where he failed to detect inaccuracies created by the particular billing system used by the company.[856] It should be noted that in France the tribunal will frequently appoint an expert to assist it in the evaluation of the *commissaire-aux-comptes*'s fault.

Even if Donna's fault is established, Paul's claim requires proof that her fault caused his damage. On more than one occasion, however, courts have shown reluctance to allow recovery in favour of third parties, such as Paul, even in the event of fault on the part of the *commissaire-aux-comptes*, by refusing the claim on the ground of causation.[857] The reasons for this restrictive tendency are partly inherent in the nature of

---

[853] Ibid. art. 457.
[854] Com. 9 février 1988, D. 1988. IF. 53; Petites Affiches, 7 mars 1988, p. 13, note Pierre Moretti.
[855] Trib. Paris, 12 juillet 1984, Bull. CNCC, 1985 – 478 Juris-Data no. 001646.
[856] Lyon, 2 juin 1994, Ibid. Petites Affiches.
[857] See L. Khoury, 'The Liability of Auditors Beyond Their Clients: A Comparative Study' (2001) 46 *McGill Law Journal* 413. Gratitude is expressed to the author for sharing her research prior to publication.

the auditor's role. The fault of the *commissaire* is usually one of omission rather than positive action, and his fault is never the only cause of the damage suffered by the company or the third person. The 'cause' of the loss is usually multiple,[858] and lies at the outset, in the fault or fraud of the administrators, and may even be attributed to plaintiff's subsequent lack of vigilance. The commentators unanimously recognize that proof of causation in this area is somewhat difficult to meet.[859] Thus third-party claims have failed where the evidence showed that the irregularities would not have been discovered even if the *commissaire* had exercised reasonable diligence;[860] when the errors did not modify substantially the results of the statements; and when the court considered that the plaintiff would have acted in the same way, had he known of the errors.

In most cases of refusal, however, the plaintiff is defeated because the evidence shows that despite the errors of the report, he knew or should have known about the real situation from other sources of information at his disposal. Often when the cession or acquisition of a company takes place, there may be several audits and financial reports other than that of the *commissaire-aux-comptes*, and these reports may well reveal the errors and discrepancies of the *commissaire*'s report. The Tribunal d'Amiens found an absence of causal connection in circumstances where it believed that these reports should have dissuaded an acquirer from taking control.[861]

Since Case 17 furnishes only the sketchiest facts about causation, in those circumstances it would be hazardous to predict the disposition that a French court might make. While the claim is reparable in principle, awards are in fact rarely made.

Apparently, the French judge's control over the causation requirement is one of the means by which the *commissaire*'s liability toward third persons is kept within reasonable bounds.

---

[858] The multiplicity of causal conditions is stressed by T. Honoré with respect to all 'interpersonal transactions'. 'Necessary and Sufficient Conditions in Tort Law', in D. G. Owen (ed.), *Philosophical Foundations of Tort Law* (Clarendon Press, Oxford, 1995) at pp. 382–3.

[859] E. du Pontavice, *Le commissaire aux comptes. Manuel pratique*, t.1 (Ormesson-sur-Marne, 1981) A. 15, 209; P. Merle, annotation to Lyon 27 jan. 1994, Bull. CNCC 1994.271; Y. Guyon and G. Coquereau, *Le commissariat aux comptes: aspects juridiques et techniques* (Litec, Paris, 1971), p. 399; D. Vidal, annotation to Cass.com., 27 octobre 1992, *Rev. Soc.* 1993.86.

[860] Aix-en-Provence, 7 juin 1985, Bull. CNCC. 1985.487.

[861] Amiens, 20 juin 1988, Bull. CNCC, no. 71, p. 317, note E. du Pontavice.

Donna is a contract auditor (*auditeur, prestataire de service*): if Donna has been hired by Caterpillar for a particular accounting purpose, her liability toward investors such as Paul is more restrained. Her responsibility toward the company basically flows from her contract, while her liability toward third persons must be resolved in terms of general tort law under articles 1382–83 CC. So long as the contract auditor accomplishes the contractual commission, they are not viewed as an adviser to the shareholders or to outside acquirers and are not obliged to advise them of a problem in the account which may cause them harm.[862]

III. Though the French delictual system takes no particular note of the type of damage which pure economic loss represents, cases such as this one furnish evidence of a subconscious concern with the question of excessive, indeterminate liability toward third persons. Some maintain that French judges are perfectly aware of these dangers.[863] However, their concern is not expressed, in the manner of the English judges, by a careful tailoring of the 'duty of care' situation so that liability is contained. In France it is believed that judges turn to a restrictive application of causal requirements as the limiting device.[864] It is difficult to observe this policy directly, since it is never avowed. Causal determinations by the lower courts lie within the theoretical control and supervision of the Cour de Cassation, but the Court has not laid down clear rules on the issue.[865] Thus considerable confusion results from this refusal to take a position. Because the notion of causation is a flexible tool that may be used subjectively, case outcomes are not as predictable as in systems that confront such issues openly and employ more precise tools.

## Belgium

I. Paul has a claim against Donna and could recover from her the damage he has suffered if that damage has not been recovered from the sellers of the shares.

---

[862] Com. 15 juin 1993, Bull. Joly 1993, p. 1130, note Michel Jeantin.
[863] B. Markesinis, 'La politique jurisprudentielle et la réparation du préjudice économique en Angleterre: Une approche comparative', (1983) *Revue Internationale de Droit Comparé* 31, 44.
[864] See Khoury, 'Liability of Auditors'.
[865] E.g. it is not clear whether France follows the theory of 'equivalence of conditions' or the theory of 'adequate causation', see G. Viney and P. Jourdain, *Traité de droit civil: Les conditions de la responsabilité* (2nd edn, LGDJ, 1998) No. 350 (*la Haute juridiction a soigneusement évité de poser des règles générales ou même susceptibles de généralisation*).

II. The audit of the accounts of a company is a mission strictly reserved to public accountants which exercise is a public function provided by law.[866]

The exercise of that function is not only made for the company but also for third parties, which shall normally rely on the audit performed.

The buyer of the shares of a company is a third party with regard to the contract made between the company and the public accountant.

If the public accountant has approved the accounts of the company, the buyer shall normally rely on these accounts to assess the value of the company.

If the buyer can prove that the value of the company has been determined in accordance with the accounts as they have been approved by the public accountant, and that that value was used to calculate the price of the shares, the buyer has a claim based on article 1382 CC against the public accountant if he committed a fault in approving the accounts.

A similar case has been recently submitted to the Brussels Tribunal of First Instance (Tribunal de Première Instance) which decided that the public accountant was liable.[867]

## Italy

I. Donna can be sued both on the grounds of article 164 *Decreto Legislativo* No. 58 of 24 February 1998 (Accountant Liability Act) and article 2043 cc.

*Decreto Legislativo, Article 164: 58/1998*

(1) The rule of article 2407, section 1, civil code, applies to accounting firms.

(2) The auditor and its employees are jointly liable with the Auditing Company, towards the client company or third parties, for damages due to their mistakes and torts.[868]

---

[866] *La révision des comptes annuels et des comptes consolidés*, Yearbook 1995 (AEBDF-Belgium, Mys & Breesch, Gand, 1995); P. Foriers and M. Van Kuegelgen, 'La responsabilité civile des réviseurs et experts comptables' (1992) 2 *Revue de Droit de l'ULB* 11–61; A. Benoît-Maury and N. Thirion, 'La responsabilité pénale du réviseur d'entreprises: Epée de Damoclès ou Tigre de papier?' RPS, 1997, p. 189.

[867] Civ. Bxl., 12 décembre 1996, TRV, 1997, p. 38.

[868] The article cancels previous art.12 d.p.r 136/75; the professional auditor subscribing the auditing relation (and its employees checking the accounts) are jointly liable with the auditing company towards client companies or third parties for damages due to their mistakes and torts.

II. *IFC v. KPMG*[869] was the first Italian case where auditors were held liable for damages suffered by investors relying on published accounts.

IFC went bankrupt shortly after it had been acquired by a new shareholder; the latter successfully sued the negligent auditors for damages suffered by the investors who relied on their statements.[870]

## Spain

I. There is no clear outcome of this case. Spanish scholars have different opinions and there are no Supreme Court decisions on the issue.

II. Spanish law on the matter is governed by the Auditing of Accounts Law no. 19 of 12 July 1988 and by its additional regulations passed by *Real Decreto* no. 1636 of 20 December 1990. As yet, there is no case law to resolve the issue in Case 17. We have to make do with contradictory doctrinal interpretations derived from this body of law.

The starting point is given by article 11.1 of the above Law: 'Account auditors shall be directly and jointly and severally liable to the audited companies or entities and to third parties, for damages derived from the nonfulfilment of their obligations.' To the last paragraph of article 15.1 of the same Law should be added: 'Civil or criminal responsibility which [auditors] may incur shall be claimed from them according to legal provisions.'

With this starting point, legal experts agree that in order to regulate the tortious responsibility of auditors with respect to third parties, the Act of 1988 establishes a cross-reference to article 1902 CC.[871] Once this idea is accepted, some authors conclude that this entails establishing wide civil liability of the auditor to any third party, and consequently

---

[869] Trib. Torino, 18.9.1993, *GI* 1994, I, 2, 655 noted by Santaroni; Cass. 9.6.1998 no. 5659, noted by Pedrazzi, *DR* 1999, 1, 59; M. Santaroni, *La responsabilità del revisore* (Milano, 1984); M. Bussoletti, *Le società di revisione* (Milano, 1985), p. 315; F. Bonelli, 'Responsabilità delle società di revisione nella certificazione obbligatoria e volontaria dei bilanci', *Riv. Soc.*, 1979, 968.

[870] Trib. Milano, 18.6.1992, *GI* 1993, I, 21; Trib Torino, 21.3.1994, *GI*, I, 1, 1106, App. Torino, 30.5.1995, *DR* 1996, 3, 367 noted by P. Valensise, 'Il revisore risponde per mancata informazione al collegio sindacale' (1996) 1 *Danno e Responsabilità*, 370 ff.; G. Romagnoli, 'Un caso di responsabilità della società di revisione nei confronti degli investitori per negligente certificazione, *Giur. Comm.* 1994, 21, II, 284.

[871] F. Pantaleón, *La responsabilidad civil de los auditores: extensión, limitación, prescripción* (1996), pp. 27 and 112; E. Petit Laval, 'El informe Cadbury: un análisis sobre la objetividad, eficacia y responsabilidad de los auditores de cuentas' (1994) 603 *Revista General de Derecho* 418.

some limits must be set.[872] Others arrive at the same conclusion which they consider to be correct.[873]

Fernando Pantaleón is of the opinion that article 11.1 of the 1988 Act establishes a cross-reference to article 1902 CC. However, he does not agree that this should entail non-contractual liability to a third party.[874] The auditor is clearly liable to a third party in the event that he acted in bad faith. Apart from such situations, auditors are only liable to a third party when the auditor's report is directed at this third party with the purpose of inducing him to carry out an operation and the auditor is aware of this at the time of agreement.[875]

Pantaleón denies that the auditor may be liable by virtue of article 1902 CC to a third party who has suffered harm due to reliance on his reports, and argues that the damage suffered by the third party cannot be objectively imputed to the auditor's conduct because it is beyond the scope of protection of the norms on auditing.[876]

**Greece**

I. Donna is not liable, unless she is obliged by law (and not by contract) to audit the accounts or unless she acted deliberately in conflict with good morals (both of which seem improbable here). Caterpillar is not liable either, unless Donna acted on behalf of it. The sale of the shares could be voidable only if caused by fraud.

II. Donna's personal liability: here the problem of Donna's liability depends on the circumstances/conditions under which she had to audit Caterpillar's accounts.

Tortious liability according to article 914 CC: if Donna has the legal duty to audit according to article 34 Royal Decree 174 of 30 March 1963 para-1 Codification of the Provisions of Law no. 2190/1920, on SA companies then her inaccurate auditing of the accounts constitutes unlawful behaviour. Thus, if the inaccuracy of the accounts was due to her fault (wilful conduct or negligence), and Paul could prove that without relying

---

[872] R. Illescas Ortiz, 'Auditoría, aprobación, depósito y publicidad de las cuentas anuales', in *Comentario al régimen legal de las sociedades mercantiles*, VIII-2 (1993) at pp. 165–9, F. J. Arana Gondra, *Ley de auditoría de cuentas* (1995), p. 430.

[873] Petit Laval, 'El informe Cadbury', pp. 12873–6 and J. Amesti Mendizábal, 'La actuación de los auditores en la sociedad anónima: la responsabilidad de los auditores de la sociedad anónima', (1995) III *Cuadernos de la Revista del Derecho Bancario y Bursátil* 99 pp. 113–116.

[874] Pantaleón, *La responsabilidad*, p. 74.    [875] Ibid. p. 121.

[876] Ibid. pp. 121–30.

on these accounts he would not have bought any shares (i.e. he could prove the causal relation between Donna's fault and his loss), then she is obliged to compensate Paul by paying him the difference between his damage, i.e. the price he paid, and the actual value of the shares, according to article 914 CC.[877]

Tortious liability according to article 919 CC: if Donna audited not as an auditor in the sense of article 34 para-1 of Law no. 2190/1920, but only by virtue of a contract with Caterpillar or anyone else, then the inaccurate auditing is not an unlawful act, but only breach of contract. Nevertheless, her behaviour could be judged as in conflict with good morals by consideration of its specific circumstances. Only in this case can Paul sue her for compensation according to article 919 CC, which lays down that whoever wilfully and immorally causes prejudice to someone else is obliged to compensate him.

Precontractual liability of Caterpillar according to articles 197–198 CC as Donna's employer: if Donna audited and published the accounts on behalf of Caterpillar, which means that she acted as an employee of this company, then the latter is liable for the former's behaviour according to articles 71[878] and 922 CC, since Donna is an organ or – at least – a servant of the company.[879] Thus Caterpillar is obliged to compensate Paul, as articles 197–198 order. Caterpillar, whose servant (according to arts. 71–922 CC) in the course of negotiations for the sale of the shares has through her fault caused prejudice to the other party, i.e. Paul, as a potential purchaser will be entitled to compensation, even if the contract has not been concluded, and even moreso if the contract has been concluded as in this case.

Voidability of the sale of shares because of error: if there is no legal ground of liability as against Donna or Caterpillar, Paul will probably suffer the risk of his purchase unless only the correct accounts of Caterpillar would have revealed some qualities of this company unknown to him. In this case Paul's error, due to which he obtained the shares, is an error as to the qualities of the vendor, as well as of the asset sold, i.e. the shares, rather than a simple error in Paul's motivation. The difference between

---

[877] About diligence in auditing, see P. Papanikolaou, *The Liability of the Bank as Underwriter* (ed. A. Sakkoulas, 1998).

[878] See J. Passias, *The Law of SA Companies*, I (1955), II (1969) par. 603.

[879] See M. Stathopoulos, *Law of Obligations, General Part* I (1979–1983) (3rd edn, 1998), p. 220. Nevertheless the Greek courts deny the implementability of art. 922 CC in the case of an *independent* person who offers his services to the master (see, e.g. AP 300/1980 EEN 47, 581; EphThes 1430/1982 Arm 38, 24; EphAth 590/1983 Arm 38, 455).

these two types of error is essential for Greek law (arts. 142 and 143 CC), insofar as only the first is stipulated as sufficient reason for the person in error to seek the retroactive annulment of the contract by the court. In such a case, the price and shares are to be reciprocally returned. However, it is to be noted that the prevailing view in Greece, especially that of Greek jurisprudence, has constantly been that the value of a thing is not a quality of it in the sense of article 142 CC (error as to the qualities).[880]

Voidability of the sale of shares because of fraud: of course, if Caterpillar knew about the inaccuracy of Donna's accounts or, *a fortiori*, if Donna was an employee of Caterpillar, Paul can claim the annulment of the sale of the shares because of fraud (according to art. 147 CC).

### England

I. Paul has no claim against Donna.

II. The case is similar to *Caparo Industries plc v. Dickman*.[881] The House of Lords held in that case that an accountant auditing the accounts of a target company owes no duty of care to a takeover bidder. It may well be different if a particular takeover bidder has emerged prior to the accountant's statements (*Morgan Crucible v. Hill Samuel Bank*).[882]

III. The decision of the House of Lords in *Caparo* was based on lack of 'proximity' between the auditor and the bidder. This concept had been criticized already in an earlier case as a concept with no ascertainable meaning, having no relation to real foreseeability.[883] Clearly, the policy of the House of Lords was to protect the accounting profession, alarmed at their increasing exposure to civil liability for negligence.

Neither the courts, nor the learned authors in England, seem to have taken into account so far, in connection with the liability of auditors, the proposed EC 5th Company Law Directive (Amended Proposal Com(91) 372 final, UJ C 321, 12 December 1991), imposing liability on auditors to third parties for loss suffered through the auditor's wrongful acts.

### Scotland

I. Paul will have no claim against Donna as she does not owe him a duty of care in the circumstances.

---

[880] See J. Spyridakis, *General Principles of Civil Law* (1990), p. 602.
[881] [1990] 2 AC 605 (HL).   [882] [1991] 1 All ER 148 (CA).
[883] See *The Aliakmon* [1985] 2 All ER 44 (CA) *per* Goff LJ as he then was.

II. We are dealing here with liability for making a negligent statement or negligent misrepresentation, written or verbal, and this is very much dependent upon the nature of the relationship between the parties, i.e. the party making the statement and the one sustaining the economic loss. *Hedley Byrne* established 'circumstances in which a party sustaining financial loss as a direct result of acting upon an incorrect statement, given by another with whom there was no contractual relationship, might sue for damages on the ground of negligence'.[884]

In *Caparo Industries plc v. Dickman*,[885] the House of Lords considered the duty of care owed by an auditor of company accounts. After reviewing the relevant cases, Lord Bridge of Harwich clearly set out the reasoning underlying the courts' approach. He stated:

The salient features of all these cases is that the defendant giving advice or information was fully aware of the nature of the transaction which the plaintiff had in contemplation, knew that the advice or information would be communicated to him directly or indirectly and knew that it was very likely that the plaintiff would rely on that advice or information in deciding whether or not to engage in the transaction in contemplation. In these circumstances the defendant could clearly be expected, subject always to the effect of any disclaimer of responsibility, specifically to anticipate that the plaintiff would rely on the advice or information given by the defendant for the very purpose for which he did in the event rely on it. So also the plaintiff, subject again to the effect of any disclaimer, would in that situation reasonably suppose that he was entitled to rely on the advice or information communicated to him for the very purpose for which he required it. The situation is entirely different where a statement is put into more or less general circulation and may foreseeably be relied on by strangers to the maker of the statement for any one of a variety of different purposes which the maker of the statement has no specific reason to anticipate. To hold the maker of the statement to be under a duty of care in respect of the accuracy of the statement to all and sundry for any purpose for which they may choose to rely on it is not only to subject him, in the classic words of Cardozo CJ, to 'liability in an indeterminate amount for an indeterminate time to an indeterminate class'... it is also to confer on the world at large a quite unwarranted entitlement to appropriate for their own purposes the benefit of the expert knowledge or professional expertise attributed to the maker of the statement... the 'limit or control mechanism... imposed on the liability of a wrongdoer towards those who have suffered economic damage in consequence of his negligence'... rested on the necessity to prove, in this category of the tort of negligence, as an essential ingredient of the 'proximity' between the plaintiff and the defendant, that the defendant knew that his statement would

---

[884] Gloag and Henderson, *The Law of Scotland* (10th edn, Green, Edinburgh, 1995), at p. 517.
[885] [1990] 2 AC 605.

be communicated to the plaintiff, either as an individual or as the member of an identifiable class, specifically in connection with a particular transaction or transactions of a particular kind (e.g. in a prospectus inviting investment) and that the plaintiff would be very likely to rely on it for the purpose of deciding whether or not to enter on that transaction or on a transaction of that kind.[886]

Applying this to the situation before him, Lord Bridge of Harwich decided the following:

These considerations amply justify the conclusion that auditors of a public company's accounts owe no duty of care to members of the public at large who rely on the accounts in deciding to buy shares in the company. If a duty of care were owed so widely, it is difficult to see any reason why it should not equally extend to all who rely on the accounts in relation to other dealings with a company as lenders or merchants extending credit to the company...In this jurisdiction I have no doubt that the creation of such an unlimited duty would be a legislative step which it would be for Parliament, not the courts, to take.[887]

The court further limited the duty of care owed. Lord Oliver of Aylmerton stated:

[T]he purpose for which the auditor's certificate is made and published is that of providing those entitled to receive the report with information to enable them to exercise in conjunction those powers which their respective proprietary interests confer on them and not for the purposes of individual speculation with the view to profit...the duty of care is one owed to the shareholders as a body and not to individual shareholders. To widen the scope of the duty to include loss caused to an individual by reliance on the accounts for a purpose for which they were not supplied and were not intended would be to extend it beyond the limits which are so far deducible from the decisions of this House...In relation to the purchase of shares of other shareholders in a company, whether in the open market or as a result of an offer made to all or a majority of the existing shareholders, I can see no sensible distinction, so far as duty of care is concerned, between a potential purchaser who is, vis-à-vis the company, a total outsider and one who is already the holder of one or more shares.[888]

As always, questions of liability depend upon the particular facts of any case. Therefore, if the auditor's report has been prepared for a specific reason known to the auditors, and they were aware that particular identified individuals will rely on it, then a duty of care would arise.[889] We are able to say that Donna would not owe a duty of care to Paul. Although *Caparo* is an English case, the *Hedley Byrne* principle on which it

---

[886] Ibid, at pp. 620–621.   [887] Ibid, at p. 623.   [888] Ibid, at p. 654.
[889] *Galoo Ltd (in liquidation)* v. *Bright Grahame Murray (a firm)* [1995] 1 All ER 16 (CA).

relies has been accepted as part of Scots law by Lord Dunpark in *Kenway (John)* v. *Orcantic Ltd*,[890] and Norrie states that there is no doubt that both of these cases represent the law of Scotland also.[891]

III. Lord Oliver of Aylmerton describes in *Caparo* the particular problem with finding liability for negligent statements and explains the courts' device for limiting a potentially limitless number of plaintiffs. He states:

> The opportunities for the infliction of pecuniary loss from the imperfect performance of everyday tasks on the proper performance of which people rely for regulating their affairs are illimitable and the effects are far reaching. A defective bottle of ginger beer may injure a single consumer but the damage stops there. A single statement may be repeated endlessly with or without the permission of its author and may be relied on in a different way by many different people. Thus the postulate of a simple duty to avoid any harm that is, with hindsight, reasonably capable of being foreseen becomes untenable without the imposition of some intelligible limits to keep the law of negligence within the bounds of common sense and practicality. Those limits have been found by the requirement of what has been called the 'relationship of proximity' between plaintiff and defendant and by the imposition of a further requirement that the attachment of liability for harm which has occurred be 'just and reasonable'... '[p]roximity' is, no doubt, a convenient expression so long as it is realised that it is no more than a label which embraces not a definable concept but merely a description of circumstances from which, pragmatically, the courts conclude that a duty of care exists.[892]

The factor upon which, more than any other, the court focused in denying 'proximity', was made by Richmond P in *Scott Group Ltd* v. *McFarlane*.[893] He stated:

> I would especially emphasise that to my mind it does not seem reasonable to attribute an assumption of responsibility unless the maker of the statement ought in all the circumstances, both in preparing himself for what he said and in saying it, to have directed his mind, and to have been able to direct his mind, to some particular and specific purpose for which he was aware that his advice or information would be relied on. In many situations that purpose will be obvious. But the annual accounts of a company can be relied on in all sorts of ways and for many purposes. It would be going too far to treat accountants as assuming a responsibility towards all persons dealing with the company or its members, in reliance to some greater or lesser degree on the accuracy of the accounts, merely

---

[890] 1979 SC 422, 1980 SLT 46, OH.
[891] *Stair Memorial Encyclopaedia, The Laws of Scotland*, vol. 15 (Law Society of Scotland, Edinburgh, 1996), p. 174, para. 277 (written by K. McK. Norrie).
[892] [1990] 2 AC 605 at pp. 632–633.   [893] [1978] 1 NZLR 553.

because it was reasonably foreseeable, in a general way, that a transaction of the kind in which the plaintiff happened to become involved might indeed take place. The relationship between the parties would, I think, be too general and not sufficiently 'special' to come within the principles underlying the decision in *Hedley Byrne*.[894]

## The Netherlands

I. Although no case law exists on this matter, it is thought possible to hold Donna liable, if she knew, or should have known, that her public statement would be relied upon by this specific party.

II. A notary public in his dealings has to take to heart the interests of third parties.[895] Undoubtedly, this duty is most convincing whenever the notary can affect the (legal) position of this third party. A (chartered) accountant may affect the position of a third party as well: the accountant's public statement that – to his best knowledge – the published accounts of the audited company are faithful and give a true report of the company's financial situation is often relied on by third parties. Therefore, the accountant should only attach his signature to the accounts when he is convinced that they contain a true report of the company's finances. If he acted negligently in verifying the accounts, in principle he can be held liable. The scope of this liability is frightfully extensive: if the accountant overlooks a detail, this might result in enormous damage. This fear has led some to press the Dutch government for the enactment of liability 'caps', but to no avail.[896]

An important question that still needs to be answered is whether the accountant owes this societal duty to *all* possible third parties, or whether it is only owed to a well-demarcated group of persons (e.g. shareholders, creditors). Surprisingly, there is little case law on this matter. In Dutch legal writing no consensus exists, but it is often said that the accountant can only be held liable by a third party if the accountant knew or could have known that the public statement would be relied upon by this specific party.[897] In the case at hand, it is not clear whether

---

[894] Ibid. at pp. 566–7.
[895] HR 15.9.1995, NJ 1996, no. 629; HR 4.10.1996, NJ 1997, no. 594.
[896] See on this subject, e.g., C. J. J. M. Stolker, *Aansprakelijkheid voor beroepsfouten – van droomcarrière naar nachtmerrie* (Ars Aequi, 1995), p. 23, and W. J. Slagter, 'Beperking van beroepsaansprakelijkheid' (1995) *TVvS (Maandblad voor ondernemingsrecht en rechtspersonen)* 178.
[897] See, e.g. H. Beckman, 'Persoonlijke aansprakelijkheid van de openbaar accountant', in J. M. M. Maeijer et al., *Aansprakelijkheid en draagplicht van bestuurders, commissarissen en*

the accountant knew or could have foreseen that the published accounts would be used by third parties for takeover bids. This would largely depend on the actual commission by Caterpillar.

It must be noted that, according to Dutch law, Paul must exercise due diligence when launching his bid. This means that he is not always allowed to rely on the accountant's reports, but – under specific circumstances – he must do his own investigations into Caterpillar's finances.[898] If found liable, Donna can possibly raise the defence of contributory negligence: had Paul exercised due diligence, the actual value of the shares would have become known. Eventually then, the claim for damages might be reduced.

## Germany

I. Paul has no claim against Donna, neither in tort nor in contract.

II. Tort claims: None of Paul's absolute rights were violated, so he cannot recover under § 823 (1) BGB.

§ 823 (2) BGB: There is no indication in the case that Donna violated a statute. Even if Donna's audit was statutorily required, the respective statute would not aim at the protection of a potential buyer of the company from overpaying.

§ 824 BGB: Paul could conceivably sue under § 824 (1) BGB which provides for liability of a 'person who declares or publishes, contrary to the truth, a statement which is likely to endanger the credit of another, or to injure his earnings or prosperity in any other manner'. It is true that Donna published inaccurate statements about Caterpillar's accounts and that, as a consequence, Paul's earnings and prosperity were injured. Nonetheless, § 824 (1) does not apply. It does not intend to hold the publisher liable for the damages of all persons who rely on the untrue statement. Instead, § 824 'was intended to protect the business reputation of persons and enterprises against infringements caused by the dissemination of untrue statements',[899] and thus applies only if the statement was made about the plaintiff or his business. In other

---

accountants; verzekeringsaspecten (Deventer, 1991), pp. 45 ff., A. T. Bolt, in A. T. Bolt and J. Spier, De uitdijende reikwijdte van de aansprakelijkheid uit onrechtmatige daad (Handelingen NJV 1996–I) (Zwolle, 1996), pp. 157–8.

[898] See, e.g. HR 22.12.1995, NJ 1996, no. 300, The Hague District Court 24.7.1991, as quoted by K. A. J. Bisschop, 'De buitencontractuele aansprakelijkheid van de accountant' (1994) Nederlands Tijdschrift voor Burgerlijk Recht 23. Compare HR 2.12.1994, NJ 1996, no. 246.

[899] BGH NJW 1963, 1871; BGH NJW 1965, 36, at 37.

words, the idea is to protect victims of an untrue statement against its economic consequences, not to protect third parties.

Contract claims: if there was a contract for services between Donna and Caterpillar, Paul could try to sue as a protected third party.[900] There are indeed cases in which the *Bundesgerichtshof* has held accountants and other experts who had made incorrect statements liable for the loss suffered by third parties who had relied on these statements.[901] But the Court has consistently required that there be special reasons to believe that the parties to the contract intended to protect the outsider in question. This requires that the statement was made, at least *inter alia*, for the benefit of the third party, and that the defendant had reason to know that.[902] Thus, errors in an audit of business accounts will trigger liability towards investors only if the audit was made with a particular view to these investors, e.g. if the company hired the accountant in order to provide potential buyers with the relevant information and if the accountant should have understood that.[903] In the present case, there is no indication that these requirements are fulfilled.

Moreover, there are two factors strongly militating against Donna's liability to Paul. First, Paul did not even receive the results of the audit from the company (as was true in virtually all cases decided in favour of the third party) but through general publication. Secondly, liability toward third parties is allowed only if the group of potential claimants is limited and predictable, not if it amounts to potential liability to every member of the public.[904] If Paul can sue Donna, virtually everyone can. Neither courts nor commentators have ever gone that far.

III. The *Bundesgerichtshof* draws the line between two kinds of cases.[905] In the first kind, accountants and other experts are hired by the business owner but their work product also serves someone else, such as

---

[900] See above, Case 13 ('Subcontractor's Liability'), sub II.
[901] See e.g. BGH NJW 1983, 1053; BGH JZ 1985, 951–2; BGH NJW-RR 1986, 1307; BGH NJW 1987, 1758.
[902] BGH NJW 1984, 355–6; BGH NJW 1995, 392; BGH NJW-RR 1993, 1497–8; BGH NJW 1987, 1758, at 1759–60; O. Palandt, *Bürgerliches Gesetzbuch* (Beck, Munich, 2000), art. 328 Rd.-Nr. 32.
[903] In at least one case, the Court also required that there be an indication that the defendant was willing to assume liability towards third parties as well, BGH NJW 1984, 354, at 355.
[904] BGH NJW-RR 1986, 484, at 486.
[905] On the liability of accountants for damages caused to third parties, see W. Ebke and H. Scheel, 'Die Haftung des Wirtschaftsprüfers für fahrlässig verursachte Vermögensschäden Dritter', WM 1991, 389–98; H. Brandner, 'Berufshaftung und Versicherung für Wirtschaftsprüfer', JZ 1985, 757–62.

a potential buyer. If they understand that, they should know that errors in their statements are likely to injury a non-party as well. In such cases, it is not unfair to hold them liable to outsiders.[906] In the second kind, they are hired for general purposes, e.g. to perform an audit which is statutorily required. In these cases, they serve only their party in contract but have nothing to do with outsiders. Holding them liable towards investors would be an unfair burden.[907] Thus, outsiders rely on these accountants at their own peril.

## Austria

I. Paul has neither a claim in tort against Donna nor a claim based on a contract with protective effects to a third party.

II. Tort claims: in recent decisions the OGH has followed the suggestions made by an influential learned scholar[908] and imposed liability on an expert *vis-à-vis* a third party according to article 1300 ABGB, if such expert has violated objective–legal duties in favour of a third party.[909] The Court saw a 'parallel situation' to that of a contract with protective effects to a third party.

However, the facts are different here: Paul relies on 'published accounts'. Whether Donna had known, or had to know, that her audit was also addressed to certain third parties who should be able to rely on its accuracy, does not follow from the hypothetical facts. Therefore, a claim has to be denied.

It has to be mentioned that the provision of article 1330(2) ABGB does not apply in this case, either. Article 1330(2) is aimed at the protection of business reputations (*wirtschaftlicher Ruf*) of persons and enterprises against infringements caused by untrue rumours. In the present case third parties are not within the scope of protection.

Contract with protective effects to third parties: the same considerations as those on the 'infringement of objective–legal duties of care in favour of a third party' (*Verletzung objektiv–rechtlicher Sorgfaltspflichten zugunsten Dritter*) directed the Court in earlier decisions. These were based on the theory of contractual protective effects in favour of third parties.[910] Courts and scholars requested that it had to be clear to the

---

[906] BGH NJW-RR 1986, 484; BGH NJW-RR 1986, 1307; BGH NJW 1987, 1758, at 1759.
[907] BGH NJW 1984, 355, at 356.
[908] See R. Welser, *Die Haftung für Rat, Auskunft und Gutachten* (1983), p. 87.
[909] Cf. OGH SZ 57/122; SV 1991/2, 22; JBl 1993, 518; see, however, OGH ÖBA 1989, 89.
[910] See OGH SZ 43/236; RdW 1985, 306.

expert that the person who ordered an expert opinion was also acting in the interest of certain third parties.[911] However, this is not the case here. Therefore, the special requirements for recovery of pure economic loss apparently are not fulfilled.

III. The OGH assumes that an expert opinion is, as a rule, established only in the interest of the person ordering it and that outsiders rely on these accountants at their own peril.

Only if it is beyond doubt that certain third persons, e.g. potential buyers of an enterprise, were entitled to rely on the opinion would protection against economic damage be expanded to such 'certain third parties', who would not have to be explicitly named. Thus, measurements (static calculations) are always made in the interest of the constructor and builder, whether or not their names are known to the engineer performing the measurement.[912]

## Portugal

I. If Caterpillar is a company listed on the stock exchange, in principle the *Código dó Mercado de Valores Mobiliários* (Stock Market Code) of 19 April 1991) is applicable, and this establishes auditor liability.[913]

If this Code is not applicable, the solution is less certain. But the doctrine has argued in favour of making auditors liable *vis-à-vis* third parties in specified circumstances, so it is likely that the court would follow this line.

II. Responsibility for the 'adequacy, objectivity, veracity and currency of information'[914] is attached not only to the company that publishes it (Caterpillar), but also to its official auditors, who have approved or certified the accounts, and to those persons, whether or not company staff, who have agreed to compile or check any information or 'any study, forecast or assessment on which such information has been based'.[915]

---

[911] See G. Wilhelm, 'Unrichtige Gutachten – Haftung für Dritte', ecolex 1991, 87.
[912] See OGH NZ 1992, 110.
[913] This question is similar to hypothesis 1 of the Tilburg Group. See the Portuguese report and the comparative law report in J. Spier *The Limits of Expanding Liability* (1998) at pp. 173 and 25 ff., respectively.
[914] Among the documents that must be published are the 'legal certification of accounts' (annual) and the 'auditors' report ...' (sub-paras. b and of art. 341, no. 1 of the Código do Mercado de Valores Mobiliários). This Code was approved by Decree-Law no. 142-A/91 of 10 April, but has subsequently been altered.
[915] Application adapted from art. 160, no. 1, sub-paras. c and e of the Código do Mercado de Valores Mobiliários, through reference to arts. 341, 340 and 333.

They are responsible whether they are auditors in the employ of the company, or 'external auditors', in the event of there being an external auditor,[916] that is to say, no matter what Donna's position may be.

The regime of liability is established in articles 161–165.[917] Damage is calculated from the difference between the acquisition price of the shares on the stock market and that for which they were later sold, 'or, where this has not yet been done, by what they could be on the date of the claim for compensation, plus the loss of justifiably expected earnings based on the contentious information…'[918] However, article 161, no. 3 (directly applicable to responsibility for the content of the prospectus in public subscription offers) does establish a maximum limit for compensation which corresponds to the price for which the shares were offered for public subscription.

Going beyond the scope of this Code, it has been argued in a recent study[919] that auditors could be held liable using the constructive route of 'liability through *culpa in contrahendo* vis-à-vis third parties', once the requirements of 'liability through trust' are present. On this or another basis (namely that of 'contracts with the effect of protecting third parties'), it is likely that the court would accept Paul's action.

**Sweden and Finland**

I. Donna will be most likely held liable.

II. Donna's liability would be affirmed on the basis of the special liability rule for auditors contained in the Swedish Companies Act 1975[920] and the Finnish Auditors' Act 1994.[921]

---

[916] In its initial wording, article 100 of the Código do Mercado de Valores Mobiliários requires a double certification of the documents relating to the rendering of accounts. Decree-Law no. 261/95 of 3 October has removed the obligation for a second auditor (from outside the company), thus enabling the services which it would have rendered to be carried out by the company's own official auditor (the audit committee or the sole auditor), once this has been registered with the Comissão dó Mercado de Valores Mobiliários.

[917] The notions that information is 'insufficient', 'unverified', lacking 'objectivity' or 'currency', are laid down in sub-paras. a and d of art. 161, no. 2 of the Código do Mercado de Valores Mobiliários.

[918] Articles 333, no. 2 and 161, no. 3, of the Código do Mercado de Valores Mobiliários.

[919] M. A. Carneiro da Frada, *Uma 'Terceira via' no Direito da responsabilidade Civil? O problema da imputação dos danos causados a terceiros por auditores de sociedades* (Almedina, Coimbra, 1997).

[920] Aktiebolagslag (1975: 385) 15 kap. 1–2 §§.    [921] Revisionslag 28.10.1994/936 44 §.

A slight margin of doubt, depending on the kind of inaccuracy resulting from Donna's action, derives from the fact that while the liability of the auditor towards the company presupposes mere negligence, that towards 'shareholders and others' also presupposes a breach of a provision of the Companies Act or of the individual company's charter. However, this should not represent a major problem, since the abovementioned Acts impose, for example, the respect of 'good auditing practice'.[922]

*Editors' comparative comments*

In most national systems (Belgium, France, Finland, Greece, Italy, Portugal, Spain, Sweden) there exist statutory rules which impose liability upon auditors. The wording and goals of these rules may be different, but their overall outcome is relevant to our issue because – as mentioned in our comment on Case 14 ('Poor Legal Services') – they enable plaintiffs to recover pure economic losses caused by auditors, regardless of the general features and traditions of a given tort law system.

In all cases where these statutes do not apply, as well as in every other legal system where no protective statute is at the plaintiff's disposal, the solution to our hypothetical case lies in the hands of scholars and judges. The problem raised by the fact that there is no direct contact between the victim and the defendant is dealt with in three different ways, although a common feature is once again an overt, or covert, concern with the issue of excessive indeterminate liability.

Some systems rely on strict scrutiny of the elements of the cause of action, whether this is the causal requirement (France and the Netherlands), the blameworthiness of the defendant's conduct (Greece and Spain), or the diligence required and actually exercised by the plaintiff when purchasing the shares (again, the Netherlands).[923]

Other systems (England and Scotland) emphasize the need for a proximity factor, understood as the obligation to prove that the defendant knew that his statement would be communicated to the plaintiff, either as an individual or as the member of an identifiable class, and that the plaintiff would be very likely to rely on this statement when deciding whether or not to undertake the transaction.[924]

---

[922] On auditor's liability, see G. Kedner, C. M. Roos and R. Skog, *Aktiebolagslagen Del II* (5th edn, Stockholm, 1996), pp. 266 ff.
[923] See our comments to Case 2 ('Cable II – Factory Shutdown').
[924] See, e.g., the ruling in *Caparo Industries plc v. Dickman* [1990] 1 All ER 568, esp. p. 576c.

This argument, adduced by English and Scottish judges in tort, lies not so far from the perspective taken by the Austrian and German legal systems – which deny a tort law remedy because an absolute right has not been violated – when dealing with a plaintiff's action grounded on the 'contract with protective effects to third party'. Indeed, the Austrian and German courts require that there be good reasons to believe that the parties to the contract intended to protect the outsider in question.[925] These good reasons are that the statement was made for the benefit of the third party as well, and that the defendant had reason to know this.[926] Thus, as our German and Austrian contributors point out, errors committed in an audit of business accounts will entail liability towards investors only if the audit was made with a particular view to these investors, e.g. if the company hired the accountant in order to provide potential buyers with the relevant information and if the accountant had agreed thereto.

---

[925] Furthermore, unlike what is statutorily established elsewhere (e.g. in France and Italy), § 323 of the German Commercial Code (HGB) is interpreted to exclude third-party liability for those carrying out statutory audits. See C. von Bar, *The Common European Law of Torts* (Clarendon Press, Oxford, 1998), p. 502, fn. 560 and p. 562.

[926] Cf. the Austrian and German solutions to Cases 14 ('Poor Legal Services') and 20 ('An Anonymous Telephone Call'), and the Austrian contributor's remarks under Case 11 ('A Maestro's Mistake'), sub II.

# Case 18: wrongful job reference

## Case

Robco Services offered a job to Peter on condition that it received a satisfactory character reference. Peter asked his former employer, David, to send such a reference. David did so but mistook Peter for another former employee who had a record of dishonesty. When Robco Services received the reference referring to 'Peter's dishonesty', it gave the job to another person. Peter wishes to sue David.

## France

I. Peter will likely recover in tort under articles 1382–83 CC.

II. Liability in tort depends upon proof of fault, damage and causal relation between the two.

David's mistake is the direct cause of Peter's non-employment. Thus, Peter is entitled to sue David and recover the amount he might have earned as Robco's employee. The damage may be based on the concept of a lost opportunity (*perte d'une chance*). The *perte d'une chance* can be certain and direct in itself when the probability of an event's realisation was diminished. Thus courts often deal with the *perte d'une chance d'évolution favorable de l'activité professionnelle*.[927] The courts decide that the *perte d'une chance* must be certain and the direct result of the damage.[928] It is also added that the chance must be serious and real.[929] Decisions of the Conseil d'Etat have also awarded compensation for the loss of a chance to obtain employment.[930]

In our case, it is obvious that if David had not mistaken Peter for an employee who had a record of dishonesty, Peter would have been hired by Robco Services. But for David's mistake, Peter would have probably obtained a job. The causal link is rather strong, although of course it is not 100 per cent certain. The chance to get the job was serious and real since a satisfactory reference was the only condition of the job offer.

---

[927] For example, Civ. 2, 9 juillet 1954, D. 1954, 627; 13 novembre 1985, Bull. 1985, II, no. 172.
[928] Civ. 2, 9 novembre 1983, JCP 1985.II.20360, note Chartier.
[929] Y. Chartier, *La réparation du préjudice dans la responsabilité civile*, éd. Dalloz 1983, nos. 22 ff., spec.
nos. 36–8 and Ibid. the relevant case law.
[930] CE 27 mai 1987, AJDA 1988, 694.

Peter should be able to recover a large part of the economic loss that he suffered.

**Belgium**

I. Peter has a claim against David, if he can prove that he was entitled to a satisfactory character reference and that if Robco Services had received that satisfactory character reference, he would have very probably or almost certainly had the job.

II. Contract claim: Peter has no contractual claim against David since there is no obligation for the employer to supply a reference for their former employee. There is therefore no breach of the employment contract.

Tort claim: Peter's claim against David can therefore rest only on article 1382 CC:

> Any act whatever of man which causes damage to another obliges him by whose fault it occurred to make reparation.

In order to hold David liable, Peter will have to prove David's fault or negligence, the damage he suffered and the causal link between the damage and the fault.

The first issue in the present case will be to prove David's fault. The fault of article 1382 CC is either a violation of law or a behaviour different from the one that the *bonus pater familias* (the normal man) would have had in the same circumstances.

Here, in the present case, it is clear that there is no violation of the law. Peter will therefore have to prove that a *bonus pater familias* would not have acted as David did in the same circumstances.

The second issue regards the damage claimed. In order to recover his damage, Peter will have to prove that he was entitled to a satisfactory character reference and that if David had sent that satisfactory character reference, he would have received the job from Robco Services.

This problem regards mostly the condition of certainty of the damage. To be recoverable, the damage must be certain.[931]

However the case law has in some cases reduced this requirement by accepting to indemnify the loss of an opportunity (*la perte d'une chance*), subject to the evidence that the opportunity was real or sufficiently certain.[932]

---

[931] R. O. Dalcq and G. Schamps, 'La responsabilité délictuelle et quasi-délictuelle, examen de jurisprudence (1987–1993)', (1995) 149 RCJB, 737; J. L. Fagnart, *La responsabilité civile – Chronique de jurisprudence 1985–1995* (Larcier, Brussels, 1997), p. 23, no. 11.

[932] Cass., 19 octobre 1937, Pas., 1937, I, p. 298; Cass., 8 décembre 1958, Pas., 1959, I, p. 354;

When the opportunity is only hypothetical, the damage resulting from its loss is not recoverable.[933]

Because of the difficulty of evaluating the damage resulting from the loss of an opportunity, the damage is mostly in such a case calculated *ex aequo ac bono*, which means repaired by the payment of a lump sum.[934]

## Italy

I. The case is not covered by any similar case law precedent. Peter can sue David on the ground of a third party's tortious interference in contractual relations – provided that David's conduct is proved to be, at least, grossly negligent – and recover damages according to the general provision of article 2043 cc.[935]

II. As a matter of principle, the amount of recovery should be determined as in *Baroncini* v. *Enel*,[936] which created a tort liability for the loss of a chance. In that case, a would-be public employee participated in two different competitions to get one of two positions. As he got the first position, he was not allowed to participate in the final exam related to the second. Baroncini was much more interested in the second position than in the first and sued for damages. The Supreme Court held in his favour, stating that an exam is a 'chance' and that to deprive the plaintiff of this chance amounts to an unjustified injury to his interests protected by the provision of article 2043 cc.

## Spain

I. Although this case may lend itself to debate, it is quite likely that under Spanish law Peter would be compensated by David.

II. Until 1994, labour law experts explained that article 75.5 of the Labour Contract Act 1944 was still in force. This precept ordered the

---

Cass., 15 octobre 1962, Pas, 1963, I, 195; Cass., 15 septembre 1972, RGAR, 1973; no. 9121; Cass., 4 mars 1975, Pas., 1975, I, 682; Cass., 19 juin 1987, RW, 1987–1988, p. 709.

[933] See, for example, Civ. Marche, 11 février 1988, RGAR, 1990, no. 11.719 – damage claimed for the loss of the opportunity to make a career in the army.

[934] See for example: Mons, 6 mai 1996, JLMB, 1997, p. 432; Anvers, 1er janvier 1996, TDRB, 1995–96, p. 271 (damage resulting from the lost opportunity to re-implant a tooth).

[935] A. Milano, 14.1.1975, AC 1975, 894; GM 1976, I, 340; A. Milano, 5.4.1957, FP I, 1248; Cass. 6.1.1984 no. 94, Rep. FI, entry 'Responsabilità Civile' no. 65, and RCP 1984, 674; Cass. 9.6.1998 no. 5659, DR 1998, 1048; Cass. 14.6.1999 no. 5880, Studium Iuris 1999, 1286; DR 1999, 1022 noted by Pedrazzi; contra Cass. SU 6.8.1998 no. 7706 CGiur. 1999, 125.

[936] Cass., SU, 19.12.1985, no. 6506, FI 1986, I, 385, noted by A. M. Princigalli.

employer, if so requested by the worker, to issue a certificate stating the time he served with the company and the kind of work that he carried out. If this certificate were incorrect and damages ensued from this error, the worker could claim compensation.[937] If the worker and employer mutually agreed that the latter would include additional information in the certificate, the employer would be liable and would have to compensate any party damaged by inaccurate information, due to bad faith or negligence (be it the worker himself or the other employer who eventually contracted with him).

At the present time, article 75.5 is no longer in force.[938] The duty of the employer to issue a certificate is not expressly contemplated as a general norm and only exists in contracts for practical experience and apprenticeship, since these have a maximum time limit which, once elapsed, prevents the worker from being hired again under those same types of contract.[939] Perhaps it is significant that in the latest editions of leading works, references to the employer's liability for issuing an incorrect certificate are either omitted or expressed in a limited manner.[940]

Case law does not abound on the subject. In fact, we have only found one Supreme Court decision of 1 June 1967, which is relevant. The facts were as follows: once the working relationship ended, the employer agreed to issue a certificate in which he affirmed that the worker had rendered services correctly. However, the employer wrote a note to another worker explaining that the termination of the first worker's services had been due to his not being fit for the job. This note came to the knowledge of a second employer who had hired the first worker. The second employer, alarmed by the note, fired the worker. The Supreme Court ordered the first employer to compensate for damages suffered by the worker as a result of this dismissal, stating that the first employer had breached the duty to ensure the effectiveness of the certificate, issued according to article 75.5 of the Labour Contract Act 1944.

This decision does not appear to be an adequate model, and is debatable from the standpoint of labour law experts. The issue is a border line case which is difficult to solve. While article 75.5 was in force, it could

---

[937] M. Alonso Olea and E. Casas Baamonde, *Derecho del trabajo* (13th edn, 1993), p. 506, G. Diéguez, *Lecciones de derecho del trabajo* (4th edn, 1995), p. 307, T. Sala Franco, *Derecho del trabajo* (7th edn, 1993), p. 530, Montoya Melgar, *Derecho del trabajo* (14th edn, 1993), p. 307.

[938] For all, see Montoya Melgar (17th edn, 1996) p. 307.  [939] Ibid., p. 590.

[940] Sala Franco, *Derecho*, p. 515, Diéguez, p. 307, Olea and Baamonde, p. 468.

be argued that the protection intended by the norm (which obligated the employer to issue a certificate) consisted in enabling the worker to draft a *curriculum vitae* for career purposes.[941] At present it concerns a duty of good faith and there would be greater scope for debate.[942] From the point of view of the duty of care[943] the issue is no clearer.

**Greece**

I. David is tortiously liable to compensate Peter for his damages, as well as his moral prejudice. David is also contractually liable to compensate Peter for his pecuniary damage.

II. Tortious liability: at the first level, the problem is again to discover an obligation for compensation between persons, regardless of whether they are bound by a contract. The main type of non-contractual liability is the tortious one, stipulated by the general clause of article 914 CC.

David's behaviour was illegal, because the law prohibits and punishes slander and the consequent unlawful harm to someone's personality (article 57 CC).[944] Greek jurisprudence considers that any unfavourable inaccurate information infringes the personality of the person and it is forbidden by law.[945] So everyone is liable for such a behaviour, even if their actions are not wilful, only negligent. In labour law, Greek courts are especially strict, in order to protect the employee's personality.[946]

The above certainly means that David should compensate Peter, not only for his pecuniary damage, but also for his moral prejudice by paying in the latter case a reasonable amount of money (as art. 932 CC

---

[941] Diéguez, *Lecciones*, p. 303.
[942] Diéguez, *Lecciones*, p. 307, Sala Franco, *Derecho*, p. 515. Perhaps it should be pointed out that the possible liability involved here should be viewed as contractual. The fact that the parties have ended their contractual relationship is not an obstacle to reach this outcome. On the other hand, it is indeed possible in the Spanish legal system to see a breach of contract even if only an accessory duty is affected. However, the way the courts have established the relationship between contractual and non-contractual responsibility (a situation quite similar to the German *Anspruchskonkurrenz*), practically allows the victim to choose between these two remedies; on this J. Lacruz, *Elementos de derecho civil* (3rd edn, Bosch, Barcelona, 1995), p. 520, R. de Ángel, *Tratado de responsabilidad civil* (3rd edn, Civitas, Madrid, 1993), p. 36.
[943] This idea is not recognized by legal experts and is only present in Pantaleón's doctrinal theory, *La responsabilidad civil de los auditores: extensión, limitación, prescripción* (1996), pp. 114–16.
[944] See A. Georgiades, *General Principles of Civil Law* (2nd edn, 1996), pp. 126–7.
[945] AP 89/ 58 EEN 25, 685; EfAth 1704/ 75 No B 23, 940.
[946] AP 2058/ 1986 NoB 35, 1236; AP 224/1990 EED.

lays down) or even taking any other appropriate measure in the circumstances (art. 59 CC).

Contractual liability: at a second level it should be pointed out, that, as the labour law specialists assume, a part of the obligations grounded in a contract for service still exists, even after the termination of this contract. Obligations of this sort are usually collateral ones. Obligations such as fidelity (burdening the employee), protection, safety (burdening the employer), etc., grounded on the good faith principle (art. 288 CC) and related to the more permanent, lifelong relationship between the two parties, continue even after the termination of their principal obligations; otherwise the conclusion of a contract for service would prove itself extremely dangerous for any one of the parties. The collateral obligation of the employer to protect his employee concerns his physical integrity, as well as his dignity, i.e. his whole personality. This has been repeatedly accepted by the Greek courts (see above).

It is to be noted that an employer is statutorily obliged to give to his former employee a 'certificate of work'. Article 678 CC, article 2 L 2112 of 12 June 1990 (Special Provisions of Labour Law) as well as Royal Decree no. 16/18 July 1920 (Special Provisions of Labour Law) lay down that the employer is obliged to give to his employee a truthful 'certificate of work'.[947] David is liable for breach by his fault of his collateral contractual obligation to protect his employee's dignity. Therefore, he is obliged to compensate him for his (pecuniary) damage (due to the loss of the job) according to article 335 CC, which is of course implemented in any case of obligation, either principal or collateral.

III. A further question is whether the employee may claim that his employer should not mention the employee's disadvantages in the 'certificate of work'. Court decisions clarify that this certificate must be truthful.[948] Furthermore, Greek doctrine argues that a truthful but unfavourable certificate is forbidden.[949]

## England

I. Peter will succeed.

II. The problem of a negligent reference was considered at great length by the House of Lords in the case of *Spring* v. *Guardian Assurance*.[950] The

---

[947] See A. Karakatsanis, *Labour Law* A, pp. 253–4.
[948] EfAth 4252/ 1970 EED 30, 1144.
[949] See, for example, K. ErmAK art. 678, no. 44; Karakatsanis, *Labour Law* A (1981), p. 254.
[950] [1995] 2 AC 296.

Lords held that there is a duty of care owed, and there should be liability in tort in the case of a negligent reference on a former employee applying for a new job, if the employee, although otherwise successful, fails to get the job because of the inaccuracy of the reference. Peter's case falls squarely under the *ratio* of *Spring*.

III. Negligent references have touched upon a sensitive chord in English judges' hearts and minds. The issue is surely moral, and there is no doubt that it can be *wrong* for the law of tort not to recognize an economic loss claim on grounds of wider legal policy, as, for example, policy dictated by predictions of adverse market repercussions of doubtful foundation.[951] As put by Lord Lowry in *Spring*:

On the one hand looms the probability, often amounting to certainty, of damage to the individual, which in some cases will be serious and may indeed be irreparable. The entire future prosperity and happiness of someone who is the subject of a damaging reference which is given carelessly but in perfectly good faith may be irreparably blighted. Against this prospect is set the possibility that some referees will be deterred from giving frank references or indeed any references... I am inclined to view this possibility as a spectre conjured up by the defendants to frighten your Lordships into submission.[952]

## Scotland

I. Peter will be able to bring an action against David for the negligently given character reference and should be successful.

II. As with Case 17 ('Auditor's Liability') we are dealing with negligent misrepresentation. In *Hedley Byrne*, the case was concerned with a negligently favourable reference; here we are dealing with a negligently unfavourable reference. In *Spring* v. *Guardian Assurance*[953] the House of Lords considered this question carefully and decided that an employer owed a duty of care when preparing a reference in respect of a former employee. Although the case had not been advanced to the Appellate Committee on the basis of a duty of care deriving from the *Hedley Byrne* principle, Lord Goff of Chieveley chose to grant the appeal on that basis. Lords Lowry, Slynn and Woolf also granted the appeal but on a different basis. However, Lord Slynn did state that he agreed with Lord Goff's interpretation of *Hedley Byrne*. Lord Goff explained his evocation of

---

[951] See E. K. Banakas, 'Civil Liability for Pure Economic Loss', in UK National Committee of Comparative Law and British Institute of International and Comparative Law (eds.), *UK Law for the Millenium* (1998), ch. 1, p. 3f.
[952] [1995] 2 AC 296 at p. 326.   [953] [1995] 2 AC 296.

the *Hedley Byrne* principle in the absence of its argument by counsel as follows:

> In these circumstances I would ordinarily have proposed that, before the appeal could be decided on a point which had not been argued, the parties should be given the opportunity of making submissions upon it. In the present case, however, I understand that a majority of your Lordships are minded to allow the appeal in any event, proceeding on a broader basis than the principle in *Hedley Byrne*...Even so, I propose to set out the reasoning upon which I, for my part, would allow the appeal. I feel it necessary to do so because I have come to the conclusion that, if the *Hedley Byrne* principle cannot here be invoked, or a contractual term to that effect cannot be relied upon by the plaintiff, the appeal ought to be dismissed; because in those circumstances it would be a simple case of the defendants having negligently made a statement damaging to the plaintiff's reputation.[954]

Lord Goff saw the issue in terms of the assumption of responsibility by the employer coupled with the reliance by the employee in a situation where the employer had particular knowledge and skill upon which the employee relied. This was an anticipation of his own key speech delivered in *Henderson v. Merrett* soon after *Spring*, but which was being considered judicially around the same time. By way of comparison, the other three Law Lords approached the issue in terms of Lord Bridge of Harwich's three-part test of the existence of a duty of care, namely: foreseeable loss, proximity of relationship and fair, just and reasonable. Lord Goff stated:

> The question whether a person who gives a reference to a third party may, if the reference is negligently prepared, be liable in damages not to the recipient but to the subject of the reference, did not arise in *Hedley Byrne* and so was not addressed in that case. That is the central question with which we are concerned in the present case...Prima facie...it is my opinion that an employer who provides a reference in respect of one of his employees to a prospective future employer will ordinarily owe a duty of care to his employee in respect of the preparation of the reference. The employer is possessed of special knowledge, derived from his experience of the employee's character, skill and diligence in the performance of his duties while working for the employer. Moreover, when the employer provides a reference to a third party in respect of his employee, he does so not only for the assistance of the third party, but also, for what it is worth, for the assistance of the employee. Indeed, nowadays it must often be very difficult for an employee to obtain fresh employment without the benefit of a reference from his present or previous employer...it is plain that the employee

---

[954] Ibid. at p. 316.

relies upon him to exercise the skill and care in preparation of the reference before making it available to the third party. In these circumstances, it seems to me that all the elements requisite for the application of the *Hedley Byrne* principle are present.[955]

The dissenting voice was that of Lord Keith of Kinkel on grounds of public policy. He stated:

If liability in negligence were to follow from a reference prepared without reasonable care, the same adverse consequences would flow as those sought to be guarded against by the defence of qualified privilege. Those asked for a reference would be inhibited from speaking frankly lest it should be found that they were liable in damages through not taking sufficient care in its preparation. They might well prefer, if under no legal duty to give a reference, to refrain from doing so at all. Any reference given might be bland and unhelpful and information which it might be in the interest of those seeking the reference to receive might be withheld.[956]

None of the other Lords found this a sufficient reason to deny liability. As to the public policy argument, Lord Lowry stated:

On the one hand looms the probability, often amounting to a certainty, of damage to the individual, which in some cases will be serious and may indeed be irreparable. The entire future prosperity and happiness of someone who is the subject of a damaging reference which is given carelessly but in perfectly good faith may be irretrievably blighted. Against this prospect is set the possibility that some referees will be deterred from giving frank references or indeed any references...I am inclined to view this possibility as a spectre conjured up by the defendants to frighten your Lordships into submission. I also believe that the courts in general and your Lordships' House in particular ought to think very carefully before resorting to public policy considerations which will defeat a claim that *ex hypothesi* is a perfectly good cause of action.[957]

So Peter should be able to successfully bring an action against David.

III. The court in such a situation must strike a balance between various competing policies and principles. This can be seen in some of the observations of Lord Woolf. He stated:

It would alter the situation, if it would be contrary to some identifiable principle of public policy for there to be a liability for negligence imposed on the giver of a negligent reference. If there were to be such a principle it would be an unusual one since, unless *Hedley Byrne*... was wrongly decided, it would apparently apply to the negligent provider of a bad but not a good reference... It is obviously in accord with public policy that references should be full and frank.

---

[955] Ibid. at p. 319.   [956] Ibid. at p. 309.   [957] Ibid. at p. 326.

It is also in accord that they should not be based upon careless investigations... the real issue is not whether there would be any adverse effect on the giving of references. Rather the issue is whether the adverse effects when balanced against the benefits which would flow from giving the subject a right of action sufficiently outweigh the benefits to justify depriving the subject of a remedy unless he can establish malice. In considering this issue it is necessary to take into account contemporary practices in the field of employment; the fact that nowadays most employment is conditional upon a reference being provided... Freedom of speech does not necessarily entitle the speaker to make a statement without exercising reasonable care. Freedom of speech has to be balanced against the equally well recognised freedom both at common law and under the conventions that an individual should not be deprived of the opportunity of earning his livelihood in his chosen occupation. A development of the law which does no more than protect an employee from being deprived of employment as a result of a negligent reference would fully justify any limited intrusion on freedom of speech.[958]

## The Netherlands

I. Peter's former employer is probably liable in tort.

II. The first thing that must be ascertained is whether it was an honest mistake. Did David regularly mistake Peter for another employee? Was it an honest mistake because the two were very much alike or had similar surnames? The nature of the mistake will be decisive. If the mistake could not have been made had David acted more cautiously, then David could be held liable in tort for the consequences of the incorrect information. Three factors are decisive:[959] was the information to be relied upon by Robco Services? Was it clear to David from the outset what the information would be used for by Peter? Was it foreseeable for David that the nature of the information might influence Robco's decision to hire? In this case all these factors indicate towards David's liability.

As a rule, Peter would have to prove that he would have got the job had the right reference been sent. However, it is not unlikely that this burden of proof would be lightened by the court, be it by way of reversal of the burden or by relaxing the standard of proof required.[960]

---

[958] Ibid. at pp. 351 ff.
[959] See, e.g., J. M. Smits, 'Aansprakelijkheid aan derden verscrafte informatie; enige dogmatische en praktische kanttekenigen bij derden-aansprakelijkheid in R. P. J. L. Tjitles and M. A. Blom (eds.), *Bank & aansprakelijkheid* (1996), at p. 91.
[960] On reversal of the burden of proof in cases such as these, see HR 26.1.1996, NJ 1996, no. 607.

## Germany

I. Peter has a claim for damages against David, possibly in tort but certainly for breach of contract.

II. Tort claim: since none of Peter's absolute rights were violated, he has no claim under § 823 (1) BGB.

Peter can sue under § 824 BGB,[961] the very point of which is to allow recovery for pure economic loss. Section 1 of this provision is clearly applicable because David has communicated a false statement about Peter which damaged Peter's reputation as an employee. The only problem is § 824 (2) which provides:

> A person who makes a communication, the untruth of which is unknown to him, does not thereby render himself liable to make compensation, if he or the receiver of the communication has a lawful interest in it.

In other words, a lawful interest of the maker or recipient can exclude liability for negligently making an untrue statement (but not for intentionally making it).

In the present case, it seems that David acted negligently (he 'mistook') and that at least Robco Services had a legitimate interest in receiving the information. Thus, it seems that David would be in the clear. Yet, § 824 (2) BGB is generally read to require a balancing of the interests and facts involved, in particular:

- the interest of the plaintiff in an unblemished reputation;
- the interest of the maker or recipient of the statement in communicating it;
- the urgency of the communication;
- the risk and magnitude of potential harm to the plaintiff;
- the ease with which the maker could have verified the information; and
- and the effort made by the maker to verify it.[962]

The present scenario contains insufficient information to perform such a balancing operation.

Nonetheless, there are two considerations supporting Peter's claim. First, it is likely that David could have easily avoided the error since

---

[961] Above, Case 17 ('Auditor's Liability'), sub II.
[962] W. Erman, *Handkommentar zum Bürgerlichen Gesetzbuch*, Band I, §§ 1–853 (9th edn, 1993), art. 824 Rd.-Nr. 11; K. Larenz and C. W. Canaris, *Lehrbuch des Schuldrechts* (13th edn, Beck, Munich, 1994), s. 79 I 4; *Münchener Kommentar zum bürgerlichen Gesetzbuch*, vol. IV (3rd edn, 1992), art. 824 Rd.-Nr. 41–44; O. Palandt, *Bürgerliches Gesetzbuch* (2000), art. 824 Rd.-Nr. 6.

the relevant information was in his records. Secondly, David carries the burden of proof under § 824 (2) BGB, i.e. he must convince the court that the balance of interests is in his favour.

Contract claim: Peter has a claim for breach of a duty implied in his employment contract with David. According to § 630 BGB, as his former employer, David is under an obligation to write him a reference at the end of the employment period. It is generally recognized that the parties of a contract owe each other an implied duty of care in the execution of all contractual obligations. The violation of this duty makes them liable for all harm proximately caused, including pure economic loss (*positive Vertragsverletzung*). Here, David breached his duty arising under § 630 BGB by providing Robco with a false reference about Peter. He is therefore liable.

It does not matter that the employment contract between Peter and David has already ended. Contractual duties of care can linger beyond the end of a contractual relationship if the principle of good faith (§ 242 BGB) requires it. Courts and commentators have recognized that this is also true in employment cases and with particular regard to references provided by the employer.[963]

III. This is one of the cases in which the broad construction of implied contractual duties of care allows the recovery of pure economic loss although tort law may not. As such, it is a fairly easy case because Peter was not a third party but David's partner in contract, because § 630 BGB expressly obliges the employer to provide a reference, and because the continuation of the duty of care beyond the life of the contract proper is particularly well established with regard to long-term relationships, such as employment contracts.

## Austria

I. Peter has a claim against David either in tort based on article 1330(2) ABGB or in contract.

II. Tort claim: Peter can sue under article 1330(2) ABGB. In mistaking Peter for another person, David has negligently given a false statement that has damaged Peter's reputation. As Peter's professional reputation is part of his absolutely protected right of personality (*Persönlichkeitsrecht*), a claim may proceed under article 1330(2) ABGB for pure economic loss.

---

[963] LAG Frankfurt BB 1980, 1160; LAG Berlin NZA 1989, 965; R. Richardi and O. Wlotzke, *Münchener Handbuch zum Arbeitsrecht Band I: Individualarbeitsrecht I* (1992), § 43 Rd.-Nr. 49; *Münchener Kommentar*, art. 630 Rd.-Nr. 51.

The last sentence of article 1330(2) which excludes negligently caused damage by someone 'making a secret communication, the untruth of which he does not know' does not apply in the present case, since a character reference is not by its nature confidential. The former employer must take into account that letters of reference always concern certain third parties.[964] Therefore, Peter's claim will succeed.

Contract claim: the contract between David, the former employer, and Peter creates an obligation for David to write a letter of reference at the end of the employment period (art. 1163 ABGB). Therefore, David's duty to deal carefully with information concerning Peter's professional performance is an implied duty of this contract. The violation of such a duty will qualify as a 'positive violation of a contract'.[965]

The breach of such collateral contractual duty by providing Robco with an incorrect reference about Peter makes David liable for all damages arising therefrom, including pure economic loss.

This result complies with the provision of article 1300, first sentence ABGB: David's letter of reference about Peter is issued 'for a consideration', since the employment contract is indeed a contract for consideration. Therefore it does not matter that the employment contract between him and Peter has already ended: post-contractual duties of care are acknowledged to a certain extent by Austrian law.

III. In addition to article 1300 ABGB, article 1330 ABGB might be an interesting foundation for the recovery of pure economic loss. Since a person's professional or economic reputation is deemed to be an absolutely protected right, violation of such right will result in a claim for compensation of the financial loss resulting therefrom.

## Portugal

I. Peter does have the right to claim compensation from David.

II. The basis lies in what is called post-contractual liability (*culpa post contractum finitum*),[966] which to some extent is the equivalent to precontractual liability (*culpa in contrahendo*).

---

[964] See OGH ZAS 1980/1.
[965] See H. Koziol, *Österreichisches Haftpflichtrecht*, vol. II (2nd edn, Vienna, 1984), p. 79; OGH EvBl 1955/22, JBl 1963, 317 SZ 57/16, SZ 64/9.
[966] In the event of cessation of a work contract, labour law establishes an obligation for the employing entity to provide the employee with a (Decree-Law no. 64-A/89 of 27 February, art. 57). But the hypothesis described in the questionnaire does not appear to be of this kind.

The second is expressly established in the law (art. 227 CC); however, the first is not, though it is unanimously accepted.[967]

The doctrine tends to set these legal figures in the category of 'obligational relationships without primary duties of performance' (*prestação*). In other words, situations where duties of performance have not yet arisen or have already been extinguished, while the parties are still bound by 'other duties of conduct' resulting mainly from the principle of good faith.

The existence of fault is necessary.

**Sweden and Finland**

I. David will most probably not be held liable.

II. Here we are again facing 'pure economic loss' in the Swedish/Finnish meaning, i.e. an economic loss arising without connection with anybody suffering personal injury or damage to things, which in principle can be recovered from the wrongdoer when it is caused through a crime, according to *SkadestL* 4:2 (Sweden) and *SkadestL* 5:1 (Finland), although the text and the preparatory works of the Tort Liability Acts 1972 and 1974 do not completely bar compensation should the courts find strong reasons for it. As mentioned earlier, courts have been very restrictive in granting exceptions to the general principle.

In cases of wrongful information given on a non-professional basis, Swedish and Finnish case law kept close to the general principle, and although there are some criticisms from scholars against this restrictive approach, there are no signs of a change in direction in the operative rules.[968]

*Editors' comparative comments*

This is another case in which the solutions, although they substantially agree on the recoverability of the employee's losses (the exceptions are Sweden and Finland, with a problematic approach taken by Spain), derive from different standpoints and are reached by different legal paths.

England and Scotland treat the case either under the '*Hedley Byrne* duty of care' rule, or under the perspective grounded on an assumption

---

[967] V. Almeida Costa, *Direito das Obrigações*, 9a Edicão Revista e Aumentada (Almedina, Coimbra, 2001), 304–6, with bibliographic references.

[968] J. Kleineman, *Ren förmögenhetsskada* (1987), pp. 513 ff.

of responsibility by the employer, coupled with the reliance placed on it by the employee.

Austria, Germany and Greece – besides a possible recovery grounded on the breach of a statutory duty – award damages to the plaintiff, considering the harm suffered by the latter to be a 'parasitic' rather than 'pure' economic loss. Indeed, these legal systems ground their solutions (in tort) upon infringement of the employee's reputation: that is, one of the absolute rights whose protection is traditionally a core aim of tort law systems.[969]

The French, Belgian and Italian legal systems treat the hypothetical case in terms of loss of a chance, to be understood here as an autonomous tort, as distinguished from cases in which the lost chance is taken into account as a specific head of damages consequent upon another tort.[970]

---

[969] See also our comments to Case 1 ('Cable I – The Blackout') and to Case 13 ('Subcontractor's Liability') *in fine*.

[970] The latter, as we have just said, is the path followed in the case under review in Austria, Germany and Greece. A further example could be that of a personal injury which prevents the victim from entering a profession: see, e.g. Limoges, 19 octobre 1995, Sem. Jur., 1996, IV, 897.

## Case 19: breach of promise

### Case

Richard is negotiating to sell his land to Sam. Sam is prepared to buy the land only if it is cleared of all buildings. The negotiations are complex and it is agreed that the contract will not be formed until it is in writing and signed by both sides. Sam assures Richard that there are only a few more details to settle, so Richard, with Sam's knowledge, clears the site. He also rejects a last-minute offer to purchase from Jane under which he would have had profits of €50,000. Sam eventually decides not to go ahead with the purchase. Richard now sues Sam for the cost of clearing the land and lost profits of €50,000.

### France

I. Richard will very likely recover the cost of clearing the land from Sam under article 1382 CC. The possibility of recovering the lost profits is less ascertainable.

II. Since the parties specified that no contract would be formed unless it was in writing and signed by both sides, we are clearly in a pre-contractual setting. It is the rule in French law that the wrongful termination of a negotiation is governed by tort law.[971] The wrongdoer can be sued under article 1382 and following.[972] This liability is based on the concept of *abus de droit de rompre* and it does not require the intention to harm, but just the proof of the bad faith of the wrongdoer. The necessity of acting in good faith during contractual negotiations is clearly a jurisprudentially developed rule.[973] For example, the termination of a negotiation may be wrongful when one side has led the other side to believe that he was about to sign the contract.[974] The further the negotiations have proceeded, the more the parties trust and rely on one another, and the more easily the court may find that the negotiation-breaker acted in bad faith.

In our case, it is clear that Richard trusted the fact that Sam would sign the contract. Sam made Richard believe he was almost ready to do

---

[971] H. Mazeaud, (1929) *Rev. trim. dr. civ.* 551; R. Savatier, *Traité de la responsabilité civile*, tome I (1949), no. 114 ff.
[972] Com., 20 mars 1972, JCP 1973.II.17543.
[973] J. Ghestin, *Traité de droit civil. La formation du contrat*, (3rd edn, LGDJ, 1993), p. 295.
[974] CA. Paris, 13 février 1883, Gaz. Pal. 1883. 2. 414.

so, subject only to a few details. Sam may have acted in bad faith, and a court might find him at fault under article 1382 CC.

Richard incurred two types of damages: (1) expenses in clearing the site; and (2) loss of profit he could have made by contracting with Jane. The first damages are certainly awarded by judges,[975] but the second have never been addressed in court decisions in cases of wrongful termination of negotiations. While, in principle, recovery under article 1382 can encompass loss of profit, nevertheless one may wonder if it would be appropriate to do so in this pre-contractual setting. To award loss of profits (as opposed to reliance losses) would be to treat the negotiations as being the equivalent of a contract, and in fact they are not. This is why doctrine suggests that the court should only take into account the reliance losses, such as Richard's expense in clearing the land.[976] On the other hand, the argument could be made that some lost profits might be recoverable under the theory of *perte d'une chance*. For example, damages were allowed in the case of a horse raiser who was injured in a car accident and thus could not train a horse he believed would have won a race. The court stated that this kind of damage is direct and certain when it is proved that the probability of a favourable event occurring has been reduced or eliminated.[977] The *juge du fond* will end up discretionarily deciding whether to award those damages or not (*appréciation souveraine des juges du fond*).

Finally, the causal link between Sam's break of the negotiations and both damages will have to be proved.

## Belgium

I. If the negotiations were broken off by Sam without any good reason, Richard will probably be able to recover from Sam the damage that he sustained, which can include part of the costs to clear the land and the lost profit he would have earned in contracting with Jane.

II. Until the contract is executed, the rule in Belgian law is that the parties can break off negotiations without incurring any liability.

However, this rule is not absolute. During the negotiations, the parties must act in good faith. Moreover, this obligation increases as long as the negotiations last.

---

[975] Com., 20 mars 1972, see above, fn. 872.
[976] G. Viney, *Introduction à la responsabilité*, Traité de droit civil (1995), p. 361, no. 198.
[977] Crim., 7 juin 1990, Bull. Crim., no. 24.

Therefore, one cannot suddenly withdraw while allowing the other party to think that the contract will be executed soon. Unless Sam had good reason to renounce the contract with Richard (because, for example, he found another party who could offer him a better deal),[978] Sam will be liable for fault through *culpa in contrahendo*.

A claim for *culpa in contrahendo* is usually based on article 1382 CC since as yet no contract has been formed:[979]

Any act whatever of man which causes damage to another obliges him by whose fault it occurred to make reparation.

To determine the amount of the damage resulting from *culpa in contrahendo*, the case law often rules that the injured party should be reinstated to the same position as if the fault had not arisen.

Therefore, the plaintiff cannot claim the profit he would have earned if the contract had been executed, but he can recover the costs that he incurred during the negotiations and also compensation for the loss of the opportunity to have executed other contracts with other persons.

Should Sam's withdrawal be considered as *culpa in contrahendo*, he can claim the recovery of the damage resulting from clearing the land if he can prove that the clearing was an essential condition of the contract and that he could legitimately think that he could do it.

He can recover the full amount of such costs only if the clearing of the land has not increased the value of the land at all. If the clearing increased the value, he will be allowed to recover only these costs reduced by the added value.

Sam is also allowed to recover the €50,000 that he would have earned if he had executed the contract with Jane. The case law will apply in such a case the theory of the 'loss of an opportunity'. The loss of an opportunity is recoverable if the opportunity was real and not only hypothetical.[980]

---

[978] See, for example Liège, 20 octobre 1989, RDC, 1990, p. 521.
[979] Cass., 10 décembre 1981, Pas., 1982, I, 494; W. De Bondt, 'Precontractuele aansprakelijkheid', RGDC, 1993, p. 116; L. Cornelis, 'La responsabilité précontractuelle, conséquence éventuelle du processus précontractuel', RGDC, 1990, p. 391; J. Herbots, 'De goede trouw in de precontractuele rechtsverhoudingen', in *Le contrat en formation* (ABJE, Bruxelles, 1987), p. 31; P. Marchandise, *La libre négociation: droits et obligations des négociation* (ABJE, Bruxelles, 1987), p. 3.
[980] Cass., 19 octobre 1937, Pas., 1937, I, p. 298; Cass., 8 décembre 1958, Pas., 1959, I, p. 354; Cass., 15 octobre 1962, Pas, 1963; I, 195; Cass., 15 septembre 1972, RGAR, 1973; no. 9121; Cass., 4 mars 1975, Pas., 1975, I, 682; Cass., 19 juin 1987, RW, 1987–88, p. 709.

Since in the present case, the opportunity to sell the land to Jane and to make a profit of €50,000 was absolutely certain, Sam can claim the full amount.

However, if the rule is in Belgian law that the damage shall be fully indemnified,[981] it is also established that the injured party shall never receive a compensation superior to the damage he suffered.

Therefore, in the present case, the allocation of $50,000 lost profit will be reduced if Jane would have paid less had the land not been cleared.

In 1988, a court decision ruled that a principal committed *culpa in contrahendo* in suddenly stopping a negotiation initiated with a potential distributor without any good reason while the negotiations were nearly complete, and while he knew that the distributor had already incurred costs to begin distribution of the products. The court ruled that the principal was liable for these useless costs.[982] The decision was confirmed by the Court of Appeal, which also granted a lump sum to the distributor to cover the lost opportunity to execute a contract with another principal.[983]

## Italy

I. In this case, Sam is liable to Richard for pre-contractual liability (art. 1337 cc), unless Sam has a substantial and just cause for breaching negotiations.

II. Article 1337, dealing with negotiation and pre-contractual liability, states that 'The parties in the conduct of negotiations and the formation of the contract, shall conduct themselves in good faith."

Sam's persistence in negotiating with Richard can be seen as a behaviour capable of inducing a reasonable reliance in Richard with regard to the sale, and Sam did not seem to have any reasonable justification for his conduct.

As to the quantum of damages, since case law maintains that pre-contractual liability concerns only negotiations, recoverable damages for unjustified withdrawal from negotiation is said[984] to consist only in the

---

[981] Cass., 13 avril 1995, JT, 1955, p. 649.
[982] Comm. Bxl., 3 février 1988, JT, 1988, p. 516.
[983] Bruxelles, 5 février 1992, JT, 1993, p. 130.
[984] See A. Luminoso, *La lesione dell'interesse negativo* (Milano, 1972). Recent decisions confirm the constant stream of Italian jurisprudence, e.g. Trib. Udine 22.4.1996; Cass., 30.8.1995, no. 9157; Cass. 13.12.1994, no. 10694; Cass. 26.10.1994, no. 8778; Cass. 25.2.1994, no. 1897; Cass. III, 30.3.1990, no. 2623; Cass. II, 11.9.1989, no. 3922.

negative interest (*interesse negativo* – *id quod interest contractus initum non fuisse*).⁹⁸⁵ Protection is provided only for costs incurred in conducting useless negotiations and for the possible loss of a chance to sign other contracts.⁹⁸⁶

III. According to case law and most of the scholars⁹⁸⁷ pre-contractual liability is a kind of tort liability.⁹⁸⁸ A party dealing with another is liable for the other party's detrimental reliance whenever he decides, without just cause, not to go ahead with the contract, and the basic elements of the contract are already defined, such as the price, the goods and the principal duties of the parties.⁹⁸⁹

Article 1337 cc provides a duty of fair play during negotiations, before reaching an agreement, under the principle of good faith (*buona fede*). The Supreme Court interpreted the article in the sense that 'pre-contractual liability occurs only when, during negotiations and before reaching an agreement, the parties have so behaved as to induce a reasonable reliance in the conclusion of the contract. Moreover, the unjustified breach of such relationship has to consist in a behaviour contrary to good faith'.⁹⁹⁰

Italian case law requires that two conditions have to be met in order to invoke pre-contractual liability: that the negotiations have induced one party to make a reasonable reliance (*affidamento*) on the conclusion of the contract; and that the party in breach did not give a reasonable motivation (*giusta causa*) capable of justifying the withdrawal from the negotiation.⁹⁹¹ The Supreme Court has recognized reliance (*affidamento*)

---

⁹⁸⁵ Positive interest (*interesse positivo*) is indeed related to the due fulfilment of the contract, and it is excluded in negotiations in order to respect the principle of freedom to withdraw from negotiations.

⁹⁸⁶ See Cass. 30.8.1995 no. 9157, according to which in the case of unjustified withdrawal from negotiation only reliance damages and the negative interests for losing other contractual opportunities are recoverable.

⁹⁸⁷ F. D. Busnelli, 'Itinerari europei nella "terra di nessuno tra contratto e fatto illecito": la responsabilità da informazioni inesatte', *CI*, 1991, 539; R. Speciale, *Contratti preliminari e intese precontrattuali* (Milano, 1990), pp. 259 ff.; F. Giardina, *Responsabilità contrattuale ed extracontrattuale* (Milano, 1988), p. 131; M. Serio, *La responsabilità complessa. Verso uno statuto unitario della civil liability* (Palermo, 1988), 45 ff.; G. Visintini, 'Responsabilità contrattuale ed extracontrattuale (Una distinzione in crisi?)', *Rassegna di diritto civile*, 1983, 1077; G. Alpa, 'Prassi negoziali d'impresa e teoria del contratto "sociale" nella elaborazione di un rapporto tra produttore e consumatore', T., 1975, 623.

⁹⁸⁸ Cass. 14.2.2000 no. 1632, DR 2000, 6, 668; Trib. Roma 28.10.1999, DR 2000, 6, 658.

⁹⁸⁹ Trib. Milano, 25.4.1954, *Nuova Revista di diritto commerciale* 1954, II, 124; Pret. Roma, 2.10.1962, RDC 1963, 72.

⁹⁹⁰ Cass. 25.11.1976, no. 4448; Cass. III, 25.10.1973, no. 2757.

⁹⁹¹ The most recent, Cass., sez. II, 14.6.1999, no. 5830; Trib. Milano, 5.5.1997.

in a wide range of situations.⁹⁹² The Italian Supreme Court usually recognizes pre-contractual liability only in negotiations (*trattative*) and in contract formation (*formazione del contratto*), excluding concluded contracts from the range of article 1337: 'The conclusion of a contract, although under conditions different to those foreseeable where the liable party had behaved according to the principle of good faith, precludes the applicability of pre-contractual liability.'⁹⁹³

## Spain

I. This situation is a clear case of pre-contractual liability. Richard is to be compensated for the cost of clearing the land. Whether he can claim for the lost profits is less obvious.

II. In order to give rise to pre-contractual liability for an unjustified breaking-off of negotiations, Spanish legal doctrine requires proof of the following:⁹⁹⁴

(1) creating reasonable confidence that the contract will be brought to term;
(2) the unjustifiable nature of the breaking-off of negotiations;
(3) causing damage to the assets of one of the parties; and
(4) a causal link between these damages and the confidence induced.

The case law has not often addressed the issue of *culpa in contrahendo*. This issue first appeard in the Supreme Court decision delivered

---

⁹⁹² For example, upon promises made in bad faith about the conclusion of the contract; or upon the agreement on minor points of a complex negotiation, such as receiving money in account for a future sale, or giving a cheque in order to fulfil an oral agreement for the sale of an immovable. See Cass., 13.12.1994, no. 10649; Cass., 25.3.1992, no. 3699; App. Milano, 15.11.1998; App. Roma, 29.10.1986; Trib. Napoli 15.11.1975; Trib. Rossano 5.7.1952.

⁹⁹³ Cass., 25.2.1992, no. 2335; App. Firenze, 17.9.1986; Cass., 22.10.1982, no. 5492; Cass., 12.7.1980, no. 4473. Although, in a recent decision the Supreme Court (Cass. 3.8.1995, no. 8501) seemed to be more flexible and open to evaluating the parties' conduct both before and after having signed the contract. It was a case concerning negotiation for renewal and modification of an existing contract.

More recently, a dissenting view (D. Caruso, *La culpa in contrahendo* (Milano, 1993) has indeed underlined that pre-contractual damages imply a 'cryptotypical restitutionary remedy' rather than the usual distinction between negative amounts (pre-contractual damages) or positive ones (contractual damages). See for the practical coincidence of pre-contractual damages with those deriving from the due fulfilment of the contract, Pret. Macerata, 7.6.1988.

⁹⁹⁴ L. Diez-Picazo, *Fundamentos de derecho civil patrimonial*, I (4th edn, Techos, Madrid, 1993), p. 278.

by the First Chamber on 16 May 1988.[995] There, the plaintiffs were a bank employee and his wife. The husband had been negotiating with his employers for his transfer to the bank's branch in Miami, FL. When the negotiations were at an advanced stage and the plaintiffs believed that the transfer was imminent, the plaintiffs sold a car and the wife requested a voluntary leave of absence from work in order to prepare for the transfer. The transfer eventually did not take place. The plaintiffs claimed compensation for material damage and pain suffered and the Supreme Court granted it on the basis of article 1902 of the CC.

This Supreme Court decision reflects an idea which is present in all doctrinal opinions: recoverable damages within the realm of pre-contractual liability include a negative interest, i.e. reimbursement of expenses incurred by relying on the intended contract.[996] Thus, it seems that in the present case Richard would have no problem in claiming the costs of clearing the site.[997]

It is more difficult to decide if Richard could additionally claim lost profits due to the rejection of Jane's offer. We have no court decisions on the matter and legal experts are divided on the issue.

For the majority, compensation for an unjustified breaking-off of negotiations should not include lost profits.[998] The essential argument, taking our case as an example, is if Jane's offer had been more beneficial than Sam's, Richard could have entered into an agreement with Jane (he would have had a justified reason for breaking off negotiations with Sam), and if he did not do so he should not complain. The alleged damages for lost profits are due to his own conduct and all negotiations entail certain risks which are assumed by both parties.

For other authors, perhaps more influenced by Italian court decisions, the negative interest to be compensated by means of *culpa in contrahendo* would include in fact both consequential damages and lost profits, cautiously estimating these lost profits.[999] They also point out the

---

[995] C. Asúa, 'Comentario a la S.T.S. de 16 de mayo de 1988', (1988) 17 *Cuadernos Civitas de Jurisprudencia Civil* 513–27, at 516.

[996] Díez-Picazo, *Fundamentos*, p. 279, C. Asúa, *La culpa in contrahendo* (1989), p. 288, R. Valpuesta, F. Blasco, F. Capilla, A. M. Lopez, V. L. Montés, J. Orduña and E. Roca, *Derecho de Obligaciones y contratos* (2nd edn, 1995), p. 382, etc.; from these expenses those which any regular negotiation entails are usually deducted: advertising costs, etc.

[997] Diez-Picazo, *Fundamentos*, p. 278 uses a similar example.

[998] Ibid., p. 280, Valpuesta et al., *Derecho de Obligaciones*, p. 382, A. Manzanares, 'La responsabilidad precontractual en la hipótesis de ruptura injustificada de las negociaciones preliminares', *Anuario de Derecho Civil*, III (1984), 747–8, B. Moreno Quesada, *La oferta de contrato: génesis y responsabilidad ante contractual* (1963), p. 232.

[999] M. Alonso Pérez, 'La responsabilidad precontractual', (1971) *Revista Crítica de Derecho Inmobiliario* 859–922, at 905, Asúa, *La culpa in contrahendo*, pp. 288–90.

difficulties of quantification and uncertainty presented by these damages and the fact that the Spanish courts appear to be quite reluctant to compensate for lost profits, even in regular situations of contractual responsibility. Furthermore, Asúa points out that there would be no problem in compensating lost profits if the party responsible acted in bad faith.

**Greece**

I. Richard has the right to claim compensation from Sam only for the cost of clearing his land and not for his lost profits of €50,000.

II. Legal ground of liability: pre-contractual fault (*culpa in contrahendo*). In the course of negotiations with Richard, Sam deliberately (i.e. by his fault) did not adopt the conduct which is dictated by good faith, as he changed his mind suddenly and without any explanation to the other party. Thus, according to articles 197–198 CC he will be liable to make good any damage that he has caused to Richard. This has been confirmed by several Greek court decisions.[1000]

Causation: the causal relation of cost of clearing the land to Sam's pre-contractual fault is arguably sufficient: if the latter had not happened, the former would not have taken place.

By way of contrast, the lost profits' causal relation to Sam's pre-contractual fault is very uncertain: as has already been stated, the indemnifiable damage in the case of pre-contractual liability is the 'negative interest' of the contract,[1001] i.e. the result of the comparison of the present value of the plaintiff's property with the value that his property would have had, if Sam had not behaved in bad faith (i.e. under a negative hypothesis). However, even if Sam had not misled Richard, it was not foreseeably certain that Richard would sell his land to Jane or to anyone else. Thus, the loss of profits of the sale to Jane is an unforeseeable damage, i.e. a damage not causally related to the legal ground of liability. Thus, it is not an idemnifiable damage.

By way of conclusion, Richard is entitled to claim compensation from Sam only for the cost of clearing his land and not for the lost profits of €50,000.

III. Can the compensation in pre-contractual liability (the contract's negative interest) be greater even than the value of the contract (the contract's positive interest)? Of course, the law does not provide here any limitation on the contract's negative interest, while in other cases the

---

[1000] AP 969/1977 NoB 26, 895; AP 1505/1988 NoB 38, 62; EfAth 4913/1991 EllDni 33, 881.
[1001] A. Georgiades, *General Principles of Civil Law* (2nd edn 1996), pp. 378–9.

law specially provides such a limitation (e.g. in arts. 145 and 231, for pre-contractual liability in cases of error or misrepresentation). Nevertheless, the increase of the indemnifiable damage over the contract's positive interest would be approached very carefully. It seems unfair to earn more by accident than by dealings.

### England

I. Richard will not be able to recover anything from Sam.

II. There is no pre-contractual liability in English law for things said or done during negotiations, if finally no contract is made. But there could be liability in tort, for things said or done during the (eventually unsuccessful) negotiations, under the principle of *Hedley Byrne v. Heller*,[1002] as affirmed and expanded in *White v. Jones*.[1003]

However, and although *White v. Jones* was itself about an omission, it is very unlikely that the courts will impose liability for things left unsaid,[1004] as opposed to things said during negotiations that proved wrong or inaccurate,[1005] unless there is a positive duty to disclose,[1006] as for example, in the case of contracts *uberrimae fidei*; a duty to disclose is entirely absent in cases of abortive pre-contractual negotiations, as far as English law is concerned.

On the facts of the present case, Sam appears to have said nothing to Richard that caused his expense in clearing the land and refusing to sell to Jane; Sam simply kept silent about his own views or feelings when he learnt of Richard's actions. Therefore, Sam cannot be liable to Richard, for by being silent he did not breach any duty of care that he might have under *Hedley Byrne*.

III. English law is wary of imposing duties of good faith and positive care upon parties during pre-contractual negotiations that fail to produce an agreement. Contract is, itself, a bargain, and this concept of contract in English law would be diluted seriously with an extension of liability to things said or done during unsuccessful negotiations. Tort liability, now possible under *Hedley Byrne*, is founded not on a duty to show good faith, but on a breach of a duty to take care in circumstances in

---

[1002] [1964] AC 465.  [1003] [1995] 2 AC 207 (HL).
[1004] See, e.g. *van Oppen v. Trustees of Bedford College* [1989] 1 All ER 273: a school does not have a duty to tell a pupil's parents that no accident insurance is carried by the school; also *Royal Bank Trust Co. v. Pampallone* [1987] 1 Lloyd's Rep. 218.
[1005] A view shared by T. Weir, *A Casebook on Tort* (9th edn, Sweet & Maxwell, London, 2000), pp. 81–2.
[1006] See *Tai Hing Cotton Mill* [1985] 2 All ER 947 at p. 959, *per* Lord Scarman.

which things actually said or done by the parties during negotiations create a relationship of reasonable reliance upon the other person's words or deeds.

## Scotland

I. Richard would have a chance of recovering his losses in contract and delict but with a stronger chance in the former than the latter.

II. First, in terms of contract, Richard has a possible action. In Scots law, '*consensus in idem* occurs when agreement has been reached upon all the essentials of the contract; what the essentials are may vary according to the particular contract under consideration'.[1007] Usually the question as to whether the parties have agreed will be based upon what a reasonable person would have concluded from the parties' words and actions. The major complicating factor for Richard is that he has agreed that the contract will not be formed until it is in writing and signed by both parties. Writing is intended to be constitutive of the contract. As a contract is dependent upon agreement, in determining whether agreement has been reached the court will look to the evidence, namely the actings of the parties. In a sense, what the parties are agreeing here is that no other form of evidence as to a concluded agreement will be acceptable. In the absence of a written and signed document, Richard is accepting that the contract is not constituted. This makes it difficult, if not impossible, for him to argue that his actions were taken in reliance upon the contract. We know that Sam has assured Richard that 'there are only a few more details to settle'; the question is whether any of these are 'essentials' to the contract which would stop it being a contract absent their agreement as to proof of its formation.

In Scots law, subject to certain exceptions, writing is not required for the constitution of a contract.[1008] Irrespective of Richard and Sam's own agreement to that effect, one of those exceptions is a contract for the transfer of an interest in land (which this appears to be). It must be in writing. Sam and Richard could not opt out of this rule by agreeing between themselves that it need not be in writing. However, under Scots law even if writing is required, in certain circumstances a contract shall not be regarded as invalid even though it is not written. The question is whether Sam and Richard's agreement that the contract must be in

---

[1007] Gloag and Henderson, *The Law of Scotland* (10th edn, Green, Edinburgh, 1995) at p. 73.
[1008] Requirements of Writing (Scotland) Act 1995, s. 1.

writing to be formed means that they can opt out of this aspect of the rule. It is assumed that they may not. Generally 'where substantial agreement has been reached, but minor details are still unsettled, it will be held that the offerer, if he knows that the other is proceeding to act in reliance on the contract, and does not interfere, has waived his objection to the terms proposed'.[1009]

One point of view is that Richard has been foolish in incurring expenditure and turning down the chance of a profit in reliance upon Sam's assurances before the contract is actually drawn up and signed, given his prior agreement as to the form of a concluded contract. Perhaps Richard deserves what has befallen him. On the other hand, Sam is relying upon the fact that, while negotiations continue and agreement is incomplete, either party may withdraw from negotiations, i.e. he has a right of *locus poenitentiae*. However, as already stated, where the party who wishes to withdraw has knowingly allowed the other party to act in reliance upon the agreement to his detriment, questions of personal bar arise and the right of *locus poenitentiae* may be lost.

In Scots law this was formerly the case with actings known as *rei interventus* under the common law. The common law rule has been replaced by a statutory one which states (as it applies to our facts) that where a contract, of which the contract for a transfer of an interest in land is one example, is not constituted in a written document but one of the parties to the contract ('the first person') has acted in reliance on the contract with the knowledge and acquiescence of the other party to the contract ('the second person'), the second person shall not be entitled to withdraw from the contract and the contract shall not be regarded as invalid on the ground that it is not so constituted if the position of the first person as a result of acting has been affected to a material extent and as a result of such a withdrawal would be adversely affected to a material extent.[1010]

That would appear to describe the factual situation here with perhaps one important exception. It begins 'where a contract', but the parties have agreed that the contract will not be formed until it is in writing and signed. If so there can be no 'contract' to be declared valid.[1011] One

---

[1009] Gloag and Henderson, *Law of Scotland* at p. 85.
[1010] Requirements of Writing (Scotland) Act 1995 s. 1(2)(3) and (4).
[1011] Here the parties have agreed there is no 'contract' until the agreement is reduced to writing, but this is also true of any agreement which *ex lege* requires writing in order to be constituted. It would perhaps have been preferable if s. 1(3) of the 1995 Act had begun 'Where an agreement...' rather than 'Where a contract...'.

possible attack upon this would be as to the form of the agreement, i.e. not to be bound in contract short of a written and signed document. Was this a legally binding agreement? For simplicity we must assume it was. Another possibility, though this is controversial, is that the new statutory form only replaces *rei interventus* in so far as it applies specifically to what the Requirements of Writing (Scotland) Act 1995 covers. Therefore, if there is not a 'contract' but merely an 'agreement', and s. 1(3) and (4) of the 1995 Act do not 'technically' apply, one may be able still to rely upon general principles of personal bar.

However, it is believed that Sam and Richard's agreement would not exclude the statutory rule. So long as none of the details left to be agreed was considered by the court to be essential to the contract then a contract would be held valid, though informal, and Sam would be barred from relying upon its informality to escape the consequences of allowing him to act to Richard's detriment. There is a possible distinction to be made between the two losses depending upon the particular facts. First, as Sam knew about and acquiesced in the clearing of the land, Richard may claim this amount. The same would apply to the loss of profit on the sale, but only if Sam knew about the other offer. However, if Sam did not know about the other offer then the rule is not satisfied in every aspect and Richard would have no action for this amount.

Secondly, in terms of delict, this would be another novel claim but with little chance of success. Richard would have to establish that Sam owed him a duty of care in the circumstances. One could characterize the situation as one where Richard has acted to his detriment in reliance upon Sam's misrepresentation of an intention to purchase. Further, one could argue that Sam has voluntarily assumed responsibility for the accuracy of his representation, knowing that Richard has relied upon it while he stands by and permits him to. The loss to Richard was reasonably foreseeable, there is proximity in the relationship and perhaps it might be fair, just and reasonable to impose a duty of care on Sam in such circumstances. However, the trouble is with the representation that he has made and whether this amounts to a negligent statement or misrepresentation. Sam has said that he will buy the site only if it is cleared. This establishes that he will not buy the site if it is not cleared. He does not, as far as we are told, say definitively that he will buy the site if it is cleared. What he has said clearly is that the contract will not be formed until it is reduced to writing and signed and, further, that the matter is not settled. Although the way he expresses it, namely, that 'there are only a few more details to settle', implies that agreement is very close, nonetheless it makes clear to Richard that agreement on all details has not been reached. Rather than breach any duty of care, if one were held to exist, he seems to have been careful to avoid doing so. Richard has been rather naive. There is 'many a slip twixt cup and lip'. Having said that, given the bare facts that we have, we are unable to gather how convincingly Sam conveyed to Richard that the deal was all but done and implied that there were really no impediments to ultimate agreement. Perhaps it was this which caused Richard to act in so trusting a way given what were, in hindsight, obvious hurdles there to surmount before a binding contract was in place. One does not usually spend large sums of money or give up the opportunity for profit on the off-chance that something may come about without very good reason so to act. If Sam could be shown to have acted reprehensibly in the circumstances, it may strengthen Richard's chances of recovering his outlay in delict by establishing the requisite degree of assumption of responsibility and proximity of relationship. The trouble is that Sam has not acted negligently. Statements of future intention do not normally amount to a misrepresentation, unless they are lies. In such a case, the misrepresentation would be fraudulent.

III. Scots law used to require writing of some type in three categories: obligations provable by writ or oath; *obligationes literis* which required formal writing; and obligations which required writing under statute.[1012] The common law rules have now been superseded by the 1995 Act. The general rule is that writing shall not be required for the constitution of a contract subject to a few exceptions. Restrictions on the forms of proof of agreement have been accordingly eased. At common law the doctrine of personal bar developed to prevent parties withdrawing from informal agreements in certain circumstances. The rationale for this is described by Lord Birkenhead in *Gatty* v. *MacLaine*, who held:

> Where A has by his words or conduct justified B in believing that a certain state of facts exists, and B has acted upon such belief to his prejudice, A is not permitted to affirm against B that a different state of facts existed at the same time.[1013]

The common law rule of *rei interventus*, which raised a personal exception to the plea of *locus poenitentiae*, has been replaced by a statutory definition which, although not identical in formulation, continues to offer possible relief to those in situations similar to Richard. Not all

---

[1012] S. Woolman, *Contract* (2nd edn, 1994), p. 57.  [1013] 1921 SC (HL) 1 at p. 7.

cases of informality are cured; it depends upon the facts of the case. As to the delictual plea, it would take an optimistic lawyer and a brave client to settle this question on these facts.

## The Netherlands

I. Sam is liable because he acted neither in good faith nor with due care *vis-à-vis* Richard.

II. The landmark case of contractor Plas versus the community of Valburg, decided by the Supreme Court in 1982, indicates that Sam is liable. In *Plas v. Valburg*,[1014] the Supreme Court decided that the process of pre-contractual negotiations can be divided into three stages. In the first stage, where the parties have only begun to negotiate, any of the parties is entitled to break off negotiations without incurring any liabilities. Breaking off in the second (intermediate) stage might oblige the party that terminates the negotiations to indemnify the other party for costs incurred as a result of negotiations. If, however, the party that terminates the negotiations has led the other party to rely on some sort of contract resulting from the negotiations, he is liable *in full* for aborting negotiations. In this final stage, neither party is allowed to withdraw from the negotiations for the simple reason that the opposite party has justifiably put his trust in the contract to be agreed upon. Although no consensus exists in doctrinal writing on the legal basis of this liability, the Supreme Court seems to base this pre-contractual liability on the principles of '*redelijkheid en billijkheid*', i.e. good faith and fair dealing.[1015]

Judging from the facts of the case, Sam had little reason to withdraw from negotiations. Because Sam had made Richard believe that a contract was forthcoming, he can be held liable for consequential damages. However, the amount of damages will most likely not be €50,000 but the amount of profit that Richard would have enjoyed had Sam concluded the contract with Richard.[1016]

---

[1014] HR 18 June 1982, NJ 1983, 723.
[1015] See J. M. van Dunné, 'Netherlands', in: E. H. Hondius (ed.), *Precontractual Liability: Reports to the XIIIth Congress, International Academy of Comparative Law, Montreal, Canada, 18–24 August 1990*, (Deventer, 1991), pp. 225 ff., and J. H. M. van Erp, 'The Formation of Contracts', in A. S. Hartkamp, M. Hesselink, E. Hondius, C. Joustra and E. du Perron (eds.), *Towards a European Civil Code* (1st edn, Nijmegen/Dordrecht 1994), pp. 129–30.
[1016] This amount can only be claimed if it was *likely* that the contract would have been concluded if Sam had not withdrawn from negotiations. See A. S. Hartkamp, *Verbintenissenrecht; deel II – Algemene leer der overeenkomsten* (Mr C. Asser's handleiding tot de beoefening van het Nederlands Burgerlijk recht) (10th edn, Zwolle, 1997), nos. 162 ff.

## Germany

I. Richard can probably recover the €50,000 lost profits from Sam for *culpa in contrahendo*. Whether he can also recover the cost of clearing the site depends on circumstances not specified.

II. Tort claims: Richard has no tort claim against Sam under § 823 (1) BGB. Sam did not violate Richard's property rights. To the extent that clearing the site caused a loss, it was self-inflicted.

§ Art. 826 BGB does not appear to help Richard either because there is no indication that Sam acted wilfully and against public policy.

Contract claims: since the parties never made a contract, Richard has no claim for breach of contractual obligation.

*Culpa in contrahendo*: Richard probably has a claim under the principle of *culpa in contrahendo*[1017] because Sam violated a pre-contractual obligation to act with due regard to Richard's interests. As a rule, parties are free to break off negotiations without incurring any liability. But even at the negotiation stage, a party must act in good faith and with due care *vis-à-vis* the other. If a party assures the other side that the deal will go ahead and then suddenly withdraws, that party is liable for the other side's reliance damages.[1018] This is the result here. Doubts about this result could arise only if Sam had cogent reasons for his behaviour, e.g. an unforeseeable last-minute change of circumstances, and no chance to give Richard advance warning.

Sam must compensate Richard for all loss incurred by relying on the future conclusion of the deal. This certainly includes the lost profits because if Richard had not relied on the deal, he would have sold the land to Jane and made €50,000. Whether the damages recoverable include the cost of clearing the land as well depends. If Jane would have bought the property (for the same price) with the buildings on it, Richard can also recover the cost of clearing the land because he would not have incurred it but for his reliance on the deal with Sam. If, however, Richard would have had to clear the land before selling it to Jane as well, he is no worse off for having relied on the deal with Sam and cannot recover the cost.

III. The issue here is essentially one of balancing the freedom to end negotiations against the principle of good faith that requires acting with due regard for the other side's interest. Where the good faith principle

---

[1017] Which is now codified in § 311 ss. 2 and 3 and in § 241 (2) BGB. See Case 11 ('A Maestro's Mistake'), sub II.
[1018] BGH NJW 1967, 2199; BGH WM 1975, 923.

prevails, as in the present case, quasi-contractual liability again covers pure economic loss not covered by tort law.

### Austria

I. Richard has a claim against Sam on the ground of a pre-contractual obligation to recover the sum of €50,000 for lost profits. He may also have a claim for the recovery of the costs of clearing the site.

II. Richard's claim under a pre-contractual obligation (*culpa in contrahendo*): it is commonly held that negotiations aiming at the conclusion of a contract create pre-contractual duties to protect and inform the other party to the negotiation.[1019] If somebody breaks off advanced negotiations without any justification and abstains from reaching a conclusion which has been previously characterized as certain to occur, or highly probable, that person is liable for damages under contract rules, if he has failed to warn his partner of a change of mind.[1020]

This appears to be the result in the current hypothetical case. If Sam is unable to show specific reasons for breaking off the negotiations and his subsequent refusal to conclude the contract, namely, reasons which were unforeseeable to him and could, therefore, create no duties *vis-à-vis* Richard to warn him, he will be liable for Richard's loss.

As a rule, Richard can only claim compensation for his reliance interest, namely, €50,000, the sum which he would have additionally received from Jane had he not relied upon Sam's assurance.[1021]

Costs of clearing the land: these are not recoverable if Richard would have been able to sell the land without clearing it. If Jane, or someone else, had not requested the clearing but would have paid the same price for the uncleared land, these expenses would also be subject to reimbursement.

III. Recovery of loss where there is a breaking-off of pre-contractual negotiations has only been generally acknowledged in Austria for a rather short period of time. Today, it is commonly held opinion that pre-contractual obligations are in many aspects to be treated as if they

---

[1019] See H. Koziol, *Österreichisches Haftpflichtrecht*, vol. II (2nd edn, Vienna, 1984), p. 70; OGH SZ 48/102, SZ 49/94, SZ 52/135.
[1020] Cf. OGH JBl 1992, 118, RdW 1992, 350; see R. Ostheim, 'Zur Haftung für culpa in contrahendo bei grundloser Ablehnung des Vertragsabschlusses', JBl 1980, 576.
[1021] Cf. H. Koziol and R. Welser, *Grundriss des bürgerlichen Rechts*, vol. II (12th edn, Vienna, 2001), pp. 18, 290; OGH SZ 46/22, SZ 52/90.

were contractual; this is in particular true with the recovery of pure economic loss.[1022]

## Portugal

I. Sam is liable for the damage suffered by Richard.

II. In accordance with article 227/1 CC:

> Whoever negotiates with another to conclude a contract must, in the preliminary stages as well as during its formation, proceed according to the rules of good faith, on pain of being liable for the damage that may be negligently caused to the other party.

One of the groups of cases of pre-contractual liability is that of improper breach of negotiations.[1023] In the present case, there are sufficient negotiations for Richard to have reasonable grounds for trusting and on that basis to make arrangements; on the other hand, the breach seems to have been arbitrary.

With respect to the damages recoverable, our personal view is that the general principles of 'obligation to compensate' should be held to apply, including the possibility of equitable reduction of compensation.[1024]

III. The differences with respect to contractual and extra-contractual liabilities are relatively small in Portuguese law. Some remain, and it is pertinent to know which rules are applied in pre-contractual liability and other parallel situations. The law does not resolve the issue, confining itself to ordering the application of the delictual limitation (art. 227/2). The interpreter is thus free to accept a 'third way', an intermediate zone where the application of rules from any of the traditional modalities of civil liability may be accepted.

## Sweden and Finland

I. The state of the law is in Sweden rather uncertain. In principle, however, Richard should be entitled to compensation for costs (more unlikely for loss of profit). This is specially true in Finland, where Richard's right to recover his expenses has a stronger statutory basis.

---

[1022] For a detailed report in English, see W. Posch, 'Austria', in E. H. Hondius (ed.), *Precontractual Liabilty, Reports to the XIIIth Congress of Comparative Law* (Deventer, 1991).

[1023] M. J. Almeida Costa, *Responsabilidade Civil pela Ruptura das Negociações Preparatórias de um Contrato* (Coimbra Editora, Coimbra, 1994).

[1024] A different view is held by Almeida Costa, *Responsabilidade*, pp. 71 ff., leading back to the problem of negative contractual interest or damage to trust, although stressing that compensation for damage arising may be at issue, as much as loss of profits.

II. Richard has no claim in torts since we are faced with a 'pure economic loss' in the Swedish/Finnish meaning, i.e. an economic loss arising without connection with anybody suffering personal injury or damage to things, which in principle can be recovered from the wrongdoer only when it is caused through a crime, on the basis of *SkadestL* 4:2 (Sweden) and *SkadestL* 5:1 (Finland), although the text and the preparatory works of the Tort Liability Acts 1972 and 1974 do not completely bar compensation should the courts find strong reasons for it. As mentioned earlier, courts have been very restrictive in granting exceptions to the general principle. In this case, a claim in contract is not possible, because of the lack of an established contractual relationship.

One way which might be open is of course *culpa in contrahendo*, which however has a rather vague basis in Swedish and Finnish law. The Swedish Supreme Court (NJA 1990 s. 24) tends to grant compensation for the consequences of negligent behaviour in negotiations up to the amount needed to restore the aggrieved party to the same economical position in which he would have been at the time before the negligent behaviour occurred. In principle, Richard should be entitled to compensation for costs if Sam has negligently given him reason to 'rely' on his words. The fact that the transaction concerns a real estate sale is a further obstacle for the application of *culpa in contrahendo*, since some scholars advocate that granting compensation on this basis would conflict with the form requirements proper to real estate sales. In Finland, the Land Act 1995[1025] prescribes that when two parties agree on a real estate sale without formalizing it, the party which subsequently refuses to complete the sale is bound to compensate the costs incurred by the prospective seller for 'advertising, becoming acquainted with the estate and for other needed interventions in connection with the negotiations'.

*Editors' comparative comments*

Once again, this is a case which cuts across the boundaries that divide tort from contract in the national legal regimes.

However, despite appearances, the core of this case lies far from most of the technical disputes – on the limits of the notion of contract, the role of good faith, the proper scope of *culpa in contrahendo* or of detrimental reliance – that might be deemed to be the key factors in the

---

[1025] Jordabalk (Land Act (Finland)), 12.4.1995/540 § 8.

solution. Comparative analysis shows that legal outcomes which allow, and those that deny, recoverability are to be divided by a line which can be drawn without having recourse to the above categories as screening devices.

The unreasonable breaking off of advanced negotiations is an issue which has arisen in every single legal system by way of adaptation.

Indeed, Austria, England, Germany, Scotland, Sweden and Finland deny recovery in tort. But only England precludes plaintiff's action no matter under what label it is brought forward. English lawyers implement their restrictive policy by drawing a sophisticated distinction between the duty to disclose (deemed absent under the circumstances) and the duty to be accurate in what has been disclosed (not violated under the circumstances). Scotland and Sweden leave room, albeit not very much, for recovery under statutory contract law and the *culpa in contrahendo* rule, respectively. Finland makes compensation possible under a statute concerned with land law. Austria and Germany allow recoverability under the *culpa in contrahendo* rule.

The other legal systems do not raise any obstacles against recoverability.

However, since this is an issue which arises between parties negotiating a contract who, by definition, are not yet parties to a contract, the comparative scenario does not reflect a clear-cut choice on the nature of the liability or legal regime to be applied. The question is particularly relevant as regards the rules governing the statute of limitations and the burden of proof.

The prevailing view in Belgium, France and Italy is that this kind of liability is extracontractual. In Greece, Portugal, Spain and the Netherlands disagreement over classification of the cause of action (whether it is grounded on tort law or contract law, or whether it represents a *tertium genus*) still divides the interpreters.

## Case 20: an anonymous telephone call

### Case

Dieter, the owner of a small business, has a longstanding agreement with First National Bank. One day, Credit, Inc., a credit rating institute, receives an anonymous phone call that Dieter's business is about to go bankrupt. Credit, Inc. makes no further inquiry and thus does not learn that the allegation is totally unfounded. Instead, Credit, Inc. calls First National Bank and reports the information. First National Bank immediately cancels all of Dieter's loans. As a result, Dieter suffers economic damages. He now sues Credit, Inc. to recover his loss.

### France

I. Assuming that credit rating institutions of this kind are in operation in France, then Dieter should be able to hold Credit, Inc. liable in tort under articles 1382–83 CC.

II. For the purposes of answering the hypothetical, we will assume that credit institutes exist in France, and that they are not ruled by a special legal regime. Thus they would be subject to general tort liability under article 1382 and following. In this case the institute has almost certainly committed a professional fault by not verifying the very suspicious information they received (via an anonymous phone call). The fact pattern states that Dieter suffered economic damages, so only the causal link is left to be proven. It is clear that Credit, Inc.'s professional mistake (together with their decision to communicate this unverified information directly to the bank) was the reason for the bank to terminate the agreement. Thus, Dieter should be able to recover his economic damages under the general rules of tort liability.

III. Credit rating institutes are not very well known in France. Banks normally conduct their own inquiries before signing longstanding loan agreements (*ouverture de crédit*), and before terminating them. Nevertheless, we are informed that large English and American credit rating institutions, such as Moody's for example, have begun operations in Paris.

### Belgium

I. Dieter has a claim against Credit, Inc.

II. Since there is no contract between Dieter and Credit, Inc., Dieter's claim rests on article 1382 CC:

Any act whatever of man which causes damage to another obliges him by whose fault it occurred to make reparation.

To hold Credit, Inc. liable, Dieter will have to prove the fault of Credit, Inc., a damage and a causal link between the fault and the damage.

The fault in the sense of article 1382 CC is either a violation of a statute or a behaviour different from the one that the *bonus pater familias* (the 'normal' man) would have had in the same circumstances.

If Credit, Inc. had acted intentionally (with intent to harm Dieter), the disclosure of false information would have been a criminal offence (calumny or defamation) punished by article 443 CC. It is therefore a violation of law.

If Credit, Inc. did not act intentionally, but in a way that a *bonus pater familias* would not have acted, it shall be liable.

First, in the present case, it is clear that a *bonus pater familias* would have checked the accuracy of the information before transmitting it to the First National Bank. Furthermore, Credit, Inc. should have known that misinformation of that sort could lead to the cancellation of the loans. The damage was therefore foreseeable.

Secondly, the issue will be for Dieter to prove the damage he suffered from the cancellation of all of his loans.

Thirdly, he will have to prove that there is a causal link between the damage he suffered and Credit, Inc.'s disclosure of the false information. Since the Cour de Cassation applies the theory of *equivalence des conditions*, Dieter will have to prove that his loans would not have been cancelled if First National Bank had not received the false information from Credit, Inc.

In the present scenario, the liability of First National Bank could also be claimed. Since there is a contract between them, the cancellation of the loans based on unreliable information could amount to a breach of contract.

III. The issue of liability for misinformation is increasing. It concerns the liability of the mass media and the problem of its compatibility with the constitutionally protected freedom of the press and broadcasting. However, if the right to issue opinions is strictly guaranteed, there is a trend to reinforce the liability for misinformation about facts.

This trend is also seen in contract law, where a duty to inform is developing rapidly.

## Italy

I. The Bank can be sued for misinformation and violation of the duty of care according to article 2043 cc and it is highly probable that Dieter could recover some damages, provided that his damage meets the causation requirement.

II. The rule can be seen as unquestionble in spite of the small number of precedents dealing with the facts of the case at issue.[1026]

A similar case worth recalling is *Fall. Codefil* v. *Fausti*,[1027] where the only difference was that the misinformation to the bank was given by another bank. The latter has been held liable to the plaintiff.

Besides, according to Italian (banking) law Credit, Inc. would have been under a special professional duty to handle business information with extreme care, a duty breached in the circumstances of the present case by the defendant's reckless behaviour.[1028]

III. Article 1337 cc imposes a duty to behave in good faith. This disposition might be read in order to oblige the parties to inform each other when they discover the other party's mistake.

Door-to-door contracts,[1029] securities sales regulations,[1030] transparency in banking and financial services,[1031] are all governed by statutes that deal with the concept of good faith and fair dealing. Other statutes ask third parties to provide the information necessary to permit the contracting party to make an informed decision when they make their decision to enter into a contract.[1032] This is the case, for example, in companies' balance certification and publication,[1033] of publication of the town zoning plan, of the duty to communicate to investors a truthful

---

[1026] A. Luminoso, 'La responsabilità della banca', *RDComm.*, 1984, I, 189 ff.; V. Roppo, 'Crisi d'impresa: la banca risponde verso i creditori? (Con postilla sugli sviluppi della responsabilità civile)', *DR* 1996, 535 ff.; Cass. 9.6.1998 no. 5659, *DR* 1999, 6, 677; Cass. 10.10.1998 no. 100067, *DR* 1999, 1, 110; M. Ronchi, 'La responsabilità della banca per false o inesatte informazioni nella giurisprudenza più recente', (2000) 65 *RCP* 593.

[1027] A. Milano, 13.3.1986, BBTC, 1987, II, 627.

[1028] Cf. *Dun Bradstreet* v. *Brechi*, Cass., 6.1.1984, no. 94, *Rep. FI*, 1984 and see also a very recent decision by the Supreme Court (unpublished) at
http://www.giustizia.it/cassazione/giurisprudenza/cass.2000/8993sen_00.html.

[1029] Law no. 216 of 7 June 1974, Decree Law no. 95 of 8 April 1974, modified by EEC Directive 89/298, enacted by d.lgvo. 25 January 1992, Law no. 74 of 29 December 1990, no. 428.

[1030] Law no. 1 of 2 January 1991, in GU 4 January 1991, no. 3.

[1031] Law no. 154 of 17 February 1992.

[1032] G. Alpa, 'La "trasparenza" del contratto nei settori bancario, finanziario e assicurativo' in GI, 1992, IV, 409, and G. De Nova, 'Informazione e contratto: il regolamento contrattuale' (1993) *Rivista trimestrale di diritto e procedura civile* 705.

[1033] D.p.r. 31 March 1975, no. 136.

prospectus of companies' assets[1034] and of the prohibition of deceptive advertising.[1035]

This statutory implementation of the good faith principle urged scholars to look for a unitary framework within which to place the various different legislative notions and wordings. Some authors propose the absorption of the pre-contractual stage into the very notion of formation of contract, thus extending contractual liability to unfair dealing during negotiations.[1036] Others stress that bad faith or negligent behaviour, contrary to good faith in negotiations, should be considered to constitute undue interference in freedom of contract. In this case it would then be possible to annul the contract and to claim damages under article 2043 cc.[1037]

### Spain

I. This case is not solved in our case law and we have no doctrinal commentary on it.

II. A Spanish court would probably grant compensation to Dieter. In this case the debate centres on ideas already mentioned in Case 17 ('Auditor's Liability'): Credit, Inc. knows that its report is directed to First National Bank in order to make a decision about Dieter's business. On the other hand, Credit, Inc. was negligent in conducting its own business. Finally, Dieter cannot protect himself contractually against Credit, Inc. reports.

### Greece

I. Credit, Inc. is tortiously liable to compensate Dieter for his damage, as well as his moral prejudice.

II. Credit, Inc. is tortiously liable according to article 914 CC, because Dieter suffered pecuniary damage, as well as a moral prejudice owing to Credit, Inc.'s fault (since it failed to make further inquiry).

---

[1034] EEC Directive 80/310, Law no. 281 of 4 June 1985, and Law no. 428 of 29 December 1990.
[1035] D.lgvo. no. 74 of 25 January 1992.
[1036] Similarly to the German model of *culpa in contrahendo* see G. Grisi, *L'obbligo precontrattuale di informazione* (Napoli, 1990); F. Nanni, *La buona fede contrattuale* (Padova 1988) pp. 1–143; F. Benatti, 'Culpa in contrahendo', *CI*, 1987, 287 ff.
[1037] R. Sacco and G. De Nova, *Il contratto* (2 vols, Turin, 1993), at p. 249; G. Visintini, *La reticenza nella formazione dei contratti* (Padova, 1972). It must be underlined that despite the deep similarity of this theory to the French position, the Italian system recognizes the possibility of cumulating extra-contractual and contractual liability.

Credit, Inc's behaviour is illegal, because the law prohibits and penally punishes slander and the consequent unlawful harm to someone's personality (art. 57 CC).[1038] Greek court decisions consider that any unfavourable inaccurate information infringes the personality of the person and it is forbidden by law.[1039] Today business people are especially protected by Law no. 2472/10 April 1997 on the protection of individuals with regard to the processing of personal data (the Greek adjustment to E/95/46C Directive of 25 October 1995 on data protection), which prohibits any conveying of inaccurate data (art. 4 para. 1 sub-para. $\gamma$) and stipulates liability for such conveying, even for negligence (art. 23).

The above certainly means that Credit, Inc. should compensate Dieter not only for his pecuniary damage, but also for his moral prejudice by paying in the latter case a reasonable amount of money (as art. 932 CC lays down) or even taking any other appropriate measure in the circumstances (art. 59 CC).

III. It is to be added that Law no. 2472 prohibits not only the untruthful, but even the truthful information about personal data of a third party without its consent. Even the simple collection of such data is prohibited, without prior announcement to a special authority protecting personal data. Is such a protection too strict? Or perhaps too tolerant, especially since companies are not protected by this law?

## England

I. Dieter is advised to sue. Whether he will recover his loss or not is, at the present time, uncertain, and this is a case in which English law may go either way, in developing new categories of actionable negligence.

II. *Murphy v. Brentwood DC*[1040] shows that English judges will consider novel claims for actionable negligence on a case-by-case basis. The line of authorities before the case of *Spring v. Guardian Assurance*,[1041] dealing with potential liability of investigators for negligence under the principle of *Hedley Byrne v. Heller*,[1042] is against recognizing a duty of care owed by an investigator to the investigated person.[1043] But *Spring* clearly established liability for negligent employment references, and one can

---

[1038] A. Georgiades, *General Principles of Civil Law* (2nd edn, 1996), p. 127.
[1039] AP 89/ 58 EEN 25, 685; EfAth 1704/ 75 NoB 23, 940; AP 297/ 1959: it is contrary to good morals for any bank to convey inaccurate financial information about a business person; nevertheless, in the last case the bank was aware of the inaccuracy.
[1040] [1991] 1 AC 398 (HL).    [1041] [1994] 3 All ER 129.    [1042] [1964] AC 465.
[1043] E.g. *Wright v. Jockey Club* [1995] *Times Law Reports* 342; *South Pacific Mfg. v. NZ Securities Investigations* [1992] 2 NZLR 282.

argue that it is only a small step for the courts to take to extend this liability to negligent credit references. This they might well do, in a case such as the present; however, notice should be taken of Lord Brandon's remarks in the House of Lords decision of *The Aliakmon*,[1044] to the effect that new formulations of principle cannot be used in novel cases to alter a previous line of decisions holding that no duty of care exists in similar circumstances. Moreover, the existence of special statutory rules providing specific remedies to consumers against incorrect entries in credit files held on them by credit agencies,[1045] or imposing special duties on holders of computerized personal data,[1046] may further discourage the courts to create a novel category of common law liability in tort.

III. The lack of direct relationship of reliance between the credit agency and the investigated individual may be seen as lack of the necessary 'close proximity', required by all cases developing in recent years the liability principle of *Hedley Byrne*[1047] for incorrect advice or information. The courts may well think that imposing liability in negligence on credit agencies will hinder their work, which is valuable for the speedy and efficient administration of private consumer credit.

## Scotland

I. It would be an extension of the law, but the courts could accept that Credit, Inc. owed Dieter a duty of care which they had breached in the circumstances. However, it may well be a step too far for the court to contemplate at this time.

II. Once more we are dealing with a negligent statement which causes economic loss. We must look to see if there is the possibility in this factual situation of another exception to the general rule of non-liability for secondary economic loss. Here we have a statement made by Credit, Inc. which is relied upon by First National Bank but which causes loss to Dieter. This is because First National Bank has relied upon the statement of Credit, Inc. to avoid it being caused loss by Dieter. First National Bank suffers no loss, even though Credit, Inc.'s statement is a misstatement. If

---

[1044] [1986] 2 All ER 145, 153.
[1045] The Consumer Credit Act 1979, s. 159, gives consumers the right to require rectification of incorrect entries and speedy notification (within 28 days) to be sent to future addressees of the information. A breach of this statutory duty by the credit agency may well lead to damages for any ensuing financial loss to the consumer.
[1046] See Data Protection Act 1998, ss. 7–15.
[1047] See above, Cases 7 ('The Careless Architect'), 11 ('A Maestro's Mistake') and 19 ('Breach of Promise').

it had been First National Bank who suffered the loss then there would have been little problem for them to recover in delict from Credit, Inc. in these circumstances. Credit, Inc. has made no representation to Dieter, but yet he suffers loss which is directly referable to and caused by their misrepresentation of a factual situation to the Bank. We appear to be outside the realm of the *Hedley Byrne* formulation which is 'to the effect that a duty of care not to cause pure economic loss arises from the making of statements which might be relied upon by others to *their* loss'.[1048] It may be stretching the interpretation of 'relied upon' to say that Dieter relies on Credit, Inc. not to make a representation to First National Bank which might cause loss to Dieter.

We cannot be in the realm of negligent interference with a contract, as discussed under Case 13 ('Subcontractor's Liability'), unless there is a contractual connection. Does the bank have a contract with Credit, Inc.? Possibly, if so it would be for the provision of credit ratings. However, missing from the *Junior Books* formulation is the element of the nominated subcontractor. Here Dieter will not even know of Credit, Inc.'s existence so the possibility of a *Junior Books* duty of care arising are negligible. That is not even taking into account the court's reluctance to extend the principle beyond the facts of the particular case and the fact that *Junior Books* was not about any form of statement.

We may not be so far outside the *Henderson v. Merrett* formulation that 'a duty of care to prevent relational economic loss will arise between A and B, if A, who renders professional or quasi-professional services, voluntarily assumes responsibility for B's economic interests, knowing that B relies upon A to provide those professional or quasi-professional services with reasonable care'.[1049] The question would be for whom the professional services are being provided. In *Caparo*, the party who sought to rely upon the information was not the one for whom it was provided. The auditors were held not to take responsibility for all who might conceivably rely on their statement. In *Caparo* it was emphasized that 'the necessary relationship of proximity could exist only between the defendant and persons in the direct contemplation of the defendant'.[1050] Here, although the service was performed for the benefit of First National Bank, it would be difficult to argue that Credit, Inc. would not have had in contemplation that their information would have serious implications

---

[1048] *Stair Memorial Encyclopaedia, The Laws of Scotland*, vol. 15 (Law Society of Scotland, Edinburgh, 1996), p. 173, para. 277 (written by K. McK. Norrie).
[1049] Ibid., p. 389, para. 587 (written by J. M. Thomson).
[1050] Ibid., p. 174, para. 277 (written by K. McK. Norrie).

for Dieter's business directly. This aspect of *Caparo* is arguably satisfied in this case.

We saw in *Spring* that Lord Goff viewed the issue in terms of the assumption of responsibility by the employer coupled with the reliance by the employee in a situation where the employer had particular knowledge and skill upon which the employee relied. Here, it could be argued that Dieter is relying upon the particular knowledge and skill that a credit rating institute professes to possess, even though he does not know about them at the time that they perform their service to the bank. But then that is in the nature of the institution. The question would be whether there was a voluntary assumption of responsibility on Credit, Inc.'s part towards Dieter's economic interests. The purpose of institutions such as Credit, Inc. is arguably to protect, and assume responsibility for, the economic interests of creditors such as First National Bank and not debtors such as Dieter. It would be the possible extension of this responsibility which may be met by a public policy objection. Credit agencies serve a useful purpose in society and it may not be in society's interests to overburden them with liability for carelessly passing on incorrect advice unless they had been reckless or even fraudulent. However, like Lord Woolf in *Spring*,[1051] the court may not be convinced by this argument. As with the employment reference, a bad credit rating can have serious consequences for a person in our society. The court may feel that it is more important that the credit agencies get their information right than that they be spared the burden of making more thorough checks on their sources of information.

III. Interestingly, this case combines features of several decisions which have helped to lay down parameters within which one might expect the courts to determine the question. It is an indication of the difficulty of the law in this area that it is not possible to anticipate which way the courts may go. Though a Scottish court may be more likely to apply principle rather than analogy with existing areas of liability, it is still very much determined not to open up Pandora's box.

### The Netherlands

I. Dieter can claim in tort.

II. Incorrect information spread by a credit rating institute is bound to damage the person that is being rated. The societal diligence that must

---

[1051] See above, Case 18 ('Wrongful Job Reference').

be exercised by these institutes is most grave. Incorrect or incomplete information can seriously damage a person. Therefore, the institute is very much to blame for the consequences. The institute is duty-bound to verify any information and not to act upon anonymous telephone calls. This damage is most foreseeable (it is foreseeable that the First National Bank will act upon alarming messages of this kind) and can be imputed to the grossly tortious act.[1052]

## Germany

I. It is likely, but not certain, that Dieter has a claim against Credit, Inc. to recover his economic damages.

II. Tort claims. § 823 (1) BGB. Dieter could arguably sue for violation of his 'right to an established and ongoing commercial enterprise'[1053] because Credit, Inc.'s conduct was directly aimed at, and concerned with, his business as such. Yet, the *Bundesgerichtshof* has construed this remedy as a secondary measure for which there is no room if a more specific one applies.[1054] § 824 BGB is such a remedy.

Dieter can sue under § 824 (1) BGB[1055] because Credit, Inc. disseminated factual information about him, causing economic damages. Yet, as in Case 18 ('Wrongful Job Reference'), the question is whether Credit, Inc. acted lawfully under § 824 (2) because it or First National Bank had a legitimate interest in the information.

In the present scenario, existing case law as well as the required balancing test[1056] suggest that Credit, Inc. may be held liable. In a case where a businessman sued a newspaper for publishing a fake advertisement falsely announcing that he was going out of business, the *Bundesgerichtshof* held the newspaper liable. The Court said that the newspaper had special reason to verify the source of the advertisement:

There is such a special reason if the advertisement obviously announces a fact with particularly important and far-reaching consequences for the person concerned, and if the possibility cannot be eliminated that it was posted by a third party, e.g. a competitor with an intent to harm...In such an exceptional case, the question whether the advertisement was posted by the person concerned

---

[1052] On the subject of liability for incorrect information, see, e.g., HR 10.12.1993, NJ 1994, no. 667 and HR 9.6.1995, NJ 1995, no. 534.
[1053] Above, Case 2 ('Cable II – Factory Shutdown'), sub II.
[1054] BGHZ 59, 76, at 79 (1972).   [1055] Above, Case 18 ('Wrongful Job Reference'), sub II.
[1056] See above, Case 18 ('Wrongful Job Reference'), sub II.

becomes paramount. Obviously, there is great risk of harm to the person concerned. Precautionary measures are called for if the advertisement is posted over the phone so that an immediate and sure identification of the person posting it is not possible...[1057]

Since there was a serious risk of harm, including cancellation of credit, the newspaper had a duty to make reasonable efforts to verify the identity of the caller.[1058] The essence of this, and similar decisions[1059] is that while the defendant is not liable for mere negligence, he must make some effort to avoid misinformation, especially if the likelihood of untruth and the potential harm are great.

According to these standards, Dieter has an even stronger case than that won by the plaintiff in the opinion cited above. Credit, Inc. relied on an anonymous phone call and thus had maximum reason to be wary. And the cancellation of the loans was not only a vaguely foreseeable consequence but the very purpose of the information given. Finally, one must not forget that Credit, Inc. bears the burden of persuasion and proof under § 824 (2) so that it will be held liable unless it persuades the court that it acted properly under the circumstances.

§ 826 does not apply because nothing in the case suggests that Credit, Inc. acted wilfully and against public policy.

Contract claims: Dieter has no claim as a third party protected under the contract (if any) between First National Bank and Credit, Inc. The credit rating institute had no intent to protect Dieter, quite to the contrary, it wanted to protect the bank as its customer.

III. Most of the case law and academic scholarship about § 824 (1) BGB is concerned with the liability of mass media. However, the media have considerably greater leeway than other defendants because the freedom of the press and of broadcasting is constitutionally protected (§ 5 (1) *Grundgesetz*). This is obviously not true for credit rating institutions. For this reason also, Dieter's claim against Credit, Inc. should be even easier to win than the plaintiff's claim in the case cited above.

## Austria

I. Dieter has a claim against Credit, Inc. based either on article 1330(2) ABGB (which is doubtful, however) or on article 1300 to recover his economic loss.

---

[1057] BGHZ 59, 76, at 81 (1972).
[1058] In a similar vein, RGZ 148, 154 (1935); BGH NJW 1957, 1149–50.
[1059] See, e.g. BGH NJW 1966, 2010, at 2011.

II. Dieter's claim according to article 1330(2) ABGB: as with Case 18, Dieter can sue under article 1330(2) ABGB because Credit, Inc. disseminated false information about him, violating his right of business reputation and thereby causing financial damage.

Unlike Case 18 ('Wrongful Job Reference'), however, the information from Credit, Inc. in the present case was confidential in the sense that it was 'non-public'. The OGH ruled in an earlier decision that confidential information given to a bank is not 'public' in terms of article 1330(2) (last sentence), notwithstanding that the information reaches several persons within the bank.[1060]

This would mean that the harmful activities of Credit, Inc. would be unlawful only if Credit, Inc. knew of the inaccuracy of its information. Thus, Dieter would have no successful claim against Credit, Inc. However, it must be taken into account that Credit, Inc. acted with gross negligence and could expect under the circumstances that the information it disseminated would have immediate and severely harmful consequences for Dieter. Gross negligence in combination with foreseeable great risk of harm would make the activities of Credit, Inc. appear to be unlawful pursuant to article 1330(2) ABGB.

Whether the claim would be successful is unsure, however, since no decisions exist on the topic.

Dieter's contract claim according to article 1300 ABGB: article 1300 ABGB is a better foundation for Dieter's claim. Pursuant to the decision of the OGH in the case of the investment consultant,[1061] Credit, Inc. gave its information doubtless 'for a consideration': it is evident that a mutual business relationship exists between Credit, Inc. and First National Bank.

It is also true, however, that there is no contract between Dieter and Credit, Inc. Nevertheless, Dieter is in the position of a 'third party' protected by the 'contract' or business relationship between First National Bank and Credit, Inc. Even if no contract (in its narrow sense) had existed between First National Bank and Credit, Inc., it is sufficient in the view of Austrian courts and scholars that objective-legal duties of care in favour of a third party may be assumed.[1062] All the more since Credit, Inc. has rendered its 'performance' (to the bank) precisely in respect of Dieter's financial reputation.

III. The balance of interests in article 1330(2) (last sentence) has not yet been made clear under Austrian law. Once again, a solution focusing

---

[1060] Cf. OGH SZ 35/82.  [1061] See above, Case 11 ('A Maestro's Mistake').
[1062] See above, Case 17 ('Auditor's Liability').

on a combination of several aspects serving as pros and cons of liability would be preferable. Instead of the positive knowledge of the untruth of a communication, grossly negligent lack of knowledge may suffice if the objective impact of the consequences upon a third person is extraordinarily high.

Portugal

I. Dieter has the right to seek compensation from Credit, Inc.

II. In accordance with article 484 CC ('offence to credit or good name'), '[w]hoever affirms or disseminates a fact capable of prejudicing the credit or good name of any person, private individual or legal person, is responsible for the damage caused'.

We are dealing with an unlawful act, specially provided for in the law.[1063] In the hypothesis given in this case, the negligent dissemination of a fact capable of harming Dieter's credit is effectively what has occurred. The obligation to compensate does not seem to be in doubt, once an adequate causality nexus has been established.[1064]

III. A subjective right to credit does not seem to exist; hence the need for a special rule to protect this good or interest. But the same cannot be said for a 'good name', protected as a personality right.[1065]

Some authors and court decisions[1066] have also understood that the affirmation or dissemination of true facts gives rise to liability (if it does not correspond to the exercise of a right or to the fulfilment of a duty). Indeed, article 484 (differing from § 824 of the BGB) makes no reference to the non-truthful nature of the facts. But this orientation is not certain.[1067]

---

[1063] Antunes Varela, *Direito das Obrigações* vol. I (10th edn, Almedina, Coimbra, 2000), p. 567 ff.

[1064] In a case decided by a judgment of the STJ of 29 June 1993 (CJSTJ II, 171) liability was excluded owing to lack of proof that the information attached to a client's file had been disseminated outside the bank.

[1065] It has been understood that art. 70 CC, by establishing that 'the law protects individuals against any unlawful offence or threat of offence to his physical or moral entity', enshrines the so-called 'general personal right'. The following articles regulate offences to deceased persons, rights to a name and to a pseudonym, confidential and non-confidential letters/missives, rights to an image and to the preservation of intimacy of private life: see O. de Carvalho, *A Teoria Geral da Relação Jurídica, 'seu sentido e limites'* (2nd edn, Coimbra, 1981), p. 83, and O. de Carvalho, *Os Direitos do Homem no Direito Civil Português* (author's edition, Coimbra, 1973), p. 27; D. Leite De Campos, *Lições de Direitos da Personalidade* (2nd edn, Coimbra, 1992), p. 49.

[1066] E.g. the judgment of the STJ of 3 October 1995, BMJ 450, 424.

[1067] See Sinde Monteiro, *Responsabilidade por Conselhor, Recomendações on Informações* (Almedina, Coimbra, 1990), pp. 208–9.

## Sweden and Finland

I. In Sweden, Dieter will certainly recover his loss. The situation in Finland is more uncertain.

II. In Sweden, Dieter would have a claim against Credit, Inc. since the activity of credit rating is presently regulated by the Act on Credit Information 1973[1068] which imposes strict liability (in the form of reversed burden of proof) on the professionals involved, who can avoid it only by showing that they have used the 'required care and attention'. Facts such as those described in the example would certainly suggest the liability of Credit, Inc.

In Finland there was no corresponding statutory provision until 1999, and liability was then very doubtful, since it was submitted to the general limitation to the compensation of 'pure economic loss' (in the Swedish/Finnish meaning of the term, i.e. economic loss arising without connection with anybody suffering personal injury or damage to things) provided in *SkadestL* 5:1, which establishes that when such damage is not caused by a criminal action it can be recovered only if there are 'special reasons'. The Act on Personal Information 1999 includes provisions establishing liability for credit rating,[1069] but it could be argued that these apply to Dieter only as a private person and not when he acts within the framework of a commercial activity.

*Editors' comparative comments*

Providers of intellectual services do so ordinarily on the basis of a contract. If the client is disappointed with the quality of the service and a financial loss is arguably attributable to the service as rendered, the client may have a cause of action for breach of contract. Sometimes, however, a person other than the client claims to have suffered a loss as a consequence of poorly and negligently rendered intellectual services. Can such a third party recover in a negligence action? This is – as it was in Cases 14 ('Poor Legal Services') and 17 ('Auditor's Liability') – the issue at stake.

The crucial test to be satisfied in any legal system is, substantially, whether the defendant supplied information for the guidance of others in their business conduct, and whether the plaintiff belongs to a group of persons which the defendant knew would be affected by the same information. An affirmative answer to both these questions suffices for

---

[1068] Kredituplyssningslagen (1973: 1173), at § 21.
[1069] Personuppgiftslag 22.4.1999/523 §§ 20–, 1, 47.

most legal systems to allow recovery of the plaintiff's loss, and even for those of England and Scotland not to deny compensation as a matter of principle – despite the unsteady finding, under the circumstances of the case, of a 'close proximity' and of a 'direct assumption of responsibility'.

Indeed, to be stressed in this case is the quantitative exposure of the defendant to a defined number of plaintiffs, or better, a single plaintiff. The danger of unbounded financial repercussion is avoided. The total liability can be calculated in advance, because the plaintiff's interests can be distinctly contemplated by the defendant at close range. The class of claimants is thereby limited, as if – to put it in common law terms – an invisible privity paradigm structured the resulting bond in tort.[1070] This is why, if we were prognostic comparativists, we would infer that England and Scotland will not delay for very long their enrolment in the liability club in the circumstances of this case.

As mentioned earlier,[1071] there is no doubt that in this field the large majority of national solutions which award plaintiffs with damages are using legal devices as a means to encourage the maintenance of a high standard of services, with a view to preventing the collapse of that service industry as a whole.

From this perspective, one might regard as merely theoretical the debate on whether a given legal system, or a future European code, should ground liability on general rules, such as the duty to inform correctly,[1072] on general standards such as good faith, or on specific norms which protect the given right (as happens in the Greek and Portuguese legal systems with their reference to personality rights); or whether it should shift the key focus of the decision to the blameworthiness of the information giver's behaviour (which is implied in Austria and the Netherlands).

---

[1070] See E. K. Banakas, 'Liability for Incorrect Financial Information: Theory and Practice in a General Clause System and in a Protected Interests System', (1999) 7 *European Review of Private Law* 261, 270–2; J. M. Thomson *Delictual Liability* (Butterworths, Edinburgh, 1994), p. 59.

[1071] See our Comments under Cases 14 ('Poor Legal Services') and 17 ('Auditor's Liability').

[1072] Bearing in mind both the problematic position currently taken by English and Scottish law and the entrepreneurial activity of the plaintiff in this hypothetical case, it is worth recalling Jane Stapleton's critical appraisal of English legal outcomes. According to Stapleton, 'In the case of pure economic loss courts do now seem to conclude that the concern about free-riding outweighs the concern to ensure the defendant is deterred, so that commercial plaintiffs who had such alternative opportunities to deter the defendant are left to use them and are denied the assistance of tort...In contrast, consumers who face inflexible standard terms and who are therefore in no danger of being encouraged by the award of a tort entitlement to change their bargaining stance...may receive support from tort', J. Stapleton, 'Tort, Insurance and Ideology', (1995) Mod. LR 820, 840.

# PART III • MUCH ADO ABOUT SOMETHING

# 8 Summary and survey of the cases and results

MAURO BUSSANI AND VERNON VALENTINE PALMER

## Introduction

Our task is now to summarize and compare the results contained in the national reports. In order to give the reader a helpful overview, we have arranged the results in a series of tables, and at the end of the section we discuss a number of findings and make comparative comments based upon them. Table 8.1 organizes the answers country-by-country, and we have continued to use the liberal, pragmatic and conservative regimes as our ordering principle. Table 8.2 compares two theories of relief, delictual and contractual, and shows the extent to which European systems make recourse to contractual ideas as an alternative to tort. Here the table shows the degree to which they rely on these two grounds instead of the single ground of tort. Table 8.3 breaks down the results for a number of widely-recognized paradigm cases (fitted to our taxonomy),[1] and once again the results are organized in terms of the liberal, pragmatic and conservative regimes.

In compiling these results, we consciously followed a conservative way of interpreting the results. We placed the responses into one of three categories: Yes, No, and Problematical. A 'yes' means that compensation for pure economic loss would be granted. (We also distinguished, however, between an affirmative grant of recovery in delict and recovery in contract or on some other basis). An answer was not considered a clear-cut yes or no, however, unless the national reporter expressed the probable outcome with clarity and confidence. If for any reason the reporter's answer indicated doubt or difficulty in predicting the outcome, the case was classified as 'problematical'. Because of the variety of reasons that may make an answer doubtful (divided jurisprudence, contrary

---
[1] See above, Part I, Chapter 1, n. 4.

Table 8.1. Country-by-country comparisons

|  | France | Belgium | Italy | Spain | Greece | England |
|---|---|---|---|---|---|---|
| Yes (delict) | 1, 2, 3, 5, 6, 7, 8, 10, 12(1), 13, 14, 15, 16, 17 (statutory auditor), 18, 19, 20 | 1, 2, 7, 8, 9, 10, 12(1), 14, 16, 17, 18, 19, 20 | 1, 2, 4, 5, 8, 9, 11, 13, 14, 16, 17, 18, 19, 20 | 1, 2, 3, 8, 9, 10, 13, 14, 16, 18, 19 | 1, 2, 6, 8, 10, 13, 14, 16, 18, 19, 20 | 7, 11, 14, 16, 18 |
| Yes (contract) | 9 |  |  |  |  |  |
| Yes (statute) | 4 | 4 |  |  | 18 |  |
| No | 12(2) | 5, 6, 12(2), 13, 15 | 3 | 15 | 3, 4, 5, 11 | 1, 2, 3, 4, 5, 6, 8, 9, 10, 12(1), 15, 17, 19 |
| Problematical | 11, 17 (contract auditor) | 3, 11 | 6, 7, 10, 12, 15 | 4, 5, 7, 11, 12, 17, 20 | 7, 9, 12, 15, 17 | 12(2), 13, 20 |

|  | Scotland | The Netherlands | Germany | Austria | Portugal | Sweden/Finland** |
|---|---|---|---|---|---|---|
| Yes (delict) | 7, 14, 18 | 1, 2, 4, 8, 10, 12(1), 13, 14, 16, 17, 18, 19, 20 | 1, 8, 9, 20 | 4, 8, 9, 10, 11, 18, 20 | 1, 8, 10, 12(1) and (2) (computer), 16, 20 | 9 |
| Yes (contract) |  |  | 13, 14, 18, 19 | 7, 13, 14, 18, 19 | 18, 19 | 19 |
| Yes (statute) |  |  | 4, 7, 14 |  | 4 | 4 (F), 17, 20 (S) |
| No | 1, 2, 3, 4, 5, 6, 8, 10, 12(1), 15, 17, 19 | 5, 7, 11, 12(2) | 2, 3, 5, 6, 10, 11, 12, 15, 17 | 1, 2, 3, 5, 6, 15, 17 | 2, 3, 5, 6, 12(2) (flat), 15 | 2, 3, 4 (S), 5, 7, 10, 12, 15, 18 |
| Problematical | 11, 12(2), 13, 16, 19, 20 | 3, 6, 7, 9, 15 | 16 | 12, 16 | 7, 9, 11, 12(1) (flat), 13, 14, 17 | 1, 6, 8, 11, 13, 14, 16, 20 (F) |

The double asterisk (**) in the Sweden and Finland box calls attention to the fact that results for the two countries are to be regarded as the same, except when an (S) or (F) has been placed next to the number of the case to indicate a divergent solution.

Table 8.2. *Comparison of type of recovery*

|  | Austria | Germany | Portugal | Sweden/ Finland | France | Greece |
|---|---|---|---|---|---|---|
| Recoveries by: | | | | | | |
| Contract action | 5 | 4 | 2 | 1 | 1 | 1 |
| Statute or other ground | 0 | 3 | 1 | 2 | 1 | 0 |
| Delict | 7 | 4 | 7 | 1 | 17 | 11 |

|  | Belgium | Scotland | England | Spain | The Netherlands | Italy |
|---|---|---|---|---|---|---|
| Recoveries by: | | | | | | |
| Contract action | 0 | 0 | 0 | 0 | 0 | 0 |
| Statute or other ground | 1 | 0 | 0 | 0 | 0 | 0 |
| Delict | 13 | 3 | 5 | 11 | 13 | 14 |

view in the doctrine, weak causal connection and so forth), this category becomes a residual one that could not be reduced to greater precision.

In choosing this conservative approach, we consciously sought to minimize the dangers of our own editorial perspective in interpreting the results. Even so, it is difficult to eliminate all chance of misclassification on our part. Naturally we submitted our compilation to the country reporters for verification, but the reader will appreciate that measuring degrees of certainty and uncertainty is a somewhat hazardous enterprise on which reasonable minds may differ.

## Reappraising the divides

The above tables bring to light a number of insights. The first is that the recoverability of pure economic loss cannot be approached in terms of some distinctive trait or characteristic of the 'legal families' of Western Europe. The question is simply not a civil law vs. common law issue. It is evident to us that common law countries, mixed jurisdictions and some civil law countries all share similar concerns about the danger of excessive liability entailed by this form of damage. The issue is the subject of thriving debate, case law development and doctrinal writings within each family, though not necessarily within every system. Thus, we respectfully disagree with Jan van Dunné's recent assertion that

Table 8.3. *Broadly recognized fact patterns*

|  | Liberal regimes (France, Belgium, Italy, Spain, Greece) | Pragmatic regimes (England, Scotland, the Netherlands) | Conservative regimes (Austria, Germany, Portugal, Sweden, Finland) |
|---|---|---|---|
| *Ricochet Damage* | | | |
| Cable Case II | Yes | No (the Netherlands: Yes) | No |
| *Ricochet Damage* | | | |
| Requiem for An Italian All Star (Meroni Case) | Yes (Belgium, Greece: No; Spain: problematical) | No | No |
| *Product Liability* | | | |
| Fire in the Projection Booth | Yes (Greece: problematical) | No (the Netherlands: problematical) | Yes (Portugal: problematical) |
| *Transferred Loss* | | | |
| The Dutiful Wife | Yes (Italy: problematical) | No (the Netherlands: Yes) | No (Portugal, Austria: Yes) |
| *Professional Services* | | | |
| Poor Legal Services (Notary) | Yes | Yes | Yes (Sweden/Finland Portugal: problematical) |
| Auditor's Liability | Yes (Spain, France, Greece: problematical) | No (the Netherlands: Yes) | No (Sweden/Finland: Yes; Portugal: problematical) |
| *Public Infrastructure* | | | |
| A Closed Motorway | No (France: Yes; Italy, Greece: problematical) | No (the Netherlands: problematical) | No |

this issue reflects a 'civil law–common law split' or a 'true Continental Divide'.[2] If we look at the results in Table 8.1, this conclusion is hardly tenable. The approach of the conservative civilian regimes and the common law as well simply contrasts with the liberalism of certain civilian

---

[2] Jan van Dunné 'Liability for Pure Economic Loss: Rule or Exception? "A Comparatist's View of the Civil Law–Common Law Split on Compensation of Non-physical Damage in Tort Law"', (1999) 4 *European Review of Private Law* 397, 399.

countries such as France and Belgium where the protection of economic loss is widespread and the issue is barely recognized. France permits (in principle) delictual recoveries in seventeen cases, but in Portugal the number is only seven. Belgium allows delictual recovery thirteen times, Austria only seven times. Italy grants recovery in fourteen cases as compared to one in Sweden. If any split is to be recognized it would appear, in our view, to lie between those countries which have an overt system of protected (vs. unprotected) interests (such as Germany and England) and those which do not.[3] It is this criterion which seems to underlie differences within the civilian camp and which draws English law conceptually closer to German law. And metalegal disagreements, not surface methodological differences, are the primary sources of a system of different protected interests.

These divergent patterns are seen most clearly in some of the more famous cases of pure economic loss. As Table 8.3 indicates, the results from Cable Case II are nearly evenly divided. Five liberal regimes, plus the Netherlands, would allow recovery of the loss, but the five conservative regimes plus England and Scotland would deny it. In the Case of The Dutiful Wife, a similar split occurs: seven yes, five no. In the *Meroni* type of case, the split widens to two yes, ten no: while two liberal regimes are positive on recovery (the exceptions are Belgium and Greece (no) and Spain (problematical)) all five conservative systems and three pragmatic systems are against a remedy. Once again, we would emphasize that these results do not correspond to an alleged common law/civil law divide. They are better described as a political divide over the appropriate areas or situations where this interest should receive selective protection. Of course, the picture is not simply one of divergence. In some selective areas the results point to a consensus. Widespread agreement exists with respect to certain paradigm cases. In the case of the defective will drafted by a negligent notary (Case 14 – 'Poor Legal Services'), there is virtual unanimity in favour of the intended beneficiary's recovery of his/her financial loss: ten countries indicate yes, none is opposed. Interestingly, eight countries reach this solution through the law of tort, while two others base it upon contract with protective effects, or upon special legislation pertaining to notarial liability. In the

---

[3] See E. K. Banakas, 'Liability for Incorrect Financial Information: Theory and Practice in a General Clause System and in a Protected Interests System,' (1999) 7 *European Review of Private Law* 261. See also K. Lipstein, 'Protected Interests in the Law of Torts', (1962–3) 21 *Cambridge Law Journal* 85.

case of The Closed Motorway, European consensus takes the opposite tack: nine systems clearly oppose relief. These selective areas of consensus confound claims of a Europe polarized along common law/civil law lines. A realistic map of pure economic loss in Europe must be more detailed and nuanced than has been supposed.

## Certainty vs. uncertainty

A second point of interest in the above tables concerns the degree of legal certainty in the answers. For example – as shown by Table 8.1 – the German system reported only one problematical case, but the Spanish report produced seven; Austria produced only two problematical cases, but Italy yielded five. Therefore, we wondered whether greater predictability and certainty (less indeterminacy) about pure economic loss seems to be characteristic of the conservative regimes and whether there is any discernible trend in the results yielded by the liberal or pragmatic regimes. As interesting as the question is, we do not think this evidence leads to any valid generalization. If there is any tendency we would have been tempted to argue that tort regimes with a structured system of 'protected interests', whether the structure results from codified texts, borrowed doctrine or case precedents (but this would include England) tend to yield more definite and predictable 'yes and no' answers from the reporters, and as a consequence fewer 'problematical' responses. However, we hesitate to call this much more than a possibility. The evidence is mixed. For example, it is difficult to explain why Portugal and Finland produced a higher number of problematical cases (seven and eight respectively) than Germany and Austria, although all these regimes adhere to a system of protected interests. It is also difficult to explain the low number of problematical cases in France and Belgium, as compared to the higher number in Spain, though these regimes do not purport to embody a system of protected interests. The reasons for these patterns can be manifold. They may stem from a variety of accidental factors, including the cautiousness of the reporter, the evolutionary stage of the question in a particular country or the variable interplay of legal formants tackling the issue within the same system.[4]

---

[4] For example, to say in a given case that the solution is not problematic in France perhaps places no stress upon the existence of covert means by which the *juges du fond*

Of course one could question whether legal certainty of the above kind is a real asset – not only for loss bearers in our societies,[5] but also in relation to the perennial need of any legal system to continue to develop new solutions that fulfil the demands of law-users. These questions, however, involve the eternal debate about the proper balance between flexibility and predictability in the law[6] (as well as between uniformity and diversity of the law, in a supranational context)[7] and might well be seen as a research issue far beyond the boundaries of our study.

---

may render an adverse or surprising judgment. A different observer might have chosen to underscore the problematical side instead of giving an affirmative answer 'in principle'. Further, the jurisprudence and/or a strand of doctrine in one jurisdiction may point to opposite outcomes (competing formants) or the precise hypothetical situation may not have been previously treated with as much clarity as in another jurisdiction.

[5] One could question the influence that some social and economic factors may have on the flowering of this issue in recent years. C. von Bar underlines the fact 'that the wealth of *modern men* consists more and more of "pure economic interests"' and that 'in our modern economy there always exists the possibility of re-acquisition, with the result that the distinction between ownership (meaning the interest in preserving individual tangible objects) and money (representing the possibility of acquiring ownership) has lost some of its importance' (emphasis added): 'Liability for Information and Opinions Causing Pure Economic Loss to Third Parties: A Comparison of English and German Case Law', in B. Markesinis (ed.), *The Gradual Convergence* (Oxford University Press, Oxford, 1994), pp. 99, 108.

[6] It would not be possible to mention the great number of reference works on this subject. See, however, as to the different legal traditions, R. von Ihering, *Der Zweck im Recht* (Leipzig, 1877); A. Hägerström, *Das Prinzip der Wissenschaft. Eine logisch-erkenntnistheoretische Untersuchung. I. Die Realität* (Uppsala, 1908); F. Gény, *Méthode d'interprétation et sources en droit privé positif* (2nd edn, Paris, 1919); R. Pound, *The Spirit of Common Law* (Harvard, 1921).

[7] See M. Bussani and U. Mattei, 'The Common Core Approach to the European Private Law', in (1997/98) 3 *Columbia Journal of European Law* (Fall/Winter) 339; M. Bussani and U. Mattei, 'Le fonds commun du droit privé Européen', in (2000) 1 *Revue Internationale De Droit Comparé* 29.

## 9 General conclusions of the study

MAURO BUSSANI AND VERNON VALENTINE PALMER

### Irrelevance of legal families

The question of the recoverability of pure economic loss is a generic question for all legal systems in Europe. As we pointed out earlier, it is not just a civil law vs. common law issue. Civil law countries are found amongst the liberal, pragmatic and conservative regimes of Europe, and thus to the extent that Europe is divided, the civil law countries are themselves divided, not *from* the common law, but *along with* the common law. An important question is how to understand the various differences and similarities between these systems, and whether there is any common core of agreement on this question, but this will have little to to with the 'legal families' in which they happen to be placed.

### Absence of methodological common core

Clearly, it is more difficult to find a common set of principles or a common set of methods when we limit our horizons to the field of tort alone. Comparisons focused solely upon tort rules and structures have a tendency to highlight (to exaggerate?) the structural and technical diversities, rather than commonalities between these systems. Anyone who collects general impressions through the monocle of delict will of course notice that liberal regimes permit recovery far more frequently than conservative regimes (e.g. France: seventeen recoveries, Belgium: thirteen compared to Sweden: one and Portugal: seven).

Methodologically speaking, the tort scene strikes us as diverse and unsettled. Our research reveals that four principal methodologies dominate the European landscape, and although some countries resort to more than one of these methods (thus adding to the complexity) generally each has one characteristic means of dealing with the issue of pure economic loss.[1] Thus the compensation issue may be left to (1) flexible causal determinations (the characteristic method found in the liberal regimes); (2) preliminary judicial screening using a 'duty of care' analysis (the approach particularly prominent in England and Scotland); (3) recourse (in Austria, Sweden and Finland) to causation techniques aiming to exclude 'third party loss'; and (4) a scheme of absolute rights that, by deliberate omission, leaves this interest unprotected (the approach of Austria, Germany and Portugal). Perhaps a simpler way to summarize all this methodological diversity is to remember the initial point of departure. The liberal regimes rely upon general clauses and start from an inclusive position, the conservative regimes impose a limited listing of protected interests and start from an exclusionary position. The first group allows recovery *in* principle, the second denies it *on* principle. One grants recoveries through tort actions, the other must deny relief in tort if it cannot find an exception, and failing that, it must turn to paracontractual actions such as *culpa in contrahendo* or contracts with protective effects for third parties. Indeed, the resort to contractual actions as a means of overcoming the narrowness of tort protection reveals *still another* methodological split in Europe: some countries deal with this issue solely in tort while others rely heavily on flexible contractual devices to palliate the sternness of their tort approach. The German courts would allow contractual recoveries of pure economic loss in about 20 per cent of our hypotheticals, which surpasses the recoveries that the BGB permits in tort.[2] In this same vein we have already seen that formal structures and legal jargon are sometimes façades which hide a deeper reality, and no great reliance should be placed upon them. French and German law may appear to have radically opposed starting points, but in both countries the practice of the courts seems to adopt a more intermediate position.[3] All in all, it is fair to conclude that there is no *methodological* common core that can be suggested by this research.

## Awareness of the time factor

Furthermore, any general assessment of common tendencies in Europe must take into account the factor of time. The attentive reader will have

---

[1] These four methods are discussed above under the editors' comparative comments to Case 2 ('Cable II – Factory Shutdown').
[2] See Table 8.2 above, for a comparison of contractual and delictual bases of recovery.
[3] K. Zweigert and H. Kötz, *Introduction to Comparative Law* (3rd edn, trans. T. Weir, Clarendon, Oxford, 1998), p. 628.

noticed that European attitudes toward pure economic loss are not always stable. Indeed, some recent developments should serve as a warning that we could be describing a 'provisional' common core in which some positions are still evolving and changing. In the past 40 years alone, Italy changed its stripes in effect from a system of 'protected interests' to a general clause system. Within that same period England admitted as many as five exceptions to the rule of no-recovery. If we take an even longer view we may note that in the twentieth century, France abandoned a more restrictive attitude that had been current throughout the previous century (based in an unlawfulness conception) in order to match more closely its codistic liberal façade.[4] Moving along an opposite path, Austrian history shows a departure from the liberal façade of the ABGB in the second half of the nineteenth century, and since then its legal system has been accepting bodily German doctrinal thought on pure economic loss together with the usual justifications for its control.[5] Our point is simply that legal positions have not stood still and some have abruptly changed and may change again. Therefore, old, and even current snapshots of the law may be of limited utility in determining the existence or non-existence of a common core.

## The substantive common core

Having concluded that methodological consensus does not exist, we now consider to what extent there is any substantive common core on pure economic loss.

Whether there is a common core of principles governing pure economic loss, however, could depend to a large extent upon our instinctual reformulation of the question by our national traditions and cultures. Yet comparative law, if it teaches anything, teaches us to resist this. Culture and tradition have summary ways of telling us to which field this question belongs (tort or contract?) and thus may project a prejudice about its proper resolution and the coherence or incoherence of national solutions. To those who believe that pure economic loss is the natural preserve of tort, there may be little common core. But to those who would say that it is the natural preserve of contract, we think there will appear to be even less common core. Our comparative and fact-based

---

[4] This historical turnabout is discussed above in Part I, Chapter 5.
[5] See above in Part I, Chapter 5, discussion of Austria's 'massive interior transplant'.

approach to the question makes us sceptical of these labels. The issue is situated at the frontier of obligations where there is both tort and contract, or where tort behaves like contract and contract behaves like tort. We believe that the existence of a common core can be discussed in factual terms.

This discussion requires us to weigh in the balance the degree of European agreement on three subjects: (1) consequential economic loss; (2) intentionally-caused economic loss; and (3) the selective protection of negligently caused economic loss. In the aggregate these elements will permit us to see the contours of a 'limited common core' on pure economic loss.

## Consequential loss

We have already highlighted that if economic loss is connected to the slightest damage to person or property of the plaintiff, the whole may be recuperated without question – provided that all the other requirements for the action to be successful are met.[6] This 'parasitic' loss is recoverable because it presupposes the existence of physical harm to the victim, whereas pure economic loss strikes the victim's wallet and nothing else. Consequential loss of this kind is protected in every European system within this study and can be seen as one area of substantive European agreement, but this generalization must be qualified in two senses. First, we are really saying that consequential loss can be unobjectionably recovered both in those countries that recognize such distinctions and in those countries that do not. Therefore, the common result is entirely distinct from the diverse reasoning which produces it. Secondly, while consequential economic loss is protected in principle in those countries that have an exclusionary rule, still the scope attributed to this causal notion varies significantly within those countries and produces some non-uniform applications.[7]

---

[6] Of course courts theoretically have a range of analytical devices at their disposal to exonerate the defendant from liability for consequential economic loss, e.g., the act was not a breach of duty, the damage was too remote, or the plaintiff had voluntarily assumed the risk. But what is worth noting is the attitudinal change that comes over the judge once the economic loss is causally connected to plaintiff's own physical harm. The importance that legal systems place on physical security from careless acts is so well recognized and accepted that courts rarely feel the need to justify or explain.

[7] For full details, see the analysis of these variations in editors' comparative comments to Case 1 ('Cable I – The Blackout').

## Intentional harm

Here is an additional building block to the common core. All systems agree that intentionally inflicted pure economic loss is recoverable in circumstances where the conduct in question is regarded as culpable, immoral or contrary to public policy. Certainly, in these kinds of cases it may not always be easy for the plaintiff to satisfy the burden of proof (although this may be reduced somewhat by the broad meaning given in some systems to the 'intention' element), but it is significant from the comparative point of view that the shift to higher degree of culpability is sufficient reason to impose liability in all systems.

## Key areas of selective protection

Earlier we noted several important areas of substantive divergence where no common core appears to exist, but we also pointed out, as an alternative perspective, that pure economic loss could also be seen as selectively protected across Europe. To see the subject as *selectively protected* is to acknowledge that there exist pockets of 'privileged' loss-types in the conservative and pragmatic countries where compensation is awarded. When these isolated recoveries are joined to the corresponding awards in the more liberal countries, a kind of 'limited common core' for negligently caused economic loss stands in relief. Admittedly this type of 'limited' common core may seem like an artificial construct, that focuses upon results alone to the exclusion of the differentiating methods and theories by which those results were reached. Yet, as stated earlier, it is in keeping with the nature of our fact-based inquiry to look behind cultural–linguistic obstacles in order to compare national solutions. In penetrating to this level, we have uncovered three areas where substantive consensus exists.

The first is when plaintiff's loss is due to negligently performed professional services. There is widespread agreement that the careless notary in Case 14 ('Poor Legal Services'), the negligent auditor in Case 17 ('Auditor's Liability') and the negligent credit rating institute in Case 20 ('An Anonymous Telephone Call') will be responsible for the economic losses of some persons (beyond their clients) with whom they had no contractual tie. Although there may be specific requirements that must be met in some systems that others do not clearly impose (for example, the German and English emphasis upon showing the 'reliance' of the third party), still it seems fair to say that in many situations (provided indeterminate and excessive liability is excluded) plaintiffs may recover losses caused by negligent professionals regardless of the general features and traditions of a given tort law system. This seems to reflect the collective view that a high standard of professional services can and ought to be maintained.[8]

A second area of agreement exists in the area of compensation for 'transferred' economic loss.[9] This agreement undoubtedly arises because jurists in both liberal and conservative countries have recognized that transferred loss is liability neutral from a tortfeasor perspective, and whatever difficulties it poses are more of a technical nature than of policy or equity. Thus in the case of the 'Convalescing Employee' (Case 4), eight countries protect the employer who is forced to continue to pay his injured worker's salary without receiving any work in return. Although that sort of loss is purely economic it is essentially the worker's claim for lost salary due to his incapacity that has been transferred, by statute or by contract, to the employer. Similarly in the case of the 'Cancelled cruise' (Case 8) the ship's lessee essentially claims the loss of profits that might have equally been lost by the ship's owner had they seen fit to operate the boat in the cruise business instead of leasing it for that purpose. Nine countries, including three conservative regimes which, as we know, do not generally protect pure economic loss in tort, would protect the economic interest of the ship's lessee in these circumstances. Many countries would also compensate the 'Dutiful Wife' (Case 10) for the reasonable value of the care that she rendered to her injured husband. Since all the countries in this study agree that a husband who receives physical injuries may seek compensation, not only for his injuries but for the reasonable cost of healthcare services, it is clear that the wife's claim can be seen as the transferred loss of the husband. Seven countries including, once again, two conservative regimes would protect the economic claims of the wife in these circumstances.

The convergence of results in these cases suggest to us that perhaps all cases of transferred loss form part of a 'limited common core'.

The third and last area of substantive agreement involves cases in which the defendant has negligently interfered with the conduct of plaintiff's business and trade (Case 16 – 'Truck Blocking Business

---

[8] We referred to this policy in our editors' comparative comments to Cases 14 ('Poor Legal Services'), 17 ('Auditor's Liability') and 20 ('An Anonymous Telephone Call').
[9] We have previously defined and classified 'transferred loss' in our Introduction. See Chapter 1, and text at notes 25–30.

Premises') or has carelessly issued an incorrect character reference (Case 18 – 'Wrongful Job Reference'). Compensation in Case 16 is allowed in eight countries and compensation in Case 18 by eleven countries, and liberal, pragmatic and conservative regimes all figure in this list. As we noted earlier in our comparative comments, in these fact situations, these results are surely influenced by the absence of any spectre of indeterminate or widespread liability.

## Summary on the 'limited common core'

When we step back from the tableau of conclusions presented above, the general contours of agreement and disagreement may be discerned. On the one hand, it is clear that Europe is particularly divided over methodology, theories of relief and causes of action. There is no methodological common core, for the systems retain their distinctive façades and their characteristic ways of controlling or regulating the issue. Further, and now approaching the question at a more substantive level, Europe is also split over the outcomes that should occur in a number of loss situations caused by negligence. Here it is apparent that metalegal factors, such as the 'floodgates', philosophical values and historical conservatism, drive the outcomes. On the other hand, we have attempted to show that a 'limited' common core deserves to be recognized at the substantive level. As just seen, Europe basically agrees to the recoverability of consequential loss, intentionally caused loss, losses due to negligent professional services and transferred losses, and perhaps in other circumstances where the risk of indeterminate liability is under control. These are the contours of selective protection. While financial interests are not as comprehensively protected as other interests, there is indeed a considerable core frame of European protection. Across façades, regimes and traditions, pure economic loss is recoverable whenever the latter is a direct consequence of the infringement of a right or of an interest that the legal system means to protect. If we judge by the developments of the past 40 years, this frame has been increasing and is likely to continue to grow.

## 10 The recoverability of pure economic loss within the perspective of a European codification

MAURO BUSSANI AND VERNON VALENTINE PALMER

### Introduction

One may wonder how this study and its results might be of possible use to the would-be codifiers of a European Code of the Law of Torts.

The comparative method on which we relied has probably unearthed many common features that were hitherto obscure in traditional legal analysis. It may also be true that our research lends itself as a valuable instrument for future legal harmonization, in the sense that it has hopefully provided reliable data for use in devising transnational solutions that may prove workable in practice.

Nevertheless, any codification attempt should be seasoned with – and this applies not simply to tort law but to all subjects – a certain amount of constructive scepticism. Leaving aside any positive or negative bias vis-à-vis the very idea of the code, as well as the many reasons put forward to deny, support or simply postpone its feasibility,[1] the point is

---

[1] On the overall aspects of the debate, see the contributions to the symposium 'Towards a European Civil Code' held in The Hague on 28 February 1997, (1997) 5 *European Review of Private Law*. A. P. Legrand, 'Sens et non-sens d'un code civil européen', (1996) 48 *RIDC* 779, 800; A. P. Legrand, 'Against a European Civil Code', (1997) 60 *Modern Law Review* 44, strongly argues in favour of legal pluralism, which provides a wealth of solutions and techniques to ensure flexibility. See also G. Alpa, 'The European Civil Code: "E Pluribus Unum"', (1999) 14 *Tulane European and Civil Law Forum* 1; H. Collins, 'European Private Law and Cultural Identity of States', (1995) 3 *European Review of Private Law* 353; B. S. Markesinis, 'Why a Code is not the Best Way to Advance the Cause of European Legal Unity', (1997) 5 *European Review of Private Law* 519; V. Zeno-Zencovich, 'The "European Civil Code". European Legal Traditions and Neo-Positivism', (1998) 6 *European Review of Private Law*; H. Kötz, 'Comparative Legal Research: Its Function in the Development of Harmonised Law. The European Perspective', in Juridiska Fakulteten I Uppsala (ed.), *Towards Universal Laws – Trends in National, European and International Law-making* (Iustus Forlag, Uppsala, 1995); T. Weir, 'Divergent Legal Systems in a Single Member States', (1998) 6 *ZEuP* 564. For a more general perspective see R. Sacco, 'La codification, forme

that the inquiry into 'pure economic loss' confirms how deeply conscious the code-drafters will need to be about the overall implications of remoulding the law of tort.

## Pure economic loss astride private law frontiers

The kind of awareness that is required in legal debate can be simply illustrated by consideration of the following. Throughout our study we have seen the conceptual dependency which exists between underlying contract and property ideas and the law of tort. Suffice it to recall, for example, the problems raised by the notion itself of pure economic loss, the flexible boundaries that comparative analysis enabled us to draw as to the so-called 'consequential' economic loss, as well as the great reliance upon contract rules to handle the issue in certain regimes. Even more strikingly than in other domains, any attempt at codification concerning pure economic loss therefore will be closely dependent on the solutions which the same code intends to offer in the other fields of private law, mainly with regard to contract and property.

To give further evidence of to what we are referring, we can return to some examples taken from our study. The first of them concerns 'The Cancelled Cruise', the second the 'Cable' cases, the third is the relevance of contract law to our issue, and finally the 'Double Sale' case.

Regarding the first case, if possession is included in the framework of property rights, or if it is at any rate protected by proprietary remedies, any infringement of possession will permit recovery of the economic loss, regardless of whether it is called consequential or pure.

---

dépassée de législation?', in *Rapports nationaux italiens au XI Congrès international de droit comparé* (Caracas, 1982, Giuffrè, Milano, 1982), p. 65; 'Symposium: Codification in the Twenty-first Century', (1998) 31 *University of California at Davis Law Review*. See also M. Bussani and U. Mattei, 'The Common Core Approach to the European Private Law', (1997/98) 3 *Columbia Journal of European Law* (Fall/Winter) 339; M. Bussani and U. Mattei, 'Le fonds commun du droit privé Européen', (2000) 1 *Revue internationale de droit comparé*, 29; M. Bussani and U. Mattei (eds.), *Making European Law: Essays on the 'Common Core' Project* (Trento, Quaderni del Dipartimento di Scienze Giuridiche, 2000); M. Bussani, 'Current Trends in European Comparative Law: The Common Core Approach', (1998) 21 *Hastings International and Comparative Law Review* 4, 785; M. Bussani, '"Integrative" Comparative Law Enterprises and the Inner Stratification of Legal Systems', (2000) 8 *European Review of Private Law*, 83; M. Bussani, 'In Search of a European Private Law', in J. Sinde Monteiro (ed.), *Um Código Civil para a Europa* (Coimbra University Press, Coimbra, 2002), pp. 79 ff.; M. Bussani, 'Before and Beyond a European Civil Code', in ERA (Europäische Rechtsakademie-Trier) (ed.), *European Civil Code(s)* (Trier, 2002), pp. 109 ff.

If possession is not included in the property framework, however, or if the power of control over the thing is not sufficient in and of itself for the holder to be deemed a possessor, then the recoverability of the economic loss caused to the holder (by interference with the thing itself) becomes an issue to be settled.[2]

Regarding the second cases, if the right to electricity (but the same could apply to Hertzian or other electromagnetic waves)[3] is deemed a right *in rem* whose transfer from the supplier to the user is completed as of the date of the agreement, any damage to the system supplying that energy (such as the cutting of power cables) will be considered an infringement of property rights and therefore will raise no problems in any of the legal systems here investigated.

Regarding the relevance of contract law, if the manner in which Austria and Germany apply the notions of *culpa in contrahendo* or the 'contract with protective effect to third parties'[4] is adopted as a model for a European code, it is beyond doubt that many of the issues raised in our hypothetical cases will be settled by contract principles, with little need to resort to tort law rules.[5]

The code's infrastructure regarding transfer of ownership would clearly have manifold effects in any 'Double Sale' such as Case 12. Indeed, the right of the first buyer (*solo consensu*) to obtain compensation depends on a variety of factors, the role of which is actually to define who has the property right in the thing. These factors include the presence of good or bad faith, the completion of delivery (for movables), compliance with formalities such as registration and recordation (for immovables) and the effects assigned to the registration itself.

---

[2] Cf. C. von Bar, *The Common European Law of Torts*, vol. II (Clarendon Press, Oxford, 2000), p. 55.

[3] For the debate on the legal nature of these entities, see U. Mattei, *Basic Principles of Property Law. A Comparative Legal and Economic Introduction* (Greenwood Press, Westport, CT/London, 2000), pp. 76 ff., 153.

[4] The same could be said for notions such as the French concept 'chaîne de contrats'. This refers to a series of contracts which, though distinct in law, form part of an economic complex. An example can be found in the chain which links a site owner to the contractor, the contractor to the subcontractor and the latter to the supplier of the building materials. See H. Kötz and A. Flessner, *European Contract Law*, I (trans. T. Weir, Oxford University Press, Oxford, 1997), pp. 255 ff. As to this technical notion and its actual impact on the recovery of pure economic losses, see G. Viney, 'Introduction à la responsabilité' (LGDJ, 1995), pp. 338 ff.

[5] Nevertheless, different technical rules could still exist in each liability regime of liability concerning, e.g., prescriptive periods or rules on the burden of proof.

## The place of pure economic loss within different possible frames of a tort law codification

The above simple remarks only hint at the web of relationships that affect our subject. The matter is far more complex. Even when all the above (and possibly other)[6] boundary issues have been clearly settled, the recoverability of pure economic loss will still depend on other critical choices. First among these is the large political choice that needs to be made at a more general level about tort law.

Any choices made by the drafters and codifiers are indeed the surrogate political acts of the legislator (whether the latter's approval of their work is one of default, rubber stamp or close consultation). Thus, any decision by the redactors to decrease, enlarge or simply maintain the existing unequal levels of protection for pure economic loss across Europe is first and foremost a political question that must be answered. For example, should Europe attempt to codify on the basis of the 'limited common core' that we have found to exist? Or would it be better to generalize from the greater protection for pure economic loss found in liberal regimes such as France? Or would it be best to reduce the level of protection to a lower common denominator to cover only intentionally inflicted loss or consequential economic loss? All questions as to the most appropriate way of stating the code's tort principles, whether via a general clause or a list of absolute rights, *initially* depend upon setting a policy with respect to the compensation issue.

Certainly, the substantive decision necessarily has implications for the draft methodology to be adopted. For example, if the decision is to protect pure economic loss *in general*, rather than in highly specific *privileged loss-type* situations, then a general clause will be the legal instrument to implement it, rather than a formula of protected interests.[7] Yet – as

---

[6] For example, our issue would certainly be affected, both theoretically and operationally, by any decision to allow or forbid the concurrence of tortious and contractual actions (see H. Beale, A. Hartkamp, H. Kötz and D. Tallon (eds.), *Contract Law* (2002), pp. 67 ff.). As mentioned (see above Part I, Chapter 5) the second alternative is better known as the French 'règle du non-cumul'. This rule clearly has a particular bearing because, if the European Code embraces it, we would predict that some cases on pure economic loss would disappear from tort law only to reappear as contract law questions.

[7] Estathios Banakas points out that '[The protected interest device does] leave it to the courts to make the social policy as they go along, with regard to liability...judges can use this device to open or close categories of liability, and create privileged loss-types, as shown in the English and German practice', S. Banakas, 'Liability for Incorrect

we suggest further on – one should have no illusions that even the clearest policies, whether stated in general clauses or protected interest formulas, will be translated into the 'law in action' without undergoing interpretative modification by judges and scholars.

## Possible basic scenarios

Our scepticism aside, however, let us try to gain better understanding of the most notable alternatives available to would-be code-drafters. This can be done by depicting the basic legal scenarios that the would-be codifiers may consider. What follows is an attempt to clarify – squaring the future (virtual) landscape with the actual results of our study – the solutions that can be supplied to the issue.

For our purposes, there are two possible frameworks that are worth taking into consideration. The first concerns a tort law system where the code-drafters cast a set of provisions in which they have predetermined (along with the other possible requirements of the cause of action) the types of harm which alone can trigger tort liability. This is a neat option which would re-enact at the European level a general feature to be found in many notable national legal systems. The second scenario considers the adoption of another distinctive feature already present in a good many national regimes: a general clause which, grounded on the requirement of culpable behaviour, leaves scholars and judges free to mark out the contours of tort law recoverability.

These two scenarios will be addressed below, but it should be noted that we will confine our discussion to negligence-based regimes.[8] We dispense with any extensive review of pure economic loss stemming

---

Financial Information: Theory and Practice in a General Clause System and in a Protected Interests System', (1999) 7 *European Review of Private Law* 261, at 284–5.

[8] Certainly, no question would arise if the inspiration for the Code were an unconditional faith in 'laissez faire' economics (for an overall assessment of the reverse perspective, see recently D. Howarth, 'Three Forms of Responsibility: On the Relationships Between Tort Law and the Welfare State', (2001) 60 CLJ 553). That would imply enactment of a regime in which, no matter what kind of interest has been infringed, only intentionally inflicted harm might give rise to liability. Accordingly the issue of compensation for pure economic loss would largely disappear from the legal debate. This hypothesis is definitely extreme and highly unlikely. It can be just added, however, that – as is well known (see above, Part I, Chapter 1 and Part III, Chapter 9) – such a codistic scenario would entail no disagreement in Europe as to compensation for pure economic loss.

from strict liability rules, because any solution would depend on the policy options taken up by the codifiers on two issues: (1) the selection of those matters to be covered by strict liability rules; and (2) the choice between a rigid typecast pattern denying the application of strict liability provisions beyond their own original scope, on the one hand, and the possibility of expanding the scope of strict liability provisions by analogy or otherwise, on the other.[9] As far as the expansion of strict liability is concerned, one should be aware that national strict liability regimes are often grounded on pieces of legislation (e.g. covering car and railway accidents, or nuclear power accidents or products liability). General policy and technical details may differ considerably across countries, thereby giving rise to difficult problems of co-ordination which might even precede the crucial selection of the harms to be compensated.[10]

---

[9] For a survey of the ongoing debate on all these points see C. von Bar, *The Common European Law of Torts* (Clarendon Press, Oxford, 1998), p. 10; W. van Gerven, J. Lever and P. Larouche, *Tort Law* (Hart, Oxford, 2000), pp. 537 ff.

[10] Moreover, throughout Western legal systems the most important economic burden of strict liability rules normally (though not always, consider, e.g., automobile liability in many countries) rests upon entrepreneurs and enterprises, that is to say, upon subjects and activities for which it is usually impossible to compress the number of accidents that they are obliged to compensate below a given threshold. See generally V. V. Palmer, 'General Theory of the Inner Structure of Strict Liability – Common Law, Civil Law, Comparative Law', (1988) 62 *Tulane Law Review* 1303. Therefore, one could at least urge a harmonization which would enable European entrepreneurs to rationalize the foreseeable cost connected with accidents that they must compensate, and European citizens not to suffer discrimination according to the place where they have suffered the damage. A discrimination which depends not only on the simple presence/absence of a strict liability regime, but also on its operative contents: e.g. the limitation period on bringing the action, or the caps imposed by legal provisions on the minimum and/or the maximum amount of damages to be recovered. Suffice it to consider that, as far as products liability is concerned, Germany, Portugal and Spain have introduced ceilings on the recoverability of loss stemming from personal injuries; or that as regards the threshold above which a loss becomes recoverable there are differences amounting to more than 200 per cent among national provisions on the matter. See G. Howells, 'Product Liability', in A. Hartkamp, M. Hesselink, E. Hondius, C. Joustra and E. du Perron (eds.), *Towards a European Civil Code* (2nd edn, Ars Aequi Libri, Nijmegen, 1998), pp. 449, 458.

On the other hand, if one considers that a defendant's 'pocket' cannot be bottomless, and if the target is to unify the treatment of European victims, whatever unified regime is adopted, it seems reasonable that it should be linked to a parallel adoption of compulsory third party insurance and a unification of standard clauses intended to cover (at least) the major risks of enterprise liability. The relevance of, and the debate on, this issue are surveyed by J. Stapleton, 'Tort, Insurance and Ideology', (1995) 58 Mod. LR 820 ff.

## A code imposing liability on the ground of a rigid typecast set of provisions

The picture would be sufficiently clear if the drafters of the code were to adopt – following the Finnish, German and Swedish, patterns, and from a different perspective the English and Scottish approach as well – some sort of *nullum crimen sine lege* principle, whereby the recoverable losses would only be those selected by the tort law provisions of the code itself. Once the infliction of pure economic loss had been included in, or excluded from, the 'crimina' cast by the code, answers would be forthcoming to most questions on recoverability.

Nevertheless, problematic in this respect would be two issues well known to the reader: (1) the need for a careful balance to be struck among the possible reasons underpinning the exclusion or the inclusion of recoverability, an undertaking which would require consideration of the various treatments made of the different cases of pure economic loss across the legal regimes of the continent; and (2) the relationship between the tort law options to be adopted and the choices made in other fields (especially in contract and property law) as to the remedies available to the victim.

Indeed, to descend from the lofty heights of theoretical speculation to the concrete reality of the 'law in action', one should bear in mind what has occurred to the BGB over the years. The restrictive wording of the German code – barring as it does the recovery of pure economic loss – has never prevented German interpreters from adding new rights to the list (as happened with the 'right of the established and ongoing commercial enterprise', *Recht am eingerichteten und ausgeübten Gewerbebetrieb*, included as 'another right' under § 823 (1)); from moulding the requirement of an 'intention contrary to good morals' (§ 826) in order to absorb a number of grossly negligent conducts; or from obtaining 'lateral support' from contractual rules in order to compensate pure economic losses otherwise unrecoverable under tort law rules.[11]

The risk which any 'typecast' choice should be ready to counter is therefore easy to detect: that system may be imposed, but there is no

---

[11] Indeed, the German, Austrian and English experiences show that there is no reason to impair privity of contract, enabling a third-party profit from this impairment, unless the given system is forced to do so by a failure of the mechanisms supplied by other legal branches of the law, namely property and contract law. For a similar cultural framework, but with different conclusions reached as to the mutual role of contract and tort rules, see von Bar, *Law of Torts* (1998), pp. 464 ff. and vol. II (2000), pp. 52–6.

guarantee it will encounter judges and scholars at the European level who are trained to use the complex machinery of weights and counterweights with which the German system and tradition are endowed.

## A tort law codification adopting a 'general clause': the selection of recoverable losses as the crucial choice

Somewhat different is the perspective that would arise, were the codifiers to fall back on the 'general clause' model found in the 'liberal' tort law regimes. In this direction, the core problem is traditionally constituted by the selection – to be made not *ex ante* by the code, as in the 'typecast' regimes, but by the interpreters *ex post* – of the recoverable losses.

Undeniably, there are many further choices which would confront the drafters of a European code: e.g. the relevance of mental capacity, the possible variety of standards of conduct, the questionable equivalence of intention to gross negligence (*culpa lata dolo aequiparatur*), and so forth. Undoubtedly, however, when one looks at the 'liberal' tort law scenario, one inevitably realises that the fundamental issue at stake is what interests are to be protected by negligence law, and to what extent.

Accordingly, one should bear in mind that whenever fault liability is controlled by general rules or general clauses, the wording of the latter has always openly delegated to scholars and judges the task of defining the scope and the technical devices to be employed in the day-to-day administration of liability issues. Hence, one should be aware of the possible outcomes that might stem from reference to such general clauses in a transnational context.

There is no doubt that open-ended rules of this kind may be of great help in overcoming the obstacles raised by local case law and/or scholars in some systems against the recoverability of pure economic loss. Nonetheless, this choice would also present a substantial risk which appears to be unavoidable. Moreover, this risk must be neutrally assessed, because any stance taken for or against it implies the answer to the broader question of the costs that one intends to reduce by means of the codification.[12]

---

[12] On this subject see, e.g. U. Mattei, 'The Issue of European Civil Codification and Legal Scholarship. Biases, Strategies and Developments,' (1998) 21 *Hastings International and Comparative Law Journal* 883; M. Bussani, '"Integrative" Comparative Law Enterprises' 83.

The risk is that, by exploiting the broad wording of the clause (such as the famous 'Any act whatever of man which causes damage to another obliges him by whose fault it occurred to make reparation': art. 1382 of the French Civil Code), national courts and scholars continue to rely on their legal culture; that is to say, on their traditional repertoire of solutions and technicalities. This may induce the interpreters of some legal systems to fulfil the general clause requirements by referring to a (hidden) protected-interest agenda by means of which they would exclude any newcomer, say, by means of causation or remoteness of damage arguments.[13] As a consequence the previous national operative rules would survive through an interpretation of the new 'written' rules built upon the old reasonings and arguments.

In other words we could have, on the one hand, 'liberal' judges and scholars who promote solutions which keep the door open to the recoverability of pure economic loss, and on the other, 'conservative' interpreters who continue to handle the issue with the technical devices to which they are accustomed, exploiting[14] any technical requirements of the cause of action that might serve to bar the recovery. Pragmatic regimes, in their turn, could still push their candour to the forefront of the debate, treating the general clause as they currently do with regard to the duty of care or causation requirements. Ultimately, policy arguments would retain their decisive role in making the compensation issue swing back and forth, according to what is felt to be 'just, fair and reasonable'[15] and not widening (too much) the 'floodgates' of recoverability.

---

[13] Cf. von Bar, *Law of Torts* (2000), pp. 52–3.

[14] This scenario would not differ greatly from either the current Austrian situation (notwithstanding § 1295 ABGB) or the one that French, Belgian and Italian interpreters arrived at in the nineteenth century and for some decades of the twentieth, despite their codistic general clauses (art. 1382 French and Belgian Codes, art. 1151 Italian Code of 1865). In the latter countries, indeed, tort liability was imposed only where a particular tort had been committed. The Codes were not read as establishing liability for any damage whatsoever caused through fault; instead: 'tort in the sense of the civil law is an act by which, intentionally or negligently, the rights of another person are unlawfully injured'. K.-S. Zachariae, *Cours de droit civil français*, (French trans. C. Aubry and C. Rau from the 5th German edn, 1839), (2nd edn, Bruxelles, 1850), II, § 444. But see also C. Aubry and C. Rau, *Cours de droit civil français*, IV (4th edn, Paris, 1871), p. 745; M. Planiol, *Traité élémentaire de droit civil*, II (8th edn, Paris, 1921), pp. 260, 275; F. Laurent, *Principes de droit civil*, XX (Bruxelles/Paris, 1887), § 401, 404. In Italy, e.g. G. Brunetti, *Il delitto civile* (Firenze, 1906), pp. 215 ff.; G. Giorgi, *Teoria delle obbligazioni nel diritto moderno italiano*, vol. V (7th edn, Firenze, 1909), p. 215; and cf. R. Sacco, 'L'ingiustizia di cui all'art. 2043', *FP*, 1960, I, c. 1420 ff.

[15] See, e.g. *Murphy* v. *Brentwood DC* [1991] 1 AC 398 (HL).

## A destiny to be interpreted

Awareness of the foregoing considerations prompts us to emphasize the extent to which the absence of a single supreme court for private law matters is bound to affect the effectiveness of a European codification. Considering the lack of a unifying institution, the codifiers might hope to capture uniformity by following the existing consensus, falling back on what our inquiry has labelled the 'limited common core' of compensation for pure economic loss.[16]

Nevertheless, even if the 'limited common core' were adopted as a legislative goal, it is worth stressing again that one should not be surprised to find that the different factors shaping liability (such as the various mouldings of the subjective element of intentional harm,[17] or the widening or narrowing of the scope of protection attributed to a

---

[16] Thus imposing liability, not only in cases of consequential economic loss and of intentionally inflicted harm, but also in some cases of 'transferred loss', on some class of professional service providers, and on defendants who have infringed a victim's right or another interest which is protected statutorily or by the legal system at large (in a continental perspective it is of no matter if the protecting rules are to be found within the national or the European Union legal system: as to the latter source of liability, see above, Part I, Chapter I, fn 16.

[17] The broad impact of this phenomenon on tort law has made it possible to state as a general proposition 'the more serious the defendant's fault, the more direct its consequences': E. K. Banakas, 'Liability for Incorrect Financial Information: Theory and Practice in a General Clause System and in a Protected Interests System', (1999) 7 *European Review of Private Law* 261, 264. But see the detailed analysis, with numerous references to the historical and comparative literature by P. Cendon, *Il dolo nella responsabilità extracontrattuale* (Torino, 1976) passim. See also, e.g., J. S. Colyer, *A Modern View of the Law of Torts* (Pergamon Press, Oxford, 1966), p. 30; H. T. Terry, 'Proximate Consequences in the Law of Torts', (1914) 28 *Harvard Law Review* 10, 15, 26; D. Payne, 'Foresight and Remoteness in Negligence', (1962) 25 *Modern Law Review* 16; W. L. Prosser and W. P. Keeton, *On Torts* (5th edn, St. Paul, MN, 1984), pp. 205 ff., 296 ff.; E. Deutsch, *Fahrlässigkeit und erforderliche Sorgfalt* (Köln, 1963), pp. 62 ff., 157 ff., 171;. J. Delyannis, *La notion d'acte illicite considéré en sa qualité d'élément de la faute délictuelle* (Paris, 1952), p. 119; C. Aubry and C. F. Rau, *Cours de droit civil français* (6th edn, ed. P. Esmein, Paris, 1956), (Eng. trans., St. Paul, MN, 1969, § 444 bis, 445). Some further examples are given in R. Demogue, *Traité des obligations*, 1, III (Paris, 1923), p. 378; J. B. Ames, (1905) 18 *Harvard Law Review* 411, 412; W. A. Seavey, 'Negligence – Subjective or Objective?', (1927) 41 *Harvard Law Review* 1, at 13; Restatement of the Law, Torts, 2d, § 298 d; H. De Page, *Traité élémentaire de droit civil belge*, II (2nd edn, Bruxelles, 1948), pp. 1012 ff.; A. Sourdat, *Traité général de la responsabilité ou de l'action en damages-intérêts en dehors des contrats*, I, 2 (2nd edn, Paris, 1872), pp. 614 ff.; J. J. Honorat, *L'idée d'acceptation des risques dans la responsabilité civile* (Paris, 1969), passim, esp. pp. 28 ff., 89, 230; G. Viney and P. Jourdain, *Les conditions de la responsabilité* (2nd edn, Paris, 1998), pp. 491 ff.; P. Cane, *Atiyah's Accidents, Compensation and the Law* (5th edn, London, 1993), pp. 5, 95; H. R. W. Hart and A. Honoré, *Causation in the Law* (2nd edn, Oxford, 1985), pp. 40 ff., 77, 149 ff., 482 ff.; F. Chabas, *L'influence de la pluralité de causes sur le droit à réparation* (Paris, 1967), pp. 92 ff.

statute, and so forth) may give rise to different outcomes in the courts of one European country as compared to another.

All this, once more, shows nothing but the real and general problem faced by tort law, no matter what the 'façade' of the code or the purposes of the debate. The problem consists in the setting of technically and socially acceptable boundaries to the shifting of losses incurred by the victim on another party.[18] Whenever this shifting is not governed by property law, nor regulated by a contract between these persons, it is up to tort law to provide the solution.[19] Consequently – and in spite of the positivistic approach that some may take – the question of whether or not to award compensation to the victim falls to the interpreter charged with making the choice, that is, the judge and the scholar.[20]

Both of these actors have crucial tasks to perform. The scholar has primarily the role of uncovering whatever specific factors in each individual case are crucial to determining the liability. While it may be acceptable for a judge to make conclusionary statements, no scholar may merely assert that the causation was proximate, that a duty was justified because the parties were in a 'special relationship', that the plaintiff had reasonably relied on the defendant or merely that it was 'just, fair and reasonable' to impose the liability. Unless given substantive content, these are just labels. In their role of decision-inspirers, scholars are bound to focus explicitly on why and whether that particular causal act was proximate, the relation was special, the reliance was reasonable, and so forth.

Of course, the judge also brings his or her own legal culture to bear. S/he has admired or criticized the judicial precedents, and s/he has learnt the opinions of the given authorities at law school. S/he has both an attitude of self-restraint and a reservoir of legal notions, 'reactions' and answers stemming from the legal tradition of the country in which s/he lives.[21] This repertoire may also comprise the role that the judiciary plays in the given legal framework: a role entailing a variable degree of respect paid to scholarly opinions, to superior court rulings, to the

---

[18] For a comparative survey of the boundaries between the law of unjust enrichment and tort law, see von Bar, *Law of Torts* (1998), pp. 525 ff.; P. Gallo, 'Unjust Enrichment. A Comparative Analysis', (1992) 40 *American Journal of Comparative Law* 431.
[19] Cf. E. K. Banakas, 'Incorrect Financial Information' 261, 280.
[20] Cf. C. von Bar, *Tort Law* at pp. 464 ff.
[21] From the comparative 'law and economics' point of view, see M. Bussani and U. Mattei, 'Making the Other Path Efficient. Economic Analysis and Tort Law in Less Developed Countries', in E. Buscaglia, W. Ratliff and R. Cooter (eds.), *The Law and Economics of Development* (Greenwich, CT/London, 1997), pp. 149 ff.

legislature's prospective or actual choices. Hence, it is no surprise to find that decisions end up being grounded on the balance between the various circumstances of the given case, as qualified, i.e. sized, in legal terms through the overall interpretative culture of the decision-maker.

All of this is possibly true of many fields of law. But within private law, and tort law in particular, it does seem to be the appropriate way to appraise what the making of law entails – thus enabling us to bridge a multi-millennial tradition over the actual answers to present needs. Some might prefer to rephrase the same concept by saying that, at the core of tort law there are policy factors which frame the technical outcomes according to changes in social demands.[22] However, the choice of how to phrase the concept is neutral to our purposes, insofar as the legal notions of change[23] and tradition are essential to our issue too.

The point is that tort law constantly reveals its interpretative fate, its interpretative mode of existence. As we have seen, the issue of recoverability of pure economic loss does not escape this fate.

---

[22] Cf. the point made by J. Stapleton, 'Tort, Insurance and Ideology', 820.
[23] As to the 'awareness of the time factor' see above, in this part, chapter 9.

# Bibliography

References to treatises and commentaries in this bibliography are to the specific editions cited by the contributors to this volume.

Accursius, *Glossa ordinaria* (1581) D. 9.2.33.
Addison, C. G., *A Treatise on the Law of Torts or Wrongs and Their Remedies* (8th edn, eds. W. E. Gordon and W. H. Griffiths, 1906)
Alarcão, R. de, *Direito das Obrigações* (with S. Ribeiro, S. Monteiro, A. de Sá and B. Proença, 1983)
Albácar Rodríguez, J. L., 'La indemnización al Estado por los sueldos pagados a sus funcionarios durante el tiempo en que estuvieron lesionados a consecuencia de un delito', in: *La Ley*, 1982, 14
Albaladejo, M., *Comentarios al Código Civil y compilaciones forales* (arts. 705 ff.), X–1 (1987)
Alcover Garau, G., *La responsabilidad civil del fabricante* (1990)
Almeida Costa, M. J. de, *Responsabilidade Civil pela Ruptura das Negociações Preparatórias de um Contrato* (1984)
Almeida Costa, M. J. de, *Direito das Obrigações*, 9 a Edição Revista e Aumentada (2001)
Alonso Olea, M. and E. Casas Baamonde, *Derecho del trabajo* (13th edn, 1993; 14th edn, 1995)
Alonso Pérez, M., 'La responsabilidad precontractual', (1971) *Revista Crítica de Derecho Inmobiliario* 859
Alpa, G., 'Prassi negoziali d'impresa e teoria del contratto "sociale" nella elaborazione di un rapporto tra produttore e consumatore', (1975) T, 623
Alpa, G., 'Costruzione di nave e responsabilità del fabbricante', (1981) RGCirc. 528
Alpa, G., 'La "trasparenza" del contratto nei settori bancario, finanziario e assicurativo', (1992) GI, IV, 409
Alpa, G., 'The European Civil Code: "E Pluribus Unum"', (1999) 14 *Tulane European and Civil Law Forum* 1

Alpa, G. and M. Bessone, 'I fatti illeciti', in *Trattato di diritto privato diretto da Rescigno* (2nd edn, 1995)
Alpa, G. and M. Bessone, *La responsabilità civile, Aggiornamento 1988–1996* (1997)
Amesti Mendizábal, J., 'La actuación de los auditores en la sociedad anónima: la responsabilidad de los auditores de la sociedad anónima', III (1995) *Cuadernos de la Revista del Derecho Bancario y Bursátil*
Ancona, *La responsabilità del professionista* (1962)
Andersson, H., *Skyydsändamål och adekvans* (1993)
Andersson, H., *Trepartselationer i skadeståndsrätten* (1997)
Andrade, M. de, *Teoria Geral das Obrigações* (with R. de Alarcão, 1963)
André, R., *La réparation du préjudice corporel* (1986)
Androulidaki-Dimitriadou, I., *The Obligations from Business Good Faith* (1972)
Angeloni, F., *La responsabilità civile del notaio* (1990)
Annis, P., 'Tort or Contract: The Question of Recovery for Economic Loss', (1981) 13 *Ottawa Law Review* 469
Antunes Varela, J. de M., *Das Obrigações em Geral*, vol. I (9th edn, 1996); vol. II (7th edn, 1997)
Aquinas, T., *Summa theologiae*, II–II, Q. 61, a. 3
Arana Gondra, F. J., *Ley de auditoría de cuentas* (1995)
Arlen, J., 'Tort Damages', in B. Bouckaert and G. De Geest (eds.), *Encyclopedia of Law and Economics*, vol. 2 (2000)
Arndts, K. L., *Lehrbuch der Pandekten* (14th edn, 1889)
Arnheim, M., *Murphy's Law*, (1990) 134 S.J. 1058
Arrowsmith, S., *Civil Liability and Public Authorities* (1992)
Arroyo, I., *Estudios de derecho marítimo*, I (1985)
Ascensão, J. de Oliveira, *Direitos Reais* (5th edn, 1993)
Asúa, C., 'Comentario a la S.T.S. de 16 de mayo de 1988', (1988) 17 *Cuadernos Civitas de Jurisprudencia Civil* 513
Asúa, C., *La culpa in contrahendo* (1989)
Atiyah, P. S., 'Negligence and Economic Loss', (1967) 83 *Law Quarterly Review* 248
Atiyah, P. S., 'Tort Law and the Alternatives: Some Anglo-American Comparisons', (1987) 36 *Duke Law Journal* 1002
Aubry, C. F. and C. Rau, *Cours de droit civil français*, IV (4th edn, 1871); (6th edn, 1956, English trans. 1969)
Augustianakis, M., *The Contesting of Fraudulent Alienation* (1991)
Azo, *Summa Codicis* (1557) D. 9.2
Backhaus, J. G., 'Sombart's Modern Capitalism', in M. Blaug (ed.), *Pioneers in Economics*, vol. 30, s. III (reprint 1992)
Backhaus, J. G. and G. Krause (eds.), *On Political Economy of Transformation: Country Studies* (1997)
Backhaus, J. G., P. Tchipev and F. Stephen (eds.), *Mass Privatisation Schemes in Central and East European Countries. Implications on Corporate Governance* (1998)

Badosa Coll, F., 'Comentario al artículo 1186', in *Comentario del Código Civil*, II (1991)
Baldassarri, A., 'La responsabilità civile', in P. Cendon (ed.), *Il diritto privato nella giurisprudenza* (1998)
Balis, G., *Law of Obligations, General Part* (3rd edn, 1960)
Banakas, E. K. (ed.), *Tortious Liability for Pure Economic Loss: A Comparative Study* (1989)
Banakas, E. K. (ed.), *Civil Liability for Pure Economic Loss* (1996)
Banakas, E. K., 'Civil Liability for Pure Economic Loss', in United Kingdom National Committee of Comparative Law and The British Institute of International and Comparative Law (eds.), *UK Law for the Millennium* (1998)
Banakas, E. K. 'Liability for Incorrect Financial Information: Theory and Practice in a General Clause System and in a Protected Interests System', (1999) 7 *European Review of Private Law* 261
Baptista Machado, J., 'A Cláusula do Razoável', (1986) 119 *Revista de Legislação e de Jurisprudência* (also (1987) 120)
Barbeyrac, J., *Le droit de la nature et des gens par le baron de Pufendorf* (5th edn, 1734)
Barendrecht, J. M., 'Pure Economic Loss in the Netherlands', in E. H. Hondius (ed.), *Netherlands Reports to the Fifteenth International Congress of Comparative Law* (1998)
Barrett, S., 'Recovery of Economic Loss in Tort for Construction Defects: A Critical Analysis', (1989) 40 S.C.L. Rev 891
Barton, R. J., 'Drowning in a Sea of Contract: Application of the Economic Loss Rule to Fraud and Negligent Misrepresentation Claims', (2000) 41 *William Mary Law Review* 1789
Bateson, D. and O. Mak, 'Has the Dust Finally Settled on Latent Damage?', (2000) 17 I.C.L. Review 675
Becker, C., 'Schutz von Forderungen durch das Deliktsrecht?', in (1996) 196 *Archiv für die civilistische Praxis* 439
Bell, C. J., *Principles of the Law of Scotland* (10th edn, reprint 1998)
Benabent, A., *Droit Civil. Les Obligations* (5th edn, 1995)
Bengtsson, B. N., K. Ulf and E. Strömbäck, *Skadestånd* (3rd edn, 1995)
Benson, P., 'The Basis for Excluding Liability for Economic Loss in Tort Law', in D. G. Owen (ed.), *The Philosophical Foundations of Tort Law* (1995)
Bernstein, R., 'Civil Liability for Pure Economic Loss Under American Tort Law', (1998) 46 *American Journal of Comparative Law* 111
Bernstein, R., *Economic Loss* (2nd edn, 1998)
Berry, M. N., 'Intentionally Causing Economic Loss by Unlawful Means: A Consideration of the Innominate Tort', (1988) 6 *Otago Law Review* 533
Bertschy, T., 'Negligent Performance of Service Contracts and the Economic Loss Doctrine', (1984) 17 *J. Marshall Law Review* 249

Bianca, M., 'Dell'inadempimento delle obbligazioni, sub art. 1218-1229', in *Commentario Scialoja e Branca* (1979)
Bianca, M., *Diritto civile. V, La responsabilità* (1994)
Birks, P. (ed.), *Wrongs and Remedies in the Twenty-First Century* (1996)
Birocchi, I., *Saggi sulla formazione storica della categoria generale del contratto* (1988)
Bishop, W., 'Economic Loss in Tort', (1982) 2 *Oxford Journal of Legal Studies* 1
Bishop, W., 'Economic Loss: A Reply to Professor Rizzo', (1982) 2 *Oxford Journal of Legal Studies* 207
Bishop, W. and J. Sutton, 'Efficiency and Justice in Tort Damages: The Shortcomings of the Pecuniary Loss Rule', (1986) 15 *Journal of Legal Studies* 347
Blankenburg, E., 'Civil Litigation Rates as Indicators of Legal Culture', in D. Nelkin (ed.), *Comparing Legal Cultures* (1997)
Blanquer Uberos, R., 'Comentario al artículo 705', *Comentario del Código Civil*, vol. I (1991)
Boecken, W., *Deliktsrechtlicher Eigentumsschutz gegen reine Nutzungsbeeinträchtigungen* (Schriften zum Bürgerlichen Recht 181), (1995)
Bolt, A. T. and J. Spier, *De uitdijende reikwijdte van de aansprakelijkheid uit onrechtmatige daad* (1996)
Bonelli, F., 'Responsabilità delle società di revisione nella certificazione obbligatoria e volontaria dei bilanci', (1979) Riv. Soc. 968
Borrell Maciá, A., *Responsabilidades derivadas de culpa extracontratual civil* (2nd edn, 1958)
Bouman, H. A. and G. M. Tilanus-van Wassenaer, *Schadevergoeding: personenschade*, Monografieën Nieuw BW no. B-37 (1998)
Brandão Proença, J. C., *A Conduta do Lesado como Pressuposto e Critério de Imputação do Dano Extracontratual* (1997)
Brandner, H., 'Berufshaftung und Versicherung für Wirtschaftsprüfer', (1985) JZ 757
Brazier, M., *The Law of Torts* (8th edn, 1988)
Bricmont, G., *La responsabilité des architecte et entrepreneur* (3rd edn, 1971)
Brodie, D., 'In Defence of Donoghue', (1997) Jur Rev 65
Brox, H., *Allgemeines Schuldrecht* (21st edn, 1996; 25th edn, 1998)
Brox, H., *Besonderes Schuldrecht* (23rd edn, 1998)
Brüggemeier, G., *Deliktsrecht* (1st edn, 1986)
Brunetti, G., *Il delitto civile* (1906)
Brunnemann, J., *Commentarius in quinquaginta libros pandectarum* (ed. novissima, 1762) to D. 2.9.7 no. 11
Buchanan, J. M., *Cost and Choice* (1966)
Bürge, A., 'Die Kabelbruchfälle. Eine rechtsvergleichende Untersuchung zum schweizerischen, österreichischen und deutschen Haftpflichtrecht', (1981) JBl 57

Busnelli, F. D., *La lesione del credito da parte di terzi* (1964)
Busnelli, F. D., 'Perdita di una chance e risarcimento del danno risarcibile', (1965) IV, FI 47
Busnelli, F. D., 'Un clamoroso révirement della Cassazione: dalla "questione di Superga" al "caso Meroni"', (1971) FI, I, 1286
Busnelli, F. D., 'Tutela risarcitoria e diritto alla salute', in F. D. Busnelli and U. Breccia (eds.), *Tutela della salute e diritto privato* (1978)
Busnelli, F. D., 'La tutela aquiliana del credito: evoluzione giurisprudenziale e significato attuale del principio', (1987) RCDP 688
Busnelli, F. D., 'Figure controverse di danno alla persona nella recente evoluzione giurisprudenziale', (1990) RCP 469
Busnelli, F. D., 'Itinerari europei nella "terra di nessuno tra contratto e fatto illecito": la responsabilità da informazioni inesatte', (1991) CI 539
Bussani, M., *La colpa soggettiva. Modelli di valutazione della condotta nella responsabilità extracontrattuale* (1991)
Bussani, M., 'Faiblesse oblige', in *Scritti in onore di Rodolfo Sacco*, vol. I (1994)
Bussani, M., 'Problemi dell'illecito: superiorità soggettive e giudizio sulla colpa', in P. Cendon (ed.), *La responsabilità extracontrattuale* (1994)
Bussani, M., 'Tort Law and Development: Insights into the Case of Ethiopia and Eritrea', (1996) 40 *Journal of African Law* 1
Bussani, M., 'Perfiles comparativos sobre la responsabilidad civil: La culpa al servicio de los débiles', in J. F. Palomino Manchego and R. Velasquez Ramirez (eds.), *Modernas tendencias del derecho en America Latina. Actas de la I Convención Latinoamericana de Derecho*, (1997) 48 *Gaceta Juridica* 41-A
Bussani, M., 'Responsabilité des sujets atteints de troubles mentaux en Italie et en common law', in F. Chabas (ed.), *Gazette du Palais numéro spécial: Responsabilité civile*, nos. 45–6 (1997), 11
Bussani, M., 'A propos d'instruments protecteurs de la liberté de contracter valablement dans la jurisprudence italienne', in *La liberté dans tous ses états. Liber Amicorum à Jacques Georgel, Apogée* (1998)
Bussani, M., 'Current Trends in European Comparative Law: The Common Core Approach', (1998) 21 *Hastings International and Comparative Law Review* 4
Bussani, M., *As peculiaridades da noção de culpa: um estudo de direito comparado* (2000)
Bussani, M., ' "Integrative" Comparative Law Enterprises and the Inner Stratification of Legal Systems', in S. Feiden and C. U. Schmid (eds.), 'Evolutionary Perspectives and Projects on Harmonisation of Private Law in the EU, Eui Working Papers. Law No. 99/7', 1999; (2000) 1 *European Review of Private Law* 83
Bussani, M., 'La malizia attira. Intenzione e nesso causale nel diritto della responsabilità', (2000) XL *Rivista di Estetica* 114
Bussani, M., 'La responsabilità della pubblica amministrazione in diritto comparato', (2000) 3 *Responsabilità civile e previdenza* 547

Bussani, M. and U. Mattei, 'Making the Other Path Efficient. Economic Analysis and Tort Law in Less Developed Countries', in E. Buscaglia, W. Ratliff and R. Cooter (eds.), *The Law and Economics of Development* (1997)
Bussani, M. and U. Mattei, 'The Common Core Approach to European Private Law', (1997/98) 3 *Columbia Journal of European Law* 3
Bussani, M. and U. Mattei, 'Le fonds commun du droit privé Européen', (2000) 7 *Revue internationale de droit comparé* 29
Bussani, M. and U. Mattei (eds.), *Making European Law. Essays on the Common Core Project* (2000)
Bussoletti, M., *Le società di revisione* (1985)
Bydlinski, F., 'Vertragliche Sorgfaltspflichten zugunsten Dritter', (1960) JBl 359
Cadarso Palau, J., *La responsabilidad decenal de arquitectos y constructores* (1976)
Cafaggi, F., 'La responsabilità dei professionisti', entry in Dig. It. IV, *Discipline Privatistiche* (1998)
Cafaggi, F., *Profili di relazionalità della colpa* (1998)
Cajetan, *Commentaria to Thomas Aquinas, Summa theologica*, II-II (1698) Q. 62, a. 2 ad 4.
Calabresi, G., *The Costs of Accidents* (1971)
Calero, G. J., *Derecho de las averías y de los accidentes marítimos* (1992)
Calrão da Silva, J., *Responsabilidade do Produtor* (1990)
Canaris, C.-W., 'Der Schutz obligatorischer Forderungen nach § 823 I BGB', *Festschrift für Erich Steffen* (1995)
Cane, P., 'Economic Loss and the Tort of Negligence', (1980) 12 *Melbourne University Law Review* 408
Cane, P., 'The Metes and Bounds of Hedley Byrne', (1981) 55 ALJ 862
Cane, P., 'Economic Loss in Tort: Is the Pendulum Out of Control?', (1989) 52 *Modern Law Review* 200
Cane, P., *Atiyah's Accidents, Compensation and the Law* (5th edn, 1993)
Cane, P., 'Economic Loss in Tort and Contract', (1994) 58 *Rabels Zeitschrift für ausländisches und internationales Privatrecht* 429
Cane, P., *Tort Law and Economic Interests* (2nd edn, 1996)
Cane, P., 'The Blight of Economic Loss: Is There Life After *Perre v. Apand*?', (2000) 8 *Tort Law Journal* 246
Cantero, G., 'Comentario a la S.T.S. de 10 de febrero de 1988', *Anuario de Derecho Civil*, I (1989), 235
Cantero, G., 'Comentario al artículo 1473', *Comentario del Código Civil*, II (1991)
Caranta, R., *La responsabilità extracontrattuale della pubblica amministrazione* (1994)
Carbonnier, J., *Droit Civil. Tome IV. Les Obligations* (1993)
Carnelutti, F., *Danno e reato* (1940)
Carpenter, C. E., 'Interference with Contractual Relations', (1928) 41 *Harvard Law Review* 728
Cartwright, J., 'Liability in Negligence: New Directions or Old?', (1997) 13 *Const. Law Journal* 3

Caruso, D., *La culpa in contrahendo* (1993)
Carvalho, O. de, *Os Direitos do Homem no Direito Civil Português* (author's edition, Coimbra, 1973)
Carvalho, O. de, *A Teoria Geral da Relação Jurídica, 'seu sentido e limites'* (2nd edn, 1981)
Castronovo, C., 'Inattuazione della prestazione di lavoro e responsabilità del terzo danneggiato', (1981) MGLav 370
Castronovo, C., *La nuova responsabilità civile* (2nd edn, 1997)
Cattaneo, G., *La responsabilità del professionista* (1958)
Cendon, P., *Il dolo nella responsabilità extracontrattuale* (1976)
Chabas, F., *L'influence de la pluralité de causes sur le droit à réparation* (1967)
Chapman, B., 'Limited Auditors Liability; Economic Analysis and the Theory of Tort Law', (1992) 20 *Canadian Business Law Journal* 180
Chartier, Y., *La réparation du préjudice dans la responsabilité civile* (1983)
Cherniak, E. A. and E. How, 'Policy and Predictability: Pure Economic Loss in the Supreme Court of Canada', (1999) 31 *Canadian Business Law Journal* 209
Cherniak, E. A. and K. Stevens, 'Two Steps Forward or One Step Back? Anns at the Crossroads in Canada', (1992) 20 *Canadian Business Law Journal* 164
Clerk, J. F. and W. H. B. Lindsell, *The Law of Torts* (3rd edn, 1904)
Coderch, S. P., 'Comentario al artículo 1591', *Comentario del Código Civil*, II (1991)
Cohen, D., 'Bleeding Hearts and Peeling Floors: Compensation for Economic Loss at the House of Lords', (1984) 18 U.B.C.L. Review 289
Collins, H., 'European Private Law and Cultural Identity of States', (1995) 3 *European Review of Private Law* 353
Colyer, J. S., *A Modern View of the Law of Torts* (1966)
Cooter, R., U. Mattei, P. G. Monateri, R. Pardolesi and T. Ulen, *Il mercato delle regole* (1999)
Cornelis, L., *Les principes de droit belge de la responsabilité extra-contractuelle*, vol. I, *L'acte illicite* (1991)
Cortez, M., *Responsabilidade Civil da Administração por Actos Administratiros Ilegais e Concurso de Omissão Culposa do Lesado* (2000)
Costales, F. J., *El contrato del arquitecto en la edificación* (1977)
Craig, P., 'Once More unto the Breach: The Community, the State and Damages Liability', (1997) 113 *Law Quarterly Review* 67
Crespo, S. J. I., 'La responsabilidad del arquitecto en la construcción. Estado de la cuestión', in *La Ley*, November 1996, no. 4163.
Cristóbal Montes, A., 'El commodum representationis del artículo 1186 del Código Civil', in *Anuario de Derecho Civil* (1979) II, 601
Cunningham, T., 'Orphans of the Economic Loss Doctrine: Tort Liability of Information Providers and Preclusion of Comparative Negligence', (1995) 8 *DePaul Business Law Journal* 41

D'Angelo, C., 'The Economic Loss Doctrine: Saving Contract Warranty Law from Drowning in a Sea of Torts', (1995) 26 U. Tol. Law Review 591

Dalcq, R. O., *Traité de la Responsabilité Civile, Tome I, Les Novelles* (1959)

Dalcq, R. O., *Traité de la Responsabilité Civile, Tome II, Le lien de causalité, le dommage et sa réparation* (1962)

Dalcq, R. O. and G. Schamps, 'La responsabilité délictuelle et quasi-délictuelle, examen de jurisprudence (1987–1993)', (1995) RCJB

De Ángel, R., 'Comentario al artículo 1903', *Comentario del Código Civil*, II (1991)

De Ángel, R., *Tratado de responsabilidad civil* (3rd edn, 1993)

De Ángel, R., *Algunas previsiones sobre el futuro de la responsabilidad civil* (1995)

De Cupis, A., *Il danno. Teoria generale della responsabilità civile* (2nd edn, 1966; 3rd edn, 1979)

De Cupis, A., 'Aspettativa legittima e risarcimento del danno', (1983) II GC 104

De Lima, P. and A. Varela, *Código Civil Anotado*, vol. I (4th edn, with M. H. Mesquita, 1997); vol. II (4th edn, 1998)

De Lugo, I., *Disputationum de iustitia et iure* (1670) disp. 18, § 4, no. 79

De Nova, G., 'Informazione e contratto: il regolamento contrattuale', (1993) *Riv. trim. dir. civ.* 705

De Page, H., *Traité élémentaire de droit civil belge*, II, (2nd edn, 1948)

De Ubaldi, B., *Commentaria Corpus iuris civilis* (1577) Dig. 9.2.41 (vulg. 9.2.42)

Del Arco, M. A. and M. Pons, *Derecho de la construcción* (1980)

Del Duca, L. F. and F. H. Del Duca, 'Section 2–314 Economic Loss Doctrine – Plaintiff Ineligible for Tort Recovery – Restrictive Definition of "Other Property" Limits Plaintiff to Warranty Theory of Recovery', in (1997) 29 *Uniform Commercial Code Law Journal* 3

Deligiannis, J. and P. Kornilakis, *Law of Obligations, Special Part I–III* (1992)

Del Olmo Garcia, P., 'Responsabilidad por daño puramente económics causado al usuario de informaciones falsas', Amuario de Derecko Civil 257–300 (2001)

Delyannis, J., *La notion d'acte illicite considéré en sa qualité d'élément de la faute délictuelle* (1952)

Demogue, R., *Traité des obligations en général*, vol. 1, Part III (1923)

Deutsch, E., *Fahrlässigkeit und erforderliche Sorgfalt* (1963)

Deutsch, E., 'Freiheit und Freiheitsverletzung im Haftungsrecht', in *Festschrift für Hauß* (1978)

Deutsch, E., *Unerlaubte Handlungen, Schadensersatz und Schmerzensgeld* (3rd edn, 1995)

Deutsch, E., 'Compensation for Pure Economic Loss in German Law (trans. T. Weir), in *United Kingdom Comparative Law Series*, vol. 16 (1996) 73

Di Majo, A., 'Il problema del danno al patrimonio', (1986) RCDP 298

Di Majo, A., *La tutela civile dei diritti* (3rd edn, 1993)

Di Staso, *I contratti in generale* (1980)

Diéguez, G., *Lecciones de derecho del trabajo* (4th edn, 1995)

Diesselhorst, M., *Die Lehre des Hugo Grotius vom Versprechen* (1959)
Díez-Picazo, L., *Estudios sobre la jurisprudencia civil*, vol. I (2nd edn, 1973)
Díez-Picazo, L., *Fundamentos de derecho civil patrimonial*, vols. I–II (4th edn, 1993)
Díez-Picazo, L. and A. Gullón, *Sistema de Derecho Civil*, vol. II (7th edn, 1995)
Dugdale, T., 'Contributory Negligence Applied to Economic Loss: Platform Home Loans and Fancy and Jackson', (1999) 62 *Modern Law Review* 2
Durandus, G., 'Speculum iuris' (1574) lib. IV, par. IV, *De iniuriis et damno dato*, § 2, no. 15
Ebke, W. and H. Scheel, 'Die Haftung des Wirtschaftsprüfers für fahrlässig verursachte Vermögensschäden Dritter', (1991) WM 389
Echevarría Rivera, L. E., *El transporte marítimo* (1973)
Eckert, J., 'Der Begriff der Freiheit im Recht der unerlaubten Handlungen', (1994) JuS 625
Englard, I., *The Philosophy of Tort Law* (1993)
Erman, W., *Handkommentar zum Bürgerlichen Gesetzbuch*, Band I, §§ 1–853 (9th edn, 1993)
Erskine, J., *An Institute of the Laws of Scotland* (8th edn, reprint 1989)
Esser, J. and H. L. Weyers, *Schuldrecht Band II, Besonderer Teil* (7th edn, 1990)
Fagnart, J. L., *Examen de la jurisprudence concernant la responsabilité civile 1968–1975*, J. T. (1976)
Fagnart, J. L., *La responsabilité civile, Chronique de jurisprudence 1985–1995*, J. T. (1997) 21
Fagnart, J. L. and R. Bogaert, *La réparation du dommage corporel* (1994)
Feenstra, R., 'Grotius' Doctrine of Unjust Enrichment as a Source of Obligation: Its Origin and its Influence on Roman-Dutch Law', in E. G. H. Shrage (ed.), *Unjust Enrichment* (1995)
Feinman J. M., *Economic Negligence* (1995)
Feldthusen, B., *Economic Negligence: The Recovery of Pure Economic Loss* (2nd edn, 1989)
Feldthusen, B., 'Dynamic Change to Maritime Law – Gracious Retreat on Relational Economic Loss', (1998) 6 *Tort Law Review* 164
Feldthusen, B., 'Liability for Pure Economic Loss: Yes, But Why?' (1999) 28 *University of Western Australia Law Review* 84
Feldthusen, B., 'Pure Economic Loss in the High Court of Australia: Reinventing the Square Wheel', (2000) 8 *Tort Law Review* 33
Fernández Hierro, J. M., *La responsabilidad por vicios de construcción* (1976)
Fezer, K.-H., *Teilhabe und Verantwortung* (1986)
Fikentscher, W., *Lehrbuch des Schuldrechts* (8th edn, 1992; 9th edn, 1997)
Filios, P., *Law of Obligations, General Part* (1987) *Special Part* (2nd edn, 1990–1992)
Forde, M., 'Liability in Damages for Strikes: A French Counter-Revolution', (1985) 33 *American Journal of Comparative Law* 447
Forrester, I. S., S. L. Goren and H. M. Ilgen, *The German Civil Code* (1975)

Forte, A. D. M., 'Reparation for Pure Economic Loss: An Historical Perspective of Scots Law in the Seventeenth and Eighteenth Centuries', (1987) 8 *Journal of Legal History* 3

Fourkiotis, G., *Greek Law of Obligations, General Part* (1964)

Frame, A., *Salmond: Southern Jurist* (1995)

Franzoni, M., 'Dei fatti illeciti', in *Commentario del Codice Civile Scialoja-Branca a cura di Galgano* (1993)

Fridman, G. H. L., 'Torts – Negligent Misstatements Causing Economic Loss – Elements of a Successful Action (1991) 70 Can. B. Rev 780

Friedman, L. M. and G. Teubner, 'Legal Education and Legal Integration: European Hopes and American Experience', in M. Cappelletti, M. Seccombe and J. Weiler (eds.), *Integration Through Law: Europe and the American Federal Experience* (1986)

Frotz, G., *Die rechtsdogmatische Einordnung der Haftung für culpa in contrahendo* (1969)

Furmston, M. (ed.), *The Law of Tort: Policies and Trends in Liability for Damage to Property and Economic Loss* (1986)

Gallo, P., *L'elemento oggettivo del tort of neglicence. Indagine sui limiti della responsabilità delittuale per neglicence nei paesi di Common Law* (1988)

Gallo, P., 'Unjust Enrichment. A Comparative Analysis', (1992) 40 *American Journal of Comparative Law* 431

Gauci, G. M., 'Ship-source Oil Pollution Damage and Recovery for Relational Economic Loss', (2000) July J.B.L. 356

Gazis, A., *Non-performance of Obligational Contract* (1940, reprint 1987)

Gazis, A. 'About the Legal Sense of "Auxiliary Performer"', in *Eranion* [Festschrift] *for G. Maridekis* (1963)

Gazzoni, F., *Manuale di diritto privato* (6th edn, 1996)

Gény, F., *Méthode d'interprétation et sources en droit privé positif* (2nd edn, 1919)

Georgakopoulos, L., *The Law of Standing Obligations* (1979)

Georgiades, A., *Problems of Civil Liability* (1972)

Georgiades, A., *Law of Obligations, A–C* (1984–1986)

Georgiades, A., *Real Law*, vol. I (1991)

Georgiades, A., *General Principles of Civil Law* (2nd edn, 1996)

Georgiades, A., *Law of Obligations* (1998)

Georgiades, A. and M. Stathopoulos, *Civil Code, Article by Article Commentary*, vols. II–IV (1978–1982)

Ghestin, J., *Traité de droit civil. La formation du contrat* (3rd edn, 1993)

Giardina, F., *Responsabilità contrattuale ed extracontrattuale* (1988)

Giorgi, G., *Teoria delle obbligazioni nel diritto moderno italiano*, vol. V (7th edn, 1909)

Gloag, W. M., *The Law of Contract – A Treatise on the Principles of Contract in the Law of Scotland* (2nd edn, 1929, reprinted 1985)

Gloag, W. M. and R. C. Henderson, *The Law of Scotland* (10th edn, 1995)

Goldberg, V. P., 'Accountable Accountants: Is Third-Party Liability Necessary?', (1988) 17 *Journal of Legal Studies* 295

Goldberg, V. P., 'Recovery for Pure Economic Loss in Tort: Another Look at *Robins Dry Dock v. Flint*', (1991) 20 *Journal of Legal Studies* 249

Goldberg, V. P., 'Recovery for Economic Loss Following the Exxon Valdez Oil Spill', (1994) 23 *Journal of Legal Studies* 1

Gomes, J. M. V., *O Conceito de Enriquecimento, O Enriquecimento Forçado e Os Vários Paradigmas do Enriquecimento Sem Causa* (1998)

Gomes Canotilho, J. and V. Moreira, *Constituição da República Portuguesa Anotada* (3rd edn, 1993)

Gómes, de la Escalera, C., *La responsabilidad civil de los promotores, constructores y técnicos por los defectos de la construcción* (1990)

Gómez Laplaza, M. C. and S. Díaz Alabart, 'Responsabilidad civil por los daños causados por productos defectuosos', in (1995) II *Actualidad Civil* 519

González Porras, J. M., *Comentarios al Código Civil y Compilaciones Forales* (arts. 694–705), IX-1-B (1987)

González Porras, J. M., *Comentarios al Código Civil y Compilaciones Forales*, XVI-1 (2nd edn, 1991)

Gordley, J., 'Contract and Delict: Toward a Unified Law of Obligations', (1997) 1 *Edinburgh Law Review* 345

Gordley, J., 'European Codes and American Restatements: Some Difficulties', (1981) 81 *Columbia Law Review* 140

Gordley, J., *The Philosophical Origins of Modern Contract Doctrine* (1991)

Gordley, J., 'Tort Law in the Aristotelian Tradition', in D. Owen (ed.), *Philosophical Foundations of Tort Law: A Collection of Essays* (1995)

Gordley, J., 'Responsibility in Crime, Tort, and Contract for the Unforeseeable Consequences of an Intentional Wrong: A Once and Future Rule?' in P. Cane and J. Stapleton (eds.), *The Law of Obligations: Essays in Celebration of John Fleming* (1998)

Gordley, J., 'The Principle Against Unjustified Enrichment', in H. Schack (ed.), *Gedächtnisschrift für Alexander Lüderitz* (2000)

Gordley, J. and U. Mattei, 'Protecting Possession', (1996) 44 *American Journal of Comparative Law* 293

Gorla, G., 'Sulla c.d. causalità giuridica: fatto dannoso e conseguenze', in *Studi in onore di A. Cicu* (1951)

Gosnell, C., 'English Courts: The Restoration of a Common Law of Pure Economic Loss', (2000) 50 *University of Toronto Law Journal* 2

Gouveia Rocha, J.-C., 'Deveres dos Notarios. Sua Responsabilidade', (1983) 6 *Revista do Notoriado*

Grisi, G., *L'obbligo precontrattuale di informazione* (1990)

Grossi, P. (ed.), *La Seconda scolastica nella formazione del diritto privato moderno* (1973)

Grossi, P., *L'ordine giuridico medievale* (1995)

Grotius, H., *De iure belli ac pacis libri tres* (1939) II.XVII.1-2.
Grunsky, W., 'Schadensersatz bei Verletzung eines Gewerbetreibenden oder Freiberuflers', DAR 57–1988, 400
Gui Mori, T., 'Daños causados por animales. Responsabilidad civil y penal', in *La Ley*, I (1992) 1055
Hägerström, A., *Das Prinzip der Wissenschaft. Eine logisch-erkenntnistheoretische Untersuchung. I. Die Realität* (1908)
Harrington, S., 'Claims in Tort for Pure Economic Loss: A Comparative View from Canada', (2000) I.J.I.L 1
Hart, H. L. A. and A. Honoré, *Causation in the Law* (2nd edn, 1985)
Hartkamp, A. S., *Verbintenissenrecht, deel II – Algemene leer der overeenkomsten* (Mr. C. Asser's handleiding tot de beoefening van het Nederlands Burgerlijk recht) (10th edn, 1997)
Hartkamp, A. S., *Verbintenissenrecht, deel III – De Verbintenis uit de wet* (Mr. C. Asser's handleiding tot de beoefening van het Nederlands Burgerlijk recht), (10th edn, 1998)
Hartkamp, A. S., 'Perspective for the Development of a European Civil Code', in M. Bussani and U. Mattei (eds.), *Making European Law: Essays on the Common Core Project* (2000)
Hartkamp, A. S., *Verbintenissenrecht, deel I – de Verbintenis in het algemeen* (Mr. C. Asser's handleiding tot de beoefening van het Nederlands Burgerlijk recht) (11th edn, 2000)
Hartkamp, A. S., M. Hesselink, E. Hondius, C. Joustra and E. du Perron (eds.), *Towards a European Civil Code* (1st edn, 1994, 2nd edn, 1998)
Hasse, J. C., *Die Culpa des Römischen Rechts* (2nd edn, 1838)
Hedley, S., 'Negligence – Pure Economic Loss – Goodbye Privity, Hello Contorts', (1995) 54 *Cambridge Law Journal* 27
Heineccius, G., *Elementa iuris civilis secundum ordinem pandectarum* (5th edn, 1772), to Dig. 9.2 § CLXXXVI
Hellner, J., *Skadeståndsrätt* (5th edn, 1995)
Herbots, J., 'Le "duty of care" et le dommage purement financier en droit comparé', (1985) *Revue de droit international et de droit comparé* 7
Herrera Catena, J., *Responsabilidades en la construcción*, I-1° (1974); I-2° (1977)
Heukels, T. and A. McDonnell (eds.), *The Action for Damages in Community Law* (1997)
Hickmott, G. J. R., *Principles and Practice of Interruption Insurance* (1982)
Hirschman, A. O., *Exit, Voice, and Loyalty: Responses to Decline in Firms, Organizations, and States* (1970)
Hodgin, R. W., 'The Law of Tort: Policies and Trends for Damage to Property and Economic Loss', (1987) 38 N.I.L. Q. 289
Honorat, J. J., *L'idée d'acceptation des risques dans la responsabilité civile* (1969)
Honoré, T., 'Necessary and Sufficient Conditions in Tort Law', in D. G. Owen (ed.), *Philosophical Foundation of Tort Law* (1995)

Hostienisis, *Summa aurea* (1556) lib. 5, rubr. 'de damno dato' no. 1.
Howarth, D., 'The General Conditions of Unlawfulness', in A. Hartkamp, M. Hesselink, E. Hondius, C. Joustra and E. du Perron (eds.), *Towards a European Civil Code* (2nd edn, 1998)
Howarth, D., 'Economic Loss in England: The Search for Coherence', in E. K. Banakas (ed.), *Civil Liability for Pure Economic Loss* (1996)
Howells, G., 'Product Liability', in A. Hartkamp, M. Hesselink, E. Hondius, C. Joustra and E. du Perron (eds.), *Towards a European Civil Code* (2nd edn, 1998)
Hutchinson, A., 'Economic Loss is Tort's Gain', (1983) 7 Can. Law. 38
Illescas Ortiz, R., 'Auditoría, aprobación, depósito y publicidad de las cuentas anuales', in *Comentario al régimen legal de las sociedades mercantiles*, VIII-2 (1993)
*Italian Civil Code and Complementary Legislation* (trans. M. Beltramo, G. E. Longo and J. H. Merryman) (1993)
Jakobs, H. H. and W. Schubert, *Die Beratung des Bürgerlichen Gesetzbuchs* (1983)
James, F. Jr., 'Limitations on Liability for Economic Loss Caused by Negligence: A Pragmatic Appraisal', (1972) 25 *Vanderbilt Law Review* 43
Jansen, N., 'The Idea of a Lost Chance', (1999) 19 *Oxford Journal of Legal Studies* 271
Jauernig, O., *Kommentar zum Bürgerlichen Gesetzbuch Unerlaubte Handlungen* (9th edn, 1999).
Jess, D. C., *The Insurance of Commercial Risks, Law and Practice* (1986)
*Jherings Jahrbücher für die Dogmatik des bürgerlichen Rechts* (Jena 1. 1857–90.1943) (1861)
Jolowicz, J. A., 'Touchstones of Tort Liability Revisited', (1991) 6 *Tulane Civil Law Forum* 157
Jones, E., 'Murphy's Law: Where Do We go from Here?', (1990) 134 S.J. 1256
Jones, W. K., 'Economic Losses Caused by Construction Deficiencies: The Competing Regimes of Contract and Tort', (1991) 59 *University of Cincinnati Law Review* 1051
Kabitsis, G., *On Precontractual Liability* (1960)
Karakostas, J., *Producer's Liability for Defective Products* (1993)
Karassis, M., *The Concept of the Joint and Several Debt* (1990)
Kaufmann, H., *Rezeption und Usus Modernus der Actio Legis Aquiliae* (1958)
Khoury, L., 'The Liability of Auditors Beyond Their Clients: A Comparative Study', (2001) 46 *McGill Law Journal* 413
Klang, H. (ed.), *Kommentar zum Allgemeinen bürgerlichen Gesetzbuch*, vol. IV/2 (2nd edn, 1978)
Kleineman, J., *Ren förmögenhetsskada* (1987)
Kohler, J., 'Recht und Process', in *Zeitschrift für das privat-öffentliche Recht der Gegenwart* 14 (1887)
Kohler, J., *Lehrbuch des bürgerlichen Rechts*, vol. 1 (1904); vol. 2 (1906)
Kornilakis, P., *Liability from Exposure to Danger* (Strict Liability) (1982)

Kottenhagen, R. J. P., 'Buiten-contractuele aansprakelijkheid voor economische schade', (1991) BR 345
Kottenhagen, R. J. P., 'Over bris de cables, Kabelbruchfälle en cable cases', (1992) BR 653
Kötz, H., 'Economic Loss in Tort and Contract', (1994) 58 Rabels Zeitschrift für ausländisches und internationales Privatrecht 3
Kötz, H., 'Comparative Legal Research: Its Function in the Development of Harmonised Law. The European Perspective', in Juridiska Fakulteten I Uppsala (ed.), Towards Universal Laws – Trends in National, European and International Law-making (1995)
Kötz, H., Deliktsrecht (8th edn, 1998)
Kötz, H. and A. Flessner, European Contract Law, I (trans. T. Weir, 1997)
Kounougeri-Manoledaki, E., 'The Problem of Hypothetical (Intervening) Causation in the Law of Compensation', (1981) 2 EEDSTh
Koziol, H., Österreichisches Haftpflichtrecht, vol. II (2nd edn, 1984)
Koziol, H. (ed.), Unification of Tort Law: Wrongfulness (1998)
Koziol, H. and R. Welser, Grundriss des bürgerlichen Rechts, vol. II (12th edn, 2001)
Lacruz, J. L., Elementos de derecho civil, II-10. (3rd edn, 1994); II-20. (3rd edn, 1995)
Landes, W. and R. A. Posner, The Economic Structure of Tort Law (1987)
Lankhorst, G. H., De relativiteit van de onrechtmatige daad (1992)
Lapoyade Deschamps, C., La réparation du préjudice économique pur en droit français (1996)
Lapoyade Deschamps, C., 'La réparation du préjudice économique pur en droit français', in E. K. Banakas (ed.), Civil Liability for Pure Economic Loss (1996)
Larenz, K., Lehrbuch des Schuldrechts, Band I, Allgemeiner Teil (14th edn, 1987)
Larenz, K. and C. W. Canaris, Lehrbuch des Schuldrechts Band II, Besonderer Teil (13th edn, 1994)
Larouche, P., 'Ius Commune Casebooks for the Common Law of Europe: Presentation, Progress, Rationale', (2000) 8 European Review of Private Law 101
Larroumet, C., Droit Civil. Tome III. Les Obligations. Le Contrat (2nd edn, 1990)
Latour Brotóns, E., 'Responsabilidad civil por los daños causados por los animales en accidentes de tráfico', Revista de Derecho de la Circulación (1979), 113
Laurent, F., Principes de droit civil, XX (1887)
Lauterbach, W. A., Collegium theorico-practici (1707) to D. 9.2 no. VII
Legrand, A. P., 'Sens et non-sens d'un code civil européen', (1996) 48 RIDC 779
Lessius, L., De iustitia et iure ceterisque virtutibus cardinalibus libri quatuor (1628) lib. 2, cap. 12, dubs. 16, 18; cap. 20, dubs. 10–11
Ligeropoulos, A., Law of Obligations (1960–1968)
Lim, R., 'Economic Loss: The New Conservatism Examined', (1988) 9 Business Law Review 222
Linehan, J., 'The Recovery of Economic Loss Damages in Tort: Pennsylvania Law And "Social Adjustment"', (1989) 51 University of Pittsburgh Law Review 203

Lipstein, K., 'Protected Interests in the Law of Torts', (1962–3) 21 *Cambridge Law Journal* 85
Llebaría, S., *Derecho de la construcción* (1993)
López Mora, L. and F. De La Cámara Mingo, *Tratado práctico del derecho referente a la construcción y a la arquitectura*, vol. IV (1964)
Lorandi, F., 'Haftung für reinen Vermögensschaden', (1990) 8 *Recht. Zeitschrift für juristische Ausbildung und Praxis* 1
Lorenz, W., 'Anwaltshaftung wegen Untätigkeit bei der Errichtung letzwilliger Verfügungen', (1995) 50 *Juristen Zeitung* 317
Löwisch, M., 'Der Deliktsschutz relativer Rechte' (1970) *Hamburger Rechtsstudien*, 63
Löwisch, M., *Arbeitsrecht* (4th edn, 1996)
Luminoso, A., *La lesione dell'interesse negativo* (1972)
Luminoso, A., 'La responsabilità della banca per false o inesatte informazioni', (1984) I *RDC* 189
Lunney, M., 'Negligence and the Recovery of Pure Economic Loss: The Re-Opening of Pandora's Box?', (1989) 19 *Queensl. L. Soc'y J.* 59
Mactavish, A., 'Tort Recovery for Economic Loss: Recent Developments', (1993) 21 *Canadian Business Law Journal* 395
Maggivas, M., *The Liability of the Producer of Standardised Goods* (1978)
Magnus, U. (ed.), *Unification of Tort Law: Damages* (2001)
Magnusson, R., 'Spring in the House of Lords', (1994) 2 *Torts Law Journal* 210
Maiorca, C., 'Colpa civile (teoria gen.)', entry in *Enciclopedia del diritto*, vol. VII (1960)
Malamud, R., 'Employee Liability for Economic Losses of the Employer's Customers: A California-Based Examination of the Question of Duty', (1994) 30 *Tort & Ins. Law Journal* 195
Malaurie, P. and L. Aynès, *Droit Civil: Les Obligations* (1st edn, 1985)
Mantzoufas, J., *Law of Obligations* (1971)
Manzanares, A., 'La responsabilidad precontractual en la hipótesis de ruptura injustificada de las negociaciones preliminares', *Anuario de Derecho Civil*, III, (1984) 687
Markesinis, B. S., 'La politique jurisprudentielle et la réparation du préjudice économique en Angleterre: Une approche comparative', (1983) RIDC 31
Markesinis, B. S., 'An Expanding Tort Law – The Price of a Rigid Contract Law', (1987) 103 LQR 354
Markesinis, B. S., 'Litigation-mania in England, Germany and the USA: Are We so very Different?', (1990) 49 *Cambridge Law Journal* 133
Markesinis, B. S., *The German Law of Obligations*, vol. II, *The Law of Torts: A Comparative Introduction* (3rd edn, 1997)
Markesinis, B. S., 'Why a Code is not the Best Way to Advance the Cause of European Legal Unity', (1997) 5 *European Review of Private Law* 519

Markesinis, B. S. and S. Deakin, 'The Random Element of Their Lordships' Infallible Judgment: An Economic and Comparative Analysis of the Tort of Negligence from *Anns* to *Murphy*', (1992) 55 *Modern Law Review* 619

Markesinis, B. S., W. Lorenz and G. Dannemann, *The German Law of Obligations*, vol. I, *The Law of Contracts and Restitution: A Comparative Introduction* (1997)

Marschall von Bieberstein, W., *Reflexschäden und Regreßrechte. Die Ersatzansprüche Dritter bei mittelbaren Vermögensschäden infolge vertraglicher und ähnlicher Beziehungen zum Verletzten* (1967)

Masel, G., 'Damages in Tort for Loss of Chance', (1995) 3 *Torts Law Journal* 43

Mattei, U., *Comparative Law and Economics* (1997)

Mattei, U., 'The Issue of European Civil Codification and Legal Scholarship. Biases, Strategies and Developments', (1998) 21 *Hastings International & Comparative Law Review* 883

Mattei, U., *Basic Principles of Property Law. A Comparative Legal and Economic Introduction* (2000)

Mattei, U. and F. Cafaggi, 'Comparative Law and Economics', *New Palgrave Dictionary of Economics and the Law* (1998)

Mayo Jáimez, F., *Abordajes y varadas* (1989)

Mazeaud, H., 'Essai de classification des obligations', *Rev. trim. dr. civ.* (1936) 1

Mazeaud, H., *Traité theorique et pratique de la responsabilité civile*, vol. I (4th edn, 1947)

Mazeaud, H., L. Mazeaud, J. Mazeaud and Chabas, F., *Leçons de Droit Civil. Tome II*, vol. 1 *Obligations. Théorie Générale* (8th edn, 1991)

McConnell, H. H., 'The Other Property Problem: Applying the Economic Loss Rule to Construction Contracting Claims', (2000) 74 Fla. B.J. 87

McDonald, B. and J. Swanton, 'Negligence in the Performance of Contractual Services – Action in Tort by a Third Party to the Contract', (1995) 69 ALJ 576

McGee, A., 'Economic Loss and the Problem of the Running of Time', (2000) 19 C.J.Q. 39

McLennan, G., 'Torts – Liability of Public Authorities – Recovery for Pure Economic Loss', (1991) 70 Can. B. Rev 175

Mead, P., 'The Impact of Contract upon Tortious Liability of Construction Professionals', (1998) 6 *Torts Law Journal* 145

Medicus, D., 'Die Forderung als "sonstiges Recht" nach § 823 I BGB?', in *Festschrift für Erich Steffen* (1995)

Medicus, D., *Bürgerliches Recht* (18th edn, 1999)

Menezes Cordeiro, A., *Direito das Obrigações* (2 vols., 1980)

Mengoni, L., 'Obbligazioni di risultato e obbligazioni di mezzi', (1954) I *RDComm*, 185

Merryman, J. H., *The Civil Law Tradition: An Introduction to the Legal Systems of Western Europe and Latin America* (2nd edn, 1985)

Mersinis, T. G. (ed.), *The Case for Contractual Solutions in the Third Party Pure Economic Loss* (1999)

Mesquita, J., M. Andrade, *Direitos Pessoais de Gozo* (1998)
Mesquita, J., M. Henrique, *Obrigacoes Reais e Ónus Reais* (1990)
Messinetti, F., 'Danno giuridico', in *Enciclopedia del diritto*, App. I.
Mevoungou-Nsana, R., 'Le préjudice causé par un ouvrage immobilier: réparation en nature ou par équivalent?', (1995) RTDCiv. 733
Michaélidès-Nouaros, G., *Law of Obligations* (1959)
Molina, L., *De iustitia et iure tractatus* (1614) disps. 315, 724
Molina García, A., *La doble venta a través de la jurisprudencia* (1975)
Monateri, P. G., 'Sintesi di informazione', (1986) II RDC 364
Monateri, P. G., *Il cumulo di responsabilità contrattuale ed extracontrattuale* (1989)
Monateri, P. G., 'Economic Loss in Italy', in E. K. Banakas (ed.), *Civil Liability for Pure Economic Loss* (Proceedings of the Annual International Colloquium of the Committee of Comparative Law, Norwich, September 1994) (1996)
Monateri, P. G., *La responsabilità civile* (1998)
Montoya Melgar, A., *Derecho del trabajo* (14th edn, 1993; 17th edn, 1996)
Morales, S., and S. Sancho, *Manual práctico de responsabilidad civil* (1993)
Moreno Quesada, B., *La oferta de contrato: génesis y responsabilidad antecontractual* (1963)
Mota Pinto, C., *Teoria Geral do Direito Civil* (3rd edn, Coimbra, 1985)
Mühlenbruch, C. F., *Doctrina Pandectarum* (1838) par. III, § 450.
Mulhern, P., 'Marine Pollution, Fishers, and the Pillars of the Land: A Tort Recovery Standard for Pure Economic Losses', (1990) 18 B.C. Envtl. Aff. L. Rev 85
Mullany, N. and A. M. Linden (eds.), *Torts Tomorrow: A Tribute to John Fleming* (1998)
Mullender, R., 'Negligent Misstatement, Threats and the Scope of the *Hedley Byrne* Principle', (1999) 62 Mod. LR 425
Mullerat Balmaña, R., 'Las enseñanzas de la S.T.S. de 19 de abril de 1977', (1979) *Revista Jurídica de Cataluña* 187
Mullerat Balmaña, R., 'La responsabilidad civil de productos en derecho español', (1995) I *Revista Jurídica de Cataluña* 9
Musy, A. M., *Il dovere di informazione. Saggio di diritto comparato* (1999)
Musy, A. M., 'Punitive damages e resistenza temeraria in giudizio: regole, definizioni e modelli istituzionali a confronto', (2000) 11 DR 1
Nanni, F., *La buona fede contrattuale* (1988)
Navarretta, E., *Diritti inviolabili e risarcimento del danno* (1996)
Nelson, G. and D. Whitman, *Real Estate Transfer, Finance, and Development* (5th edn, 1998)
Netto, A. M. and A. Christudason, 'Junior Books Extended', (1999) 5 Const. L.J. 3
Nicoll, C., 'Pure Economic Loss – A New Zealand Perspective', (1997) 4 Int. M.L. 233
Norrie, K. McK., 'Liability of Solicitors to Third Parties', (1988) SLT (News) 309

Norrie, K. McK., ' "Binding" Precedent and Disappointed Beneficiaries', (1990) Jur Rev 107

Nussbaum, F., 'The Economic Loss Rule and Intentional Torts: A Shield or a Sword?', (1996) 8 *St. Thomas Law Review* 473

Odofredus, *Summa de formandis libellis in Refugium advocatorum* (1510)

Ogilvie, M. H., 'The Law of Tort: Policies and Trends in Liability for Damage to Property and Economic Loss', (1987) 66 Can. B. Rev 851

Ogilvie, M. H., 'Concurrent Liability in Contract and Tort: Cautionary Tales from the Supreme Court of Canada', (1997) J.B.L. 372

Ostheim, R., 'Zur Haftung für culpa in contrahendo bei grundloser Ablehnung des Vertragsabschlusses', (1980) JBl 576

O'Sullivan, J., 'Negligence Liability of Auditors to Third Parties and the Role of Assumption of Responsibility', (1998) 14 P.N. 195

Oughton, D., 'Liability in Tort for Economic Loss Suffered by the Consumer of Defective Goods', (1987) J.B.L. 370

Owles, D., 'A Tool of the Trade – Strict Liability and Economic Loss', (1982) 132 N.L.J. 470

Palmer, V. V., *The Roman-Dutch and Sesotho Law of Delict* (1970)

Palmer, V. V., 'In Quest of a Strict Liability Standard Under the Code', (1975) 56 *Tulane Law Review* 1

Palmer, V. V., 'Contractual Negligence in the Civil Law', (1982) 50 *Tulane Law Review* 1317

Palmer, V. V., 'Why Privity Entered Tort – An Historical Re-examination of *Winterbottom v. Wright*', (1983) 27 *American Journal of Legal History* 85

Palmer, V. V., 'Trois Principes de la Responsabilité Sans Faute', (1987) *Revue Internationale de Droit Comparé* 825

Palmer, V. V., 'General Theory of the Inner Structure of Strict Liability: Common Law, Civil Law, Comparative Law', (1988) 62 *Tulane Law Review* 1303

Palmer, V. V., 'Tortious Interference with Contract at French Law: An Excursion Along a Road Not Taken', (1991/92) 6/7 *Tulane Civil Law Forum* 131

Palmer, V. V., 'A Comparative Study (From a Common Law Perspective) of the French Action for Wrongful Interference with Contract', (1992) 40 *American Journal of Comparative Law* 297

Palmer, V. V., 'Fault in Tort (Delict)', in *Encyclopedia of Philosophy of Law* (1999)

Palmer, V. V., *Louisiana: Microcosm of a Mixed Jurisdiction* (1999)

Palmer, V. V., 'The Fate of the General Clause in a Cross-Cultural Setting: The Tort Experience of Louisiana', (2000) 46 *Loyola Law Review* 535

Palmer, V. V., (ed.), *Mixed Jurisdictions Worldwide: The Third Legal Family* (2001)

Pantaleón, F., 'Comentario a la S.T.S. de 25 de junio de 1983', *Cuadernos Civitas de Jurisprudencia Civil*, no. 3 (1983) 789

Pantaleón, F., 'Comentario a la S.T.S. de 10 de mayo de 1984', *Cuadernos Civitas de Jurisprudencia Civil*, no. 5 (1984) 1645

Pantaleón, F., *Responsabilidad civil: conflictos de jurisdicción* (1985)

Pantaleón, F., 'La indemnización por causa de lesiones o de muerte', *Anuario de Derecho Civil*, April-June (1989) 613
Pantaleón, F., 'Causalidad e imputación objetiva: criterios de imputación', *Centenario del Código Civil*, II (1990)
Pantaleón, F., 'Comentario al artículo 1902', in *Comentario del Código Civil*, II (1991)
Pantaleón, F., 'Comentario a la S.T.S. de 30 de julio de 1991', *Cuadernos Civitas de Jurisprudencia Civil*, no. 27 (1991) 871
Pantaleón, F., 'Perseverare diabolicum (¿Otra vez la responsabilidad civil en el Código Penal?)', in *Jueces para la Democracia*, II (1993) 6
Pantaleón, F., 'Notas a la Ley 22/94, de 6 de julio, de responsabilidad civil por los daños causados por productos defectuosos', in *Actualidad Civil*, IV (1995) 723
Pantaleón, F., *La responsabilidad civil de los auditores: extensión, limitación, prescripción* (1996)
Parra Lucán, M. A., *Daños por productos y protección del consumidor* (1990)
Parra Lucán, M. A., 'Notas a la Ley 22/94, de 6 julio, de responsabilidad civil por los daños causados por productos defectuosos', 1995-IV, *Actualidad Civil*
Pascual Estevill, L., 'La perturbación del derecho de crédito y las cuestiones de la imputabilidad, causalidad y tipicidad en el derecho civil', in *Revista Crítica de Derecho Inmobiliario* (1989) 1183
Pascual Estevill, L., *La responsabilidad extracontractual, aquiliana o delictual* (1990)
Passias, J., *The Law of JA Companies*, vol. I (1955), vol. II (1969)
Payne, D., 'Foresight and Remoteness in Negligence', (1962) 25 Mod. LR 16
Pereira Coelho, F. M., *O Problema da Causa Virtual na Responsabilidade Civil* (reprint 1998)
Pessoa Jorge, F., *Ensaio sobre os Pressupostos da Responsabilidade Civil* (1968)
Peterson, C. H. and J. Zekoll, 'Mass Torts', (1994) 42 American Journal of Comparative Law 79
Petit Laval, E., 'El informe Cadbury: un análisis sobre la objetividad, eficacia y responsabilidad de los auditores de cuentas', in (1994) *Revista General de Derecho*, no. 603
Petrelli, P., *Il danno non patrimoniale* (1997)
Planiol, M., *Traité élémentaire de droit civil*, vol. II (8th edn, 1921; trans. Louisiana Law Institute, 12th edn, 1959)
Plum, W., 'Zur Abgrenzung des Eigentums-vom Vermögensschaden', in *Archiv für die civilistische Praxis* 181 (1981), 68
Ponzanelli, G., *Le clausole di esonero dalla responsabilità civile* (1984)
Ponzanelli, G., 'Il Tort of interference nei rapporti contrattuali: le esperienze nordamericana e italiana a confronto', (1989) Q 69
Ponzanelli, G., *La responsabilità civile. Profili di diritto comparato* (1992)
Ponzanelli, G., 'Il risarcimento del danno meramente patrimoniale nel diritto italiano', (1998) 8-9 DR 729

Ponzanelli, G., 'The Compensation of Pure Economic Loss in Italian Law', in *Rapports Nationaux Italiens au XVème Congrès International de Droit Comparé* (1998) (Rassegna forense – Quaderni, 2, 1998)
Posch, W., 'Der ungeschützte Strombezieher als Fall des "mittelbaren Schadens" in der Rechtsprechung des OGH', (1973) JBl 564
Posch, W., 'Austria' in E. H. Hondius (ed.), *Precontractual Liability, Reports to the XIIIth Congress of Comparative Law* (1991)
Posner, R. A., *Economic Analysis of Law* (3rd edn, 1986)
Pouliades, A., *Collective Action and Consumer's Protection* (1990)
Pound, R., *The Spirit of Common Law* (1921)
Prata, A., *Notas sobre a Responsabilidade Pré-Contratual* (1991)
Prosser, W. L. and W. P. Keeton, *On the Law of Torts* (5th edn, 1984)
Pufendorf, S., *De iure naturae et gentium libri octo* (1688) III.i.2, III.i.3; III.i.6.
Puig Brutau, J., *Fundamentos de derecho civil*, II, 3d. (1983)
Pulignano, N. Jr. and L. Studdard, 'Reining in Tort Liability Claims Based on Breach of Contract – The Economic Loss Rule', (1996) 46 *Federation of Insurance and Corporate Counsel Quarterly* 259
Rabin, R. L., 'Tort Liability for Negligently Inflicted Economic Loss: A Reassessment', (1985) 37 *Stanford Law Review* 1513
Rafferty, N., 'Recovery in Tort for Purely Economic Loss: Contract Law on the Retreat', (1986) 35 U.N.B. L.J. 111
Rafferty, N., 'Torts – Negligent Misstatement – Recovery for Purely Economic Loss', (1991) 70 Can. B. Rev. 381
Rafferty, N., '*Winnipeg Condominium* v. *Bird Construction* – Recovery of Purely Economic Loss in the Tort of Negligence: Liability of Builders to Subsequent Purchasers for Construction Defects', (1996) 34 Alta. *Law Review* 472
Ragatz, R., 'Drawing the Line Between Contract and Tort Theories Under the Economic Loss Doctrine', (1998) 71 Wis. Law. 20
Ranieri, F., '"Cable cases" e responsabilità per danni puramente economici: Il "Case Method" come esempio di approccio didattico nell'insegnamento del diritto civile europeo', in A. Jannarelli, G. Piepoli and N. Scannicchio (eds.), *Quaderni di diritto privato europeo*, no. 2 (1998) 151
Reece, H., 'Loss of Chances in the Law', (1996) 59 Mod. LR 188
Reischauer, R., 'Commentary', in P. Rummel (ed.), *Commentary on the General Civil Code*, vols. 1–2 (1992)
Richardi, R. and O. Wlotzke, *Münchener Handbuch zum Arbeitsrecht Band I: Individualarbeitsrecht*, vol. I (1992)
Rizzo, M. J., 'A Theory of Economic Loss in the Law of Torts', (1982) 11 *Journal of Legal Studies* 281
Rizzo, M. J., 'The Economic Loss Problem: A Comment On Bishop', (1982) 2 *Oxford Journal of Legal Studies* 197

Roca-Sastre Muncunill, L., 'El perjuicio del derecho de crédito por acto de tercero', in (1962) Revista Jurídica de Cataluña 571

Roca Trias, E., 'Naturaleza de la relación entre el arquitecto y los clientes. Responsabilidad extracontractual de los arquitectos', (1975), Revista de Derecho Privado 783

Rodger, A., 'Lord MacMillan's Speech in Donoghue v. Stevenson' (1992) 108 LQR 236

Rodotà, S., Il problema della responsabilità civile (1967)

Rogel Vide, C., La responsabilidad civil extracontractual en el derecho español (1977)

Rogers, W. V. H., Winfield and Jolowicz on Tort (15th edn, 1998)

Rojo Fernández-del Rió, A., La responsabilidad civil del fabricante (1974)

Roppo, V., 'Crisi d'impresa: la banca risponde verso i creditori? (Con postilla sugli sviluppi della responsabilità civile)', (1996) DR 535

Roppo, V. and G. Benedetti, 'La responsabilità professionale del notaio', (2000) 8–9 DR 801

Roujou de Boubee, M.-E., Essai sur la notion de réparation (1974)

Roussos, K., Schaden und Folgenschaden (1992)

Rubio San Román, J. I., La responsabilidad civil en la construcción (1987)

Rudden, B., 'Torticles', (1991–1992) 6/7 Tulane Civil Law Forum 126

Rummel, P. (ed.), Commentary on the General Civil Code, vol. 2 (2nd edn, 1992)

Rummel, P., 'Wettbewerb durch Umweltschutz – Überlegungen zum Mißbrauch subjektiver öffentlicher Rechte', (1993) RZ 36

Rumrell, R. G., 'Bad Faith and the Economic Loss Rule: the Thin Grey Line', (1998) 6 Int.I.L.R. 158

Ryan, T., 'Recovery of Economic Loss in Tort', (1986) 59 Wis. B. Bull. 19

Sacco, R., 'L'ingiustizia del danno di cui all'art. 2043 cc.', (1960) I FP 1420

Sacco, R., 'Comparazione giuridica e conoscenza del dato giuridico positivo', in R. Sacco (ed.), L'apporto della comparazione alla scienza giuridica (1980)

Sacco, R., 'La codification, forme dépassée de législation?', in Rapports Nat. It. au XI Congrès Int. Dr. Comp. (1982)

Sacco, R., 'Legal Formants: A Dynamic Approach to Comparative Law (Installments I and II)', (1991) 39 American Journal of Comparative Law 1, 349

Sacco, R., A. Gambaro, Sistemi giuridici comparati, in R. Sacco (ed.), Tr. dir. comp. (1996)

Sacco, R. and R. Caterina, 'Il possesso', in L. Mengoni (ed.), Trattato di diritto Civile e commerciale, Cicu-Messineo (2nd edn, 2000)

Sacco, R. and G. De Nova, Il contratto (2 vols, 1993)

Sala Franco, T., Derecho del trabajo (7th edn, 1993; 10th edn, 1996)

Salmond, J. W., Jurisprudence, or the Theory of the Law (1902)

Salmond, J. W., The Law of Torts: A Treatise on the English Law of Liability for Civil Injuries (2nd edn, 1910; 8th edn, 1934)

Salmond, J. W. and R. F. V. Heuston, Law of Torts (20th edn, 1992)

Salomons, R. A., Schadevergoeding: zaakschade (Monografieën Nieuw BW no. B-38) (2nd edn, 1993)

Salvi, C., *Il danno extracontrattuale* (1985)
Sánchez Calero, F., *El contrato de obra* (1978)
Santaroni, M., *La responsabilità del revisore* (1984)
Santos Briz, J., 'La responsabilidad del fabricante frente a terceros en el derecho moderno', in *Estudios de Derecho Civil en Honor del Prof. Castán* (1969)
Santos Briz, J., 'El contrato de ejcución de obra y su problemática jurídica', (1972), *Revista de Derecho Privado* 379
Santos Briz, J., *La responsabilidad civil: derecho sustantivo y derecho procesal* (6th edn, 2 vols, 1991)
Savatier, R., *Traité de la responsabilité civile* (1949)
Saxén, H., *Adekvans och skada* (1962)
Saxén, H., *Skadeståndsrätt* (1975)
Saxén, H., *Tillägg till Skadeståndsrätt* (1983)
Schilcher, B. and W. Holzer, 'Der schadenersatzrechtliche Schutz des Traditionserwerbers bei Doppelveräußerung von Liegenschaften', (1974) JBl 445
Schilcher, B. and W. Posch, 'Civil Liability for Pure Economic Loss: An Austrian Perspective', in E. K. Banakas (ed.), *Civil Liability for Pure Economic Loss* (1996)
Schlechtriem, P., 'The Borderland of Tort and Contract – Opening a New Frontier?', (1988) 21 *Cornell International Law Journal* 467
Schlesinger, P., *L'ingiustizia del danno nell'illecito civile* (1960)
Schlesinger, R. (ed.), *Formation of Contracts* (1968)
Schlesinger, R. 'The Past and Future of Comparative Law', (1995) 43 *American Journal of Comparative Law* 477
Schlesinger, R., Baade, H. W., Damaska, M. R. and P. E. Herzog, *Comparative Law. Cases-Text-Materials* (5th edn, 1988).
Schmiedel, B., *Deliktsobligationen nach deutschem Kartellrecht*, vol. 1 (1974)
Schubert, W. (ed.), *Die Vorlagen der Redaktoren für die erste Kommission zur Ausarbeitung des Entwurfs eines Bürgerlichen Gesetzbuches, Recht der Schuldverhältnisse, Teil 1, Allgemeiner Teil I* (1980)
Schwartz, G. T., 'Economic Loss in American Tort Law: The Examples of J'Aire and of Products Liability', (1986) 23 *San Diego Law Review* 37
Schwartz, G. T., 'The Economic Loss Doctrine in American Tort Law: Assessing the Recent Experience', in E. K. Banakas (ed.), *Civil Liability for Pure Economic Loss* (1996)
Schwartz, G. T., 'Tobacco, Liability and *Viscusi*', (1999) 29 *Cumberland Law Review* 555
Schwiep, P., 'The Economic Loss Rule Outbreak: The Monster that Ate Commercial Torts', (1995) 69 Fla. B. J. 34
Schwimann, M. (ed.), *ABGB*, vol. 7 (2nd edn, 1997)
Schwitansky, H. G., *Deliktsrecht, Unternehmenschutz und Arbeitskampfrecht* (1986)
Sériaux, A., *Droit des Obligations* (1992)

Serio, M., *La responsabilità complessa. Verso uno statuto unitario della civil liability* (1988)
Seybold, K., H. Schippel and U. Bracker, *Bundesnotarordnung Kommentar* (6th edn, 1995)
Shavell, S., *Economic Analysis of Accident Law* (1987)
Shephard, J., 'The Murky Waters of *Robins Dry Dock*: A Comparative Analysis of Economic Loss in Maritime Law', (1986) 60 *Tulane Law Review* 995
Siebrasse, N., 'The Choice Between Implied Warranty and Tort Liability for Recovery of Pure Economic Loss in Contract-Torts: A Comparison of Judicial and Private Ordering in the Real Property Market', (1996) 19 *Dalhousie Law Journal* 247
Silciano, J., 'Negligent Accounting and the Limits of Instrumental Tort Reform', (1988) 86 *Michigan Law Review* 1929
Silverstein, E., 'On Recovery in Tort for Pure Economic Loss', (1999) 32 *University of Michigan Journal of Law Reform* 403
Sinde Monteiro, J. F., 'Medical Responsibility in Portugal' (with J. F. Dias) in E. Deutsch and H-L. Schreiber (eds.), *Medical Responsibility in Western Europe* (1985)
Sinde Monteiro, J. F., *Responsabilidade por Conselhos, Recomendações ou Informações* (1990)
Sinde Monteiro, J. F., *Deliktsrecht in Europa, Landesbericht Portugal* (with R. M. Ramos and H. E. Hörster, 1994)
Sinde Monteiro, J. F., 'Genome Analysis and Civil Liability in Portugal', in *Genome Analysis. Legal Rules – Practical Application. Reports of the Workshop 11–14 June 1992* (1994)
Sirvent, J., *La acción subrogatoria* (1996)
Smith, J. C., 'Economic Loss and the Common Law Marriage of Contracts and Torts', (1984) 18 U.B.C. L. Rev. 95
Smith, T. B., '*Jus Quaesitum Tertio*: Remedies of the Tertius in Scottish Law', in T. B. Smith (ed.), *Studies Critical and Comparative* (1962)
Smits, J. M., 'Aansprakelijkheid voor aan derden verscrafte informatie; enige dogmatische en praktische kanttekeningen bij derden-aansprakelijkheid', in R. P. J. L. Tjittes and M. A. Blom (eds.), *Bank & aansprakelijkheid* (1996)
Sombart, W., *Der moderne Kapitalismus*, vols. I–III (1928)
Soto, D., *De iustitia et iure libri decem* (1553) lib. 4, q. 6, a. 5
Sourdat, A., *Traité général de la responsabilité ou de l'action en dommages-intérêts en dehors des contrats*, vol. 1, Part II (2nd edn, 1872)
Sourlas, P., *Adaequanztheorie und Normzwecklehre bei der Begruendung der Haftung nach § 823 Abs.1 BGB* (1974)
Speciale, R., *Contratti preliminari entire precontrattuali* (1990)
Spier, J. (ed), *The Limits of Liability: Keeping the Floodgates Shut* (1996)
Spier, J. (ed), *The Limits of Expanding Liability: Eight Fundamental Cases in a Comparative Perspective* (1998)

Spier, J. and C. H. W. M. Sterk, *Rope-dancing Dutch Tort Law, Schriftenreihe deutscher Jura-Studenten in Genf* (1993)
Spyridakis, J., *General Principles of Civil Law* (1990)
St Cyr, G., 'Torts – Recovery of Economic Losses Absent Personal Injury or Property Damage Allowed', (1986) 20 Suffolk U. L. Rev. 732
Stair, *The Institutions of the Law of Scotland* (reprint 1981).
*Stair Memorial Encyclopaedia of the Laws of Scotland*, vol. 14 (1988); vol. 15 (1996)
Stamoulis, G., *The Problem of Causal Cohesion in Law* (1961)
Stanton, K. M., *The Modern Law of Tort* (1994)
Stapleton, J., 'Duty of Care and Economic Loss: A Wider Agenda', (1991) 107 *Law Quarterly Review* 249
Stapleton, J., 'Tort, Insurance and Ideology' (1995) 58 Mod. LR 820
Stapleton, J., 'Duty of Care Factors: A Selection from the Judicial Menus', in P. Cane and J. Stapleton (eds.), *The Law of Obligations: Essays in Celebration of John Fleming* (1998)
Stapleton, J., 'Legal Cause: Cause-in-Fact and the Scope of Liability for Consequences', (2001) 54 *Vanderbilt Law Review* 941
Starck, B., H. Roland and L. Boyer, *Droit Civil. Obligations* (2nd edn, 1985)
Stathopoulos, M., *Staudinger Kommentar zum Bürgerlichen Gesetzbuch* (12th edn, 1986)
Stathopoulos, M., *Contract Law in Hellas* (1995)
Stathopoulos, M., *Law of Obligations, General Part I–III* (1979–83), (3rd edn, 1998)
Stewart, W. J., *Delict and Related Obligations* (2nd edn, 1993)
Stollner, C. J. J. M., *Aansprakelijkheid voor beroeps-towten – van carriere naar nachkmerrie* (1995)
Stone, J., *Legal Systems and Lawyers' Reasonings* (1964)
Stör, U., *Die Haftung für Drittschäden beim Gefahrguttransport, Ein Vergleich der CRTD mit deutschem und portugiesischem Recht* (1997)
Storch, H., *Cours d'économie politique*, I–V (1823–1824)
Storch De Gracia, J. G., 'Daños causados por los productos elaborados', in: *La Ley*, 1985-I, 615
Street, *On Torts* (9th edn, 1993)
Struvius, G. A., *Syntagma iurisprudentiae secundum ordinem pandectarum* (1692) Exerc. XIV, lib. 9, tit. 2, no. XX
Taveira Machado, S. F., 'Pressupostos da responsabilidade civil dos notários', (1986) 7 *Revista do Notariado*
Telles, I. Galvâo., *Direito das Obrigações* (7th edn, 1997)
Terry, H. T., 'Proximate Consequences in the Law of Torts', (1914) 28 *Harvard Law Review* 10
Tettenborn, A., 'Tort: Pragmatism and Abstraction where Ship Hits Ship', (1986) 45 *Cambridge Law Journal* 10
Tettenborn, A., 'Components and Product Liability: Damage to "Other Property"', (2000) 3 L.M.C.L.Q. 338

Theime, H., 'Qu'est-ce que nous, les juristes, devons à la seconde scolastique espagnole?', in P. Grossi (ed.), *La seconda scolastica nella formazione del diritto privato moderno* (1973) 20

Thivaeos, P., *On the Negative Interest of the Contract* (1931)

Thomson, J. M., 'A Prophet not Rejected in his Own Land', (1994) 110 LQR 361

Thomson, J. M., 'Delictual Liability for Pure Economic Loss: Recent Developments', (1995) SLT 139

Thomson, J. M., 'Damages for Nuisance', (1997) SLT 177

Thomson, J. M., *Delictual Liability* (1999)

Thomson, J. M. and M. Tilbury, 'Purely Economic Loss in the Supreme Court of Canada', (1994) 2 *Torts Law Journal* 1

Torralba Soriano, O. V., 'La responsabilidad por los auxiliares en el cumplimiento de las obligaciones', Anuario de Derecho Civil, (1971) II, 1143

Treitel, G., *The Law of Contract* (9th edn, 1995)

Triantaphyllopoulos, K., *Law of Obligations* (1935)

Trimarchi, P., *Rischio e responsabilità oggettiva* (1961)

Trimarchi, P., *Causalità e danno* (1967)

Trimarchi, P., 'Sulla responsabilità del terzo per pregiudizio al diritto di credito', (1983) I *Riv. dir. civ.* 29

Trindade, F., 'Commercial Morality and the Tort of Negligence', (1989) 105 *Law Quarterly Review* 19

Vaggelas, K., 'Proximity, Economic Loss and the High Court of Australia', (1997) 5 *Tort Law Review* 127

Valpuesta, R., F. Blasco, F. Capilla, A. M. Lopez, V. L. Montés, J. O Orduña and E. Roca, *Derecho de obligaciones y contratos* (2nd edn, 1995)

Van Dunné, J. M., 'Liability for Pure Economic Loss: Rule or Exception? A Comparatist's View of the Civil Law–Common Law Split on Compensation of Non-physical Damage in Tort Law', (1999) 4 *European Review of Private Law* 397

Van Gerven, W., 'Bridging the Unbridgeable: Community and National Tort Laws after *Francovich* and *Brasserie*', (1996) 45 ICLQ 507

Van Gerven, W., 'Casebooks for the Common Law of Europe: Presentation of the Project', (1996) 4 *European Review of Private Law* 67

Van Gerven, W., J. Lever, and P. Larouche, *Tort Law: Scope of Protection* (1st edn, 1998; 2nd edn, 2000)

Van Vliet, L. P. W., *Transfer of Movables* (2000)

Vaz Serra, A. P. S., 'Responsabilidade Civil (Requisitos), *Boletim do Ministério da Justiça* No. 92

Vaz Serra, A. P. S., 'O Abuso do Direito (em Matéria de Responsabilidade Civil)', *Boletim do Ministério da Justica*, No. 85

Vettori, 'La violazione del contratto', in G. Alpa and M. Bessone (eds.), *La responsabilità civile* (1987)

Viney, G., 'La responsabilité: conditions', in J. Ghestin (ed.), *Traité de droit civil* (1982)

Viney, G., 'L'indemnisation des victimes de dommages causés par le "fait d'une chose" apres l'arrêt de la Cour de Cassation, Civ 2, 21 juillet 1982', (1982) D. Chr. 201

Viney, G., 'La réparation des dommages causés sous l'empire d'un état d'inconscience: un transfert necessaire de la responsabilité vers l'assurance', (1985) I JCP 3189

Viney, G., *La responsabilité: effets, Traité de droit civil* (1988)

Viney, G., *Introduction à la responsabilité, Traité de droit civil*, (1995)

Viney, G., 'Pour ou contre un principe général de responsabilité pour faute?', (2002) 49 *Osaka University Law Review* 33

Viney, G. and P. Jourdain, *Traité de droit civil: Les conditions de la responsabilité* (2nd edn, 1998)

Vinnius, A., *In quatuor libros Institutionem Imperialium commentarius* (4th edn, 1665), to I. 4.3 pr.

Visintini, G., *La reticenza nella formazione dei contratti* (1972)

Visintini, G., 'Responsabilità contrattuale ed extracontrattuale (Una distinzione in crisi?), *Rass. DC* (1983), 1077.

Visintini, G., 'Risarcimento del danno', (1983) I RDC 811

Visintini, G., *I fatti illeciti*, I, *L'ingiustizia del danno* (1987)

Von Bar, C., 'Negligence, Eigentumsverletzung und reiner Vermögensschaden. Zu den Grenzen der Fahrlässigkeitshaftung für reine Vermögensschäden in der neueren Entwicklung des common law', in (1992) 56 *Rabels Zeitschrift für ausländisches und internationales Privatrecht* 410

Von Bar, C., 'Liability for Information and Opinions Causing Pure Economic Loss to Third Parties: A Comparison of English and German Case Law', in B. S. Markesinis (ed.), *The Gradual Convergence* (1994)

Von Bar, C., *The Common European Law of Torts*, vol. I (1998)

Von Bar, C., *The Common European Law of Torts*, vol. II (2000)

Von Gierke, O., Culpa in contrahendo oder Schadensersatz bei nichtigen oder nicht zur Perfektion gelangten Verträgen, *Jherings Jahrbücher* 4 (1861)

Von Gierke, O., *Der Entwurf eines bürgerlichen Gesetzbuch und das deutsche Recht* (1889)

Von Gierke, O., *Deutsches Privatrecht*, vol. 3 (1917).

Von Ihering, R., *Der Zweck im Recht* (1877)

Von Lillienskiold, M., *Aktuelle Probleme des portugiesischen Delikts- und Schadensersatzrechts* (1975)

Von Staudinger, J., *Kommentar zum Bürgerlichen Gesetzbuch* (12th edn, 1986)

Von Vangerow, K. A., *Lehrbuch der Pandekten*, vol. 3 (6th edn, 1863)

Vranken, M., 'Negligent Solicitors and Compensation for Economic Loss: *Hill* v. *Van Erp*', (1997) 5 *Torts Law Journal* 1

Wagner, K. and G. Knechtel, *Notariatsordnung* (5th edn, 2000)

Waldron, J., 'Moments of Carelessness and Massive Loss', in D. Owen (ed.), *Philosophical Foundations of Tort Law* (1995)
Walker, D. M., *The Law of Delict in Scotland* (2nd edn, 1981)
Wallace, I. N. D., '*Junior Books* Extended: A Short Commentary', (1999) 15 *Constable Law Journal* 218
Watson, S. and A. Willekes, 'Economic Loss and Directors' Negligence', (2001) J.B.L. 217
Weir, T., 'Complex Liabilities', in XI *International Encyclopedia of Comparative Law*, no. 52 (1976)
Weir, T., *Economic Torts* (1997)
Weir, T., *A Casebook on Tort* (9th edn, 2000)
Welser, R., 'Der OGH und der Rechtswidrigkeitszusammenhang', (1975) ÖJZ 37
Welser, R., *Die Haftung für Rat, Auskunft und Gutachten* (1983)
Werro, F., 'Tort Liability for Pure Economic Loss: A Critique of Current Trends in Swiss Law', in E. K. Banakas (ed.), *Civil Liability for Pure Economic Loss* (1996)
Weston, C. A. R., 'Suing in Tort for Loss of Computer Data', (1999) 58 *Cambridge Law Journal* 67
Wilhelm, G., *Unrichtige Gutachten – Haftung für Dritte* (1991) ecolex
Windscheid, B., 'Die Voraussetzung', (1892) 78 *Archiv für die civilistische Praxis* 161
Windscheid, B., *Lehrbuch des Pandektenrechts*, vol. 2 (7th edn, 1891)
Woolman, S., *Contract* (2nd edn, 1994)
Yeager, L. B., 'Deregulation and Monetary Reform', in *American Economic Review, Papers and Proceedings* 75.2 (1985)
Zachariae, K.-S., *Cours de droit civil français*, vol. II (2nd edn, 1850) (French trans. C. Aubry and C. Rau from the 5th German edn, 1839)
Zasius, U., 'Commentaria seu Lecturas eiusdem in titulos primae Pandectarum ad Dig. 9.2 no. 1 39', in *Opera omnia*, vol. 1 (1550, reprinted 1966).
Zeno-Zencovich, V., 'The "European Civil Code". European Legal Traditions and Neo-Positivism', (1998) 6 *European Review of Private Law*
Zepos, P., *Greek Law of Obligations, General Part* (1955), *Special Part* (1965)
Ziccardi, F., *L'induzione all'inadempimento* (1979)
Zimmermann, R., *The Law of Obligations: Roman Foundations of the Civil Law Tradition* (1990)
Zimmermann, R., 'Breach of Contract and Remedies under the New German Law of Obligations', in Centro di studie ricerche di diritto comparato e straniero (ed.), 48 *Saggi, conferente e seminari* (2002)
Zimmermann, R. and S. Whittaker (eds.), *Good Faith in European Contract Law*, in *The Common Core of European Private Law Project – Cambridge Studies in International and Comparative Law* (2000)
Zuckerman, A. A. S. (ed.), *Civil Justice in Crisis* (1999)
Zweigert, K. and H. Kötz, *Introduction to Comparative Law* (3rd edn, trans. T. Weir, 1998)

# Index

Accursius, 27
Addison, C. G., 48, 54
adjudication costs, 78
adoption agencies, 113–14
advice. *See* reliance on professional advice
agency, Netherlands, 395
alcohol tests, employees, 112
animals. *See also* Case 6
  Austria, 267
  Finland and Sweden, 269
  Portugal, 268
  strict liability, 258, 264, 269–70
antitrust law, 8
Aquinas, Thomas, 30, 31, 32, 33
architects. *See also* Case 7
  professional ethics, Portugal, 287
  regulation, Belgium, 272
  standard of care, 286
Aristotle, 30
asbestos, 19
Atiyah, P. S., 51
auditors' regulation. *See also* Case 17
  Belgium, 457
  EC Directive, 461
  France, 453–5
  Greece, 459–60
  Italy, 457
  Portugal, 469
  Spain, 458
  Sweden and Finland, 470
Austria
  Case 1, 186–7
  Case 2, 202
  Case 3, 218–19
  Case 4, 235–6
  Case 5, 251

  Case 6, 267–8
  Case 7, 285–6
  Case 8, 302–3
  Case 9, 323–4
  Case 10, 339–40
  Case 11, 356–7
  Case 12, 378–80
  Case 13, 398–9
  Case 14, 413–14
  Case 15, 429–30
  Case 16, 448–9
  Case 17, 468–9
  Case 18, 484–5
  Case 19, 503–4
  Case 20, 516–18
  conservative regime, 125, 152–4
  contract. *See* contract
  façade, 126–7
  floodgates argument, 20, 21, 303
  labour law, 219
  pre-contractual duties, 154, 356, 503–4
  transferred loss, 302–3, 339, 340

Baldus de Ubaldi, 29
Belgium
  *bonus pater familias*, 474, 508
  Case 1, 173–4
  Case 2, 192–3
  Case 3, 209–11
  Case 4, 223–4
  Case 5, 242–3
  Case 6, 256–7
  Case 7, 272–3
  Case 8, 292–3
  Case 9, 310–11
  Case 10, 328–30

Case 11, 345–6
Case 12, 363–4
Case 13, 386
Case 14, 404–5
Case 15, 420–1
Case 16, 436
Case 17, 456–7
Case 18, 474–5
Case 19, 489–91
Case 20, 507–8
causation, 132–3, 210–11, 257, 420–1, 508
Criminal Code, 173
employers' liability, 173, 192–3, 223
*force majeure*, 293
liberal regime, 123, 131–3
recoverability of pure economic loss, 22
Bell, G. J., 441
Bernstein, Robby, 47, 52
Bhopal gas leak, 19
Brunnemann, J., 27, 29
Buchanan, James M., 61
building defects. See also Case 13
US cases, 114–18

cables. See Case 1; Case 2; Case 3
Cajetan, 30, 32–3, 36, 46
Calabresi, Guido, 71
cancellations. See Case 8
Carbonnier, Jean, 120
carers. See Case 10
Case 1 (Cable I – Blackout)
Austria, 186–7
Belgium, 173–4
comparative law, 189–91
economic approach, 70
England, 179–80
facts, 171
Finland, 188–9
France, 172–3
Germany, 185
Greece, 177–9
Italy, 174–6
Netherlands, 183–5
Portugal, 187–8
Scotland, 180–3
Spain, 176–7
Sweden, 188–9
Case 2 (Cable II – Factory Shutdown)
Austria, 202
Belgium, 192–3

comparative law, 205–7, 527
economic approach, 70
England, 196
facts, 192
Finland, 204–5
France, 192
Germany, 200–2
Greece, 138, 195–6
Italy, 193–4
Netherlands, 198–200
nightmare scenario, 207
Portugal, 202–4
private and social loss, 87
Scotland, 196–8
Spain, 195
Sweden, 204–5
Case 3 (Cable III – Day-to-Day Workers)
Austria, 218–19
Belgium, 209–11
comparative law, 220–1
economic approach, 71, 87
England, 214–15
facts, 208
Finland, 219–20
France, 208–9
Germany, 218
Greece, 213–14
Italy, 211–12
Netherlands, 147, 216–17
Portugal, 219
Scotland, 215–16
Spain, 212
Sweden, 219–20
Case 4 (Convalescing Employee)
Austria, 235–6
Belgium, 223–4
comparative law, 239–40
economic approach, 71
England, 231
facts, 222
Finland, 238–9
France, 222–3
Germany, 234–5
Greece, 229–31
Italy, 224–5
Netherlands, 233–4
Portugal, 236–8
private and social loss, 87–8
Scotland, 231–3
Spain, 225–9
Sweden, 238–9

Case 5 (Requiem for an Italian All Star)
  Austria, 251
  Belgium, 222–4
  comparative law, 254, 527
  economic approach, 71, 88–9
  England, 247–8
  facts, 221
  Finland, 253
  France, 221–2
  Germany, 250
  Greece, 246–7
  Italy, 224–5
  Netherlands, 147, 249–50
  Portugal, 251–3
  Scotland, 248–9
  Spain, 225–8
  Sweden, 253
Case 6 (Infected Cow)
  Austria, 267–8
  Belgium, 256–7
  comparative law, 269–70
  economic approach, 71–2
  England, 260–2
  facts, 255
  Finland, 268–9
  France, 255–6
  Germany, 151, 266–7
  Greece, 259–60
  Italy, 138, 257–8
  Netherlands, 263–5
  Portugal, 268
  Scotland, 262–3
  Spain, 258–9
  Sweden, 268–9
Case 7 (Careless Architect)
  Austria, 285–6
  Belgium, 272–3
  comparative law, 289–90
  economic approach, 72
  England, 277–8
  facts, 271
  Finland, 288–9
  France, 271–2
  Germany, 284–5
  Greece, 276–7
  Italy, 273–4
  Netherlands, 283–4
  Portugal, 286–8
  Scotland, 278–83
  Spain, 274–6
  Sweden, 288–9
Case 8 (Cancelled Cruise)
  Austria, 302–3
  Belgium, 292–3
  comparative law, 305–7
  economic approach, 72
  England, 296–7
  facts, 291
  Finland, 304–5
  France, 291–2
  Germany, 301–2
  Greece, 295–6
  Italy, 294
  Netherlands, 300–1
  Portugal, 303–4
  Scotland, 297–9
  Spain, 294–5
  Sweden, 304–5
Case 9 (Fire in Projection Booth)
  Austria, 323–4
  Belgium, 310–11
  comparative law, 326–7
  economic approach, 72
  England, 316–17
  facts, 308
  Finland, 326
  France, 308–10
  Germany, 321–3
  Greece, 314–16
  Italy, 311–12
  Netherlands, 147, 320–1
  Portugal, 324–6
  Scotland, 317–20
  Spain, 312–14
  Sweden, 326
Case 10 (Dutiful Wife)
  Austria, 339–40
  Belgium, 328–30
  comparative law, 341–3, 527
  economic approach, 72
  England, 333
  facts, 328
  Finland, 341
  France, 328
  Germany, 338–9
  Greece, 331–2
  Italy, 330
  Netherlands, 147, 336–8
  Portugal, 340
  Scotland, 333–6
  Spain, 330–1
  Sweden, 341

Case 11 (Maestro's Mistake)
  Austria, 356-7
  Belgium, 345-6
  comparative law, 360-1
  economic approach, 72-3
  England, 348-9, 350
  facts, 344
  Finland, 359-60
  France, 344-5
  Germany, 354-6
  Greece, 347-8
  Italy, 346-7
  Netherlands, 353-4
  Portugal, 357-9
  Scotland, 350-3
  Spain, 347
  Sweden, 359-60
Case 12 (Double Sale)
  Austria, 378-80
  Belgium, 363-4
  comparative law, 383-4
  England, 368-70
  facts, 362
  Finland, 382
  France, 362-3
  Germany, 377-8
  Greece, 367-8
  Italy, 364-5
  Netherlands, 375-7
  Portugal, 380-2
  Scotland, 370-5
  Spain, 365-7
  Sweden, 382
Case 13 (Subcontractor's Liability)
  Austria, 398-9
  Belgium, 386
  comparative law, 401-2
  England, 390
  facts, 385
  Finland, 401
  France, 385-6
  Germany, 396-8
  Greece, 389-90
  Italy, 387
  Netherlands, 395-6
  Portugal, 399-401
  Scotland, 390-5
  Spain, 387-9
  Sweden, 401
Case 14 (Poor Legal Services)
  Austria, 413-14
  Belgium, 404-5
  comparative law, 417, 528
  England, 407
  facts, 403
  Finland, 416-17
  France, 403
  Germany, 413
  Greece, 406-7
  Italy, 405
  Netherlands, 412
  Portugal, 414-16
  Scotland, 407-11
  Spain, 405-6
  Sweden, 416-17
Case 15 (Closed Motorway)
  Austria, 429-30
  Belgium, 420-1
  comparative law, 432-4, 528
  England, 423-4
  facts, 418
  Finland, 431-2
  France, 418-20
  Germany, 427-9
  Greece, 422-3
  Italy, 421
  Netherlands, 147, 424-5
  Portugal, 430-1
  Scotland, 424-5
  Spain, 421-2
  Sweden, 431-2
Case 16 (Blocking Truck)
  Austria, 448-9
  Belgium, 436
  comparative law, 451-2
  England, 439-40
  facts, 435
  Finland, 451
  France, 435-6
  Germany, 447-8
  Greece, 438-9
  Italy, 437
  Netherlands, 446-7
  Portugal, 449-51
  Scotland, 440-6
  Spain, 437-8
  Sweden, 451
Case 17 (Auditor's Liability)
  Austria, 468-9
  Belgium, 456-7
  comparative law, 471-2
  England, 461

Case 17 (Auditor's Liability) (cont.)
   facts, 453
   Finland, 470–1
   France, 453–6
   Germany, 466–8
   Greece, 459–61
   Italy, 457–8
   Netherlands, 465–6
   Portugal, 469–70
   Scotland, 461–5
   Spain, 458–9
   Sweden, 470–1
Case 18 (Wrongful Job Reference)
   Austria, 484–5
   Belgium, 474–5
   comparative law, 486–7
   England, 478–9
   facts, 473
   Finland, 486
   France, 473
   Germany, 483–4
   Greece, 477–8
   Italy, 475
   Netherlands, 482
   Portugal, 485–6
   Scotland, 479–82
   Spain, 475–7
   Sweden, 486
Case 19 (Breach of Promise)
   Austria, 503–4
   Belgium, 489–91
   comparative law, 505–6
   England, 496–7
   facts, 488
   Finland, 504–5
   France, 488
   Germany, 502–3
   Greece, 495–6
   Italy, 491–3
   Netherlands, 501
   Portugal, 504
   Scotland, 497–501
   Spain, 493–5
   Sweden, 504–5
Case 20 (Anonymous Telephone Call)
   Austria, 516–18
   Belgium, 507–8
   comparative law, 519–20
   England, 511–12
   facts, 507
   Finland, 519
   France, 507
   Germany, 515–16
   Greece, 510–11
   Italy, 509–10
   Netherlands, 514–15
   Portugal, 518
   Scotland, 512–14
   Spain, 510
   Sweden, 519
case studies
   metalegal formants, 170
   methodology, 163
   operative rules, 169–70
   purpose, 163
   questionnaire, 166–70
causation
   Belgium, 132–3, 210–11, 257, 420–1, 508
   Case 4, 239
   Case 5, 254
   France, 127, 172, 454–5, 456
   Germany, 185
   Greece, 138, 178, 332, 422–3, 438–9
   Italy, 175, 211
   liberal regimes, 205–6, 220–1
   Netherlands, 147–8, 184–5, 199–200, 300
   reliance on advice, 13
   Spain, 136–7, 258–9
chances. See lost opportunities
citizens, relationships with public bodies, 65
civil or common law regimes, irrelevance, 530
Clerk, J. F., 48, 54
Coderch, Salvador, 388
codification. See European civil code
collateral benefits
common core
   absence, 158, 530–1
   approach, 163–6
   Common Core Project, 163
   consequential loss, 533
   intentional harm, 534
   interference with business, 535–6
   professional services, 534–5
   purpose of case studies, 163
   questionnaire, 166–70
   search for, 121
   selective protected areas, 534–6
   substantive common core, 532–6
   transferred losses, 535

common or civil law regimes, irrelevance, 530
commutative justice, 30–1, 33, 34
competition, 66–8
consequential economic loss
    common core, 533
    recoverability, 7
    vs. pure economic loss, 5–8
conservative regimes, 125, 148–58, 206–7, 526
conspiracy, 139, 372–3
contract
    chain of contracts, France, 309
    changed circumstances, Germany, 25
    England, 142
    freedom, 58–9
    interference. *See* interference with contractual relations
    positive violation of contract, 154
    pre-contractual liability. *See also* Case 19
        Austria, 154, 356, 503–4
        Belgium, 489
        England, 496–7
        France, 488–9
        Germany, 151, 355–6, 502
        Greece, 495–6
        Italy, 491–3
        Netherlands, 501
        Portugal, 470, 485–6, 504
        Spain, 493–5
        Sweden and Finland, 505
    privity. *See* privity of contract
    Scotland, 144, 497–8
    third parties
        Austria, 154, 398–9, 413–14, 468–9, 517
        Germany, 150–1, 396–8, 467–8
        Greece, 315
        Portugal, 286–8
        US, 104
contributory negligence, 285–6, 321, 466
copyright, 8
Cornell methodology, 4
*Corpus iuris civilis*, 26–7
credit reference agencies. *See* Case 20
*culpa in contrahendo*
    Austria, 154, 356, 503–4
    Belgium, 490
    European codification, 539
    Germany, 151, 355–6, 502
    Greece, 495–6
    Portugal, 470, 485–6

Spain, 493–5
Sweden and Finland, 505
currency stability, 63–4

damage, meaning, 23, 31
De Ángel, R., 437
deceit, 139
defamation. *See also* Case 20
    Belgium, 508
    England, 139
    Greece, 477
    Scotland, 144
defects. *See* Case 9
derivative litigation, 90–2
descriptive formants, 170
Díez-Picazo, L., 245
disclaimers, US, 102–3
discrimination, and market economy, 59
distributive justice, 30
drug tests, employees, 112
due process, 65
Durandus, 29
duty of care
    Belgium, 131–2
    Case 2, 206
    England, 140, 142
    Greece, 138
    Netherlands, 146
    Scotland, 145, 232–3
    screening mechanism, 124–5

economics approach, 77–81
    private and social loss, 81–5
    pure economic loss, 57, 81
education, freedom, 64
employment. *See also* Case 4
    Austria, 485
    Belgium, 209
    drug/alcohol tests, 112
    employers' liability, 173, 192–3, 223, 460
    France, 208
    Germany, 484
    Greece, 478
    Spain, 475–6
England
    *Caparo Industries*, 461
    Case 1, 179–80
    Case 2, 196
    Case 3, 214–15
    Case 4, 231
    Case 5, 247–8

England (cont.)
    Case 6, 260–2
    Case 7, 277–8
    Case 8, 296–7
    Case 9, 316–17
    Case 10, 333
    Case 11, 348–9, 350
    Case 12, 368–70
    Case 13, 390
    Case 14, 407
    Case 15, 423–4
    Case 16, 439–40
    Case 17, 461
    Case 18, 478–9
    Case 19, 496–7
    Case 20, 511–12
    case law, 46–55
    complex structures, 316
    contract law, 142, 496–7
    exclusionary rule, 25, 46–54, 55
    floodgates argument, 20–1
    *Hedley Byrne*, 52, 277, 349
    *Junior Books*, 390
    legal policy, 142, 180
    nightmare scenario, 261, 424
    pragmatic regime, 124, 139–42
    primary purpose of law, 23
    pure economic loss, 6, 46–55
    *Rylands* v. *Fletcher*, 260–1
    *Spartan Steel*, 47, 53, 54, 179–80, 196, 261–2, 296
    *Spring* v. *Guardian Assurance*, 478–9, 511–12
    *White* v. *Jones*, 407
equity, 231
*erga omnes* rights, 4, 127
Erskine, 371
Esmein, 420
European civil code, 75
    Study Group, 164–5
    tort law, 537–8
        place of pure economic loss, 540–1
        possible scenarios, 541–5
European Law casebooks, 165–6
European regimes. *See also* specific countries
    common core. *See* common core
    conservative regimes, 125, 148–58, 206–7, 526
    liberal regimes, 123–4, 126–38, 205–6, 220–1, 526
    no common theoretical matrix, 158
    pragmatic regimes, 124–5, 139–48, 526
    types of regimes, 123–5
European Union law, breach, 8–9
evidence, negligent spoliation, 112–13
exclusionary rules, 16–24
    floodgates argument, 16–21
    historical perspective, 23–4, 25
    lack of coherence, 92–3
    scale of human values, 21–3
    United States
        cases, 108–18
        product liability exception, 96–101
        rationale, 101–7
        relative unimportance, 94–6
expected value, 35
externalities, 65–70, 77–8, 81–5
Exxon Valdez oil spill, 19

façades, 122–3
fairness, floodgates, 17
Feinman, Jay M., 96
Finland
    Case 1, 188–9
    Case 2, 204–5
    Case 3, 219–20
    Case 4, 238–9
    Case 5, 253
    Case 6, 268–9
    Case 7, 288–9
    Case 8, 304–5
    Case 9, 326
    Case 10, 341
    Case 11, 359–60
    Case 12, 382
    Case 13, 401
    Case 14, 416–17
    Case 15, 431–2
    Case 16, 451
    Case 17, 470–1
    Case 18, 486
    Case 19, 504–5
    Case 20, 519
    conservative regime, 125, 156–8
floodgates argument
    Austria, 17, 21, 303
    Case 3, 221
    comparative law, 432–4
    England, 20–1
    France, 21, 131
    generally, 16–21

Germany, 20, 21, 428–9
Netherlands, 20, 264–5, 301, 426–7
Portugal, 21
public infrastructure closures, 13
Scotland, 20–1
foot and mouth disease, 19, 61–2, 71
*force majeure*, 208, 222, 258, 293
foreseeability, 17, 52
  Austria, 448–9
  Greece, 213, 422–3, 438–9
  Netherlands, 184, 199, 217, 264, 321, 425–7, 515
  problem, 89–92
  rules, workability, 23
  Scotland, 232, 248, 334, 393–4, 499
  United States, 89, 106
forgery. *See* Case 11
France
  Case 1, 172–3
  Case 2, 192
  Case 3, 208–9
  Case 4, 222–3
  Case 5, 240–1
  Case 6, 255–6
  Case 7, 271–2
  Case 8, 291–2
  Case 9, 308–10
  Case 10, 328
  Case 11, 344–5
  Case 12, 362–3
  Case 13, 385–6
  Case 14, 403
  Case 15, 418–20
  Case 16, 435–6
  Case 17, 453–6
  Case 18, 473
  Case 19, 488
  Case 20, 507
  causation, 127, 172, 454–5, 456
  *chômage technique*, 208
  contract. *See* contract
  credit reference agencies, 507
  damages, 292
    mitigation, 328
  *dommages matériels*, 173, 271
  floodgates argument, 21, 131
  *Football Club de Metz*, 241
  judicial policy, 128–9
  Labour Code, 208
  liberal regime, 123, 126–31
  loss of economic expectations, 15
  *neminem laedere*, 121, 126
  recoverability of pure economic loss, 22
  tort and contract, 129–30, 271–2, 310
fraud, 43, 371–2, 461
freedom of expression, 64, 516
freedom of religion, 64

gambling, 108–9
Germany
  before codification, 36–8
  *Begriffsjurisprudenz*, 46
  Case 1, 185
  Case 2, 200–2
  Case 3, 218
  Case 4, 234–5
  Case 5, 250
  Case 6, 266–7
  Case 7, 284–5
  Case 8, 301–2
  Case 9, 321–3
  Case 10, 338–9
  Case 11, 354–6
  Case 12, 377–8
  Case 13, 396–8
  Case 14, 413
  Case 15, 427–9
  Case 16, 447–8
  Case 17, 466–8
  Case 18, 483–4
  Case 19, 502–3
  Case 20, 515–16
  causation, 185
  Civil Code
    interpretation, 543
    codification, 38–46
    cases, 44–5
  conservative regime, 125, 148–51
  contract. *See* contract
  damages, 302
  established commercial enterprises, 201–2, 448, 515
  exclusionary rule, history, 25
  floodgates argument, 20, 21, 428–9
  fraud, 43
  joint liability, 284–5
  loss of economic expectations, 15
  necessary services, 339
  pay continuation statute, 71, 234–5, 250
  primary purpose of law, 23
  *Schuldrechts modernisierung* 151, 354–5

Gloag, W. M., 281
Goldberg, Victor, 96
Gordon, William, 48, 54
Greece
  burden of proof, 315–16
  Case 1, 177–9
  Case 2, 195–6
  Case 3, 213–14
  Case 4, 229–31
  Case 5, 246–7
  Case 6, 259–60
  Case 7, 276–7
  Case 8, 295–6
  Case 9, 314–16
  Case 10, 331–2
  Case 11, 347–8
  Case 12, 367–8
  Case 13, 389–90
  Case 14, 406–7
  Case 15, 422–3
  Case 16, 438–9
  Case 17, 459–61
  Case 18, 477–8
  Case 19, 495–6
  Case 20, 510–11
  causation, 138, 178, 332, 422–3, 438–9
  joint and several debts, 276–7
  liberal regime, 123, 137–8
  professional sport, 247
Griffith, Walter, 48, 54
Grotius, Hugo, 23, 30, 31
guarantee funds, notaries, 403
guarantees, procedural guarantees, 64–70
Guatemala, 111

Harberger triangle, 67–8
historical perspective, 23–4
human rights, basic freedoms, 64

immovable property rights. *See also* Case 12
  England, 369
  France, 362
  Greece, 367
  Italy, 364–5
  Netherlands, 376
  Portugal, 380
  Scotland, 371, 374
  Spain, 365–7
inequality, and market economy, 59

insurance
  business interruption insurance, 24
  maritime insurance, 296–7
  professional indemnity, 403
  subrogation, 110
  transferred losses, 11
intangible wealth, 21–3
intentional wrongdoing
  common core, 534
  or negligence, 9, 22
    Germany, 37, 40, 201
  Portugal, 253
interference with contractual relations
  Belgium, 364
  comparative law, 383
  England, 139, 214
  France, 363
  Italy, 346–7
  Portugal, 252–3
  Scotland, 370–1, 373
  United States, 94
interference with trade, 139, 535–6
intimidation, England, 139
intoxication, 108–9
Italy
  *Baroncini* v. *Enel*, 211, 475
  Case 1, 174–6
  Case 2, 193–4
  Case 3, 211–12
  Case 4, 224–5
  Case 5, 243–4
  Case 6, 257–8
  Case 7, 273–4
  Case 8, 294
  Case 9, 311–12
  Case 10, 330
  Case 11, 346–7
  Case 12, 364–5
  Case 13, 387
  Case 14, 405
  Case 15, 421
  Case 16, 437
  Case 17, 457–8
  Case 18, 475
  Case 19, 491–3
  Case 20, 509–10
  causation, 175, 211
  liberal regime, 123, 133–5
  *Meroni*, 134–5, 251, 254
  *Puddu & Enel* v. *Ditta Giampaoli*, 175–6, 194

James, Fleming, 95
joint and several liability
  Germany, 284–5
  Greece, 276–7
  Italy, 387
  Netherlands, 283
  Spain, 388, 458
*ius*, meaning, 33
*ius quaesitum tertio*, 278, 280–2
Justinian, 26

Kaufmann, Horst, 29
Kohler, Josef, 38
Kötz, H., 23, 144

Lacruz, J. L., 437
latent defects, Scotland, 317–18
Lauterbach, W. A., 29
leases, transferred losses, 11, 302–3
legal environment, stability, 63
legal harmonization, 164
legal policy
  England, 142, 180, 214, 296–7
  Portugal, 268
  Scotland, 183
legal regimes, irrelevance, 530
legal services. *See* Case 14
Lessius, Leonard, 30, 33, 34
*lex Aquilia*, 26, 29, 37, 127
liability
  generally, 61–2
  open-ended liability, 90–2
  optimum scope, 78
  rules
    application, 86
    practical problems, 85–9
    social and private costs, 84–5
liberal regimes
  characteristics, 123–4
  chart, 526
  control of issue, 124
  flexible causal determinations, 205–6, 220–21
  generally, 126–38
limitation periods
  Germany, contract, 150
  United States, 102, 105
Lindsell, W. H. B., 48, 54
litigation rates, 20, 90–2
lost opportunities. *See also* Case 16; Case 18

Belgium, 436, 475
France, 473
generally, 14
Italy, 212, 475
Lugo, Juan de, 30, 34, 35–6

maritime law. *See also* Case 8
  France, 291
  United Kingdom, 298
market economy
  basic requirements, 58–64
  currency stability, 63–4
  freedom of contract, 58–9
  liability, 61–2
  market dynamics, 69–70
  open markets, 64
  private property, 59–61
  stable legal environment, 63
mayhem, England, 139
medical treatment, consent, 62
*Meroni* case, 134–5, 251, 254
metalegal formants, 170
methodology
  case studies, 163
  questionnaire, 166–70
Middle Ages, just price, 67
misfeasance in public office, 139
mitigation of damages, 328, 438
Molière, 129
Molina, Luis de, 30, 33, 34–5
monopolies, 67
movable property rights
  England, 369–70
  France, 363
  Germany, 378
  Italy, 365
  Netherlands, 376–7
  Portugal, 381
  Scotland, 374–5

natural law, 29–36
negligence
  England, 139–40, 179, 214–15, 261, 277–8, 423–4
  or intentional wrongdoing, 9, 22
  France, 345
  Germany, 37, 40
  Scotland, 144
negligent misrepresentation, 114
negligent spoliation of evidence, 112–13

neighbourhood principle
  England, 140, 142
  Scotland, 145
neighbours, 52
*neminem laedere*, 121, 126, 136
nervous shock, 17, 55
Netherlands
  Case 1, 183–5
  Case 2, 198–200
  Case 3, 216–17
  Case 4, 233–4
  Case 5, 249–50
  Case 6, 263–5
  Case 7, 283–4
  Case 8, 300–1
  Case 9, 320–1
  Case 10, 336–8
  Case 11, 353–4
  Case 12, 375–7
  Case 13, 395–6
  Case 14, 412
  Case 15, 424–5
  Case 16, 446–7
  Case 17, 465–6
  Case 18, 482
  Case 19, 501
  Case 20, 514–15
  causation, 147–8, 184–5, 199–200, 300
  floodgates argument, 20, 264–5, 301, 426–7
  joint and several liability, 283
  ordinary business risks, 265
  *Plas v. Valburg*, 501
  pragmatic regime, 124, 145–8
nightmare scenarios, 207, 261, 420–1
Norrie, Kenneth, 144–5, 282, 320, 409, 410
notaries. *See also* Case 14
  Belgium, 404–5
  France, 403
  Germany, 413
  Greece, 406–7
  Italy, 405
  Netherlands, 412, 465
  Portugal, 414–15
  Spain, 405–6
nuisance
  private nuisance, 439–43
  public nuisance, 260–1, 423

Odofredus, 27
open markets, 64
operative rules, 169–70

Pantaleón, F., 227, 437, 459
parasitic loss. *See* consequential economic loss
passing off, 139, 144
patents, 8, 68
pharmaceutical products, 68
philosophical values, 21–3
Pollock, Sir Frederick, 48
Portugal
  Case 1, 187–8
  Case 2, 202–4
  Case 3, 219
  Case 4, 236–8
  Case 5, 251–3
  Case 6, 268
  Case 7, 286–8
  Case 8, 303–4
  Case 9, 324–6
  Case 10, 340
  Case 11, 357–9
  Case 12, 380–2
  Case 13, 399–401
  Case 14, 414–16
  Case 15, 430–1
  Case 16, 449–51
  Case 17, 469–70
  Case 18, 485–6
  Case 19, 504
  Case 20, 518
  conservative regime, 125, 154–6
  contract. *See* contract
  floodgates argument, 21
  manifest abuses, 358–9, 381
  personal right of enjoyment, 304
Posch, W., 152
Posner, R. A.
possession, Germany, 302
potential property. *See also* lost opportunities
  Aquinas, 32
  Cajetan, 32–3
  compensation, 33–6
  Lessius, 33
  Molina, 33
pragmatic regimes
  characteristics, 124–5
  chart, 526
  generally, 139–48
precautionary measures, 176, 194
press freedom, 64, 516
private nuisance, 439–43
private property, 59–61

privity of contract
  France, 172
  Germany, 150–1
  Greece, 276, 367–8, 389
  Scotland, 280
  Spain, 388
  United States, 104
procedural guarantees, 64–70
product liability. *See also* Case 9
  Austria, 324
  Belgium, 310
  comparative law, 326–7
  England, 316
  France, 308–9
  Germany, 322–3
  Greece, 314
  Italy, 311
  Netherlands, 321
  Portugal, 324–5
  Spain, 312
  Sweden and Finland, 326
  United States, 96–101
professional advice. *See* reliance on professional advice
professional services. *See also* Case 14; Case 17
  common core, 534–5
  freedom, 64
  indemnity insurance, 403
  liability, Italy, 273–4
  misconduct, US, 105
property rights. *See also* Case 12
  Austria, 448
  exercise, 63
  framework, 538
  France, 362
  Germany, 447–8
  guarantee, 59–61
  immovable. *See* immovable property
  movable. *See* movable property rights
  potential property. *See* potential property
  private property, 59–61
proximity
  England, 277, 349, 461
  Netherlands, 426
  proximate cause, 110–11
  Scotland, 181–3, 279, 393, 464–5
  United States, 106
public bodies
  relationships between, 64–5
  relationships with citizens, 65

public infrastructure closures, 16. *See also* Case 15
public nuisance, England, 260–1, 423
public policy
  Case 3, 221
  exclusion of pure economic loss, 53–4
  Scotland, 215–16, 233, 263
Pufendorf, Samuel, 30

Rabin, Robert, 96
reduction, 374
relational economic loss. *See* ricochet losses
reliance on professional advice. *See also* Case 11
  causation, 13
  England, 277–8, 349–50
  generally, 13–14
  Greece, 347–8
  Portugal, 287–8
  Scotland, 280
religious freedom, 64
remoteness of damage
  Case 2, 206
  English cases, 47, 54, 55
  Italy, 257–8, 330
  Scotland, 181–3, 197, 262–3
rent seeking, 69
ricochet losses
  France, 127
  generally, 10–11
  Greece, 138
  Netherlands, 147, 336
rights
  absolute and relative, 45
  *in personam*, 218, 227, 378–9
  *in rem*, 381, 539
  meaning, 33
road traffic accidents. *See also* Case 15
  Austria, 430
  France, 222, 418–20
  Germany, 428
Roman law, 26–9, 121, 143–4
Rudden, Bernard, 131

Sacco, Rodolfo, 120, 133, 167, 365, 382
sale of goods, implied warranty of fitness, 102
Salmond, J. W., 48–9, 54
Santos Briz, J., 245
scale of human values, 21–3
Schwartz, Gary T., 96

Schilcher, B., 152
Schlesinger, Rudolf, 167
scholastics, 30, 46
Scotland
  *Caparo Industries*, 279, 462–4
  Case 1, 180–3
  Case 2, 196–8
  Case 3, 215–16
  Case 4, 231–3
  Case 5, 248–9
  Case 6, 262–3
  Case 7, 278–83
  Case 8, 297–9
  Case 9, 317–20
  Case 10, 333–6
  Case 11, 350–3
  Case 12, 370–5
  Case 13, 390–5
  Case 14, 407–11
  Case 15, 424–5
  Case 16, 440–6
  Case 17, 461–5
  Case 18, 479–82
  Case 19, 497–501
  Case 20, 512–14
  contract, 144, 497–8
  *Donoghue v. Stevenson*, 317–18
  *Dynamco*, 196–7, 215, 297
  floodgates argument, 20–1
  *Hedley Byrne*, 278–9, 282, 350–3
  *Henderson v. Merrett*, 280, 351–2, 391
  *Junior Books*, 390–3, 394–5
  *jus quaesitum tertio*, 278, 280–2
  mixed jurisdiction, 143
  *Nacap*, 297–9
  necessary services, 335–6
  pragmatic regime, 124, 142–5
  sequestration, 317
  *Spring v. Guardian Assurance*, 479–80, 514
  *White v. Jones*, 407, 409–10
Serra, Vaz, 155
Shavell, Steven
Sirvent, J., 389
slander of title, 139
Smith, Adam, 58
smoking, 109–12
Soto, Domingo de, 30, 34
sources of law, 168
Spain
  *a non domino* dispositions, 367
  Case 1, 176–7
  Case 2, 195
  Case 3, 212
  Case 4, 225–9
  Case 5, 244–6
  Case 6, 258–9
  Case 7, 274–6
  Case 8, 294–5
  Case 9, 312–14
  Case 10, 330–1
  Case 11, 347
  Case 12, 365–7
  Case 13, 387–9
  Case 14, 405–6
  Case 15, 421–2
  Case 16, 437–8
  Case 17, 458–9
  Case 18, 475–7
  Case 19, 493–5
  Case 20, 510
  causation, 136–7, 258–9
  general risks of life, 259
  liberal regime, 123, 135–7
  *neminem laedere*, 136
sport, Greece, 247
spouses, mutual assistance, 328, 338, 340
standard of care, architects, 286
strict liability
  animals, 258, 264, 269–70
  France, 222, 435–6
  product liability, 97–8, 316
  road traffic, Austria, 430
  sale of goods, US, 102
  Sweden, 519
subcontractors. *See* Case 13
subrogation
  Austria, 235–6
  Case 4, 239–40
  England, 231
  Finland, 238–9
  France, 222
  Germany, 234–5
  health costs, 111
  insurance, 110
  Portugal, 236–8, 400–1
  Spain, 389
  Sweden, 238–9
Sweden
  Case 1, 188–9
  Case 2, 204–5
  Case 3, 219–20
  Case 4, 238–9

Case 5, 253
Case 6, 268–9
Case 7, 288–9
Case 8, 304–5
Case 9, 326
Case 10, 341
Case 11, 359–60
Case 12, 382
Case 13, 401
Case 14, 416–17
Case 15, 431–2
Case 16, 451
Case 17, 470–1
Case 18, 486
Case 19, 504–5
Case 20, 519
conservative regime, 125, 156–8
pure economic loss, 6

Thomson, J. M., 282–3, 392, 394, 441, 442
Tilburg Group, 18
title to sue, Scotland, 197–8
tobacco damage, 109–12
tortious liability
  limits, 22
  or contractual liability
    Austria, 154, 187
    Case 7, 289–90
    France, 129–30, 271–2, 310
    Germany, 150–1, 201, 396–8
    loss of economic expectations, 15–16
    United States, 101–5, 108
  rights and legitimate interests, 210
transaction costs, 65–6
transfer of title, 381–2, 535. *See also* Case 12
transferred losses
  Austria, 302–3, 339, 340
  common core, 535

comparative law, 342–3
generally, 11–12, 307
trends, greater tort liability, 18
trespass, 139, 144
Tunc, André, 223

unemployment, France, 208
United States
  contract or tort, 101–5, 108
  contract, third parties, 104
  exclusionary rule
    cases, 108–18
    product liability exception, 96–101
    rationale, 101–7
    relative unimportance, 94–6
  foreseeability, 89, 106
  Restatement of Torts, 94–5, 104, 110
  tort law, 94–5
  Uniform Commercial Code, 101–3
unjust enrichment

Van Dunné, Jan, 525
vehicles, keepers, 435–6, 446
vicarious liability, Greece, 195, 389
Viney, G., 420
Vio, Tomasso de. *See* Cajetan
von Bar, C., 12, 145
von Gierke, Otto, 38
von Jhering, Rudolph, 16, 37, 120

Walker, D. M., 144, 373
wills, 14, 16. *See also* Case 14
Windscheid, Bernard, 25
wrongful adoption cases, 113–14
wrongful job references. *See* Case 18

Zasius, 29
Zweigert, K., 144

For EU product safety concerns, contact us at Calle de José Abascal, 56–1°,
28003 Madrid, Spain or eugpsr@cambridge.org.

www.ingramcontent.com/pod-product-compliance
Ingram Content Group UK Ltd.
Pitfield, Milton Keynes, MK11 3LW, UK
UKHW012004090825
461507UK00013B/757